50
GREAT
JOURNEYS

50
GREAT
JOURNEYS

Edited by John Canning

First published in 1968 by The Hamlyn Publishing Group Ltd
for Odhams Books

This 2003 edition published by
Bounty Books, a division of
Octopus Publishing Group Ltd,
2-4 Heron Quays, London E14 4JP

ISBN 0 7537 0864 7

Contents

CONTENTS

CONTENTS

CONTENTS

CONTENTS

9

EDITOR'S NOTE

There is a tremendous aura of excitement and promise about the word "journey": the thrill of possible adventure, the stimulus of broadening mental horizons, the fascination of the unknown, the growth of sympathy to embrace new people and places.

People today, especially the younger ones, are travelling more than ever before. And a very good thing it is, too. Although there is no simple formula which will instil in men a love of peace, there is to my mind no doubt that travel with its widening insights is one of the basic factors required to produce the changed attitude in men if they are to pursue permanently the paths of peace.

But perhaps this is to strike too serious a note; the travel undertaken by most people today is, after all, almost wholly pleasurable. However, even with the vast and ever-growing facilities available there will still be more beckoning places in the world than most travellers, even the keenest, will ever be able to visit. Moreover, unless he is one of a very few he will not want (or have the courage, the energy, or the determination) to travel in the original and trail-blazing way of a Waterton, a Burkhardt, a Casteret or a Fawcett.

There will always be, therefore, a large area of travel possibilities that the individual will be able to encompass only vicariously, through the experiences of others.

And added to this is the great world of the past: how many of us have not thought how marvellous it would be if we could by some magical means be present at this or that event in history, or have lived during a period that has always drawn and intrigued us? Here again, although magic is not available to us (or at any rate to this editor) we can draw upon the first-hand accounts of many gifted observers of the past.

To try to do a little towards bridging this gap between what can be experienced directly and what must be learnt from others in this fascinating area of travel is my modest aim in this volume.

To this end I have brought together re-tellings of fifty of the great classics of travel in man's history. They range in time through

11

two and a half thousand years, in space through every continent and ocean from mountainous heights to submarine depths, and in mood from a brooding Chinese mystic in the tents of Jenghiz Khan to the roistering good nature of the crew of the *Kon-Tiki*.

If these accounts, then, can do a little towards adding to the wonder, enjoyment or wisdom of the traveller-at-heart, be he as static as a mollusc, I shall be well content.

John Canning
April, 1968

HERODOTUS'S GREAT JOURNEY
THROUGH THE LAND OF EGYPT

WHEN HERODOTUS was a boy in Halicarnassus, a Greek city in the southwest corner of Asia Minor, he must often have gone down to the quay to see the ships come in from all the ports and harbours of the eastern Mediterranean, and watched them sail away into the sunset, beyond the fringe of rock-bound islands.

What strange-looking men they were who worked the sails or pushed their oars through the blue waters, what strange merchandise they produced from their holds, rich stuffs and pottery of exotic designs, spices and gold, and dusky-complexioned slaves! The busy scene filled his mind with a sense of wonder, ideas as yet vague and unformulated possessed him, venturesome urgings, daring imaginations. Very early (we may be sure) he formed the intention of stepping aboard one of those thrusting vessels and let it take him to what mysterious realms of history and romance.

There came at length the day when he was enabled to set out on his travels. We may see him going down the plank gangway on to the ship's deck and wriggling his way among the piles of merchandize, coils of rope, rough-handed and rough-voiced sailors. He strikes us as being a young man, perhaps little more than a youth, and we are surely justified in assuming that round his neck

13

is hanging a little packet of wax-covered tablets on which he is to note down everything that strikes his fancy and seems worth recording.

This gives us the key to the "why" of his adventure, but there is a whole heap more of questions – "when?" "where?", "how?", to which no satisfactory answer is forthcoming. It is a thousand pities that in the many hundreds of pages of the *History* that he wrote years later, when his travelling days were over and done with, he saw fit to include practically nothing about his own journeys.

We know some of the places he reached, for he mentions their names in connexion with some such phrase as "I was told by the priests when I was there . . .", but for the rest we are left guessing. How did he get to Babylon? Did he go on foot across the mountains of Anatolia and down the valley of the Euphrates, or was he carried in a mule-drawn litter? Did he ride across the Scythian steppes on some mettlesome steed, in the company of splendidly ferocious nomads? And when he traversed the sands of the Libyan desert, were his heels gripping the sides and neck of a grunting camel? And how did he pay his way? There were no travellers' cheques in those days, no banks in every town, and to carry his money in a bag round his waist would surely have been asking for trouble? One guess is that he "worked his passage" by giving Greek lessons to foreigners in the places he visited.

Born in about 480 B.C., Herodotus is believed to have started on his journeyings when he was in his early or middle twenties. Very probably Egypt was the first country he visited, situated as it was within a few days' easy sailing, and moreover because its immense historical and religious appeal made it a most obvious "must" for the inquiring tourist. And for once we are given a clue as to the date.

In the third book of his *History* he tells us that when he was in Egypt he visited the battlefield of Papremis, and saw the skulls of the men who had been slain there. The battle in question was fought between the Persian forces – Egypt had been conquered by the Persians under Cambyses in about 525 B.C. — and a host of "rebel" Egyptians under the command of one Inaros, a Libyan. The latter had had the best of it, and among the slain was the Persian satrap, or governor, of Egypt, a man whom the Greeks knew as Achaimenes. This battle has been more or less certainly dated to 455 B.C., although some Egyptologists have preferred to put it some five years earlier.

14

With characteristic inquisitiveness, Herodotus examined the bones of the fallen. The Persians' bones lay in one place, and those of the Egyptians in another, and Herodotus was quick to notice a "very surprising fact" about them: the skulls of the Persians were so thin that if you struck them, even with a pebble, it was quite easy to knock a hole in them, whereas the Egyptians' skulls were so thick that you had to hit them really hard with a heavy stone before you could break them. Turning to his guides he asked them the reason, and this is what they told him. The men of Egyptian race were in the habit of shaving their heads from childhood, and so the bones of the skull were hardened by constant exposure to the sun. But the Persians always made a point of wearing hats or turbans, and in consequence their skulls were thin and weak... "This seemed to me likely enough", he tells us, and so he noted it down.

Round about 455 B.C., then, we may suppose that Herodotus crossed the sea from Halicarnassus and arrived in the land of Egypt, about which he had heard and read so much. We may assume that his port of disembarkation was Naucratis, some thirty miles upstream on one of the western branches of the Nile that cut across the muddy plains of the Delta. We may imagine him going ashore for the first time, the young Greek making contact with a foreign world. He books a bed in one of the inns – perhaps the pilot has given him the address of one he can recommend: he has his dinner of fish and meal-cakes and fresh fruit, with a cup of the local wine to wash it down – and then he sallies forth to see the sights. And very soon he has arrived at the conclusion that "there is no country in the world which is so full of wonderful things as Egypt, so many and so wonderful that really they defy description". Through street after street he wanders, along the banks of the sail-studded Nile, past splendid temples through whose pillared porticoes comes the sound of solemn music, and down alley-ways where such vice as he has never dreamed of in his home-town revels in unashamed abandon.

"Not only is the climate of Egypt different from that of the rest of the world," he notes, "and their river different from all other rivers, but the people have adopted manners and customs which, many of them, are so peculiar as to be exactly the reverse of those of all other peoples. Thus the women go to market and engage in trade, while the men stay at home and do the weaving. The men carry burdens on their heads, the women on their shoulders. The women stand up to make water, but the men do it sitting down. They have their meals out of doors, but relieve themselves indoors, since they hold that whatever is necessary but indecent ought to be done in private, but what is not indecent should be performed in the full sight of everybody. A woman cannot become a priest, even of a goddess. Sons are not obliged to contribute something to their parents' support, but daughters must do so, whether they want to or not.

"In other countries priests have long hair, but in Egypt they shave their heads; the only time when Egyptian men wear their hair long is when they are in mourning — just the opposite to what the men of other nations do. All other men keep their animals in stables, but Egyptians have them in their own homes. Other people make barley and wheat their food, but Egyptians would be ashamed to eat them; they make their bread from spelt, which they call *zea*. Dough they knead with their feet, but they have no hesitation in picking up mud and even manure with their hands. Other men leave their private parts as they are formed in nature, but Egyptian males are circumcised. The men wear two garments apiece, the women only one. When they write or do sums, the Egyptian moves his hand from right to left, instead of as the Greeks do, from left to right. They have two quite different sorts of writing [in fact, they had *three*], one of which is called sacred and the other common."

Religion is one of the subjects that interested Herodotus most deeply, and he gives us many pages descriptive of the peculiar customs and ceremonies of the Egyptian worship. He treats it with reticence, because of its sacred character. He seems never to have appreciated the fact that by his time the age-old religion of the gods and goddesses had degenerated into magic and superstition, and that the wily priesthood were primarily concerned with their own vested interest.

"The Egyptians are far more religious than any other people", he asserts, and he frequently acknowledges the information he received on the subject from the priests. On the whole he seems to have got on well with them, and doubtless they were no worse than the priests he had met with at home. The Egyptian priests, he writes, "wear linen garments, which they are very careful to wash frequently. They practise circumcision, thinking it better to be clean than handsome. They wash themselves twice a day in cold water, and twice every night. They shave their bodies every other day, so that no lice or other impure thing may adhere to them when they are engaged in the service of the gods. On the other hand, they enjoy quite a number of privileges. Thus their housekeeping costs them nothing, since everything is provided for them free; every day bread is baked for them of the corn in the sacred granary, a plentiful supply of beef and poultry is assigned to each, and also a portion of wine of the grape. Each temple has a number of priests attached to it, and the priestly career is an hereditary one, sons succeeding their fathers in due course."

The Egyptians, Herodotus informs us, were great ones for festivals. "They were the first to introduce solemn assemblies, processions, and litanies to the gods", and there must have been as many "holy-days" among them as in medieval Europe. Each of the principal towns had its great temple, dedicated to one or other of the divinities in the immensely numerous pantheon–gods and goddesses that were human or animal, half-human half-animal–and pilgrimages were arranged to these temples on certain days of the year.

Not far from Naucratis was the city of Sais, which boasted of a famous temple dedicated to the goddess Neith and in which there was to be seen the tomb of Osiris, the greatest and most revered of all the Egyptian divinities. "On one night in the year," Herodotus writes, and doubtless he was writing of what he had actually witnessed, "all the inhabitants light a great number of lamps which they place in the open outside their doors. These lamps are like flat saucers, and they contain a mixture of oil and salt, on which the wick floats. These they keep burning all through the night, for which reason it is called the Feast of Lamps".

All the pharaohs or kings of one of the Egyptian dynasties were buried in the royal tomb-house at Sais, and Herodotus of course went to see it. But the great object of devotion was the tomb of Osiris, and Herodotus says that the priests at certain times performed "mysteries" on the neighbouring lake in which the sufferings of the god were represented. "I know well the whole course of the proceedings, but no account of them shall pass my lips."

At On (Heliopolis), not far from the present Cairo, he noted the "magnificent obelisks" of red granite which stood at the entrance to the temple; and perhaps he may have actually set eyes on the one that is known to Londoners as "Cleopatra's Needle" which, like its fellow in New York's Central Park, originally stood in the temple precincts there. Then at Bubastis (which has been identified with the Pibeseth mentioned by the Prophet Ezekiel in the Old Testament) he visited the extensive cemetery for embalmed cats and the magnificent temple, set on an island between two tributaries of the Nile, where Ubastet, or Bast, the great cat-headed goddess, was specially worshipped.

Of all the religious festivals the one held at Bubastis was the most popular, and Herodotus joined the crowds of merry-making pilgrims. They went there by boat from all the towns in the Delta, and his description is particularly vivid, as will be seen from this extract taken (like our earlier quotations) from Henry Cary's translation of the *History*.

"Now, when they are being conveyed to the city Bubastis, they act as follows. Men and women embark together, and great numbers of both sexes in every barge. Some of the women have castanets on which they play, and the men play on the flute the whole voyage. The rest of the women and men clap their hands together at the same time. When in the course of their passage they come to any town, they lay their barge near to land, and ... some of the women do as I have described; others shout and scoff at the women of the place; some dance, and others pull up their clothes: this do they at every town by the riverside. When they arrive at Bubastis, they celebrate the feast, offering up great sacrifices; and more wine is consumed at this festival than in all the rest of the year. What with men and women, besides children, they congregate, as the inhabitants say, to the number of seven hundred thousand."

Moving upstream from the Delta, Herodotus came to Memphis, where "I got much information from conversation with the priests". Of course he went to see the Pyramids, and he carefully noted down what his priestly guides told him. Standing before the Great Pyramid, they informed him that it had been constructed to the orders of Pharaoh Cheops. When Herodotus saw it, the Pyramid was already much more than two thousand years old, and nearly another fifteen hundred years have been added to it since.

The priests gave a very unfavourable account of Cheops. He was a terrible fellow, they asserted; he had plunged into all manner of wickedness and had even closed the temples and put an end to the temple worships! Instead of sacrificing to the gods, the Egyptians had been compelled to labour, one and all, in the king's service. Some were required to drag huge blocks of stone from the quarries in the Arabian hills down to the banks of the Nile, where others ferried them across and then drew them to the building site.

A hundred thousand men were employed constantly, working in relays, three months at a time. Why, it had taken ten years to make the causeway along which the stones were hauled; "a work not much inferior, in my judgment", commented Herodotus, "to the pyramid itself." The pyramid was twenty years in building.

How did they manage to get the great stones up to the top, asked Herodotus. The priests explained it to him. They built the pyramid in steps, they said; they used wooden machines to lift the stones from the ground to the first step or terrace, where other machines raised them to the second step, and so on. "I couldn't quite make out," says Herodotus, "whether they used the same machines on every step, or had a fresh machine standing ready on each one." Having received the information and explanations he sought, Herodotus moved over to the pyramid to take a closer look. "On the pyramid I noticed an inscription in Egyptian characters, recording the quantity of radishes, onions, and garlic consumed by the workmen who constructed it; and I perfectly remember the interpreter who read the inscription for me, telling me that these had cost sixteen hundred talents of silver. If this really be the case, what an immense sum must have been spent on the iron tools used in the work, the food and clothing of the workmen, and so on!"

Yes, agreed the guides, it was indeed a colossal sum, and it is no wonder that Cheops's treasury was exhausted in the process. And did Herodotus know how the wicked king had met the deficiency? He had "prostituted his own daughter in a brothel", and ordered her to extort from her customers – they did not know exactly how much, but it was sufficient to meet her father's demands. And then, wishing to leave a monument of herself, she required each man who came to her to give her a stone towards the edifice she had designed. They did as she bade them, and with the stones thus collected she was able to build the pyramid that stands in the middle of the three, immediately in front of the Great Pyramid! "And if you don't believe me," we can almost hear the guide saying, "there is the pyramid itself, and what better proof can you have than *that*?"

Leaving Cheops's pyramid, Herodotus went across to take a look at the one that was built by Chephren, his successor. "This isn't as big as the other," writes Herodotus, "and I know what I am saying, for I measured them both myself." He also inspected the third pyramid, the one called after the pharaoh Menkaura, or Mycerinus to use his Greek style. "Some of the Greeks say this pyramid was built by Rhodopis the courtesan, who carried on her business in Naucratis. But this is absurd. Rhodopis was very beautiful and amassed a great fortune, but you can be sure that it was nothing like enough to pay for the erection of such a building as this. We are told that, wishing to leave something of a memorial to herself in Greece, she expended a tenth of her wealth on providing the temple at Delphi with a quantity of iron spits, such as are used for roasting oxen whole. Anyone who wishes to know how much a tenth of her property comprised has only to go to Delphi to see for himself, for the spits are still there, lying in a heap behind the altar. Clearly, if *these* cost a tenth, the rest of her wealth would be nothing like enough to pay for this pyramid ..."

One remarkable omission on Herodotus's part may be noted in this description of the "sights" of Memphis and its neighbourhood. There is no mention of the Sphinx. And yet it was certainly there, and had been there, staring out with its blind eyes over the desert, for a thousand years.

From the Delta Herodotus went up the Nile to Thebes – nine days' sail, and a distance of between four and five hundred miles. He went by boat, of course – a boat made of planks of wood pegged together and tied to the ribs with ropes made of papyrus fibre. These boats were provided with sails, but often the crew had to help them along with their wooden paddles or tow them from the shore by ropes. Perhaps now and again Herodotus gave them a hand, but we may imagine him for the most part lying beneath an awning on deck and scratching away on his tablets as interesting people and things came into view.

The gnats (or mosquitoes) seem to have bothered him, since he writes very feelingly about them, as something "with which the country swarms". In those parts of Egypt above the Delta (he says) the inhabitants pass the night upon lofty towers, where the gnats are unable to reach them on account of the wind; but in the marshlands "each man possesses a net, which during the day he uses to catch fish and at night spreads over his bed". This is much more effective than just wrapping yourself in your clothes, he explains: "The gnats would bite through *them*, but they do not so much as attempt to bite through the net."

Arrived at Thebes, Herodotus must have spent some time in this great centre of royalty and religion. There were splendid palaces to visit, magnificent temples and shrines, tremendous statues, walls covered with carvings, avenues of sphinxes. Herodotus must have seen all these, and yet, strangely enough, he passes most of them by without so much as a mention. The one construction that did arouse his admiration was what he calls the Labyrinth. "I visited this place," he says, "and found it to surpass description. If all the great architectural works of the Greeks be put together, they would not equal this, either for labour or expense. The temple at Ephesus is worthy of remembrance, and likewise the one at Samos. The Pyramids beggar description – but the Labyrinth puts the Pyramids in the shade. It has twelve courts, all of them roofed, and it contains three thousand chambers – fifteen hundred above ground and fifteen hundred underground. I visited the former myself, but of the latter I can speak only from what others told me, for the keepers could not be persuaded to show them. They contained, they said, the sepulchres of the kings, and also those of the sacred crocodiles."

Crocodiles? Yes, crocodiles, for Thebes was "the City of Crocodiles". Now here was something really wonderful! "They are four-footed, and live indifferently on land or in water. The crocodile has the eyes of a pig, big teeth resembling tusks, strong claws and a skin covered with scales, so hard that they cannot be broken. It is the only animal that hasn't got a tongue; and the only one, too, that cannot move its lower jaw but brings the upper jaw down to the lower. It is blind in the water, but very keen sighted on land ... In some parts of Egypt the crocodile is treated as an enemy, but at Thebes it is sacred. The people adorn it with golden earrings and put bracelets on its forepaws, furnish it with a daily supply of bread, treat it with the greatest possible respect when it is alive and when it dies embalm its body and bury it in a sacred repository." The people of Elephantine, on the other hand, "are so far from considering these animals sacred that they even eat their flesh ..."

This is one of several indications Herodotus gives us that he reached this frontier city high up the Nile Valley, at the First Cataract (where there is the great dam of Assuan), representing a journey of well over a thousand miles from the Delta. The ancient Egyptians called the place Yebu, i. e., "Elephant City", and in the hieroglyphs of the name we may see the neat little figure of an elephant. It is unlikely, however, that Herodotus actually saw an elephant; elephants play no part in the Egyptian mythology, and there is no Egyptian deity with an elephant head, from which it is

21

deduced that they had retreated far to the south long before his time.

But surely he had seen wonders enough, and had travelled far enough. He listened to the tales told him by venturesome boatmen who had gone a long way beyond Elephantine, into the land of the Pygmies and even the mysterious region of Ethiopia; but now he turned back, back down the river to the Delta, back across the Mediterranean to his homeland. He must have spent at least a couple of years in Egypt, and what he had managed to accomplish was something that was never surpassed, hardly approached even, until the days of modern travel and scientific investigation.

ALEXANDER THE GREAT'S
MARCH TO INDIA–AND BACK

WHAT HAD the young Alexander in mind on those spring mornings in 334 B.C. when he watched his troops cross the Dardanelles into Asia? A missionary expedition to broadcast Greek culture and civilization among the "Barbarians" who occupied the countries to the east? A war to avenge the Persian invasions of Greece a hundred and fifty years before, in the course of which Athens, finest flower of Greek cities, had suffered from the destroyer's torch? A freebooting raid on the fabulously wealthy centres of Oriental magnificence and unparalleled luxury? A journey of exploration, inspired perhaps by his old teacher Aristotle, into the vast spaces of the unknown and allegedly inaccessible? An adventure born of a brilliant youth's megalomania, a most daring challenge flung at the fates who control human destiny, or just an endeavour to win for himself a crown of immortal glory?

Perhaps something of each of these ideas and objectives, confused and conflicting, jostled in the brain of the twenty-two-year-old king of Macedon and Captain-General of the Greek Confederation as he stood there on the bank, watching his armies stepping down to the boats and being ferried across to the farther shore. Of one thing we can be sure, that he was proud, very proud, for this

23

was the finest fighting force that had ever been assembled in any European kingdom. Thirty thousand foot and something over five thousand horse... Splendidly equipped and mounted "Companions", two thousand strong, who were the royal bodyguard; a corps of Thessalian light horse; regiment upon regiment of sturdy Macedonian mountaineers; nine thousand infantrymen whose spears, eighteen or twenty feet long, presented an impenetrable thicket of shafts as the phalanx delivered its tremendous charge; thousands of Greeks from the allied cities, javelin-men, archers from Crete, light-armed skirmishers... Behind these came a host of army engineers and surveyors, the legions of the commissariat, the professional philosophers who were the army chaplains of the day, clerks and secretaries, and an uncountable number of camp-followers, not men only but women and children who were to share the ardours and dangers of the campaign.

Among the leaders were men whose names live in history as the founders of dynasties and kingdoms, but there was none so famous as Alexander himself, whom sober historians, carried away by the splendour of his achievement and the yet more thrilling legend, have acclaimed as the greatest man that the human race has as yet produced. There we may catch a glimpse of him, striding down to the water's edge, while his groom leads beside him the prancing steed Bucephalus, which likewise has a place in the enthralling record.

Did Alexander look back as he stepped aboard? He can hardly have suspected that he was never to see his homeland again, never again tread a European strand. Ahead lay a long, long road which he and his valiant comrades were to follow to the farthest limits of the then known world, although they never reached the shore of that globe-encircling Ocean of which the poets and philosophers had told them.

When his galley was in mid-channel, Alexander ordered it to be stopped while he offered a sacrifice to Poseidon, the god of the sea, and poured out a libation to the Nereids, the beautiful and gracious sea-maidens. Then, as they neared the shore, he leaped into the shallows and, striding up the beach, flung his spear far ahead into the thickets, crying as he did so that this was a sign and symbol of the conquest of Asia.

While his forces were completing their assembly, he went on a pilgrimage to the traditional site of ancient Troy. As a Greek he had learnt the stories of the *Iliad* at his mother's knee, and to him Achilles and Hector were not creatures of the poet's fancy but real historical figures who had gone before him on the heroes' path. Achilles, indeed, had a place in his family's pedigree; and his mother Olympias, who as a girl had been initiated into the Dionysian mystery-cult, had whispered to him that his father had been not King Philip of Macedon but none other than Zeus, the Great King of the Gods... Arrived at the small village known as New Ilium, Alexander made his way into the shrine of the goddess Athene Polias and offered a sacrifice on the altar before which, so ran the legend, Priam, the Trojan king, had been cut down by his pursuers. A soothsayer assured him that the goddess had accepted his offering. Whereupon he dedicated his armour to her, and was handed from behind the altar an ancient shield, which was supposed to be charged with supernatural power. This shield was carried before him in all the ensuing battles, and on one occasion in India it was believed to have saved his life.

After this pious excursion, Alexander returned to his camp, and shortly afterwards encountered the first of the armies that the Persians sent against him. The so-called Battle of the Granicus, fought on the banks of a stream a few miles inland from the Sea of Marmora, was not much more than a skirmish. The disciplined Macedonians made short work of their opponents, who were mainly drawn from the local militia, and Alexander marched on into the heart of enemy country.

On the face of it, it was a desperate adventure on which he was now embarked. The Persian empire which he was invading was by far the greatest in extent that the world had seen, extending as it did in an immense arc from northern Africa to the valley of the Indus at the foot of the Himalayas. Within its bounds were included Egypt and Libya, Palestine and Syria, Asia Minor with the string of Greek towns along the Ionian shore, Assyria and Mesopotamia, Persia (where at Susa was the imperial capital), and those countries to the east which we know as Afghanistan and Baluchistan, and so on into the north-western regions of India. But it was a ramshackle empire at best, loosely governed and with large local autonomies, and its then emperor was a rather weak and ineffectual figure known as Darius Codomanus, who proved no match at all for his vigorous young opponent.

Before Alexander's onset the Persian empire was toppled into hopeless and helpless ruin. A few cities – Tyre, for instance, which stood a siege of seven months – put up a considerable resistance, and terrible was the price they were condemned to pay, expressed in terms of slaughter and rapine and the enslavement of whole peoples. Most of them capitulated without striking a blow, and in many Alexander was received as a welcome liberator. There were great battles — Issus in 333 B.C., Gaugamela two years later — in which Alexander triumphed, and by 330 B.C. Darius was a fugitive. Alexander sat on the throne of the "King of Kings and Lord of Lords", and the whole Persian world paid him homage.

This career of unparalleled conquest has been a favourite subject with historians from Alexander's time to ours, and there is no call to repeat the story here. What draws our attention is not Alexander the world-conqueror but Alexander the world-traveller, the man who sent the streams of European intelligence and enterprise into the stagnant pools of Egypt and the near and middle east.

Alexander was in Egypt for less than a year, but this was long enough for him to choose the site and see to the laying of the foundations of the great city which ever since has borne his name. Long enough, too, for him to be acclaimed as king of Egypt, crowned with the most solemn and splendid ceremonial by the priests at Memphis, and accepted by priests and people as the latest addition to the crowded ranks of the Egyptian pantheon.

It is not recorded whether he smiled when he heard himself acclaimed as a god: there was a mystical streak in his character – something that he had inherited through his mother – and he may well have seen nothing strange in the idea. It *is* recorded that when he was at Memphis he was "seized with a yearning", as had happened to him once or twice before, and this time the inward voice told him to make a pilgrimage to the most renowned and remote of the Egyptian oracles, the shrine of Ammon in the Siwah oasis, deep in the sands of the Sahara. So, leaving his architects and builders to get on with the job at Alexandria, he set out along the coast road to the west, accompanied by only a handful of followers. A week's riding would have brought the party to the small town of Paraetonium, on the border between Egypt and Cyrene (Libya). Here their route turned southwards across the desert, and the travellers would exchange their horses for camels. Now Plutarch may take up the tale.

"It was a long and laborious journey; and besides the fatigue, there were two great dangers attending it. The one was, that their water might fail, in a desert of many days' journey which afforded no supply; and the other, that they might be surprised by a violent south wind amidst the wastes of sand, as had happened long before to the army of Cambyses – the wind raised the sand, and rolled it in such waves, that it devoured full fifty thousand men. These difficulties were considered and represented to Alexander; but it was not easy to divert him from any of his purposes. Fortune had supported him in such a manner, that his resolutions were become invincibly strong; and his courage inspired him with such a spirit of adventure, that he thought it not enough to be victorious in the field, but so must conquer both time and place."

Nor was Alexander wrong in trusting to his "star". As Plutarch continues: "The divine assurances which Alexander experienced in his march, met with more credit that the oracles delivered at the end of it ... In the first place, Jupiter sent such a copious and constant rain, as not only delivered them from all fear of suffering by thirst but moistened the sand, making it firm to the foot and made the air clear and fit for respiration. In the next place, when they found the marks which were to serve for guides to travellers removed or defaced, and in consequence wandered up and down without any certain route, a flock of crows made their appearance, and directed them in the way. When they marched briskly on, the crows flew with equal alacrity; when they lagged behind or halted, the crows also stopped. What is still stranger, when they happened to be gone wrong, these birds called them by their croaking, and put them right again."

When Alexander "had passed the desert and was arrived at the place, the minister of Ammon received him with salutations from the god, as from a father". He inquired of the oracle whether the men who had murdered his father, King Philip, had been sufficiently punished? The oracle, speaking through the priests, assured him that this was the case. Then he was informed that the god wished to speak with him in private, and Alexander entered the innermost shrine, alone. What happened to him there he never disclosed. But, reports Plutarch, in a letter which he wrote to his mother Olympias, he informed her that "he had received certain private answers from the oracle, which he would communicate to her, and her only, at his return". It has been conjectured that the wily priests had arranged that the young conqueror should have been assured by the oracle that his father was indeed Zeus, as his mother had hinted. Perhaps Olympias guessed as much when she received her son's letter. But she was destined never to hear from his own lips what had occurred in that mysterious sanctum in the African desert.

From Siwah Alexander returned to Memphis by the direct caravan route across the desert. He did not remain there long, but in the summer or autumn of 331 B.C. started for the heart of the Persian empire. He soon reached it. Up the Mediterranean coast to Alexandretta, the port he had established and given his name to after his victory at Issus, across country to Assyria, through the "land of the two rivers" to Babylon, and thence down the Tigris to near the head of the Persian Gulf, from where he struck eastwards into Persia, and occupied in turn the ancient seats of the Persian monarchy: Susa, Persepolis, and Pasargadae.

Here his soldiers no doubt thought they had reached the end of the road; why go farther, when here they might enjoy the spoils of the victory they had won? Wine and women, immense treasures, quarters provided with every luxury, hosts of slaves to do their bidding... As it was now mid-winter Alexander allowed them a few months of respite and relaxation, while he himself went off on plundering raids into the surrounding country. In the spring of 330 B.C. he collected his forces and resumed the pursuit of the unhappy Darius, who when last heard of was at Ecbatana (the modern Hamadan) where he was making vain efforts to raise another army.

Marching across the Iranian plateau, Alexander reached Ecbatana (where, we may be sure, he observed the great rock-sculpture put up by the first Darius nearly two hundred years before), and found that the Persian monarch had fled eastward, hoping to find a safe refuge in the remote province of Bactria, of which his kinsman Bessus was the satrap, or governor. Alexander pursued him to Ragae, south of the Caspian, and at length came upon his murdered corpse. Bessus, it appeared, finding that the pursuers were gaining upon them, had stabbed the unfortunate king and made off into the hills.

Alexander gave orders that the body of Darius should be taken back to Pasargadae and given honourable interment in the sepulchre of the Persian kings. He then resumed his march, with the intention of catching up with Bessus and his fellow conspirators and inflicting on them the punishment they deserved. This was his ostensible objective, but that he was inspired by something more than the avenging of the murdered monarch is clear from the fact that even when Bessus had been captured and, after mutilation, sent back to Ecbatana for execution, Alexander continued his journeyings. For three years he moved here and there across the Iranian plateau and then among the peaks and passes of the knot of the Hindu Kush in the heart of Asia.

It is impossible to follow his march with any degree of certainty. Quite a number of accounts have come down to us, but they are conflicting and incomplete, and in any case most were written long after the event. Some of the routes he attempted were impassable or blind alleys, and he had to turn back. Others led him into inhospitable wastes where his men suffered greatly from thirst and hunger and exposure. What he was trying to accomplish it is impossible to determine: very likely he was not too clear himself.

But while we cannot trace his wanderings, we are able to put our finger on the map – he had no maps, of course – and say that here Alexander came and conquered and for a time stayed. This is because he established a number of "cities" to which his own name was given. One Alexandreia was in the neighbourhood of Herat, in Afghanistan; another was at Kandahar, which may be a corruption of Alexander; a third was in the Peshawar district; and a fourth was north of Maracanda (Samarkand), on the River Jaxartes in the territory of the Scythian nomads. This was called by the Greeks, for distinction's sake, Alexandreia Eschate, or "the Extreme", since it marked the extreme limit to which Alexander penetrated into central Asia. It is supposed to have been situated near where Khojend now stands, in the Soviet republic of Uzbekistan.

After these three years of apparently aimless wanderings, Alexander determined on something which no doubt he had had long in mind, the invasion of India. And here it should be understood that by "India" the Greek geographers had in mind nothing more than the plains of the Indus and its tributaries. Of what lay beyond they had no knowledge; and if asked, they would probably have replied that beyond the Indus lay the all-surrounding Ocean.

In the late summer of 327 B.C. Alexander crossed the Hindu Kush for the second time, and while part of his army took the route of the Khyber Pass he entered the country to the north of Kashmir, where he was engaged for nine months in subduing the fierce native tribes before he could fight his way down on to the plain.

On the way occurred a romantic adventure, a delightful interlude in the campaign of rapine and slaughter. After much hard marching, the column under Alexander's own command arrived at a small fortified town called Nysa, at the foot of Mt. Meros (the place has been identified, more or less probably, with the neighbourhood of Jalalabad, between Kabul and the frontier of Afghanistan with Pakistan). The townsfolk placed themselves under Alexander's protection, and he was deeply interested to learn that the "city" had been founded in the long ago by the Greek deity Dionysos, or Bacchus, whose ecstatic rites were still celebrated on the slopes of the mountain. "Alexander felt a strong desire to see the place where the Nysaians boasted to have certain memorials of Dionysos," writes Arrian, a Greek author of the second century A.D., among whose works is a valuable account of Alexander's Indian expedition.

"So he went (it is said) to Mount Meros with some of his Companions and foot-guards, and found that the mountain abounded with ivy and laurel and groves of all kinds of trees, and that there were animals of the chase in plenty. The Macedonians in particular were delighted to see the ivy, as they had not seen any for such a long time, and they are said to have set themselves immediately to weave ivy chaplets which they placed round their heads, and then they danced around, singing hymns to Dionysos the while and calling on the god by the different names they knew him by. Alexander, for his part, offered up sacrifices to Dionysos, and then feasted with his friends. Some even go so far as to state that many of his courtiers, Macedonians of quite high rank, while invoking Dionysos and dancing about wearing their ivy vrowns, were seized with ecstatic madness, and revelled in the Bacchanalian orgies he was supposed to have inspired."

After this brief interlude of peaceful celebration there came one of the most hard-fought incidents of the campaign – the storming of the "Rock Aornos", the "birdless rock". A number of the "Barbarians" had entrenched themselves on this summit, and for long they successfully resisted every effort of the attackers. At length Alexander himself took command of the scaling-party and fought his way to the top and put the enemy to flight. The identification of Aornos has been the subject of much controversy among archaeologists, but the matter seems to have been determined by Sir Aurel Stein, who professed to have located it in the mountains above Peshawar.

Now the two sections of the expeditionary force were rejoined, and Alexander prepared to descend on the plains of the Indus. His army is said to have numbered about 35,000 men, although some of the Greek chroniclers make it very much larger. But even this figure seems impossibly large when we consider the difficulties of keeping so large a force supplied with the necessaries of life and military existence; and yet there is no doubt that the army was large enough to meet and put to utter rout the much more numerous armies of the Indian kings or rajahs that were sent against it. Whatever the actual figure, there can have been very few of the original Macedonians left, what with the losses suffered in battle and through sickness, and also the large numbers of colonists who had been left behind *en route* to establish the cities that Alexander had founded and which bore his name.

For a few days the troops celebrated their reunion with military games, horse races, and religious festivals, and then, on a morning in the spring of 326 B.C., the vanguard of Alexander's army crossed the Indus by a bridge of boats in the neighbourhood of the present-day Attock. Here fortune favoured them, for there was disunion in the Indian camp, and negotiations had already been opened with the king of Taxila, described as a great and flourishing city in the heart of a rich and fertile countryside.

The Greeks and Macedonians were given a warm welcome in Taxila; the king supplied them with 3,000 oxen and more than 10,000 sheep for their commissariat, as well as a contingent of 5,000 troops as allies. The invaders thoroughly enjoyed themselves, and there was also much in their new surroundings that they found of deep interest. Fortunately for us, there was in Alexander's entourage a Greek scribe named Aristoboulos, who kept notes of what he had seen and heard which, centuries later, were incorporated in Arrian's narrative, as well as in the *Geographica* of Strabo (a contemporary of Julius Caesar), foremost geographer of antiquity.

Among the "strange and unusual" customs that Aristoboulos remarked upon was that "those people who are too poor to provide their daughters with dowries, expose them for sale in the market-place, in the flower of their age. When a possible purchaser steps forward, first the back of the girl down to her shoulders is exposed for his examination and then her bosom: and if she pleases him and is herself willing to be persuaded, they come together upon such terms as may be agreed upon". Other novelties noted were that the bodies of the dead were thrown out to be devoured by vultures, and that "some wives allowed themselves to be burned alive with their deceased husbands, and that gladly, and that those women who refused to do so were held in disgrace". So that even so early the custom of suttee was being practised.

From Taxila Alexander marched to meet Poros, the king of the land between the Hydaspes (River Jhelum) and the Acesines (Chenab), who had mustered an army of more than 30,000 men, with 300 chariots and 200 war-elephants. Poros was the one Indian prince who put up a strong resistance, and Alexander's victory was no easy one. At length, however, the Macedonian phalanx carried all before it, the Indian host was swept away in utter rout, and Poros himself was taken prisoner. Covered with wounds, he was brought before his conqueror, who demanded of him how he expected to be treated? "Like a king, of course", he proudly replied, and Alexander's response evinced a nobility that he did not always show. Poros was spared, and reinstated on his throne as Alexander's vassal.

After the battle of the Hydaspes, as it is called, Alexander resumed his march through the Punjab. Resistance was slight and ineffectual, and the Greeks reached the Hyphasis (identified with the Beas). Alexander was planning to push on across the deserts to the Ganges, of which he had now heard, probably for the first time, but it was not to be. Whatever *he* had in mind, his soldiers had had enough: they refused, point blank, to go any farther – they struck. In vain he ordered them, pleaded with them, stormed and threatened, appealed to their fighting spirit, reminded them of all the wonderful things they had done together and promised them greater glories in the future. With sullen determination they maintained their refusal. In the past eight years they had come twelve thousand miles – and what miles! They had fought, and won, how many battles – and what battles! Glory? They had had their fill: all they wanted now was to go back home, and as soon as possible. Alexander for the first time in his life had to give way. In July, 326 B.C., the Graeco-Macedonian army turned their faces westward.

Little did they know how many months filled with hardship and danger lay before them. As the boats packed with soldiers moved down-stream they were attacked by hordes of tribesmen. Towns blocked their progress, and had to be stormed; in one of these encounters Alexander was wounded and nearly killed. At the junction of the Chenab with the Indus another Alexandreia was founded, and the voyage down the Indus was continued. In July, 325, Alexander reached the head of the delta at Patala (Hyderabad), whence he sailed down the eastern mouth to what Arrian calls the "Great Sea". This was his first glimpse of the Indian Ocean, and on the beach he offered up sacrifices to the gods as (so Arrian tells us) the priests of Ammon had enjoined upon him years before. Then in one of his galleys he sailed out to sea with a view to ascertaining whether there was any land lying to the west. To his great joy there was nothing ahead of him but an apparently limitless expanse of ocean. So he returned to his camp and made preparations for the homeward journey.

As he planned it, his famous admiral Nearchos, who had been in charge of the transports during the river passage, should conduct the fleet of some hundred and fifty ships along the coast to the west, while he with the army should march on a more or less parallel route on shore. In September, 325, therefore, Alexander and the army set out from Patala, heading for what we know as Baluchistan. Nearchos had intended to wait for the monsoon, but the tribesfolk became threatening and he sailed forthwith for a haven near the present Karachi, where he was delayed for several months because of contrary winds.

Meanwhile Alexander was making progress across country. Somewhere on his route he founded one more Alexandreia, and then entered the country of the Ichthyophagi, "the fish-eaters", who are described by another of the ancient chroniclers, Q. Curtius Rufus, as "having long nails like claws and long shaggy hair, dwelling in huts constructed of shells and other off scourings of the sea, their clothing the skins of wild beasts, and their food fish dried in the sun and the flesh of sea monsters".

Thence they passed into the Gedrosian desert. It was a dreadful place. "Most of the historians of Alexander's career", says Arrian, "admit that all the hardships which the army endured in Asia were as nothing compared with the miseries which they now experienced." A large part of the army was destroyed by the blazing heat and want of water. Many of the baggage animals sank into the sand, "which was like deep mud or untrodden snow", and it was impossible to extricate them. Many more had to be killed for food, so that it was soon impossible to transport the wounded and sick, who had to be left behind to their fate. Then overnight the streams became converted into raging torrents, and "most of the women and children of the camp-followers, the royal baggage and such of the beasts as were left, were swept away. The soldiers themselves, after a hard struggle, barely escaped with their lives, and left many of their weapons behind. Many of them besides came to their death through drinking with insatiable avidity the first water they came to after marching for hours in the broiling heat. Because of this Alexander generally pitched his camp at some little distance from the watering-places, in order to prevent men and beasts from rushing in crowds into the water to the danger of their lives, as well as to prohibit those who had no self-control from pulluting the water for the rest by stepping into the stream".

Only a fraction of the army emerged at length into the fertile country of Carmania, where Alexander allowed them a short period of rest and enjoyment of every kind. Then they resumed their march, and in February, 324 B.C., contact was re-established with Nearchos, who had successfully completed one of the great voyages of antiquity by sailing into the Persian Gulf and up the Tigris.

Little more than a year later, in June, 323 B.C., Alexander the great captain, who had led his army through such immense dangers and tremendous trials, across how many thousands of miles, lay dead of a fever at Babylon. For him there were no more marches, except through the pages of unforgettable history...

HANNIBAL CROSSES THE ALPS

A Journey into War

HAMILCAR BARCA the great Carthaginian general, stared up at the huge bull-headed figure of Baal, dimly seen through the grey twisting smoke of incense. His face reflected the bitter, deep-seated pain with which he had lived for years, then softened as he lowered his eyes and looked at the nine-year-old boy standing at his side. Taking the boy gently by the arm, he led him forward and watched as the lad placed his hand on the altar and began to repeat a solemn oath of enmity against the country which had so humiliated his own.

"I, Hannibal, swear that so soon as age will permit, I will follow the Romans both at sea and on land. I will use fire and steel to arrest the destiny of Rome!"

When this oath had been sworn, father and son walked from the gloom of the temple into the eye-narrowing brightness of the afternoon sun. As they went, Hamilcar's face again reflected the dark thoughts which the recent ceremony had so vividly recalled.

For six centuries Carthage (sited near the modern city of Tunis) had been the undisputed centre of Mediterranean trade; into her bustling harbours had come the wealth of the then known world. It was this wealth, inevitably, which had attracted the envy of the rising Roman nation. Rome had had a chequered history. Founded about 750 B.C., a century or so after Carthage, it had been invaded and plundered by several nations; yet, despite these set-backs – or perhaps because of them – she had grown steadily stronger and her frontiers had continued to widen.

All Italy had come under her control and then, in the middle of the third century B.C., the two great nations clashed at last.

At the outbreak of hostilities Carthage was at the height of her powers, her people boasting that "no Roman might even wash his hands in the Mediterranean" without their permission. She had thriving colonies also in Spain, in the islands of the Mediterranean, and along the coast of northern Africa.

War began in 264 B.C. and the Carthaginian army, handicapped by a vacillating government, reeled from one disaster to another. Even the appointment of Hamilcar Barca could not stop the reversals, and when what was to become known as the First Punic War ended in 241 Carthage had lost Sicily, Corsica and Sardinia, and was compelled to pay an enormous sum to Rome as reparation.

Hamilcar, brooding upon revenge, took his hate with him when he went to Spain to command the colony from New Carthage (now Cartagena) and spent many hours with his young son discussing, scheming and planning for the war which both knew must come. In 228, however, Hamilcar died and his adopted son-in-law Hasdrubal took command. He proved to be as adroit a diplomat as he was skilful general and, playing for time, he continued to negotiate with Rome whilst extending the powers of his own country by treaties with the surrounding tribes.

The Romans, naturally, kept a wary eye on their late opponents and, seeking to extend their influence westwards, established a close link with the Greek colony at Massilia (Marseilles). Also, to have a military post *inside* Spain, they strengthened the defences of Saguntum (now Sagunto) which lay well within the agreed Carthaginian territory, for the River Ebro, more than one hundred and forty miles to the north-east, had been established as a demarcation line between the two countries.

Hasdrubal, well aware of the Roman encroachment, continued his policy of friendship with other tribes and those who would not co-operate he subdued by force. Hannibal, now in his early twenties, took part in a great deal of fighting and proved himself a courageous warrior and a brilliant tactician. Livy says of him:

"There never was a genius more fitted for the two most opposite duties of obeying and commanding, so that you could not easily decide whether he was dearer to the general (Hasdrubal) or the army."

When Hasdrubal suddenly died, Hannibal took over his command and, true to the oath he had sworn when a youth, immediately began preparations for war. His aim was a dramatically simple one – to march along the coast into Gaul, over the Alps, and to invade Italy from the north; but first he had to mislead the enemy into thinking he was going to confine his activities to Spain. He did this by leading an army against Saguntum which he besieged for eight months before it capitulated. It is said that when the fall of the city was inevitable, many of the townspeople deliberately burned themselves to death rather than be taken prisoner. The city was very rich and Hannibal sent much of the wealth to Carthage, knowing that such a gesture would influence the government in his favour.

His decision proved a wise one, for when an embassy from Rome arrived in Carthage to demand that Hannibal be surrendered to them, they left again bearing a declaration of war.

Hannibal was now ready for the great adventure. He brought some troops over from Carthage to Spain, putting them under the command of his brother to protect his rear, for he knew that Rome would use her command of the Mediterranean to send an army to Spain in order to crush the uprising.

The winter was spent in preparation and in May, 218 B.C., the great army began to move slowly out of New Carthage. It was composed of 90,000 infantry – many from Spanish tribes – and 12,000 cavalry, which included the Numidians from the desert, considered the finest horsemen in the world. Behind the plodding infantry and the wheeling cavalry which screened their flanks came Hannibal's "heavies" — thirty-seven great elephants whose tough hides and earth-shaking, ponderous charge brought terror to the enemy. In the rear of this vast cavalcade came the baggage-trains – slow-moving wagons and sumpter mules.

They followed the coast road mainly, moving north-eastwards, making friends with some of the tribes through whose territory they passed, fighting with others. The River Ebro was reached and crossed; then they moved on until they reached the foot-hills of the Pyrenees. Here Hannibal parted with Hanno – another brother – giving him 11,000 men to help protect his rear.

Then, leading an army that had now dwindled to 50,000 infantry and about 9,000 cavalry, Hannibal moved out of Spain and into Gaul. More days of marching brought the army to the first great natural barrier — the fast-flowing River Rhône — which, from its source in the ice of the Swiss Alps, flows for five-hundred miles until it reaches the warm waters of the Mediterranean. The army followed the river, moving northwards, trudging through the desolate salt marshes and pastures of the Camargue until Hannibal decided it was time to cross, although strong currents and a powerful Gallic tribe called the Volcae which awaited him on the eastern bank promised a difficult and dangerous attempt.

Two days passed in a frenzy of activity. Some boats and canoes were bought from local tribes, but many others, as well as rafts, were knocked together by the soldiers. Elaborate building was not required. As long as they would float and get across the river with men and materials, that was sufficient.

On the third day, whilst it was still dark, Hannibal sent his cavalry upstream where, in the biggest boats and rafts, they began to pour across the river. The men paddled desperately; their horses, already saddled and bridled, swam behind, tethered to the rocking and spinning craft. Their passage, however, helped smooth the turbulence of the river, making it safer for the thousands of boats and canoes which were pushed off farther down river and which carried the infantry. The first force of Carthaginians drew near to the opposite shore and the massed Gauls, shouting their war-cries and shaking their long spears, crowded down to the water's edge to await its coming.

Then, as the first boat ran into the swirling shallows, there came a sudden crash and a wild yell of triumph. The Gauls had been too busy watching the enemy before them to pay any attention to what was happening elsewhere and the terrible Numidian cavalry had burst upon their right flank, smashing it in, and throwing the whole Gallic army into a confused and struggling mass. Warriors in the rear ranks turned and saw tall columns of smoke rising into the morning air – their tents had been fired. Some ran back to save what they could, others turned to meet the attack of the Numidians who, screaming and whooping, were driving deep into their ranks. Others stood to meet the attack of the Carthaginian infantry who, leaping from their boats, were wading ashore, their shields together and their iron-tipped spears glinting in the bright sunlight.

More and more men were pouring across, more cavalry was

swinging in from the right and within minutes it was all over. The Gauls broke and ran, the cavalry picking off those who lagged behind until recalled by their officers.

Hannibal was now in control of the river bank and his next task was to get the elephants across. The army camped and waited whilst he and his officers went back across the river to supervise the building of some huge rafts, two hundred feet long and fifty feet wide. These were lashed to the bank by stout ropes, then others, only half the length, were floated out and moored to them. Two cow elephants were led onto the rafts and some of the huge males, weighing about seven tons, dutifully followed. The lashings of the smaller rafts were then cut and, with their strange freight, they began to move sluggishly across the river. The elephants became terror-stricken at the insecurity of the ground beneath their great feet and, with much trumpeting and squealing, began to stamp and move about. Some, indeed, fell into the water but, following the rest, struggled into the shallows and thence ashore.

This strange ferrying was repeated until all thirty-seven of the precious pachyderms had been carried safely to the other side. The only casualties – although very serious – were amongst the mahouts, some of whom were drowned or were trampled to death by their terrified charges.

During this operation a party of scouts came racing into the camp with disturbing news. A fleet of Roman warships had arrived at Massilia with a full legion commanded by Publius Cornelius Scipio. Hannibal at once sent five hundred of his best horsemen to make contact with the enemy and to find out, if possible, what was happening. They galloped off, and came upon a smaller number of Roman cavalry riding towards their own lines for the same purpose. After a short but bloody action, during which both sides lost half their men, the remainder drew away and galloped off to report to their respective commanders.

Publius realized that Hannibal's army outnumbered his own but he drew his legion into marching order and headed for the western bank of the Rhône. He arrived there to find the camp deserted and only the litter of boats along the water's edge and the churned and muddy ground showing where the army had been. It had left three days earlier, going away from the Rhône, heading eastwards towards the Alps.

On hearing this news from some Volcae tribesmen, Publius shivered with apprehension. His guess had been wrong. Hannibal had never intended to restrict his activities to Spain – he was after something far bigger ... Rome itself!

He ordered his legion to wheel about and hurried back to Massilia and the ships. A few days later the white sails of the galleys were speeding them back to Italy. Realizing that it was Hannibal's intention to invade Italy from the north, Publius hoped to station his legion at the southern foot of the Alps to await his arrival.

For a while Hannibal's army followed the river, covering some ten miles a day, making camp at night. When the junction of the Rhône and Drome was reached, the army paused, as if to gather strength for the ordeal ahead; then the 60,000 men that remained of the 110,000 who had left New Carthage swung due east along the banks of the smaller but even faster-flowing river. In the distance, as they went, they began to see the high peaks of the Alps, swathed in veils and banks of soft mist that shifted and changed colour, for only rarely did they emerge starkly visible in their entirety.

For a while the going was easy and even pleasant, the long winding column of men and animals moving through flat, fertile country. Then, almost imperceptibly, the terrain began to change. The track began to ascend, becoming more twisting and tortuous, the going harder. The hills began to crowd in on them, with tall rocky crags that towered upwards on either side. The summer was slipping away now and the grass-covered slopes were covered with the gentians and sun roses of autumn. Higher up, the grass was short and scanty, ending in the screes of the upper slopes which were already dusted with the first powdery snow of winter.

The trudging army had little time to enjoy the beauties of an Alpine autumn, for now, ominously, groups of men were seen to be watching their progress from high overhead and the scouts rode back with news of gathering bands of tribesmen ahead of them, in a narrow gorge that had high cliffs on one side and a precipice on the other.

It was obvious that they were awaiting the arrival of the main body of the army which, strung out for miles, would be terribly vulnerable to an attack from above.

One piece of information that his scouts brought back, however, gave Hannibal an idea. He learned that the waiting tribesmen – known as Allobroges – only took up their positions by day; at night they returned to their homes. He therefore led his army into the entrance to the gorge, then gave the order to camp for the night. Soon hundreds of fires were blazing and his men gathered round them thankfully, for the air was steadily becoming colder. As soon as it was dark, Hannibal led out a band of picked men which, on horseback, made for the heights where the enemy had last been seen. At dawn, the main body of the army began to move off again and, at the same time, the Allobroges returned to take up their former positions. They were furious when they saw their places filled with a compact group of warriers whilst the rest of the Carthaginian army – and especially its baggage train – was below them moving past to safety.

For a time they hung back; then, realizing that the opportunity for plunder would soon be gone, they screamed out their war-cry and began to scamper down the rocky slopes, by-passing Hannibal and his men, to fall upon the mule-drivers and the men protecting the rear. It was a fierce and desperate fight. The tribesmen went smashing in at several points at once, grappling with the drivers who, with their heavily loaded mules, were frequently swept off the narrow track to crash on to the sharp rocks below. The infantry, farther along the column, tried to turn and go back to help their comrades, but the confined space — for in places only four men could move abreast — and an avalanche of bounding, crushing rocks from above, added to the tremendous confusion.

Hannibal, although very aware that the men surrounding him were awaiting the order to attack, continued to stare down, watching the slaughter that was going on below him. Then he gave the order at last, whipped out his sword and, sliding and slithering down the slope, led his men to the rescue. The air was filled with screams, cries and groans as, pressed together in a space that hardly allowed them to use their spears or swords, the men fought and died. As the battle progressed the better-trained Carthaginians proved too much for the Allobroges who began to hang back and then, breaking at last, scrambled away up the slopes to safety.

Hannibal climbed wearily from his horse and walked slowly along the whole line of his army, watching with a grim face as his men tended the injuries of their comrades, many of whom lay in contorted attitudes along the gorge. Others fought to recover packs from dead and dying mules, knowing that every ounce of food was vital to their enterprise.

Slowly and painfully the army was got back into column of route and the grim gorge was left behind at last. The road still climbed upwards until it ran through a wide and splendid pass that led through the first great mountain chain. The army marched through this, then saw, with great relief, that the road now descended into the broad and fertile valley of the Durance. Here lay the town of the Allobroges and Hannibal was able to recover many of his pack animals and also free some of his men who had been taken prisoner. He also found a generous supply of food and fodder with which to replace part of that which had been lost in the recent battle.

Hannibal led his men forward again, the road climbing steadily through the massive ranges of the Alps whose snow-capped peaks stretched farther and farther into the grey distance. The air was loud with the sound of rushing mountain streams which smashed against the shiny black bases of the rocky banks and frothed in white fury at obstacles caused by fallen rocks and trees. The long tired columns plodded on, threading their way through the narrow valleys until another gorge was reached.

With the memory of the other ambush still fresh in his mind, Hannibal looked about him and upwards to the dark, craggy heights which towered on either side. Then, with a nerve-tingling suddenness, there came a series of dull crashes from the rear of the column, followed by the harsh screams of men and animals. Great rocks, some weighing several tons, came hurtling from above, crushing everything in their path. At the same time, at the head of the column, a great mass of screaming Gauls, carving red arcs with their heavy swords, began to thrust the leading ranks of the Carthaginians back against themselves.

Hannibal desperately pushed his way through the press with his bodyguard of picked warriors and, in a wild frenzy of hacking, stabbing and thrusting, managed to throw back the Gauls to allow the following ranks, which also contained the elephants, to push ahead. It was virtually a case of every man for himself as, slipping and sliding over the wet rocky path and over the bodies of the dead and dying, the army somehow managed to push itself forward.

The leading columns broke free of the gorge at last and almost immediately found themselves in another where, once again, the boulders came bounding from above, sweeping away men and animals in their deadly path. Behind them came the battle-crazed Gauls, hacking their way into the tired, struggling mass of their enemy. Ambush followed ambush, but somehow the Carthaginians fought their way on, Hannibal and his escort always at their head, clearing the path, rallying the men, keeping them moving, always moving.

During the night Hannibal found a tall, flat-crested plateau and, urgently throwing up defences, waited anxiously for what the dawn would bring. From time to time, detachments of his army came staggering wearily out of the defile to sink exhausted within the safety of its hastily constructed walls.

The morning light saw a long dark column of his men moving painfully towards the encampment. Some staggered along, using their spears as staffs or, in some cases, as stretchers for their desperately wounded comrades. Others dragged themselves forward as if asleep, supporting themselves against the flanks of mules and horses which already carried two or three men.

They continued to arrive until Hannibal felt that he could hardly bear to see more. It was the greatest disaster of the crossing which, altogether, accounted for nearly a third of his earlier force of 60,000 men.

After a brief pause to re-group and minister to the wounded, the army set out again. Now the enemy was not human, but of Nature herself. They climbed upwards, following a track that led inexorably to the snowline. The oaks and pines of the lower areas thinned and disappeared, and only sparse scrub dotted the white landscape. A fierce, penetrating wind howled incessantly around them, causing the men from the warm climates of Africa and Spain to huddle into their cloaks by day and around the fires during the desperate chill of night.

The elephants were also suffering terribly, for there was not sufficient leaves or bark with which to feed them. Slowly the great, uncomplaining animals began to pitch forward into the snow to shudder and to die.

The nightmare of snow, wind and piercing cold continued for nine days and nights, and what was left of the army stumbled along a narrow, wind-swept track. Then weak cheering drifted back to those toiling in the centre and rear. The sound became blanketed by a flurry of fresh snow which covered the struggling, starving men with a white shroud, yet it still persisted. Others, reaching the end of a tortuous pass, began to take up the cheering. Hannibal, who had ridden in the centre of his army, moved through the long column until he reached the vanguard which had encamped upon a narrow ridge.

He slid stiffly from his tired horse and staggered forward, his cloak held tight around him to give some protection from the biting wind. He looked down. Eight thousand feet below he saw a gentle green plain, clearly visible in the afternoon light. He blinked his frost-caked eyelids and looked again.

There was no mistake, before him lay Italy... and the road to Rome.

A TAOIST SAGE TRAVELS ACROSS ASIA

A Visit to Jenghiz Khan

THE JOURNEY of the Taoist philosopher Kiu Chang Chun took place at the beginning of the thirteenth century of our era. There were then three living centres of civilization in the Old World: Christian Europe, of which France was the most powerful nation; the world of Islam, already sinking into decay but which was still master of most of Spain and which embraced North Africa and all the Near East and had pushed far into Central Asia; and, cut off from close contact with its rivals, the civilization of China.

China was not an imperial power, though in Roman times her frontiers had once been in the neighbourhood of Tashkent and Samarkand. Under the Tang Dynasty of the sixth and ninth centuries A.D. the Chinese of the South, Middle and Northern kingdoms had become one people with a benevolent and highly organized administration. The great poets of the period, such as Po Chui and Li Po, had completed the work of making a Chinese national consciousness begun a thousand years before them by Confucius and Lao-tye.

The Chinese had developed a stable political society with religious toleration and a fairly widespread culture long before the

45

time of Charlemagne. Hundreds of thousands of Chinese lived in large cities, built mainly with bricks, of between forty an fifty thousand people, with a well-developed sea and land trade, at a time when the people of Europe were living either in hovels in the country, in small walled towns or feudal fortresses. Painting on wood blocks, the use of gunpowder, the making of silks and the drinking of tea were all common in China. Under the Sung Dynasty in the thirteenth century, one of whose emperors was a pioneer socialist, China lost North and a part of Western China to the Tatar peoples beyond the Great Wall; but the invading barbarians quickly adopted the way of life of the conquered, avidly reading Chinese books.

Chang Chun lived in the Middle kingdom which belonged to the Sung emperors. He had already visited the Kin Tatar King of Northern China and his life had not been disturbed even when other Barbarians, the Mongols of Jenghiz Khan, had conquered the Kin kingdom with its capital, Peking, in A.D. 1214, and had for a time made incursions even into the Sung land. These men were not really strangers either, even though their habits were uncouth and they were always dashing about on small horses and living in tents or wagons. Chinese, Tatars and Mongols were of the same race.

In 1219, Chang Chun received a strange and, for him, rather disquieting letter from Jenghiz Khan, the great Mongol leader, asking him to visit him at his camp, which was then near the Hindu Kush on the borders of the western part of Afghanistan. Chang Chun was then sixty-one, but his very ascetic way of life had made him appear frail and ethereal, though not lacking in vigour. Chang Chun was believed by the credulous to be no less than three hundred years old and as wise as he was old.

A contemporary wrote of him: "The adept Chang Chun was certainly a possessor of the 'secret way'. By the time I reached middle age I made sure that this old man must long ago have flown aloft and in some new guise be communing with the divinities of the clouds; and it grieved me to think that I had never met him. But one winter day a rumour reached me that he was living near the coast and had just received an invitation to make a long journey. In the Spring of the following year he actually arrived in Peking and put up in the Monastery of Jade Emptiness. I saw at my first meeting with him that he was by no means an ordinary person; conversation showed me that his learning was tremendous; there seemed to be no book he had not read. Henceforward my admiration for his genius continually increased. He sat with the rigidity of a corpse, stood with a stiffness of a tree, moved as swift as lightning and walked like a whirlwind."

Jenghiz Khan wrote: "I have succeeded in accomplishing a great work – uniting the whole world in one empire. I have not myself distinguished qualities; but as my calling is high, the obligations incumbent on me are also heavy and I fear that in my ruling there may be something wanting. To cross a river we make boats and rudders; likewise we invite sage men and choose assistants for keeping the empire in good order. I have heard that thou, Master, hast penetrated the truth and that thou walkest in the path of right. Thy sanctity is become manifest. We are separated by mountains and plains of great extent and I cannot meet thee. I implore thee to move thy sainted steps. Do not think of the extent of the sandy desert. Have pity upon me and communicate to me the means of preserving life. I shall serve thee myself. I hope that at least thou wilt leave me a trifle of thy wisdom. Say only one word to me and I shall be happy."

The humility and respect for learning which the letter shows comes strangely from a man who, though one of the greatest military leaders of the world, was also reported to have been one of the most savage, a greater object of terror than his forebear Attila, the Hun leader, whose troops had broken into Europe seven centuries before.

His boast at the beginning of the letter that, in seven years, he had united the world was not at all far-fetched. At his birth in A.D. 1156 he was the leader of a large tribe of Central Asiatic peoples whose principal camping ground was on the Argun river in eastern Siberia. He had conquered and peacefully united the neighbouring tribes of Mongolia and Manchuria and his army had then easily conquered the Northern kingdom of China. From northern China he had swept easily across eastern and central Asia whose Turkish and Tatar tribes were akin to the Mongols, and come to the borders of what is now the Soviet Republics of Uzbekistan, Kirghizia and Tadyhikistan. He would have stopped on the limits of the Tatar world but for the treachery of the Mohammedan Shah, who accepted peace from Jenghiz's Mongol envoys but then cut off their heads. The war that followed saw the victorious Mongol armies on the Indus, on the borders of the Caspian Sea, and northern raiding forces on the banks of the Dneiper. So when Jenghiz Khan wrote to Chang Chun, he ruled from the Caspian Sea to the Pacific and over a large part of India and northern China.

Nothing could have been more bloodthirsty than the Mongol conquest of western Asia; but afterwards peace was kept everywhere on the roads of the empire. Whilst the Mongols ruled, travellers from Europe could make, in comparative safety, the long overland journey from Europe to Asia, as did the celebrated Marco Polo a few years later. When the rule of the Mongol Khans came to an end in central Asia in the middle of the fourteenth century, China was once more separated from the Western and Islamic worlds. The Mongols were a tolerant people, interested in all religions and all men. Their attitude towards the outside world was one of intelligent curiosity. Though the Mongols were nomadic and the Chinese a sedentary people, they belonged to the same world. It was a matter of course that Chinese methods and officials should be used in administering their conquests. Indeed, the man who wrote to Chang Chun on Jenghiz Khan's behalf was a high Chinese official in the Mongol service, and so too was Liu Chung Lu, described as "a herbalist" who brought the letter and accompanied the Taoist sage on his arduous journey.

The commander of the Mongol escort, Prince Chinkai, was a Mongol from northern Mongolia whose tribe had been converted to Christianity in the eleventh century. Chang Chun travelled from Shantung to Peking and hoped that he might be allowed to await Jenghiz Khan's return from the East there. But an answer quickly came that the Khan expected him to make the journey at all costs. There was another difficulty. Liu Chung Lu had also been ordered to bring back with him a number of girls for the Khan's harem. Chang Chun protested that though he was only "a savage from the mountains" he could not be expected to travel with harem girls. Some other arrangements were made for the girls and finally, with nineteen disciples and his Mongol escort, he set off on a bright day of May, 1220.

They did not go very far, and at Te-Hsing (about a month's journey from Peking) they stayed at a Taoist temple all summer. The master was still expecting communication from Jenghiz that he might give him permission after all to stay in China. But the invitation to come to Hindu Kush was repeated in the most flattering but also its most commanding tones. Winter was now coming on and Chang Chun suggested that they should pass the season as they were. So the journey really began in March, 1221.

Friends and disciples were in tears as they stood round Chang Chun's horse. "Master," they said, "you are starting on a journey of several tens of thousand li—when shall we have the happiness of again bowing before you?" The Master replied: "If you be strong in the faith I shall meet you again." Again the friends pressed the question and he said evasively: "Our staying and our going do not depend on our own will." But the friends would not desist; they wanted a decisive answer. Finally the old man said: "I will be back in three years, three years."

After two days' travelling they came to a great battlefield still covered with bleached human bones, the place where Jenghiz Khan's army had crushed the Kin Tatars ten years before. "Here China and its customs and its climate suddenly came to an end," wrote the disciple who kept the record of Chang Chun's journey. They were to cross a great deal of sandy desert and barren hills before arriving at the royal encampment of Prince Tamoga, a younger brother of Jenghiz. They noticed although it was the end of March, and yet the ice had not begun to melt and there was no sign whatever of spring. How different it would have been in Shantung.

On 23 April, after travelling through its Gobi desert, they reached the tents of Prince Tamoga as the grass was beginning to grow green and winter to disappear. There was a wedding and many Mongol chiefs had arrived and they saw several thousand black carts and felt tents drawn up in rows. Chang Chun wrote: "The Mongols live in black carts and white tents; they breed cattle and hunt, dress in furs and leather, and live upon fermented milk and meat. The men and unmarried young women wear their hair in two braids that hang down over their ears. The married women wear a head-dress made out of birch bark; it is two feet high and sometimes is covered with a woollen cloth or, if the woman is rich, with red silk. Attached to the head-dress is a long goose-shaped tail which they call a Kuku. The women are always apprehensive that someone will knock into it accidentally and this makes them cautious when they enter a tent; they usually back in and lower their heads. These people have no writing. Their agreements are all verbal and contracts are recorded by marks cut in wood. They are never disobedient to orders, nor do they ever break their word once it is given. They have preserved the values of earlier ages."

From Prince Tamoga's encampment it was to take them seven

months of constant travel to reach Samarkand and the rich territories which Jenghiz Khan had just won from the Abbasid Caliph.
The names of places, of mountains and deserts in Chang Chun's
narrative do not enable the reader, unless he is very well informed,
to follow his journey and it is necessary to adopt modern place
names. Prince Tamoga's encampment was near Lake Bor. The party
then travelled up the Kerulen river, crossing the region of Karakorum in north-central Mongolia, coming to the great Altai
mountains, probably passing near the modern city of Uliassutai.
The party then crossed the Altai mountains, visiting what is now
the city of Urunsti in Sinkiang and then moving along the north
of the Tien Shan mountains into what is now Kirghizia and the
region of Tashkent. Then they turned south to Samarkand. Chang
Chun was to go farther south across the Iron Gates of Termit, to
cross the Oxus and to join Jenghiz Khan finally in his camp in the
Hindu Kush, near Kabul in Afghanistan.

Desert and mountains–but after their stop with Prince Tamoga
mostly mountains with icy rivers and rain which always turned to
hail. But in the bleak upland country there were Mongol *ordos* or
camps with richly tapestried tents which were the temporary
palaces of Mongol, Tatar or Chinese princes. Here they were received with honour. In August, before they had to cross the Altai
mountains, two concubines of the Chinese Emperor Chang Sung,
who had died in 1208, greeted the Master at one such camp with
tears of joy, one of theam saying: "I have heard of your holy reputation and virtues for a long time and always grieved at never having seen you. And now unexpectedly I meet you in this strange
country."

A little later the Master suggested to Prince Chinkai that he
should remain where he was until the next winter was over. This
was not to be. The Mongol leader advised him to leave some of
his disciples behind because the country was so rough that it could
not be crossed with heavy wagons carrying supplies for such a
large number of people. A monastery was built for the disciples–
everyone worked at its construction, the rich gave money and the
workmen their labour. In less than a month the different parts, the
monks' cells, the kitchens at the east end and the cloisters on the
west end, the cloud chambers on the sides and the Hall of Saints
were completed.

The crossing of the Altai mountains was very difficult. The
Mongol horsemen escorting the party had to haul the wagons up

by ropes and lower them when the descent started. But it was after this that the most difficult part of the journey began, a desert to cross before they reached the northern slopes of the Tien Shan range.

They travelled a great deal by night, smearing their horses' heads with blood. When the Master noticed what was being done he smiled and said: "Evil spirits and ghosts fly when they see a good man. We all know that to be true and it certainly does not become a Taoist to be afraid." In crossing the desert they were obliged to leave wagons, starving horses and oxen behind to die. What a relief it was to move westward.

In September they came to Bishbalig, the modern town of Urumsti and a country with grape wine, onions, excellent fruit and Persian leather. At Bishbalig they camped comparatively comfortably in a vineyard, being visited by the ruler and by his Buddhist and Taoist monks.

They had many further hardships to face before reaching Kirghizia but at least they came, every few days, to rich Moslem cities and civilization. At Almaliq, near Lake Kulja, they obtained cloth made from "vegetable wool". The Chinese believed that when a lamb died it was buried like a seed and bore a crop of fresh young lambs. The writer of the travel diary says that they obtained seven pieces of this cloth to be made into winter clothes. The hair of the cloth resembled the down in which willow seeds are wrapped; it is very clean, fine and soft and it is used for making thread, ropes, cloth and wadding.

They reached the great city of Samarkand on 3 December, but it was not until April that they began the final lap of their journey to Jenghiz Khan's encampment near Kabul. On arrival Jenghiz Khan received the Master at once, saying: "You were invited by rulers of other courts but you refused. Yet you have journeyed ten thousand li to see me. I am deeply gratified." The Master answered: "That I, a hermit of the mountains, responded to your majesty's request was the will of heaven."

Food was brought and almost at once the Khan asked him: "Adept, what medicine of immortality have you brought me from your distant home?" The Master answered that he had no elixir for immortal life, but that by his teaching he could show how life could be protected. If Jenghiz Khan had had at the back of his mind the idea that Chang Chun had a magic formula—in fact in his letter he had used the phrase "Have pity upon me and commu-

51

nicate to me the means of preserving life"–he showed no sign of disappointment but praised the Master for his frankness. He conferred on him at once the title of Heavenly Eternal Man.

The Khan was a seeker after wisdom. During the nine months which Chang Chun spent with him, first at Hindu Kush, then in Samarkand, he found time for many long conversations with the Master about the doctrine of Tao. Along with explanations about the nature of the Universe and the necessity of detachment from material things, the Master gave Jenghiz Khan a great deal of advice about the conduct of his life which the Khan received with gratitude and even humility.

One day the Khan had a mishap when hunting; his horse stumbled and fell after he had wounded a wild boar. When the Master heard what had happened he scolded the Khan and cautioned him to hunt as little as possible since he was far too old. He went on to explain that the fall from the horse was a warning, and that the boar's failure to gore him showed that the Khan had been saved by the intervention of Heaven. "Your advice is no doubt wise and good," Jenghiz Khan answered, "but it is hard not to hunt. We Mongols are brought up to ride and shoot arrows–a habit not easily given up. But I will take your advice to heart and from now on do as the Holy Immortal advises".

The Master also warned him against his carnal desires. "Try," he said, "sleeping by yourself for a month. You will be surprised at the improvement there will be in your spirits and energy." There was a great deal of political advice, too, some of it to us of a rather curious character. For instance, the Master said to Jenghiz: "I have heard that in order to avoid the wrath of Heaven, you forbid your countrymen during the summer to bathe in rivers, wash their clothes, make fresh felt or gather mushrooms. This is not the way to serve Heaven." The Master also said: "It is said that of the three thousand sins the worst is ill-treatment of one's father and mother. Now in this respect I believe your subjects to be greatly at fault and it would be well if your Majesty would use your influence to reform them." The Master continued to please the Khan. To a gathering of all the princes, including his sons and many high officials, he announced that "The Chinese reverence this Holy Mortal just as you revere Heaven and I am more than ever convinced that he is indeed a being from Heaven."

When Jenghiz Khan went on a campaign in the mountains of Afghanistan, the Master insisted on returning to Samarkand. He said that armies and fighting were not for him. Nevertheless, he could not altogether avoid the atmosphere of war. Unlike Mongolia or Singkiang, which were Tatar lands, the western provinces of the Mongol empire were enemy country, seething with revolt. The Master was given an escort of a thousand horsemen for his return to Samarkand. They passed at night through the great city of Balkh, once the rival of Nineveh and Babylon, and, under the Arabs in the twelfth century, still a great trading centre of the Middle East, and heard no sign of life except for the barking of famished dogs. Balkh had recently risen against the Mongols and all its inhabitants had been put to the sword.

In Samarkand the people were restless and parts of the city were often being set on fire by rioters. Before the Mongols took the city in 1221 it was said to have a population of over one million, with students from far afield coming to its renowned Moslem university. After the sack, which so often followed capture by force, barely a quarter remained alive. The Master was lodged in a palace on a hundred-foot hill in what was considered a dangerous quarter of the city. Asked if he minded living there, the Master answered: "The Man of Tao lets fate lead him where it will. How should he be in a panic about a rising that has not taken place?"

He loved the palace and the views from his upper room of snow-capped mountains. He loved walking in the gardens and shady groves laid out by Persian designers which surrounded the city to a depth of thirty miles in all directions. The writer of the travel diary gives some long decriptions of the Moslem inhabitants of Samarkand, including a, to us, quite commonplace description of the call to prayer from the muezzin. He also wrote: "There is one thing very strange about these people, some of the women have beards and moustaches."

In March, 1223, the Khan at last allowed Chang Chun and his party to leave for China, showing himself to the end eager to absorb Taoist wisdom. The Master refused all gifts; Jenghiz Khan thereupon exempted all the Master's disciples in Tatary or China from taxation for ever. The journey back was, of course, exhausting. The party arrived in Peking in January, 1224. The Master was to live for another three years in Peking. In his memory, Jenghiz Khan made over a part of the Imperial Gardens to a large Taoist monastery. The sources from which a non-Chinese reader, incapable of reading Chinese, can obtain a picture of Chang Chun do not present the Master with the vividness of an Saint Francis or a

Socrates. The great Taoist makes, on most of us, a shadowy impression although a charming one. At Bishbalig, in the course of his long and hazardous journey he wrote a poem, one of many, which seems to express the spirit in which he made his long and hazardous journey:

Suddenly in the sky heavy clouds massed,
And a tempest shook the leaves of the great tree;
You speak of voyages of ten thousand li;
Already we are come where the winter knows no chill.
Whether I live or die what matters it now?
Like thistledown, I will go where I am blown.

TO THE COURT OF KUBLAI KHAN
The Travels of Marco Polo

THE SITUATION which enabled Marco Polo to make his famous journey across the great spaces of central Asia to the court of Kublai Khan was a peculiar one which existed for about a century in the Middle Ages. He could not have made the journey before the thirteenth century and he probably could not have made it afterwards. It is certain that he could not have made it today.

The circumstances which made this great journey possible were created by the Mongol conquests of Asia and eastern Europe. Although the Mongol hordes ravaged the countries they invaded, and caused great terror, the subsequent empire into which they welded the subjugated territories—far greater in extent than that of Rome or Alexander the Great—was neither oppressive nor unenlightened.

Kublai, who became the Grand Khan of all the Tatars in 1259, was a wise and revered ruler with a love of culture and an inquiring mind. During the golden age when he ruled his vast domain, which stretched from the Black Sea to the Pacific Ocean and as far south as the Himalayas, the barriers between East and West were lowered, and for a few enlightened decades all of Asia was open to intercourse with western Europe. Representatives of every nation were invited to the court of Kublai Khan, and all the roads and

trade routes of Asia were open to travellers. A handbook for merchants, written by an Italian about the year 1340, said: "The road
you travel from Tana (a port on the Black Sea) to Cathay (northern
China) is perfectly safe whether by day or by night, according to
what the merchants say who have used it." This could hardly be
said for travel in Europe at that time. But under the Mongol Dynasty, which lasted until 1368, the roads were safe and the whole
of Asia was open. It was like a shaft of light between the dark centuries which went before and which followed.

A number of European missions of a religious and diplomatic
nature were sent to distant Cathay, among them William of Rub-
ruquis (or Rubrouck), a Franciscan friar who visited the court of
the Grand Khan at Karakorum in 1253.

About the year 1255, Nicolo Polo and his brother Maffeo went to
Constantinople. The Polos were wealthy traders descended from a
noble Venetian family. Nicolo was married and he had left his
wife with child. Their business took them to the Crimea. They were
away for fifteen years, during which Nicolo Polo's wife died, and
her son Marco—our traveller—passed his childhood in the mansion
of the Polo family at Venice. He was fifteen when his father
and uncle returned to Venice with a wondrous tale of travel to
tell.

From the Crimea they had travelled to Kazan, being prevented
from returning westwards owing to a Tatar war which had broken
out. In an attempt to circumvent the war which was raging across
the routes which led back to Constantinople, they had made a wide
detour which took them to Bokhara, well beyond the Caspian Sea.
Bokhara was ruled by a prince who was a direct descendant of
Jenghiz Khan. Unable to proceed farther, the Polo brothers were
forced to stay in Bokhara for three years, during which time they
thoroughly learned the Tatar language.

A diplomatic mission on its way from Persia to the court of the
Grand Khan, at that time near Peking, stopped at Bokhara. Kublai
Khan's envoys were greatly taken by the two Italian travellers
marooned in Bokhara, and they told them that the Khan very much
wanted to meet Italians, as he was greatly interested in the Christian religion of which Italy was the spiritual home. Nicolo and
Maffeo Polo were strongly pressed to accompany the envoys to the
Khan's court, where they were assured they would be honourably
received and recompensed with many gifts.

The journey was a full three thousand miles across deserts and mountains and was not one to be undertaken lightly, even by such inveterate travellers as the Polo brothers. But they were convinced that to return to Constantinople would expose them to risks far greater than those involved in this mammoth trans-Asian journey. They were curious, too, about the fabled wonders of the court of Kublai Khan, so they went with the envoys. The caravan travelled northwards to Otrar, and then in a north-easterly direction to Pekin. The journey took a year, the travellers being delayed by flooding and the snow-blocked passes in the Tien Shan mountains.

The Polo brothers were fêted when they got to the court of Kublai Khan. They were the first Latins the Khan had met, and this intelligent, inquiring and humane man was greatly interested in their country and particularly their religion. Kublai had been rather impressed by what he had seen of Christianity, and was shrewd enough to see the value of it politically and economically as a means of opening up his vast dominions to the culture and trade of Europe. He therefore proposed to the Polo brothers that they should go to the Pope at Rome as his ambassadors with a request that a hundred scholars should be dispatched to the Khan to instruct the Tatar people in Christianity and the liberal arts. He also asked for a quantity of the holy oil from the lamp of the Sepulchre of Our Lord in Jerusalem.

The Polo brothers were pleased to undertake the journey, and Kublai Khan furnished them with a royal tablet of honour, which not only guaranteed them safe passage and escort throughout the whole of his dominions, but also provided them with accommodation and provisions from the public funds such as they required for the whole of their journey.

The Khan's tablet, however, was no protection against the hazards of climate and terrain which they encountered on their return journey. Extreme cold, snow, ice and floods considerably delayed them, and it was three years before they arrived at the Armenian coastal town of Layas. They took ship to Acre in Palestine, where they arrived in April, 1269, to learn from the Papal Legate there that the Pope had died and his successor had not yet been chosen.

The two brothers then returned to Venice to await the decision of the College of Cardinals at Rome. There Nicolo found that his wife had died and that he was the father of a fine, manly son, Marco.

When young Marco heard the fabulous stories his father and his uncle had to tell, he begged to go with them on their return journey, and the fact that his wish was granted resulted in an historic book of travel which greatly advanced medieval Europe's knowledge of Asia.

There was an unusually long delay in electing the new Pope, owing to serious disagreements in the Sacred College. The Polo brothers waited for two years and, as there was still no Pope to receive the request of Kublai Khan, they decided to return to the East and report the failure of their mission.

And so, accompanied by Marco, they embarked again on the long journey to distant Cathay. They sailed from Venice to Acre in 1271. At Acre they went to the Papal Legate and obtained from him documents authenticating the delay and also his permission to get oil from the lamp of the holy sepulchre. Thus equipped, they set out by sea for Layas, then a great Armenian trading city from which merchants journeying to the East generally started.

The Papal Legate at Acre, embroiled in a crusade led by Edward of England, who had his headquarters at Acre, then heard that he had been elected Pope. The first thing he did was to take the style Gregory X. He then sent a swift messenger after the Polos commanding them to return so that he could fully satisfy the wishes of Kublai Khan.

The Polos hastened back to Acre in an armed galley furnished by the king of Armenia, and Gregory gave them letters papal to transmit to Kublai Khan. However, there were no hundred scholars prepared to journey across Asia in accordance with the Khan's wishes, merely two Dominican friars who were directed to accompany the Polos.

Gregory then departed from Acre to sit upon the Papal throne at Rome, and the English prince abandoned his crusade when he heard that his father, Henry III, had just died, and set out in state to occupy the English throne as Edward I.

The Polos returned to Layas. Armenia at that time was under attack from the armies of Bundokdari, the warlike Sultan of Egypt, who had already conquered the greater part of Syria. The two friars turned out to be faint-hearted, and fearing for their lives at the hands of Bundokdari's men, who slaughtered all Christians on sight, turned back. The theologians anyway had no stomach for the immense journey which lay before them. Delivering over to the Venetians their sacred mission and the Papal gifts and letters, the friars sought the protection of the Knights Templars who were stationed in Armenia.

Nicolo and Maffeo Polo were used to the dangers and alarms of Asian travel, and young Marco was inspired with a fearless sense of adventure. They pushed on and saw nothing of Bundokdari's men. At first they went north across the eastern part of modern Turkey. They passed Mount Ararat, where Noah's Ark was supposed to have rested. It is not clear whether they got as far as Trebizond on their outward journey, but hereabouts they turned south-eastward.

Here they heard stories of the oil-fields of Baku. The oil, says Marco Polo, was used as an "unguent for the cure of cutaneous distempers in men and cattle, as well as other complaints, and it is also good for burning". All the surrounding countries used oil-burning lamps and the Baku oilfields were a fruitful source of trade, then as now.

They now followed the course of the Tigris through Mesopotamia to the mouth of the Persian Gulf. This unnecessary detour leads one to suppose that they intended to make the journey to China by sea. It is probable that they took ship at the mouth of the Tigris, from which merchant ships regularly sailed to India, but they went only as far as Ormuz, on the southern coast of Persia. Here they met and talked with merchants from India.

They abandoned the plan of going by sea, probably because they considered the dangers greater than those of the overland route. The elder Polos knew Asia and were land travellers. The Ormuz merchants may well have taken them safely to India, and even the spice islands of what we now know as Indonesia. But the voyage from there to China was still long, perilous, uncharted and largely unknown. In any case the Venetians did not take a good view of the ships they saw at Ormuz, and considered them unseaworthy. They had no iron anchors, and used instead a kind of ground tackle, "the consequence of which is", said Marco, "that in bad weather–and the seas here are very tempestuous–they are frequently driven on the shore and lost".

They decided, therefore, to keep to dry land, and once more turned north towards the vast hinterlands of Asia. They crossed the terrible salt desert near Kerman, where the streams were liquid salt and where they travelled for days without seeing a sign of life. After a brief rest at the town of Kobiam, they crossed the Dasht-e-Kavir Desert and reached Damghan, in the most northern part of

Persia, a pleasant place separated from the unhealthy shores of the Caspian Sea by the Elburz mountains, and where the women, declared young Marco, were the most beautiful in the world.

Here, not inappropriately, he heard the story of the Old Man of the Mountains, the head of a fanatical sect of Assassins, who were young men who blindly obeyed their leader's orders to commit murder. The sect existed from the eleventh to the thirteenth centuries in Syria and Persia. Marco Polo's version was that this chief, whose name was Alo-eddin, kept a castle in the mountains where he had caused springs to run with milk and honey and where he kept many beautiful damsels. In order to alleviate the consciences of the young men who became his assassins, he had them drugged and transported to the castle where they enjoyed all the promised fruits of Paradise, after which they were drugged again and brought away. Thenceforth they were the creatures of Alo-eddin, for they had no reason to fear the hereafter in the service of a man who could send them to Paradise at will. So great was the resulting scandal of murder and rapine at the hands of these Paradise-intoxicated young assassins, that the Mongol rulers sent an army to destroy the Old Man of the Mountains, together with his castle and Garden of Paradise.

From Damghan the travellers turned east to Khorasan, the most north-easterly province of Persia, visiting the once magnificent city of Balkh, its marble palaces and spacious squares still in a state of ruin from the assault of Jenghiz Khan in 1221, when every one of its inhabitants were massacred.

The route now led through Badakshan, then an extensive kingdom which stretched across the upper reaches of the River Oxus (now the Amu Darya) between the mountain ranges of the Pamirs on the north and the Hindu Kush on the south. According to Marco Polo, Badakshan's royal family were directly descended from Alexander the Great and a daughter of Darius, King of the Persians. All of its kings bore the title of Zalkarnen, the Saracen form of Alexander.

Marco Polo, his father and uncle stayed for some time in Badakshan. Young Marco fell ill at this point of their mammoth journey, and declared that the pure mountain air of this salubrious country contributed greatly to his recovery.

It was months later when the party was ready to proceed on the most formidable and difficult part of their journey—the ascent of the Pamirs and the crossing of the great Sinkiang plateau. For weeks they travelled across the mountain passes–"where you might suppose the surrounding summits to be the highest lands in the world". The name Pamir for this vast mountain region was first used in Marco's book. No other European travellers went there again until the expedition of Lt. John Wood of the Indian Navy in 1838.

Having crossed the Pamirs, they descended to Kashgar, then went in a south-easterly direction along the southern edge of the Takla Makan desert to Khotan, a green oasis in the endless sands where Marco found farms, vineyards and pleasant gardens, and inhabitants who were industrious and unwarlike.

The great Gobi Desert now lay before them. Marco calls it the Desert of Lop, and he said that the town of Lop is situated "near the commencement of the great desert". It is clear that he passed the vicinity of Lop-Nor, whose lakes, fed by the Tarim river, have been shifting for centuries under the influence of wind and sandstorms. Marco Polo makes no mention of the famous lakes for the reason that they were probably not there in his day. It is believed that they were formed about 1750. After the Polos had passed through, it was six hundred years before another European reached Lop-Nor.

It took them thirty days to cross the narrowest part of the immense Gobi Desert, halting each night by the brackish ponds which made it possible for them to survive the passage of this terrible desert.

There were other terrors, besides thirst, and the awful sandstorms. The Gobi Desert was renowned for being the abode of many evil spirits "which bemuse the travellers to their destruction". Marco described the many weird and dangerous illusions which overtook travellers crossing the fearful wastes of Gobi–strange voices, the sound of marching cavalcades, unnerving music and the clash of arms. Travellers had been attacked by ghostly armed bands, taken flight and lost their way, afterwards perishing miserably of thirst.

Marco did not say whether his party experienced these assaults from the spirits of the desert, and the likelihood is that he copied his description from the account of the superstitious terrors of Suan T'sang who had crossed the desert six hundred years earlier. These stories were widely believed in this part of Asia.

Having crossed the great desert, they came to the upper reaches of the Hwang-ho and the Great Wall (which in the Polos' time was an ancient monument fifteen hundred years old), and found themselves in the middle of the greatest civilization they had ever seen. They quickly learned that the Grand Khan was at his summer pleasure palace at Kai-ping-fu, to which place they now eagerly directed their steps.

Their journey had taken three and a half years, and they had covered several thousand miles on foot. They had suffered delays of months at a time during the winter. Travellers across the roof of the world in those days were often held up for as long as four months at a time.

Over his vast dominions Kublai Khan had organized an efficient intelligence service, and he knew about the approach of the travellers, and had been kept informed of their progress, even when they were in the remotest part of his great empire. Their return had been long awaited, and as soon as they came within the confines of China proper he sent envoys to meet them, and in every place through which they passed they were received with honour and found every comfort awaiting them.

To be treated thus after the hardships and sufferings of their immeasurable journey, to find themselves the personal concern of this man, who was in his day the mightiest ruler on the face of the earth, created a deep impression in the minds of those tough, hard-bitten Venetians, the most travelled men of their time. By Kublai Khan they were received with more than the honour due to them as ambassadors from the Pope of Rome. At his summer palace he greeted them warmly, almost as friends, and he took a particular fancy to young Marco, a handsome, intelligent, prepossessing youth, as tough as nails, his clean-cut Latin face tanned like leather by the endless winds of high Asia.

Kublai Khan received the Pope's letters and the holy oil with due interest and reverence, but no mention was made of the hundred teachers he had asked for. He was pleased enough that the Polo brothers had returned, and was delighted to see young Marco. He immediately enrolled them in his imperial service, and gave them places of honour and importance in his empire. He expected them to stay, and for years they were happy to do so, becoming persons of wealth and distinction.

Marco in particular had great success. With complete mastery of more than one of the Tatar languages, he distinguished himself in the Khan's service. Kublai sent him on several important missions, chiefly in South-west China, and in his book his account of the vast stretches of smiling and prosperous country, with on every road excellent hostelries for travellers, of the fine vineyards and gardens, of the industries making cloth of silk and gold and fine taffetas, of the many splendid abbeys of the Buddhist monks, and the constant succession of cities and boroughs, was later read in Europe with wonder and incredulity.

When Marco Polo went to the East it was at its most splendid and most magnificent. He saw it in all its wonder, and the tale he had to tell remained a dream in men's minds for centuries.

His romantic narrative is dominated by the remarkable figure of Kublai Khan, for whom he felt something like reverence. Marco Polo makes Kublai a noble and splendid monarch, a king of legend. He made him live in history. But for these dusty Venetians who came to his court from the unknown after wandering across the world, Kublai Khan would be just another name in half-forgotten annals.

Marco Polo was sent on other missions to Karakorum, to India, Cochin-China, Japan. For three years he was governor of Yang-chow, where he probably impressed the Chinese inhabitants as being no more of a foreigner than a Tatar governor would have been. Chinese records state that a certain Polo was attached to the Imperial Council in 1277, a fact which has been taken as a confirmation of the general truth of the Polo story.

His father and his uncle also rendered great service to Kublai Khan, particularly in military matters. All of them became rich, and after seventeen years they began to think about returning home to Venice. Kublai Khan was in his late seventies, and they were greatly concerned about what would happen to them after his death. But Kublai would not hear of their going, and was even hurt at the suggestion.

However, a felicitous request from Persia came to their aid. Envoys arrived from Arghun, Khan of Persia, whose favourite wife, a relation of Kublai Khan, had just died, with the last wish on her lips that her place should only be filled by a lady of her own family. Arghun's envoys now begged the Grand Khan to grant Bolgana's dying request, and Kublai chose the Lady Kogatin, an accomplished and beautiful girl of seventeen, to go to Persia.

Tatar wars had broken out, making the overland route unsafe, and so it was decided to spare the lady both the dangers and the rigours of the caravan journey across Asia, and send her by sea. The Persian envoys then begged Kublai to let the three Venetians sail with them in the ships, "as being persons well skilled in the practice of navigation". Reluctantly Kublai Khan agreed. But he would only let them go after they had promised to return to him after visiting their homeland. When he bade them farewell, he loaded them with presents and jewels of great value.

The expedition sailed from Zaitum, probably the modern Changchow, in 1292, hugged the coast of China for a while to avoid the reefs, then crossed the Gulf of Tonkin to Cambodia. The ships then made for Borneo, where they stayed a while before proceeding to Sumatra. Another long delay, and then they got a fair wind which took them past the Nicobar and Andaman Islands to Ceylon. From here they hugged the western coast of India and arrived finally at Ormuz in the Persian Gulf.

The voyage lasted two years and involved considerable delays in Sumatra and South India. Two of the three Persian envoys and most of their suite died during the voyage. So did many of the crew. But the intended bride survived and only one of her female attendants died. This kind of mortality was not unusual in small vessels crowded with people unaccustomed to voyages of such duration and was experienced by European navigators of the seventeenth and eighteenth centuries. The long stops ashore were necessary in order for the passengers to recover from the rigours of shipboard life.

When they reached Persia they found that Arghun had died and the Lady Kogatin was delivered to his son and successor, who dutifully married her.

Nicolo, Maffeo and Marco Polo then set out for home, travelling through Persia to Tabriz and Trebizond. They had not gone far before they learned that Kublai Khan had died in 1294 in his 80th year. From Trebizond on the Black Sea they took ship and sailed home to Venice, via Constantinople and Negropont.

At the end of 1295 they arrived at their family mansion in the parish of St John Chrysostom, Venice, dressed in shabby, outlandish Tatar garb. Here their identity was scornfully denied by their relatives, and it was not until they had ripped the seams of their clothes and produced quantities of precious jewels that their relatives decided to acknowledge them, and they were finally received back into Venetian society.

Marco Polo immediately launched into another adventure which led directly to the writing of his famous book. Venice was at war with Genoa and the Polo family, being rich, was called upon to furnish and equip a galley. Marco sailed in command of the Polo galley. The Venetian fleet was defeated and Marco Polo taken prisoner to Genoa, where he languished in jail for three years, despite efforts to ransom him. During this time he dictated an account of his travels to a fellow prisoner named Rusticano, an author who came from Pisa.

Little is known of Marco Polo's life after he came out of prison. He is presumed to have died in 1324. He was nicknamed Marco Millioni on account of his wondrous tales of the East.

Though his book was disbelieved by his contemporaries, it remained for six centuries the chief authority for parts of central Asia and of the vast Chinese empire.

THE CHINESE CRUSADER

Rabban Sauma's Pilgrimage to Jerusalem

IT WAS not until the twelfth century, when the Crusaders discovered in the markets of the Middle East all the exotic luxuries of Cathay–spices, silks, ivories, perfumes and jewels–that Europeans really became interested in the world beyond their own limited horizons. In the year 1261, the Venetian merchants Nicolo and Maffeo Polo (the forerunners of Marco Polo) arrived at the court of Kublai Khan in Peking. Their coming was a great event. Kublai Khan, the powerful emperor of China, was intensely interested in these two visitors from the remote western lands, and he was also fascinated by Christianity. When, after spending several years in China, the Polos returned to Italy, Kublai Khan asked them to come back again and bring with them a hundred priests to teach the Christian religion.

The visit of the Polos and Kublai Khan's obvious sympathy towards Christianity may have been what inspired two Chinese Nestorian monks (followers of Nestorius, a disciple of St. Chrysolstom, Patriarch of Constantinople) to leave their homeland and make a pilgrimage to Jerusalem. Rabban Sauma, the elder of the two monks, was a man famed in China for his wisdom and piety. Mark, ten years younger, had been a pupil of Rabban Sauma for many years.

66

When they announced their plan, their Christian friends in Peking were horrified, for in those days such a journey was regarded as almost to the ends of the earth, with unimaginable hazards *en route*. But the monks were not to be dissuaded. Armed only with a safe-conduct note from Kublai Khan and a letter from their superior in Peking commending them to other Nestorians they might meet on their journey, the two determined pilgrims set off.

The account of Rabban Sauma's travels during the next fifteen years is laconic in the extreme, for he was far more interested in the holy places he visited and the unique relics he saw than in the dangers and difficulties of his itinerary. Regardless of hardship, he and his companion persevered towards their objective, Jerusalem, although they never actually reached it.

The travellers passed through the relative civilization of Kublai Khan's kingdom, where there were paved roads, with comfortable post-stations every twenty-five miles to provide fresh horses for the regular messengers and envoys of the Khan, where law and order prevailed and travel was swift and easy. They then entered a wild and difficult country of harsh terrain. It was essential to travel with the caravans, following the route which Chinese merchants had used for hundreds of years, for there was always the danger of attack by bandits and wild tribesmen. The caravans consisted of a hundred or more camels, horses and donkeys, and the travellers had to carry with them all the tents, food and water that they might need.

Slowly they made their way across hills and rivers, and the vast sand wastes and barren mountains of the Gobi Desert, where, it was said, spirits filled the air with strange and terrible sounds. At that time the rebellion of a petty chieftain had made the caravan trail even more dangerous, and had ruined and impoverished the oasis towns. And later, in the rugged territories north of what is now the Indian border, the constant danger from barbarous tribes was added to by marauding wolves.

In due course, exhausted but thankful, the two monks reached Khorassan, and here there were Nestorian monks to help them and monasteries where they could rest for a while. When they had recovered their strength they continued their long journey to Baghdad, the seat of the Patriarch of the Eastern Church. However, while travelling down the western side of the Caspian Sea the monks came to Maraghah, the capital of Azerbaijan, and were delighted to learn that the Patriarch was staying in the city at that time. He greeted the Chinese travellers kindly, and gave his gracious approval to their journey.

Jerusalem was still the ultimate destination, but the pilgrims made slow progress, for they took the opportunity to visit many holy places on the way. Though travel was easier now, the danger of attack or ambush by outlaws remained as great as ever. In addition, unforeseen diversions occurred to impede their advance upon the holy city, the first of which was initiated when they stayed for a while at the monastery of Mar Michael. Before they could depart, the Patriarch sent them on a special mission to Tauris, some two hundred miles north of Baghdad, to the court of the Tatar ruler of Persia, Abaga, King of Kings. Rabban Sauma and Mark were well qualified for such a mission for they were travelling under the protection of the great Kublai Khan; furthermore, they were familiar with Mongol customs and they could speak and write both Chinese and Persian.

Once the mission was accomplished, the pilgrims attempted once more to reach Jerusalem, but they were forced to return to Baghdad, for the route through Syria was unsafe. Although they made a long detour northward, through Christian Armenia and Georgia, with a view to getting a ship at a Black Sea port, they found that even this roundabout route was impassable because the mountains flanking the road were infested by murderous robbers, and only armed parties of travellers could hope to get through.

On their re-appearance in Baghdad, the Patriarch decided that they could be of greater use to him in helping to govern the Nestorian church in China, and accordingly they were promoted to high office. Despite their earnest desire to remain simple monks, Mark was renamed Yahbhallaha (meaning "God have him") and ordained as Bishop of Cathay and Mang, two districts in northern China, while Rabban Sauma, aged about forty-five, was ordained Visitor-General.

Thus honoured, but disappointed at not completing their long pilgrimage, the two men reluctantly started their return journey to China. But once again they were forced to retreat, for vicious fighting had broken out between Tatar tribes on both sides of the Oxus river which lay across their road, and the caravan routes were cut. They had no alternative but to go back to the monastery of Mar Michael, where they stayed and lived in peace for two years.

Almost at the time when they were planning to resume their homeward journey, the Patriarch died. Yahbhallaha (i.e., Mark, now aged thirty-seven) was unanimously elected his successor by his Fellow bishops, and the appointment was duly confirmed by King Abaga, who was friendly towards the Nestorians. But King Abaga himself died soon afterwards. His place was taken by his brother who, although baptised in the Nestorian faith, leaned towards Islam. When he was in due course actually converted to the Islam religion, he made a treaty with the Sultan at Cairo which so antagonized the powerful Mongols at his court that they revolted and overthrew him. The late King Abaga's son, Arghun, was placed on the throne.

The scene was now set for Rabban Sauma's historic journey into Europe at the instigation of his old colleague, Mark, now the Patriarch. The position was that although King Arghun's own inclinations were towards Buddhism, the Patriarch remained his best friend. Their experiences under Abaga's brother had given the Nestorians a foretaste of what could happen to them if Islam were to triumph. Apart from which the young king, like his father, longed to conquer Syria and Palestine, and capture Jerusalem. Such a conquest, he believed, vould only succeed if the western kings could be persuaded to start an offensive in the threatened Crusader kingdoms. By acting together they had a chance to destroy the Muslim wedge that separated them and was therefore a danger to them both.

So King Arghun asked his friend the Patriarch to suggest a wise man who could act as an ambassador and visit the western kings to seek their help. The Patriarch recommended his old friend Rabban Sauma, for he spoke the language; and Sauma expressed his willingness to undertake such an important diplomatic mission. The king then gave him letters of authority addressed to the kings of the Greeks and the Franks, together with personal gifts for the kings. He also gave Sauma gold worth about £1,000 for his journey, thirty riding animals, and a gold tablet inscribed with a warrant that the bearer was deputed to act for the king and should be treated by those he met as though he were himself royal. The Patriarch also gave him letters and gifts for the Pope, and, weeping, the two friends said good-bye.

Rabban Sauma set out on his journey early in 1287. Accompanying him were a number of priests and deacons from the house of the Patriarch. At the Black Sea he took a ship from Trebizond and spent the days of the long voyage preaching to the three hundred assorted passengers aboard. He amazed them all by his wisdom, and–one hopes–took their minds off the discomforts and, indeed, perils of the journey in the primitive ships of the day, the planks of which were stitched together with twine and smeared with redolent fish-oil instead of pitch, and which had no decks and only one sail.

At about Easter of that year, Rabban Sauma and his retinue arrived at the great city of Constantinople. The king, Andronicus II, sent his courtiers out to escort Sauma into the city and gave him a mansion in which to stay. Sauma then dined with the king, and after they had eaten he asked if he might be allowed to see the churches and shrines and other holy places and sights for which the city was famous.

The king handed Rabban Sauma over to a selected group of his nobles who were assigned to escort him on a tour of the city. They took him first to the Church of Divine Wisdom with its three hundred and sixty marble pillars and an enormous dome above the altar which, by its height and spaciousness, defied description. In this church Sauma was shown a picture of the Virgin Mary which Luke the Evangelist had painted, and also the hand of John the Baptist, and parts of the bodies of Mary Magdalene and Lazarus, who was raised from the dead. He saw also the stone which sealed off the entrance to Christ's tomb which even to that day, he was told, was still wet with the tears of Mary; the stone bowl in which Christ changed water into wine at Cana of Galilee; the stone on which Simon Peter was allegedly sitting when the cock crowed thrice; and the tombs of King Constantin and Justinian, and of over three hundred bishops whose bodies, it was said, had not suffered corruption because they had confirmed the true faith.

Sauma saw also many other shrines and religious relics. Then, having completed his tour, he set off for the territory of the Franks to fulfil his mission, taking with him gifts of gold and silver from King Andronicus.

The destination was Italy, and the sea journey lasted for two wearying months. Approaching Naples he saw a great mountain from which fire and smoke ascended–this, in fact, was the great eruption of Mount Etna which took place on 18 June, 1287. Sailing on through the sulphurous volcanic fumes, Rabban Sauma duly landed at Naples.

He presented himself to King Charles II, and was welcomed with suitable ceremony. At that time Charles was at war with King James II of Aragon, and one of Sauma's first entertainments as a holy visitor to Italy was to sit on the roof of the mansion to which he and his retinue had been assigned and watch a major naval battle in the Bay of Sorrento. What he thought about it is not known, except that he "admired the way in which the Franks waged war, for they attacked none of the people except those who were actually combatants".

From Naples Rabban Sauma and his company travelled northwards on horseback in the direction of Rome. During their journey they received the news that the Pope, Honorious IV, had died. This was depressing in the extreme, for it was part of Sauma's mission to discuss with the Pope the matter of Jerusalem, and whether it should be taken by force by King Arghun.

When Rabban Sauma called at the Vatican he saw the twelve cardinals who were administering the papal throne and engaged in the complex process of electing a new Pope. Although they greeted their eminent visitor cordially, they clearly had not the time nor the inclination to discuss Jerusalem on that occasion, even though Sauma was an ambassador of the Patriarch. His status had not made its proper impact.

However, three days later the cardinals sent for him, and questioned him about his mission and his position in the establishment of the Patriarch. They were astonished that a Chinese Christian should have come on such a long and difficult journey as the representative of the King of the Mongols. He told them the story of how the Christian religion had come to be established in the East, and mentioned the desire of King Arghun of the Mongols to take Palestine and Syria by force.

The cardinals, though impressed by Sauma's powers of persuasive argument, had neither the authority nor the inclination to make a political decision, particularly on the question of a religious war. They therefore decided to arrange a tour of the churches and holy shrines for Sauma and his colleagues, a diversion which they rightly supposed would be welcomed by Sauma. Although a high-ranking envoy, he was also very much of a tourist.

Rabban Sauma made the round of the many impressive spectacles and exhibits, some of which today might be regarded as of dubious authenticity. He visited the church of Peter and Paul, containing the tomb and throne of Saint Peter, and then the church of Paul the Apostle, with the tomb under the altar, and also the chain with which Paul was bound when he was dragged there. There, too, was the head of Stephen the Martyr, and the hand of

71

Ananias who baptized Paul. There was also the staff of Paul, and on the spot where Paul was martyred had been erected a shrine containing the bones of martyrs.

Visits to other churches followed, and the catalogue of holy relics grew longer and longer. Sauma was shown what was said to be the seamless robe of Christ; a piece of wood on which Christ had lain as a child; the dress of Miriam; the head of Matthew the Apostle, and parts of the bodies of various saints and martyrs. The tour continued with visits to historical buildings which were secular rather than sacred, and at the end of it Sauma and his party were exhausted as well as exalted. But the political matter of the fate of Jerusalem, which was the principal object of the mission, remained unresolved, for the cardinals had still not elected a new Pope and therefore could give no answer. Rabban Sauma asked permission to continue his journey.

The delegation journeyed north through Tuscany to Genoa, where a great throng of people, having learned that he was an ambassador of King Arghun, gave him an enthusiastic welcome. In Genoa there was no king and consequently no possibility of political negotiations, but there were the sights to be seen and, inevitably, Sauma and his party started on a new round of sight-seeing. In the great church of San Lorenzo they saw the body of John the Baptist in a silver coffin—even though they had already seen a piece of him in Constantinople. And they were shown the six-sided emerald platter off which Christ ate the Passover with His disciples. Various legends have been told of this dish, known as the *Sacro Catino*, which had been seized by the Genoese in Jerusalem in the year 1101, and all agreed that it was made of a single flawless emerald. But in 1809 Napoleon brought it to Paris, and in 1815 it was accidentally broken and found to have been made of opaque green glass.

From Genoa Rabban Sauma and his followers journeyed through the plain of Lombardy into France and the vast territories of King Philippe IV. They travelled on horseback along what were only the vestiges of roads, and stayed at the most primitive of wayside inns. Bandits proliferated, so that travel was dangerous as well as difficult. Rabban Sauma was astonished to discover that conditions in these western lands of which he had heard so much were so uncivilized compared with his Chinese homeland. The journey took four weeks.

King Philippe received Sauma with great courtesy, and gave him a house in which to live. Three days later he summoned him to court for talks. Sauma explained his mission, and the king promptly pledged his support. If the Mongols were prepared to fight against the Arabs for Jerusalem, then it seemed only right to him that the French should fight, too.

Sauma was no doubt very pleased to hear such a ready declaration of support. After the success of his mission to King Philippe he could continue his tourism with a clear conscience. His request for a guide was promptly granted. The king appointed a courtier to conduct Sauma and his party on a sight-seeing tour of France's ecclesiastical and cultural shrines and institutions, after which they were to return to the king who would show them his own personal holy relics which had been brought back from the Third Crusade in 1204.

For a whole month Sauma and his companions stayed in Paris. They were shown the famous theological schools in which thirty thousand pupils studied the holy scriptures, as well as philosophy, logic and the sciences, with financial support from the king. In the burial palace of the French kings they were awed by the magnificent tombs bearing gold and silver statues of the royal dead, with their crowns, robes and armour. In this great church five hundred monks were maintained by the king to perform continual commemoration services, with unending prayers and periods of fasting.

The vast number of people directly supported by the king in the interests of religion and culture seems to have impressed Rabban Sauma far more than the relics and curiosities that Paris had to offer, for these are barely mentioned in his account of his European travels. But after the Paris excursion was over, Sauma was summoned by the king, who gleefully informed him that he had not yet seen everything. The king took Sauma into an upper chamber of gold and produced a coffer made of transparent beryl in which was the Crown of Thorns which the Jews had placed on the head of Christ. (There were, at that time, about twelve such crowns circulating in Europe and the Middle East, all trophies of various Crusades.) Also in the coffer was a piece of wood from the Cross. The king explained that these holy relics had been brought to Paris after Constantinople had been taken and Jerusalem sacked in the Third Crusade.

Sauma and his retinue finally left Paris bearing costly gifts and apparel, and accompanied by a councillor who was to convey King Philippe's answer to King Arghun. Now their destination was

Bordeaux in Gascony, where the King of England, Edward I, had his court at that time.

Entering Bordeaux (and possibly they were the first Chinese who had ever been seen in that part of the world) they were welcomed first by the townspeople, who came out in throngs to greet the strangers from the Orient, and then by King Edward himself. This was as near as Rabban Sauma ever got to England. The king was overjoyed when Sauma presented his credentials and explained the purpose of his mission, for Edward was the last of the distinguished Crusaders. He said that the thought of Jerusalem was always foremost in his mind, and that he was pleased to learn that King Arghun had the same ideas on the subject as himself. In this mutual atmosphere of goodwill Sauma celebrated the Eucharist and then made his usual request for a guide to arrange a tour of the local churches and shrines. Burgundy, however, did not have much to offer in the way of holy relics. The king suggested to Sauma that he had already seen in the country of the Franks something which was more remarkable than any church or shrine or relic, namely, that, unlike in the East, there was only one religion and confession of faith, and that was the Christian.

Perhaps as compensation for the lack of sight-seeing opportunities, the king gave many gifts to Rabban Sauma as well as money for the long journey back to Rome to call on the new Pope.

The Sauma delegation stopped in Genoa and were so impressed by its mild climate that they decided to spend the winter there rather than go to Rome, where, as Rabban Sauma learned to his dismay, a new Pope had still not been appointed. It was not until winter was almost over, towards the end of February in 1928, that Nicholas IV was elected Pope. Sauma, who was still in Genoa, was summoned to Rome.

He set off immediately and arrived in Rome after a fifteen-day journey. There he was met by a bishop and a large company of escorts to take him straight to the Vatican for an audience with the Pope. Sauma was quite overwhelmed when he was finally able to complete his mission by meeting the Pope and presenting to him the gifts and letters of King Arghun and the Patriarch. The Pope in return paid Sauma the high compliment of asking him to stay on to keep the festival in Rome; it was then half-way through Lent. Sauma was given a mansion in which to live, with servants to look after him and his needs.

A few days later, Rabban Sauma was granted permission to

74

perform the Eucharist so that the Pope could witness the customs of the Christian church of the East. A vast congregation gathered to see how the ambassador of the Mongols would celebrate the mass. They found that though the language was different the usage was the same, and after Sauma had received the offering from the Pope's hands the rites ended in mutual satisfaction.

On Palm Sunday thousands of people attended the ceremony in which the Pope blessed olive branches and distributed them to the priests and the populace. Then, during mass, the Pope gave the Eucharistic mystery to Rabban Sauma first of all, who received the honour with tears and sobs. Later, on the day of the Passover, Sauma again attended the ceremonies in the Church of St John the Baptist and saw the Pope wash the feet of the people of his household. And all through the days of Easter, until Resurrection Sunday, Sauma and his companions attended the religious services and rites, observing the customs of the western church and sharing the festivals.

When the Easter ceremonies were over, Rabban Sauma asked the Pope for permission to return to his own people, but the Pope insisted that he wanted Sauma to stay in Rome, and promised that he would guard his guest "like the pupil of his eye". But Sauma, politely but firmly was equally insistent that he must return, having completed his mission, in order to present his report to King Arghun. He asked the Pope for some holy relics of the saints which he could take back with him.

The Pope explained that he was not in the habit of giving away relics to everybody who visited Rome, but since Rabban Sauma had come from a far country he would make an exception. So he gave him a small fragment of the apparel of Christ, a piece of the handkerchief of the Virgin Mary, and some small fragments from the bodies of the saints. He also sent to the Patriarch a golden crown inlaid with precious stones, a gown woven with threads of gold, sandals sewn with pearls, a ring, and a papal "bull" or edict authorizing him to exercise patriarchal domination over the East.

And to Rabban Sauma he also gave an authorization for him to act as Visitor-General over all Christians—and money for his return journey. Finally he gave Sauma gifts for King Arghun, then embraced his visitor, blessed him, and sent him on his way.

Thus Rabban Sauma returned to Baghdad, re-crossing the lands and seas he had traversed on his outward journey more than a year previously. He arrived to find King Arghun safe and well, and handed over to him all the letters and gifts he had brought from the Pope and the Frankish kings. He told Arghun the full story of his astonishing journey, stressing how warmly he had been received, and relating in detail his many visits to see churches, shrines and relics.

King Arghun was pleased and satisfied, and as a recompense for Rabban Sauma's arduous journey promised that he would not in future allow Sauma to leave him, and that he would build a church at the gate of his palace which Rabban Sauma would minister. The king commanded the Patriarch to come and receive the gifts which had been sent to him by the Pope—and at the same time to set up and consecrate the new church. And there Rabban Sauma remained and lived in peace for the rest of his days.

THE GREAT MISTAKE

The Triumph of Christopher Columbus

STRONG APRIL sunshine flooded the streets of Barcelona as thousands of boisterous, jostling townsfolk pushed and pressed their way into positions of advantage. There was an air of excitement, of carnival, as the trill of flutes and throb of drums showed that a procession was drawing near. It had been long awaited in the city for it had started from Seville, crossed Andalusia in the glory of springtime and then, having wound along the coastal road through Taragonna, had at last reached the outskirts of Barcelona where later, in the royal palace, it would proudly march past the king and queen of Spain.

There was a roar of cheering as the head of the procession came into view and the eager townspeople craned forward to see sights that no other Europeans had seen until this time. Some mounted soldiers were in the van and behind them came six natives, each wearing strange costumes with barbaric ornaments and with belts studded with polished fish bones and small pieces of gold. They were followed by attendants carrying bright-plumaged parrots in cages, strange plants and the skins of unknown animals.

Finally, leading a cavalcade of Spanish soldiers, rode the man who alone had made all this possible. He sat tall and dignified, his face only slightly tanned, his hair grey, although he was but a little over forty years of age. His light, piercing eyes moved from side to side as his horse carried him forward and a slightly cynical smile touched his lips, although he was obviously savouring every moment of this tumultuous welcome.

He had every right to do so, for if ever a man had been ridiculed by the foolish, deluded by false promises and dismissed as unpractical by the "wise" it was this man–Christopher Columbus.

This was his moment of triumph, the culmination of years of struggle and disappointment, of insults and poverty – years that stretched back to 1474 when he had first become obsessed with the idea that a western route to the Indies was practicable. The idea had come to him when poring over some maps and charts left to him by his father-in-law, one of Prince Henry the Navigator's captains, and from that moment nothing was going to stop him from proving his theory right.

As a loyal Genoese he had offered his scheme to Genoa, but his countrymen refused to listen to him. Then, confident that Portugal, anxious to find a new sea route to India, would give him a hearing, he went to that country and obtained an audience with King John II. He put forward his plan which, simplified, meant that he would sail *westward*, leaving Africa and Europe behind him, and would sail on until India and the Orient was reached. The king was impressed and the scheme was submitted to the royal councillors. The king was not satisfied with their unfavourable report and called a council of other "experts". This one decided to keep Columbus hanging about whilst they secretly fitted out a ship which would find out whether the theory was feasible.

The expedition was a failure and Columbus, furious at such treatment, left Portugal and went to live in Spain. Here, for eight long years, he tried to interest the royal court and, as an insurance, also sent his brother Bartholomew to England to similarly try to interest King Henry VII.

After a series of irritating delays, Columbus was summoned to Cordova where he gained an audience with Queen Isabella. Unfortunately the time was not opportune, for the united kingdoms of Castile and Aragon were involved in a bitter struggle against the Moors, and their wealth and energies were, for the time at least, fully devoted to obtaining a victory over the infidel. Even so, some interest was shown in the scheme and a council consisting of theologians, astronomers and savants discussed and dissected, summoning

Columbus before them on several occasions until his persistence and arguments finally persuaded them that there might be something in the scheme after all. He was referred back to the queen who, somewhat reluctantly, was forced to tell him that the time was not right for such a project.

Back where he had been eight years earlier, Columbus decided to leave Spain and try the court of King Charles VII of France. On his way out of the country he stopped at La Rabida to collect his eleven-year-old son from a monastery, and the friar, Juan Perez, pleaded with him to stay for a while until he himself could send an urgent message to the queen. Within two weeks a reply was received—Columbus was to report to the court once more. In August, 1491, he was before Isabella once more and was elated when told that the matter was at that very moment being dealt with by a committee which would, she felt sure, reach a favourable verdict.

After more weeks of waiting the blow fell with a crushing finality—the whole scheme was to be rejected once and for all. This decision was due, in part, to the fact that Columbus, irritated by the wasted years in Spain, was now demanding to be created admiral, to be made vice-ruler of all the lands he discovered, and to have one-tenth of all the profit that might be gained from the expedition.

For the last time, as he thought, Columbus quitted the Spanish court and took the road to Cordova and a ship for France. But a powerful voice was being raised on his behalf—that of Luis de Santangel, keeper of the privy purse. He told the queen that she was throwing away the opportunity to promote an enterprise that would be beneficial, not only to Spain but to the Holy Church as well, adding that if she still persisted in her refusal to help Columbus he would finance the whole thing himself.

The queen listened, was convinced, and yet another messenger went galloping after Columbus, summoning him back to court. This time he heard, almost with incredulity, that all his demands were to be met and that a squadron of three ships was to be made ready to sail from the port of Palos de la Frontera.

He went straightway to Palos, but found that the news of his enterprise had preceeded him and that no one could be found who was prepared to sail westwards with him where, or so it was said, lay the regions of perpetual darkness and even the edge of the world. Four months were to pass until, with pressed men, the tiny squadron of three diminutive ships was ready for sea. It consisted of the flagship, the *Santa Maria*, a ship of 100 tons and a crew of

50, commanded by Columbus himself, who had several officials with him whose presence gave royal authority to the expedition. The second ship was the *Pinta*, of 50 tons and a crew of 30, commanded by Martin Pinzon and his brother Francisco. The third was the *Nina*, a lateen-rigged vessel of 40 tons, a crew of 24, commanded by another brother, Vincente Pinzon, who, in later years, was to discover Brazil.

The three ships set sail on 3 August, 1492, on what was to become the most famous voyage in history. Their first landfall was to be the Canaries, but before they reached these islands the rudder of the *Pinta* began to give trouble. The ships anchored on 9 August but were delayed for nearly a month whilst repairs were made. At the same time, *Nina's* lateen rig was altered to a square one, more suited to the Atlantic crossing ahead.

The three ships took in water, stores and wine, and on 9 September, 1492, headed westwards into the unknown.

At first the voyage was very pleasant. The trade wind blew steadily, the sky and sea were blue and with little or no need for alteration of sails the men lounged about the deck in what was almost a holiday mood. The presence of birds, also, gave them the feeling that they were still quite near land. Then, quite suddenly, the atmosphere changed. The knowledge that they were sailing farther and farther in uncharted and unknown seas began to work on their superstitious minds and they began to grumble and complain.

At sunset on 25 September there came an excited shout from the *Pinta's* masthead—*"Tierra! Tierra!"*—Land, Land! This news spread around the squadron and everyone fell on their knees to sing a hymn in praise of God who had brought them safely to their journey's end. The ship's bows were turned towards the distant land and the men looked forward to the morning. At first light everyone was on deck and staring eagerly ahead. But there was no land. What had been seen was merely a cloud on the horizon which, at sunset, had the appearance of a solid mass—a common occurrence at sea.

The grumbling increased, provoked by the discovery that the compass had ceased to point to the North star and had changed to the westward. Then the wind dropped and, after drifting for several days, the ships ran into a floating bed of weeds, so thick that it was difficult for them to maintain steerage way. At this the men in the *Santa Maria* broke out into open mutiny and, advancing on the admiral, standing wide-legged and stubborn at the break of the poop, demanded that the ship be turned about and headed back towards Spain.

It was an ugly moment, but Columbus was able to calm his men by promising to do as they said if after three days land had not been sighted. In any case, he pointed out, with the easterly trade wind filling their sails again, and a steadily rising sea, the ships would not be able to follow a course for home.

The next day, 11 October, the wind had freshened and the sea was building up alarmingly. But signs of the proximity of land were becoming more and more plentiful–land birds were wheeling and calling overhead, a branch with berries still upon it floated past and, as if to clinch the matter, a little stick with a carving upon it which had obviously been fashioned by a human hand was fished out of the sea.

With the sunset, Columbus summoned his crew aft to promise them land very soon, ordering them to be particularly vigilant so that they did not run aground during the night. He then offered a silken doublet in addition to the reward that the king of Spain had promised to the first person to sight land.

No one slept that night. Columbus himself paced up and down his small poop, his eyes constantly turned to the west. At about ten o'clock he thought he saw a tiny light shining in the distance like a torch being carried by someone on shore, but his officers dismissed it as fancy.

At 2 a.m. on the morning of 12 October, under a bright moon, there came the shout which echoed through the squadron, *"Tierra! Tierra!"* This time there was no doubt–it really *was* land!

The fleet was plainly heading towards a lee shore and Columbus ordered all the ships to close up, shorten sail, and lay-to until morning light. When day broke at last there, ahead of them, was a low, tree-covered island. All signs of mutiny disappeared with the morning mist, the crew begged forgiveness and a hymn of praise and thanksgiving was sung. Soon, when the ships were close enough inshore, Columbus was ready to take possession of the New World on behalf of the kingdoms of Castile and Aragon.

There have been many claimants for the honour of being the first landfall to be made by Columbus in the New World, but today there is no doubt of its identity. It was an island in the Bahamas group, originally known as Guanahaní and now called San Salvador or Watlings Island. Lying to the east of Cuba, it is a coral island some 13 miles long by 6 wide and is situated 24 °N, longitude 74°30″W.

The boats were swung into the water and Columbus, richly dressed in scarlet, as befitted his new rank of Governor, was rowed ashore, and despite a crowd of naked people who peered inquisitively at the strangers from the undergrowth, kissed the beach, then erected the standard of Spain. The Pinzon brothers also put up their banners and after Columbus had named the island San Salvador the natives hesitantly came forward.

He named them "Indians", for he was confident that he had arrived at one of the islands in the fabulous Indies, a mistake he perpetuated when he named other islands in the group with the collective name of the "West Indies".

It was soon noticed that some of the natives were wearing golden ornaments and, in answer to their eager questions, the Spaniards were told by signs that the metal came from the south. Columbus was anxious to find the source of this precious metal. He was equally anxious to find a place that had more obvious signs of civilization and, two days later, he was at sea again, carrying with him some of the natives as guides, heading towards some other islands.

The ships slipped along under easy sail and reached a large island which Columbus named Santa Maria de la Concepcion (now Rum Cay). The ships kept raising other islands as they cruised through the Bahamas and, as each was reached, the inhabitants informed him that there was another island, still farther to the south, which had a king who was immensely rich and powerful. This person, Columbus decided, must be a great noble of Cathay—if not the king himself—and he set course to the south-south-west. On the morning of 28 October, a long range of mountains was seen ahead and the ships entered a magnificent harbour. The island bore the native name of Cuba, but he renamed it Juana in honour of the heir to the thrones of Castile and Aragon.

Columbus stared ashore at the lush greenery, his brows creased in doubt. If this was Cathay, where were the golden-domed temples and palaces? Where, indeed, were the elegant silk-clad ladies and gentlemen who should be waiting to greet their friends from overseas? There were no braying trumpets, or welcoming crash of cannons, only the singing of thousands of birds in the tall trees that lined the water's edge. Greatly disappointed, Columbus went ashore and found a few deserted fishermen's huts, a few strange yellow dogs that grunted instead of barked, and that was about all.

The squadron continued to sail around the island, exploring as it went, but the gold for which the men were now desperately seeking continued to elude them, although the guides, ever seeking to be helpful, kept promising that there was plenty "just around the corner". Columbus learned that a chief lived in the interior and sent off two of his men to pay a courtesy visit and to find out what they could. They returned with little to add about the whereabouts of the great cities spoken of by Marco Polo. They did, however, report an interesting and strange local custom. They had seen "several of the natives going about with Firebrands in their hands, and certain dried herbs which they rolled up in a leaf, and lighting one end, put the other in their mouths, and continued exhaling and puffing out the smoke".

They were the first white men to see tobacco in use.

The exploration—and naming—of the islands continued until, during the night of 22 November, the *Pinta* altered course to the eastward and was soon out of sight. The Admiral waited for the missing ship, then, realizing that Martin Pinzon had sailed off without orders, continued with the other two ships. He was not to learn until later that Pinzon had heard tales of a vast treasure in gold at Babeque (Great Inagua) and had sailed off to have first pick.

Columbus, furious at such insubordination, continued to sail amongst the islands and, on 5 December, sighted the bulk of Haiti. He was fascinated by its beauty, declaring the climate was like that of Cordova in May and its hills and valleys rivalling in loveliness those of Castile: so he called the island Española. Here he met and dined with a young king and decided that the island possessed more culture, if of a primitive kind, than any of the islands so far visited.

The two ships explored other parts of the island and then, on Christmas Eve, 1492, the officers and crews had their evening meal, sang a carol in honour of the occasion and retired to rest, leaving only the watch on deck. The night was dark and warm and soon almost all the watch were snoozing. Even the helmsman had handed over the tiller to one of the ship's boys, and settled down for a nap.

The *Santa Maria* was moving slowly along, the gentle wind barely filling her sails, the *Nina* some distance astern. Then, as midnight brought in Christmas Day, the flagship edged imperceptibly onto a coral reef. For a while the sleepy boy at the tiller did not appreciate what had happened; then, as he realized that the ship was no longer moving and that the pounding sound he heard was that of waves breaking on a reef, he gave a shout of alarm. The watch was soon awake and, as it stood irresolute, Columbus came running on to the deck. He saw at once what was to be done–the ship must be kedged off by dropping an ancher astern, then heaving at the cable by the main windlass.

He ordered the master, Juan de la Cosa, to take the anchor and cable into the ship's boat and drop the former into deep water, but the master ignored the order and the boat–it was the only one the flagship possessed–was rowed across to the *Nina*. Vincent Pinzon, the *Nina*'s Captain, was furious when he saw La Cosa coming aboard his ship and immediately ordered him back to the *Santa Maria* whilst sending his own boat to help.

The delay had proved fatal, however. Long swells, rolling in from the open sea, were driving the ship farther on to the reef, lifting her up with each surge, then letting her crash down again with a sickening thump onto the sharp-pointed coral. Soon the ship was holed in several places and water was flooding into her. Columbus decided nothing could be done until daylight and had himself and his crew rowed across to the *Nina* where, pacing the deck, he waited miserably for the dawn.

Christmas Day was spent in a desperate attempt to save the *Santa Maria* and to salvage her stores, much of the latter work being done by willing natives who set off from the island in their canoes. By noon it was obvious that the ship was a total wreck. Columbus was heart-broken at the loss, but still went ashore to thank the chief for the help his men had given him and, ironically, found that this place was richer in gold than any he had visited so far. Relations were so pleasant and cordial that Columbus decided to raise a settlement on the island and leave some of his men there until his next visit–for the *Nina*, with accommodation for about thirty men, could not accommodate the extra forty from the wrecked ship–and no one knew what had happened to the *Pinta*.

A fort and settlement were built and named La Navidad–in memory of the day on which the disaster had occurred–and on 4 January, 1493, and after touching farewells, the little *Nina* weighed and stood out to sea. Two of the forty men who stayed behind in this, the first settlement in the New World, were an Englishman named Tallarte, or Allard, and an Irishman who was entered on the ship's books as William of Galway. How these two adventurous seamen came to be at Palos when the squadron sailed is still a mystery. They may well have been amongst those "pressed" into service.

After several days' sailing a lookout cried out in amazement. Heading straight for them was the missing *Pinta*! Columbus was still angry at Martin Pinzon's desertion but restrained his temper, not wishing to cause more friction than necessary. He welcomed the other, listened to his lame excuses, and the two ships turned for home in company.

Five weeks later the ships ran into the first real storm of the expedition, the little vessels began to be tossed and battered by the pummelling waves, pitching and rolling under bare poles, shuddering under the tons of water that came crashing on to their decks. They finally lost sight of each other during the night of the 14th and the *Nina* struggled on alone until, after days and nights of great peril, she limped into the deceptive shelter of the Portuguese harbour of Santa Maria in the Azores. Deceptive it was indeed, for when half of the *Nina*'s crew were kneeling in the church ashore to give thanks for their deliverance, they were taken captive by an armed body of men. Columbus was making plans to rescue them when his cables parted and he was forced to run before a rising storm. He managed to claw his ship back to the island however, and prise his men out of the grasp of their captors.

Another storm met him when on course for home, and unable to make a Spanish port he was forced to run into the Portuguese harbour at the mouth of the Tagus. There was irony in the fact that the Portuguese should be the first to learn of the success of the expedition which could well have been accomplished under their own flag, had not their king rejected Columbus's overtures.

The storm-battered *Nina* came to ancher in the outer harbour of Lisbon and a few days later the Admiral received an invitation from the king of Portugal to visit him and tell him of his adventures. Some of the courtiers whispered to their royal master that Columbus should be assassinated before he was allowed to return to his ship, but the king refused, although he was sufficiently angry with himself to exclaim, "Why did I let slip an enterprise of so great importance?"

Columbus returned to his ship to find that his crew had been working hard during his absence and had repaired most of the storm damage. They sailed on 13 March, and at midday on Friday the 15th entered the harbour from which they had set sail thirty-two weeks earlier. Unknown to them, almost in their wake came the *Pinta,* and as Martin Pinzon brought his ship round the promontory that guarded the harbour there before him lay the *Nina,* swinging gently at her anchors.

A few days later Columbus received a letter from the king and queen which began: "Don Christobel Colon, Admiral of the Ocean Sea, Viceroy and Governor of the Islands that he hath discovered in the Indies."

A great moment of triumph; a moment that must have made the years of frustration and waiting seem worth while.

THE NEW-FOUND LAND

John Cabot, Merchant and Explorer

GIOVANNI CABOTO or more familiarly, John Cabot, was first and foremost a merchant, for ever seeking new ways to encourage and increase international commerce. He was born in Genoa but, when 21, moved to Venice, one of the great trading centres of the world, and at that time in control of all the eastern Mediterranean trade. Her title of "Mistress of the Sea" was no idle boast and Cabot, wishing to gain first-hand experience of the steadily growing markets, began to visit neighbouring countries to investigate conditions and assess their potential. He also visited Mecca in Arabia, the great trading centre where goods from the West and the Orient were collected and exchanged.

Cabot studied the writings of Marco Polo and Sir John Mandeville, who had both described the glories of the Celestial Land, its immense cities, its gold-roofed palaces, and the great wealth that it possessed. He knew of the vast distances that the goods had to travel by the overland route and began to consider how these long and arduous routes could be shortened and the inconvenience of the middlemen obviated. His voyages had given him considerable navigational experience and, seated in his house in Venice, and with the primitive and highly imaginative maps of the time spread before him, he came to the logical conclusion that ships reaching the Far East by a voyage to the *west* would bring the centres of trade closer and more economically together.

Like his contemporary Columbus, however, his schemes met with a cool response in his own country. In 1484, when he was in his mid-thirties, he sold his house in Venice and, with his family, came to England–the home of the "nation of shopkeepers" who, he hoped, would more readily appreciate his plans. He settled in Bristol, and very soon this young and earnest foreigner was introducing something that the seaport had lacked until then: an appreciation of the new ideas concerning exploration that were spreading along the Mediterranean coast, and a sense of the adventure–and profits–that such dreams aroused.

His personal knowledge of the fabulous spice islands of the Orient, and his skill in map-reading and navigation, kept his audiences enthralled, and promising financial support. Considerably encouraged, for he had had nothing like this in his own country, he began to finalize his plans. His course was quite different to that of Columbus, for he laid out one that lay close to the 60° meridian which, because of the curvature of the earth, was a much shorter route than that which Columbus planned across the 30° meridian.

The project was beginning to take shape when Henry VII visited the city on a tour in 1496. Cabot was presented to him and had an opportunity to put forward his plans. Henry was impressed and Cabot soon afterwards received letters patent which authorized him and his three sons to sail in the "Eastern, Western and Northern Seas" and the right to discover "Isles, Countries, Regions or Provinces of the Heathen and Infidels which before this time have been unkown to all Christians". The Cabots were promised that they would have the undisputed right to trade with any lands that they discovered, provided they took possession of them in the name of the King of England and that all merchandise was brought in by the port of Bristol. Not for nothing had King Henry earned a reputation as the craftiest and stingiest prince in Europe. He contributed nothing towards Cabot's expedition except the effort of appending his seal to the letters patent, yet he assured himself of increased revenues and new territories should it prove successful.

News of Columbus's successful voyage on behalf of Spain gave impetus to the English expedition. Other merchants contributed what was outstanding and a ship was made ready. Cabot's original plan had not been influenced by what he had learned from Spain. He was sure that Columbus had not reached the mainland but had stopped at some islands well away from the shore—an appreciation that was later proved correct. Cabot also believed that the nearest part of Cathay was opposite Britain and that the shortest route would be straight across the ocean—winds and currents permitting! He also estimated that from that point the continent bore away to the south-west, well beyond those islands discovered by Columbus. It was his intention, once he had made a landfall, to follow the coast towards the equator, sailing *between* the mainland and the islands that Columbus had christened the West Indies.

On 2 May, 1497, the little *Matthew* set sail from Bristol. She was no larger than a fishing smack and had a crew of only eighteen men, but she was making history, for she was the first English ship to cross the Atlantic.

The passage westwards was very stormy but otherwise un-eventful, the small ship rolling violently in heavy seas, the masts showing but a bare scrap of canvas and her crew soon exhausted from days and nights of misery. Land was sighted on the morning of 24 June, a blessed sight to the weary men. Cabot had reached the coast of North America, the first European to do so since the days of the Vikings, of Lief Ericsson and his brother Thorwald, who had first sighted Labrador (which they called Hellu-land), Nova Scotia (Nark-land) and the area around Boston (Vinland).

Cabot named his first landfall Prima Vista, or First Seen, and was rowed ashore to stand on what is now Cape Breton Island and to take possession of it in the name of King Henry and of England. He then took his ships across to the larger island which he named New-found-land and then, turning north, cruised along the coast of Labrador.

He sailed in what is now Cabot Straight and did a great deal of naming, although nearly all his names have since been changed. His "christenings" include Cape Discovery (now Cape Ray), the Trinity Islands (St. Pierre and the Miquelons) and England's Cape (Cape Race).

He returned to England in triumph and was soon in London, recounting his adventures to Henry VII. He was confident that he had reached the mainland of Asia and visited the territory of the Grand Khan. Whilst in London he was visited by the Venetian ambassador, who later wrote to the Doge, saying: "Our Venetian, who sailed from Bristol some while ago in a small vessel, is now back and relates that he reached the continent under the sovreignty of the Great Khan seven hundred Italian miles away. He sailed along three hundred miles of the coast of this land and saw no man. Nevertheless he gave the king of that place several traps for catching wild beasts and a needle for making nets. Moreover he found trees bearing notches. From this he concluded that the territory is not uninhabited.

"For reasons of prudence he re-embarked. He was away three months. This is reliable. He lives in Bristol with his wife and sons. He bears the title of Grand Admiral and is treated with great honour. He dresses in Silk and the English run after him like fools. He, however, wants nothing to do with them. The discoverer of this territory hoisted the English flag there, but also the flag of St. Mark, since he is a Venetian. So our banner has been planted in a far-off land."

The Spanish ambassador must also have reported to *his* master for, very shortly, he was examining maps prepared by Cabot and declaring them to be entirely false. What Cabot had discovered lay well within that territory already discovered by Columbus and which now was the proud possession of Spain. Henry VII, for his part, chose to ignore the protest and, generous as ever, awarded Cabot £10 for his discoveries although he subsequently made him an admiral and granted him an annuity of £20. No doubt the king was impressed with Cabot's promises that on his next voyage he would find the rich islands of the Orient, and that gold, pearls and spices would soon be pouring into the port of Bristol. Cabot had, as it happened, already given concrete proof of the wealth of the new land, for, during the first voyage, they had sailed through waters teeming with fish that could be caught simply by lowering weighted buckets over the side and scooping them up. This in itself was a worthwhile discovery, for England had become dependent on Iceland for much of its fish.

The new expedition got under way, and there was no lack of support for the venture. Merchants were anxious to invest in something that would bring the wealth of the Orient tumbling into their coffers. The king, eager as the rest, issued new letters patent on 3 February, 1498. This time, Cabot decided, the expedition would be mounted in style, and he travelled to Lisbon and Seville to sign on experienced navigators. At home, London provided a large ship, Bristol four more.

Cabot set out again in May, 1498, commanding the squadron of five ships and about three hundred men. Out in St. George's Channel they ran into a storm. One of the ships was almost dismasted and had to make for the safety of an Irish anchorage. The remainder fought their way to the latitude of northern Scotland, then steered north-westward until the coast of Greenland loomed up early in June. Cabot then led his ships north-eastward until great masses of ice forced him to turn southwards along the coast. He passed the southern tip of Greenland, then moved through the Davis Strait and into Baffin Bay. He traded with natives on the coast of Labrador, of whom a chronicle said:

"The inhabitants of this Island used to wear beasts skinnes, and have them in as great estimation as we have our finest garments. In their warres they use bowes, arrowes, pikes, darts, woodden clubs, and slings. The soil is barren in some places, and yieldeth little fruit, but it is full of white bears, and stagges far greater than ours. It yieldeth plenty of fish, and those very great, as seales, and those which commonly we call salmons: there are soles also above a yard in length: but especially there is a great abundance of that kind of fish which the natives call baccalos (cod). In the same Island also there breed hauks, but they are so blacke that they are very like to ravens, as also their partridges, and eagles, which are in like sort blacke."

Cabot continued cruising to the south, missing the Gulf of St. Lawrence and, not surprisingly, quite unable to discover the oriental trade route. Finally, as his supplies were running low, he turned back when in the latitude of Chesapeake Bay. From that moment he disappears from history. A contemporary historian, Polydore Vergil, states that Cabot and his ship went down with all hands, but there is no mention of the other four ships of the expedition. Perhaps the flagship was wrecked and Cabot himself was rescued to return to England in another ship, but at this period of time no one can say with any accuracy. What is definite, however, is that the voyage seemed to be a complete failure to the promoters of those days who were interested only in profits, not in geography!

The tremendous importance of his discoveries became apparent later when England was able to claim the whole of North America on the ground that John Cabot was the first European to reach the mainland and had claimed it in the name of the kingdom of England.

Cabot's work was carried on by his son, Sebastian, who became a renowned navigator and map-maker. His career, however, was more spectacular—and certainly more exciting— than that of his father. When still young he accompanied the English army, which had been sent by Henry VIll to the aid of his father-in-law, Ferdinand of Aragon, to fight the French. Whilst there, Sebastian's voyages with his now famous father became known to Ferdinand's councillors and he was appointed a captain in the navy of Aragon.

He later returned to England and was offered the command of five ships by Cardinal Wolsey to explore the coast of Newfoundland but declined the offer and went instead to Spain where he was appointed commander of an expedition to discover "the Moluccas, Tarsis, Ophir, Ciphango and Cathay".

He sailed with three ships in April, 1525 and two months later was off the coast of Brazil. Here he met three Spaniards who gave him such a glowing account of the riches of the country that he immediately abandoned the search for the Moluccas and the rest and spent some months exploring the area. On his return to Spain he was tried for neglecting his duty and banished to Oran in Africa. He returned after three years in exile and ended his days in England where he became a Governor of the Merchant Adventurers under Edward VI, and did much to open trade between England and Russia.

THE DISASTROUS VISIT OF JOHN
HAWKINS TO SAN JUAN DE ULUA

ON GOOD FRIDAY, 1519, the Spanish adventurer Hernan Cortes
had the good fortune to be taken for a god. Mexican prophecy had
foretold that a great god would arrive in that year, sailing in from
the east: he would have a pale complexion and be dressed in black:
the day of his arrival would be a special one in the Mexican
calendar, a day somewhat like our 29th of February, styled a "Nine
Wind Day in a One Reed Year".

In 1519, the Day fell on 22 April. So did Good Friday, when
every devout Spaniard would be wearing black, and it was on this
day that Cortes disembarked, with his handful of men. He was
immediately taken for the great god Quetzalcoatl: a little later,
Mexico was his.

The harbour at which he landed was given the Spanish name of
San Juan de Ulua. In a few years' time it had became a busy New
World port, jealously guarded by an Old World power, with a
Pope's blessing.

After his dramatic exit mary years later, from this same San Juan
de Ulua, John Hawkins wrote:

"If all the miseries and troublesome affairs of this sorrowful voyage should be perfectly and thoroughly written, there should need a painful man with his pen, and as great a time as he had that wrote the lives and deaths of the martyrs."

It was toward the close of the year 1567 that Hawkins had set out from Plymouth, in command of a slaving expedition to West Africa. He had already acquired the dubious reputation of being the first Englishman to traffic in slaves and would later achieve the pleasanter one of being knighted by his queen for bravery against the Spanish Armada.

The Armada, for John Hawkins, was merely the settling, by him, of an old, old score.

But the first disaster that befell him on his slaving expedition had nothing to do with Spaniards. His little fleet had only been at sea for seven days when a terrible storm struck it and sank the largest ships. The survivors, of which the *Jesus* was the only vessel of any size, set course for home, hoping to reach there before that ship also disintegrated and sank.

Yet, after four days on the homeward journey, the weather changed so dramatically for the better that they decided to resume their original journey: they would repair the *Jesus* themselves, on the African coast.

Luck—for a brief spell—was with them, and they were able to patch her up in a convenient harbour of one of the Canary Islands, at the same time taking on food and water. They then sailed southward to the Cape Verde Islands and thence to the mainland cape from which they take their name, a promontory now the site of the port of Dakar, in Senegal. Here they landed a hundred and fifty men—and their troubles began all over again. The negroes they tried so unsuccessfully to capture were more than a match for Englishmen: their arrowheads were tipped with filth to infect flesh with the dreadful disease of tetanus, and John Hawkins's account of the symptoms is probably the first in medical history: "The hurt and damage to our men chiefly proceeded of their envenomed arrows: and although in the beginning they seemed to be but small hurts, yet there hardly escaped any that had blood drawn of them, but died in strange sort, with their mouths shut some ten days before they died, and after their wounds were whole; where I myself had one of the greatest wounds, yet thanks be to God escaped."

There were at this stage six vessels surviving the original storm: the *Jesus*, and five smaller. These now continued down the coast of West Africa, putting occasional parties ashore to buy or capture negroes. The intention was, even now, to gather at least five hundred of these unfortunates, then sail as swiftly as wind and weather permitted to the West Indies, selling the human cargo at a profit before heading for home. But by the twelfth of January in the new year, 1568, they had picked up rather less than a hundred and fifty, and were considering a search for gold instead.

"But even in that present instant, there came to us a negro, sent from a king, oppressed by other kings his neighbours, desiring our aid, with promise that as many negroes as by these wars might be obtained, as well of his part as of ours, should be at our pleasure: whereupon we concluded to give aid, and sent one hundred and twenty of our men which, the 15 of January, assaulted a town of the negroes of our ally's adversaries, which had in it eight thousand inhabitants, being very strongly impaled and fenced after their manner, but it was so well defended that our men prevailed not, but lost six men and forty hurt: so that our men sent forthwith to me for more help: whereupon considering that the good success of this enterprise might highly further the commodity of our voyage, I went myself, and with the help of the king of our side, assaulted the town, both by land and sea, and very hardly with fire (their houses being covered with dry palm leaves) obtained the town, put the inhabitants to flight, where we took two hundred and fifty persons, men, women and children, and by our friend the king of our side, there were taken six hundred prisoners, whereof we hoped to have had our choice: but the negro (in which nation is seldom or never found truth) meant nothing less: for that night he removed his camp and prisoners, so that we were fain to content us with those few which we had gotten ourselves."

But those few brought the total up to between four and five hundred: they decided to head west, make a quick sale and get home.

They left the African coast on 3 February, and after a long and hard journey sighted the island of Dominica in the West Indies. They sailed from island to island, selling a dozen slaves here, twenty there, and making a reasonable profit despite the strict order which had gone out from the King of Spain, forbidding any of his subjects to trade with Englishmen. At almost every port of call the Spaniards seemed friendly, anxious to do business: at Rio de la Hacha, however–a town which Hawkins describes with a fine, inaccurate, flourish as the one "whence come all the pearls"–they ran into a spot of difficulty. The Spanish commander refused to allow them to take on food and water, or to disembark: he trained the arquebuses of a hundred men against the English ships. His intention, Hawkins surmised, was to force them, by starvation, to put the negroes on shore, a free, unsolicited, gift from England.

The Spaniard might have achieved this design, for water in particular had run dangerously low, but Hawkins decided to open fire and land his men. He did so, and with a landing party of two hundred look Rio de la Hacha, "with the loss of only two men of our part, and no hurt done to the Spaniards because after their volley of shot discharged, they all fled".

The vanquished garrison maintained (as vanquished garrisons do) that the whole thing had been an embarrassing mistake. No one had any idea who gave the order to resist an English landing: Englishmen, particularly these splendid fellows here, were the friends of Spain; all those who fired upon them would be punished and any man who raised his hand against an Englishman would be shot, with the blessing of King and Pope. And in the meantime, they would like to buy two hundred negroes.

His stock almost exhausted, a tidy profit in hand, Hawkins decided on 24 July to set sail for England. He hoped that by leaving then they would avoid the worst of the late summer storms which afflict that region.

Once again they were mistaken. On 12 August they encountered an appalling storm; leaks appeared in all six vessels and the *Jesus* lost its mast. At this point they were somewhere between the north coast of Cuba and the southern tip of Florida, heading east: there was no chance of getting across the Atlantic without considerable repair, and they made for the coast of Florida.

But there "we found no place nor haven for our ships, because of the shallowness of the coast: thus, being in greater despair, and taken with a new storm which continued other three days, we were forced to take for our succour the port which serveth the city of Mexico, called San Juan de Ulua, which standeth in 19 degrees."

They arrived there 16 September.

The local Spanish garrison, believing them to be a part of the Spanish fleet, cheered as the six vessels sailed in and dropped anchor. A party of important men went aboard and were "greatly dismayed" to find they had made a foolish mistake–and greatly relieved at finding themselves not clapped in irons.

(The early history of Mexico is studded with these jewels of misapprehension: from the deification of Cortes to the Latinizing of Hawkins, via a whole series of muddled comings and goings.)

Hawkins explained that he had come for repairs and victualling. As the Spanish fleet, for which he has already been mistaken, was expected any day, he made haste to secure the goodwill of the Governor of Mexico, two hundred miles inland in his mountain capital. He sent two men to Mexico City, craving permission for a stay long enough to complete his repairs, and assured the King of Spain of his friendship. He requested that there should be no misunderstanding on this score when the larger Spanish fleet arrived.

And arrive it did, the very next morning. Thirteen great ships appeared, each of them dwarfing the crippled *Jesus*, largest vessel of Hawkins's six. It would require many days for a message to come back from Mexico City, so Hawkins "sent immediately to advertise the General of the fleet of my being there, doing him to understand that before I would suffer them to enter the port, there should some order of conditions pass between us for our safe being there, and maintenance of peace. Now it is to be understood that this port is made by a little island of stones not three foot above the water in the highest place, and but a bow-shoot of length any way; this island standeth from the mainland two bow-shoots or more, also it is to be understood that there is not in all this coast any other place for ships to arrive in safety, because the north wind hath there such violence, that unless the ships be very safely moored with their anchors fastened upon this island, there is no remedy for these north winds but death".

A reply came back from the "General" of the Spanish fleet, agreeing, with the utmost courtesy, to the English conditions. Indeed, the Spaniards claimed to have had good report of Hawkins's honest behaviour towards the inhabitants of the West Indies, and they professed gratitude. They agreed to exchange hostages, and to regard the small island in the harbour as English territory for the duration of the English fleet's stay. After three days of amicable discussion the Spanish fleet sailed, salutes being exchanged.

Yet Hawkins had doubts. Quite a number of men seemed to be embarking from the mainland into the Spanish vessels, rather than the reverse, and as he watched his suspicions mounted. The date was Thursday, 23 September.

"The same Thursday, in the morning, the treason being at hand, some appearance showed, as shifting of weapon from ship to ship,

97

planting and bending of ordinance from the ships to the island where our men warded, passing to and fro of companies of men more than required for their necessary business, and many other ill likelihoods, which caused us to have a vehement suspicion, and therewithall sent to the Viceroy to enquire what was meant by it, which sent immediately straight commandment to unplant all things suspicious, and also sent word that he, in the faith of a Viceroy, would be our defence from all villainies. Yet we being not satisfied with this answer, because we suspected a great number of men to be hid in a great ship of 900 tons, which was moored next to our *Minion*, sent again to the Viceroy the master of the *Jesus*, which had the Spanish tongue, and required to be satisfied if any such thing were or not."

And now the Viceroy, seeing that his treason is about to be discovered, gives the order. Most of the Englishmen are ashore on the little island and the whole Spanish fleet opens up on them with its ordinance, while Spanish soldiers, who have been secreted aboard the ships, wade through shallow water to the island and proceed to hack up the greatly outnumbered English.

The nine-hundred-tonner, which has had three hundred men secreted in her hold, now bears down upon the far smaller *Minion*, but in the half-hour which has elapsed since English suspicion was first roused the *Minion* has been made ready for sea: she is able to avoid capture and to slaughter a great many Spaniards on the decks of the larger ship.

The Spaniards board the crippled *Jesus*, hundred upon hundred of them struggling aboard under artillery support from other Spanish ships. Yet somehow these are repulsed, and though the English ship has been still further crippled by artillery fire from the island (which the Spaniards captured at the outset) she manages to get clear.

It is a remarkable testimony to English seamanship and courage that within a few minutes of Hawkins having got both the *Minion* and the *Jesus* a few lengths clear of the Spanish fleet, these two badly damaged vessels have sunk the two largest Spanish vessels and a number of smaller ones. But while this is going on, more and more damage is being done to the *Jesus*: Hawkins decides he must abandon her and transfer men and armament to the other, smaller ship. He manoeuvres the bigger vessel so she lies, a battered hulk, between the *Minion* and the frantically firing guns on shore.

Suddenly he sees two huge Spanish ships, blazing from stem to sterm, being headed in his direction.

There is panic for a moment, but the *Minion* is manoeuvred out of the way of the flames. She drifts away, heavily overloaded and followed by a still more heavily laden long-boat with survivors from the abandoned *Jesus* who have not been able to get aboard. The *Minion* and the still smaller *Judith* are now the sole British survivors of six ships which entered San Juan de Ulua and the much greater fleet which left Plymouth painful months ago.

Night falls: the *Judith* disappears. The next day a strong wind seizes the *Minion* and, though it nearly wrecks her, she gets safe out of the harbour, into the open sea.

"Having a great number of men and little victuals, our hope of life waxed less and less: some desired to yield to the Spaniards, some rather desired to obtain a place where they might give themselves to the Infidels, and some had rather abide with a little pittance the mercy of God at Sea: so thus, with many sorrowful hearts we wandered in an unknown sea by the space of fourteen days, till hunger enforced us to seek the land, for hides were thought very good meat, rats, cats, mice and dogs, none escaped that might be gotten. Parrots and monkeys that were had in great price, were thought there very profitable if they served the turn one dinner: thus in the end, the 8 day of October we came to the land in the bottom of the same bay of Mexico in twenty-three degrees and a half, where we hoped to have found inhabitants of the Spaniards, relief of victuals and place for the repair of our ship, which was so sore beaten with shot from our enemies and bruised with shooting off our own ordinance, that our weary and weak arms were scarce able to defend and keep out water. But all things happened to the contrary, for we found neither people, victual nor haven of relief, but a place where, having fair weather, with some peril we might land a boat. Our people being forced with hunger desired to be set on land, whereunto I consented."

Only two hundred men have survived the disastrous year, two hundred out of thousands, and half these now demand to be left on this alien coast, rather than attempt the voyage back to England in an overloaded, under-victualled, badly damaged ship. Hawkins agrees and a hundred men are ferried ashore to vanish in the undergrowth.

The next day Hawkins himself lands, with fifty of his remaining hundred men, to carry back water for the ship. There is little enough to eat, but they manage to kill a few small animals and gather some unappetizing plants a mile inland.

And once again storm strikes. For three days Hawkins and his fifty are marooned ashore, unable to regain their ship, certain every hour that she will be dashed ashore and wrecked.

"But yet again God had mercy on us, and sent fair weather, we had aboard our water, and departed the sixteenth day of October, after which day we had fair and prosperous weather till the 16th day of November, which day God be praised we were clear from the coast of the Indies, and out of the channel and gulf of Bahama, which is between the Cape of Florida and the islands of Lucayo."

God has been briefly merciful to them, but soon they are back in a cold northern climate; and as October, 1568, gives way to November, men start dying of famine and disease. The wind alters dramatically, making it all but impossible for them to regain England. As men die, day after day, they are left with scarcely enough to man the ship. They make a desperate bid to gain the coast of Spain, and get there, on the last day of the year.

One might have thought that with this arrival on a more or less familiar coast, not far from home, their troubles would be nearly over. Yet though there is food to be had in plenty, and the local people seem friendly, the sickness rate doubles from an apparent "excess of fresh meat". Soon there is no one fit enough to go ashore and replenish the water for the last leg home. Hawkins, who with good reason trusts no Spaniard, goes to pains to ensure that this "feebleness" of his crew is not discovered, lest the locals try and attack him. As at San Juan de Ulua, his suspicions mount and finally he lifts anchor at dead of night and sails down the coast to the port of Vigo.

Here, to his profound relief, he finds a number of English ships, and with their help manages to assemble a working crew with sufficient rations and water to get home. They arrive off Cornwall, a tiny fragment of the proud fleet which had sailed more than a year previously. It is 25 January, 1569.

This was the third slave-trading voyage of John Hawkins and it is one of the most disastrous journeys on record. Yet Hawkins did not leave the sea: mineteen years later he was commanding the *Victory* during the defeat of the Spanish Armada, a defeat which he helped bring about with such deadly–and justified–zeal that he was awarded a knighthood by his Sovereign.

Hawkins was criticized by some for "abandoning" half his men in the New World, but it is interesting to study the account of this abandonment, as told by one of the survivors, Job Hortop. To be sure, Hortop must many times have wished that he might perish with so many of his companions, but he was spared to endure twenty-three long years out of England, returning eventually in 1590, just five years before the death of Hawkins, to give his account.

According to Hortop, when the *Minion* had escaped from San Juan de Ulua and made a landfall, Hawkins "asked them, who would go on shore, and who would tarry on shipboard: those that would go on shore he wills to go on foremast, and those that would tarry, on baftmast: fourscore and sixteen of us were willing to depart. Our General gave unto every one of us six yards of cloth, and money to them that demanded it. When we were landed, he came unto us, where friendly embracing every one of us. He was greatly grieved that he was forced to leave us behind him, he counselled us to serve God, and to love one another, and thus courteously he gave us a sorrowful farewell, and promised if God sent him safe home he would do what he could, that so many of us as lived should by some means be brought into England, and so he did."

But it was many years before Hortop saw England. Almost immediately after having been left on shore, he and his ninety-five companions were captured by Indians, stripped naked and left to fend for themselves. Some died, some including Hortop survived to be handed over to the Spaniards, who threatened to hang the lot of them, even erecting a new gallows for the purpose. They were miraculously reprieved, then shuttled from one place of imprisonment within Mexico to another, for two years before being shipped to Spain. Some were executed on arrival; some, like Hortop, spent two years in Seville prison before being tried by the Inquisition. On being convicted these were brought out in procession, "every one of us having a candle in his hand, and the coat with St Andrews crosses on our backs: they brought us up on an high scaffold, that was set up in the place of St Francis, which is in the chief street of Seville: there they set us down upon benches, every one in his degree, and against us on other scaffolds sat all the judges, and the clergy on their benches. The people wondered and gazed on us, some pitying our cases, others said 'Burn those heretics'".

Some where indeed burned, there and then: but Hortop and his friend John Bone were sentenced instead to ten years' hard labour, rowing in the galleys. For some reason Hortop had to serve an extra two years, making a total of twelve, chained with the other men, "four and four together", living on black bread and water, having head and beard shaved every month.

From this he was returned to prison, succeeded in buying himself out with borrowed money, for which he had to serve the usurer another three years. Making a total, with periods in prison and on trial, of twenty-three.

And at last Tob Hartop, last man to return from the ill-fated voyage of John Hawkins, was loaded on a ship for England, *"where they set me on land the 2 day of December last past, 1590"*.

MAGELLAN'S DREAM

The Naming of the World's Largest Ocean

JOHN CABOT, an Italian, gained North America for England because his own country was not interested. Columbus, also an Italian, discovered the West Indies whilst sailing under the Spanish flag. Portuguese-born Ferdinand Magellan sailed into history under the same flag to prove beyond question that the world is round, and that it is possible to reach the east by sailing to the west, something that Cabot and Columbus tried, but failed, to achieve.

Magellan transferred his allegiance to Spain because of a sense of injustice. He was born in 1480, a member of an ancient and noble Portuguese family, and was brought up in the royal palace as page to the queen. He was destined for high rank in court circles until, when twenty-five years old, he decided to lead a more adventurous and exciting life. He went to sea and sailed to the Indies, then helped his country in the quick-moving events of the Portuguese conquests in India. He was promoted to captain and sailed with a fleet that was sent to Malacca and Ceylon in 1508-9. Whilst in Indian seas he began to dream—as had so many before him—of the great advantages of the western route to the East.

This dream went with him when he accompanied a Portuguese expedition to Morocco. He was wounded in a fight against the Moors and on his return to Portugal applied for an increase of pay which, to his chagrin, was refused. He also learned that proceedings were to be taken against him for illicit trading with the enemy. This charge was never proved, but the suspicion was enough to lose him the royal favour. Furious at such treatment, he renounced his nationality and offered his services to Charles V of Spain. He found a powerful ally in Juan Rodriguez de Fonseca, Bishop of Burgos, formerly the implacable enemy of Christopher Columbus, through whose aid he was able to present his scheme for royal approval. He planned to sail westwards and reach the Spice Islands (the Moluccas) either through a passage that might exist somewhere in South America or, if this was found to be impossible, by a route that would take him around the extreme southerly tip of the great landmass. To do this he was prepared to sail southward as far as 75° if necessary. At the same time he would establish, once and for all, the ownership of the recently discovered lands that lay on the "Spanish" side of the line of demarcation laid down by the Pope in 1494.

The king listened, was convinced, and gave his consent. Five ships were allocated which, though pitifully small by modern standards—their combined tonnage was less than that of a modern tug—were considered adequate for a voyage into the unknown. They were *Trinity*, 110 tons; *San Antonio*, 120 tons; *Victoria*, 85 tons; *Conception*, 90 tons, and the *Santiago* of 75 tons.

By midsummer the ships were ready for the great adventure and, on 10 August, 1519, they sailed from Seville with trumpets blaring and banners flying, dropping down to the mouth of the Guadalquivir.

News of the expedition had travelled throughout Europe and, not unnaturally, gave rise to a great deal of resentment in Portugal. Now that the squadron was about to leave, King Manoel of Portugal was beginning to wonder whether he should, after all, have granted Magellan the half-ducat a month rise for which he had asked and which, having been refused, had caused him to offer his allegiance elsewhere. Hoping to alleviate his master's heart-searching the Portuguese Ambassador to Spain sent back a despatch in which he described the ships:

"They are very old and patched up. I saw them when they were beached for repairs. It is eleven months since they were repaired, and they are now afloat and they are caulking them in the water. I went on board of them a few times and I assure your Highness that I should be ill-inclined to sail in them for the Canaries because their knees are of touchwood. The artillery which they all carry are of eighty guns, of a very small size: only in the largest ship, in which Magellan is, there are four very good iron cannon. All the crews they take, in all the five vessels, are 230 men, and they carry provisions for two years."

Magellan was having trouble enough, for he had received a warning from his father-in-law who had learned of intended treachery of some of his captains. These men it was said, were in the pay of Manoel and had pledged themselves to take over the command at the first suitable opportunity. Attempts were also made on Magellan's life whilst in Spain, and, being forewarned, he was determined to crush any signs of mutiny with the utmost severity.

With so much at stake, Magellan must have been relieved when the squadron sailed at last on 20 September, and he was able to hoist his "admiral's" flag in *Trinity*. The ships reached the Cape Verde Islands to a very cool reception from the Portuguese, then headed south-westwards for the coast of South America. All the captains had been given careful sailing instructions, especially those dealing with the alteration of course or taking in sail during the night, such changes to be signified by combinations of lights hoisted in the flagship's rigging.

Cape St. Augustine, near Pernambuco, Brazil, was sighted on 29 November and the ships turned to the south, following the coastline of the New World down to Rio de Janeiro, where Pigafetta described the inhabitants as living in long houses, each of which contained a hundred people.

The squadron sailed on until it reached the La Plata estuary. Magellan spent some days in exploring it, for he hoped that it would provide the passage across the continent for which he was searching. Disappointed, he led his ships still further southwards, sailing along the coast on a voyage of some 4,000 miles which were full of interest. The credulous sailors saw islands populated by "geese" (which must have been penguins) and with "sea wolves" (which can only have been sea lions). Of these latter, the imaginative Pigafetta, main chronicler of the voyage, says: "If these animals could run they would be very bad and cruel, but they do not stir from the water, and swim and live upon fish."

On 3 March, 1520, the ships arrived at what is now Port St. Julian. Magellan was farther south than any explorer had ever been and having been at sea for six months, decided to lay up for a while and refit. His orders to this effect were badly received by his captains and pilots, most of whom were in favour of returning home without delay. They obviously did not relish the prospect of spending the winter in such a cold, dreary and barren place, so different from their own sunny Spain.

Three of the five ships rebelled against Magellan's authority and the ringleaders of what had now become open mutiny, Luis de Mendoza and Gasper Quesada, vowed that they would not only take their ships home but would carry Magellan with them in chains, as he was obviously intent on leading them all to their deaths. They sent an insolent message to him to this effect, demanding a conference. In Magellan, however, they had someone who was not to be frightened by such threats–he had been through too much for that–but, pretending to fall in with their wishes, stipulated that the conference should be held in his flagship. This condition was curtly refused by the mutineers and Magellan decided to act at once.

He sent a boat to Mendoza's ship and his men were allowed to board and approach the captain. Mendoza asked them what they wanted, was told that they had come to take him to the flagship, and when he bluntly refused to go was stabbed several times with a dagger. As his own crew hung back, irresolute without a leader, more of Magellan's men came pouring over the ship's side from a boat which had crept up unobserved. The ship was taken, giving Magellan three against two, for his own and another had remained loyal. The mutiny was crushed almost as soon as it was begun and the body of Mendoza was beheaded and quartered, whilst Quesada and one of his lieutenants were condemned to the same fate.

The expedition, however, did not possess an executioner and the lieutenant was given the choice–kill his own captain or be killed himself. He did not hesitate and Quesada was hanged and then quartered. Cartagena, the captain of the third ship, had been personally appointed to his command by Charles V and, in deference to his royal master, Magellan ordered him to be set ashore with provisions, a priest, and the remains of his two former partners in the mutiny.

Soon after this incident, *Santiago*, which was exploring farther along the coast, ran aground, and although her crew was saved she became a total loss.

The long winter passed, the snows gradually melted and vegetation began to show once again. Magellan decided it was time to set sail again, but before he left he ordered a huge cross to be set up on top of a high mountain as a sign that the country was now a Spanish possession. During their stay the explorers had come into contact with some of the natives who were so tall and well-muscled that they seemed like giants. Everything about them was so large that Magellan gave their country the name of Patagonia, or "Big Feet". Several of these newly named Patagonians were lured aboard and sailed with the squadron when it cleared the harbour on 24 August 1520. Still heading south it arrived two months later at the Cape of the Eleven Thousand Virgins, after a continuous battle with adverse winds and rough seas.

A few miles farther on a large bay was discovered where three separate channels ran westwards into the interior. The *San Antonio* and *Conception* were sent off to explore and returned with the exciting news–they had found the long-sought passage. Magellan now revealed his plans, which he had kept secret from his officers until that moment. He was going to sail through this strait, come out into the sea on the other side and, by sailing westwards, come eventually to the Spice Islands and the great wealth of the Indies. It was the fulfilment of his dream.

To his officers, however, the scheme savoured more of a nightmare, and they begged him to return to Spain with the news that the strait had been discovered and then organize a new expedition that could sail directly to it, without the time-consuming search down the coast that they had undergone. In any case, they pointed out, their provisions were running out and their ships were in no condition for such a venture. But Magellan would not listen. He had sailed expressly to find a short route to the South Seas, he was confident that the strait before him *was* that route, and he declared that if anyone dared to mention anything about going home again he would be severely punished.

The captain of *San Antonio* returned to his ship with this ultimatum. He was immediately bundled below and chained, and in the darkness the ship slipped her cable and headed eastwards for Spain.

Magellan was now reduced to three ships, but, still determined, insisted on leading them westwards into the unknown. The nightmare journey began. The ships sailed only by day, groping their way along channels that were narrow and tortuous. Sometimes they were faced with several channels and the boats had to go ahead and reconnoitre. This strait (now called the Strait of Magellan) was 360 miles long. Barren, snow-covered mountains loomed high above the three tiny ships as they made their slow and painful way to the west. Although no people were to be seen on the shore, they obviously existed, for at night the glow of fires lit up the dark sky, prompting Magellan to name the region as Tierra del Fuego.

On 28 November, 1520, the squadron broke free of the mountains and sailed past a point which Magellan named Cape Desiderate—the "Desired". Before them lay the vast expanse of the waters of the Great South Sea, first sighted by Balboa and which, from the steady and gentle winds which thrust them along, Magellan renamed the "Pacific". This was the greatest discovery since Columbus first set foot on an island off the New World. Magellan's long-cherished dream had become a reality. He had proved that the land-mass of the Americas did not provide an impassable barrier to the Orient. He had also proved that Columbus was wrong-that the land was not part of the continent of Asia.

But the worst part of the voyage was now beginning. "They now sailed three months and twenty days before they saw any land; and having in this time consumed all their biscuit and other victuals they fell into such necessity that they were enforced to eat the powder that remained thereof, being now full of worms. Their fresh water was also putrefied and became yellow. They did eat skin and pieces of leather, which were folded about certain great ropes of the ships; but these skins being made very hard by reason of the sun, rain, and wind, they hung them by a cord in the sea, for the space of four or five days, to mollify them, and ate them."

Many died, including one of the Patagonian giants, whom Magellan had kidnapped with the idea of exhibiting him in Spain, to the regret also of the indefatigable Pigafetta, who had made a start at setting down the Patagonian language. Those who still lived had difficulty in keeping the ships together and on course. Yet, even despite these hardships, there were some who could still take an interest in what they saw. Several marked the position of a collection of stars "like to two clouds" which are known today as the Magellanic Clouds.

The ships ploughed on until, on 24 January, 1521, they made landfall at last—one of the islands in the Tuamotu group. On 6 March they reached Guam in the Marianas, although Magellan named them the Ladrones (or Thieves) Islands, because of the "taking ways" of the inhabitants. This pilfering finally became such a nuisance that Magellan had to teach the natives a lesson. He landed an armed force which rapidly dispersed them, although when one of the natives was wounded by a Spanish arrow he pulled it out and stared at it in surprise, never having seen anything like it before!

The islands had plenty of fruit and fresh water, whilst the sea teemed with fish, and the starving, exhausted sailors were able to feed well and rest themselves. Then the ships sailed on again, passing the southern point of Samar Island on 16 March. On 7 April they dropped anchor at Cebu, in the heart of the Philippines. At last Magellan fully realized the magnitude of his achievement, for here he met merchants from Asia, and now knew that his ultimate goal was quite near. He began trading with the natives—for Cebu was rich in spices—and, as a devout Catholic, to convert them to Christianity. Soon the king of Cebu and all his court became converts, and accepted the King of Spain as their overlord.

The inhabitants of the nearby island of Mactan, however, refused to trade with the Europeans or to listen to them when they attempted conversion. When Magellan learned that the king of Cebu was planning an attack on them, he offered to lead his own men into battle on the king's behalf. The other all too readily agreed, and Magellan, with forty-eight of his men, landed on Mactan where, drawn up to oppose him, were fifteen hundred of the enemy. He refused to be daunted by such superiority of numbers and led his men forward. By sheer weight, however, the Europeans were pushed back, and as they retreated the enemy followed and, picking up the spears they had already cast, threw them again.

Magellan was quickly singled out for attack and one of the natives pushed the sharpened end of his cane lance into Magellan's face. Magellan thrust with his own lance, striking his assailant in the breast. He then began to draw his sword, but whilst it was still half-way out of the scabbard received another thrust through his right arm, so that he could not draw it properly. At this the enemy gave a great shout and rushed at him. One swung at his leg with a scimitar-like weapon which caused him to stumble and fall into the shallows and the natives swarmed around him, thrusting their lances into his helpless body.

Thus, in a senseless local squabble, on 27 April, 1521, died one of history's greatest explorers.

The remainder of his men managed to scramble back on board

their ships and return to Cebu. Two of the officers were elected in Magellan's place and were invited to a feast at the royal palace before returning to Spain. They went, not knowing that their recent defeat had made the king regret his conversion. As soon as they entered, both were treacherously murdered.

The three ships hurriedly left harbour and headed for the Moluccas, on the way calling at Borneo (9 July–27 September). There they decided to burn *Conception*, for there were not enough men to man three ships. In *Trinity* and *Victoria* they headed for the rich and fabulous Spice Islands. They reached Timor on 8 November and soon filled their holds with the sweet-smelling spices. When they prepared for sea, however, *Trinity* was found to be leaky and desperately in need of repair and she was left behind to follow later. On her way home she was captured by the Portuguese and the greater part of her crew perished.

Now commanded by Juan Sebastian del Cano, *Victoria* set off for the Cape of Good Hope but, over-reaching it, arrived at the Cape Verde Islands on 9 July, 1522. A crew of only forty-seven Europeans and a few natives remained, for on the way scurvy had accounted for the lives of another twenty-five. The remainder had been continually at the pumps, working in relays, to keep down the level of the water in the hold. As the travel-weary ship limped into harbour, the survivors learned that the news of their achievements had gone ahead of them. Twelve of the crew were seized by the Portuguese authorities when they attempted to land at Santiago, and the remainder had to leave harbour immediately before their ship was captured.

The *Victoria* finally dropped anchor at Seville on 6 September, with only 17 Europeans remaining from the 230 who had sailed with Magellan three years earlier. News of her arrival ran through the city and the little ship was almost sunk at her moorings by the thousands who flocked to see her and congratulate the survivors. It was a proud moment for Spain for, under her flag, a ship had circumnavigated the world for the first time, the western route to the east had been proved possible and many of the previous misconceptions had been swept away. Only the death of the gallant leader marred the rejoicings that followed, for it was due to him, and him alone, that triumph had been wrested from near failure.

To del Cano went the immediate glory. He was presented to the emperor and received an augmentation to his coat of arms, a globe of the world with the apt description *Primum circumdedisti me* –

"You were the first to encircle me". The other sixteen Europeans, together with four Indians who also returned with him "weaker than men have ever been before", were also honoured.

But to Ferdinand Magellan has gone the lasting glory. He may well be considered the first man ever to sail around the world, for on a previous voyage he had sailed eastward to 130°, and when he was killed he was in 124° west longitude. In the whole history of maritime exploration, no name ranks higher than his. He had done what Columbus had set out to do—to sail westward to the Spice Islands and to prove, once and for all, that the world is round and that it is possible to reach the east by sailing to the west.

Part of the route he took is still known as Magellan's Strait; he was the first man to cross the Pacific Ocean from west to east and, indeed, that very ocean upon which he first sailed still bears the flattering name which he gave to it. And it was this vast ocean that he opened to the civilized world.

111

THE TRAVELS OF MONTAIGNE

In Switzerland, Germany and Italy

IF SHAKESPEARE is the greatest genius of the sixteenth century, Michel de Montaigne was perhaps the most intelligent man of that time, or at least the most intelligent man the world knows anything about. His Essays, written in an unbuttoned-up, racy and anecdotal style, give the best picture ever of Man as he is, and not as he likes to think he is, and deals with man's most trivial and often comic habits as closely as with his thoughts about religion, philosophy and friendship.

In the eighteenth century a manuscript account was found in Montaigne's château of a two-year journey he made in Germany, Switzerland and Italy, mainly in the last country. At the time, the manuscript was not very highly thought of, perhaps because scholars were expecting something different. It was written, in part, by Montaigne's secretary, then by Montaigne himself, partly in Italian and partly in French, and it consisted of notes often carelessly put together and often very detailed about subjects such as the mechanism used by the city of Augsburg whereby men could be admitted by mechanical contrivances to the city at night. Now this and many other curious descriptions in which the travel diary abounds, such as a detailed account of a Jewish circumcision ceremony in Rome which Montaigne witnessed, did not interest the intellectuals of the eighteenth century, nor most of the literary critics of the nineteenth century, with the exception of Saint Beuve. This was a strangely blind view. The travel diary appears today as a unique, at times almost sensational, document throwing far more light on what life was like in Europe four hundred years ago than most historical records or treatises.

Wandering about in a casual manner, Montaigne was able to note a very large number of things we so rarely know concerning the past—about food, drink, beds and prices of hotels, about police regulations and many kinds of doctors. He is received by the Pope, and has long conversations of a very frank kind with high Roman Catholic ecclesiastics, Lutheran, Calvinist and Zwinglian ministers; he goes to dances at various public bathing establishments, where men and women, as Montaigne himself, seek to cure various ills and to amuse themselves doing it; he is entertained by dukes, princes and merchants, he mingles with peasants and shopkeepers, he witnesses public executions and many curious religious practices.

Montaigne adored travelling and no observer was more intelligent or more free from any kind of prejudice. "Nature," he once wrote, "put us into the world free and unfettered and yet we imprison ourselves in narrow districts." He said he also felt as much akin to a Pole as to a Frenchman, so when, on his travels, he was asked if he wanted to be served in the French manner, he would laugh at the idea and make straight for the table thickest with foreigners.

Montaigne began his journey at the age of forty-seven, after having lived the previous ten years in retirement at his château at Montaigne, some thirty miles west of Bordeaux. During the period he had written two-thirds of his Essays, and had them published in Bordeaux. Just before he left for Switzerland and Germany he had presented them to King Henry III, who had admired them. "Sire," said Montaigne, "thus it seems that I too must necessarily please your Majesty if my book is agreeable, for it is nought but discourse on my life and actions."

Montaigne stood well with the king, as he had done with his predecessor, Henry II. Montaigne was a Catholic Loyalist who had, at the parliament of Bordeaux of which he was a Councillor, and on various missions to Paris, served the monarchy well. France, all through Montaigne's adult life, was in the throes of the wars of religion in which the French monarchy was striving to keep the peace between, and to exert its influence against, the extreme Catholic faction, the League, headed by the Duke of Guise on the one hand and the Protestants or Huguenots, headed by Henry of Navarre, afterwards King Henry IV, on the other. Shortly after the massacre of Saint Bartholomew in Paris, in 1572, Montaigne had attempted unsuccessfully to bring together the Duke of Guise and Henry of Navarre whom he knew as a friend.

It is probable that one of the reasons why Montaigne decided on a long journey away from France was his increasing disgust with a spirit of intolerance that existed in France at that time. He was tired of civil wars and did not want to think about politics. Loyally he attended, on the eve of his departure, the siege of a Protestant fortress at La Fère by the Royal Army, temporarily at peace with the Catholic League, and saw one of his friends have his right arm blown off by a cannon-ball and die of gangrene. Montaigne was also sick of too much domesticity, too much chat from his wife and mother about housekeeping and possessions. Travel meant freedom from politics and domestic duties. So off he went at the end of September, 1580, accompanied by a small retinue of servants for himself and four young noblemen, three from Gascogne, one his son-in-law, who were going to taste the delights of civilized Italy and to perfect themselves in fencing, at which the Italians excelled, as they did in all the social arts as well. These young men do not seem to have minded the slow going, with detours to visit this or that curiosity, which Montaigne insisted on, nor the long sojourns at the thermal establishments or baths at various cities.

Another reason for Montaigne to travel was to visit these numerous mineral springs and baths, spas as they are called today, of Switzerland and Italy. Montaigne's health until 1576 was excellent, but he had begun to suffer from bladderstones, a disease which had killed his father, and which was to torment him to an appalling extent. He had little faith in physicians and believed he could purge his stones, to some extent, by drinking the health-giving waters and by bathing. During his journey his disease at times was at its worst and Saint Beuve says "he strewed his stone and sands along the roads of Italy". So we find him sojourning long at thermal stations and particularly at the baths of La Villa near Lucca, where he spent, in two visits, at least seventy-four days. In the sixteenth century in Italy these baths were agreeable social centres, frequented by men and women of the best society and also by courtesans, travelling musicians and gipsies.

The first stop of any length made by the travellers was at Plombières in the Franche Comté. The secretary who, until they reached Rome, kept the travel diary wrote that the people of Plombières considered Montaigne's practice strange, for, without previous medicine, he would drink nine glasses of the water, which came to about one pot, every morning at seven and dined at noon. On the days when he bathed, which was every other day, he did so at about four o'clock, staying in the bath only about an hour. Other people only sipped the waters but remained for a long time in the baths. Unlike the baths at La Villa, where men and women bathed together and the most beautiful Venetian courtesans were often present, there were strict regulations at Plombières. "All prostitutes and shameless girls are forbidden to enter the said baths or to approach within five hundred paces of them, on pain of being whipped to the four corners of the said baths; and on pain, for the hosts who have received or harboured them, of imprisonment of their persons and arbitrary fine."

The travel diary is full of details concerning Montaigne's sufferings, like this one at Lucca in 1581 when he records constant stomach trouble, headaches, vomiting and even toothache, which resulted from his disease and which lasted ten days. Then suddenly: "On the 24th in the morning I pushed down a stone that stopped in the passage, I remained from that moment until dinner-time without urinating, in order to increase my desire to do so. Then I got my stone out, not without pain and bleeding, both before and after; as big and long as a pine-nut, but as thick as a bean at one end. It was a very fortunate thing for me to be able to get it out. I have never ejected one comparable in size to this one." Nothing shows more what a real philosopher Montaigne was than that in spite of his suffering the tone of the whole diary is animated and gay—so gay indeed that Saint Beuve writes that travelling for Montaigne was like a story from The Thousand and One Nights.

On the subject of what the French call *les moeurs* Montaigne noted a curious story at the very beginning of his journey in France. Seven or eight girls had plotted together a few years before to dress up as males and thus make their life in the world. One of them came to Vitry under the name Mary, earning her living as a weaver, a well-disposed young man who made friends with everybody.

"At the said Vitry he became engaged to a woman who is still alive, but because of some disagreement that arose between them, their compact went no further. Later he went to a place called Montier, still earning his living as a weaver, and fell in love with a woman whom he married and with whom he lived for four or five months, to her satisfaction, so they say. But she was recognized by someone from her home area, the matter was brought before the Justices and she was condemned to be hanged, which she said she would rather undergo than return to a girl's status. She was hanged for using illicit devices to supply her defect in sex."

Montaigne liked the Swiss, found their food excellent but their beds uncomfortable and noted that, in various towns where one or the other predominated, Catholics and Lutherans lived amicably together and frequently intermarried, each party preserving their own religion. Whenever he arrived in a town or village one of his first visits was always to the priest or minister whom he would invariably interrogate, no doubt lightly and quizzically, about his flock and about his views on religion. Montaigne was a practising Catholic but he was also a sceptic and his *Essays* mocked at the intellectual pretensions of Catholic as well as Protestant intellectuals. Above all, he was intensely interested in finding out the real views of Protestants of all kinds and the views of the members of various strange sects that abounded in the sixteenth century.

He spent a long time in Augsburg, reputed to be the finest and richest town in Germany. He stayed at an hostelry near the great palace of the Fuggers, merchant bankers, known from the Baltic to the Nile, to whom most of the kings of Europe, including Philip II of Spain and Henry III of France, were heavily indebted. Montaigne and his company, on arriving at their inn and taking their first supper, received a present from the lords of the city of fourteen large vessels full of local wine which was offered them by seven sergeants dressed in livery with an eminent officer of the town. The officer, whom they invited to sup with them, told Montaigne that there were three such officers in the town who were responsible for honouring strangers of some quality. To a duke, one of the burgomasters came in person to make the present; they took Montaigne and his company for barons and knights.

The travellers went to see, in the church of the Holy Virgin, the marriage ceremony of a rich and ugly girl of the town with one of the Venetian agents of the Fuggers. Montaigne notes that they saw not one beautiful woman there. They were curious about the way the company danced. They broke off at the end of each number, and ladies returned to their seats, which were benches ranged along the side of the room in two rows, covered with red cloth. The men did not mingle with the women. After a short pause they would go and fetch them again; the man kisses his hand to the lady; the lady receives him without kissing hers, and then, putting his hand under her armpit, she embraces him cheek to cheek and puts his right hand on her shoulder.

Montaigne was much struck by the practical inventiveness of the Germans in Augsburg for, in addition to the mechanical postern and gate of which Queen Elizabeth of England had asked particulars but had been refused, Montaigne noticed clocks worked by water, ingenious fountains, gardeners who stored artichokes, cabbage, spinach and endives in earth against the cold. People, he noted, were extravagantly clean and cloths were placed on the staircase of their hotel lest the steps should be stained. He noted that in many rooms there were curtains for those who wanted to draw them over the windows. There were hardly any tables in the bedrooms, except those that were attached to the foot of each bed, which hung by hinges and could be raised or lowered. He also noticed that in the inns, beside the beds, linen and curtains were hung so that people could not dirty the wall by spitting. He also noticed, as a curiosity, that in Augsburg they dusted their glassware with a hair duster, attached to the end of a stick.

The travel diary is relatively brief regarding their journey through northern Italy, through Verona where Montaigne visited a synagogue, Vicenza, Padua and Venice which Montaigne found slightly less admirable than he had imagined. Later, in France, to return to Venice became one of his keenest desires. The diary notes that the inns in Italy are inferior to those of Switzerland and Germany, but they were at least one-third cheaper and were roughly similar in price to those in France. They were struck by the level roads of northern Italy and the great extent of cultivated fields.

In Ferrara, Montaigne was received by the Duke, and noted the extremely rich costumes of the Duke's courtiers. Great care was taken in this city against travellers who might bring the Plague or other infectious diseases, and no one could enter in until he had been given permission by the magistrates. On the door of every room in the inn was a notice stating "Remember your health certificate".

As they approached the towns of Tuscany they noticed the custom of sending agents some eight or nine miles from the city to meet strangers and to conjure them to choose their inns. "You would," the travel diary states, "often find the landlord himself on horseback, and in various places many well-dressed men in wait for you." Montaigne, who wanted to amuse himself, was much entertained with the various offers which these people made him. One man, for instance, offered him a hare, purely as a gift, if he was willing just to visit his inn.

Montaigne's first impressions of Florence, perhaps because of the fatigue of travelling, were less favourable than when he came there on his return journey. He writes that he does not know why the city should be privileged to be surnamed "The Beautiful". It was indeed beautiful, but without any advantage over Bologna or even over Ferrara he thinks, and he found it incomparably inferior to Venice.

At last they reached the Eternal City, where they were to stay five months and where Montaigne's companions were to remain. At the gates of Rome, they had a tiresome medical examination to submit to, on account of the plague then raging in northern Italy. Some manuscripts and books on religion which Montaigne had collected in Switzerland were taken away for examination, which annoyed him; they were politely returned later with the exception of one work by a Swiss Catholic which the Vatican officials considered gave too much attention to heretical notions.

As soon as they arrived Montaigne spent his days studying the ancient and modern city, traces of the former being harder to find than they are today. At the beginning, writes the secretary, Montaigne took a French guide; but when this man quit, he made it a point of pride to learn all about Rome by his own study, aided by maps and books that he had read to him in the evening; and in the day-time he would go on the spot to put his apprenticeship into practice, so that in a few days he could have guided his guide.

On Christmas Day, 1580, he went to hear the Pope's mass at St. Peter's, where he had a convenient place for seeing all the ceremonies at ease. The Pope gave communion to several and with him at this service there were a number of cardinals. There was a certain instrument for drinking from the chalice in order to provide safety from poison. It seemed novel to Montaigne that both at this mass and others the Pope, cardinals and other prelates are seated and, almost all through the mass, with their heads covered, chatting and talking together. The ceremony seemed to him more magnificent than devout.

Montaigne was received by the Pope and describes the extremely intricate ceremonial, including various tentative steps into the chamber, the waiting on your knees, the ringing of the bell for a further advance. At the edge of the carpet, on which the Pope's chair is placed, the visitors go down on both knees. Then the ambassador who was presenting them knelt on one knee and pulled back the Pope's robe from his right foot, on which there is a red slipper with a white cross on it. Those who are on their knees drag themselves in this position up to his foot and lean down on the ground to kiss it. Montaigne said that the Pope raised the end of his foot a little. He described the Pope as a very handsome old man with a long white beard, of middle height, erect, his face full of majesty. He was more than eighty years old and as healthy and vigorous for his age as anyone could wish, "without gout, colic, stomach trouble and not subject to any ailment".

The Pope, Gregory XVIII, was of a very gentle nature, not very passionate about the affairs of the world, a great builder. He gave as many audiences as anyone wanted. His replies were invariably short and decided and you waste your time if you combat his reply with new arguments. He gave advancement to his relations, says Montaigne, but without any prejudice to the rights of the Church which he preserves inviolably. He was very lavish in public buildings and in the improvement of the city streets, but in truth, says Montaigne, his life and conduct have nothing very extraordinary about them one way or the other, but inclined much more to the good than to the bad. From the window of his hotel Montaigne watched the Pope pass in solemn state, accompanied by some two hundred horsemen, the persons of his court and the cardinals.

A few days later he saw a very different kind of procession. Catena, a famous robber and bandit, was being led to execution. They carried in front of the criminal a big red crucifix covered with a black curtain and on foot there were a large number of men dressed and masked in linen who, apparently, were gentlemen and other prominent people of Rome who devote themselves to the service of accompanying criminals led to execution. There were two or three monks dressed and masked in the same way who attended the criminal on the cart and preached to him. And one of them continually held before his face a picture on which is a portrait of Our Lord and the criminal was made to kiss it incessantly. With this it is impossible to see the criminal's face from the street. At the gallows, a beam between two supports, they still kept this pic-

ture against Catena's face until he was hung. He met an ordinary
death, without movement or words.

After this, Montaigne noted, they cut him into four quarters.
They hardly ever killed men except by a simple death, and exercised their severity after death. As soon as the criminal is dead, he
goes on, one or several priests, usually Jesuits, get up on some high
spot and shout to the people—one in this direction and the other in
that—and preach to them to make them take note of this example. A
few days later Montaigne saw the execution of two friars who had
murdered an important ecclesiastic. They were taken to the spot
where they had committed the murder, torn with red-hot pincers
and then had their fists cut off. Over the bleeding stumps they put
capons on the wounds. They were then executed on a scaffold; but
first they were clubbed with a big wooden mace, and then their
throats were cut. This was a punishment adapted to the crime, since
they had killed their master in that way.

Of Roman women, Montaigne at one time found that they were
no more beautiful than those of Paris, but you saw fewer ugly women
in Rome than in France. The heads of Roman women, he said, were
more advantageously dressed, and so is the lower part below the
girdle. The body, Montaigne says, is better in France; for in Rome
"they are too loose around the girdle and carry that part as though
like our pregnant women". Their countenance, he writes, has more
majesty, softness, and sweetness. "There is no comparison between
the richness of their apparel and of ours. Theirs is full of pearls
and precious stones. Wherever they let themselves be seen in public,
whether in a coach, at a festival, or in the theatre, they are apart
from the men; however, at dances they intermingle freely enough,
where there are occasions for talking and touching hands."

Rome he found very international, with French spoken commonly in the streets, Spaniards, Portuguese and men of other
nationalities everywhere. There was a great and pompous display
of Spanish horsemen and archers with many drums, conducting the
Spanish Ambassador to the Vatican. The Ambassador from Moscow who watched this said he expected to see a great gathering of
soldiers but had been very disappointed. In his country when there
was a ceremonial parade it was a matter of twenty or thirty thousand cavalry at the very least.

If Rome was a cosmopolis it was also to an extraordinary degree
an ecclesiastical city, without much evidence of trade or industry,
its streets continually full of religious gatherings and demonstra-

tions. Montaigne observed the procession of Flagellants, five hundred or so at one time, whipping themselves with cords and bleeding pitifully. Yet he noted that though these men were torn and cruelly wounded, their bearing was calm, their speech was firm and their faces did not appear as though they were in the middle of a painful or indeed a serious action. Close to Montaigne was a young man who had a pleasant face; a young woman lamented to see him wound himself so. He turned towards her and said, laughing: "That's enough, remember I'm doing this for your sins not for mine." Not only, said Montaigne, did they show no distress in their actions, but they did them cheerfully or at least with such nonchalance that you might see them talk with one another about other matters. To see their shoes, however, it was plain that they were people of very little means who probably sold themselves for this service; at least, some of them did. Indeed, he was told that they greased their shoulders with something. But Montaigne writes that he had seen their wounds so raw, the beating so lengthy, that there is no medicament that could take away the feeling of it.

Among the curious things Montaigne reports is the following. On Palm Sunday he saw in a church, at Vespers, a boy sitting beside the altar on a chair, dressed in a great new robe of blue taffeta, head bare, with a crown of olive branches, holding in his hand a lighted torch of white wax. He was a boy of fifteen or thereabouts, who, by order of the Pope, had been delivered from prison that day. He had killed another boy.

The officials of the Curia and the great ecclesiastics are quite exempt from the emotional fanaticism which marks the Roman population. Montaigne had submitted his *Essays* to the papal censorship. The authorities are most polite, excuse themselves for certain animadversions which the censors had made on the book. Montaigne writes: "The Master of the Sacred Palace and his colleague urge me not to make use of the censorship of my book, saying that they honoured both my intention and affection for the Church and my ability, and thought so well of my frankness and conscience that they left it to myself to cut out of my book, when I wanted to republish it, whatever I found too licentious in it." Largely on the Pope's recommendation Montaigne was made a Roman citizen, an honour which he deeply appreciated. He was admitted to the Vatican library, an honour which was not normally given even to the French Ambassador. The liberal attitude which the Church took to the *Essays* at the time contrasts with the very wary and critical view taken of Montaigne's work in the seventeenth century.

From Rome, Montaigne again travelled north, re-visiting Florence, which this time he decided is worthily called "The Beautiful", and the baths near Lucca where he spent a long time. What he found most attractive about Italy was the natural elegance and culture of the peasants, the effect of an old civilization. In the fields of Tuscany he had often seen hay-makers and shepherds with lutes and heard many poor people recite poetry. At the La Villa baths it was customary for visitors of note to give dances to the guests and the people of the neighbourhood. Montaigne did this. He noted that the peasants and their wives were dressed like gentlefolk.

"You never saw a peasant who did not wear white shoes, fine thread stockings, a coloured apron of light silk taffeta. They danced and pirouetted admirably as quite the equal of high-born ladies." Of his entertainment he notes: "I invited them all to supper, for the banquets in Italy are nothing but a very light meal by French standards—a few cuts of veal and one or two brace of chicken is all. There stayed to supper at my table a poor peasant woman of the neighbourhood, living about two miles from the baths, who, like her husband, had no way of earning her living except by the work of her own hands. She was ugly, thirty-seven years old with a swollen neck. She could neither read nor write. But in her youth there was an uncle in her father's house who was always reading Ariosto and other poets in her presence, and her mind was found to be so born to poetry that she not only composes verses with the most wonderful readiness possible, but also brings in to them ancient fables, names of gods, countries, sciences, famous men as if she had been brought up to study. She delivered a number of verses in my honour. To tell the truth, they were nothing but verses and rhymes. But her delivery was very elegant and very rapid."

It was during his last sojourn at Lucca baths that he received a letter from France stating that the king had nominated him Mayor of Bordeaux, a most important post in view of the Civil Wars and the strategic importance of the city. Montaigne's first inclination was to decline this honour. He returned to Rome to discuss this with the French Ambassador, who was a friend of his, and finally obeyed what amounted to a Royal Command to return as soon as possible. He was never to see Naples or to make a return visit to Venice.

Just as Montaigne obviously wanted to go on travelling, so the reader puts down this travel diary wishing for more. The Europe he has been introduced to—Europe at the time of Elizabethans—is rather different from what people imagine. In spite of the slowness of travel and the absence of communications, it is much more one world than it is today. The unity given to Europe by the Roman Church had not passed away; the increasing separateness between peoples as a result of the growth of nationalism had not yet come about.

What a pity that Montaigne never came to London; it was in England that he was to know his most fervent admirers during his lifetime—Shakespeare, Ben Jonson, Bacon read him avidly. But instead of travelling further, Montaigne was to be Mayor of Bordeaux and to write his last group of *Essays* which are perhaps the best. He died in 1591. Strangly enough, he did not die of stones in the bladder; he was in fact carried off by a form of pneumonia. In his final years Montaigne had come to think of pain and pleasure as equally necessary to man and indeed interdependent. As he was to write: "I have seen the grass, the flower and the fruit; now I see dryness—happily, since it is naturally."

SIR HUMPHREY GILBERT'S EXPEDITION

The First Attempt to Colonize North America

RICHARD HAKLUYT, whose name was pronounced, in his day, "Haklit" and spelt in a dozen different ways, was a clergyman. Had he stuck to his pulpit we would never have heard of him. As it is, he is the compiler of one of the great prose epics in our language, a tome with the awesome title, *The Principal Navigations, Voyages, Traffics and Discoveries of the English Nation.*

An ambitious project–and faithfully carried out. Hakluyt had entertained himself by translating, almost from childhood, works on discovery and exploration. As far as we know he did little voyaging himself, a spell in Paris as Chaplain to the British Embassy being virtually all his foreign travel. Yet seldom can man have read more assiduously, listened more keenly to travellers' tales, than Richard Hakluyt.

The first edition of this huge labour of love was published in 1589. The second, twice its length, came out in three volumes over the years 1598, 1599 and 1600. By this time Hakluyt, returned from France, had held a benefice in Suffolk and been made Canon of Westminster. We have no evidence to suggest that his writings were responsible for such an elevation in the hierarchy, but without doubt they occasioned, a year or two later, his appointment as

"Consultant on Eastern Problems" to the East India Company. It was a remarkable appointment for a man who had never ventured farther east than the capital of France.

But as we read through the tales of exploration and travel, some of them exciting, some thrilling, some dull, which Hakluyt investigated, edited and assembled into his monster work, we realize that there can hardly have been another man more knowledgeable about travel. Almost certainly Shakespeare, who was his contemporary and died in the same year, drew upon Hakluyt's *Voyages* for the background to some of his writing.

What size of a world did these two giants inhabit?

A little one. Yet a world which, at the time of their birth, midway through the sixteenth century, was expanding crazily. Until 1550 the English had been remarkably uninterested in travel beyond the confines of Europe. Foreigners–who in English eyes were even more foreign than they are today–had explored the Atlantic. Uncouth, untrustworthy, Spaniards, Portuguese had discovered places in the West Indies, southern Africa, the American continent and India– and the lands had rather ludicrously, it was felt in England, been divided between them by the Pope. The English, unimpressed, were content with their trade to Europe.

But in the middle of the sixteenth century there came economic depression at home, and unsettled conditions on the Continent, which seriously hindered European trade. The English were forced at last to consider markets farther afield. As these had been fairly well exploited by the South Europeans, and trading expeditions to West Africa and America, though possible, were hazardous under the scrutiny of Spanish and Portuguese gunboats–and the Pope–it was decided to explore farther north.

Almost overnight the English, previously so lacking in enterprise, were swarming all over the globe, backed by the merchants of London and the monarch herself. Though London was the greatest port in the country and the richest, dwarfing the others, with men-of-war and merchant ships by the dozen at anchor in the Thames, it was usually from the West Country and particularly from Plymouth that great voyages of exploration began. Stukely sailed for Florida, Grenville for Virginia, Frobisher for the North-west Passage, Walter Raleigh for Guiana and Gilbert for Newfoundland, to name a few.

And it is with Gilbert–Sir Humphrey–that we are here concerned. A brave man, as most were who ventured abroad in the sixteenth century, with a dream. A dream which led him to his death, and which so enthralled Richard Hakluyt that one of the longest, most thrilling tales in his work is that of Sir Humphrey Gilbert's voyage to Newfoundland.

Like almost everything else in the *Voyages*, it is written by another hand than Hakluyt's, but carefully checked, cross-checked, edited. It is a "report of the voyage and success thereof, attempted in the year of our Lord 1583, by Sir Humphrey Gilbert, knight, with other gentlemen assisting him in that action, intended to discover and to plant Christian inhabitants in place convenient upon those large and ample countries extending northward from the cape of Florida, lying under very temperate climes, esteemed fertile and rich in minerals, yet not in the actual possession of any Christian prince..."

It was originally written, as Hakluyt points out, by "Mr. Edward Haie, gentleman and principal actor in the same voyage, who alone continued unto the end and by God's special assistance returned home with his retinue safe and entire". This, then, was Gilbert's dream: to colonize North America. Had his luck held, the first colony on that continent would have taken root a quarter of a century earlier than the one in Virginia, and earlier still than the famous *Mayflower* exploit of 1620. The history of North America, the United States, might to this day have been different.

And yet, had geography been better understood in the sixteenth century, it seems unlikely that such an attempt at colonization would have been made so far north. The behaviour of the Gulf Stream, which makes Britain a temperate country in a latitude between fifty and sixty degrees north–that of Labrador and the Aleutian Islands–was not understood. Men believed fondly that Newfoundland, ten degrees to the south, *must* be at least as temperate. Evidence pointed to the contrary, but was disregarded. The *Voyages* points out carefully that Newfoundland is at about the latitude of Brittany, and therefore "cannot much differ from the temperature of that country: unless upon the outcoast, lying open unto the Ocean and sharp winds, it must indeed be subject to more cold than further within the land, where the mountains are interposed as walls and bulwarks to defend and resist the asperities and rigour of sea and weather".

And to Sir Humphrey Gilbert, who was aware that Newfoundland had been discovered by John Cabot and "Sebastian his son, an Englishman born", and that the Spaniards had failed singularly in their attempts to explore north of Florida–and knew nothing of the great eastern seaboard lying in between (nor did anyone else)–the New Found Land was the obvious place to plant a Christan colony in the queen's name.

His determination was great, and the failure of a first expedition, thanks to the faint-heartedness of his companions, did nothing to discourage him. He persuaded his sovereign to grant a commission entitling him to form a Christian colony in this new land, and for that colony to embrace "an area extending every way two hundred leagues". The commission was valid only for six years: he made haste to equip a second expedition and this time, because he resolved it should be as perfect as human ingenuity could make it, he took two years in the preparation, "shipping, munition, victual, men and things requisite". All this required money, which, as he had expended much in the first, unsuccessful, venture, was not easy to acquire. But gradually, "other gentlemen to their ability joined unto him, resolving to adventure their substance and lives in the same cause".

And at last, on Tuesday, 11 June, 1583, the expedition sailed from Plymouth. It was led by the *Delight*, of 120 tons, in which Sir Humphrey was travelling, and which for that reason was appointed "Admiral". (In those distant days the title belonged to the vessel, not the man.) With her were *Raleigh* (owned by Sir Walter, though he was not present), of 200 tons; *Golden Hind*, 40 tons; *Swallow*, 40 tons; and the tiny *Squirrel*, 10 tons. The expedition numbered two hundred and sixty men, "among whom we had of every faculty good choice, as shipwrights, masons, carpenters, smiths and such like, requisite to such an action: also mineral men and refiners. Besides, for solace of our people, and allurement of the savages, we were provided of music in good variety: not omitting the least toys, as Morris dancers, hobby horses, and May-like conceits to delight the savage people, whom we intended to win by all fair means possible. And to that end we were indifferently furnished of all petty haberdashery wares to barter with those simple people."

They sailed on Tuesday, and the first cruel blow struck just forty-eight hours later. The magnificent *Raleigh*, "most puissant ship in our fleet", was forced back into Plymouth owing to a sudden and violent outbreak of some mysterious disease among the crew. The expedition sailed on without her.

Then the weather. From 15 June until 28 June they endured the most appalling conditions of fog and rain, alternating with winds of hurricane force. The remaining four vessels were separated one from the other, none knowing whether the others had survived. They kept on course as best they could in conditions of zero visibility, but the winds were so adverse that in order to do so they had to travel huge distances in the wrong direction, tacking for hundreds of miles, many degrees off course, swinging between latitudes 41 and 51 North. They came to sudden and terrifying "mountains of ice" and miraculously escaped shipwreck against them.

On Tuesday, 30 July, exactly seven weeks after setting out from Plymouth, they caught sight of land. It was an unappetizing sight, even for men who had begun to wonder if they would ever see land again. "So great haze and fog did hang upon the coast, as neither we might discern the land well, nor take the sun's height. But by our best computations we .were then in the 51 degree of latitude.

"Forsaking this bay and uncomfortable coast (nothing appearing unto us but hideous rocks and mountains, bare of trees and devoid of any green herb) we followed the coast to the south."

The commentary–as edited by Hakluyt–is from Edward Haie who is travelling in *Golden Hind* (indeed, he owns it) and those taking passage in that vessel have little idea of the whereabouts of the others. But, to their delight, as they sail slowly down the coast in search of a place to land, they come upon *Swallow*.

We can get some idea of the problems facing a sixteenth-century seafarer from the description of this encounter. The captain of that vessel was an upright character who had been encumbered with a crew of cut-throats, most of whom had in fact been pirates before being "persuaded" to join the expedition. Habits die hard, and those on board *Golden Hind* were at first startled to see the crew of *Swallow* in completely new clothes, "apparel whereof it seemed their store was so amended they spared not to cast up into the air and overboard their caps and hats in plenty". They had looted a passing vessel, having received their helpless captain's permission to go aboard and "borrow food", on the grounds that the other ship was sailing towards England and they away from it. They boarded the other ship and promptly attacked the much smaller crew, "not sparing by torture (winding cords about their heads) to draw out what they thought good". And then, getting aboard their ship's boat to regain *Swallow*, they were capsized by a monster wave. One might imagine that the looted sailors watching their departure might have welcomed this development; but no: the thieves are rescued from the sea, "preserved even by those silly souls whom they had before spoiled, who saved and delivered them aboard the *Swallow*".

One can only assume the massive bulk of *Swallow* intimidated the simple fishermen on board the smaller vessel, for they returned the thieves to her, complete with all their loot. What became of the fishing vessel, Hakluyt surmises, "destitute of sails and furniture sufficient to carry them home (whither they had not less to run than 700 leagues) God alone knoweth". But he points out a Divine vengeance, approaching.

A little later *Golden Hind* and *Swallow* reached the harbour of St John's and there found the diminutive, ten-ton, *Squirrel*. She had been refused entry by the few fishermen and merchants who were already there with their own ships.

Sir Humphrey went ashore, armed with the Commission from Her Majesty, and all three of his ships were allowed in. The merchants–adventurers who were here for a week or two–greeted this ambitious attempt to make a permanent settlement, by firing off all the guns of their vessels. In those days it was a foolish trader who wandered abroad on the high seas without a battery of muzzle-loading guns.

The next day, Sunday, 4 August, Sir Humphrey and his associates landed for a tour of the area. He stayed on land and the following day took possession of it, his promised "two hundred leagues in every direction". Of this he could dispose as he saw fit, so long as it remained a territory "appertaining to the Queen of England", with laws "agreeable, so near as conveniently might be, unto the laws of England". Quite a few of these laws were publicly proclaimed by Sir Humphrey, ending with the warning that "if any person should utter words sounding to the dishonour of Her Majesty, he should lose his ears and have his ship and goods confiscate".

Haie (and Hakluyt) go on to describe the New Found Land in great detail, "situate in the North regions of America, upon the gulf and entrance of the great river called St Lawrence in Canada. The island round about hath very many goodly bays and harbours, safe road for ships, the like not to be found in any part of the known world". They go on to explain (with their ignorance of the Gulf Stream) exactly why Newfoundland *must* be as temperate and attractive as England, and probably more so, even if first impressions have been misleading. They point out the extraordinary wealth of the land, with its wood, both for masts and hulls, its hides, flax, hemp, corn and metals, plus endless varieties of fruit and "roses passing sweet". This of course is August, and it would appear that the land becomes highly inhospitable in winter, though even then there is no limit to the variety of birds and beasts with which a man may feed and clothe himself.

Sir Humphrey–who as colonizer is nobody's fool–had brought a metallurgist with him, "a Saxon born, honest and religious, named Daniel". Samples of ore were brought to this expert who pronounced it good, to the great satisfaction of Sir Humphrey. Indeed, Sir Humphrey admits that "were it but to satisfy my private humour, I would proceed no farther". He had, however, a duty to his queen to explore farther and find the most perfect spot from which his colony could grow. He loaded his ship with samples of the ore, in the greatest secrecy, for "I would have no speech to be made so long as we remain in harbour, here being Portugals, Spaniards and Frenchmen, not far off, from whom must be kept any bruit or muttering of such matter".

Daniel had given good report of the land's mineral wealth– though precisely what he told his leader we will never know, for both were soon to perish–and it became clear that the expedition, quite apart from having established a new English realm, would go home with its pockets full. Morale is high.

But once again comes the weakness, the avarice, of man. Some of the crew members wanted to seize a vessel for themselves, fill it with loot and then, having murdered their officers, sail home with a tale of shipwreck. While awaiting opportunity for their crime, they seized a fishing boat while Gilbert was ashore and dumped its unhappy crew on a deserted part of the coast. They then transfered its cargo to one of their own vessels and cast the fishing boat adrift.

Quarrels broke out over loot, men were killed, and others, deciding they could do better for themselves alone in this country than as members of the expedition, deserted and vanished into the tall evergreen forest, intending to plunder merchants and eventually get passage home. But, apart from these deserters, a number of good and honest men were "sick of fluxes and many dead: and, in brief, by one means or other our company was diminished". So much so that Sir Humphrey was forced to leave *Swallow* behind for lack of crew to man her.

Captain Maurice Brown, a good and highly respected man who

had, as far as was humanly possible, kept his crew of cut-throats under control, was not too upset at having his charge taken from him. Most of the deserters had been members of the *Swallow*'s crew of erstwhile pirates and he was now placed, by Sir Humphrey, in command of *Delight*, the "Admiral" of the diminished fleet. There now remained *Delight*, *Golden Hind* and *Squirrel*: the worst was yet to come.

Sir Humphrey transferred to the ten-ton *Squirrel* as being the most suitable vessel for exploring the narrow inlets of the coast. The intention was to press on round the island.

"We departed from this harbour upon Tuesday the twentieth of August, which we found by exact measurement to be in 47 degrees 40 minutes. And the next day by night we were at Cape Race, 25 leagues from the same harbour." They carried on south-west, west, north-west, north, trying to circumnavigate their island. On Tuesday (and so much, in this venture, seems to happen on Tuesdays), the 27 August, Sir Humphrey from his tiny craft watched with mingled amusement and concern as the ship's company of *Delight* staged an impromptu concert, "sounding trumpets, with drums and fifes, also winding the cornets, oboes". There seems to have been little enough reason for such a celebration, particularly as the weather was closing in, making their task of exploration more difficult, more hazardous.

And, as Hakluyt points out, the event was much like "the swan that singeth before her death".

They carried on happily singing throughout the Wednesday. Singing, that is, on board *Delight*: not on the other two vessels, which kept their distance and wondered.

Suddenly, on the Thursday, came a blinding, terrifying storm, which whipped up gigantic seas, followed by a fog so thick that, they might have been dropped in a bowl of porridge. And yet, through it all, those on board *Squirrel* and *Golden Hind* could hear the fools on board *Delight* singing and playing their instruments.

The lookout on the *Golden Hind* roars out "Land!"

Too late. The *Delight*, near enough to hear the cry but in no shape to do anything about it, runs aground. Within minutes she has been beaten to pieces on the savage rocks of the Newfoundland coast. One cannot help feeling that the unfortunate Captain Maurice Brown, who now perishes with his entire ship's company, has had remarkably little control over his crews in either *Swallow*

131

or *Delight*. And yet Hakluyt goes to some trouble to praise him as a fine and worthy man, a staunch commander—and a tragic loss.

And in this wreck perished, too, the metallurgist Daniel, taking his secret with him, for it was shared by only one other man, Sir Humphrey himself, soon to follow him. It was a shocking loss, "to lose at one blow our chief ship freighted with great provision, gathered together with much travel, care, long time and difficulty. But more was the loss of our men, which perished to the number of almost a hundred souls. Amongst whom was drowned a learned man, an Hungarian, born in the city of Buda, called thereof Budaeus, who of piety and zeal to good attempts, adventured in this action, minding to record in the Latin tongue the things worthy of remembrance happening in this discovery, to the honour of our nation, the same being adorned with the eloquent style of this orator and rare poet of our time."

The Latin record was not to be.

"Our people lost courage daily after this ill-success, the weather continuing thick and blustering, with increase of cold, winter drawing on, which took from them all hope of amendment, settling an assurance of worse weather to grow upon us every day... Those in the *Squirrel* were already pinched with spare allowance and want of clothes chiefly. Whereupon they besought Sir Humphrey to return for England, before they all perished. And to them of the *Golden Hind* they made signs of their distress, pointing to their mouths, and to their clothes, thin and ragged: then immediately they also of the *Golden Hind* grew to be of the same opinion and desire to return home."

Sir Humphrey agrees. They will set course for England—and he will return the following summer. Most of his party are overjoyed at the decision and they expect him to transfer to the mighty *Golden Hind* for the journey across the Atlantic: the weather is growing daily worse and *Squirrel* will receive a tremendous buffeting. There is even talk of abandoning her, transferring her men to *Hind*, but Gilbert scoffs at this: *Squirrel* will make the passage, and he will travel in her. He has been with her gallant company for many weeks; he has no intention of deserting them now.

They set course, and the weather grows steadily worse. On Monday, 9 September, *Squirrel* can hardly be made out from *Hind*, through fog and mountainous waves. Then they see Sir Humphrey, setting an example of courage to his crew and "sitting abaft with a book in his hand, who cried out unto us in the *Hind*, so oft as we did approach within hearing, 'We are as near to heaven by sea as by land!' Reiterating the same speech, well beseeming a soldier, resolute in Jesus Christ, as I can testify he was."

But suddenly, shortly after midnight on the Tuesday morning, 10 September, *Squirrel* vanishes. Just that. Her lights, so close one moment, have gone forever the next.

Surely, when dawn breaks, they will find their leader's ship? Or at least its wreckage?

They never do. Not a spar or rag of sail is ever seen again. With heavy hearts the survivors of this ill-fated expedition, the crew of *Golden Hind*, pile on sail for home. Perhaps there, by some miracle, they will find *Squirrel*, saved by God's mercy.

They reach Falmouth on 22 September: *Squirrel* never does.

And so perished a brave man–indeed, many brave men–and a bold venture. The Newfoundland colony grew into being many years later, and not as one of the first or most important in North America. Sir Humphrey Gilbert's dream died with him.

TAVERNIER, THE "WANDERING JEWELLER"

Travels in Persia, Turkey and India

WHEN HE was on the verge of seventy and had thus reached an age when he might well suppose that his travelling days were over, J. B. Tavernier sat down to write the story of his forty years of wanderings. And what a story it turned out to be! The vast distances covered–"sixty-thousand leagues" (say a hundred and fifty thousand miles) by land alone, not counting the long sea voyages; the countries visited–"the whole of Turkey, all Persia, and all India", not to mention much the greater part of Europe; the strange peoples and places, not least "the famous mines of diamonds, where no European had been before me..." In a rather condescending footnote, Gibbon refers to "that wandering jeweller, who had read nothing, but had seen so much and so well", and the tribute, grudging though it may appear, is no more than Tavernier's due.

As his name indicates, Jean Baptiste Tavernier was a Frenchman. He was born in 1605 at Paris, where his father Gabriel and his uncle Melchior, Protestant refugees from Antwerp, were doing very well as geographers and map-engravers. With such surroundings it is not difficult to account for Tavernier's bent, and

134

indeed he himself is quite explicit. "The interviews which many learned men had daily with my father upon geographical matters, which he had the reputation of understanding well, and to which, young as I was, I listened with pleasure, inspired me at an early age with the desire to go to see some of the countries shown to me in the maps, which I could not then tire of gazing at."

Before he was sixteen he had made his "first sortie", this being to England, and by the time he was twenty-two he "had seen the best parts of Europe, France, England, Holland, Germany, Switzerland, Poland, Hungary, and Italy, and I spoke fairly the languages which are the most necessary, and which have the greatest currency". One of the first places he visited was Amsterdam, and it was probably then that he laid the foundations of the specialized knowledge which made it possible for him to follow the career of a high-class dealer in pearls and diamonds and other precious stones.

Very early in life he had some under the spell of the Orient, and in 1631 he made the first of his many trips into Asia. In the company of two French Jesuit fathers he reached Constantinople early in that year, and, after spending the best part of the next twelve months there, proceeded across Asia Minor into Persia, as far as Ispahan; the return journey was made by way of Baghdad, Aleppo, Malta, and Italy, and he was not back home in Paris till 1633. In his baggage were some Turkish turquoises, which he was able to dispose of to excellent profit.

This was the first of what became celebrated as "Tavernier's Six Voyages". The Second Voyage, begun about five years after his return to Paris, took him again to Persia, whence he proceeded into India, but it is not clear how he got there. At Agra he visited the court of the Great Mogul, Shah Jahan, and he also seems to have visited the famous diamond mines at Golconda. He returned to Paris, but after a very short stay he was off again to the East on his Third Voyage, in the course of which he visited India and Persia, and also the Dutch colonies in the East Indies. After being away for five years and more he was back in Paris in the spring of 1649. Two years later, and he was off again, and on this Fourth Voyage he went again to Persia and India, where he engaged in some profitable business at the Golconda diamond-mines.

Apparently he returned to Paris in 1655, and he started on his Fifth Voyage some eighteen months later. Shortly after leaving Marseilles the vessel in which he had taken passage was chased by pirates, and had to take refuge in a port near Toulon. Tavernier was carrying a number of jewels which he hoped to sell in the East, and he was careful to keep them on his person. He now took an English ship for Italy, and thence sailed in a Dutch vessel for Smyrna, where he rested for some time while his servant proceeded to Constantinople to purchase some pearls to be added to his master's stock. From 1657 to 1659 Tavernier was in Persia, and then he went on to India, where he seems to have spent several years. Towards the end of 1662 he was back in Paris, and now, at the mature age of fifty-six, he thought it time he settled down and got married. Madeleine Goisse, daughter of a jeweller with whom he had had some business transactions, became his wife.

Instead of settling down, however, Tavernier was off again, towards the end of 1663, on his Sixth Voyage. Smyrna, Persia (where he disposed of a large stock of jewels, at good prices), India (where he was received in audience by the Great Mogul, the Emperor Aurangzeb, who sold him a number of his most precious stones, and was privileged to be shown the Emperor's own collection), Persia again, and so home by way of Constantinople and the Mediterranean. Now he must have thought he must really call a halt. He was wealthy, he was sixty-three, and he was famous. King Louis XIV sent for him, bought some of his diamonds and other precious stones, and conferred on him a patent of nobility. In 1670 Tavernier purchased the barony of Aubonne, near Geneva, and henceforth was known as the Seigneur Baron d'Aubonne.

For the next fourteen years or so Tavernier led a quiet life, at least we are not told very much about him. He restored the castle on his estate, and set about preparing his voluminous notes of travel for publication in book form. The volume containing the account of his "Six Voyages" was published in 1676, and was soon translated into the principal European languages.

As a topographical handbook the "Six Voyages" has its defects, since the several journeys are not clearly distinguished, and sometimes the places referred to cannot be properly identified. But what makes the book so valuable is its information on the life of the countries visited, India in particular, and also the sidelights on the business activities with which Tavernier was so chiefly concerned. The Indian chapters are likely to appeal most to the English reader, and we have the assurance that Tavernier knew what he was writing about. "The routes to all the principal towns of India are not less well known to me than are those of Turkey and of Persia (he informs us), and, for six journeys which I have made from Paris to Ispahan, I have made double the number from Ispahan to Agra, and to several other places in the Empire of the Great Mogul." But (he continues) "it would weary the reader to cause him to pass more than once by the same roads while giving him an account of these different journeys", and so he proceeds to give an "exact description of each route", without indicating the actual times at which he followed them.

As a fair specimen we may take the Route from Surat (on the west coast of India, north of Bombay) to Agra, via Burhanpur and Sironj. All the principal towns *en route* are listed and something is said about each, but we will concentrate on the more interesting features, more especially the "human" ones.

Navapoura is a large village full of weavers, but rice constitutes the principal article of commerce in the place. All the rice which grows in this country possesses a particular quality, causing it to be much esteemed. When you wish to make an acceptable present to anyone in Persia you take him a sack of this rice.

Brampour is a large, much-ruined town, the houses of which are for the most part thatched. Both at Brampour and in all the province an enormous quantity of very transparent muslins are made, which are exported to Persia, Turkey, Muscovie (Russia), Poland, Arabia, Grand Cairo, and other places. Some of these are dyed various colours and ornamented with flowers, and women make veils and scarves of them; they also serve for the covers of beds, and for handkerchiefs, such as we see in Europe with those that take snuff.

Sironj is a large town, of which the majority of the inhabitants are Banian merchants and artisans, who have dwelt there from father to son, which is the reason why it contains some houses of stone and brick. There is a large trade there in all kinds of coloured calicoes, with which all the common people of Persia and Turkey are clad. They make similar calicoes in other places besides Sironj, but the colours are not so lively, and they disappear when washed several times. It is different with those of Sironj; the more they are washed, the more beautiful they become...

Callabas is a large town, where formerly a great Rajah resided who paid tribute to the Great Mogul. Generally, when caravans passed it, the merchants were robbed, and he exacted from them excessive dues. But since Aurangzeb came to the throne he cut off the Rajah's head, and those of a large number of his subjects. "On my last journey, in 1665, it was not long since this execution had taken place, for all the heads were still entire", set in the windows of towers near the town, "and they gave out an unpleasant odour".

Gate is a pass in the mountains, and the road is so narrow that chariots can pass one another only with the greatest difficulty. At the Agra end there are five or six shops of Banians, who sell flour, butter, rice, herbs, and vegetables. "On my last journey I halted at one of these shops while awaiting the coaches and carts, the passengers having descended from them for this transit. Close by them was a large store full of sacks of rice and corn, and behind these sacks a snake of thirteen or fourteen feet in length, and of proportionate girth, was concealed. A woman while taking some grain from the sacks was bitten on the arm by this snake and, feeling herself wounded, left the shop, crying 'Ram, Ram!' that is to say, 'Oh God! Oh God!' Immediately several Banians, men and women, ran to her aid, and they tied the arm above the wound, thinking they could prevent the poison from ascending higher. But it was unavailing, for immediately her face swelled, and then became blue, and she died in less than an hour. As she was on the point of death, four Rajput soldiers, who make no scruple of killing when it is a question of attacking or defending, having learnt what had happened, entered the store, each with a sword and a short pike in his hand, and slew the serpent... I was compelled to remain two days in this place, because there is a river to cross, which increased from hour to hour on account of the rains, so that I had to cross it half a league lower down."

An alternative route from Surat to Agra was by way of Ahmadabad, and this likewise Tavernier sometimes followed. The first town he mentions is Baroche, "a large town, in which the English have a very fine dwelling. I remember that one day on arriving there together with the English President [of the 'factory' or trading station] some jugglers came up and asked him whether he desired them to show some examples of their art. These he was curious to see. The first thing they did was to kindle a large fire, and heat iron chains to redness; these they wound round their bodies, making believe that they experienced some pain, but not really receiving any injury. Next, having taken a small piece of stick and planting it in the ground, they asked one of the company what fruit he wished to have? He replied that he desired mangoes, whereupon one of the conjurors, covering himself with a sheet, stooped to the ground five or six times. I had the curiosity to ascend into a room in order to see from above, through an opening of the sheet, what this man did, and I saw that he cut himself under his armpits with a razor, and anointed the piece of wood with his blood. At each time that he raised himself, the stick increased under the eye, and at the third time it put forth branches and buds. At the fourth time the tree was covered with leaves, and at the fifth we saw the flowers themselves". This is one of the earliest accounts by an eye-witness of a performance of the "mango trick".

Passing through Cambay (Tavernier continues), you reach a village where there is a pagoda to which the majority of Indian courtesans make offerings. "This pagoda contains many nude figures, and among others a large figure like an Apollo, which has all the private parts uncovered. When the old courtesans have amassed a sum of money in their youth, they buy young female slaves, to whom they teach dances and lascivious songs, and all the tricks of their infamous trade. When these young girls have reached the age of eleven or twelve years their mistresses take them to this pagoda, as they believe it will be good fortune to them to be offered and abandoned to this idol."

So on to Ahmadabad, "where I have been ten or twelve times". It is one of the largest towns in India, with a considerable trade in silken stuffs, tapestries, and others mixed with silk. A river flows past it on the north-west, during the rainy season becoming very wide and rapid and doing great damage every year. There is no bridge, so you may have to wait six weeks or two months before it is possible to ford it. There are two or three boats which one can use when the river falls, but even so it takes much time to make the crossing. "The peasants do not stand on ceremony, for in order to get from one bank to the other they make use of the skin of a goat, which they fill with air and tie on between the chest and the ab- domen. It is thus that the poor, both men and women, cross, and when they wish to take their children across with them they make use of round earthen pots, and placing a child in one of these pots they push it before them while swimming."

There are in Ahmadabad (Tavernier goes on) two or three houses which serve as hospitals, especially for cows, oxen, monkeys, and other sick and disabled animals. On every Tuesday and Friday all the monkeys in the neighbourhood, of their own instinct, come in a body to the town and ascend the houses, each of which has a small terrace where the occupants sleep during the great heat.

This reminds him of an incident that occurred when one day he was riding in the neighbourhood with the "English Chief or President". "We saw overhead numbers of large monkeys, male and female, and several of the latter carried their young ones in their arms. We each had our carriage, and the English President stopped his to tell me that he had an excellent and curious gun which the [Portuguese] Governor of Daman had presented to him, and, knowing that I was a good shot, he asked me to prove it upon one of these monkeys. One of my attendants, who was of the country, signed to me not to risk it, and I sought to dissuade the President from his intention, but it was impossible; so taking his gun he shot a female monkey, which remained extended between two branches and let her young ones fall to the ground. What my attendant had foreseen followed at once. All the monkeys on the trees, to the number of more than sixty, descended immediately in a rage, and jumped on the carriage of the President, and would have strangled him, but for the prompt assistance that some gave by closing the windows, while the crowd of attendants who were present drove them off... So much were the monkeys enraged that they pursued the carriage of the President for nearly a league."

From Ahmadabad we are transported to Agra; and although Tavernier found the heat there most oppressive, there was much in the city that he admired, particularly the palace of the emperors and the tomb of the "Begum, or sultan queen" of Emperor Shah Jahan, which is as famous as the Taj Mahal. "Of all the tombs at Agra," says Tavernier, "this is the most splendid." It is at the east end of the town by the side of the river, in a large square which is "divided into compartments like our parterres, but in the places where we put gravel there is white and black marble". In the middle of the square are three great platforms with towers at the corners. "There is a dome above, which is scarcely less magnificent than that of the Val de Grace at Paris. It is covered within and without with white marble, the centre being of brick. Under this dome there is an empty tomb, for the Begum is interred under a vault beneath the first platform... I witnessed the commencement and accomplishment of this great work, on which twenty-two years have been spent, during which twenty thousand men worked incessantly; this is sufficient to enable one to realize that the cost of it has been enormous."

So richly informative are Tavernier's descriptions of the towns he visited in the course of his travels in India that it is difficult to know where to stop, but we should remember that he was not just a sightseeing tourist but a keen businessman. What he was after were precious stones, which he might purchase and sell at a profit. One of his most interesting chapters tells of his excursions to the diamond-mines.

"The diamond is the most precious of all stones," he begins, "and it is the article of trade to which I am most devoted. In order to acquire a thorough knowledge of it I resolved to visit all the mines. The terrible picture that was drawn of these mines, situated in barbarous countries to which one could not travel except by the most dangerous routes, served neither to terrify me nor to turn me from my intention. I have accordingly been at four mines, and at one of the two rivers whence diamonds are obtained, and I have encountered there neither the difficulties nor the barbarities with which those imperfectly acquainted with the country had sought to terrify me."

The first of the mines he visited was situated "in the territory of the king of Bijapur in the Province of the Carnatic... five days journey from Golkonda and eight or nine from Bijapur"; the site has been identified as 20 miles south of Kurnool. Tavernier says that "all round the place where the diamonds are found the soil is sandy, full of rocks and jungle, somewhat comparable to the neighbourhood of Fontainebleau. There are in these rocks many veins, some of them half a finger and some of a whole finger in width; and the miners have small irons, crooked at the ends, which they thrust into the veins to draw from them the sand or earth, which they place in vessels; it is in this earth that they afterwards find the diamonds."

At this mine, he further states, there are numerous diamond-cutters, each with a steel wheel "of about the size of our plates. They place but one stone on each wheel, and pour water incessantly on the wheel until they have found the 'grain' of the stone. The 'grain' being found, they pour on oil, and do not spare diamond dust, although it is expensive, in order to make the stone run faster, and they weight it much more heavily than we do". He watched the process with intense interest, and concluded that "the Indians are unable to give the stones such a lively polish as we give them in Europe... due to the fact that their wheels do not run so smoothly as ours". He had nothing but praise for the management. "Business is conducted with freedom and fidelity", and he had no difficulty in paying for his purchases with bills of exchange on Agra, Golkonda, or Bijapur.

From all that may be gathered, Tavernier was most highly regarded in India, as a merchant and as a man, and he was selected for the most signal exhibition of royal favour. What must have been the red-letter day in his career was 2 November, 1665, when he went to the palace at Jahanabad to take leave of the Emperor Aurangzeb. "Early in the morning five or six of the Emperor's officers announced that the Emperor wished to see me. Immediately on my arrival at the Court the two custodians of the royal jewels accompanied me into the presence of His Majesty; and after I had made him the customary salutation, they conducted me into a small apartment, which is at one of the ends of the hall where the Emperor was seated on his throne, and whence he was able to see us. I found in this apartment Akil Khan, chief of the jewel treasury, who, when he saw us, commanded four of the imperial eunuchs to bring the jewels, which were carried in two large wooden trays lacquered with gold leaf, and covered with small cloths expressly made for the purpose—one of red and the other of green brocaded velvet. After these trays were uncovered, and all the pieces had been counted three times over, a list was prepared by three scribes who were present."

Then the finest pieces were passed to Tavernier for his examination, and "the first piece which Akil Khan placed in my hands was the great diamond, which is a round rose, very high at one side. At the basal margin it has a small notch and flaw inside. Its water is beautiful, and it weighs 319½ ratis, which are equal to 280 of our carats ..." Tavernier describes it as a "splendid stone", and well he might, for there is good reason to believe that this was the Koh-i-noor itself.

When Tavernier published his "Six Travels" in 1676 he had said that he was "now too old to undertake fresh voyages". But he had under-estimated his powers of endurance, his undaunted love of adventure. His last years are obscure; but this we know, that in 1687, when over eighty, he set out on a seventh journey to the East, and he died two years later in Moscow and was buried in the Protestant cemetery there.

Defoe

DANIEL DEFOE FINDS ADVENTURE
AT HOME

A Tour of England and Wales

ON 3RD APRIL, 1722, "a middle-sized, spare man of a brown complexion with dark-brown coloured hair but wearing a wig, with a hooked nose, sharp chin, grey eyes and a large mole near his mouth" started on the first of a series of journeys which was to cover the whole of Britain and Wales, and his account of which was to constitute the first Guide Book ever written. His name was Daniel Defoe, the author, among a very large batch of books and innumerable tracts, of *Robinson Crusoe, Moll Flanders* and *Roxana.*

Born in London in 1660, Defoe was the son of a butcher of Flemish extraction. He was well educated, at a Non-Conformist school, and had taken to writing political pamphlets in favour of the Non-Conformists, and of liberal political causes. He went into business himself–building and marine insurance–and was once bankrupted. His religious pamphlets had got him into trouble with the authorities and he had sat in the stocks at Temple Bar–where, however, the crowd had applauded him. The description of Defoe quoted above, the only one known to posterity, was one circulated by the magistrates when they were looking for him. After his release from prison, Robert Harley, who was one of Queen Anne's Prime Ministers, took the perhaps wise step from the point of view of the government, employing Defoe as a journalist. Defoe probably received a pension for the rest of his life from the government and he seems to have been regularly employed by both Whig and Tory government, as a journalistic agent. When he went to Scotland it was with the aim of finding out the reactions of the Scots to the Act of Union, which was passed in 1707. It was towards the end of his life that he wrote the literary works for which he is famous: he had made his peace with society but not in any way dishonourable to himself.

He left London on 3 April by Bow Bridge, where the county of Essex began, and about the first thing he noted was something which has been happening ever since–though never so fast as today–London was growing. During the past twenty years or so, all the villages had been doubling or trebling their populations–Stratford, Ilford, Woodford, Epping–all becoming joined to the metropolis in spite of marshes, rivers and canals. The Londoners going to the country were of the richer sort, either retired people or those who could afford town houses, and, Defoe says, there were no less than two hundred coaches kept by the inhabitants within the small circumference of these villages.

He travelled towards Colchester, making a detour towards Barking, Dagenham and the Essex marshes. Here he notes a curious thing. "All along this country it was frequent to meet with men that had from 5 or 6 to 14 or 15 wives; nay, and some more; and I was informed that in the marshes on the other side of the river near the Candy Island there was a farmer who was then living with his 25th wife, and that his son who was about 35 years old had already had 14 wives". He enquired the reason for this and found, from one "merry fellow" who claimed to have had 12 wives himself, that the men, accustomed to the foul air of the marshes, do well but look for their wives from the hilly country. The poor women, of course, leaving their native, healthy country air quickly sicken and die off among the fogs and damps.

Defoe has many such a story to tell; like all good journalists he has an eye for the human. He describes the antiquities of the regions he passes through, not always with great accuracy, and the great houses, at immense length, for he liked splendour although he was a Puritan. He is fascinated by the English Civil War, which was after all only fifty years ago; at Colchester he finds a diary written by one of the inhabitants during the siege of that time in 1648 and he reproduces this in his book.

But, above all, Defoe had an interest which literary men do not usually have–he was concerned about how men earned their living–he was interested in new trades and inventions, in farming and in the customs of seafarers. He is also, of course, interested in the highways and notes with approval the construction of turnpike roads for travellers. In those days, one of the main functions of the roads was to facilitate the passage of huge herds of fat cattle, pigs and sheep travelling from as far away as Leicestershire to the London market. The animals, needless to say, particularly during their winter journeys, made the highways almost impassable for the ordinary traveller. Every day, travelling towards Suffolk, Defoe would meet several droves of turkeys or geese, a drove of turkeys amounting to some five or six hundred birds and of geese upwards of two thousand. Recently the farmers of Suffolk had invented a cart with four wooden storeys, by means of which many thousands of fowls could be carried in a couple of days and a night to the London market. To-day's parallel is the storeyed lorry invented by motor manufacturers for getting their cars to London and ports.

In Suffolk and Norfolk, Defoe saw that already the best farmers were growing turnips and clover; England is already beginning to be the leader of the world in farming. Coming back to London, he watched the horse races at Newmarket. He saw the nobility and gentry, all so eager at placing their wagers and bets that they seemed to Defoe like a lot of common "sharpers" from Smithfield, losing all their high dignity. Of one noble and successful race-horse breeder Defoe says, "his horses were all cheats however honest their master was; for he scarce ever produced a horse that he looked like what he was not, and was what nobody could expect him to be. If he was as light as the wind and could fly like a meteor, he was sure to look as clumsy and as dirty and as much like a cart-horse as all the cunning of his master and the grooms could make him".

Defoe's next circuit was to the south-west, going to Cornwall and returning to London by Gloucestershire and Wiltshire. He leaves by Hampton Court, of which he makes, as he has done of Oxford and Cambridge, a laborious, long and not very interesting catalogue. He also describes in great detail the beautiful house at Wilton belonging to the Earl of Pembroke. Apropos of Stonehenge he makes a disclaimer of his competence to talk about antiquities, noting that "it is indeed a reverent piece of antiquity and it is a great loss as to the true history of it, it is not known". He strikes the coast at Christchurch, which he thinks an inconsiderable place. Of Bournemouth, a tiny village, there is no mention, but Poole is described as a very important seaport, which among other things fits out ships for the Newfoundland fishing every year. The oysters of Poole were the biggest in all England and were pickled, barrelled and sent not only to London but to the West Indies, Spain and Italy. He keeps close to the ports. Saltash, his first Cornish port, he finds to be the ruins of a much larger place and he saw many houses falling down and did not doubt that the rats and mice had abandoned many more. Yet he notes that Saltash has a mayor and alderman, many other privileges, and sends members to the House of Commons. Falmouth, he notes, has taken the trade of Truro except for the tin, and specializes in exchanges with Portugal. Padstow has much of the trade with Ireland.

In Defoe's time Bristol was a rapidly rising port with a population of over fifty thousand. Defoe gives it as double this figure. Bristol, he says, is the greatest, richest and the best port in Great Britain, London only excepted. Nor is it only its great sea-borne trade that is important. Bristol's trade and commerce is supplemented by an important inland waterway and, by rivers and canals, it supplies goods as far afield as Nottingham and the cities on the Trent. In the West Country, he describes the various prosperous textile undertakings–the serges of Exeter and Taunton, the stockings, principally for trade with Spain, which are produced in Wells and Glastonbury, and the druggets, cantaloons and other stuffs from the neighbourhood of Bristol.

This part of the West Country was one of the great manufacturing centres of England at this time. At Taunton he notes approvingly that "there was not a child in the town or in the villages round about of above five years which could not, untaught, earn its own bread in industry". He is somewhat censorious about the goings-on in Bath, writing "the whole time is a round of the utmost diversion. In the morning you, supposing you to be a young lady, are fetched in a chair, dressed in your bathing clothes, that is, stripped to the smock, to the Crossbath. There the music plays you into the bath, and the women that tend you present you with a little floating wooden dish like a basin; in which the lady puts a hankerchief and a nose-gay and a snuff-box and some patches; then the ladies and the gentlemen pretend to keep some distance, and each to their proper side, but frequently mingle; and the place being but narrow, they converse freely, and talk, rally, make vows, and sometimes love; and having thus amused themselves an hour or two they call their chairs and return to their lodgings."

It is impossible to follow Defoe everywhere and so, after noting some aspects of his journey in Wales, it is perhaps good to concentrate on Yorkshire and Lancashire and then on Defoe's account of the country surrounding London.

He started on his tour of Wales from Hereford, passing through the Black Mountains which he describes as a ridge of horrid rocks and precipices between and over which, if he had not had trusty guides, he would never have found his way: at one moment indeed Defoe thought of turning back. South Wales, he found, was a pleasant, agreeable place, highly populated, with a good fertile soil stocked with cattle which supplied Bristol with butter done up in barrels and salted just as Suffolk did for London. At Swansea he noted the great coal trade and says sometimes one could see a hundred ships coaling there at one time.

He passed through Pembrokeshire to Cardigan, which he describes as a nursery of cattle for all England. In North Wales he observes the immense quantities of great standing stones and dolmens, which, he thinks, would make the traveller no longer consider Stonehenge a wonder. Of the mountains of North Wales he writes that "they are so like the Alps that, except for the language of the people, the traveller could hardly avoid thinking he is going from Grenoble to Susa". He found the journey laborious, relieved only by the fact that provisions were everywhere cheap and inns usually good. Also he found the Welsh gentlemen very civil, hospitable and kind. When Defoe let people know that he was travelling out of curiosity to view the country and to be able to talk about it to strangers, their civility was heightened to such a degree that nothing could be more friendly.

Defoe spent a great deal of time in Lancashire and Yorkshire and made innumerable journeys. He was well aware that this was the part of the country where the population of England was increasing the most rapidly. Passing into Yorkshire from Rochdale, crossing Blackstone Edge, they met a high wind with snow on the top of the Pennines although it was August, and heard a sudden clap of thunder which frightened them considerably. It is eight miles from Blackstone Edge to Halifax, and all the way, Defoe says, "it is up hill and down so that, I suppose, we mounted to the clouds and descended to the water level about eight times in that little part of that journey".

As they came nearer to Halifax they noted that the houses clustered thicker and thicker up and down the sides of the steep hills. Defoe was in the middle of one of the great clothing trade districts of England, and though, as they passed, they scarcely saw anyone about in the streets or fields, all the houses were full of people and "all full of business with not an idle person or a beggar anywhere, except perhaps in the alms houses where were the aged and decrepit". The reason for the growth of this industry in the Pennines was that the hills were full of springs of clear water and also of surface coal.

Defoe describes the cloth market in Leeds, the largest in England, where, in a broad street lined with trestle tables, foreign and English merchants would buy goods worth twenty thousand pounds, all in an hour between the ringing of the opening and closing bells. After the closing bell has rung, nobody stays a moment in the market but carries his cloth back if it is not sold. And what is most admirable, he says, "is that it is all managed in the most profound silence, and you cannot hear a word spoken in the whole market by the persons buying and selling. It is all done in whisper".

In Lancashire he finds that Manchester is still a mere village with a constable or "head borough" as its highest magistrate. Manchester sent no members to Parliament. Yet he thinks that it had a population of over fifty thousand people. It had undoubtedly a hospital, a college, a free-school and, what was even rarer, a public library. Its trade was increasing by leaps and bounds. Liverpool he describes as a very flourishing port and city with the finest buildings in England, with the exception of London. Defoe is not at all interested in natural beauty and, though he loves the sight of well-farmed valleys and trim villages, he is as insensitive as was Dr. Johnson to wild nature. Defoe notices, for instance, that fish from Lake Windermere are potted and sent far and wide as dainties. But his general attitude to the Lake District is "a country eminent only for being the wildest, most barren and frightful of any I have passed over in England or even in Wales".

The descriptions of London and its environs make the most fascinating reading. Hampstead had risen from a little country village to what Defoe calls a town, partly because of the fame of its waters (Well Walk reminds one of this). Defoe himself is surprised by the popularity of Hampstead and that the "uneven surface, inconvenient for building, uncompact, unpleasant" did not deter people from flocking there and new buildings arising even up the steepest sides of the hills.

"On the top of the hill there is a very pleasant plain called the Heath of about a mile every way; and in good weather it is pleasant airing upon it. Some of the streets are extended so far as they begin to build even on the highest spot of the hill. But it must be confessed it is so near heaven that I dare not say it to be a proper situation for any but a race of mountaineers, whose lungs have been used to a rarefied air." The view he admits is very fine and he states that once he saw Hanslope steeple, which is only eight miles from Northampton. At the foot of the hill there stood a large house, which belonged to the Earl of Chesterfield, called Belsize, which had been turned into a house of pleasure; to which he notes "the wicked part had given the tone" and the house had been shut by orders of the magistrates.

To the west of London he describes the great houses and palaces of Kensington and Chelsea which latter has the best foundation of its kind in the world for the entertainment of maimed and old soldiers. He noted that Chelsea promises soon to be joined to London. What impresses Defoe is the immense amount of building by the nobility and gentry everywhere to the west of London; to the south of London he observes that new houses are built by the citizens of London. Croydon, Carshalton and Beddington, with the River Wandle and proximity to the Downs, he thinks is the best spot in all London.

The great races on Banstead Downs add to the popularity of this area, as does the Spa of Epsom. This is a place, he says, wholly adapted to pleasure, where you can take your lodgings and go out to see "who and who is together". He makes an idyllic picture of life at Epsom Spa. "Those that had coaches or horses, as soon as the sun declines, take the air on the Downs and those that have not content themselves with staying a little later and, when the air grows cool and the sun low, they walk out under the shade of the hedges and trees. In the meantime, towards evening, the bowling-green begins to fill, the music strikes up in the Great Room and company draws together apace. Here they never fail of abundance of mirth, every night being a kind of ball. The day closes with good wishes and appointments to meet the next morning at the baths or somewhere else." This is altogether, in Defoe's mind, a more obviously salubrious place than the fashionable Bath.

Elegant buildings and jollity characterize the south of London; to the south-east, down the Kentish coast, we come to the serious business of shipping. At Gravesend Reach, all vessels coming up or down the river must anchor for the customs which are managed by soldiers. They are entitled to rummage throughout the ship, but this they very rarely do, though they don't mind taking a tip for their civility. When a ship approaches Gravesend Reach, a sentinel fires his musket as a warning to stop; and perhaps has to do this three times. If the ship takes no notice, a gunner from the fort fires a shot without ball—twice. If this doesn't work, then all the guns from Tilbury Fort, and any others which can be brought to bear on the ship, let fly. Whilst Defoe was at Gravesend he saw a ship deliberateley run the gauntlet and get away from guns and police boats, and also, he learnt, thanks to a fine breeze and a strong tide, to escape from the men-at-war at the Nore.

His tour in Kent included Rochester, with its great naval shipping yards, and Sheerness, which was not only a fortress but a kind of town inhabited by officers of the Ordinance. South-west of the Isle of Sheppey, Defoe writes, "there stands a town memorable for nothing but that which is rather a dishonour to our country than otherwise—namely Queenborough, a miserable, dirty, decayed, poor, pitiful fishing-town. Yet it is vested with Corporation privileges, has a Mayor, and His Worship the Mayor has his Mace carried before him to church and attended in as much state and ceremony as the Mayor of a town twenty times as good". This disgraceful town sends two members to Parliament—as many as the City of Westminster. Yet Defoe notes that all its inhabitants are not worth in hard cash the value of one good estate in Westminster.

An enemy of the pretensions of the aristocracy and of the Church, Defoe, it is plain, has his own social prejudices. He rejoices at seeing merchants becoming gentlemen and living in fine houses. But he has a distinct distaste for neighbourhoods such as the Kent Marshes where laborious people live in what he thinks unhealthy surroundings. So it is with great relief that, when he is touring Kent, he reaches Maidstone and notes that "you begin to converse with gentlemen and persons of rank of both sexes". This makes Maidstone an agreeable place to live in and where a man of letters and of manners will always find a suitable society, both to divert and to improve himself.

Defoe is in fact the great advocate of the decent middle-classes who can be confused with "the gentry". He knows much about low life, as his great novel *Moll Flanders* shows, but he does not like it. This does not prevent him having great sympathy for men and women of all classes whom he knows something about. Defoe, in fact, was no idealistic social reformer, but, genius apart, a very ordinary Englishman with all his prejudices.

Many pages of his Guide Book are of course devoted to London, the great city which swallows up the oysters and cherries of Kent, together with the large all-red Kentish bullocks with their inward-turning horns, the sheep of Leicestershire and the turkeys and poultry of East Anglia. At that time there was not a region within a hundred and fifty miles of the metropolis that did not live by supplying it with necessities or luxuries. Even more than today, the London at the beginning of the eighteenth century dominated the economic life of the country.

Just as today nine people out of ten would be foxed if they had to describe not merely the limits of Greater London but even of Inner London, so Defoe's London is a very vague concept. It includes Deptford and Islington, Marylebone and Tottenham Court. He puts its population at one million five hundred thousand, and considering that the population of all England and Wales was only five and a half million around 1714, this is certainly an over-estimate. Of the spread of London he writes: "It is the disaster of London, as to the beauty of its figure, that it is thus stretched out in buildings, just at the pleasure of every builder or undertaker of buildings, and as the convenience of the people directs, whether for trade or otherwise; and this has spread the face of it in the most straggling, confused manner, out of all shape, uncompact and unequal; neither long or broad, round or square. Whereas the city of Rome, though a monster for its greatness, yet was in a manner round with very few irregularities in its shape."

Defoe catalogues the great public and private buildings of the city. He thinks that men other than those engaged in Government or public business are drawn to live in London by the pressure of life, the need to make more money. Oddly enough, he thought that, with good management of the nation's affairs, which he saw beginning, the public debt would be reduced and so would be taxes. Then, Defoe thought, the reason for the ever-increasing influx of people to London would be removed and many would go back to the quiet towns and the countryside where they could live so much better and more cheaply. A curious thought—and it must be said that neither the public debt nor the taxes nor the rates were ever likely to be reduced as the eighteenth century went on, any more than they are today. Defoe for all his admiration of his own city was, like most Englishmen, someone who believed that the best of England was in the country.

It has been possible only to give a fragmentry glimpse of this book compiled with so much care and enthusiasm and ceaseless travel. The writer of this essay has tried to bring out some of the more picturesque aspects of what Defoe observed. Defoe's whole account of his travels provides a living picture of life at the beginning of the eighteenth century, fifty years before the industrial revolution began. As well as being amusing, it is therefore a most important and unique social document.

THE ACAPULCO GALLEON

George Anson Puts to Sea

COMMODORE GEORGE ANSON stared glumly at Funchal beach, watching the surf beating violently on the stony shore. Desperate as he was for fresh water, he was not prepared to risk his longboats, and ordered a signal to be made to the ships of his small squadron to employ the local Portuguese boats whose owners knew how to avoid the dangers of the coast. That done, he stumped down from the quarterdeck of his flagship, *Centurion*, entered his day cabin and, with hands clasped behind his back, paced up and down, reviewing the situation.

Had Anson been a superstitious man–which he was not–he would have been convinced that some malignant spirit was determined that this present expedition was to be a continuous series of disasters and setbacks. He recalled, with some bitterness, the summons which had sent him hurrying to Whitehall on a cold November day in 1739 and the excitement he had felt when told he was to take command of a squadron of ships and sail to the Philippines without delay. Victualling had begun immediately, but then, at the beginning of January, 1740, he had been informed that the original plans had been changed–he was now to sail for the Pacific.

The conflict which was to become known as the war of Jenkins's

Ear had just begun, and England was at war with Spain. Anson's new commission instructed him to: "Sail around Cape Horn into the South Seas to Annoy and Distress the Spaniards there, whether on the Sea or on the Land, to the Utmost of your Power." It went on to say that he was also expected to locate the Acapulco galleon which sailed to and from Manila once a year and, if possible, capture it and the fabulous treasure it always carried.

He hoisted his flag in *Centurion*, a 4th-rate of just over 1,000 tons. He was eager to sail but, from that day, everything began to go wrong. His sailing orders did not materialize and he could not leave without them; stores were hard to come by and, when obtained, were usually mouldy or rotten; his ships were painfully undermanned and, although he had press-gangs sweeping the district, the miserable creatures they collected soon deserted or went sick.

Month followed month until Anson began to fear he would never sail. He had been promised prime seamen and a regiment of soldiers. He finally got invalids newly discharged from hospital, old Chelsea pensioners, tottering sexagenarians and raw soldier recruits who had never fired a gun in their lives. Those sailors who had enough strength to walk out of Portsmouth deserted as soon as they could, leaving Anson with a squadron whose crews were mainly invalids and cripples.

And still the little squadron was not allowed to leave, for Anson next received orders to wait for a convoy that was preparing to sail for the West Indies. Finally, the long-awaited sailing day arrived and, after three false starts, the convoy put to sea on 18 September, 1740. When two days out of Portsmouth they were joined by another convoy, and the fleet, which numbered more than a hundred and sixty ships, sailed as far as the latitude of Gibraltar. By 29 September both convoys had gone their separate ways, and on a sea that seemed suddenly empty, Anson led his ships towards their first landfall–Madeira.

His squadron consisted of six warships: *Centurion*, 60, two other 4th-raters, *Gloucester*, 50, and *Severn*, 50, and three smaller vessels, *Pearle*, 40, *Wager*, 24, and a sloop, *Tryall*, 8. There were also two store-ships, *Anna* and *Industry*, which were to sail with them until the warships could take the extra stores they carried into their own holds.

Soon after the squadron parted from the second convoy the north-east trade wind failed and the ships drifted through calms or beat against irritating head-winds until, on 25 October, and after a journey that had taken thirty-eight days (three times as long as the average passage) Madeira was sighted at last.

A week later, before leaving the island, Anson heard very disquieting news. A powerful Spanish fleet had been sighted in the neighbourhood and it was obvious that the delays in starting the expedition had lost the element of surprise and given the enemy the opportunity to mount strong opposition.

The British ships cleared the harbour on 3 November, and in light and fickle airs began their slow slog to the south. The ships were so deeply laden that their lower-deck ports could not be opened, and in the stifling, oven-like holds men sickened and died. Anson tried to alieviate the situation, cutting ventilating shafts in decks and sides, but men still died. Then, on 18 December, the Brazilian coast was sighted and the squadron dropped anchor behind the island of Santa Catherina. Boats began to ferry the sick from ship to shore whilst the rest of the crews set to and cleaned the ships with vinegar and fumigated them with smoke–the primitive disinfectants of the time.

Anson stayed in this anchorage for a month whilst his ships were readied for the long voyage ahead. He believed himself to be on good terms with the Portuguese Governor of the island, but that worthy secretly sent a message to the Admiral of the Spanish fleet, then lying in the River Plate, some five hundred miles to the south. The Admiral received the news and led his fleet out to do battle, but the British were already heading for Cape Horn and the Pacific. The ships ran down to the Straits of le Maire, a strong wind and southerly current sweeping them between the snow-covered coast of Tierra del Fuego and Staten Island. Then, as they cleared the Straits, they ran into the full fury of a westerly gale and, reeling and tossing under scraps of canvas, clawed their way to the southward.

After days of hideous battering, when men working aloft had to cling desperately with frost-bitten fingers to avoid being plucked from the yards and thrown to certain death, they ran into a blessed moment of calm. Hardly had the most urgent repairs been done than the wind was shrieking about them once more and the nightmare began again. Another calm, and then the ships were hit by a storm worse than any that they had previously encountered. The battered, struggling ships were unable to keep in company, and after a violent snowstorm had enclosed each vessel in a shroud of whirling white flakes, *Severn* and *Pearle* were nowhere to be seen.

A few days later the little *Anna (Industry* had already left the squadron) was scouting ahead when her look-outs sighted land. It was the jagged black cliff of Tierra del Fuego again. Storms, misery and near despair had brought them back to where they had been five weeks earlier!

The depleted squadron drove to the south-west and, after another vicious storm had sent them cowering under bare poles, morning broke to reveal *Centurion* alone on a heaving, white-capped sea. Anson, desperately tired from days and nights without sleep, was in a critical situation with his squadron scattered and his crew dying of scurvy. After several days of hopeless search he set course for the agreed rendezvous at Juan Fernandez Island. The day before, however, on 22 May, 1741, *Centurion* was struck by a hurricane which blew her sails to tatters, shifted her ballast and stores and threw her on her side. It was only by a miracle that she survived for, with most of her crew sick with scurvy, her numbers were so reduced that the master and chaplain had to take the wheel whilst the few fit men worked frantically to replace her rigging and bend on new sails.

At last they reached the rendezvous of Juan Fernandez–Robinson Crusoe's Island–and with only 200 men left out of her original complement of 521, and most of those that remained both ill and weak, they dropped anchor and struggled ashore. Here fresh water, green grass and vegetables awaited the weary, salt-encrusted seamen. Hardly had they reached the shore, however, when there was an excited cry of "Sail ho!", and soon afterwards *Tryall*, the smallest warship in the squadron, came limping into harbour. Some days later another ship was sighted–the *Gloucester*. Scurvy had so decimated her crew, however, that there was hardly an able man left to work the ship and it was nearly a month before she was finally brought to anchor near the other, and then only after Anson had sent boats' crews out to help fetch her in. Of her original crew of 400 she had few men able to walk and 80 who were so ill that they had to be carried ashore.

Whilst the invalids slowly recovered from the terrible scourge, the rest were kept busy felling trees to make good the damage caused by the storms. In the middle of this work, to everyone's surprise, the tiny *Anna* sailed in, without a single man ill from scurvy, although those on board her had several narrow escapes during the passage, including a brush with Indians. But the ship had been badly strained and Anson reluctantly took everything usable from her, then ordered her to be burnt.

Whilst the repairs on the rest were being carried out, Anson's thoughts kept returning to the pursuing Spanish fleet. If it arrived now and caught him at anchor, with three damaged ships and with most of his men still recovering ashore, he would have stood no chance at all. He was to learn later, however, that he need not have worried. The storm that had blown his ships eastwards had scattered the Spaniards so that finally, of the six ships that had been searching for him, only one eventually struggled back to Spain.

Anson naturally did not know of this at the time, and when a sail was sighted he hurriedly put to sea in *Centurion*, thinking that the stranger was a man-of-war. Closer inspection showed it to be a merchantman which surrendered after a few shots had been put through her rigging. She was found to be carrying a valuable cargo and chests and casks crammed with silver dollars and plate. Her frightened crew also told their captors that the Spanish fleet, as such, no longer existed, to Anson's great delight. Although his squadron was now reduced to three, it was the only force of warships in the area, even though his men together numbered less than the full crew of one 4th-rate, and with not enough men to handle all *Centurion*'s guns. His soldiers also had dwindled to four officers, a sergeant and eighteen men, but never once did he think about sailing home. He was in enemy waters, he had ships and men, and he was determined to capture the treasure ship and make all the suffering and hardships worth while.

Until the galleon sailed, however, he was still under orders to "annoy and distress" the enemy, and this he was about to do. He cruised along the western coast of South America, taking several more prizes, and then, on the night of 12 November, he sent in a force of fifty-six men in armed pinnaces to capture the town of Payta. His men landed, advanced through fire from the guns of a fort, then chased the entire population—many of them still in their nightshirts—out of the town and into the hills beyond. Everything valuable was taken off and, as the absent Governor did not appear anxious to ransom the town, Anson ordered it to be burned to the ground.

A month later *Centurion* made rendezvous with *Gloucester*, which had gone off on an independent cruise, and knowing that the treasure galleon was due to arrive at Acapulco some time in February, squared away for the coast of Mexico. Lack of wind delayed him, and when the squadron arrived off the port Anson learned that the galleon had actually arrived a month earlier. He also learned that the galleon would set sail for Spain earlier than usual, during the first week in March. Although she would be mounting fifty guns and have a full complement of well-trained soldiers, she would also have her hatches crammed with virgin silver.

But news of the presence of the hated English on the coast got back to the authorities in Acapulco and the sailing was cancelled. Anson did not hear of this at once and spent the spring and summer of 1742 cruising along the coast, waiting for her to arrive. In time his ships had become rotten and foul, rigging was spliced and re-spliced, sails were patched and stores were running low. *Gloucester* was even beginning to fall apart until, very reluctantly, Anson ordered her to be burned, after her spars, sails and stores had been taken out and transferred to *Centurion*. The smoke from her burning hulk was still drifting upwards when, on 16 August, he ordered his ships's bows to be pointed towards the south.

Centurion passed through some small islands and then, when the water was running low and scurvy was breaking out again, they reached the island of Tinian. It seemed a veritable paradise. There was plenty of fresh water, fruit and vegetables, whilst cattle, pigs and wild-fowl were there for the killing. The sick–at least a hundred and twenty-eight could not even walk–were ferried ashore and made comfortable, and although twenty-one died, the remainder soon recovered. The ship was made secure and her leaks were plugged and caulked, a working party of fit men sleeping aboard her. On the night of 22 September a full gale came howling from the east, and whilst Anson and the others on shore watched in helpless horror the ship's cables snapped. By morning she had gone.

The rest were marooned and, without papers or even uniforms, could be hung as pirates if captured by the Spaniards. Anson immediately set his men to building another ship, and although they had only a few tools it gradually began to take shape. Then, on 11 October, a sailor glanced out to sea and yelled, "The ship! The ship!"

There was no mistaking the lines of the old *Centurion* and, as the chronicler of the voyage says, Anson was so thrilled that "his joy broke through for the first time the equable and unvaried character which he had hitherto preserved". Work on the *Centurion* went on faster now, although the old ship was desperately in need of a proper dockyard refit. She still leaked, her masts were very shaky and she had only one anchor left out of the original four. Anson therefore decided to make for China where, with luck, he could effect his repairs and return in time to waylay the treasure galleon.

They set sail and on 8 November, after passing through the islands between Formosa and the Philippines, dropped anchor in the Canton River, some twenty-five miles from the Portuguese town of Macao. The ship then sailed for Canton, where she could be properly repaired. At first there were delays, for *Centurion* was the first warship ever to visit China and the local mandarins did not understand that such ships were not liable for harbour dues. Gradually losing his patience, Anson finally solved the difficulties by inviting the mandarins on board, showing them his rows of guns, then casually remarking that, unless he received stores very quickly, his starving sailors might soon become cannibals and they would surely prefer the plump Chinese to their emaciated comrades!

The impressed mandarins left hurriedly and both the stores and facilities for repair were granted immediately. Work began on 7 January, 1743, and were completed within three months. On 19 April *Centurion*–almost as good as new–made sail and stood out to sea.

The waiting game began again. Keen-eyed look-outs stared into the blue distance, hoping to be the first to glimpse the topsails of the Acapulco galleon lifting above the horizon. Days passed, then weeks, and still there was no sign of their quarry. Then, on 20 June, a midshipman looked to the south-east, rubbed his eyes in disbelief, and looked again. There was no doubt about it–the galleon had arrived at last. Anson immediately stood towards her and shortly before dusk the galleon fired a gun, thinking the other to be her consort. Anson calmly returned the salute and kept company with her throughout the night.

By noon of the next day both ships were close and Anson waited, his men at their stations, two seamen to each gun, the rest acting as loaders. He also sent thirty of his best marksmen aloft. At one o'clock *Centurion* hoisted her colours and the Spaniards, taken by surprise, were seen frantically throwing cattle and lumber overboard to clear their guns. The battle lasted for nearly two hours, by the end of which all but one of the Spaniard's officers had been killed or wounded and she was forced to strike. Anson lost no time in transferring most of the galleon's treasure to the hold of his own, a task that took some time, for the other was truly crammed with treasure—130,000 pieces of silver, worth, by today's values, about five million pounds.

Centurion and her prize turned and made for Macao, anchoring there on 11 July, 1743, moving up-river to Canton a few days later. Anson, who had suffered from the prejudices and dilatory customs of the Chinese on his previous visit was more experienced this time and, after some initial arguing, received everything he wanted. *Centurion* was repaired, the galleon sold and, on 15 December, the gallant old ship heaved her anchor for the last time from the muddy water of Macao harbour and pointed her bluff bows for home.

Two weeks later she arrived at Java; then, after taking in wood and water, sailed for Capetown. Leaving there on 3 April she sailed well out into mid-Atlantic and entered the English Channel on 10 June.

Anson's "luck" held to the last. An outward-bound ship informed him that England had been at war with France for nearly three months. Some time later a thick fog came down and *Centurion*, groping her way through it, sailed right through a strong French fleet which was coming down Channel. Anson did not learn of his lucky escape until some time later. How ironic it would have been if the treasure, which had cost so much in effort and lives, had been snatched from him at the last moment!

On 15 June, 1744, *Centurion*'s anchor splashed into the waters off St. Helens, Isle of Wight. The voyage, which had lasted three years and nine months, was over.

THE DANISH EXPEDITION TO ARABIA

Carsten Niebuhr, Sole Survivor

IT WAS a winter's evening when Carsten Niebuhr got back to Copenhagen. By the time he reached the city itself the sky was splashed with a million stars: he interested himself, as he had done almost nightly for the last six years, in taking a few astronomical observations.

Then he rode the last mile home.

Time, they say, heals all things, and the young German geographer was content with his lot. He was home, for though German by birth and speaking only that language, he had come to regard himself as a Dane. He had lived much of his life in Denmark, it had been good to him, he was grateful. Had it not been for the wisdom and generosity of Denmark's king he, a simple country youth from the plains of Friesland, would never have had his opportunity. And an extraordinary, unique opportunity it had been.

Apart from what he himself had learnt from the experience, he had brought back a deal of scientific information for others to ponder and had supervised the dispatch from those distant lands of far, far more. Time had obliterated the accidents, the tragedies, of the past few years. In his own eyes he had achieved what he had set out to do.

Carsten Niebuhr was the sole survivor of the six men who had set out from Copenhagen seven years before: The eyes of Europe had been fixed on these men; their names headline material for every newspaper in every country. It was thought that their brilliance and scientific wisdom would bring back from "Arabia Felix" information to electrify the greedy "Age of Enlightenment", and at the same time raise high the prestige of the northern monarch who had conceived the plan.

For this was the Danish Scientific Expedition, the most stupendous ever undertaken: Marco Polo all over again—but with the marvels of eighteenth-century science to help.

It was 20 November, 1767, when Carsten Niebuhr returned to the Denmark which had sent him off, almost seven years before. And Denmark turned her back. Perhaps that proud, small, northern country had reason to do so. It was not only that the expedition had fallen short of Europe's expectations: the only two members of it who were in fact Danish had failed, more disastrously than their comrades, in everything they had set out to do. And they had perished.

Of the two Danish-born explorers, one—the querulous von Haven—had sent back a small amount of subjective comment on a part of the journey, all of it bemoaning his own problems and hardships. The other—a canary-fancying physician, Kramer—had never put pen to paper, save for a few signatures appended to round-robin letters in which all of them—save von Haven—complained about von Haven.

Small wonder, then, that not a word was written about the Great Scientific Expedition until a very few years ago, two hundred years after the expedition had set sail. Then, in 1962, there appeared in Copenhagen a remarkable book.

If Denmark has little reason to be proud of the original exploit, she can take pride in the twentieth-century work of scholarship and research which has told the story for the first time of the Great Scientific Expedition to "Arabia Felix".

Why "Arabia Felix"? Why "Happy Arabia" for the Yemen, a land whose eighteenth-century horrors took the lives of five men out of six? The name, like the expedition itself, was a mistake. For "Yemen" in the ancient Arabic meant merely "right" as opposed to "left": not "right" against "wrong". But to six young men who set sail from Copenhagen on 4 January, 1761, though their enthusiams differed in type and degree, it was a pleasing place, a happy place to which they were heading, this "Arabia Felix". Though their private greeds and quarrels helped obscure the objective, they were optimistic.

As we have seen, only two of the six were Danish. Two more were Germans: the artist Baurenfeind and the geographer destined to be sole survivor, Niebuhr. There was a second professor, a jealous foil to Professor von Haven, the Swede Forsskal, who would write, on von Haven's death, that it "made the expedition incomparably easier for the rest of us".

There was, too, the nuggety little servant–also a Swede–Berggren.

The expedition had been in the making for no less than five years. The concept had been a German one, passed to the Danish Foreign Minister in the hope that Denmark, which had missionaries all over the Near East and India, might like to arrange it. Professor Michaelis of Hanover suggested that a journey into Arabia would illuminate many problems connected with the Bible: animals, plants, might be identified which were mentioned in Holy Scripture; the geography of Arabia could be studied at first hand; in particular the Red Sea tides with their important bearing on the Israelite exodus from Egypt. The languages and customs of the Arabs themselves could be studied, and in all probability would not have changed overmuch from the day of Moses himself. Palestine had been exposed to all manner of foreign influence and–so the savants reckoned–there was a better chance of finding a modern Moses in "Arabia Felix" than in the Israelite homeland itself.

The expedition set off and–a week later–the *Copenhagen Post* made this announcement:

"As His Majesty, despite the heavy cares of government in these evil times, strives indefatigably for the furtherance of knowledge and of science and for the greater glory of his people, he has dispatched a few days ago by the vessel *Greenland* a group of scholars who will travel by way of the Mediterranean to Constantinople, and thence through Egypt to Arabia Felix, and subsequently return by way of Syria to Europe; they will on all occasions seek to make new discoveries and observations for the benefit of scholarship, and will also collect and dispatch hither valuable Oriental manuscripts, together with other specimens and rarities of the East... These men will remain for several years in the Orient, and as they have already spent several years in careful preparation for this undertaking, it can be confidently expected that their industry and their abilities will, with God's blessing, have happy consequences both for the advancement of knowledge in general and for the more accurate interpretation of the Holy Scriptures in particular..."

But no sooner had *Greenland* set sail than she ran into trouble–a thoroughly frightening storm. One sailor ("only one sailor", as Niebuhr tells thankfully in his diary) was blown from the yardarm and drowned during the first night: a few days later another joined him.

Captain Fisker, in command of *Greenland*, took his battered vessel back to Copenhagen.

At this point Professor von Haven, who had complained bitterly at not being given command of the expedition (the Danish Government ordained that all members would be equal in status and that the canny geologist Niebuhr would act as treasurer), refused to travel farther in northern waters. To von Haven's rage, Captain Fisker would not let him disembark without express government order, but after a pitiful letter from the frightened professor to his king the royal wish was made known that Professor von Haven would travel overland to Marseilles and join *Greenland* there. While the others watched in mingled puzzlement and contempt, the professor was rowed to the Danish shore.

And in the fullness of time *Greenland* arrived off the French south coast. She had been stormbound in Danish waters throughout the winter and von Haven had been able to spend the time pleasantly, moving south to join her. By May, when the party was re-united at Marseilles, his self-esteem had returned: his hatred of Professor Forsskal reasserted itself immediately. During dinner at the captain's table the two men had to be forcibly separated.

By the end of June the vessel with its five "wise men" and their simple, shared, servant, reached Turkey. Von Haven had neither will nor opportunity to do research in his chosen subjects of language and literature, but Niebuhr interested himself greatly in astronomical observation; he had by now checked latitude and longitude of every port they visited, with an accuracy which resulted in some of them being moved on the map. Professor Forsskal had filled many jars with fishy life and he now set off with enthusiasm for the hinterland of Turkey to collect plants, soil, seed. The artist Baurenfeind settled down to sketch as much of the country as time would permit. The physician Kramer had nothing to do and nothing which seemed to catch his fancy: it had transpired during the voyage that he was an expert on the care and breeding of canaries.

The servant Berggren did his job cheerfully and well: these brainy gentlemen, his masters, might find foreign lands stimulating and alarming by turns, but Berggren was an old soldier, he had seen and done more than any of these ever would. He shrugged his shoulders and went on cleaning his masters' boots.

But each day tension between von Haven and Forsskal mounted. And in Constantinople someone discovered that the Dane had purchased a very large quantity of arsenic. Aware that the others had found out and were shocked, von Haven handed it to his compatriot Kramer for safe-keeping: the Professor would ask for it when needed.

With misgiving, simple fear mounting steadily, the expedition sailed from Constantinople. It was September now and the greatly relieved Captain Fisker had sailed for home in his warship: the expedition was aboard a Turkish vessel. At Rhodes his companions signed a joint letter expressing grave anxiety about the behaviour of von Haven. The letter was addressed to the Danish Ambassador in Constantinople, whose acquaintance they had made, and this diplomat watered down their straightforward request that Professor van Haven be removed to a suggestion that nerves were frayed and it would be foolish to split up the party now.

The Danish Foreign Minister replied that the expedition would carry on, exactly as constituted. But by the time the Foreign Minister's letter was received von Haven was dead. Indeed, so long did correspondence take to be considered and replied to that letters addressed to members of the Great Scientific Expedition were received long after they were dead.

By now all were worried about death, in all its forms: death from conspiracy within the group, from robbers, epidemics. The diaries that survived show a constant pre-occupation with it. Fortunately for their sanity, there was much to do from the moment of arrival in Egypt; manuscripts to be bought and studied, plants to collect, maps and sketches to be made. The plan had been for the team to spend only the month in Egypt needed to traverse the country and get out again, but there was now so much material that had to be gathered that the months rushed by.

Niebuhr, who perhaps achieved throughout the trip rather more than anyone else, wrote some hundred and fifty quarto pages on the subject of Cairo alone, while mapping with great accuracy a considerable part of northern Egypt. He also calculated the height of the pyramids.

Within a week of arrival in Egypt our distinguished travellers had adopted Arab dress, though only Niebuhr seems to have carried it off with *panache*. His modest, frank bearing usually won the grudging friendship of the Arabs they encountered, whereas the overbearing attitudes of Professors von Haven and Forsskal landed them in a whole series of unpleasant situations. Fortunately for von Haven there was a deal of "necessary social life", contacting, visiting, dining with governors and diplomats. As for his other work, he referred in a letter to Denmark to "fifty or so manuscripts" which he had obtained and was studying, though he omitted to describe any one of them. He did manage to undertake a short journey in the Sinai peninsula "in the footsteps of Moses". This was in fact one of the more important tasks of the expedition, but by neglecting to obtain a letter of introduction from the Archbishop of Sinai, and by antagonizing his Arab guides, he managed to see precisely nothing. He dismissed the failure as a trivial one, pointed out that there would be no time to make a second attempt: in any case, like the fox's grapes, any possible discovery or revelation would not be of importance.

Early in October, 1762, our friends sailed from Suez towards Djidda, the port of Mecca. They had mellowed, and von Haven had so often been made to seem a fool and a coward that he was quite subdued. The threat of arsenic poisoning still existed, but it was no longer in the forefront of their minds. There had been some illness. Niebuhr, destined to be sole survivor, had succumbed first, but made a good recovery.

On 29 October they anchored off Djidda. Pilgrims had accompanied them south across Egypt and on board the vessel: here the pilgrims left them, headed inland to Mecca. There was a long halt off Djidda, for winds were unfavourable, but by the end of 1762 the six men were safely ashore in their intended "Arabia Felix", scrambling to dry land at the port of Loheia.

Yemen, as they had ascertained, is in two parts: a long flat coastline from this northern port to Mocha in the south, and a mountainous fertile area inland, containing the capital, Sana.

Their first reactions were favourable; they were delighted that people seemed to "become more courteous the farther we got from Egypt". They headed inland to Beit-el-Fakih. An objective at this point was to trace a rare balsam tree, and after some vicissitude Forsskal found one. He was able to get one flowering stalk and this–despite the Danish Government's insistence that everything be sent to Copenhagen–he dispatched to Sweden.

By the time the dried stalk reached there Forsskal was dead. But when it was sent, early in 1763, both he and von Haven, sworn enemies, were alive.

On 6 April of that year, Niebuhr recorded in his diary that von Haven was sick with what seemed a severe stomach complaint, though the frequent bouts of shivering bore a resemblance to the ailment Niebuhr himself had shaken off. Perhaps, he wrote, they were all eating too much meat: this was the only foodstuff their cook seemed able to serve in European style and they were accord—ingly getting little else.

And at this juncture the natives, so friendly at first, turned suddenly, inexplicably, nasty. Petty officials came from nowhere to demand that the expedition's equipment be checked. Alcohol from Forsskal's specimen bottles was dumped on the sand, leaving the specimens to rot. To the rage and despair of the visitors, and the equal annoyance of self-styled "Customs Officers" the neighbourhood was suddenly filled with the stink of alcohol and rotten fish.

At Mocha, which they reached after Beit-el-Fakih, von Haven's condition grew worse. Throughout the voyage he had written to the Danish Foreign Minister complaining of his health: now, when he was really ill, he wrote nothing.

On 25 May–the year is still 1763 and they have been rather more than two years out of Denmark–von Haven died. There was very great difficulty in obtaining a coffin, but eventually to the great relief of his companions–relief of several sorts–he was interred in the small Christian cemetery outside Mocha.

On 9 June the five survivors left Mocha for the inland, highland, capital, Sana. Soon they reached the town of Taaes and there another tiresome functionary ordered them back to the coast. They demurred, were deprived of more goods, more money. Eventually, much poorer–they had lost more goods and money since arriving in "Arabia Felix" than in the previous two years–they were allowed to keep going towards Sana. But here Forsskal was struck down by illness. He trembled violently; he vomited: he fell down. And though he shivered like a naked man in a thunderstorm, it was obvious that he was suffering from high fever.

The party had already decided that they must reach the capital, Sana, carry out the research they had planned, and leave from the port of Mocha by mid-August, when some English ships were due to sail for Bombay. To this end Forsskal demanded he be strapped to the back of a donkey–he was too weak now to sit up–and the party make its way with all speed to Sana. They agreed, for there was little alternative, half-way between coast and capital.

By the time they reached the city of Perim, Forsskal was obviously dying, just as von Haven had died. Seeing the travellers' distress, Arabs flocked round to extort what they could. Money was much desired, but Niebuhr's great problem was the retention of his telescope. This was a wonderful, magic device to the Arabs: why, it turned people upside down, quite apart from what it did in the way of making them bigger. A woman moved by at the end of the street and the magic tube turned her literally upside down, she waddled by with her feet in the air. And her clothes did not fall down.

Somehow Niebuhr managed to retain his magic tube, but by now they were surrounded day and night by grasping Arabs. Arabs who invaded the inn at Perim, stumbled over the dying man on the floor in an effort to find and steal new wonders. At last, literally in order to find solitude in which Forsskal could die, Niebuhr as treasurer of the ill-starred group rented a house for a month, though they would probably require it for a day or two at most. Sick, exhausted, denied help by the locals, they picked up the dying man's bed, staggered through the streets with it. In the process they knocked over an urchin and were stoned by the crowd: they just managed to get into their rented hovel and draw shutters in time to avoid being killed in the street.

For a day or two in this darkened room Forsskal appeared to rally. The others took turns sitting with him, and Niebuhr and Baurenfeind, while the Swedish professor lay back, eyes closed, would sketch the town of Perim through a window which they had finally dared to open. Some of these superb sketches remain.

On 11 July Forsskal died, in that darkened room at Perim. By now death seemed familiar, inevitable; and business-like steps were taken. There was the same trouble about obtaining a coffin, but the body was eventually buried a foot below the surface of the ground, and an hour before dawn, when a burial party would not be disturbed.

A day later grave-robbers dug it up. Finding only a body, they left coffin and corpse on the ground. A local official ordered a man to re-bury the body, and gave him the coffin as payment.

Despite the pillaging and destruction of so many botanical and biological specimens in Arabia, the survivors were now able to send a large collection off to the coast. This included 1300 different plants and seven packets of manuscript. It even reached Copenhagen.

And there, incredible as it may seem, it was left to rot. Alcohol was not replaced, boxes were left unopened, their contents to be consumed by worms and insects. A combination of apathy—the Great Expedition had been away so long—and jealousy over the fact that a Swede had made a large part of this astonishing collection, resulted in the loss of almost all of it. Most had to be thrown away. Today there is but a small collection of non-perishable shellfish and coral surviving in the Copenhagen Museum. A few of Forsskal's manuscripts saw the light of day, and in 1950, after almost two centuries had elapsed, his notebook was published with its important information two hundred years out of date.

But all this was in the future. The four survivors pushed on with all speed to Sana.

And here they found only delight, after the horrors of the journey. The Imam made them greatly welcome, they ate good food, slept in comfort. They were able to fill notebooks, sketchbooks, with information; their every request was granted. The Imam urged them to spend a year as his guests.

They refused. With two of their number already victims of the country and its sinister illness, they decided to make for Mocha and catch the English vessels in August rather than wait a twelvemonth, which they could have done, and catch the same ships a year later on the next, monsoon-speeded, voyage. The deciding factor in their decision was that both Professors, whose researches into philology and science were so much a reason for mounting an expedition in the first place, were gone.

Once away from Sana they ran into more perils on the way to Mocha. And when they reached the port the English vessels had sailed. This, to sick, exhausted, men, was almost the *coup de grâce*. They had left the comfort and safety of Sana to sink again into the hellhole of Mocha—and now they might well stay there a year. Few of them expected to survive that long.

Fate smiled, if only for a moment: one English vessel had been delayed in loading, it was still available to take them to Bombay. On 21 August, 1763, four men embarked on it, three of them having to be carried.

A week later, both Baurenfeind and the servant Berggren had perished. They were buried at sea. The two survivors, physician

Kramer, geographer Niebuhr, reached Bombay 11 September, 1763. Their chief interest was, understandably, to get home, via London, as this would be the easiest route and neither had strength or will to carry out the planned last half of the journey, overland through Syria. But sailing vessels have to travel with the monsoon wind, and when this was blowing the right way, from India towards Africa, Kramer was far too ill to be moved. Niebuhr nursed the helpless healer till he died on 10 February, 1764.

As Thorkild Hansen, a fellow-Dane, points out in his description of the fantastic journey, "Kramer did not leave behind him a single word. That enigmatic person made the whole of the journey from Copenhagen to Bombay without so much as writing a letter or making a note. In all the pile of documents on the Arabian journey in the State Archives there is not a word in Kramer's hand. If we did not have his signature as a witness on some of the letters sent by the others we might well doubt that he had ever been on the expedition. His only message to posterity is a few words of advice on the proper care of canaries."

By the time Kramer died the monsoon had switched direction again: it would be six months before Niebuhr could set sail for London.

His health had improved and he decided to implement the original plan, travel home overland.

Before he set off he completed a monster work on Bombay. Then, 8 December, 1764, the lone geologist boarded an English warship for the port of Muscat in South-east Arabia.

One might expect his enthusiasm to be at an end: not a bit of it. The long trip home, via Persepolis, which Alexander had burnt down after defeating the Persians, and a host of other places, was the most rewarding part of his whole journey. Perhaps the absence of his companions helped toward this. He never regretted the fact that copying a cuneiform alphabet in blinding sunlight, off shimmering, glaring rocks, so damaged his eyes that, years later, he went blind.

And so, slowly but lovingly across Asia Minor and into eastern Europe, Carsten Niebuhr made his return journey, keeping up the diary which is one of the few worthwhile legacies the Great Expedition left behind. He reached Germany and wrote: "There are such comprehensive maps of all the regions between Breslau and Copenhagen already in existence that it would be superfluous to continue any further with these records."

It was 6 September, 1767. Carsten Niebuhr closed his diary. On 20 October he rode into Denmark.

He was glad to be home, to be greeted by the now greatly aged Foreign Minister, Bernstorff. He was not resentful when the Minister found something urgent to do and left him.

Niebuhr and his Great Expedition were forgotten. Nobody, anywhere, cared.

He tidied up his accounts, financial and otherwise, and submitted them. There was no comment.

Carsten Niebuhr died, blind but otherwise fit and strong, on 26 April, 1815. He had published a few works on his research, none of which set the Kattegat on fire, and he was content. He had done his duty.

"Arabia Felix" kept her secrets.

CAPTAIN COOK'S FIRST VOYAGE

By *Endeavour* to Australia

In 1768 the scientific world of the time awaited an astronomical phenomenon with great enthusiasm, for the following year the transit of Venus across the sun's disc was due to take place on 3 June. Observations would, it was hoped, determine the distance between the earth and sun, and England's Royal Society decided to fit out an expedition to observe the transit in the opposite hemisphere.

They chose Dalrymple, Chief Hydrographer to the Admiralty, to lead this expedition, but as he had no experience of naval discipline and refused to serve in a subordinate capacity someone else was required.

From a list of "possibles" the Society unanimously chose James Cook, a comparatively unknown warrant officer in the Royal Navy: but, as it turned out, the ideal choice. Cook was one of nine children and the son of a farm labourer. When the boy was thirteen years old he was apprenticed to a Yorkshire shopkeeper in Staiths, but at eighteen he turned sailor and went to sea in a collier trading out of Whitby, rising to the rank of mate. He was in the Thames in 1755 when the press gangs were very active and, to anticipate the inevitable, volunteered for the Navy as an able seaman.

Later, having risen to the rank of master of a small vessel, the

Mercury, he joined Sir Charles Saunders's fleet in the Gulf of St Lawrence. He undertook the survey of the river and his brilliant work greatly assisted General Wolfe to capture Quebec.

He continued with his survey work and charted more of the St Lawrence as well as part of the coast of Newfoundland and Labrador. His work, together with a short paper on astronomical mathematics which he had submitted earlier to the Royal Society, earned him the command of the expedition to the South Seas.

He was promoted to Lieutenant and, typically, chose his own vessel, a 370-ton sturdy collier with a draught of only thirteen and a half feet. It was named *Endeavour*. Before the preparations were completed, Captain Wallis returned from a voyage around the world (1766-68) in *Dolphin* and, on being asked for the most suitable spot in the South Seas from which to observe the transit of Venus, named an island which he had visited called King George the Third's Island.

Cook sailed from Plymouth on 26 August, 1768, with, as his journal says, "94 persons including officers, seamen, Gentlemen and their servants, near 18 months' provisions, 10 carriage guns, 12 swivels, with good store of ammunition and stores of all kinds".

Sailing with him as "Gentlemen" were Charles Green, astronomer to the expedition; Dr Daniel Solander, a distinguished botanist, and artists and naturalists headed by Joseph Banks, a young and wealthy man who was nevertheless a dedicated botanist and who later, as Sir Joseph, became President of the Royal Society. His personal wealth was put to practical use, for he helped equip the ship with "all sorts of machines for catching and preserving insects; all kinds of nets, trawls, drags and hooks for coral fishing", and a curious sort of telescope which enabled the bottom of the sea to be seen, even at a great depth.

Thus equipped, and with Cook ensuring that by a balanced diet the dreaded scurvy would be prevented, *Endeavour* touched at Rio de Janeiro and Tierra del Fuego, then headed for the Straits of Le Maire and Cape Horn. As they went, the scientists on board were busy pulling in specimens from the sea or collecting them from their landfalls, drawing and classifying them and putting some into preserving bottles.

The passage around Cape Horn and into the Pacific beyond took thirty-four days, and Cook, who was fortunate with the weather, stated that the route he took was preferable to that through the Straits of Magellan. At daybreak on the morning of 11 April, look-outs reported the island then known as King George the Third's Island, and by the following day the ship had drawn close to the land. She was greeted by the occupants of native canoes who waved green branches, signifying welcome. They followed the ship as she stood on under easy sail and, as Banks wrote: "Before the anchor was down we were surrounded by large numbers of canoes, the people trading very quietly and civilly, chiefly for beads, in exchange for which they gave coconuts, breadfruit both roasted and raw, some small fish and apples. They had one pig with them which they refused to sell for nails upon any account, but repeatedly offered it for a hatchet; of these we had very few on board, so thought it better to let the pig go than to give one of them in exchange, knowing on the authority of those who had been here before, that if we did so they would never lower their price."

The ship swung to her anchor and John Gore, the third officer, who had sailed with Wallis in *Dolphin*, recognized several old friends amongst the natives and led a party ashore. He was very much on his guard, for Wallis had received rough handling at the same place two years earlier. Nevertheless, he ordered his men to try and cultivate a friendship with the natives and to treat them with all humanity. This insistence on generous and proper respect for others showed that Cook possessed traits rare in sailors of those days.

He and his men found themselves in a veritable Arcadia. Over their heads was a profusion of breadfruit and coconuts: yams, bananas and sugar-cane grew wild: the island had ample fresh water: there were pigs, wildfowl and chickens, and specially bred dogs for eating, whilst the encircling sea teemed with fish. There were no snakes or, in fact, anything dangerous on the island, and as there was no winter the native huts, made from tree-bark beaten into cloth, were open to the warm, gentle breezes. Life on the island was a continual round of fishing and swimming, feasting and love-making. An idyllic existence, it might be thought.

With few possessions of their own, however, the natives were soon trying to acquire some of the—to them—treasures of the white men. Trouble began early. Some of the "Gentlemen" were being entertained in a chief's hut on the day after their arrival, and Banks, a very personable young man of twenty-five, found himself seated next to the chief's middle-aged wife, who began to pester him with her attentions. He, quite naturally, was more interested in a pretty young girl seated opposite and, calling her to his side, began to give her some beads and other showy trifles. The situation became interesting, with the wife showing her irritation at such flagrant rivalry, when there came a serious interruption: Dr. Solander and Mr. Monkhouse, the ship's surgeon, both complained that they had been robbed; Solander of his spy-glass, the other of his snuff-box.

Banks demanded the return of the stolen articles, and although the worried chiefs made a counter-offer of a large quantity of cloth, would not be satisfied until they were given back. After complicated and lengthy dealings with various people, the articles were returned at last and, when they were handed over, everyone became good friends again and began to press gifts upon each other. Such incidents were continually repeated; the natives' hands were constantly dipping into the white men's pockets and frequently only the threat of firearms would end the arguments that arose.

Cook meanwhile had been planning a permanent settlement on the island which he now learned was called Otaheite by the natives, and which today is known as Tahiti. He chose a part of the sandy beach on the north-east point of the bay and erected a tent to mark where a fort would be built. Then, leaving a midshipman and some marines to guard it, he, Banks and others went exploring. As they went, a number of ducks flew overhead and Banks, firing at them, happened to kill three with one shot. "This," says Cook, "struck the natives with the utmost terror, so that most of them fell suddenly to the ground as if they had also been shot at the same discharge."

They soon recovered and the party strolled on. Back at the tent, however, things had become ugly. Some natives had collected around it, and whilst the sentry's attention was distracted one seized his musket and began to run away with it. The midshipman ordered the marines to open fire and the thief was shot dead. When Cook returned he had great difficulty in persuading the scared Tahitians to come out of hiding, but eventually peace was restored and the natives were soon carrying on as if nothing had happened.

As if in compensation, a few days later the expedition lost its best landscape painter, Mr Buchan. He had been subject to epileptic fits and died after a severe bilious complaint which had begun on board ship. To avoid offending the natives, he was buried at sea with full honours.

The thefts continued, disturbing the otherwise tranquil existence on the island. On one occasion a chief came to Banks in great distress, claiming that the ship's butcher had threatened to cut his wife's throat. Investigation showed this accusation to be true. The butcher had taken a fancy to a stone hatchet which he had seen in the chief's house and had offered the woman an iron nail (much used as currency) and, when she refused his offer, seized the hatchet and threatened to cut her throat if she offered resistance. When Cook heard of the trouble he ordered the butcher to be tied to the ship's grating, stripped and flogged. The chief, his wife and other natives were called to the ship to watch the punishment, but as soon as the first stroke was given they pleaded that the flogging should stop. Cook was determined to set an example, however, and, to an accompaniment of tears and sobs from the natives, the butcher received his full two-dozen.

On the whole, however, the seamen and natives got on well together, both being amused and intrigued by the customs and habits of the other. The seamen were especially fascinated by the tattooing on many of the Tahitians and, despite the pain, had themselves similarly decorated.

Work on the fort went on. High walls were raised around it and six swivel guns and two 4-pounders were moved into position. Joseph Banks also set up a kind of store at the fort's entrance and soon found that for an axe, hatchet, large nails and knives, almost anything could be obtained from the natives. The observatory was set up on 1 May; two smaller observatories were created on the other islands and on 4 June the transit of Venus was checked by Dr Solander, Mr Green and Cook from these three stations.

That done, Cook set off in the ship's pinnace and made a circuit of the island, charting and surveying as he went. Other islands were similarly charted and then, his work done on Tahiti, Cook decided it was time to leave the island and fulfil the second part of his mission—to proceed to the South Pacific and ascertain whether a great southern continent existed which, as many believed, was created to "balance" the huge land-mass of Asia.

The fort was dismantled, and although the thefts still went on most of what was stolen was later recovered. Then a more serious incident occurred. Beguiled by conditions on the island, and not relishing a return to the rigours of life at sea, two of the marines deserted, hiding themselves in the mountains. Realizing that it would take weeks to find them, Cook took several of the leading Tahitians hostage, vowing that they would not be released until his marines were tracked down, captured and returned. The natives were naturally put out by his action, for they had nothing to do with the desertions, but agreed to help. The men were finally rounded up and confined until *Endeavour* was at sea again, when both were given two dozen lashes.

When the time came for parting, the grief of the islanders was very apparent. Indeed, one of the chiefs, Tupia, insisted on sailing with the expedition and Cook agreed to him joining them, and also allowed him to take his 13-year-old servant. The anchor was weighed, and at noon *Endeavour* moved slowly out of the bay. She was surrounded by hundreds of canoes filled with loudly sobbing natives until, as more sail was made, the canoes were left bobbing in the ship's wake. Tupia, at the masthead, continued to wave to his friends as long as they were in sight.

On leaving Tahiti, Cook visited the neighbouring islands, the first white man to do so, and gave the group the collective name of the Society Islands.

Four day's sailing to the west and south-west brought him to another island which Tupia informed him was called Oheteroa. As the ship drew nearer, Cook could see a large number of warlike natives drawn up on the beach and several war-canoes lurking nearby ready to dash out if he attempted to land. Accepting the situation with a shrug, he ordered his helmsman to bear away and, for the next six weeks, *Endeavour* sailed on and on, without any signs of the southern continent.

Finally, on 6 October, land was seen stretching away to the horizon, with ranges of hills rising one above the other and with a chain of high mountains beyond. It was realized that this was part of New Zealand, which had been discovered by Abel Tasman in 1642. A party went ashore but found the native New Zealanders fierce and hostile. Although several attempts were made to overcome this attitude, they were unsuccessful. Unable to obtain any provisions whilst he lay in harbour, Cook named it Poverty Bay and at sea again began to follow the coast northwards.

Having finished the examination of the north-western shore of New Zealand, *Endeavour* ran into fierce gales, and Cook was glad to reach the safety of a large and protected harbour which he named Charlotte's Sound. Whilst the storms raged outside, Cook took possession of the territory and carefully surveyed it. Whilst doing so he climbed a hill and, looking to the south-east, was surprised to see water when he had, from what Tasman had said, expected land. It was obvious that the land mass was not continuous but divided by a passage of some kind. When the storms abated he took *Endeavour* through the channel he had sighted earlier, a strait between North and South Islands and which today bears his name. By sailing through this strait and between the two islands, Cook destroyed once and for all the myth of the great and unknown continent–Terra Australis–in the South Pacific, a continent that was believed to extend all the way to the South Pole.

Still loath to sail for home, Cook now decided to make for the eastern coast of New Holland (Australia) and its uncharted and unnamed coast. April 28, and twenty day's sailing, brought him to the coast of Australia and the point where Tasman's survey had ended. The next day Cook and some of his "Gentlemen" went ashore in a large bay which they named Sting Ray Bay. Banks, however, found so many botanical treasures there that he insisted that it be renamed Botany Bay.

Cook was still trying to make friends with the natives, but although they did not appear warlike they refused to converse by signs, and seemed completely indifferent to the beads and other trinkets offered them–trinkets which had been so eagerly sought after by the natives of Tahiti.

Endeavour moved slowly along the east coast of Australia and Cook solemnly claimed the country in the name of Great Britain. He also surveyed and charted as he went and continued to do so until the middle of June. So far no accident had yet occurred in a voyage of 2,000 miles along a hitherto unexplored coast but, on a clear moonlight night, the ship ran up on a sharp coral reef and stuck fast. Indeed, so great was the initial impact that several planks which formed her sheathing floated off and the water began to flood in through a large rent in her hull.

The pumps were manned, and although the men toiled through the night in relays the leak could hardly be kept under. When day broke, Cook was rowed around the ship and realized that, tight-fixed as she was, the only way to get her off was to lighten her. Overboard went guns, iron and stone ballast, casks, hoop staves, "Oil Jarrs, decay'd Stores etc.", but she still stuck fast. Cook then decided to heave her off, although, once she was free and in deep water, she would very probably founder. He sent as many of his hands as could be spared from the pumps to the capstan and windlass and she was finally prized loose from the reef.

To everyone's surprise the depth of water in her hold remained level and she was edged across to the mainland where, in a convenient harbour, she was beached and repaired. It was found that a large piece of coral had forced its way through her timbers and acted as a plug, otherwise she would have undoubtedly sunk the moment she had been freed from the reef. The site where the ship was beached was fed by a stream which Cook named the Endeavour River. Here the natives were more friendly than any they had met in this region, but still showed complete indifference to anything but food.

Banks and his colleagues were kept very busy during the stay, for almost everything they examined, whether animal or vegetable, seemed new or unusual. "They were particularly pleased with the animal called by the natives, kangaroo. They saw several at a distance, but a long time elapsed before they could succeed in shooting one."

The repairs finished, *Endeavour* made for the open sea once more, but a sudden calm sent her drifting towards other reefs near the shore, reefs which had the large waves of the Southern Ocean breaking over them. When it seemed inevitable that she would run upon one of these, a narrow channel was sighted and the ship edged her way through in safety. Soon afterwards Cook reached a point of land from which he could see open water to the south-west and, landing on an island, took possession in the name of his king and country of the immense coast-line he had discovered, giving it the name of New South Wales. The island on which the ceremony was performed he called Possession Island.

By this time the crew of *Endeavour* were worn out from sickness and fatigue and Cook decided not to examine the coasts of New Guinea as he had hoped, but to head for England. The bluff, salt-stained bows of the ship were turned for home, but not before Cook had taken her through the Torres Strait to prove that Australia and New Guinea were separate land masses. He held course for Batavia, where he hoped for a refit, but the climate there proved more fatal than all the other hardships of the voyage combined. His men began to sicken and soon there were only ten who remained immune. Tupia and his young servant had been afflicted with scurvy from the time they had left their own island and were the first to die from the "pestilential air" of Batavia.

Others died on the passage from Batavia to the Cape of Good Hope, thirty being buried at sea, including Mr Green and Mr Monkhouse, the surgeon.

On 10 June, 1771, the Lizard was sighted by the same look-out who had first seen New Zealand, and two days later Cook "came to an anchor in the Downs, having been employed two years and eleven months in his voyage round the earth".

This was the most important and productive journey of exploration that the world had ever known, and for this alone Cook must rate as the greatest navigator and explorer in history. He was not content with what he had done, however, for a second voyage of exploration (1772–75) took him to the far north. He sailed for the Antarctic, covering more than 75,000 miles, and passed right around the world. The Antarctic Circle was crossed for the first time and he was able to delete from the maps the imaginary continent that was supposed to lie to the far south of Australia.

The most significant achievement of this second journey, however, was the fact that in an exhausting journey of three years he lost only one man and proved that it was possible to remain at sea for long periods without suffering the ravages of scurvy which previously had decimated so many ships' companies. This success was made possible by careful attention to diet and hygiene; and by his great example–which opened the world to extended maritime exploration–he received the Copley gold medal of the Royal Society.

On his third journey he sailed once more to the Pacific and rediscovered the Hawaiian Islands, then sailed northwards along the North American coast as far as Bering Strait until he found his way barred by ice, which ended his hope of finding the elusive North-west Passage from the Atlantic to the Pacific. He returned to Hawaii where he was killed on 14 February, 1779, in a senseless squabble with the natives.

MUNGO PARK IN WEST AFRICA

The Exploration of the Niger Region

MUNGO PARK was perhaps the most remarkable of explorers. His amazing adventures in eighteenth-century Africa made his name a legend in that largely unknown continent. During his relatively short life–he died when he was 35–he made two memorable journeys to explore the Niger.

It had long been known that this great river had its source a mere 150 miles from the Atlantic coast, and that it flowed not westwards to the ocean, but eastwards and northwards towards the great Sahara Desert. This gave rise to much speculation about the unknown interior of Africa. It was not then known that the Niger made a great detour south-eastwards and entered the Atlantic in the Gulf of Guinea, disguising its mighty outflow in a huge delta swamp, which early explorers did not suspect was the mouth of the third greatest river of Africa.

The learned men of the eighteenth century believed that they possessed nearly the sum total of human knowledge. But the mystery of Africa, and particularly that of the Niger, was still unrevealed. And so in London the African Association was formed in 1788, and this Association sent out Mungo Park to explore the Niger region.

Mungo Park was born in 1771 at Foulshiels, near Selkirk, the son of a prosperous Scottish farmer, who had thirteen children, only eight of whom reached maturity. Mungo was sent to Edinburgh University where he studied medicine and took his surgeon's diploma. In 1791 he went to London seeking a medical post. There he was introduced to Sir Joseph Banks, President of the Royal Society, and Treasurer of the African Association, who was so taken by this "upstanding, well-built young Scotsman, six foot high", that he recommended him to the Association as the man to continue the search for the course of the Niger. Major Daniel Houghton had already penetrated well into the interior but had been killed after sending back much useful information–robbed and left to die in the desert in Ludamar, the place where Mungo Park was to suffer his greatest tribulation.

Mungo Park went out to West Africa on the brig *Endeavour*. His mission was to find his way to the Niger by any route which served him best, discover its source and its mouth, and plot its course. The Association gave him a letter of credit for £200 with a Dr Laidley, a well-established trader at Pisania, on the River Gambia. The trading was mainly in slaves, but the good doctor was apparently a genial and friendly man, despite his grisly and disreputable trade, and a good Christian to boot, by the standards of the day. Mungo Park himself saw nothing wrong in the slave trade, though he was later to be horrified by his own experiences in close contact with it.

Mungo Park left Pisania on his first terrible journey on 2 December, 1795. He rode on a horse, a small, hardy beast to which he was to owe his life. His party consisted of two Africans, Johnson, a freed slave, and Demba, a slave boy who had been promised his freedom if the expedition should be a success. Four African slave merchants accompanied them part of the way. The journey was beset with difficulties from the start. Crossing the upper Senegal basin into the semi-desert region of Kaarta, Mungo found himself among the African Moors. With the simple and, in the main, friendly negroes he usually got on well. He spoke their Mandingo language, was always ready to doctor them, and was, it seems, very popular with the African women. But with the Moors, who lived on the fringes of the great desert, it was a different matter. He found them inherently cruel and indifferent to human life. They regarded the negroes as animals and were the greatest slave traders in Africa. Europeans they hated and despised as infidels.

Already the news of the white man's progress through the various African kingdoms, some at war with each other, had spread far and wide. He was regarded with a mixture of curiosity and suspicion, and the fact that he travelled alone, apart from his two negroes, made him an easy prey for robbers, and one of the first things he learned about Africans was that they were inveterate thieves and robbers. He was robbed over and over again, forcibly and quite openly, often with jeers and insults, until finally he had little more than he stood up in.

Mungo Park suffered all this with an iron patience and an imperturbable endurance which makes his story an epic in the annals of exploration. He was prepared to suffer anything, believing that beyond the pain and the torments, on the other side of the dark horizon, lay his bright goal, the magic River Niger.

Shamed, insulted, imprisoned, robbed, the long-suffering young explorer travelled on with nothing but his two slaves, his horse, a few tattered clothes, a beaver hat in which he kept hidden his precious diary, and two compasses. When he arrived at Kemmoo, the capital of Kaarta, his bedraggled and truly fearsome appearance—so different from what was expected—was greeted with something like horror, though the king of Kaarta received him well, and provided him with an escort to lead him on his way to the neighbouring Moorish kingdom of Ludamar. The route was a scene of confusion, Kaarta being at war with Bambarra, a half-Moorish, half-negro kingdom to the south of Ludamar.

Beyond Ludamar—he did not know how far to the east—lay the Niger, and the intrepid Scot could not know the terrors and sufferings which awaited him in this Moorish state. As he passed through the Moslem crowds they hissed and spat upon the hated Christian, robbed and abused him, his property being lawful plunder for the followers of Mohammed. He made his way south, trying to reach Bambarra, through which country the magic river Niger was reputed to run. He came to a part of Ludamar where the negroes outnumbered the fanatical Moors, and was staying at Dalli in friendly surroundings, with bright hopes of at last reaching his goal, when a party of Moorish horsemen descended upon the village with orders from Ali, Emir of Ludamar, to take the white man to Benowm, the camp where the Emir held court. If he did not go peaceably, he would be taken there by force.

Thus, as he puts it, was his golden dream shattered. It was a terrible moment. Resistance was of no avail. Once more he must fall back on his patience and his hope, and perhaps rarely, in the long and miserable weeks and months which were to come, were these qualities so strained in a human being.

Ali's men told him he had nothing to fear, but he knew the Moors better than that. At Benowm the white traveller was treated as an object of great curiosity, as well as scorn and contempt. They fingered his clothes and poked his flesh, threatening him with all kinds of unspeakable things if he did not acknowledge Allah and his Prophet.

Half fainting through ill-treatment, lack of food and water, he was finally dragged before Emir Ali, who was an old man with an Arab cast of face and a long white beard, and whose expression was marked with sullenness and cruelty. Ali regarded him with more suspicion than curiosity. White men were very unwelcome in this part of Africa. What were the Emir's intentions towards him was unclear, but plainly he had no intention of letting him go.

Mungo Park could do nothing but wait, and endure what befell him. Teased, tormented, exhibited by the Moors, whose curiosity was mingled with a cruel sense of humour, he just set himself the task of waiting and enduring with a patience which was truly Christian, as well as being the only course in the circumstances if he wished to survive.

Day after day he had to endure this humiliating and demoralizing treatment. "They asked a thousand questions," he wrote, "inspected every part of my apparel, searching my pockets, and obliged me to unbutton my waistcoat and display the whiteness of my skin. They even counted my toes and fingers, as if they doubted whether I was in truth a human being."

The women were more inquisitive than the men. "Anxious to conciliate favour," he said, "and if possible afford the Moors no pretence for ill-treating me, I readily complied with every command, and patiently bore every insult; but never did any period of my life pass away so heavily; from sunrise to sunset I was obliged to suffer, with an unruffled countenance, the insults of the rudest savages in the world." It was little wonder that Mungo Park hated and despised the Moors and reckoned the negroes greatly their superiors.

They put him in a tent, outside which was tethered a wild pig, a form of insult, the pig being considered unclean by the Moors. Mungo wrote: "The boys assembled to beat the hog and the men and women to plague the Christian. It is impossible for me to describe the behaviour of a people who study mischief as a science and exult in the miseries and misfortunes of their fellow creatures."

Ali was being strongly urged to put the white man to death as a spy, but his brother came forward with a less humane suggestion that his eyes should be put out. The malevolent Ali agreed to this, but suspended the sentence until Fatima, the queen, who was away in the north, had had an opportunity of inspecting this human curiosity.

The inquisitiveness of the Moorish ladies remained unabated, and went to limits which had a not unexpected and even amusing turn. One evening, wrote Mungo: "A party of them came into my hut, and gave me plainly to understand that the object of their visit was to ascertain, by actual inspection, whether the rite of circumcision extended to the Nazarenes as well as to the followers of Mohammed. The reader will easily judge of my surprise at this unexpected declaration; and in order to avoid the proposed scrutiny, I thought it best to treat the business jocularly. I observed to them that it was not customary in my country to give ocular demonstration in such cases, before so many beautiful women; but if all of them would retire, except the young lady to whom I pointed (selecting the youngest and handsomest), I would satisfy her curiosity. The ladies enjoyed the jest and went away laughing heartily; and the young damsel herself to whom I had given the preference (though she did not avail herself of the privilege of inspection) seemed in no way displeased at the compliment, for she soon afterwards sent me some meal and milk for my supper."

Mungo was a tall, very handsome young man in his twenties, and there is no doubt that the Moorish women's interest in him was a fundamental and natural one. After this incident he was taken to be inspected by some of the ladies of Ali's harem. They examined his hair and skin with great attention, "but affected to consider me as a sort of inferior being to themselves and would knit their brows and seem to shudder when they looked at the whiteness of my skin". Doubtless their natural propensities were inhibited by the presence of the watching guards and eunuchs.

The magnificent beard which Mungo had grown was an object of great curiosity and comment, and he was remembered for over a hundred years in that part of Africa as "Big Beard".

But there was little enough to find amusing in his situation and in the way he was treated by his cruel and unpredictable captors, who kept him short of food and water, and who refused him even the most elementary privacy. As the miserable days passed, the blackness of the prospect before him began to cloud even his sanguine temperament. Escape was impossible. It was the middle of the hot season. He had been deprived of every possession. His distress was merely a matter of sport to the Moors. His one consolation was the faithful boy slave, Demba, whose courage and companionship helped him to bear the long months of torture.

One day he left his tent and walked to some shady trees a short distance away, where he lay down in the hope of obtaining a little solitude. Here he was discovered by Ali's son and a band of horsemen who ordered him to get up and follow them back to the camp. When he begged to be allowed to stay for a few hours, one of the horsemen drew his pistol, pressed it to Mungo's temple and pulled the trigger. The gun failed to go off. Again the Moor pressed the trigger and again the gun failed to fire. After such a providential escape, Mungo returned to Benowm in the firm belief that he was spared to complete his mission.

He was taken before Ali, who told him that the next time he was found wandering outside the camp he would be shot forthwith. Despite his resolute indifference to what they did to him, the Emir and his men continued to play cat-and-mouse with Mungo. Ali went north to fetch his queen, and after the lady had inspected her lord's plaything it was proposed that his eyes should be put out.

Meanwhile his capricious captors gave him back his horse, but only in order to make sport of him the more. He was made to ride about Benowm to show himself to the women, and during these enforced peregrinations on his bony little horse the enfeebled, listless white man would be charged by the Arabs on their magnificent steeds and used as a target for their furious and terrifying riding exercises.

During the fearful heat of the Saharan day he was not allowed to go inside the tent which had been allotted to him and his slaves, and was forced to remain outside in the terrible sun so that he could always be on show to anyone who might pass.

A sudden threat of war from Bambarra brought about a quick change in the course of events. Ali's son ordered the whole of the tented city of Benowm to be moved northwards to where the Emir was encamped. It was a complete exodus—men, women and cattle, the men on their horses, the women on bullock carts, the Emir's favourite concubines on camels fitted with sun canopies. The prisoners had to follow as best they could, without rations and scrabbling for water along with the cattle, for the wells were only for the faithful, and Christians and negro pigs were not allowed to drink at them.

When they got to Ali's camp, Mungo was presented to Queen Fatima, "a woman of Arab caste with long black hair and remarkably corpulent", who at first appeared rather shocked at the thought of having a Christian so near her. But Fatima was a kindly woman and undoubtedly Mungo Park owed his deliverance to her. The question of having his eyes put out was quietly dropped, probably at her insistence.

Ali's thoughts were now fully occupied with the war with Bambarra, and he decided to take his horsemen to Jarra, on the borders of Ludamar. Through the intervention of Fatima, Mungo was allowed to accompany the expedition. Not only that, all his possessions were suddenly returned to him, and he was allowed to keep his horse. The sudden *volte face* on the part of Ali could only have been due to the influence of Fatima behind the throne.

And so on 26 May, 1796, his stout heart once more bright with hope, Mungo Park and his two slaves, Demba and Johnson, set out with the Moors for Jarra.

But the evil old Ali had not finished with him yet. He and his two slaves were under heavy guard all the time. They had not gone far before Ali sent his chief slave to Mungo Park with the instruction that the boy Demba was to be sent back to Bubaker as a slave. This was the last straw. He had grown very fond of Demba, who had been a true and faithful companion and his only solace during their long and terrible months of captivity. He went straight in to Ali and made a passionate and angry plea for Demba, but to no avail. Ali, "with a haughty and malignant smile", told him that if he did not mount his horse and go he too would be sent back to Bubaker as a slave.

Mungo could only submit. He said goodbye to the weeping boy, and indeed wept too and promised to try and redeem him. But even though he later offered many times Demba's value on the slave market the ill-natured old Ali refused to let the boy go. Mungo never saw him again.

Ali still played cat-and-mouse with him, as he endeavoured to hide in Jarra, which was swarming with refugees from the war. He heard through Johnson, his remaining slave, that Ali planned to take him back to Bubaker.

Mungo would rather have died than this. He made desperate and secret plans to escape, and left at dead of night for Bambarra, alone, without provisions and money. Speed was impossible, as his horse was reduced to skin and bone. It was scrub and forest country and infested with elephant, lion and leopard, but even though he had no weapon of any kind, none of these wild animals, some of whom he met face to face, attacked him, and at night he slept unprotected in the open in perfect safety. Mungo Park's story of his African travels seems to suggest that the wild animals of that continent are not so dangerous as they are alleged to be, and will only attack man if they have reason to fear him. Generations of hunters and travellers have much exaggerated the dangers of African travel.

For three weeks he plodded on. In Bambarra he met with friendly negroes who helped him on his way and directed him to the Jolibar, the Mandingo name for the Niger.

Finally, early in the morning of 21 July, 1796, he stood on the banks of this long-sought river of mystery, and saw indeed that its majestic stream swept on towards the east, into the very eye of the newly risen sun. He was the first white man to gaze upon this great river of legend.

His ecstasy was short-lived, for his troubles now began again. An object of curiosity, a white beggar with barely a possession to his name, he was in a difficult position in Bambarra. In the more sophisticated regions of the African townships he did not encounter the same friendship and hospitality as he had done from the simple folk of the country districts. He went to Segu and tried to see Mansong, the king of Bambarra, but Mansong would not see him, though he sent him a present of cowrie shells which he was able to use as currency.

He continued eastward, following the course of the Niger, often on the brink of starvation, always an object of curiosity, often derision, this white waif, emaciated, bearded, on his scraggy little horse, meekly enduring all for the sake of his great mission.

But sometimes he was the recipient of the most touching kindness and hospitality, always from the African women, and indeed his story is an undying tribute to their infinite compassion. No one who had read it can forget the incident when, shunned at a village, he sat dejected by a tree, was found by a negress, who took him to her hut, cooked him supper, fed his horse, gave him a warm bed and then, with the other women of her household, sang him to sleep with an extemporary song which went: "The poor white man, faint and weary, came and sat under our tree. He has no mother to bring him milk, no wife to grind his corn. Let us pity the white man. No mother has he."

Mungo was so deeply moved by this that, he said, sleep fled from his eyes. In the morning he gave her the two remaining brass buttons of his waistcoat, "the only recompense I could make her". It was a gift she doubtless treasured.

Mungo traced the Niger for 300 miles as far as Bamako, before he turned back westwards, suffering fever, robbery and semi-starvation. He reached Kamalia in the middle of September, and fell in with an African slaver named Karfa, who gave him the hospitality of his house and probably saved his life.

He stayed with Karfa until April, 1797, when the slaver set out with a *coffle* of "black ivory" for Pisania. The slaves, individually manacled, were yoked together, making it difficult for them to walk. To add to their burden, loads were put on their heads, and they were driven on at a relentless pace under the constant stimulation of the lash. No mercy was shown to the weak. Those who fell by the wayside were left to die and be devoured by wild beasts.

Mungo Park records all this without too much compassion, despite his love of the negro peoples. He accepted slavery as part of the African way of life. He said that all the internal African wars were fought for the acquisition of slaves, and it had always been so. He did not believe it would make much difference if the Europeans discontinued their slave traffic.

At Pisania, Mungo received a hero's welcome, but his troubles and adventures were by no means over. He was unable to get a ship back to England, and none was expected. The only vessel available was an American slave ship, *Charlestown*, and he decided to sail in her to America where he could more easily get a ship to England.

In the long crossing of the Atlantic in a ship packed with slaves, Mungo Park experienced the worst horrors of this abominable trade. The sufferings of the unhappy slaves were indescribable. The wretched ship was unseaworthy and was leaking like a sieve, and it was only kept afloat by the slaves working at the pumps day and night and flogged towards superhuman efforts.

Mungo acted as ship's doctor and worked in the fetid hold among the manacled human cargo, doing his best to alleviate the general sickness brought on by their unspeakable conditions. Many of the Africans knew him or knew of him, for his fame had spread far and wide, and he was able to talk to them in their own language and bring some slight comfort to them in their miserable fate.

The leak gained and the ship hurriedly put into Antigua, where Mungo boarded a passing mail ship for Falmouth.

His account of his travels, published in 1799 *(Travels in the Interior of Africa)*, was extremely popular, and for some years he settled down in England and married. He lived at Foulshiels where he became friendly with Sir Walter Scott.

In 1803 the British Government invited him to lead another expedition to the Niger. Two years later, with his brother-in-law, Alexander Anderson, as his second-in-command, he sailed at the head of a large expedition, composed mainly of soldiers.

It was one of the most disastrous and ill-conceived expeditions on record, and it is difficult to understand why Mungo Park had anything to do with it. It was in fact a different Mungo Park to the meek, long-suffering lone-traveller of the first journey to the Niger. Now at the head of a strong force, he marched his men ruthlessly into the African jungle. The soldiers wore full uniform, and carried packs and rifles, and the result in the intolerable heat of Central Africa can be imagined.

One by one the men fell sick and died. The expedition was followed by bands of robbers who stole the muskets and the very clothes off the backs of the dying stragglers, while at night wild beasts killed their pack animals. Mungo Park has been accused of inhumanity on this march, of leaving his men to die, and of not giving them the medical attnetion which he as a doctor was able to give them. He was certainly a changed man, a fanatic determined to reach his goal at whatever the cost.

Eventually, sick, exhausted, the shattered remnant of the party got to the Niger. Only 11 Europeans were left alive of the 45 who started. But Park was not dismayed. He converted two canoes into a 40-foot boat which he christened *Jolibar*, and in it, with the surviving members of his party, he set sail downstream from the town of Sansandig, a little below Segu, with the intention of following the course of the river to the coast. The date was 19 November, 1805. Nothing more was heard of the party, until months later reports of disaster reached the settlements on the Gambia.

The British Government sent a relief expedition which discovered that Mungo Park had descended the river a thousand miles to the Bussa rapids, well below Yauri, where the *Jolibar* struck a rock and was attacked by natives. Under a hail of spears and arrows, the remnants of the brave expedition perished either in the *Jolibar* or in the river. Mungo Park himself leaped into the swirling waters of his beloved Niger and was seen no more.

His wife refused to accept that he was dead, and to her dying day, thirty years later, clung to the belief that her husband was yet alive and would some day be found. His second son, Thomas, also clung to this belief, and in 1827 went to Africa in search of his father whom he believed to be held a prisoner. He started off into the bush towards the Niger and was never heard of again.

JOURNEY TO THE WESTERN ISLANDS

Dr Samuel Johnson and Mr Boswell

IN MID-AUGUST, 1773, Doctor Samuel Johnson, the great literary lion of London and the author of the famous dictionary, then aged sixty-four, and James Boswell, often known as Bozzy, a comparatively young man of forty-three or so, rode out of Edinburgh towards St Andrews on a tour of the North and West of Scotland, with a visit to the Hebrides as their main objective.

Doctor Johnson was visiting Scotland for the first time. Already in the Scottish capital, he had talked his way through a number of dinner parties, routing those who argued with him by well-drawn arguments, seasoned, when the arguments were not too good, with a truculent ridicule of his opponent. The Scottish nobility and intelligentsia had admired him, laughed with him and no doubt at him, as people did in London. His alleged poor opinion of the Scots and Scotland—"the best prospect that a Scotsman sees is the road that leads him to London", he had said—was only one of his foibles, not one of his deeply ingrained prejudices.

The doctor was in high fettle and astonishingly prepared to face the rigours of their journey, which was to last for ninety-four days. The north of Scotland and the Hebrides were wild regions visited seldom by anyone. They were to travel mostly on horseback, or rather on highland ponies, and in rough boats across stormy seas. Occasionally, up the east coast, Johnson rode in a post-chaise with Bozzy and his servant, John Ritter, who accompanied them on their journey, cantering alongside. It was to be an uncomfortable rather than perilous venture, though once the travellers were nearly drowned off the coast of Mull. The most common peril of the eighteenth century, the highwayman, did not afflict the roads of Scotland, and Dr Johnson left behind in Edinburgh, on his friends' advice, the pair of pistols, gunpowder and bullets which he had brought from London. Presumably there were insufficient people to rob in the wild country they were going to.

Boswell draws a picture of his companion as they left that morning: "His person was large, robust and I may say approaching to the gigantic, and grown unwieldy from corpulency. His countenance was naturally of the cast of an ancient statue, but somewhat disfigured by the scars of that evil which, it was formally imagined, the Royal touch could cure. He was now become a little dull of hearing. His sight had always been somewhat weak; yet so much does mind govern, and even supply, the deficiency of organs, that his perceptions were uncommonly quick and accurate. His head and sometimes also his body shook with a kind of motion like the effect of a palsy: he appeared to be frequently disturbed by cramps or convulsive contractions of the nature of that distemper called St Vitus' Dance. He wore a full suit of plain brown clothes, with twisted hair buttons of the same colour, a large bushy greyish wig, plain shirt, black worsted stockings and silver buckles. Upon this tour, when journeying, he wore boots and a very wide brown greatcoat with pockets which might almost have held the two volumes of his folio dictionary; and he carried in his hand a large English oak stick."

Countless times Boswell, who was to write his monumental biography of the doctor, the best of all biographies in the English language, described aspects of Johnson's mind. He never wrote a truer thing than when at the beginning of this journey he described Johnson as "at bottom much of a John Bull, much of a blunt true-born Englishman. There was a stratum of common clay under the rock of marble. He was voraciously fond of good eating; and he had a great deal of that quality called humour, which gives an oiliness and a gloss to every other quality".

The young Scottish nobleman was a bird of a different feather. Frank and gay in manner–"this", as Dr Johnson remarked "helped draw out people during their journey"–he was treated with amused contempt by most of those who knew him and only Johnson's redoubtable character had obtained Boswell's entry to the great literary club in London which included men such as Burke, Goldsmith, Sir Joshua Reynolds and the great historian Gibbon.

Boswell was excessively vain, full of foolish fancies, a gossip and a liar. He was a great frequenter of loose women, and though not a drunkard was very much more frequently drunk than most men were even in the eighteenth century. He was also at times very pious, and then he repented of his follies and told the world about these and other foolish aspects of his behaviour without the slightest reticence. He was passionately fond of notoriety and, having been in Corsica and met General Paoli, the Corsican leader in the fight for independence against the French, went to Stratford-on-Avon once with a placard on his back stating "This is Corsican Boswell". Macaulay wondered how such a foolish man could have written such a great book as his *Life of Johnson*. In truth, Boswell was perceptive about people to the point of genius, and in his admiration of great men and particularly of Johnson found the way to express his personal genius. His weaknesses served his pen, for he would never accept a snub, never minded the most ill-humoured talk so long as he got answers to his questions.

Johnson was often cross with him. "Sir," he once said, "you appear to have only two subjects; yourself and me and I am tired of both." But Johnson was extremely fond of Boswell. He liked first of all men of noble families, he found Boswell extremely amusing and could not help but be affected by his admiration. Johnson had a very kind heart and was himself very religious; he knew he exerted a very strong influence on his young friend. He once explained to Boswell why he liked him. "Sir, I love the acquaintance of young people; because, in the first place, I don't like to think myself growing old. In the next place, young acquaintances last longest if they do last; and then, sir, young men have more virtue than old men; they have more generous sentiments in every respect. I love the young dogs of this age; they have more wit and humour and knowledge of life than we had; but then the dogs are not so good scholars."

Not surprisingly, Boswell's family did not take to Johnson, whom they had just met in Edinburgh. Boswell's father, a learned man and very Scottish, did not share the reverence for Johnson which was felt in London, and once said that his son was a foolish fellow, had first of all taken up with a Corsican General and now with an "ould dominie that once kept a schaale and called it an acaademie". Boswell's wife said once that she had often seen a man leading a bear but never before a bear leading a man.

What was their journey for? Doctor Johnson's admiration as a young man had been stirred by the Hebrides and he desired to make contact with an ancient and aristocratic form of society to which he felt akin. He had no doubt a book in mind and he also wanted to fill-in his ignorance of this benighted part of the British Isles. It was not at all to enjoy the beauties of nature; neither cared a straw for them. On the shores of Loch Ness, Johnson was to say: "It will very readily occur that this uniformity of barrenness can afford very little amusement to the traveller; that it is easy to sit at home and consider rocks and heath and waterfalls; and that these journeys are useless labours, which neither impregnate the imagination nor enlarge the understanding." When Boswell, who was the more romantic of the two, once called a mountain "immense", his mentor rebuked him and said it was only a "considerable protuberance".

In St Andrews, Dr Johnson, a great reverencer of the past, took off his hat when he sat or walked on any part of the ruins where the ancient cathedral had once stood. They visited all the authorities and were most politely received by the professors of the university. Their journey proceeded uneventfully with visits here and there to well-known personages, to Aberdeen and to Fores in the north. At a small place north of Aberdeen, where they breakfasted, the landlady of the house said to Boswell "is not this the great doctor who is going about the country?" Boswell answered "yes" and the landlady said she had heard of him, had made an errand into the room on purpose to see him, that such a man in one's house does the whole establishment much good. "If I had thought of it," she said, "I would have shown him a child of mine who has had a lump in his throat for some time." Boswell answered that he was not a doctor of physic. "He is only," said Boswell, "a very learned man." Then the landlord piped up and said: "They say he is the greatest man in England except Lord Mansfield." Doctor Johnson was pleased with this and said that the exception marked that the praise was in earnest.

It was not until they left Inverness that they came really into the wilds and were for a time out of touch with the society and hospitality of educated men. On this shore of Loch Ness they come on a wretched hovel made of earth, with an old woman squatting by its door. The only window was a small hole which was stopped with a piece of turf which was taken out occasionally to let in the light. Doctor Johnson was curious to know where she slept. At his question the old woman displayed some emotion and appeared afraid that they had designs on her virtue. However, they managed to reassure her. She offered them whisky and begged for snuff. She had an elderly husband, six young children and about sixty goats. On leaving they gave her a shilling. They were struck by the extreme poverty of the highlanders and, though they were treated with civility everywhere, Boswell, at least once, had fears that the landlord of one of the tough inns where they stayed might murder him to get his money.

At Auchnashiel, between Fort Augustus and the sea coast, they stayed to drink milk in the morning and eat some wheat bread which they had brought with them. They soon had a circle all about them, men, women and children. Not one of these could speak English and Boswell said to Johnson that it was the same as being with a tribe of Indians. "Yes," said he, "but not so terrifying." Boswell distributed snuff and tobacco and gave a penny apiece to each child. Then Johnson said he would distribute pennies to the children. Upon this there was a great stir; not only did some children come running down from neighbouring huts but one blackheaded man went and fetched his young child. Boswell notes that there was a great diversity in the faces of the circle around them. Some were as black and wild in their appearance as any American savages whatever. One woman was as comely as the figure of Sappho, he notes. They asked the old woman, the mistress of the house where they had had the milk, what they should pay. She answered, whatever they pleased. One man asked her in Erse if a shilling was enough. She said yes. But some of the men told her to ask for more. Boswell finally gave her half a crown and the people were much pleased, gave them many blessings and said they had not had such a day since the old laird had come to visit them.

When they reached Glenelg, on the seashore, opposite to the Isle of Skye, they were weary and peevish. Coming down the hills to Glenelg, the doctor's horse had staggered and nearly thrown him over the mountainside. They had quarrelled, too, because Boswell wished to ride on in advance to find them lodging. At the inn there was no meat, no milk, no eggs, no wine and only bread to eat and a freshly killed fowl which was very tough. Nor were there any beds and the doctor slept in all his clothes on a bundle of hay, whilst Boswell, as Johnson says, being more delicate, laid himself sheets of hay over and under him and "lay in his linen like a gentleman". But before they went to sleep they had a pleasant surprise. Their arrival had been noticed by a highland gentleman who lived in a house with a slate roof and glass in the windows and who sent them rum and sugar. In spite of this, as he went to sleep that night Doctor Johnson may have found confirmation of his retort to a remark made to him–"Well, sir, God made Scotland"–"Certainly," he had replied; "but we must always remember that he made it for Scotsmen; and comparisons are odious, but God also made Hell."

Sir Alexander Macdonald had a ship sent over to Glenelg to take them to Armidale in Skye the next morning. He was dressed in tartan clothes and Boswell notes that his wife, who was a cousin of Boswell's, stood on the top of a bank and made "a kind of jumping for joy to welcome them". Sir Alexander and his wife, who were on the point of leaving for Edinburgh, received their guests in a house belonging to one of his tenants. The travellers were at once somewhat critical of the meanness of Sir Alexander's way of life. They quickly learned from people in the house that the tenants and crofters of the Macdonald clan were discontented and mourned the previous laird, Sir James Macdonald. Boswell thought that their dinner was ill-dressed, noted that there was no claret and that, when two gentlemen came into the room after they had sat down to dinner, Sir Alexander let them stand around and stuck his fork into a liver pudding instead of getting room made for them. Boswell apparently took care to act as the host ought to have done. When Johnson and Boswell retired for rest the Doctor said it grieved him to see the chief of a great clan in such a state and that he was just as one in a lodging house in London. The only sign of being in a house of a highland chief was that a piper played below stairs at breakfast and dinner.

Johnson and Boswell, both of them high Tories, did not scruple to criticize Sir Alexander Macdonald, who seems to have been a very mild man, for his lack of dignity. Boswell reproached him to his face with his behaviour to his people, with the meanness of his appearance here and with the fact that his wife had neither a maid nor was any better dressed than a servant. "In short," Boswell says, "I gave him a volley." Not surprisingly, Sir Alexander flew into a violent temper, but by evening came round and, as Boswell

FIFTY GREAT JOURNEYS

said, they had moor-fowl for supper that night. Dr Johnson also set-on his host and told him that in seven years he would make Skye an independent island, that he'd roast oxen whole and hang out a flag as a signal to the Macdonalds on the mainland to come over to Skye and get beef and whisky. Sir Alexander made some difficulties. "Nay," said Johnson, "if you're born to object I have done with you." He said he would have a magazine of arms. Sir Alexander said the arms would rust. To which Doctor Johnson replied: "Let there be men to keep them clean. Your ancestors did not use to let their arms rust."

Lady Macdonald was the subject of their private ridicule. Johnson said of her: "This woman would sink a ninety-gun ship. She is so dull and heavy." Later, when they were staying in a more comfortable and much more sympathetic house, with much better food, in Skye with Coriechatachan, another of Macdonald's tenant farmers, Doctor Johnson called Boswell to his bedroom in the morning and there, in Boswell's words: "He took-off Lady Macdonald leaning foreward with a hand on each cheek and her mouth open–insipidity on a monument grinning at sense and spirit".

It must not be thought that either Johnson or Boswell were habitually as rude as they seem to have been to Sir Alexander Macdonald. On the contrary, they habitually behaved with great politeness and understanding of the people they met. But Sir Alexander had straight away upset their ideas of what a highland chief should be and they could not forgive him this. On the Isle of Raasay, which they visited from Skye, they were far better pleased by a chief of the McCleod clan whose father had been "out" for Bonnie Prince Charlie in 1745. Boswell and Raasay had "a quiet feudal chat". Doctor Johnson, who was in high spirits, said: "This is truly the patriarchal life. This is what we came to find." Boswell explains the attitude of the great Doctor, which was more or less his own, to the Stuarts and their cause, which, of course, was still dear to the hearts of many highlanders. "We are both," he writes, "lovers of that reverence and affection for sovereigns which constitute loyalty, a principle which I take to be absolutely extinguished in Britain and which is one of the worst consequences of the revolution in 1688. Doctor Johnson is not properly a Jacobite. He does not believe in the Divine Right of Kings. He founds their right on long possession which ought not to be disturbed on slight grounds. He would not involve the nation in a civil war to restore the Stuarts. Nay, I have heard him say he was so dubious that if holding up his right hand

198

would have gained the victory to the highland army in 1745, he does not know if he would have done it ... But with all this, he and I have a kind of liking for Jacobitism that it is not easy to define."

Back in Skye with Coriechatachan, the travellers lived most convivially, Boswell frequently getting drunk and repenting of it. They made many journeys, often in rainstorms–it was now the end of September–and the travellers were beginning to think of getting to the large island of Mull and thence to the mainland. They moved back to Armidale on the coast which they liked much better and found more comfortable without Sir Alexander.

From different parts of the highlands young chiefs and old ministers came to visit them. On Saturday, 3 October, they set sail on a windy afternoon for Mull in a fishing boat accompanied by a young man, the son of the laird of Col, Mr Donald Maclean, and one of his friends, together with two or three dogs. The crew was an old captain, a man with one eye and one other sailor. The weather got rougher and rougher towards evening and when it was dark there was talk of running first of all to the mainland, then for one or two islands which were rather nearer than Mull. Much time was lost in straining against the storm, first in one direction and then in another. The captain was at a loss and finally it was Mr Donald Maclean–a "col" as he was called–who undertook to get them into this island. A peat fire was lit in the vessel in order to guide a smaller wherry, also making sad head against wind and waves. Johnson had suffered from sea-sickness early in the afternoon but had recovered and lay all through the evening and the night on a bed of straw with Donald Maclean's greyhound at his back keeping him warm.

As they made, in the darkness, for the rocky shores of Col, Boswell was much alarmed by the peat fire in the boat which flew terribly about; he thought that since Col had powder on board for his shotguns they might be blown up. Col, his friend, and the captain, appeared a little frightened, which made Boswell even more so, and the perpetual talking or rather shouting in Erse also alarmed him considerably. He writes: "The boat often lay so much to a side that I trembled lest she should be over-set; and indeed they told me afterwards that they had run her sometimes to within an inch of the water, so anxious were they to make what haste they could before the storm became worse. I saw tonight what I never saw before, a prodigious sea with immense billows coming upon a vessel so that it seemed hardly possible to escape. Amidst all these terrifying circumstances I endeavoured to compose my mind. It was not easy to do it, for all the stories that I had heard of the dangerous sailing among the Hebrides, which is proverbial, came full upon my recollection. It distressed me to think how much my dearest wife would suffer should I now be lost, and in what a destitute, or at least wretchedly dependent, state she would be left. Piety afforded me a good deal of comfort. I prayed fervently to God, but I was confused for I remember I used a strange expression; that if it should please Him to preserve me, I would behave myself ten times the better."

They made the harbour and anchored but there was no question of going ashore until the morrow. Boswell, soaked to the skin and very sea-sick, wrapped his overcoat round his head in order to snatch a few fitful slumbers. The Doctor was very much more comfortable.

They were more than a week in Col, so stormy was the weather. They thought of returning as soon as possible to Boswell's father's house in Ayrshire, but then they decided they could not leave the Hebrides without visiting Iona. They finally sailed for Mull with the ever-obliging Donald Maclean. Of him Doctor Johnson said: "He is a noble animal. He is as complete an islander as mortality can figure. He is a farmer, a sailor, a hunter, a fisher; he will run you down a dog. If any man has a tail, it is Col. He is hospitable; and he has an intrepidity of talk whether he understands the subject or not".

In Mull young Col presented them to the chief of his clan, Sir Alan Maclean, who had served as a soldier in America and who was very kind and took the travellers under his wing. He accompanied them to Iona where, after warming themselves at the house of the most substantial man in the island, the chief and his guests were conducted to a barn where they were to sleep. There was a fire in the middle of the floor, but the smoke was drawn off when they went into the barn. They were given oysters boiled in butter. Doctor Johnson ate none of that dish. They then had roast potatoes and the fire was carefully removed and good hay strewed at one end of the barn. Doctor Johnson lay down with all his clothes and greatcoat on. Sir Alan and Boswell took off their coats and lay them at their feet. Doctor Johnson lay next to one wall, Boswell next to the other and Sir Alan in the middle. Boswell could not help thinking in the night how curious it was to see the chief of the Macleans, Doctor Samuel Johnson and James Boswell, Esq., lying thus.

Doctor Johnson describes the ruins of Iona at some length. He also makes some interesting remarks about the people, noting that: "The inhabitants are remarkably gross, and remarkably neglected; I know not if they are visited by any Minister. The island which was once the metropolis of learning and piety, has now no school for education nor temple for worship, only two inhabitants that can speak English and not one that can write or read. Though Sir Alan had not been in the place for many years, he was received with all the reverence due to their chieftain."

Johnson's book, of course, is much less amusing than that of Boswell, but it contains a great many reflections on the lot of the people. He dwells constantly on the great poverty which, supervening on the decay of the clan solidarity which had been preserved because of war and clan conflicts, now leads the population to emigrate in ever-greater numbers, particularly to America. Peace and a gradual beginning of a money economy Doctor Johnson considered as one of the main causes of the depopulation of the highlands. Land was now let for money to strangers because the chiefs no longer attach the same value as in the past to clan loyalty. Divested of their ancient prerogatives as lords and judges the chiefs now turned their thoughts to the improvement of their revenues and expected more rent as they received less homage. The authorities in England and Scotland, never forgetting the troubles of the '45, had done nothing to stop emigration, Doctor Johnson notes. He has a splendid paragraph of typical Johnsonian prose:

"To hinder insurrection by driving away the people and to govern peaceably by having no subjects is an expedient that argues no great profundity of politics. To soften the obdurate, to convince the mistaken, to mollify the resentful, are worthy of a statesman; but it affords a legislator little self-applause to consider that where there was formally an insurrection, there is now a wilderness."

It was not until 2 November that Johnson and Boswell arrived at Auchinleck. For three days Johnson, and Boswell's sardonic father, were exceedingly amicable, but a clash between two strong and intransigent characters, one a high Tory and a fervent Episcopalian, the other a Whig and a Presbyterian, was bound to come. It came when the conversation turned by accident to Oliver Cromwell. "What, Sir, had Cromwell ever done for his country?" asked Johnson. "God doctor, he gart kings ken that they had a lith in their necks," retorted the laird. (He made kings learn that they had a joint in their necks.) The next day was Sunday and matters were not made better by Doctor Johnson refusing to attend the Presbyterian kirk. Notwithstanding what had happened, Lord Auchinleck behaved with the dignified courtesy of the time, was very civil to Doctor Johnson and attended him to the post-chaise which was conveying him and his son to Edinburgh. "Thus," writes Boswell, "they parted–they are now in another and a higher state of existence; and as they were both Christian men, I trust they have met in happiness. But I must observe, in justice to my friend's political principles and my own, that they have met in a place where there is no room for Whiggism."

For more than a year Boswell was allowed no more roaming after his tour of the Hebrides. His wife had not been sorry to see Doctor Johnson go, disliking his uncouth habits and particularly no doubt his habit of turning candles head-down over the drawing-room carpet to make them burn brighter. Doctor Johnson in a letter to Boswell from London remarks on Lady Boswell's willingness to see him depart; he asks his friend to: "Make my compliments to Mrs Boswell and tell her that I do not love her the less for wishing me away. I gave her trouble enough, and should be glad in recompense, to give her any pleasure."

Doctor Johnson's book was received with general acclaim, even in Scotland, though not surprisingly a few individuals bitterly resented some parts of it. His real thoughts about Scotland were expressed to a gentleman he met at Lord Auchinleck's at a rather dull tea-party at which nobody spoke very much. The gentleman asked Doctor Johnson how he liked the highlands. The question seemed to irritate Johnson; he answered: "How, Sir, can you ask me what obliges me to speak unfavourably of a country where I have been hospitably entertained? Who can like the highlands? I like the inhabitants very well." The gentleman asked no more questions.

TRAVELLING UP

The First Ascent of Mont Blanc

WHO WAS the first man to set foot on the summit of Mont Blanc? That this 15,771-ft. peak, highest in the Western Alps, was mastered on 8 August, 1786, by two doughty climbers is indisputable, but the actual circumstances of their triumph have been partly shrouded in mystery ever since.

The two men were Dr Michel Gabriel Paccard, a Chamonix physician, and a picturesque local character named Jacques Balmat, who accompanied the doctor as his porter.

Behind the scenes, as prime inspirer of the venture, was Professor Horace Bénédict de Saussure, a wealthy aristocrat from Geneva, a botanist, physicist and geologist, who had visited Chamonix in 1760 and had spent some time exploring the lower slopes of Mont Blanc. The mountain cast something of a spell upon him. Gazing up wistfully at the majestic crest, he felt suddenly moved to offer a prize for the first person to succeed in reaching the summit. Subsequently, de Saussure became a frequent visitor to Chamonix, itself 3,445 feet above sea-level. He made seven trips in all, but always he was content to confine his excursions to the lower slopes, where he spent most of his time studying geology and collecting crystals.

Jacques Balmat knew all about the reward, of course, and often went out climbing upon the lower slopes, sometimes tacking himself on to parties of other climbers as an uninvited extra. Judging from various accounts that have been published he does not appear to have been very welcome. He was liable to leave a climbing party just as suddenly as he had joined it and to go tramping off on his own, being, as will become apparent, a moody, eccentric individual and very much a creature of impulse.

On one occasion, it is recorded, Balmat startled his wife in the middle of the night by suddenly clutching hold of her and yelling out in fright. He had been dreaming that he was out climbing, had lost his foothold and was slipping over an icy precipice. In his dream he made a frantic grab at a bough and had then wakened to hear his wife yelling to him to let go of her ear. Possibly to escape her understandable fury at being so rudely disturbed, Balmat had leapt straight out of bed, announcing that he was going out to search for crystals. He stuffed some bread and a flask of brandy into his pockets, and, as he reached for his stout, ironshod walking-stick, he called back to his still-protesting wife that if he had not returned by the following morning she would know that he had slept somewhere on the mountain-side.

Anecdotes like these serve to indicate Balmat's impulsive, feckless, happy-go-lucky nature. A further example of his exhibitionist streak is afforded by his amusing habit of suddenly giving voice to his innermost thoughts in whimsically dramatic fashion. Once, when driving sleet was whipping savagely into his face, he wound a large handkerchief round his head and shouted defiantly: "Fire away! You're not hurting *me*!"

He was also endowed with a droll sense of humour, and during another excursion he cheerfully pictured fellow villagers grouped snugly round their firesides in Chamonix saying to themselves: "That ass Jacques is wearing out his shoe leather!" And, to spur himself on, he added: "Courage, Balmat!"

No doubt he was a man of great courage and fine physique, which is probably why the practical Dr Paccard selected him to be his companion on the ultimate prize-winning climb. They were two very contrasting men. The doctor refined, scholarly, more interested in the challenge than the now half-forgotten reward.

Dr Paccard was, in fact, a climber of proven prowess. He had ventured upon numerous serious excursions from Chamonix; had himself scaled the Buet, had climbed some way up the icy slopes towards the Grands Mulets, and had explored the Geant glacier. Apart from this store of practical experience, Dr Paccard spent hours studying the mountain-side through field glasses, and he had worked out in his own mind what he was sure would be the most practical route to the summit of Mont Blanc, a way leading up from the Grand Plateau, between the two Rochers Rouges. Long years of thought and planning, therefore, lay behind Dr Paccard's dreams of ultimate conquest.

In his 70th year, Jacques Balmat gave a highly-coloured version of the joint conquest of the summit of Mont Blanc to Alexandre Dumas, the elder, in which he explained wistfully that he had been only twenty-five at the time of this triumph, but omitted to mention that his companion was then thirty.

"What a fellow I was!" he told Dumas, his old eyes doubtless flashing with pride. "With the devil's own calves and hell's own stomach, I could have gone three days without bite or sup—and had to, once, when I got lost on the Buet. I just munched a little snow, and that was all.

"And, from time to time, I looked across at Mont Blanc saying: 'Say what you like, my beauty, and do what you like. Some day I shall climb you.' "

In this Walter Mitty-like vein Jacques Balmat cheerfully claimed all credit, in his narrative to Dumas, for having initiated the climb and for accomplishing the final successful assault. He told how he had called upon Dr Paccard and had put the proposition to him on the spur of the moment.

"Look here, doctor. Are you afraid of cold, and snow, and precipices? Speak out and tell me like a man!"

And he quoted the doctor as replying instantly: "With you, Balmat, I am afraid of nothing."

"Very well," Balmat told him. "Now is the moment to climb the molehill."

This kind of zestful braggadocio characterizes Balmat's whole reminiscence of the prize-winning climb as recounted to Alexandre Dumas. All through the breezy recital the worthy village doctor is casually relegated to a very minor role, a "bit" player, and made to move more or less as a foil to Balmat's self-claimed heroic star quality.

This strangely contrasting pair, then, set off at about 5 p.m. on 7 August, and slept that night at the top of Montagne de la Côte, forcing themselves to rouse up again at 2 a.m. to resume their climbing until they came eventually to the Glacier de Taconnay.

Mont Blanc covers more than 38.6 square miles, literally over-flowing with ice. Seven great glaciers, bright green and shimmering in the Alpine sunshine, stream down below the 4,000-foot level. There are wide seas of ice which Balmat described as cloven with immense crevasses which apparently stretched down to unplumbed depths. There were also treacherous ice-bridges which had to be tested with caution. According to Balmat these could sometimes be heard cracking ominously beneath their feet.

But the two climbers braved these and other hazards and pressed on determinedly to scale the Grands Mulets. Balmat, according to this particular version, was always in the van, showing immense prowess and superb qualities of leadership, while the village doctor, often referred to in belittling terms, was presumably trailing in docile fashion in the narrator's wake.

As they gained the higher zones they must often have gazed up at the beckoning peak which had to be approached by walls of barren rock where snow had failed to find a lodging-place. By now their endurance must have been sorely taxed. The rarefied air made breathing progressively more difficult, and they began to suffer considerably from biting winds, driving sleet and snow and intense cold.

Dr Paccard, again according to Balmat, was now very near to the point of exhaustion and was obliged to pause and rest. Balmat, however, still full of determination, decided to press on by himself, confident, no doubt, that his "devil's own calves" would sustain him. On and on he climbed, heedless of the ice and snow. The challenge of suffering seemed only to stimulate him, and it is conceivable that he bolstered his resolution by recalling that vow he had shouted to Mont Blanc across the echoing valley so long ago from the safer slopes below: "Some day I'll climb you!"

Anyway, he kept on, though he confessed to Dumas how he had faltered for one brief instant to look round after stumbling to the summit, harbouring a secret dread that there might be yet one more ridge to be scaled. But his fear was groundless; he had indeed reached the final peak, and the discovery forced him to yell aloud in ecstasy.

"I was the King of Mont Blanc!" he told Dumas.

Then, to follow this same version, Balmat picked his way down the treacherous frozen slopes to the point where he had left Dr Paccard resting. He said he found him dazed and half-conscious.

Balmat told Dumas how he rallied his fainting companion, helped him to his feet and led him, tottering, to the summit to share the triumph of conquest. Balmat's recollection was that it was then past 6 p.m.

The two weary, yet elated, climbers stayed on the crest of Mont Blanc for something like half an hour, and one can picture them surveying the magnificent vistas of Alpine scenery that presented themselves on every side. When they finally started upon their return journey they calculated that they would have at least two and a half hours of daylight left to them in which to accomplish what they knew must be the most difficult and treacherous part of the descent.

Almost immediately they made the disconcerting discovery that the tracks they had left on their upward climb had been almost entirely obliterated by fresh falls of snow which had already frozen hard. But, by peering very closely, they found that they were just able to discern faint traces of occasional holes that had been left here and there by the sharp spikes of their sticks.

Progress was inevitably slow and, according to the doughty Balmat, the doctor was now weakening and seemed to have become almost completely devoid of will-power and energy. Balmat claimed that he had to rally his companion and to assist him from then onward. "I had," he said, "to guide in easy places, and to carry in the hard ones and to force him on." The sun sank behind the mountains and darkness fell swiftly. Its dying glow had long since vanished when they finally left the dangerous regions of ice behind them.

Both men were by this time severely afflicted by cold and suffering and had become greatly weakened as the result of their exertions. Dr Paccard's hands were tormenting him and when he removed his gloves it was seen that the flesh had turned white, as if dead. One of Balmat's hands had also gone completely numb. Describing this, Balmat indulged in one of his characteristic bits of whimsy, remarking wryly that he had "three frost-bitten hands".

In his narrative he stated at this point that Dr Paccard now appeared to desire nothing but to pause and sleep. Yet the doctor seems to have been sufficiently alert to offer advice on the best action to take in their predicament. He told his companion to start rubbing their hands with snow, and Balmat promptly set to work with his one unafflicted hand to massage their frozen fingers with snow under the doctor's direction. It was soon found that this treatment was helpful in bringing back circulation. But as the blood began to flow again in their benumbed fingers after the snow treatment they both suffered from acute pain, which Balmat described as feeling "as if every vein had been pierced with needles".

Both men badly needed to rest. According to Balmat he now wrapped Dr Paccard in a blanket and rolled him gently under a sheltering ledge of rock, making him as comfortable as possible. They then took a little food and drink to sustain them through the night and, huddling closely together for warmth, managed at last to fall asleep.

Dr Paccard was the first to return to wakefulness and he at once roused his companion with a cry of alarm. "It's strange, Balmat, I hear the birds singing and don't see the daylight. I suppose I can't open my eyes." Balmat immediately sat up and examined his companion's frost-encrusted eyelids. Recalling the snow treatment that had proved so successful when applied to their frozen hands, he now took up some snow and began gently to massage the doctor's eyelids. The only effect, it seems, was to make the afflicted eyes still more painful, so the treatment had to be abandoned. Balmat consulted his watch and saw that it was just 6 a.m.

They struggled up and set off down the mountain again, the handicapped Paccard, under Balmat's instructions, hanging on to the strap of his companion's knapsack and following closely upon his heels. Slowly and patiently they managed in this fashion to complete without mishap the remaining part of their descent.

The two men parted as soon as they reached the village of La Côte, the doctor being now sufficiently recovered to grope his way homeward with the help of his stick. Jacques Balmat also made straight for his home. How his wife received him we can only guess. Balmat was fond of relating that his very first act on reaching home was to make for a mirror and to stand gazing in amazement at his frightening reflection.

"I received a staggering surprise," he said. "My eyes were red; my face black; my lips were blue. Whenever I laughed or yawned the blood spurted from my lips and cheeks, and I could only see in a dark room."

But he was still "King of Mont Blanc" and he apparently collected the prize offered by de Saussure, as well as a gratuity which the King of Sardinia instructed should be sent to him. A subscription was also opened for him by a keen supporter of mountain climbing, Baron von Gersdorff.

For some time after the epic climb a great controversy concerning the details of the achievement raged in the columns of the *Gazette de Lausanne*, and during that time Jacques Balmat gave a very different version of the adventure to the one recalled so colourfully in his old age and reeled off so fluently to Alexandre Dumas. But as he was then seventy and reciting an oft-told tale after an interval of fifty-four years, some allowances may perhaps be made for his braggadocio and for the scant credit he then allowed to his climbing companion. Possibly other allowances should also be made, for some scholars have expressed the opinion that his interviewer may have been partly responsible for embroidering certain highly-coloured passages in his flowery narrative. Certainly, Dumas plied Balmat generously with wine and encouraged him to "let himself go".

Be that as it may, Dr Paccard had in his possession a long document signed by Jacques Balmat in which the mountaineer adopted a much more modest tone and gave the doctor full credit for having been the initiator of the enterprise. He also admitted quite frankly that he himself had been engaged by the doctor for the occasion merely as an assistant.

One passage in this interesting document runs:

"I declare that, except for the steady manner in which he proceeded we should never have succeeded; that he shared my labour."

Balmat, it seems certain, was given the responsibility for choosing camping sites during the climb, and doubtless the experience he had gained during his many climbs and his frequent habit of sleeping in the open must have proved invaluable. But this statement emphatically credits Dr Paccard with having found their route to the summit of Mont Blanc. Balmat also confessed that in the final assault he himself had veered away to the right in order to avoid a particularly repellent snow slope, whereas the doctor had insisted upon sticking to the more direct and more difficult route he had already mapped out in theory after intensive study. Paccard did, indeed, press on and courageously scale the forbidding peak the hard way to get straight to the summit ahead of his companion.

As this statement is actually dated 25 March, 1787, less than eight months after the historic climb had been made, it may not be too fanciful to surmise that the ebullient Jacques had, even at that early date, been gaily "drawing the long bow" to impress the local villagers. After all, had he not been granted de Saussure's award and other cash tributes? The temptation to claim more than his fair share of adulation must have been irresistible to a spirited youngster of twenty-five.

The significant fact that Dr Paccard went to all the trouble of getting the precise details set forth in the form of a semi-legal document, signed by Jacques Balmat before two witnesses, would seem to indicate pretty clearly that the statement was expressly designed to put an end to an embarrassing controversy and perhaps to place a curb upon his almost irrepressible companion's loquacious tongue. But, according to one leading authority, T. Graham Brown, F.R.S., "Balmat's account of the ascent grew with the years", and he thinks that Dr Paccard was dead when the "fantasy" gathered by Dumas was published. At any rate, it was allowed to go unchallenged for years.

A contemporary climber, Marc Bourrit, also published an account of the first ascent which, says Brown, "distorted the facts and gave the credit of the achievement to Balmat". T. Graham Brown, on the other hand, unhesitatingly gives full honours to Dr Paccard as acknowledged initiator of the enterprise, not only in his thoughtful planning of the route, but in leading the ascent itself.

By any standards the joint achievement of Paccard and Balmat was a remarkable one, for they were seventy years ahead of the day when mountaineering first developed as an organized sport. Their triumph is all the more astonishing when it is considered that these men accomplished their ascent without any of the elaborate scientific devices and paraphernalia now considered as an indispensable part of the average mountaineer's equipment. With nothing, in fact, but their blankets and knapsacks, their stout sticks and stout hearts, they set forth in the confident belief that success must crown their efforts.

Dr Paccard may not have shared Balmat's contemptuous view that they had only a "molehill" to master; but he was armed, at least, with the fruits of long, painstaking study and observation and carefully considered calculations of all the risks involved.

Once they had demonstrated that the feat could be done, de Saussure was sufficiently heartened to attempt the climb himself. He did so a year later, 1787, thus becoming the third man to set foot on the summit of Mont Blanc.

Visitors to Chamonix today can see a joint monument to Bénédict de Saussure and Jacques Balmat.

And Dr Paccard? He was well content to have accomplished

what he had set out to do, and he sought no limelight. The snow blindness he had endured on the descent had no lasting effect upon his eyes. He lived to a ripe old age, still able to read without glasses.

Mention was made at the outset of this account of the historic climb of the atmosphere of mystery that has partly shrouded it ever since. It is a most tantalizing mystery because it is known that Dr Paccard did eventually get down to the task of writing out his own detailed recollections of the climb under the simple title of: "The First Ascent of the Highest Mountain on the Continent". No doubt this account would have cleared up a great many vital points; but, unhappily, this precious manuscript was mysteriously lost before it could be published.

There was a time when ardent researchers advertised widely in the eager hope that the manuscript might still be in existence somewhere, or that someone might possibly come forward who could shed some light upon it.

But no one ever did respond to these appeals. The rest is silence; silence—and endless speculation. A priceless literary treasure must thus be assumed to have been lost to the world; and a gap in the annals of mountain climbing remains that can never be satisfactorily filled.

AN ECCENTRIC IN SOUTH AMERICA

Squire Waterson's Travels

This account is based on *The Strange Life of Charles Waterton* by Richard Aldington (Evans Bros). The copyright owner is Madame Catherine Guillaume. – Ed.

SOME OF the greatest travellers had a touch of eccentricity about them. Explorers like Mungo Park and Colonel Fawcett, who suffered sickness and privation and eagerly faced unknown dangers, were considered to be a little mad.

But few travellers have shared the eccentricities of Charles Waterton who nearly killed himself with his brutal self-doctoring in the wild jungles of South America in the early nineteenth century. He was a fearless traveller, and he endeared himself to his age by his eccentricities as much as by his dashing exploits.

Born in 1782, he was the twenty-seventh lord of Walton Hall, a position, however, which did not carry a title, although the Waterton family was more ancient and noble than that of many who were titled. He was always known throughout his life as the Squire, and a squire in the literal meaning of the word he was. His ancestors were related to the royal houses of Europe. One of them was mentioned in Shakespeare's play *Richard II*.

212

I have from Port le Blanc, a bay
In Brittany, received intelligence
That Harry, Duke of Hereford, Rainold, Lord Cobham,
That late broke from the Duke of Exeter,
His brother, Archbishop late of Canterbury,
Sir Thomas Erpingham, Sir John Ramston,
Sir John Norbery, Sir Robert Waterton, and Francis Quoint . . .

After the Reformation the Watertons obstinately refused to adopt the new religion. Remaining Roman Catholics resulted in their losing much of their property and suffering many legal penalties. Their title-less state was doubtless due to this also. In the eighteenth century Catholics had to pay double land taxes and £20 a month for not attending church. They could not be Justices of the Peace and were barred from entering Parliament. A Catholic could not go to an English University as subscribing to the Thirty-nine Articles of the Church of England was one of the conditions of entry.

The Watertons were all fanatical Romanists, and the Squire was more fanatical than any of them. "I would rather," he declared, "run the risk of going to hell with St Edward the Confessor, Venerable Bede and St Thomas of Canterbury, than make a dash at heaven in company with Henry VIII, Queen Bess and Dutch William".

Squire Waterton, however, was not re-fighting the arid battles of the Reformation all his life. He found something more interesting to do. His parents sent him abroad to keep him out of mischief. He went to Spain and then to Guiana to manage one of the Waterton plantations there. However, he showed more interest in the fauna and flora of the country than he did in the three large plantations upon which a thousand slaves worked to produce coffee, sugar and cotton.

In his famous book, *Wanderings*, he gives his opinion on many things, including that of slavery, a wretched trade which he said can never be defended. But he denied the stories that the condition of the plantation slaves was wretched or that they were subjected to cruelty. Britons are the same all the world over, he declared, and the Englishman who runs a plantation "cheers his negroes in labour, comforts them in sickness, is kind to them in old age and never forgets that they are his fellow-creatures".

The Squire certainly did not fall into the kind of life which most young men adpoted when they came from Europe to manage these plantations. He took neither to rum nor to coloured women, but went barefoot and bareheaded in search of ornithological specimens in the steaming, malaria-ridden jungles of Guiana. His father died in 1805, when he returned to England to take his patrimony, but he was soon back in Guiana where for a few years he divided his time between managing the family plantations and pursuing the wild life of the tropical hinterland.

His relations with the Colonial authorities administering the country were not always of the best. The Squire never took well to authority, especially Protestant authority, and he had a habit of aiding the outlaws of the colony, which did not endear him to the representatives of law and order. The Squire's temperament was such that when he was planning to explore the unknown interior of the country, for which he would require a passport from the Governor, General Carmichael, he went out of his way to offend that official by engineering the successful escape of a wanted man for whose apprehension Carmichael had offered £500 reward.

Naturally enough the Squire was peremptorily invited to Government House to explain himself. The Waterton charm triumphed in the end. The cool irrelevance of the Squire's explanation had a certain fascination for General Carmichael, a fiery man whose ire quickly subsided. Something of an eccentric himself, he instantly perceived that Waterton was not only a fellow eccentric, but also a man of rare genius. Instead of having him arrested, the Governor entered into a long conversation with him on the subject of the Squire's project of exploring the then unknown inland regions of British Guiana as far as the borders of Brazil, at the end of which the official passport was no longer in doubt.

The Squire's object was to search for a drug called curare which was used by the South American Indians. This extremely powerful drug was made by the Macusi Indians of the Guiana highlands. They bartered the stuff with the warring tribes who tipped the small arrows of their blow-guns with it, making them into very lethal darts.

There was great scientific curiosity about curare and Waterton's object was to bring back sufficient of the drug for experimentation. He was not to know that curare was to become one of the most important drugs known to medical science. Certain of its curious qualities, however, were known at the time—its ability to cause rapid paralysis and muscular spasm, and also the fact that the flesh of animals killed by it was not poisoned and remained wholesome and edible.

In its modern application, curare is used to relieve spastic paralysis and in the shock therapy of schizophrenia and manic-depressive psychoses. One of its most important uses is in anaesthesia when it causes the extreme muscular relaxation necessary for surgery. Curare is now a vital component of modern anaesthetics. Everyone who has an operation has reason to bless curare, and to thank Squire Waterton for being the first person to bring the drug to civilization.

In his day, however, it was just a barbaric poison with the most remarkable effects, and one of his objects was to seek an antidote for it. He had no idea that the poison itself would prove such a valuable aid to medicine.

By modern standards the equipment with which the Squire set off into the unknown and dangerous jungles of the interior of Guiana was laughable. He intended to go most of the way by water, so he took a canoe and several Indians to paddle it. His clothes consisted of a hat, a pair of light trousers, and a thin flannel waistcoat under a check shirt. He took shoes and stockings, though he seldom wore them, preferring to go barefoot even through the jungle. He did not believe in encumbering himself with clothes. He slept in a hammock over which he fixed a thin waterproof sheet tied to two trees. This was to keep off the rain.

With his usual disregard for both comfort and safety, he had elected to travel in the rainy season, when the whole country was a dripping swamp, and it was nearly impossible to distinguish the river courses from the surrounding floodland. He took with him a shot-gun and ammunition and equipment for preserving and transporting the specimens of animals and birds he sought.

Perhaps the most important, but useless, part of his equipment was what he called his physic—bark, laudanum, calomel, jalap and a lancet. The Squire was his own doctor and a savage and punishing physician he proved to be. Only the stoutest physique could have survived the fearsome doctoring which he inflicted upon himself. When he caught malaria he made himself much worse by violent purging and continuous blood-letting.

His advice on the subject was as follows: "Shouldst thou ever wander through these remote and dreary wilds, forget not to carry with thee bark, laudanum, calomel and jalap, and the lancet. There are no druggist shops here, nor sons of Galen to apply to in time

of need." He added: "I never go encumbered with many clothes...
Shoes and stockings I seldom had on. In dry weather they would
have irritated the feet and retarded me in the chase of wild beasts;
and in the rainy season they would have kept me in a perpetual
state of damp and moisture. I eat moderately, and never drink
wine, spirits or fermented liquors in any climate."

Thus inadequately equipped, the barefoot explorer set out from
Georgetown in April, 1812 (at about the same time as Napoleon was
setting out to conquer Russia), and made his way up the flooded
Demerara River through the ferocious rains till he was halted by
the Demerara Falls.

In his book, *Wanderings*, he wrote vividly of the jungle scene
during this journey:

"At sundown the vampires, bats and goat-suckers dart from their
lonely retreat and skim along the trees on the river's bank. The
different kinds of frogs almost stun the ear with their hoarse and
hollow-sounding croaking, while the owls and goat-suckers lament
and mourn all night long. About two hours before daybreak you
will hear the red monkey moaning as though in deep distress; the
houtou, a solitary bird, and only found in the thickest recesses of
the forest, distinctly articulates 'houtou, houtou' in a low and plaintive tone an hour before sunrise..."

Waterton had his own names for the various animals of the
South American jungle, but he was the first traveller to conjure
up the tropical forest scene with any vividness, as when he writes:

"Every now and then the maam or tinamou sends forth one long
and plaintive whistle from the depths of the forest, and then stops;
whilst the yelping of the toucan and the shrill voice of the bird
called pi-pi-yo is heard during the interval. The campanero never
fails to attract the attention of the passenger; at a distance of nearly
three miles you may hear this snow-white bird tolling every four
or five minutes, like the distant convent-bell. From six to nine in
the morning the forests resound with the mingled cries and strains
of the feathered race; after this they gradually die away. From
eleven to three all nature is hushed as in a midnight silence, and
scarce a note is heard, saving that of the campanero and the pi-
pi-yo; it is then that, oppressed by the solar heat, the birds retire
to the thickest shade and wait for the refreshing cool of evening."

At the Demerara Falls he bought some curare from an Indian.
Anxious to assure himself that it was the real thing, he immediately
proceeded to test it. He purchased a dog, smeared some curare on

an arrow point which he then jabbed into the dog's thigh and watched the result with some callousness, recording it thus later:

"In three or four minutes he began to be affected, smelt at every little thing on the ground around him, and looked wistfully at the wounded part. Soon after this he staggered, laid himself down and never rose more. He barked once, though not as if in pain. His voice was low and weak; and in a second attempt it quite failed him. He now put his head betwixt his fore-legs, and raising it slowly again he fell over on his side. His eye immediately became fixed, and though his extremities every now and then shot convulsively, he never showed the least desire to raise up his head. His heart fluttered much from the time he laid down, and at intervals beat very strong; then stopped for a moment or two, and then beat again; and continued faintly beating several minutes after every other part of his body seemed dead. In a quarter of an hour after he had received the poison he was quite motionless."

This unfeeling experiment satisfied him that the curious powers and qualities of curare had not been exaggerated, and he continued his quest, leaving the Demerara River and continuing up the Essequibo and its tributaries. Then he marched barefoot across dense forests and tropical swampland to the Brazilian frontier. Here he bought more curare, which he stored in balls of wax for transportation back to civilization. He watched the Indians collect and prepare the poison from various plants.

The basic poison was obtained from a plant called *strychnos toxifera*. The Indians added various ingredients to this, such as two kinds of ants with vicious stings, strong Indian pepper and the fangs of deadly snakes, all pounded up and boiled with the basic poison. The result was a glutinous juice. The additional ingredients were added for the purposes of sympathetic magic, for the whole business of manufacture was surrounded by various taboos. No female can be present, the pot used must be a new one, the man making the curare must not eat during the whole process of manufacture, and afterwards the shed where the poison is made must be abandoned for ever.

Waterton's investigation into the making of curare was a contribution to scientific knowledge of some importance, though he is hardly ever credited with it.

He continued towards the Brazilian frontier, then in Portuguese hands. Here he was suddenly overwhelmed with a severe attack of malaria, which he immediately proceeded to worsen by copiously "tapping his claret", and violently purging himself. He would probably have killed himself with his ferocious doctoring had he not fallen in with the commander of a Portuguese frontier post who almost certainly saved his life.

The Portuguese was under orders not to admit any foreigner to the fort, but as he put it to the Squire: "The orders I have received forbidding the admission of strangers were never intended to be put in force against a sick English gentleman." At the fort there was no doctor, but the kindly Portuguese put the sick man to bed and gave him more suitable medical treatment than the punishment Waterton had been inflicting upon himself.

After a week's rest with proper food and no blood-letting the Squire had recovered sufficiently to make the return journey. Characteristically, he chose the most dangerous and foolhardy way back–by shooting the rapids of the Essequibo, then in full roaring flood after the rains. Though weakened by this violent attack of malaria, the Squire braved the dangerous rapids with reckless abandon, and he and his party of terrified Indians time and again escaped death by a hairsbreadth in the boiling cataracts amid the hidden boulders and perilous rocks.

After he had survived the rapids by some chance of fate, the malaria returned worse than before. Sick, exhausted, racked with fever, he sought refuge in the hut of an Indian who took pity on him. The Indian noticed that on Waterton's back were "nine thriving nests of chegoes"–West Indian fleas which had an unpleasant and painful habit of burrowing underneath the skin.

The Squire did not hesitate. He handed the Indian his penknife and told him to dig the fleas out of his bare flesh. This the Indian did. Later the Squire wrote of this incident in characteristic style:

"Sick though I was, I wished an artist were present at the operation. The Indian's hut, with its scanty furniture and bows and arrows hanging round; the deep verdure of the adjoining forest; the river flowing rapidly by; myself wasted to a shadow; and the negro grinning with exultation as he showed me the chegoes' nests which he had grubbed out, would have formed a scene of no ordinary variety."

His return to Georgetown was something of a triumph. He had blazed a pioneer trail across what was then a totally unknown part of Guiana. His journey was a valuable contribution to the scanty information available about conditions in the interior of this newly-acquired British colony.

Not content to rest upon his laurels, he ardently pursued the life of the successful explorer-naturalist, recklessly and with never a thought for his own comfort and safety. Searching for specimens in the Brazilian jungle, he saw what he took to be a pale green grasshopper fluttering in the undergrowth. Net in hand, he pursued it with his usual recklessness, and was right on top of it and about to pounce when he saw that it was the head of a large rattlesnake. Only a sudden leap backwards saved his life.

He had a way with animals, especially reptiles. He was utterly fearless of snakes and alligators, and the most famous Watertonian episode was his ride on the back of a cayman—the South American alligator.

This celebrated event took place during one of his many determined encounters with the wild life of Guiana. He went cayman-catching with some friendly Indians in the interior who reckoned to be experts at this perilous game. The Squire devised a special hook which was baited and secured firmly by a rope. When the cayman took the bait he was like a fish, unable to get the hook out of his mouth.

Finding one of these formidable creatures, all of ten and a half feet long, firmly secured by the rope near the river bank, the Squire directed his natives, seven in all, to haul on the rope and drag the angry, struggling beast away from the river. The Indians hauled away and the fearful though unequal struggle (it could hardly be otherwise with Waterton there) was climaxed by the Squire in a moment of wild inspiration jumping on the back of the alligator and seizing the creature's fore-legs, twisting them upwards and backwards as though they were a bridle. Robbed of his fore-feet, the cayman was helpless to resist the heaving Indians who were thus able to drag the Squire on his strange steed for a full forty yards. The creature was finally tied up and then despatched by having its throat cut by its rider.

"Should it be asked how I managed to keep my seat," remarked the Squire later of this remarkable ride, "I would answer I hunted some years with Lord Darlington's fox-hounds."

Equally fearless and stirring were his encounters with the deadly snakes of South America, many of which he captured with his bare hands. His method was to approach the reptile cautiously but fearlessly, slide a firm hand along its back, then grasp it quickly by the neck. He took a number of such snakes back to England.

The extraordinary power he had over these highly dangerous

219

snakes required courage of the highest order. On one occasion he grabbed hold of the tail of a ten-foot boa, which not unnaturally turned angrily on him. The Squire dealt with it summarily by a punch to the jaw which apparently knocked the snake out. This extraordinary man then allowed the partly conscious boa to coil itself around his body and then he walked off with it as his prize. The snake squeezed him hard, he said, "but not alarmingly so". It obviously knew it had met its master.

On one occasion, being told that a dreaded anaconda had been sighted, the Squire resolved to take this largest and most formidable of Amazonian snakes alive. The thing was fourteen feet long and the fearless traveller took it on, armed with a bayonet mounted on a stick. With this he pinned the anaconda to the ground, but found himself unable to hold down his viciously writhing victim. His Indians, inspired by their master's intrepidity and determination, flung themselves upon the deadly monster. The Squire, with great cunning, persuaded the anaconda to wrap itself around the lance instead of around the men. He then tied up its mouth with his braces. They eventually carried the still-fighting snake home in triumph, and not until later did the Squire despatch the beast by cutting its throat. He said that when the snake was skinned, its open jaws were large enough for a man's head to go into.

Among Squire Waterton's lesser but more widely observed exploits was the ascent of the façade of St Peter's during a visit to Rome in 1817. He climbed right to the top and affixed a pair of gloves to the points of the lightning conductor. His Holiness was not amused and immediately ordered that the gloves should be removed. But there was none among his entourage able to perform such a feat, and so Squire Waterton was approached. He then repeated his climb before a vast audience and removed the offending gloves to the cheers of the faithful.

When he was in his forties, Waterton married a girl of seventeen named Anne Edmondstone. The marriage took place at 4 a.m. on 11 May, 1829. Anne died a year later, shortly after the birth of their son. After that the grieving widower vowed that he would never again enter a bed. For the rest of his life he always slept on the floor, his only covering being a cloak and a napless blanket, his pillow a block of beechwood with a slight hollow for his head.

His later life was that of a true ascetic, and he greatly resented being called an eccentric. He always went to bed at nine and rose at three in the morning. Wherever he went he lit a fire, no matter what the time of the year. He became a true nineteenth-century character and as he grew older legends gathered around his name. His books of travel brought him fame, although many found some of his exploits hard to believe.

He lived until he was 83, retaining his boundless health right to the end. In his eighties he was still able to perform remarkable feats of climbing and acrobatics. He died as the result of a fall in 1865 and was buried in a lonely grave beside the lake in his family home of Walton Hall.

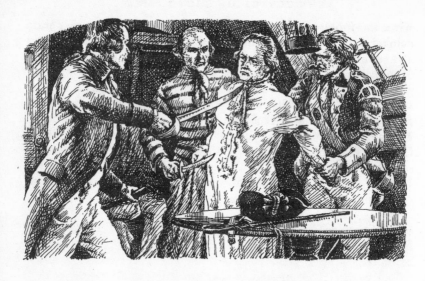

THE VOYAGE OF THE *BOUNTY*

William Bligh's Command

IN THE autumn of 1787, H.M. Armed Merchant Vessel *Bounty*, a full-rigger of 215 tons, lay anchored at Spithead. *Bounty* had been commissioned for a unique expedition which would take many months to complete: she was to sail to the Society Islands to collect breadfruit cuttings, and thence to the West Indies where it was hoped to establish these remarkable trees. The ship's main cabin had been converted into a greenhouse, and two experts, David Nelson, a botanist, and William Brown, a gardener from Kew, had been appointed by Sir Joseph Banks, President of the Royal Society, to tend and water the delicate shoots.

The command of *Bounty* had been given to William Bligh, a naval lieutenant, who had sailed under Captain Cook, the great explorer of the Pacific, and had spent a considerable time on Otaheite (Tahiti). As master of *Resolution* he had given ample proof of his genius for navigation, his skill in drawing charts and taking soundings in unknown waters. Bligh, who was 33 at the time, was somewhat below average height, thickset and inclined to corpulence; in contrast with his black hair and the pallor of his complexion, his eyes were almost startlingly blue. Born in Plymouth, he came from a good-class family, and had joined the Navy at sixteen. Unlike most seafaring men, he was only a moderate drinker, but he had an ungovernable temper, and when he was in a rage, his language was unspeakably foul. As was usual in those days, Bligh, as well as being the captain of *Bounty*, was also the purser.

Bligh had personally selected several members of the crew, amongst them Fletcher Christian, the mate. Christian, who was 24, was even better-born than Bligh; his people owned large estates in Cumberland and the Isle of Man. Short, dark-haired, swarthy-skinned, his open expression and pleasant manner made up for his lack of good looks. Christian had the kind of personality that commands both liking and respect.

While Bligh was awaiting his sailing orders, two men deserted. He chose as replacements a surgeon, Ledward (it had not taken Bligh long to note the fact that *Bounty*'s surgeon, Huggan, was a drunken sot), and a half-blind fiddler, Michael Byrne, both of whom were signed on as able seamen. Bligh had been extremely anxious to have a musician aboard, for in his view there was nothing like dancing to keep a crew fit.

The personnel of *Bounty* was as follows: the captain, two midshipmen and 8 warrant officers, 23 able seamen, 3 carpenters, 1 sailmaker, 1 gunner, 1 gunner's mate, 1 armourer, 1 corporal, 1 surgeon, 1 clerk; Nelson, the botanist, and William Brown, the gardener. As regards the able seamen, nine most certainly did not answer this description: Ledward, Byrne, three superfluous midshipmen who had been foisted on Bligh, his steward, two cooks, and the master's brother-in-law, Mr Tinkler, a young gentleman who could only be described as a kind of reserve midshipman. *Bounty* was thus very definitely undermanned.

On 24 November, Bligh's long-awaited sailing orders arrived. The voyage to the Society Islands was to be made without stopping *en route* via Cape Horn; when the breadfruit cuttings had been collected, *Bounty* was to proceed by way of the Torres Straits and the Cape of Good Hope to the West Indies, putting in at Java to replace any shoots that had died with valuable plants for Kew. One-half of the surviving breadfruit shoots was to be delivered to the Botanical Gardens at St Vincent, the other half to the Botanical Gardens at Jamaica. This accomplished, it was England, Home and Beauty.

On 23 December the *Bounty* sailed from Portsmouth, and almost at once ran into exceptionally dirty weather. She was buffeted by a gale-force wind, and the heavy seas which broke over her smashed her stern superstructure, flooding the small hold below, ruining such provisions as were stored there and shattering several casks of beer. On 6 January, 1798, Bligh put in at Vera Cruz where the damage was repaired and fresh supplies laid in. These included a quantity of pumpkins.

On the day *Bounty* left Tenerife, Bligh cut the bread ration by one-third, and made good the difference with an allowance of pumpkins. The crew, who regarded their rations as sacred, protested, but were pacified when Bligh told them that as it might prove a lengthy business to round Cape Horn, it was necessary to ensure that the provisions would be adequate. They had, however, no sooner crossed the Equator than the entire bread ration was replaced by the pumpkins, which were beginning to go rotten. Naturally, the men complained bitterly. "You damned infernal scoundrels, I'll make you eat grass or anything else you can snatch before I've finished with you!" Bligh roared in reply.

Towards the end of February, *Bounty* made contact with a British whaler, and Bligh took the opportunity to send home a report which ran: "My men share in all but the poultry [*Bounty* carried a large number of live chickens, pigs and sheep] and show much content and cheerfulness, dancing from four till eight at night. I am happy that I shall bring them all back safe and well."

Bounty's crew, it need hardly be said, were anything but contented and cheerful. As the ship was undermanned, jigging and hornpiping for four hours non-stop was hardly likely to raise the spirits of overworked seamen; moreover, their rations were always short, for Bligh had taken advantage of the fact that he was the purser to add to his meagre pay. Proof of this was afforded when, according to custom, a barrel of provisions was opened in the presence of the entire personnel. This particular barrel contained cheeses, two of which were found to be missing. Bligh immediately feigned anger and declared that the cask had been got at, only to be reminded by one of the seamen that the cask had been broached at the order of his clerk while *Bounty* was still in the Thames estuary, and that two of the cheeses had been delivered to his residence. Bligh silenced him with a stream of filthy expletives, and without further enquiry ordered the cheese ration to be withdrawn until the deficiency had been made good.

There is much that must be put to Bligh's credit, the hygienic measures, for instance, that made him so unpopular with his crew, but nothing can excuse his behaviour to his officers. With the exception of fourteen-year-old Midshipman Peter Heywood, to whom he was always kindly, and, on the voyage to the Society Islands, Fletcher Christian, he treated them abominably. When they dined at his table Bligh took a sadistic delight in insulting them and making them writhe. He held John Fryer, the master, in particular contempt, and duly humiliated him by promoting Christian, twelve years Fryer's junior, over his head to second-in-command. Naturally, the master lost face, and when he reported a seaman, Matthew Quintal, for insolence to him, Bligh, to show his low opinion of Fryer, sentenced Quintal to a mere dozen lashes.

On 22 March really bad weather set in, but thanks to Bligh's masterly handling *Bounty* succeeded in rounding Cape Horn. On 9 April she passed the 77th parallel of longitude, and would soon have been on the right course for Otaheite had she not been hit by an almost unbelievably violent squall.

Conditions now became frightful. Far from making headway, *Bounty* was forced back and back, and on 23 April she was swept past Staten Island which she had sighted a month earlier. It was piercingly cold, and ice formed on the men's saturated clothing. To add to their misery the ship sprang a leak, and as it was quite impossible to repair the sprung planking, it was all hands to the pumps. In spite of the safety line that had been fastened with the greatest difficulty across the deck, the crew were in constant danger of being washed overboard by the mountainous waves; some were injured, others fell ill, and the situation became so desperate that Bligh was forced to put about, and make for Cape Town, the nearest port. *Bounty* was thus to sail half-way round the world before she reached Otaheite.

Bounty limped into Cape Town at the end of May, and so extensively had she been damaged that, even with the help of Dutch shipwrights, it took a full two months to repair her. Throughout the stay in Cape Town, Bligh provided the crew with a generous allowance of fresh meat, fruit and vegetables, and all were fit and well when the ship sailed on 1 July.

After 51 days at sea *Bounty* sighted Brunio Island, off the coast of Tasmania, and Bligh dropped anchor in Adventure Bay, which he had visited eleven years earlier with Captain Cook. When the water casks had been filled and a fresh supply of wood collected, *Bounty* resumed her voyage.

At the beginning of October there was a head-on clash between Bligh and Fryer. When the ship's accounts were submitted to the master, instead of signing them he wrote out a testimonial for himself which included a statement that he had "done nothing amiss" while on board, and requested the captain to put his name to the document. Bligh, fully alive to the fact that this was Fryer's way of accusing him of falsifying the books, charged him with blackmail—which makes it pretty obvious that he *had* juggled with the figures—immediately summoned everyone on deck, read out the list of dire punishments he could inflict for disobedience, and again confronted the master with the accounts. Fryer lost his nerve and signed, but from this time forth he obstinately declined to dine at the captain's table.

On 28 October, at sunrise, *Bounty*, after a voyage of over 27,000 nautical miles, at last reached Otaheite, and dropped anchor in Matavei Bay. Bathed in the glowing colours of a tropic dawn, with surf breaking in lacy patterns on the black lava shore, the island was so breathtakingly beautiful that the crew forgot all the hardships they had endured. When the entire personnel had assembled, Bligh read out the list of rules that were to be observed on Otaheite, and stated that on no account must the islanders be told of Captain Cook's death; it was vital, he said, that they should continue to believe he was alive and well. Scarcely had he finished speaking than a fleet of canoes appeared in the bay and drew alongside. At once a delighted cry went up: "*To amtou taio Parai*—it's our friend Bligh!", and the next moment the Otaheitans began scrambling aboard. Men, women and children crowded on to the deck, pressing presents of sucking-pigs, fresh fruit and coconuts on one and all, and eagerly enquiring about Cook. The islanders spent the day on the ship, but while Bligh ordered the men to leave at sunset, he allowed those women who were unwilling to go to remain for the night.

On the following morning, Bligh sent Fletcher Christian with a party of four ashore where they were to put up a tent for themselves, build a temporary greenhouse, and help Nelson and Brown collect the breadfruit cuttings. The breadfruit patrol led an idyllic existence; the work was light, the islanders showered hospitality on them, and they were surrounded by graceful, warm-blooded young women. The rest of the crew who slept on *Bounty* were almost as fortunate, for Bligh made no objection to their sharing their bunks with charming bedfellows.

Within three weeks Nelson and Brown had as many cuttings as they needed, yet *Bounty* was to remain at Otaheite for almost five months. While it is not known for certain why Bligh made such a prolonged stay, it was probably because he knew that if he sailed immediately he would encounter unfavourable westerly head-winds, which would make it extremely difficult for him to navigate the treacherous Torres Straits.

Bligh, being the kind of man he was, soon introduced unpleasant elements into Eden. He insisted, for instance, that half the transplanted cuttings were dead and ordered them to be replaced, but when they were pulled up he was forced to concede that only one had failed to root. As he could not bear to see the men idle for as much as an hour he set them useless tasks, such as making tubs for which there was no room on *Bounty*; far worse, he confiscated the pigs the seamen had bought—everything brought aboard was his he told them, and they counted themselves lucky if they received as much as a pound of their own meat.

On 5 January, 1789, Midshipman Heywood fell asleep on watch, and three men took the opportunity to desert in the ship's cutter. They were eventually found and brought back, and Bligh sentenced them to 48 lashes, an extraordinarily light punishment for such a serious offence.* Bligh dealt severely with Heywood, however (the wretched boy was clapped into irons and confined for eleven weeks), and wrote in his log: "Such neglectful and worthless petty officers I believe never were as are in this ship."

For some inexplicable reason, Bligh's feeling for Fletcher Christian cooled and died on the island, but while they remained there he gave the latter no cause to suspect his change of heart.

On 4 April *Bounty* bade farewell to Otaheite. Far from regretting their departure, however, the men were in high spirits—already they were thinking of the jollifications they would have when they were back in England. Bligh's mood was very different; from the outset of the voyage to the West Indies he was in a black rage. Almost immediately he turned on the astonished Christian and let loose on him a torrent of abuse. Day after day he hurled imprecations at his second-in-command and insulted him in every possible way. Christian was stunned. What had he done to deserve such cruel treatment? Hourly, he grew more wretched.

As for the crew, Bligh cursed them up and down, and swore time

* The popular belief that Bligh flogged his men brutally is quite untrue.

and again that when they reached the Torres Strait, he would "kill half the people and make the officers jump overboard".

For almost three weeks Christian suffered in silence, but the moment came when he could control himself no longer. "Sir," he burst out, "your abuse of me is so bad that I cannot do my duty with any pleasure. I am in hell–in hell!"

On 23 April *Bounty* reached the Tonga Islands, and Bligh anchored off Annamooka. A party of eleven men with Christian in charge was sent ashore to fill the water casks and collect wood, and while they were given muskets Bligh ordered these to be left in the boat, as they were on no account to open fire unless a dire emergency arose. The patrol rowed to the island, but had hardly set foot on shore when a band of natives, brandishing clubs and spears, appeared, and rushed towards them. After the first shock of surprise, the men of *Bounty* succeeded in beating them off, but not before their assailants had snatched from them an adze and an axe. When they returned to the ship, Christian reported the loss of these tools to Bligh, who instantly damned him as a cowardly dog, afraid to tackle naked savages although he had muskets to hand. "Sir," answered Christian indignantly, "The muskets served no purpose since your orders were not to use them."

On 26 April *Bounty* left Annamooka, her last Pacific port of call, with a large supply of provisions: live pigs, yams, fresh fruit and coconuts. The coconuts were piled up on the deck between the guns, and Bligh ordered a strict watch to be kept on the heap. On the following afternoon it seemed to him that this heap had diminished, and summoning the officers he asked them if they had seen any of the men helping themselves to the coconuts. No, they had not, they replied, whereupon he shouted furiously: "Then you must have taken them yourselves!" Determined to get to the bottom of the matter, he asked each officer in turn how many coconuts he had purchased for himself and how many of them he had eaten. When Christian was questioned, he answered: "I do not know, sir, but I hope you do not think me so mean as to be guilty of stealing yours." "Yes, you damned hound, I do!" roared Bligh. "You must have stolen them or you would be able to give a better account of your own!" Christian turned deathly white. To be called a thief–a thief! The cup of bitterness he had been forced to drink overflowed; he could not, would not bear any more, and in his despair he resolved that, come what might, he would leave *Bounty* that night.

Before another hour had passed there was a second passage between the captain and his second-in-command. What Bligh said to Christian is not known, but it reduced him to tears. Incredibly, a little later on, Bligh asked Christian to dine with him. Possibly he felt that he had gone too far; be that as it may, Christian refused the invitation point-blank.

Christian made no attempt to conceal from the crew the fact that he intended to desert. Feverishly he began to nail together planks and poles, and the men who knew full well that Bligh had driven him to the desperate step he was about to take, willingly lent him a hand and helped him to construct a crude raft. As soon as the raft had been built, Christian filled a sack with provisions and bartering goods. All was now ready, but he decided to delay his departure from *Bounty* until the morning when she would be quite close to the island of Tofua. He crawled into his bunk and fell into a fitful sleep.

At 4 a.m. he was roused by Midshipman Stewart to set the watch. Stewart did his utmost to persuade him to give up his desperate scheme. "Remember you are not the only sufferer, Mr Christian," he said, "Indeed, Captain Bligh has driven the men so far that they are ripe for anything."

The mutiny was unconsciously triggered off by Midshipman Heywood who, for the second time, had fallen asleep on watch. The moment Christian saw his recumbent form the wild idea of seizing *Bounty* flashed into his disordered mind. Stewart's words echoed in his ears: *the men are ripe for anything* ...

In his unbalanced state Christian did not even pause to think. Instead, he rushed off to the men on watch and asked them if they would help him to take the ship. One of them roused the rest of the crew who were asleep in the fo'c'sle—the decision to rally round Christian was unanimous.

Christian next woke the bosun, Cole, who kept the key of the chest where the arms were stored, and told him he needed a musket to shoot a shark which was following *Bounty*. Suspecting nothing amiss, Cole handed it to him.

As soon as the weapons had been distributed, Christian told Quintal and another man to go below and seize the master, Fryer. At 5. 30 a.m., Christian, together with Churchill, the corporal, and a seaman named Burkitt, entered the captain's cabin. Bligh was asleep. Christian woke him, and said: "Mr Bligh, you are my prisoner." At once Bligh shouted for help and began to struggle, but

Churchill and Burkitt overpowered him and bound his hands behind his back with a length of rope.

Bligh's shouts had roused the officers, who stumbled up on deck where they were immediately confronted by some of the mutineers. True, the latter were armed and they were not, but they did not put up as much as a token resistance; even Christian was surprised at the ease with which he was able to take possession of *Bounty*.

Bligh was brought on deck and stood against the mizzen mast with his hands tied behind his back. A cry went up of "Kill the bastard!", but Christian immediately silenced it and ordered the cutter to be launched. He then gave the entire personnel the choice of going with Bligh in the cutter or remaining on *Bounty*, and when the loyalists had declared themselves (they were loyal, not to the captain, but to king and country), told them to go below to collect Bligh's uniform and their own possessions. Christian freed Bligh's hands so that he could dress himself, and as man after man stepped into the cutter she sank lower and lower into the water. "You can't all get in, my lads," exclaimed Bligh. "I'll see that justice is done to you if ever I reach England." He now turned to Christian and appealed to him, for the sake of his wife and children, to drop what he was doing, swearing on his honour that he would hold nothing against him. "If you had any honour, any regard for your family, you should have thought of them before and not acted like a villain," Christian replied, and ordered him to take his place in the cutter.

Christian, far from turning Bligh and the eighteen men with him adrift and consigning them to almost certain death, did everything he could to ensure their survival. The sea was calm, the weather set fair, the island of Kotu was in sight. He handed Bligh his sextant, and, when he asked for arms, gave him five cutlasses. He then put into the cutter enough provisions and water for the first few days, and offered to tow it to the island where he was certain that Bligh, knowing the natives as he did, would find a safe refuge. Bligh agreed to Christian's proposal, but *Bounty* had not towed the cutter far before one of the mutineers with a shout of: "Blow the bastard's brains out!" fired a shot over the captain's head. Fearing further violence, Christian cut the tow-rope, and as the loyalists took out the oars and began to row away he gazed in silence at the receding cutter. Already he was torn with remorse–indeed, he was never to know another happy moment.

Twenty-four men remained on *Bounty* with Christian. Seven

were loyalists, and amongst these were young Peter Heywood who had been too dazed to get into the cutter, and James Morrison, the bosun's mate, who had recorded in his journal all the events that had occurred on the ship on the outward journey, on Otaheite, and on the ill-fated voyage that had ended with the mutiny.

Christian decided that it would be highly imprudent to return to Otaheite, and he therefore set course for the remote island of Tupuai, of which he had read in Captain Cook's accounts of his voyages.

The attempt to colonize Tupuai, where the natives were unfriendly, ended in failure. In September, 1789, sixteen men announced that they wished to settle on Otaheite, and Christian agreed to take them there, but said that he himself intended to sail on and seek for some uninhabited island. "I'll go with you, Mr Christian," cried Midshipman Young, and seven others, Quintal, Smith, Mills, Martin, Mickey, Brown and Williams followed suit. Three of the islanders of Tupuai also decided to throw in their lot with Christian.

The sixteen separatists were left on Otaheite, and with twelve women, one for each man aboard, *Bounty* sailed from the island on the quest for a new home. Disastrously, as it was to turn out, three Otaheitan stowaways were discovered on the ship: the balance of the sexes was now upset.

Christian cruised amongst the atolls until November without finding one that was suitable for colonization. Where to go? He pored over Bligh's books and maps, and at length, in Carteret's *Travels*, read of an uninhabited island, Pitcairn, which seemed ideal in every way. The distance to Pitcairn was over 3,000 nautical miles, and it was not until 15 January, 1790, that the exhausted voyagers reached their destination. After the stores had been taken ashore and the ship stripped of everything that might be of use, Christian decided to burn her as there was always the danger that she might be sighted by a passing vessel. On his order, one of the men rowed out at night and set fire to her. Soon *Bounty* was ablaze from stem to stern, and as he gazed at the awe-inspiring sight, Christian could not refrain from weeping.

There is no space to relate here Bligh's epic journey of 3,701 nautical miles to Kupang on the Timor Sea, a journey he accomplished with the loss of only one man. On his return to England, H.M.S. *Pandora* was despatched to Otaheite where the loyalists welcomed her and the mutineers gave themselves up without a struggle. Four of them were drowned when *Pandora* was wrecked, and of those who stood trial, Peter Heywood, Morrison, Ellison, Burkitt, Millward and Muspratt were sentenced to death. At the eleventh hour, Peter Heywood and Morrison were reprieved.

In 1814, when the memory of *Bounty* had grown dim, the captains of two British frigates who were cruising in the Pacific, decided to find out if Pitcairn really was uninhabited. When they landed they were met by a band of youngsters, much lighter-skinned than the Polynesians, who took them to a hut where an old man was sitting—to their amazement, he was white. He told them he was Smith, the sole survivor of the *Bounty* mutineers, and related the following story:

Christian selected a suitable spot on the island for the colony and divided the land into nine lots. The six Polynesians were left to fend for themselves, and as they had only three women between them violent quarrels soon resulted in the deaths of two of them. Christian's elder son, Thursday October Christian, was the first child to be born on Pitcairn—others rapidly followed. Christian himself was sunk in melancholy; always religious, he prayed daily for forgiveness. After the birth of his second son, the wives of Williams and Smith both died, and they took two women from the four remaining Polynesians. Smarting at this injustice they ran amok, and in a single day murdered Christian, Mills, Williams, Brown and Martin. The bereaved wives avenged them, however, and in a horrific manner slew the assassins. Mickey discovered that alcohol could be distilled from a certain root, and in a very short time drank himself to death. Quintal, always a vicious character, became so bestial in his cups that Smith, fearing for the women and little ones, split his skull in two with an axe. After Quintal had been disposed of, Young started a school, and under his wise guidance peace and happiness came to Pitcairn. After a long illness Young died, and Smith was left alone to care for the little colony. He had carried on the good work which Young had initiated, and was honoured and loved by all on the island.

Smith told the two captains that he was ready to accompany them back to England and stand trial, but at the prospect of losing him his little flock had shown such grief that they decided to leave him on Pitcairn to end his days in tranquillity.

A last word about Bligh. He served with distinction under Nelson at the Battle of Copenhagen, but in 1804 was court-martialled and severely reprimanded for "tyranny, unofficer-like conduct, and ungentlemanly behaviour". In 1806 he was appointed Governor of New South Wales, where he was embroiled in a second mutiny; he was seized by rebel colonists and held prisoner for two years. On his release he returned to England, was promoted to vice-admiral, and died in London in 1817.

Smith outlived him by twelve years. After the patriarch's death some of the descendants of the mutineers remained on Pitcairn, others settled on Norfolk Island. Today the Christians, Quintals, Youngs and the rest are proud of the names they bear, the names that link them to one of the most colourful ships in the annals of the British Navy: H.M.S. *Bounty*.

ARTHUR YOUNG, THE IDEAL OBSERVER

Through Revolutionary France

EYE-WITNESSES of revolutions usually have an interesting story
to tell, and it is liable to be the better story if, instead of being obsessed with trying to interpret political happenings, they recount
what they see and hear from the people they mix with. Of course,
there are people so stupid that, fate having taken them to Paris on
17 July, 1789, when the Bastille fell to the Paris mob, they would not
even be curious but remain interested only in trivialities. Arthur
Young, however, was the ideal observer. He spoke French well,
liked the French, and had many connections with French noblemen
and men of science.

Arthur Young was a great expert in farming and he was in 1789
starting on the third of his tours of French agricultural areas which
was to take him to eastern and southern France, to Marseilles and
Nice, and back to Paris by Savoy. His journey, in fact, could be
said to be more concerned with turnips than politics. But he left
London on 4 June for Dover in the stage-coach, which he called
"The Machine", extremely aware of the significance of the fact
that the French King Louis XVI had called together the States
General of the realm for the first time since early in the seventeenth
century. It meant, he foresaw, the end of the Absolute Monarchy
and a new epoch in French and European affairs.

From the start his ears are pricked. From Dover to Calais he travels on "a vehicle which does not allow one the power to reflect". In a stage-coach from Dieppe to Abbeville he meets no kindred spirit but watches a French couple fleece a young French teacher from Ireland of a largish sum of money. Young was accustomed to travel in private carriages, as he did during most of his journey, or on horseback. He was in a raspish mood when he wrote his diary in Paris on 8 June and had liked the company he met on the journey from Abbeville to Paris–102 miles–no better than the card players. Of the company he met on the way to Paris he writes: "These men and women, girls and boys, think themselves very cheerful because very noisy; they have stunned me with singing, my ears have been so tormented with French airs that I would almost have soon have rode the journey blindfold on an ass. This is what the French call good spirits; no truly cheerful emotion in their bosoms; but of conversation they had none. I lose all patience in such company."

Arthur Young was a very earnest and ever so slightly priggish man, more typical one would say of the Victorian Age than the time of Doctor Johnson. He was forty-eight years old and already an acknowledged expert on farming and agricultural economy, which was the reigning passion of so much of the English aristocracy. King George III considered him one of the most valuable men in his kingdom, and under the name of "Ralph Robinson" he contributed to the *Annals of Agriculture* which Young had started to publish in 1784.

Young was the son of a well-off parson, the rector of Bradfield in Suffolk, who had been Chaplain to the Speaker of the House of Commons. At an early age Arthur Young was placed in business at King's Lynn; he did not like business, went to London where he wrote four novels, and then, on his father's death, took up farming on his own estate and in Essex. He was the squire of Bradfield and possessed a reasonable fortune. Like some other good writers on agriculture, Young was a failure as a farmer. He experimented in every modern method of farming and stock-breeding, and though most of what he tried out was to prove itself good, his experiments nearly brought Young to financial disaster.

He had married, not too happily, and his friends considered it fortunate that the four children of his marriage were beneficiaries of a trust-fund which he could not touch. Having still some money left, and not having mortgaged his estate at Bradfield, Young took to travelling all over England and Ireland and observing the practices of farmers, passing on what was good and successful in extremely well-written articles. He took a very serious attitude to his role as an "improver". Whenever he practised farming he nearly ruined himself and his family; whenever he put pen to paper, his success was immediate and acknowledged. His books were widely translated and well known in France and Germany. He was an inspiring person and men took note of what he said. After the Battle of Waterloo, in 1815, an English officer happened to visit a nearby farm which struck him as first-class in every way, with a mixed system of stock and arable on the English model. The farmer told the officer that his success was entirely due to advice given him by an English visitor, a Mr Arthur Young.

Young's great friends in France were members of the La Rochefoucauld family, particularly the eldest son, the Duke of Liancourt, one of the first of the King of France's subjects and a man who, from the start, took the side of the reformers, being anxious to see a constitutional monarchy formed. The king had summoned the States-General in order to raise money to avoid bankruptcy. What happened at once–and what everyone was discussing when Young arrived in Paris–was that the Commons or the Third Estate in the States-General demanded that there should be one House and that they and the clergy and the nobility should sit and legislate together. Many of the nobility, and among them the Duke of Liancourt, were in favour of this; but the king, dominated by Queen Marie Antoinette, failed to see that he should give way graciously to the Commons, and so, on 23 June, a National Assembly was created, after the celebrated oath on the tennis courts of Versailles, in spite of the king.

France, as Young notes, had formed its own Long Parliament and Louis XVI was now in the position of Charles I after the first Civil War. The Revolution was now to begin. It was to begin in real earnest on 14 July, 1789, when the Royal prison of the Bastille surrendered to the mob who slaughtered its defenders. Arthur Young was then far away in eastern France, but during this month of June, when the revolution was still comparatively respectable, Young, who was a liberal-minded conservative Englishman, understood the forces in play very accurately. He saw the court ladies in Versailles hiss the wife of Necker, the finance minister whom the king hoped would save the realm. Indeed, he saw the king and queen booed as they drove to Paris from Versailles. While the Assembly and the cafés of Paris were at fever-heat of excitement, the nobility preserved an artificial calm. Young notes: "Amongst a class so much higher as those I dine with, I was struck with the difference. There were not, in thirty persons, five in whose countenances you could guess that any extraordinary event was going forward; more of the conversation was unexcited than I should have expected. They eat, drink, sit, walk, loiter, smirk, smile and chat with an easy indifference which made me stare at their insipidity. Perhaps there is a certain nonchalance that is natural to people of fashion from long habit, and which marks them from the vulgar."

Young's attitude to the Revolution was founded on a conviction that the middle classes must be given a share of power in government such as they already enjoyed in England. He hoped and expected that France would evolve a constitutional monarchy and that a House of Lords would be created to act as a check on parliament. He was a great admirer of the British Constitution and a believer in the gradual expansion of liberties, civil and religious. Young hoped that France would evolve on the British pattern. He had a clearer vision, drawn from his extensive travelling in France, than many of his French friends, and he saw the "other" Revolution which was breaking out in France among the peasants and the town artisans and which was certainly not a respectable bourgeois revolution aiming at a constitutional monarchy.

Young had seen bread riots in 1787 in France and was well acquainted with a bitterness with which the peasants now resented the feudal rights which the nobility exercised over them. He was convinced that the condition of the artisans and peasants must be changed. But he felt that the respectable forces in France, King and Court, Church, Army and the Regional Parliaments and the Liberal Reformers must check the mobs or disaster would follow. In 1789, and indeed until 1792 when the king and queen were guillotined and the Terror began, Young was passionately in favour of the new forces. He did not think it in Britain's interest that Prussians, Austrians and Russians should control French after a counter-revolution. Property at all costs must in his view be safe-guarded; but there must be progress. His attitude to the "other" Revolution is well shown when, at Liancourt, on the estate of his patron and friend, he saw that the peasants had seized some waste land belonging to the duke and were cultivating it. He saw some men very busy at work on this waste land, hedging it in, in small divisions, levelling and digging and bestowing much labour on this poor land. He was told by the steward that the poor people in the town, when the revolution began, had declared that the poor were the nation, that the waste belonged to the nation and, proceeding from theory to practice, had taken possession without any further authority and begun to cultivate. The duke showed no opposition and was clearly not displeased. Young states:

"This circumstance shows the universal spirit that is gone forth and proves that, were it pushed a little farther, it might prove a serious matter for all the property in the nation. In this case, however, I cannot but commend it; for if there be one public nuisance greater than another it is a man preserving the possession of waste land which he will neither cultivate himself nor let others cultivate. The miserable people die for want of bread, in spite of wastes that would feed thousands. I think them wise and rational in seizing such tracts, and I heartily wish there was a law in England for making this action of the French peasants a legal one with us."

Young left Paris at the beginning of July and for a while the Revolution takes second place in his mind. He is observing French life and gathering together those practical observations of how people live which made the great success of his writings. He spends a day with a gentleman farmer at Meaux, noticing that this man, whose wealth all comes from the plough, was of noble birth and lived in a chateau yet his daily life was simple, his wife preparing the table for dinner and his bailiff and female domestic dining with the family. At Epernay he is busy with getting information about the making of champagne. He finds that drinking champagne cures his rheumatism of which he "had had some writhes".

His diary for a while is more full of pleasant contacts with farmers and men of science; the only constant undertone is some alarm which everybody expresses at the price of bread and its scarcity. It is not until 20 July that, at Strasbourg, he learns about the taking of the Bastille, the setting up of a National Guard and the overthrow of the old government. He remains optimistic, writing: "It will be a great spectacle for the world to view, in this enlightened age, the representatives of twenty-five million people sitting down to construct a new and better order. It will now be seen whether they will copy the constitution of England, free from its faults, or attempt, from theory, to frame something absolutely speculative; in the former case they will prove a blessing to their country; in the latter they will probably involve it in inextricable confusions and civil wars, perhaps not in the present period but certainly at some future one."

That night in Strasbourg he witnessed a scene curious to a foreigner but dreadful, he thinks, to a Frenchman. The mob were breaking the windows of the town hall with stones whilst a detachment of soldiers, with an officer at its head, stood by watching. The mob grew bolder and broke open the doors and some magistrates and clerks flew out, panic-stricken, from the back. The mob dashed into the town hall and threw out of the windows chairs, tables, sofas, books, papers, pictures, skirting boards, bannisters, framework and every part of the building which force could detach. The troops were now reinforced but still did not interfere. Young even saw some common soldiers, with their white cockades, among the plunderers instigating the mob even in sight of the officers of the detachment. He was surprised to see people who were well-dressed participating in this sacking of the town hall.

Shortly after, Young was surrounded, in a small village, by a mob of young men who asked him why he had no Tricolour cockade in his hat. He was about to explain that he was an Englishman when a parish priest vigorously addressed the mob, told them to avoid violence and said it was their duty, for the time being, to pay all taxes. After the priest had gone, Young was still in some danger, various people suggesting he was a Seigneur and ought to be hanged. Then Young gave them a discourse on English taxation, pointing out that in his country the poor escaped lightly from taxes, and the well-off paid a great deal. They listened, approved, and gave him an huzza. Young was careful, thereafter, to wear a cockade wherever he went.

One of the things most wrong with France, Young decided, was the chaos in men's minds which resulted from the absence of news or information about what was happening. Not until he had reached Strasbourg was he able to read newspapers, and he noted, for instance, at Chateau Thierry that there was no coffee-house and no newspapers to be got in this town. Here was a place with some thousands of inhabitants and not a newspaper to be seen by a traveller, even in a moment when everybody obviously wanted to read one. In England news travelled rapidly from one end of the kingdom to the other and men at once got together to defend their principles or their interests or to preserve order. In France there are no such spontaneous associations. He writes: "Thus it may be said perhaps with truth that the fall of the King, Court, Lords, Nobles, Army, Church and Parliaments is owing to a want of intelligence being quickly circulated, consequently is owing to the very effects of a thraldom in which they held the people; it is therefore a retribution rather than a punishment."

The responsibility of "Absolutist" government or the stupidity of people generally is constantly a theme of Arthur Young. Thus in Metz he noted that at the officers' dining tables in the inns there was a "voluble garniture of bawdry or nonsense; at those of merchants, a mournful and stupid silence. Take the mass of mankind, and you have more good sense in half an hour in England than in half a year in France–Government". Nor is it only stupidity for which Young finds government responsible.

He travels on the roads awhile with a poor woman who complains of the taxes and the exactions imposed on her by the landlords, and writes: "This woman might have been taken for sixty or seventy, her figure was so bent, and her face so furrowed and hardened by labour; but she said she was only twenty-eight. An Englishman who has not travelled cannot imagine the figure made by the greater part of the country-women in France. It speaks at first sight of hard and severe labour. I am inclined to think that they work harder than the men; this, united with the miserable labour of bringing a new race of slaves into the world, destroys absolutely all symmetry of person and every feminine appearance. To what are we to attribute this difference in the manners of the lower classes in the two kingdoms? The Government."

Despite the lack of newspapers, much of the news, all the same, became known. In some cities the National Guard, the vanguard of the Revolution, was employed in repressing the plundering and murder of aristocrats by the mobs. At an inn in Burgundy, Young met an unfortunate gentleman of rank, his wife, a few-months-old child and servants who had just escaped, a night or two before, from their burnt-out chateau, all property lost. On enquiry, Young discovered that the gentleman had passed for being well liked by his tenants and peasants and had a benevolent disposition.

At Moulins, in central France, Young learned of the abolition of all feudal rights enjoyed by the nobility–tithes, forced labour of all kinds and game-preserves. Near Clermont Ferrand, Young hired an elderly peasant woman to lead him to some mineral springs of volcanic origin which he wished to see, high up in the mountains. On her return with Young, the woman was arrested and conducted to a heap of stones which had once been a chateau and where the village council was assembled. The woman was accused of the grave crime of conducting a stranger about the country at a time when everyone knew the Queen of France was conspiring with foreigners against the Revolution. Young spoke in her defence, of course, and the council asked him why he had been asking so many questions about prices, values and products of the land. What had that got to do with springs or volcanoes? They suggested he was either a Royalist spy–or else, equally damnable, a commissioner from Paris sent to find out what was the wealth of the district. He and the woman were finally let off with a caution.

At Clermont Ferrand he dined or supped five times at the principal inn with from twenty to thirty merchants, tradesmen, officers, etc. It was not easy for Young to express what he calls the insignificance and inanity of the conversation. "Scarcely any politics at a moment when every bosom ought to beat with none but political sensations. The ignorance or the stupidity of these people must be absolutely incredible; not a week passes without their country abounding with events that are analysed and debated by the carpenters and blacksmiths of England."

Farther south Young was again arrested by the National Guard who could not understand why he was travelling about the district and visiting farmers. He was taken before another town council. They too had never heard of any man travelling for agriculture. But all this was said in the most polite and liberal manner and the council obligingly took the trouble to put Arthur Young in touch with a local agricultural historian whom he wished to see. Another time, Young had been examining, in the half-dark, a small field of land said by its owner to produce mulberries in great quantities for the silk-worms. The National Guards came up into his bedroom in the inn when he was falling asleep, roused him up, examined his letters and papers, but finally left him as he said "to the bugs which swarm in my bed like flies in a honey-pot".

In Marseilles, Young found plenty of newspapers and a large coterie of intelligent men, such as the Abbé Raynal, a well-known economist. Generally speaking, in Provence Young spent his time examining the estates of noblemen rather than thinking about the Revolution. In the neighbourhood of Aix-en-Provence, Young was pestered with what he called "the mob of country shooting", and he thought that every rusty gun in the whole of Provence was popping off at every kind of bird. Five or six times shot fell into his carriage and about his ears. The National Assembly's declaration that every man had a right to shoot game on his own land had filled all the fields of France with sportsmen who have become a public nuisance.

At the Tour d'Aigues, twenty miles north of Aix on the Durance river, Young called on the baron of that name, President of the Parliament of Aix and a great landowner and tree-planter. The baron was going to suffer greatly from the Revolution, for a great extent of country around the chateau, which had belonged to him absolutely, now became the property of his tenants. There was no compensation. Young found the company in the chateau alarmed by the state of society, many of them having had their houses burnt or damaged and gardens trampled on by local mobs; but none the less the atmosphere was cheerful and agreeable. The baron had a large library, one part of which was entirely devoted to books, brochures and tracts on farming published in every country of Europe.

Antibes was, at that time, the frontier, and Nice, to which Arthur Young now directed his steps, was an Italian city. For Young this part of the Côte-d'Azur was indeed Italy, and he writes, as he approached Nice: "The first approach to that country so long and justly celebrated that has produced those who have conquered and those who have decorated the world, fills the bosom with too many throbbing feelings to permit a bush, a stone, a clod to be uninteresting." He arrived in time to dine at the inn. The price for his apartment, which was exceedingly moderate, and for dinner and supper was five Piedmontese livres a day, that is five shillings in English money. There were several Frenchmen and more Italians in the dining-room and only the French Revolution was talked of. The Frenchmen were all in favour of it and the Italians all against it and, according to Arthur Young, the latter were absolute victors in the argument. The number of new streets, squares and buildings in the town was, according to Young, evidence that the place was flourishing. This was already owing to the resort of foreigners, principally English, who passed the winter in Nice on account of the climate. The inhabitants were very much dismayed by the disturbances in France, which they believed would prevent many of the English from coming that winter.

Young travelled back to Lyons over the Mt. Cenis Pass on a mule, and in Lyons he had many conversations about industry and trade and much to say about prices and food. Of French cooking he says there is but one opinion; "every man in Europe that can afford a great table, either keeps a French cook or one instructed in the same manner. In England," he goes on, "we have about half a dozen real English dishes that exceed anything in my opinion to be met with in France; by English dishes I mean a turbot and

lobster sauce–ham and chicken–turtle–a haunch of venison–a turkey and oysters–and after these there is an end of an English table.
It is idle prejudice to class roast beef among them, for there is no
better beef in the world than at Paris. The variety given by their
cooks to the same thing is astonishing; they dress a hundred dishes
in a hundred different ways and most of them excellent and all
sorts of vegetables have a savouriness and flavour from rich sauces
that are absolutely wanted to our greens boiled in water. This
variety is not striking any comparison of a great table in France
with another in England; it is manifest in an instant between the
tables of a French and English family of small fortune."

Like many foreigners, yesterday and today, Young noticed that
French families, consisting of several sons with their wives, all tended to live with the paternal family. This, he argues, is not because
of economy, for many of the richest families in France live together;
but because of the French character. Much as he criticizes French
government which has produced a breed of people who take no
interest in public affairs, he is full of praise for the French character,
which he considers good-humoured and good-tempered. It is this
which makes the families live together; but, he states, it would never
work in England.

He notes that whilst the French make the fashions both male and
female of the civilized world, neither French men nor women dress
with the same extravagance as the English upper and upper-middle
classes. The French as a whole live better than the English because
in his view they do not live beyond their means. Where one gentleman of property in the French provinces is so foolish as to run
through his fortune, there are a dozen such in England. Nothing,
he thinks, contributes more to making the French a happy people
than the cheerful and facile disposition with which they adapt
themselves to the circumstances of life. This disposition they possess
much more than the volatile high spirits which are attributed to
them.

Whilst Young had been away from Paris the Paris mob had
stormed the Palace of Versailles, killing the King's Guards, and
brought back "the baker, the baker's wife and the baker's brat"
to Paris as virtual prisoners. Young, after breakfast, walked in the
Tuileries Gardens and saw the most extraordinary sight. The king
was walking in a part of the garden with six National Guards, a
page and an officer of his household. The doors of the gardens were
kept shut in respect to him in order to exclude anybody but Depu-

ties or those who had admission tickets. When the king entered the palace, Young noted that the doors of the gardens were thrown open to all without distinction, although the queen was still walking with a lady of her court. She also was attended so closely by the National Guard that she had to speak in a low voice to avoid being overheard by them. A crowd followed her, talking very loudly and paying no other apparent respect than of taking off their hats whenever she passed, which was indeed more than Young expected.

He felt the queen did not appear to be in health and seemed much affected and showed it in her face. But the king seemed as plump as ever. There was a little garden railed off for the Dauphin to amuse himself in and a small room to retire to in case of rain. Here the Dauphin was at work with a little hoe and rake; he also had a guard of two Grenadiers. He seemed a very pretty, good-natured little boy, five or six years old, with an agreeable countenance. Young was also glad to note that people took off their hats when the Dauphin passed.

In Paris there was constant talk of counter-revolution and the nobility were beginning to emigrate in large numbers. The National Assembly was becoming increasingly in the hands of the extremists. On his journey back to London, Young had no alternative but the hateful public stage-coach. "Passing from the first company of Paris to the rabble which one sometimes meets in diligences is contrast sufficient—but the idea of returning to England, to my family and friends made all things appear smooth." The two hundred and seventy-two miles of land and sea from Paris to London took him the best part of five days.

Young's accounts of his travels in France, and particularly that of the year 1789, increased his fame. From the United States Washington corresponded with him as did the presidents of most of the learned societies of Europe. He was made President of the Board of Agriculture set up in 1791 and King George III gave him a black merino ram. After the execution of the King of France and the triumph of the Jacobins, and Robespierre's reign of terror, Arthur Young changed his view about the Revolution, as did the majority of Englishmen. But his diary remains today as an example of cool-headed thinking. All that he saw and learnt in France gave him the conviction that change was necessary; a change which would limit the royal authority, restrain the feudal tyranny of the nobles, correct the abuses of arbitrary finance and purify justice. But whether to effect these things it was necessary to experience the excesses of the Terror was another matter.

Young argued that evils such as the Terror are surely more imputable to the tyranny of the master than to the cruelty of the former servant. He writes: "The murder of a Seigneur or a chateau in flames is recorded in every newspaper; the rank of a person who suffers attracts notice; but where do we find the register of that Seigneur's oppression of his peasantry and his exactions of feudal services from those whose children were dying around them for want of bread? In these cases the sufferers are too ignoble to be known and the mass too indiscriminate to be pitied."

These are noble sentiments and the fruit of a mind which lacked class prejudice and also of a man who had seen events close-to and had really examined what he was writing about. His journey in 1789 was not the arduous exploit of an explorer of unknown countries; but it took a great deal of courage to travel alone through the most isolated regions of France whilst the chateaux were going up in flames.

ROAD WITH A LOAD OF MISCHIEF

By Coach from London to Bath

"IF GOD permit." These three qualifying words appear prominently in an old coaching bill addressed "To all those desirous to pass from London to Bath." They let intending passengers know, if they did not know already, that the road to Bath–all 107 odd miles of it–was paved with peril.

The promoters who catered so enterprisingly for eighteenth-century passengers took no chances. They claimed that their coach would perform the whole advertised journey between La Belle Sauvage, on Ludgate Hill, and the White Lion, in Bath, within three days, but safeguarded themselves with the proviso: "If God Permit." No qualification was ever more aptly applied.

Wags of those days dubbed coach passengers "Godpermits". But the "desirous" ones were not to be put off. A coach left for Bath every Monday, Wednesday and Friday. "Passengers to pay one pound five shillings each, who are allowed to carry fourteen Pounds weight–for all above to pay three-half-pence per Pound." Departure time was 5 a.m.

The picturesque appeal of the great stage-coach is with us yet, for in spite of the growing fashion for strangely off-beat Christmas cards, nothing can wholly oust the traditional favourite–the mail-coach theme, with bluff, hearty, rosy-cheeked coachmen and equally rosy passengers, convulsed with merriment as their gaily-painted vehicle, drawn by four or even six plunging horses, ploughs bravely along snow-clad country roads.

Yet, in a way, the coaching card is as strangely off-beat as the ultra-modern interlopers in the card catalogues. No doubt our ancestors were hardy and bluff and hearty and full of merriment, but the scenes convey no hint of the hazard and discomfort involved in any long journey by stage-coach. When the Bath coach encountered heavy snow, a not uncommon occurrence in winter, strong cart-horses had to be found to help heave it clear of drifts; and passengers frequently had to get out to lighten the load and perhaps to put their shoulders to the wheels as well. But that is only one of the minor troubles that assailed the coach travellers. Whether it took three days or a week or more, the journey by road from London to Bath could provide thrills and spills and adventure in full measure.

It was a Member of Parliament, John Palmer, manager of the Bath Theatre, who, in 1784, put the first mail-coach into regular service as an alternative to relays of post-boys, by inaugurating a run between London and Bristol. In spite of much initial opposition, the idea so caught on with the public that by 1797 there were at least 80 passenger-carrying coaches operating on various routes in England. Their number increased yearly until, by 1835, there were more than 700 passenger coaches on the roads of Britain. They throve until the coming of the railways, in 1840, demonstrated conclusively that their days of usefulness were done.

In its heyday, the London to Bath coach enjoyed unique popularity, for the magnetic lure of Bath as a centre of fashion was never stronger than in the eighteenth century. In *Coaching Days and Coaching Ways*, William Tristram writes: "Old, young, beautiful, decrepit, bent on health, pleasure, scandal, wine or the waters," all flocked to Bath. Thackeray tells us that: "All history went and bathed and drank there . . . scarce a character one can mention but was seen in that famous pump room."

It was the celebrated Beau Nash who really put Bath firmly on the map as a place that had to be visited, and, fortunately for us, the engaging story of his life has been told most felicitously by Oliver Goldsmith. He was a man with many delightful facets to his character, as one short anecdote reveals. Asked to explain an item in his expenses which ran, "For making one man happy, £10", he told how, overhearing a stranger saying: "If only I could

247

get £10 I'd be happy," he had impetuously thrust that sum into the astonished fellow's hand.

In his reign at Bath, Nash made countless men and women happy. He organized everything on regal lines, imposed dignity and discipline, put down duelling, drew up his own rules for social conduct and behaviour, studied the welfare and happiness of a growing swarm of visitors, and earned for himself the nickname "King of Bath".

He lived up to his nickname, for when he rode from London to Bath it was in his own magnificent equipage. "Sumptuous" is Goldsmith's word for it, a post-chariot drawn by six greys, with outriders, footmen, French horns "and every other appendage of expensive parade". He wore a white hat—as a safeguard against its being stolen, he said—though it was also a mark of distinction that his countless admirers could not miss.

The departure of the Bath coach from La Belle Sauvage was invariably a colourful and exciting event, even though at 5 a.m. some passengers might be bleary-eyed and yawning. There would be plenty to stir them into wakefulness as the bustling and jostling mounted; there would be the stamping of hooves, the jingle of harness, the shouts and oaths of the ostlers and other servants in the busy inn yard. Mingling with these would be the cries of eager hawkers offering a variety of wares to forgetful travellers who might be in need of pencils and penknives or kerchiefs. There would likewise be the excited chatter of travellers taking their seats, inside or out, according to their inclination and purse. There would be the exhortations and lamentations of relatives and friends who had come to wish them god-speed.

Then, suddenly, almost miraculously, the clamour would subside and a moment of hush would descend, as it nearly always did, to mark the appearance of the coachman, lordly in bearing, multi-garmented, rosy in face and most likely wearing a fresh buttonhole or bearing a nosegay—parting gift from some admiring damsel. Like the proverbial sailor, the mail-coach driver was reputed to have girl friends at every stage along the road.

All eyes would turn upon him as he made his swaggering progress across the inn yard and people would step aside in deference. Ceremoniously he would mount to his high perch; ceremoniously he would settle himself to his satisfaction; ceremoniously he would accept the reins; then, with a quick nod and a crack of the whip, the Bath coach would rumble out of the yard to a chorus of cheers and parting cries from innkeeper, ostlers, waiters, maidservants, post-boys, friends, hawkers and urchins and all.

A punctual start, on the very minute, was the coaching rule; but the prevailing English weather. There are those today who like to tell us that our weather has deteriorated and is growing worse because of the price that must always be paid for progress, if you can describe atomic explosions as progressive. But long before Hiroshima the English weather was being its own capricious, frustrating, unpredictable self, witness this report from a newspaper of nearly one hundred years ago:

"The eccentricity of English weather is likely to be mentioned to the close of the year. We had winter up to August, a fortnight of summer in September, after which we had a return of cold weather and an occasional fog; but for a month past we have had as near an approach to summer in December as we had to winter in July . . ."

So the coach travellers had to be prepared for anything. In foggy weather the start of the journey to Bath might well begin at funereal pace, the driver's language as sulphuric as the atmosphere, as men bearing torches escorted the Bath Mail out of London at three miles an hour.

But assuming the weather to be benign at the time of departure, there would be other things to cause concern, especially among the first-timers. There would almost certainly be a seasoned traveller aboard, ready enough to set timid hearts a-flutter with tales of "gentlemen of the road", or "the road inspectors" as highwaymen were sometimes facetiously termed. But, even without such unsolicited running commentary, passengers would behold visual evidence of the "gentlemen" quite early in their journey.

After highwaymen, a numerous breed, had paid the penalty at Tyburn it was customary for them to be cut down so that their bodies could be taken to Hounslow Heath, there to be suspended in chains from roadside gibbets till nothing but their skeletons remained. Cecil Roberts mentions in his pleasantly discursive *And So To Bath* (the record of a leisurely pilgrimage to historical and literary shrines *en route*) that as late as 1800 there were thirteen gibbets to be seen between Hounslow and Heston.

The grisly exhibits in chains were meant to be a deterrent to those "gentlemen" still at large, and possibly some travellers may have drawn some crumb of comfort from such reminders that the law was on their side. But it could only have been a crumb, for the highwaymen formed a daring, ruthless fraternity, and as coaching traffic increased so the potential spoils to be gathered from wealthier passengers became more numerous and more tempting.

Besides, there were so many spots that provided an abundance of cover for any marauder. Gibbets or no gibbets, Hounslow Heath and Maidenhead Thicket remained favourite lurking places for the bold, romantic outlaws, who made themselves familiar with every inch of the ground, used many a hidden way as escape routes in emergency, while also cultivating the friendship of numerous confederates among rascally innkeepers or their servants, many of whom provided safe hideouts.

Many highwaymen were indeed gentlemen down on their luck or men of adventurous spirit who probably started on their marauding career "for kicks" and then found it impossible to get out of the game. Others were survivors of recent wars, cast aside, perhaps, by a thoughtless country and left to fend for themselves by exacting toll from society.

Whatever their origin, the leading exponents had their look-outs posted at strategic points. These were hand-picked scouts who were capable of taking the measure of passengers as the different coaches stopped at a wayside inn to rest or to obtain a change of horses. Having marked down likely victims, the spies would confirm their estimates by ogling chambermaids or other servants and inducing them to talk about the transitory guests. In this way they would gather inside information about the passengers, their position in life, how long they proposed to stay in Bath and what the women-folk were carrying in the way of jewellery.

Long before the Bath coach was clear of Knightsbridge some highwayman's scout had probably gathered all the information he desired and would be riding ahead at speed to pass on the good news to his master. The "gentleman" would thus have ample time to select the ideal place at which to intercept the coach, would be able to identify his most promising victims on sight and have a pretty fair idea of the kind of booty he could expect.

There is a record of at least one Old Etonian highwayman. Macaulay has pictured the "gentlemen" as being bold and skilful horsemen. John Gay is said to have devised his conception of the swaggering, swashbuckling Captain MacHeath during a gossip about the "gentlemen" with the poet Pope at the latter's villa in Twickenham.

In *The Beggar's Opera* Gay painted his hero as such a romantic, impudently successful womanizer, that the celebrated magistrate, Sir John Fielding, protested that the opera was never presented without producing a crop of increased robberies on Hounslow Heath—just as our current television programmes get blamed for encouraging crime and seduction and infidelity. But wise old Dr Johnson prophesied that Mr Gay had devised a new-style production that would hold the stage for many a year to come. Hogarth, too, lent the opera and swaggering MacHeath an additional lease of immortality in his matchless paintings of the opera's principal scenes.

How much does the memory of the "gentlemen" of the road owe to art, literature and poetry? Were they twopence coloured or penny plain? Were they as romantic in real life? Dick Turpin and Black Bess are immortal, as is the imaginary MacHeath. So is Claude Du Vall, the courteous Frenchman who impudently persuaded a lady of fashion to descend from her coach after he had held it up and to dance a few steps with him on the roadside verge. Even if that be true, the legend that he also handed back two-thirds of his booty for the privilege takes some swallowing.

Dick Turpin's famous ride to York is enshrouded in myth. He rode to York, certainly—to be hanged there for slaying a keeper in far-away Epping Forest in an affray in which he accidentally shot a fellow highwayman, Tom King. As for Claude Du Vall, "the Ladies' Joy, the Ladies' Grief", he got himself into a drunken brawl and ended his short career in his twenty-seventh year.

In the coaching days such "gentlemen" were menacing enough, and besides the lone riders there were bands of desperadoes who also frequented Hounslow Heath and other lonely stretches on the long road to Bath. There would be plenty of stories of such outlaws to keep the travellers in a state of constant perturbation.

Macaulay has recorded how one gang, lying in ambush for nobility returning from junketings at Windsor, actually held up thirty or forty coaches in succession "and rode off with great booty in guineas, watches and jewellery".

But even if fashionable travellers to Bath were lucky enough to escape the attentions of highwaymen, there were other aspects of the trip to plague them. The caprice of weather conditions has been mentioned, and outside passengers doubtless suffered intensely from wind and rain and sleet or snow. There was little they could do in inclement weather except to wrap up as warmly as they could and to huddle together on their exposed perches. Sometimes a chilled passenger was known to creep into the luggage basket for shelter, a move not likely to be repeated, for anyone who tried it found himself buffeted by pieces of luggage which were apt to shift on hills to the increasing discomfort of the human occupant.

The inside of the coach, if sheltered, can never have been truly comfortable, for passengers would be jolted incessantly in an atmosphere stuffy with the odours of pomade, powder and perfume, and dust. Dust especially, for the roads were rough in the extreme. There were stretches where the passage of a coach-and-six could stir up dense clouds of choking, blinding dust which powdered and plagued passengers and horses alike. In wet weather those same roads could be reduced to a quagmire in the space of a few minutes; progress could be reduced to a treacherous, slithering crawl and a coach could easily end up in a deep, waterlogged ditch.

The strain upon coaches and harness and passengers and horses and driver and guard were great at all times. The battle to keep to a scheduled thirty or thirty-five miles a day can never have been easy. Mishaps were plentiful; traces might snap and horses bolt; wheels might become overheated; fire was not unknown; axles might snap or buckle under strain. Nor was the menace of highwaymen confined to the notorious Hounslow and Maidenhead belt. An encounter was possible on almost any stage of that long, lonely road. Yet, on the whole, it is said that the mail coaches kept pretty good time and their proprietors were ever striving after improved performance.

It must have been a great relief at the end of a stage to rumble into the yard of some well-known coaching inn for food and rest and shelter; to rid oneself of some of the grime of travel and to gather strength for the next day's run. But it must be borne in mind that the old hostels that modern travellers find so charmingly picturesque and romantic, and which look so attractive in old prints, were often large, draughty, barnlike places within, sparsely furnished, with no hot water laid on, no central heating, no electric light. As now, there were good inns and bad, and all throve on the growing custom assured by the constant comings and goings on the great Bath road.

All along the route, through Brentford, Hounslow, Slough, Windsor, Reading, Newbury, Hungerford, Marlborough, Devizes, Calne, Chippenham and Bath, these inns were to be found. Fanny

Burney, the diarist and brilliant author of *Evelina* and other novels, who won the esteem of the great Doctor Johnson, was just one among the thousands who braved the journey to Bath in her day, 1780. Her stages were Maidenhead (where she stayed at the popular Bear Inn), Speen Hill and Devizes. A lively young lady who took life in her stride, she seems to have arrived at journey's end fresh, bright and with energy to spare.

Arrival in Bath was a signal for plunging forthwith into the gaiety of the exciting centre. A visitor upon entering the city would be welcomed by a peal of the Abbey bells and the city waits would attend at his lodgings to greet his party with music and song—provided he rewarded the ringers with half a guinea, and stumped up half a crown apiece for the waits. Visitors of all ranks were delighted to advertise their arrival in this fashion.

It was the custom for the head of the family to make the rounds of all the public places. He needed a full purse for this formality, for there was a two-guinea fee to be paid to the Assembly Rooms towards the cost of balls and music in the Pump Room, and the privilege of being sure of three tickets for every ball night.

There were also fees ranging from a crown to half a guinea or one guinea, according to the visitor's rank or quality, for the use of private walks belonging to Simpson's Assembly House. A crown or half a guinea was payable to the booksellers if a visitor wished to have library books in his lodgings. Yet another subscription to the Coffee House entitled visitors to the use of pen, ink and paper during the period of their stay in Bath. There was also a Reading Room where newspapers, pamphlets, etc., could be perused.

Lively accounts of all these formalities and the resultant pleasures are to be found in *Humphry Clinker*, whose epistolary style enables Smollet to put extravagant descriptions into the letters his amusing characters pen to their various relatives and friends. Thus, Winifrid Jenkins, Tabitha Bramble's rustic maidservant, tells a friend that those who live in other parts "could have no deception of our doings at Bath. Here is such dressing and fidling and dancing, and gadding, and courting and plotting.—O gracious! If God had not given me a good stock of discretion, what a power of things might I not reveal, consarning old mistress and young mistress . . . "

For the young mistress in question, Lydia Melford, Tabitha Bramble's niece, Bath was a new world, all "gaiety, good-humour, and diversion". She was dazzled by the splendour of dress and equipage she saw, and thrilled by the merry bells ringing from morn till night, the music in the Pump Room, the lively cotillons in the forenoon, the concerts every other night and the grand balls twice a week. She found Spring Gardens "a sweet retreat, laid out in walks and ponds and parterres of flowers", with a long room for breakfasting and dancing. She wrote enthusiastically to her friends of the great scenes of entertainment in the spacious rooms, so very strinking when lighted up, where visitors assembled in parties for tea-drinking, card parties or gossip.

In common with other visitors, Lydia made the full round of the baths, pump room, coffee-houses, and booksellers, usually finishing up with a call at "Mr Gill's, the pastry-cook, to take a jelly, a tart, or small bason of vermicelli". Lydia records the genteel side of Bath; Winifrid, the maid, her frankly earthy impressions of all she sees and hears. Quests innumerable drew all kinds of folk to Bath. Besides the gouty, rheumaticky, obese invalids and victims of over-indulgence seeking a "cure", there were gamesters, sharpers, tricksters, quacks, pimps, courtesans, fortune-hunters seeking an heiress with a rich dowry; philanderers and professional seducers, adventurers, idlers, hangers-on and just plain pleasure-seekers.

Intrigues and scandals were plentiful; many an innocent was ruined; many a fool parted from his money; many a romantic maiden deceived and abandoned. But still the coaches bore eager visitors along the Bath road in increasing numbers, to empty their purses and to depart to face all the dangers and discomforts of the long journey home.

It was on the return journey that Matthew Bramble befriended Humphry Clinker (a Wiltshire lad so down on his luck that he lacked a shirt to his back), making him a postilion. When a mishap occurs and the coach lands in a ditch, poor Humphry's poverty is revealed, for his breeches split to affront Tabitha Bramble with the spectacle of his bare posterior!

Smollett, as a humorist, wrung much hilarity from coaching; but for the average passenger returning from Bath the long journey to London can only have been a repetition of the outward trip without the expectation. In place of thoughts of the delights of Bath, a renewal of anxiety, ordeal and discomfort. The only compensation, perhaps, might lie in the reflection that there would be much less booty for any marauding highwayman.

And, whatever they were destined to endure, London and home would be reached in time–"If God permit".

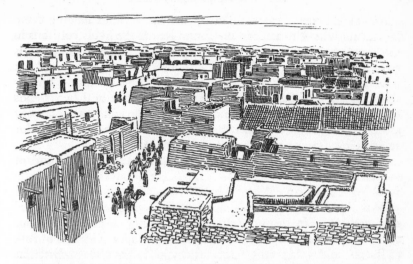

THE MAN WHO UNVEILED TIMBUKTU

The Journey of René Caillié

TIMBUKTU! For hundreds of years the name of this city of Africa, on the farthest edge of the Sahara, was a synonym for what was mysterious, hidden, almost inaccessible and almost never approached. Ibn Batuta managed to reach it in the middle of the fourteenth century–but where did this venturesome Moor fail to get to in his years of wandering between Tangier and Bokhara, China and the Indies? The first European to walk its dusty lanes seems to have been the Scottish explorer, Alexander Gordon Laing, who was there in 1826. But though he got there he did not come back, for he was murdered through the treachery of his servant. Two years later a young Frenchman followed in his footsteps. He got to Timbuktu, and he returned to tell the tale. His name was René Caillié.

Explorers are strange creatures, but surely Caillié's career is among the most improbable. Born in 1800 in a small village in the west of France, he was the son of poor parents, whom he lost in his childhood. The only education he received was in the charity-school of his native village, and as soon as he could read and write he was put to a trade, which he heartily detested. All his leisure moments were taken up with reading books of voyages and travels, and in a fortunate moment he came across a copy of a French translation

255

of *Robinson Crusoe*. This so inflamed his imagination, he says, that: "I was impatient to encounter adventures like his–already I felt an ambition to signalize myself by some important discovery springing up in my heart."

Geographical books and maps were lent him by kindly neighbours, and it was the map of Africa which enthralled him above all others. It was so empty, or in the middle of the great blank spaces were the words "desert" or "unknown". Why should not he do something to fill in those gaps? He told his uncle of his itch to travel, and the answer he got was most discouraging. But nothing could alter the resolution he had formed. He *would* travel, he would do as Robinson Crusoe had done–and who knows?

"All that I possessed was sixty francs, and with this trifle I proceeded to Rochefort in 1816, and embarked in the brig *La Loire*, bound to Senegal." He arrived at St Louis, tramped across country to Dakar, and was then offered a passage to the West Indies. In 1818 he was back again in West Africa and saw service with an English expedition into the interior. Then in 1824 he set out on an expedition of his own, "among the people who inhabit the smiling banks of the Senegal", which sounds much pleasanter than it proved in actual fact. This but whetted his appetite, and he formed the plan of penetrating into the interior of the continent. But when he put his proposals before the French authorities in Senegal they almost laughed at him. He thereupon went to Sierra Leone, to seek the support of the English Governor–and he, too, discounted the idea as altogether impractical.

He was disappointed, but not downhearted, and in 1826 he happened to be shown a notice issued by the Geographical Society of Paris, in which they offered a "premium" or prize of several thousand francs to the first European who should succeed in reaching Timbuktu, preferably from the direction of the French possessions in Senegal. What the Society required, it appeared, was: "A manuscript narrative, with a geographical map. The author shall observe the nature of the soil, the depth of the wells, the width and rapidity of the rivers, the productions of the countries which they irrigate. He shall make remarks upon the climate. In observing the people, he shall take care to examine their manners, ceremonies, customs, weapons, laws, religion, food, diseases, the colour of their skin, the form of their face, the nature of their hair and also the different articles of their commerce. It is desirable that he should form vocabularies of their idioms, compared with the French language;

finally, he should make drawings of the details of their habitations, and make plans of the towns wherever it is possible to do so."

A tall order, one might think; but Caillié was not in the least put off. At that time he had no more than two thousand francs, which he had saved from his salary as manager of an indigo plantation, but "this treasure seemed to me to be sufficient to carry me all over the world". Since he had been unable to obtain any official backing, his journey would have to be made entirely at his own expense, but he hoped that when he returned–and of course he had no doubts about that!–the French Government, "ever just in its appreciation of courageous exertion", would reward fittingly the services he had rendererd to geographical science.

So he resigned his job on the plantation, and expended his small resources on the essential articles of travel, and, since he hoped to pay his way at least in part as a trader, in such trifles as glass beads and trinkets which he supposed might appeal to the peoples he encountered. Then he made sure of his disguise. He assumed Arab dress, and with it the character of a young man who had been born in Egypt, of Arabian parents, and who had been carried into France in his infancy by some soldiers of the French Army under Napoleon which had invaded Egypt. Afterwards, his story ran, he had been brought to the Senegal by his master, who in consideration of his services had given him his liberty. Now he felt a natural inclination to return to his relations in Egypt and adopt the Mohammedan religion. This account of himself he maintained throughout his travels, with an occasional variation, such as that he was making the pilgrimage, as a devout Muslim, to the holy cities of Arabia.

Leaving Sierra Leone towards the end of March, 1827, he arrived at Kakondy, at the mouth of the Rio Nunez, where he completed his preparations. Then on 19 April he started off into the virtually unknown, as one of a caravan consisting of five Mandingo negroes, three slaves, a porter of the Foulah tribe, his guide and the latter's wife. "All except the last two and myself carried enormous burdens" on their backs as they trudged along through the bush.

For the next couple of months they moved on steadily into and across the mountainous interior of Senegambia. His record is one of constant plodding, weary arrivals at remote villages, and almost as weary startings off again in the morning. The travellers suffered greatly from the heat, the rains, and insufficient food and rest. At every opportunity he jotted down details of their journey in his note-books, and so far as human relations are concerned he seems to have had little to complain of.

Sometimes his real character came under suspicion, but he was always successful in putting doubts to rest. Often he met with real kindness from the Mandingoes and Foulahs at whose villages he stopped for the night. To quote one of many examples: "The wife of the chief kindly asked me to take a little milk, and then she went to gather some figs and bananas, and put them into a clean calabash, which she gave to me and my guide. This woman had a pleasing countenance, and her dress, which was very clean, consisted of two breadths of cotton cloth of the manufacture of the country. She had not the offensive smell of the roving Foulahs of Irnanké. The hut was large and in good order; the floor was adorned with handsome designs, made of earth..."

From the highlands they descended to the open country, and pushed on steadily. Caillié had a new guide now, since the man he had started out with had reached his home village and stayed there. He joined a small caravan and in August arrived at a village called Timé. Here misfortune overtook him. He had a terrible sore on one of his feet, through the incessant marching; the bad food had brought on dysentery, and he had a severe attack of fever. For a month he was laid up in the hut which the village chief put at his disposal, and an old negress acted as his nurse. "This good creature was very kind and attentive to me. She brought me herself twice a day a little rice, dressed my foot morning and evening, and often consoled me with the hope of a speedy cure." In gratitude for her attention he gave her a piece of coloured cloth, which pleased her exceedingly. "She had probably never before possessed anything so beautiful." Her son, remarking on the flowers of the pattern, said that "none but God could have made anything so beautiful".

For weeks he lay in his hut, but at length his foot was almost healed and he was confidently looking forward to a speedy resumption of his journey, when: "Alas! violent pains in my jaw informed me that I was attacked with scurvy, and I soon experienced all the horrors of that dreadful disease. The roof of my mouth became quite bare, a part of the bones exfoliated and fell away, and my teeth seemed ready to drop out of their sockets. I feared that my brain would be affected by the agonizing pains I felt in my head, and I was more than a fortnight without sleep." It was one of the worst periods of his long adventure; and to crown his misery the sore in his foot broke out afresh and all hope of early departure vanished.

"The horror of my situation may be more easily imagined than described—alone, in the interior of a wild country, stretched on the damp ground, with no pillow but the leather bag which contained my baggage, with no medicine and no attendant but Baba's old mother. This good creature brought me twice a day a little rice-water, which she forced me to drink, for I could eat nothing. I was soon reduced to a skeleton . . ."

But the dark moment passed. He was on the road to recovery, thanks to the attentions of his negro nurses, but it was not until January, 1828, that he was able to get moving again. It tells us something of the quality of the man that, even when on the bed of sickness, he kept his notebooks handy, and some of the most interesting pages in his account describe the manners and customs of the Mandingoes among whom he remained so long. The women in particular aroused his concern and admiration. They did all the hard work of the community, while their menfolk lolled at their ease. "While pregnant they continue to perform the severest labours until the very last moment of their time. They give birth to children without uttering a complaint, and resume their usual occupations on the following day. The mothers watch over their infants with great tenderness, seldom trusting them to the care of others. They always suckle them themselves, and they carry them everywhere on their backs."

The male Mandingoes were circumcised between the ages of fifteen and twenty, and the women, too, were required to submit to an excision before they might marry, or at least have children.

Three months elapsed in almost uninterrupted travel, and then on the morning of 10 March, 1828, Caillié and his party arrived on the banks of the Dhioliba, as he calls the great river which we know was the Niger. The river's water was tolerably clear (he reports), but with a whitish tint. It seemed to be coming from west-north-west, and to be running at about a knot and a half an hour. The river banks were for the most part low and open, and in mid-stream was an island. We may imagine the traveller's emotion when he understood that this broad and impressive stream was flowing in the direction of Timbuktu.

Crossing the Niger in "frail canoes, about thirty feet long and very narrow, which every moment threatened to upset", he pressed on to Jenné, a largish town, peopled by Mohammedans, situated on an island on a branch of the great river. Here he rested for about a fortnight, being well treated by the Moors and engaging with them in the ritual of the month of Ramadan; and then on 23 March he embarked on a boat which shortly carried them to the Niger again. "Majestic," he calls it now, flowing slowly and very deep, "about three times the width of the Seine in Paris at the Pont-Neuf". The canoe in which he was a passenger was a vessel of 60 or 90 tons burthen, 90 or 100 feet long, and of very light build, and yet capable of carrying an astonishing amount of cargo as well as a consignment of forty or fifty slaves. It was unprovided with sails, but was propelled by poles or paddles. Sometimes, he says: "The rowers stand up close against the side of the vessel, and at other times sit upon the merchandise, having scarcely room to turn themselves round. These men are naked; they row very fast, and keep time."

More weeks slipped away in their slow but steady passage, until on 19 April they drew near to Cabra, which he was given to understand was the port for Timbuktu. They put in at the quay, and he was glad to be able to stretch his legs. He wandered through the market-place, and made a hearty breakfast of a little milk and a loaf of wheaten flour. "I was a little tormented by the mosquitoes, which, however, are not so common on the banks of the Dhioliba as on those of the Senegal."

The next morning he set out to walk the few miles to Timbuktu, and at length he arrived there, just as the sun was setting. "On entering this mysterious city, to reach which had so long been the object of my wishes, I experienced an indescribable satisfaction. I never before felt a similar emotion and my transport was extreme. I was obliged, however, to restrain my feelings, and to God alone to confide my joy. With what gratitude did I return thanks to Heaven, for the happy result which attended my enterprise!"

All the same, first impressions were uninviting. There was none of the grandeur and wealth that he had anticipated. "The city presented, at first view, nothing but a mass of ill-looking houses, built of earth. Nothing was to be seen in all directions but immense plains of quicksand of a yellowish white colour. The sky was pale red as far as the horizon; all nature wore a dreary aspect, and the most profound silence prevailed; not even the warbling of a bird was to be heard."

Before he had left Jenné he had been provided by a good friend there with a letter of introduction to a well-to-do citizen of Timbuktu, one Sidi-Abdallahi; on presenting this he was made most welcome and given lodging in a house near the market-place and opposite to the one which had been occupied by Major Laing. (Early in the present century, when the French occupied Timbuktu, they put up tablets on Caillié's house and on Laing's, commemorating their stay there.) "Often, when seated before my door, I thought of the fate of that unfortunate traveller, who, after surmounting numberless dangers and privations, was cruelly assassinated when on the eve of returning to his country. In the course of these reflections I could not repress a feeling of apprehension, lest, should I be discovered, I might be doomed to a fate more horrible than death–to slavery!"

Behaving with the utmost caution Caillié was able to move about the city at his leisure, storing his mind with impressions and putting down on paper such details as could not be left to his memory. He also ventured on a few sketches, as on the occasion of his visit to the Great Mosque. "To make my sketch," he says, "I sat down in the street in front of it, and, covering myself in my large wrapper which I folded over my knees, I held in my hand a sheet of white paper close to a leaf of the Koran. When I perceived any one approaching, I hid my drawing, and looking at the leaf of the Koran I appeared to be absorbed in devotion. The passers-by, far from suspecting me, regarded me as one of the elect, and applauded my zeal."

The people of the city were composed of Moors and negroes. The former were mostly traders who, like Europeans in the colonies, had gone there with the intention of making their fortunes, when they would return to their own country beyond the Sahara. The prince, Osman by name, was a negro. When Caillié was received in audience, he came away with the impression of a man of very amiable disposition. He seemed to be much respected by his subjects, and very simple in his manners. He was of middling height, jet black in colour, with hair that was white and curly. On his head was a red cap, bound round with a large piece of muslin to form a turban, and his shoes were of morocco leather, shaped like slippers and of native manufacture. His house seemed to be no better furnished than those of the Moorish merchants, but Caillié was disappointed in not being invited to take a closer look. He had four wives, besides an infinite number of slaves of both sexes, and was a zealous Mohammedan.

The native inhabitants were likewise zealous Mohammedans, and like the Moors they had four wives each. The women attended to their domestic occupations, and Caillié notes with approval that, unlike the females of the Mandingo tribes among whom he had passed, they were not subject to beating. "I have constantly observed in my travels," he remarks, "that in proportion as a people are uncivilized the women were always more enslaved", so that "the female sex in Africa have reason to pray for the progress of cultivation". But the people of Timbuktu, being in constant contact with the half-civilized inhabitants of the Mediterranean, "have some idea of the dignity of human nature".

The women were not veiled like those of Morocco; they were allowed to go out when they pleased, and were at liberty to see anyone. He saw some women who might be considered pretty. The women of the better class at least were very neatly dressed. Their hair was beautifully plaited, and they wore nose-rings and a great number of glass beads round about their necks and in their ears. It was a common practice for the people to anoint their heads and bodies with butter: "the great heat, which is augmented by the scorching east wind, renders this custom necessary." The female slaves of rich masters wore gold ornaments about their necks, and instead of ear-rings little plates in the form of a necklace.

Caillié reports that the dwellings of the Timbuktu inhabitants were as exceedingly neat as their persons. They had wooden platters, and were unacquainted with the use of knives and forks, believing that all people in the world ate with their fingers, as they did. Their furniture consisted of mats for sitting on, and their beds were frames of sticks, over which were stretched some mats or a cow-hide. The rich might have cotton mattresses, which the neighbouring Moors manufactured from camel's hair and sheep's wool.

When he had been in Timbuktu a matter of a few days, Caillié learn that a caravan of Moorish merchants was planning to set out for the north on 4 May, and that it would be three months before the next. He resolved to join it, and the necessary arrangements were made for him by "this excellent man", as he terms Sidi-Abdallahi. He had disposed of all that remained of his small stock of goods, and the proceeds were little more than enough to pay for a camel, with something for the guide who should see him across the desert. In gratitude Caillié persuaded his kind host to accept from him as a parting-gift his woollen robe and drinking vessel—about all he had to give—but in return he was given another robe, a change of clothes, and a small sum of money to defray his expenses as far as the first stage. On the morning of departure: "Sidi Abdallahi accompanied me to some distance from his house, and, at parting from me, he affectionately pressed my hand and wished me a good journey."

The caravan with which he was now travelling consisted of nearly six hundred camels. Leaving Timbuktu on 4 May they halted at El-Arawan, near where Caillié was shown the spot where Major Laing had been murdered by the tribesmen, and stayed there some days. On 19 May they resumed their journey, and now the caravan had been greatly augmented, consisting as it did of fourteen hundred camels, laden with the various productions of the Sudan–gold, slaves, ivory, gum, ostrich-feathers, and pieces of cloth.

Before long they came to some deep wells, and here they "stopped and took a hearty draught, for we were about to enter upon a part of the desert where we should find no water for the space of eight days". Then they moved off again. "A boundless horizon was spread before us, and we could distinguish nothing but an immense plain of shining sand, and over it a burning sky. At this sight the camels uttered long moans, the slaves became sullen and silent, and, with their eyes turned towards heaven, they appeared to be tortured with regret for the loss of their country, and with the recollection of the verdant plains from which avarice and cruelty had snatched them."

All their miserable forebodings were more than justified. It is clear from Caillié's journal that this was by far the worst part of his tremendous journeyings. He was so poor that he could hardly buy sufficient to keep himself alive, and he soon found that the Moors had no pity to spare for a man whom they suspected of being an "infidel" and in any case despised. Thirst, hunger, intense heat, a terrible weariness ... still they plodded doggedly on. One "horrible day" they were assailed by pillars of sand, one of which crossed their camp, blew over all the tents, and whirled men and beasts about like straws. "We knew not where we were, and could distinguish nothing at the distance of a foot. The sand wrapped us in darkness like a thick fog, and heaven and earth seemed confounded and blended into one." On another day–or rather night, since they were travelling in the dark to avoid the heat–his camel threw him and he thought his skull was fractured: "I felt the effects of this fall for more than two months." There were other days when the more malicious-minded of the party, men and women alike, teased and taunted him and made him the butt of their cruel jokes. There came the time when he was subsisting on a handful of dates a day and a few sips of milk.

July was well advanced when they emerged at length from the ocean of sand and found themselves among "the beautiful and majestic palm-trees of the country of Tafilet". Here he exchanged his camel for an ass, and joined another caravan (of mules this time) which was heading for Fez, in Morocco. He arrived there on 12 August, and reports that it was the finest town he had seen in Africa. But the state of his purse made it absolutely necessary that he should push on, and he had barely sufficient to hire a mule to carry him to Mequinaz. On 14 August he resumed his journey, almost penniless and very depressed.

By a fortunate chance, however, there were in his company a couple of Moorish women "who, being under no restraint, shewed but little solicitude to conceal their fair complexions and pretty faces beneath their veils. One of them rode on my mule behind me; and I presume that my attentions were agreeable to her, as she offered me a slice of melon and a bit of bread which I accepted with pleasure."

From Mequinaz he made his way on to Rabat, and then along the seashore "until at length, ill, and worn out with fatigue, I arrived in Tangier on the 7th of September, at nightfall". As soon as possible he made himself known to the French Vice-Consul in the town, who was staggered—as well he might be—by the appearance on his doorstep of a fellow countrymen who said he had arrived from Timbuktu. Moreover, Caillié was still in native dress, and even then, if his true identity had been revealed, he might have been seized by the fanatical mob and murdered or enslaved. But all went well. M. Dalaporte, the Vice-Consul, presented him with a European dress "which I gladly exchanged for the dirty rags I had so long worn", and eventually he was able to arrange his passage in a French sloop to Toulon and thence to Paris.

"Those who have been long absent from their native land," he wrote at the end of his account of his travels, "and have good cause to fear that they may never return, can alone form an idea of my sensations on my restoration to my beloved country." He made a full report to the Geographical Society, and "it was not long before I enjoyed the glorious reward of its merited approbation. The Society applauded my zeal, and awarded to me the recompense promised to the first traveller who should penetrate to the mysterious town of Timbuctoo, and bring from thence his authentic observations."

These "observations" formed the substance of Caillié's *Travels through Central Africa to Timbuctoo, and across the Great Desert, to Morocco, performed in the years 1824–1828,* which was published in Paris in 1830 and at once translated into English. Of Caillié himself there is little more to be said. In 1838, still under forty, he died near Paris of a malady he had contracted in that epic journey of his in which he had "unveiled" the mysterious city of Timbuktu.

MASS MOVEMENT

The Mormons Move to Utah

AN HOUR before dawn the first of them set off from their homes in Nauvoo, the Zion they had built for themselves, which had become so hostile, untenable. They got to the river, were able to scramble a part of the way across the mighty Mississippi on ice, before getting into the ferries which awaited them, which would take them on the first stage of a journey to a new, divinely chosen land.

The organizer of this, one of the greatest mass movements in modern times, was Brigham Young, on whom the mantle of Mormon leader had fallen after the assassination of the Prophet, Joseph Smith. He was not with this advance party across the Mississippi, for he had work to do organizing the main group, but his son, aged ten, was with the first ferry-load. Years later, the son was to write:

"Such a scene" (as he looked around him on the farther bank), "such a scene of misery and desolation met the gaze as never will be forgotten: dogs, chickens, cows and children by the thousand ran hither and thither in the utmost confusion. Wagons were scattered about; here was one hitched up, the driver cracking his whip and pushing recklessly through the crowd. Babies were screaming for their mothers, and mothers calling piteously for lost babies and children. Weeping, groaning, sick ones lay here and there, while anxiety was in every heart. A yoke of oxen were drowned in the river. One of the animals was recovered. Some men tore off the hide and told the people that anyone who lacked provisions was welcome to use the meat thus obtained."

A bad start, it would seem, to a long, long journey. But why should these people, industrious and God-fearing Americans like the neighbours they were so precipitately deserting, choose to make it? To find the answer, we must look more closely at their religion—for it was this which estranged them from neighbours as devout as themselves. They were Mormons, pioneers of a new faith, whose Prophet, had he lived, would have been forty-one years old as they set out towards his promised land.

That Prophet, self-styled, had been born at the start of the nineteenth century, in a village in Vermont. As a child he had moved down to New York State with his parents, and it was there in the ferment of immigrant religion, that he began to have ideas of his own. He was to write, years later: "I often said to myself, what is to be done? Who of all these parties be right—or are they all wrong together?" And it was in the midst of this uncertainly that, according to the young man—whose name was Joseph Smith—an angel came to him. The angel was the son of "Mormon" and he had been sent to tempt and try young Joseph, to see if he were a worthy recipient of Mormon's scriptures. According to Smith, the tempting, the assessment, lasted four years. Then the angel handed over the scriptures, engraved on plates of gold.

With the aid of a scribe—who has to report that he himself was not allowed to gaze on the plates, that quite often Smith seemed to dictate without looking at them—The Book of Mormon took shape. The golden plates have now vanished like King Arthur's sword, but a number of witnesses were produced to give sworn evidence that they had seen them, that "an angel of the Lord came down from heaven and he brought and laid before our eyes, that we beheld and saw the plates, and the engravings thereon".

So began the religion of Mormon. It was not the only new faith springing up in the eastern United States, but it most successfully captured the imagination of the people; fitted in with their lives, the future they saw for themselves in this best of all possible lands, where it was man's duty to himself and to his God to build and prosper and reproduce. It has been called a grossly materialistic religion, and certainly its founders had considerable business interests; but it had and has a strict moral code. It also encouraged polygamy—which made sense in an under-populated country—so that a contemporary critic could describe the Mormons as men with a creed which was singular, wives who were plural.

The Book of Mormon—consisting like the Bible of a number of books, fourteen in all—is believed by its adherents to be the true story of ancient America and its aboriginal inhabitants, during a period of roughly half a millennium before the birth of Christ to half a millennium after. According to Mormon, these aboriginal inhabitants were Hebrews who left Jerusalem at the time of the Babylonian captivity and, instructed by their God, built a ship and sailed it to a new land across the sea. This, of course, explained the presence of the Red Indian, a problem which had exercised men's minds for some time. The theory, dazzling in its lucidity and revealed through the exciting agency of a Prophet with golden plates, ensured that the new religion, unlike its contemporaries, would prosper and grow. Cynics scoffed at the apparent attempt by Smith (or was it Mormon?) to imitate the language of the English bible, scoffed at anachronisms like steel swords in 600 B.C., the finding of horses and cattle on the American continent by the first arrivals. But to the ever-increasing band of adherents, these were petty faults, easily explained away. The followers of the Mormon prophet grew mightily in numbers, and soon—remarkably soon—had sent missionaries and literature not only over the east of America, but by sea to England, where a number of converts was being made and prepared for shipping over to the promised land. This zeal for evangelism still characterizes the Mormon church.

But there were some—and their numbers too were growing—who distrusted the new creed. They watched with dismay as the church centre, now in Kirtland, Ohio, drew more and more followers, and missionaries spread out to recruit the Indians. There was more than a suspicion that these peaceful Mormon neighbours planned to abolish slavery, that they regarded themselves as divinely entitled to any land they chose to settle. They were also—like the Jews and persecuted for the reason—very industrious, with a system of beliefs which urged them to amass land and wealth, while paying large tithes to their church, so that it prospered with them. Certainly there was much talk of "building temples".

Suspicion, misunderstanding, led to violence. Smith, on more than one occasion, was tarred and feathered, even had nitric acid poured into his mouth so that he would be unable to preach—though he did so through swollen lips, and earned still greater respect from his followers. He had by now gathered about him Twelve

Apostles, one of whom was Brigham Young, a dedicated evangelist who would soon have to give over the harvesting of souls and prepare to lead the Mormon people to safety.

Gradually the movement spread westward, largely as a result of persecution and hostility from the eastern communities in which it had been born. In June, 1839, the Mormon church bought a large tract of land in Hancock County, Illinois, and started to build a city, the new Jerusalem, which they would call "Nauvoo", meaning, in their scriptures, Beautiful. With Nauvoo rapidly taking shape, Brigham Young and a few others set out for England; it is a measure of the zeal with which they proselytized and the attraction of their new faith, that in twelve months they not only recruited and baptized eight thousand people, but had five thousand copies of the Book of Mormon, three thousand copies of their hymnal, printed in England, with countless thousands of religious tracts.

Young returned to receive the congratulations of his leader, and a little later the first of a growing band of European converts set sail for the United States. But by now the patience of the people of Illinois was wearing thin. Some apostates from the Mormon church set up their own newspaper, the Nauvoo *Expositor*, and announced in its columns that they believed Joseph Smith an impostor: at the same time they drew attention to the polygamy in which so many members of the faith indulged. This would and did come as a shock not only to outsiders but to many calling themselves Mormons. Smith was enraged and promptly took matters into his own hands, sending a posse of his own "legion" to destroy the *Expositor* press. The owners brought action against him in the courts and the Governor of Illinois declared that Smith must surrender himself for trial. The Prophet, after considering escape, an idea which fitted in with a long-held, long-term, plan to build a still finer New Jerusalem in the west of the continent, gave himself up.

This was an error of judgment—but it has provided the Mormon church with a real and gallant martyr. On 27 June, 1844, while Joseph, his brother Hyrum and two others sat in their cell, they were attacked by a mob of a hundred and fifty men with blackened faces who stormed into the prison, unhindered by the guards. Joseph, after wounding several of them with a six-shooter, tried to jump the twenty-five feet to the ground from his upstairs window, but was killed by shots from behind and below in the street. He fell and the lynchers propped his body up against a wall, riddled it with bullets.

The Prophet was dead, aged thirty-eight.

For a time, with grieving on one side, satisfied blood-lust on the other, there was peace. It was not to last long. Burnings, lootings, began all over again, and now Brigham Young, who had been chosen leader in succession to the Prophet, decided that a mass exodus to the far west would be the only solution. Here, alone, the Mormon people would be able to build for themselves the life they wanted.

Word spread through the community and soon Young had the names of over two thousand families who professed themselves willing and ready for immediate flight. Many, he found, were by no means ready, and he laid down strict instructions that each family have one wagon, three yoke of cattle, two cows, three sheep, a thousand pounds of flour, twenty pounds of sugar, a rifle, ammunition, a tent and at least ten pounds of seed. Working day and night, supervising the bulding of wagons, the assembling of stores, Young ensured that this was done. And knowing that man does not live by bread alone, he brought choir leaders, entertainers and two professional bands into his party.

A notice was printed in the Nauvoo periodical, *Times and Seasons*: "The Exodus of the only true Israel from these United States to a far distant region of the West, where bigotry and insatiable oppression will have lost its power over them, forms a new epoch, not only in the history of the Church, but of this nation." It was signed by Brigham Young and the Twelve Apostles.

And so on 4 February, 1846, the great exodus began. Young stayed behind for a further eleven days to get the whole party clear of Nauvoo before he set off to join the leaders. The going was worse than they had feared, and for the first weeks they never made more than six miles in a day. They trudged on through snow, mud and ice and at last, after four and a half months, attained what is now Omaha, Nebraska. Here Young decided to halt the column and build an encampment on a grand scale, a "winter quarters" for the thousands who would be following on behind. They built a fine town during the summer and autumn of 1846, with log houses laid out neatly in avenues, and spent the winter there. They had planted seed on arrival—indeed, had planted seed the whole way across Iowa for those who would follow, and the harvest was a good one, filling the granaries of "winter quarters". The granaries were needed, for soon more parties trickled in from the east. By the end of the year "winter quarters" had a population of fifteen thousand.

But the journey took so long: it was obvious to Brigham Young that at this rate of travel his Mormons would take years to arrive at the promised land which he now believed, pending word from his God, to lie in the Great Basin of the Rocky Mountains. Without Young it certainly would have taken years, but he now planned the next stage with great care, profiting from the errors of the first. He sent to England for theodolites and sextants so that navigation across the broad, featureless plains would be dead accurate, and he organized each party so that it contained not only these instruments and men to work them, but blacksmiths, builders, farmers, engineers and "a cannon to over-awe the Indians".

Meanwhile war broke out between the United States and Mexico; and Young, who was a patriot as well as a shrewd leader, urged that a Mormon battalion be raised from those at winter quarters and sent to California. The President of the United States welcomed the offer, there was no shortage of volunteers, and soon the battalion was marching into the south-west, fortified by the promise of their leader that not a man would fall in battle. He and the rest of the community at winter quarters were fortified by the knowledge that these brave men would send back their pay and allowances, for the good of the community.

Young's promise, which he represented as divine revelation, came true. The Mormon battalion, marching at the limit of its endurance, lost men through illness and exhaustion–but it arrived too late to be put into the firing line.

Early 1847 found the main group preparing to leave winter quarters; there were six hundred bodies in the cemetery.

It was 1 April when Brigham Young set off with the first party, consisting of one hundred and forty-eight people in seventy-two wagons. They were strong, confident in their faith, for doubters and backsliders had been sloughed off during the passage across Iowa. They were, as we have seen, strictly organized: reveille was blown at five every morning, the halt signal at exactly four in the afternoon. Bed, after prayers, was at eight-thirty. They made excellent progress now, leaving rudimentary habitations behind for those following on, as well as crops for them to harvest, and they mapped their way with great accuracy using not only sextant and theodolite but the wagon wheel itself. As William Clayton, "Clerk" to the advance party, wrote on 8 May, he had: "Measured the circumference of one of the hind wheels of Brother Kimball's wagon (being the one I sleep in), in charge of Philo Johnson. I found the

wheel exactly fourteen feet eight inches in circumference, not varying one eighth of an inch. I then calculated how many revolutions it
would require for one mile and found it precisely 360, not varying
one fraction, which somewhat astonished me. I have counted
all the revolutions during the day's travel and find it to be a little
over 11¾ miles. According to my previous calculations, we were
285 miles from winter quarters this morning before we started,
and after travelling ten miles I placed a small cedar post in the
ground with these words inscribed on it with a pencil: 'From winter quarters 295 miles, May 8th, 1847. Camp, all well. William
Clayton'".

When posts were not available, they used the bleached skulls of
buffalo, often with the interior as a sort of post-box where letters
could be left.

The route Young took was entirely uncharted between winter
quarters and Laramie, five hundred miles farther west. He had
been advised to follow the so-called "Oregon Trail" south of the
Platte River, along which others were emigrating to the far north-
west, but he decided, and probably wisely, to avoid his fellow-whites
and take his chance with Indians to the north of the river. Certainly
the Mormons were more than a match for the Indians, able to
defend themselves when necessary, but eager and able to win them
over with talk and presents. (This route, hacked out and "navigated"
by the Mormons, was later chosen by engineers as the shortest and
best for their Union Pacific Railway.)

But now the question grew more urgent: just where were they
going? As the question was asked him each day, Young replied that
God would answer, in God's good time: On they went.

His forty-sixth birthday was on 1 June, and on that night he and
his party camped near Laramie. The next day they ran into a group
of hunters, led by one Moses Harris, who had been living in the west
for twenty-five years, earning a precarious but satisfying living
with gun and traps. He urged them not to consider settling in the
Rocky Mountain Basin: it was arid, inhospitable, had no timber. California—now *that* was a place. In fact there was already a
small Mormon settlement there; they would feel at home.

This was true, for on the same day in 1846 that Young's exodus
began from Nauvoo, a party of Mormons sailed from the east coast
to head round the Horn and make a new life for themselves in a
legendary California. They had prospered, and a week after Moses
Harris had gone, a messenger arrived from them, urging the

marchers to carry on to the west coast where they would be made welcome.

Young brushed aside the offer. By now his vision had told him where he must settle. He was ill, unable to stand, but he summoned Apostle Orson Pratt and ordered him on at full speed with a fast party of twenty-three wagons. They must go on to the great Salt Lake.

Pratt set out immediately, making good speed. Late in July a messenger caught up with him to report that Brigham Young was still a sick man, but slowly mending, and on no account must the advance party wait for him: When they reached the valley of the Salt Lake they were to bear up to the north where they would find a stream of water, and here they should camp. They should also build a dam so that the bone-dry, rock-hard, soil be irrigated. Here they should plant the first crops of the new land.

Orson Pratt and this messenger, Erasmus Snow, now pushed on ahead of the wagons, travelling horseback. A few days later they climbed the steep hill which they expected, would command, a view of the valley. It would be an arid, depressing place, and they were without enthusiasm. But to their unspeakable joy, the valley was radiant with a vast blue lake. They feasted their eyes on it for a few minutes, then wheeled round, galloped back towards the rest of the party.

A few days later they had led them to the lake, thence to the promised creek in the north, which they attained on 22 July. And, wrote Orson Pratt, "about two hours after our arrival we began to plough, and the same afternoon built a dam to irrigate the sod, which at the place where we were ploughing was exceedingly dry".

Surely no settlers in history have settled faster.

On this same day the main party, with Young almost recovered in health, had moved on to "East Canyon". Faster and faster they travelled, and two days later, on the 24th, they reached the Lake. Pratt's men had formed an encampment, soon to become Salt Lake City, and their wagons were in a long rectangle about the sweet-water stream.

One gets an insight into the thinking, the determination, of these pioneers, the reasons for their success, if one considers the comment of Wilford Woodruff who was driving the wagon in which Young travelled. "When we arrived on the ground, the brethren had commenced ploughing. I had a bushel of potatoes with me and I resolved that I would neither eat nor drink until I had planted them.

I got them into the ground by one o'clock and these, with the potatoes that the other brethren had planted, became the foundation for
the future potato crops of Utah."

Not everyone saw the spot in the same light as Orson Pratt and
Erasmus Snow. One young woman gasped with horror. "Weak and
weary as I am, I would rather go a thousand miles farther than remain in such a forsaken place as this." She was persuaded to change
her mind, perhaps by Brigham's wife, who declared staunchly, on
dismounting from her wagon, "I am satisfied. We enjoyed the
social life of winter quarters; but things do not look dreary to me
here. There are no trees, but they can be planted."

The day of this arrival, 24 June, has, ever since, been celebrated as
Pioneer Day in Utah. It is a major holiday in the Mormon church.

Young quickly laid out his new city, with a well-defined site for
its first temple, and construction began immediately. A month after
his arrival, with adobe houses springing up on all sides, he set off
for winter quarters, some 1,031 miles, as recorded by the Clayton
wagon-wheel meter. To his joy he ran into another large party
moving west, following his trail to the new land. The party consisted of 1,540 people in 540 wagons, bringing with them 124 horses,
9 mules, 2,213 oxen, 887 cows, 358 sheep, 35 hogs and 716 chickens.
Only seven of the humans had died *en route* and the survivors were
in good heart.

Back in winter quarters, a bustling community, but soon to be
dwarfed by the new city a thousand miles to the west, Young drew
up rules for the running of the new community. At the same time
he had himself proclaimed President of the church, "Prophet, Seer
and Revelator".

By May of 1848 he was riding westward again, at the head of a
further 2,417 settlers.

And so the Mormons, driven out of an America in which most of
them had been reared, hacked their way into a new one which they
were able to call their own. It was a wilderness, but they made it
bloom. Brigham Young had been right in refusing to move to California: had the Mormons done so, the natural charms of that more
hospitable region would have brought over thousands of other
settlers—as indeed they did—and the community would once again
have become a hated, feared, minority.

Now, strong, secure—and therefore respected—in the State of
Utah, they remain an object lesson in what faith and determination
can achieve.

LIVINGSTONE'S LAST JOURNEY

A Pioneer in the Heart of Africa

BORN AT Blantyre in Lanarkshire on 19 March, 1813, David
Livingstone was the son of a retail tea-dealer who had all the religious fervour and proselytizing zeal of a missionary. In a household where every penny counted, it is not surprising that the boy's
scholastic career ended prematurely at the age of ten, so that David
could contribute to the family income. First as a piecer, then as a
spinner in the local cotton mill, young Livingstone had to work
about twelve to fourteen hours a day. Such were his powers of concentration and his determination to improve himself that even
under those conditions he managed to read an astonishingly
large number of books, mainly concerned with travel and natural
history.

It was the story of a German missionary, however, that told David
beyond all doubt where his future lay. He would carry the word of
God to the unenlightened, knowledge to the ignorant, healing to
the sick. He would be a missionary.

After an intensive period of study he qualified in divinity and
medicine, and by 1840 was ready for his first assignment overseas.
Prevented by the Opium War from playing an operational role in
China, Livingstone was sent instead to Africa, landing in Algoa
Bay at the end of a long sea voyage. A seven-hundred-mile trek

took him to the Missionary Society's headquarters at Kuruman in Bechuanaland.

It may have been as an enthusiastic missionary that David Livingstone started his journeys into the interior, but he must have realized very early that there was a great deal more to his travels than curing diseases and saving souls. The deeper he plunged into the heart of that vast continent, the greater became his geographical curiosity. He wanted to know about the land itself, its mountains and valleys, its dense forests and boundless plains, its lakes and rivers.

A real pioneer, Livingstone made it his business to open up the unexplored centre of Africa to other missionaries. He travelled westwards to the River Kolobeng and was the inspiration behind the prosperous agricultural colony that sprang up there. It was Livingstone who, along with William Oswell and Mungo Murray, crossed the Kalahari desert, followed the course of the Zonga and discovered Lake Ngami. His next exploit was to cross Africa from ocean to ocean, canoeing part of the way up the Zambezi among hostile tribes, pushing on through the Kioko country in spite of fever and physical exhaustion, and not stopping until he reached his objective, Sao Paula de Loanda and the waters of the Atlantic. Then, four months later, this indefatigable traveller refused a passage back by sea because he had promised his native bearers that he would ensure their safe return along the way they had come. Livingstone prided himself on being a man of his word.

Towards the end of 1856 Livingstone was back in England, the focal point of the nation's esteem and admiration. Published the following year, his account of his journeys, *Missionary Travels and Researches in South Africa,* proved so popular that if he had wished to do so he could have retired on the proceeds. But already preparations were afoot for another expedition, financed by the British Government to the tune of five thousand pounds. This time Livingstone was to explore the Zambezi valley and examine the possibilities of establishing a colonial settlement in that area. Covering the five years from 1858 to 1863, the enterprise was not entirely successful. Although he discovered lakes Shirwa and Nyasa, Livingstone emerged from the experience a sad and disappointed man. For one thing, his wife, who had insisted on joining the venture, had succumbed to malaria and had died at Shupanga, on the Lower Zambezi. For another, he had seen for the first time a region devastated by the slave trade and the sight had sickened him. From then on,

Livingstone was determined to do everything in his power to stamp out the horrible traffic in human flesh.

One of his motives for going back to England in 1864 had been to draw public attention to the iniquity of slavery in Africa. Although the British Government evinced little genuine enthusiasm, people flocked to his lectures up and down the country and listened to his views with respect. A talk he delivered to the British Association at Bath made a profound impression and it was not long before the Royal Geographical Society decided that Livingstone was the ideal man to resolve the vexing question of the central watershed of the African continent.

The whereabouts of the source of the Nile had long been a subject of speculation. Livingstone, who was already chafing to get back to Africa, eagerly seized the opportunity of defining for all time the upper waters of Africa's three great rivers–the Nile, the Zambezi and the Congo. As soon as the Royal Geographical Society's proposition was put before him, he agreed to undertake the formidable task. Government sanction was quickly forthcoming and Livingstone began the preparations for what was to be his last journey.

Neither the Government nor the Royal Geographical Society was willing to give the explorer enough financial backing, so when Livingstone reached Bombay *en route* for Africa in 1865, he could only just about afford to fit out the expedition.

His first recruits were a number of African boys trained at the Nassick Mission near Bombay, a dozen sepoys and a *havildar*. The whole party then went to Zanzibar, where ten Johanna men were engaged. Livingstone's small task force now numbered thirty-six, including two devoted followers who had shared his long trek from Zanzibar–Wikitani and Chuma. In Zanzibar he also bought half a dozen camels, four donkeys, two mules and four Indian buffaloes. He had chosen Zanzibar as his start point for various reasons, but principally because it was near to the operational area and because he considered the Sultan's approval and support essential to the unimpeded progress of the expedition. Then again, with a British official stationed there, he would never be completely cut off from the outside world.

Provided by the Sultan with letters of introduction to the influential Arabs of the interior, Livingstone sailed on his birthday, 19 March, 1866, in H.M.S. *Penguin*, bound for the Rovuma river. To avoid the many sandbanks in the mouth of the Rovuma, the vessel landed about twenty-five miles up the coast at Mikindani Bay. With the departure of the *Penguin*, Livingstone's third and most important journey really began.

After hiring more porters in Mikindani, he set out full of hope and enthusiasm. He was glad to be on the move again. "The effect of travel on a man," he wrote in his *Journal*, "whose heart is in the right place is that the mind is made more self-reliant... The body is soon well-knit; the muscles of the limbs grow as hard as a board and seem to have no fat; the countenance is bronzed, and there is no dyspepsia... No one can truly appreciate the charm of repose unless he has undergone severe exertion."

The country fringing the East African coast is fairly level, but farther inland the vast central plateau rises to an average height of three thousand feet, and broken here and there by snow-capped mountains and split by the Great Rift Valley, with its immense lakes, stretches right across the continent. Although the mountain and lake scenery is superb, the savannah region is mostly bleak, barren and unattractive. The nervous traveller probably needs convincing that the wild animals he encounters are comparatively harmless if left alone, but in time he learns to keep his camp fires burning at night to scare away inquisitive tigers or leopards or even elephants. Experience also teaches him that his most dangerous enemies are mosquitoes, ants and tsetse flies.

Livingstone was well aware of the many difficulties that would have to be overcome. He knew that no other white man had set foot on the route he proposed to follow. He knew, too, that the Bantus, through whose primitive villages he would have to pass, would be curious about him and possibly suspicious and frightened. He could only hope that they would not be hostile.

It was early April when he set out from Mikindani and marched south towards the Rovuma river. Two months later, after a slow but determined advance westwards to the edge of the Waiyau territory, the porters he had recently taken on refused to go any farther. Livingstone paid them off and sent them back, but his troubles were by no means over. Ever since the expedition started, the sepoys had been lazy, quarrelsome and cruel to the animals. When Livingstone discovered that they had tried to persuade the Nassick boys to desert, his only recourse was to dismiss them. With a mere handful of porters and the faithful Nassick boys he reached the shore of Lake Nyasa, which he could not cross because no dhows were available.

Forced to travel round the south end of the lake, Livingstone made for Mponda's village. There he reluctantly parted with Wikitani, who returned to his old home in that locality. After reaching Marenga's village shortly afterwards, most of his other bearers (who had been stealing attractive items from their own loads all along) announced that they had had enough. They were not prepared to risk their lives in the country ahead which was, they insisted, full of hostile Mazitus. Their defection left Livingstone with the loyal Nassick boys and such porters as he had managed to hire in the villages *en route*.

Depressed but undaunted, Livingstone pressed on relentlessly, past Mount Mulundini, across the highlands of north-eastern Rhodesia and dropping down thereafter into the valley of the Loangwa river. Reasonable progress was made until 29 October when a sudden thunderstorm heralded the beginning of another rainy season. The daily downpours that followed were bad enough; a far more serious matter was the worsening food situation. Early in the New Year, Livingstone made this significant entry in his *Journal*: "We have neither sugar nor salt... I feel always hungry, and am constantly dreaming of food when I am not sleeping. Savoury viands of former days come vividly before the imagination even in waking hours."

But the greatest disaster of all was reserved for 20 January. On that fatal day two Waiyau boys decamped with the medicine chest containing his entire stock of quinine and other essential remedies. Livingstone felt that he had "received the sentence of death".

Nevertheless, although he fully appreciated that he was gambling with his life, he refused to swerve from his avowed purpose. Soaked to the skin, with very little to eat and with no medical supplies whatsoever, he plunged deeper into the unknown. He had already marched eight hundred miles from Mikindani and was determined to attain his goal.

By the time the expedition reached the southern end of Lake Tanganyika, Livingstone could hardly stand upright. Burning with fever he collapsed and lay dangerously ill for some weeks. Not until the beginning of May was he in a fit state to continue his journey. His intention was to move westwards to examine the waters of Lake Mweru, but fortunately he fell in with a party of friendly Arab traders who told him there was trouble in the territory towards which he was heading. If he carried on, they warned him, he would surely be murdered. He would be well advised to wait in Chitamba's village until conditions were more favourable.

After rather more than three months' delay, Livingstone moved on, first to Lake Mweru and then veering west via Casembé's village as far as the Lualaba river. It was there, in Mpwéto's village, that he heard of Lake Bemba (Bangweolo) and decided it had to be explored and mapped, but his men were strongly opposed to such a project. In the end only five faithful attendants accompanied him when he crossed the hilly country on his way to the lake. With very few provisions and no resources he was compelled to rely on the good-will of the inhabitants. It was a near thing on 13 July when Livingstone and his porters were surrounded by a horde of intoxicated savages armed with spears, axes, and bows and arrows. Only by keeping a cool head did the explorer avert a certain massacre.

Eager now to get to Ujiji, where he believed stores, drugs and news would be awaiting him, Livingstone had to be satisfied with no more than a cursory examination of the lake. He hurried back to Mpwéto's, found his rebellious porters still in the village, all apparently most penitent, and promptly re-engaged them. Joining an Arab caravan for protection, Livingstone and his men set out for Ujiji on 11 December.

The New Year, 1869, started badly for the explorer. The back-breaking trek to Lake Tanganyika and the long exposure to drenching rains had reduced him to a physical wreck. Coughing day and night, with pneumonia of the right lung, he could no longer walk. As he was borne along helpless on a litter, he lost all sense of time and was clearly on the verge of delirium. If the leader of the Arab caravan had not cooked for him and treated him with Arab medicines, it is doubtful if even his tough constitution would have survived the winter.

The entry in his *Journal* for 8 March runs: "I have a good appetite, and sleep well, but am dreadfully thin, and I have no medicine. Sputa increases. Hope to hold out to Ujiji. Cough worse. Hope to go tomorrow."

This indomitable traveller *did* hold on. Another Arab merchant provided canoes and six days later he reached Ujiji. There was, however, nothing to reward him at his advanced base. Most of the supplies he had expected to find there had been stolen. The items of food that would have strengthened him physically, the drugs that would have eased his aches and pains, the letters that would have boosted his morale–all had gone. It was the cruellest blow he had so far suffered.

It speaks much for the courage and endurance of the man that at the beginning of July he was off again, this time risking his life in Manyema territory. He wanted another opportunity of exploring the Lualaba river, hoping that it would lead him to the sources of the Nile. Indeed, his original desire to discover the Nile's head waters was fast becoming an obsession with him.

The weary frustrating months that followed must have brought Livingstone very close to despair. He had to endure incessant rain, unreliable porters and servants, the sight of broken-hearted slaves, hostile natives, gnawing ulcers, endless delays and exasperating detours. He had estimated that the Manyema expedition would take him four or five months. Altogether he was in that sadly exploited area for the space of two years. Sometimes wading through a sea of mud, sometimes negotiating flooded rivers, Livingstone staggered along, always seeking but never finding, drawing what comfort he could from the Bible. In his Bible readings he had also come across references to yet another riddle that his explorations in Africa might solve, for now he was dreaming of locating the ruins of Meroc, the city Moses had founded in Inner Ethiopia. In his *Journal* he declares that "an eager desire to discover any evidence of the great Moses having visited those parts bound me, spell-bound me, I may say; for if I could bring to light anything to confirm the Sacred Oracles, I should not grudge one whit all the labour expended".

On New Year's Day, 1871, he was at Bambarré, depressed, disillusioned and longing for home. Then, before the month ended, his spirits revived when he heard that the men and supplies he needed had arrived at Ujiji. Ten of the men joined him in early February, but they soon made it clear that they were there to escort him back to Zanzibar, not to follow him farther into the wilderness. Only when Livingstone agreed to increase their wages would they consent to go on.

Then came the blood-bath at Nyangwé market and in neighbouring villages, where nearly four hundred unarmed natives were massacred by a party of Arab traders. The sight of these wanton killings persuaded Livingstone to quit the Manyema country. In any event, he was suffering from "a severe headache, which might have been serious had it not been relieved by a copious discharge of blood". On 20 July he started back to Ujiji.

Every step of the journey was now an agony to the thwarted explorer. Weakened by an attack of dysentery, he was hungry but dared not touch food. Footsore, feverish, a walking skeleton, he felt unutterably depressed. The Arab slave-traders had all returned with something from the interior. He alone had brought back nothing. He saw himself as an abject failure.

Nor was there anything waiting for him in Ujiji, for a rascally Arab half-caste had sold all the goods sent to Livingstone from Zanzibar. All he could count on were a few miscellaneous items he had providentially deposited with an Arab trader before setting out. Only by practising the most rigorous economy could he hope to keep going for another month.

Several wealthy Arab merchants offered to help him, but Livingstone stubbornly refused to accept charity. By denying himself the nourishing foods that might have given him a new lease on life, he grew more and more morose and despondent. Then, towards the end of October, when his spirits had sunk to their lowest ebb, came a totally unexpected change in his fortunes. On the morning of 28 October his devoted attendant Susi rushed into his hut with the thrilling news that an Englishman had entered Ujiji at the head of a well-laden caravan.

The newcomer was Henry Morton Stanley, an American by adoption, who had been sent to Central Africa by his employer, the editor of *The New York Herald*, to "obtain accurate information about Dr Livingstone". That meeting between the two white men on the eastern shore of Lake Tanganyika must have been the most dramatic encounter in history.

Stanley's timely arrival acted as a tonic on Livingstone. The explorer was soon eating normally again, building up his strength and enjoying the lively company of the man who had undoubtedly saved his life. Within three weeks he and his deliverer were investigating the northern end of Lake Tanganyika. Although Stanley was obviously eager to return to civilization to publish his incredible story, he could not resist the opportunity of spending a few months with the famous doctor-missionary.

At last, on 14 March, Stanley bade Livingstone farewell, taking with him the explorer's correspondence and journals and heading for Zanzibar. He reckoned that Livingstone had sufficient supplies at that time to support him for about four years. As porters were unobtainable locally, he said he would enlist fifty when he reached the coast and send them inland. He did his best to persuade Livingstone to abandon his quest for the Nile sources, but the explorer knew that if he went home he would never again be fit enough to venture into Central Africa.

It was his last chance to complete the Royal Geographical Society's assignment. Besides, after the barbarities he had witnessed, he was more than ever concerned to bring about the abolition of the slave trade. An important discovery would help publicize his activities and attract more attention to his reports on how African men, women and children were being systematically bartered for guns and rolls of cloth. His strong feelings on the subject were expressed in a letter he sent to *The New York Herald*. "All I can say in my solitude," he wrote, "is may Heaven's rich blessing come down on every one–American, English, Turk–who will help to heal this open sore of the world."

On 15 August, 1872, Stanley's promised porters joined Livingstone's party in Unyanyembé. Ten days later the expedition moved off, swinging south-west to avoid a tribal war in the Ujiji area. Travelling conditions soon became intolerable. Tsetse flies and incompetent handling were killing off the transport animals, while the sun's intense heat was making "the soil so hot that the radiation is as if it came from a furnace. It burns the feet of the people and knocks them up".

Although Livingstone's health was clearly not up to the task, he never dreamed of calling a halt. Weakened by a fresh bout of dysentery and loss of blood, he continued his gruelling journey through the mountainous Fipa country, across the Lopanza, and headed for Lake Bangweolo at the worst possible time of the year, during the period of heavy rains. As often as not the track he was following would vanish under water, food was getting scarcer, and at the turn of the year the whole party found itself bogged down in flood and mud. It was not long before Livingstone's last ounce of strength oozed away. His men had to take it in turns to carry him pick-a-back, splashing through rivers, squelching across morasses and sometimes groping blindly through cold wet fog. The rate of advance was reduced to a mile and a half a day.

Never free from dysentery, steadily growing weaker, Livingstone nevertheless contrived to jot down his observations in his *Journal*. The miracle was that he could still describe the exotic flowers and trees, the snakes and leeches, the vicious red ants. "The first came on my foot quietly," he noted, "then some began to bite between the toes, then the larger ones swarmed over the foot and bit furiously and made the blood start out."

Not even the dismal prospect before him at the beginning of February could daunt this most valiant of travellers. The party had stopped on the desolate shore of Lake Bangweolo, not far from the swollen waters of the River Chambesi. All round them stretched illimitable floods. With no canoes to transport them across the lake, they were stranded on a "miserable, dirty, fishy island called Motovinza". Racked with pain though he was, Livingstone could still summon up sufficient energy to negotiate with an unfriendly tribal chief for canoes and food.

In pelting rain the little party crossed the Chambesi, camped for the night in Kabinga's territory, then turned south-west towards the Muanakazi. On 12 April, the day they reached the river, Livingstone made the following ominous entry in his *Journal*: "I could hardly walk, but tottered along nearly two hours, and then lay down, quite done."

After a long rest he staggered to his feet, stumbled along the muddy tracks for some distance and then collapsed again. Once more the men had to carry him part of the way in relays. Continuing south-west they crossed the Lombatwa and Kazya rivers and two extensive patches of spongy marshland. Now bleeding profusely, Livingstone was too feeble to record his observations. He made a superhuman effort to ride a donkey, but fell to the ground exhausted. His men then constructed a wooden framework, made it as comfortable as they could with grass and a blanket, and fitted it with a sort of canopy to keep off the pitiless heat of the sun. On this improvised litter they bore him as far as Ilala, a village close to the southern tip of Lake Bangweolo. There they built a hut and laid him inside.

Livingstone had reached the end of his long journey.

Shortly afterwards, on 1 May, 1873, the great explorer died. He had not discovered the sources of the Nile, but according to another distinguished explorer, Sir Harry Hamilton Johnson, it was thanks to Livingstone that: "Central Africa, in its main geographical features, its marvels, its riches, and its horrors, has been completely laid bare to the contemplation of the white man."

But perhaps the finest tribute was paid him by his own fellow travellers, the African boys who had accompanied him on his courageous journey into the heart of Africa. Such was their high regard for their intrepid leader that they carried his body and belongings all the way back to the coast through fifteen-hundred miles of hostile territory. Their devotion made it possible for the explorer's remains to find a fitting resting-place in Westminster Abbey. The story of his life is surely summarized on his tombstone:

> For 30 years his life was spent
> In an untiring effort
> To evangelise the native races
> To explore the undiscovered secrets
> To abolish the desolating slave-trade
> Of Central Africa.

PILGRIMAGE TO MECCA

John Lewis Burckhardt Travels in Disguise

MECCA AT last! It had taken him a long time, and he had come a very long way round. While his companions led the camels away and went in search of quarters for the night, he wrapped his robes about him and slowly made his way along the dusty streets, between rows of shops and many-storeyed houses, to a vast, colonnaded and cupolaed space. And there, not far from the entrance gate, rose the black mass of the most sacred object of the Faith that he had made his own. The Kaaba ... he flung himself on his knees before it, recited the prescribed prayers of thankfulness, walked round it, ran round it, kissed the Black Stone as millions had done before him and millions more have done since.

None who have in mind the circumstances of the time, the dangers and difficulties he had to encounter, will deny to John Lewis Burckhardt the honour of being one of the world's foremost travellers. He was a Swiss, born at Lausanne in 1784, and his youth was passed in a period of revolutionary troubles which culminated in a Napoleon-dominated continent. Young Burckhardt would have liked to have embarked on a military career, but he could never get himself to serve under a man whom he regarded as a despotic destroyer of the people's liberties. So, after some years studying at universities in Germany, he managed to get to London, where he presented letters of introduction to Sir Joseph Banks, the eminent scientist.

Banks was, among many other things, one of the most active members of the committee of the association for promoting discoveries in the interior of Africa; he was on the look-out for likely recruits, and twenty-two-year-old Burckhardt seemed to fill the bill. It was no easy assignment, as we may be sure Sir Joseph was careful to make plain: several young men who had been sent out to explore the unmapped wastes of North and West and Central Africa had perished in the attempt, or had not been heard from for years. Burckhardt was joung and eager, however, and he offered his services, which were promptly accepted.

But first he had to train, and after studying Arabic at London and Cambridge, he left London in 1809 for Syria, where he was to spend a couple of years perfecting himself in the language and in acquiring Oriental aptitudes. Realizing that he would never be able to make much headway unless he personated a Mussulman, or Moslem as we should say, he soaked himself in the Koran, allowed his beard to grow to a prophetic length, assumed eastern dress, and made himself physically fit and hard by long journeys on foot, in the heat of the noonday sun, sleeping at night on the hard ground and subsisting for days and weeks on nothing but vegetables and water.

After a time his disguise was so complete that he was able to travel across Asia Minor as a Mohammedan merchant from India, and the descriptions that "Ibrahim ibn Abdullah" was able to give of Indian places and personages were so convincing that his true character was never even suspected. He traversed Syria and Palestine, and at length arrived in Egypt, where it was intended that he should make a start with his African explorations. From the committee in London came the suggestion that he should endeavour to cross Africa from Egypt to the Niger, that mysterious river which (such was the knowledge, or lack of knowledge, of African geography at that time) some believed might be a branch of the Nile! With this end in view, Burckhardt sought an opportunity to join one of the caravans which from time to time moved southwards into the Sahara from Fezzan, in Libya. He heard of one, but since it was not to start for some time he decided to employ the interval in making a journey up the Nile, perhaps as far as Nubia.

With this in mind he quitted Cairo early in January, 1813, and got as far as Assouan without much difficulty. Then, in the character of a humble Syrian merchant, without a servant and with a single ass to carry his provisions and little stock in trade–and of course on the face of it a devout Moslem–he pushed on into the Nubian desert, through which the great Scottish traveller James Bruce had made his way some forty years before. At Berber he regained the Nile, and moved along it to Shendy. Here there was a great slave-mart; and having disposed of the remainder of his wares, he bought a slave with the proceeds–a boy of fourteen–and together they set out with a caravan which was moving in the direction of Suakin, on the Red Sea. He was now on one of the regular routes followed by the pilgrim bands to the holy cities of Arabia, and Burckhardt thought the opportunity of making the pilgrimage with them too good to be missed. So when, after a journey of thirteen days, he and his black slave-boy arrived at Suakin, they took boat and crossed the Red Sea to Jiddah, then as now the principal port of arrival for pilgrims making for Mecca, the Prophet Mohammed's birthplace, and Medina, where he was buried.

This brings us to the opening page of Burckhardt's *Travels in Arabia, comprehending an Account of those Territories in the Hedjaz which the Mohammedans regard as sacred*. He wrote this book after his return to Egypt, basing it on the notes he made when he was actually in the places he describes, but it was not published until 1829, "under the authority of the Association for promoting the Discovery of the Interior of Africa". It was at once recognized as a classic of African travel and exploration, a worthy successor to Burckhardt's *Travels in Nubia* and *Travels in Syria and the Holy Land* which had appeared under the same auspices some years earlier. Since his time there have been other accounts of visits to the holy cities of the Mohammedan faith and world, but Burckhardt's holds an unchallengeable position as the first really comprehensive and authoritative description by a European.

"My arrival in the Hedjaz," he begins, "was attended with some unfavourable circumstances. On entering the town of Djidda (as he spells it), in the morning of the 15th of July, 1814, I went to the house of a person on whom I had a letter of credit, delivered to me, at my departure from Cairo, in January, 1813, when I had not yet fully resolved to extend my travels into Arabia. From this person I met with a very cold reception; the letter was thought to be of too old a date to deserve notice: indeed, my ragged appearance might have rendered any one cautious how he committed himself with his correspondents, in paying me a large sum of money on their account ... and I thus experienced a flat refusal, accompanied, however, with an offer of lodgings in the man's house."

This offer he accepted, thinking that a closer acquaintance might convince the man that he was neither an adventurer nor an impostor; but this did not happen, and after a couple of days Burckhardt removed to one of the public khans (inn, or caravanserai) in the town, since the whole stock of money in his possession was two dollars and a few sequins (Italian gold coins of lesser value) sewed up in an amulet which he wore on his arm.

"I had little time to make melancholy reflections upon my situation (he writes); for on the fourth day after my arrival, I was attacked by a violent fever, occasioned, probably, by indulging too freely in the fine fruits which were then in the Djidda market; an imprudence, which my abstemious diet for the last twelve months rendered, perhaps, less inexcusable, but certainly of less consequence."

For several days he was delirious, and he might well have died but for the aid rendered him by a Greek captain, who had been a fellow-passenger from Suakin. This man attended Burckhardt in his lucid intervals, and at his request procured a barber, or country physician, who bled him copiously, "though with much reluctance, as he insisted that a potion, made up of ginger, nutmeg, and cinnamon, was the only remedy adapted to my case".

In a fortnight Burckhardt was able to get about again, but his little stock of money was now all gone and he was compelled to sell his slave-boy, much as he regretted the necessity of parting from him, "as I knew he had some affection for me, and he was very desirous to remain with me". But at least Burckhardt had the satisfaction of making a profit, since he had bought the boy at Shendy for sixteen dollars and now disposed of him for forty-eight.

With a little money in his purse, he came to the conclusion that he would do better to abandon his disguise of a beggar, and "equipped myself anew, in the dress of a reduced Egyptian gentleman". This done, he wrote to Cairo for a further supply of cash, but he could hardly expect to receive this in less than three or four months. In these circumstances he had no resource but to apply for assistance to Ali Pasha, the governor of the district, whom he had met in Cairo. Ali Pasha's headquarters were then at Tayf, a town to the east of Mecca and about five days' journey from Jiddah, but communications were slow and uncertain and it might be that he would have to wait perhaps twenty days for a reply.

While waiting, Burckhardt remained in the khan, still feeling so weak from his illness and finding the heat so oppressive that except for a few hours early in the morning, spent in transcribing the notes of his travels in Nubia, he passed the rest of the day in the cool shade of the khan's great archway. Now his luck began to turn. First, his plight came to the notice of one Yahya Effendi, physician of Toussoun Pasha, Ali Pasha's son, in Jiddah, whom he had also met some time before at Cairo. This man was good enough to negotiate a bill for him to the amount of about a hundred pounds. Then a reply from Ali Pasha came to hand, brought by a messenger with two camels, a new suit of clothes, and a small sum of money, in which he was invited to visit the Pasha forthwith at Tayf. "The invitation of a Turkish Pasha is a polite command," Burckhardt explains, and he at once set out for Tayf, where he was received in the most friendly fashion.

The Pasha clearly did not quite know what to make of him. When he had met Burckhardt in Cairo he had been given to understand that he was an English gentleman travelling for pleasure, and he may well have suspected that he was some sort of English spy; if so, he should be treated with respect, since news of the British defeat of Napoleon had reached even this out-of-the-way quarter of the world. But Burckhardt was insisting that he was a true Moslem, and there was no doubt of the fact that he could speak the most excellent Arabic.

"It is not the beard alone which proves a man to be a true Moslem," remarked the Pasha once to his guest who was fingering his beard in the most approved fashion. However, to resolve the matter, he arranged that Burckhardt should be examined by some of the most learned *cadis*, or exponents of the Mohammedan laws and customs. Burckhardt had not the slightest objection, and accordingly two of the most learned professors then in Arabia were directed to examine him on his knowledge of the Koran and of the practical as well as the devotional precepts of their creed. The result was a complete conviction in the minds of his questioners that he was not only a true Moslem but a very well informed one.

After one of these encounters, Burckhardt remarks with some naïveté: "I supped with the Kadhy, and afterwards performed the evening prayers in his company, when I took great care to chaunt as long a chapter of the Koran as my memory furnished at the moment..." As for the Pasha, Burckhardt says: "I am still ignorant of his real opinion concerning my sincerity in professing the Mohammedan faith," but "he certainly treated me as a muselman, and I flattered myself that the boldness of my conduct at Tayf had convinced him that I was a true proselyte."

However that may be, there was no doubt that Burckhardt had come through the test with flying colours, and at length "Sheikh Ibrahim", as he was then known, was allowed to leave Tayf and made his way to Mecca. He arrived there on 9 September, 1814, and as already indicated proceeded at once to carry out the prescribed ritual in its every detail.

For the best part of three months–September, October, November of 1814–Burckhardt was in Mecca, ample time for him to observe the appearance of the city and its sacred edifices, its people in their social and religious activities, its environs associated with the various incidents of the great pilgrimage. His account of what he had seen and heard has the ring of indubitable truth, and the information he gathered is conveyed in a prose that is vivid and picturesque. And there is the added interest that he was the first European Christian to mingle freely in the sacred ceremonies of the holiest shrine of the Mohammedan world.

Immediately after his arrival he hired decent apartments in a not much frequented quarter of the town, where "I had the advantage of several large trees growing before my windows, the verdure of which, among the barren and sun-burnt rocks of Mekka, was to me more exhilarating than the finest landscapes could have been under different circumstances." He chose his own company, mixing with pilgrims from all parts of the world. If any question arose as to his origin–which rarely happened in a place that abounded with strangers–he gave out that he was a gentleman in reduced circumstances from Egypt. Even had he been "found out" it would not have mattered very much, "for the assumption of a false character is frequent among all eastern travellers, and especially at Mekka, where every one affects poverty in order to escape imposition, or being led into great expenses." During all his eastern journeys, he says, he never enjoyed such perfect ease as in Mecca, and he retained the most pleasing recollections of his prolonged stay there.

"During the mid-day hours I staid at home: the first part of the night I passed in the great square of the mosque, where a cooling breeze always reigns; here, seated upon a carpet, which my slave (he had purchased another to replace the one he had disposed of at Jiddah) spread for me, I indulged in recollections of far-distant regions, while the pilgrims were busily engaged in praying and walking round the Kaaba."

Of course he made a point of visiting all the places and objects of religious devotion. His description of the Great Mosque is exact and intimately detailed: he had no measuring-tape with him, but he paced out the distances with the utmost care. He counted the number of pillars in the surrounding arcade, noted what they are made of, and studied the designs of their capitals. Towards the middle of the central area was the Kaaba, "an oblong massive structure, eighteen paces in length, fourteen in breadth, and from thirty-five to forty feet in height... constructed of the grey Mekka stone, in large blocks of different sizes, joined together in a very rough manner, and with bad cement".

At the Kaaba's north-east corner, "near the door, is the famous 'Black Stone'; it forms a part of the sharp angle of the building at four or five feet above the ground. It is an irregular oval, about seven inches in diameter, with an undulated surface, composed of about a dozen smaller stones of different sizes and shapes, well joined together with a small quantity of cement, and perfectly smoothed; it looks as if the whole had been broken into many pieces by a violent blow, and then united again. It is very difficult to determine accurately the quality of this stone, which has been worn to its present surface by the millions of touches and kisses it has received. It appeared to me like a lava... Its colour is now a deep reddish brown, approaching to black; it is surrounded on all sides by a border, composed of a substance which I took to be a close cement of pitch and gravel... Both the border and the stone itself are encircled by a silver band, broader below than above and on the two sides, with a considerable swelling below, as if a part of the stone were hidden under it. The lower part of the border is studded with silver nails."

On only three days in the year the Kaaba was open to the public, and we may be sure that Burckhardt made a careful note of the days. He certainly took advantage of the occasion. "The opening takes place one hour after sunrise," he begins his account, "when the steps are wheeled up to the gate of the building; as soon as they touch the wall, immense crowds rush upon them, and in a moment fill the whole interior of the Kaaba. The steps are lined by the eunuchs of the mosque, who endeavour in vain to keep order, and whose sticks fall heavy upon those who do not drop a fee into their hand; many of the crowd, however, are unmercifully crushed."

In the interior every visitor was supposed to pray a certain number of times and make a certain number of prostrations, "but it may easily be conceived how these prayers are performed, and that while one is bowing down, another walks over him. After the prayers are finished, the visitor is to lean with extended arms against any part of the wall, with his face pressed against it, and thus to recite two pious ejaculations. Sobbing and moaning fill the room; and I thought I perceived most heartfelt emotions and sincere repentance in many of the visitors: the following, and other similar ejaculations are heard, and many faces are bedewed with tears: 'O God of the house, O God forgive me, and forgive my parents, and my children! O God, admit me into paradise! O God, deliver our necks from hell-fire, O thou God of the old house!' I could not stay longer than five minutes; the heat was so great that I almost fainted, and several persons were carried out with great difficulty, quite senseless."

As he left the crowded little room and descended the steps into the sun-baked courtyard, Burckhardt was hailed by a "sherif" who held out to him the silver key of the Kaaba for him to kiss – for a gratuity, of course. Gratuities had also to be given to a number of other eunuches and minor officiales and servants of the holy place.

Hard by the Kaaba is the Well Zem-Zem, a square building containing the well from which water is drawn in leathern buckets throughout the day. "I have been more than once in the room a quarter of an hour," says Burckhardt, "before I could get a draught of the water, so great was the crowd." The water, he goes on, "is regarded as an infallible cure for all diseases; and the devotees believe that the more they drink of it, the better their health will be, and their prayers the more acceptable to the Deity. I have seen some of them at the well swallowing such a quantity of it as I should hardly have thought possible ... Few pilgrims quit Mekka without carrying away some of this water in copper or tin bottles, either for the purpose of making presents, or for their own use in case of illness, when they drink it, or for ablution after death. I carried away four small bottles, with the intention of offering them as presents to the Mohammedan kings in the Black countries."

Burckhardt happened to be at Mecca in the month of Ramadan, that month in the Moslem calendar when believers are forbidden to eat or drink anything between the hours of daybreak and sunset. It was the hottest time of the year, and great crowds assembled in the mosque, anxiously waiting for the call to evening prayers, when they might at length break their fast and partake of a cooling drink. Every one, he tells us, carried in his handkerchief a few dates, a little bread and cheese, or some grapes, which he placed on the ground before him, together with a flask of Zem-Zem water. As soon as the imam on the top of the well-house began his cry of *"Allahou Akbar!"* ("God is most great!"), they all hastened to take a drink of the water, and to eat something, previous to joining in the prayers, after which they all returned home for supper. But they were back again for the evening orisons, at which time the whole square and colonnade were illuminated with thousands of lamps; and in addition each of the hadjis, or pilgrims, had his own lantern standing on the ground before him. "The brilliancy of this spectacle, and the cool breeze pervading the square, caused multitudes to linger here till midnight."

Then he spied, coming through the gate, a black-skinned pilgrim who had come all the way from Darfur, in the Sudan. "After his long journey across barren and solitary deserts, on his entering the illuminated temple he was so much struck with its appearance, and overawed by the black Kaaba, that he fell prostrate by the place where I was sitting, and remained long in that posture of adoration. He then rose, burst into a flood of tears, and in the height of his emotion, instead of reciting the usual prayers of the visitor, only exclaimed, 'O God, now take my soul, for this is Paradise!'"

But the Kaaba, Burckhardt feels obliged to state, is not always regarded with such reverence; on the contrary, "it is rendered the scene of such indecencies and criminal acts, as cannot with propriety be more particularly noticed. They are not only practised here with impunity, but, it may be said, almost publicly; and my indignation has often been excited, on witnessing abominations which called forth from other passing spectators nothing more than a laugh or a slight reprimand".

Then he draws a pitiful picture of the temple courts when the time of the pilgrimage has come to an end. On every hand might be seen dead bodies, the corpses of those who had succumbed to the trials of the long journey, the light covering of the *ihram* (pilgrim's robe), unhealthy lodgings in Mecca, the bad fare, and sometimes absolute want; or as was very often the case, they had been already sick and near to death when they had been brought to the holy place, in the hope that they might be cured by a sight of the Kaaba, or at least have the satisfaction of expiring within the sacred enclosure.

For a month subsequent to the conclusion of the Hadj (pilgrimage) he found, almost every morning, corpses of pilgrims lying in the mosque, and once he and a Greek *hadji*, whom accident had brought to the spot, closed the eyes of a poor pilgrim from North Africa, "who had crawled into the neighbourhood of the Kaaba, to breathe his last, as the Moslems say, 'in the arms of the Prophet and of the guardian angels'. He intimated by signs his wish that we should sprinkle Zem-Zem water over him, and while we were doing so, he expired; half an hour afterwards he was buried."

Burckhardt estimated the number of pilgrims in that year to be in the neighbourhood of 80,000, and yet, strangely enough, he was of the opinion that "the time has passed, and probably for ever, when pilgrims from all regions of the Muselman world came every year in multitudes, that they might visit devotionally the sacred places of the Hedjaz". A hundred and fifty years after his own visit, the holy places of Arabia still draw immense crowds, and they come no longer on foot or on camels, as in his time, but by motor and aircraft. He for his part did all that was required of him. He visited Arafat and the other sacred sites, and then accompanied those pilgrims who added to their good works by going on to Medina, and paying their devotions in the mosque where is the Prophet's tomb.

Arriving at Medina towards the end of January, 1815, he spent about three weeks there, performing all the ceremonies that were customary, and then planned to take the overland route to Egypt. But again he was struck down by illness, a kind of tertiary ague, which kept him confined to his bed, or rather carpet, until April. This caused him to abandon his idea of the overland route; and as soon as he could support the motion of a camel he went to Yenbo, on the Red Sea, and took a passage on a boat that after twenty days landed him at Ras Mohammed, on the tip of the Sinai peninsula. Again he suffered a bout of illness, but at last he arrived back in Cairo, on 19 June, 1815. He had been absent nearly two years and a half.

At Cairo he recruited the strength which had been so sorely tried by the long marches and privations, and worked on his journals, which he sent home to the Africa Association as they were completed. In 1816 he was once more on his travels; this time to Sinai, where he endeavoured to decide the route which the Israelites had taken when they left the Land of Egypt for the Promised Land. Returning to Cairo in June, he busied himself with preparations for his long-intended visit to Fezzan, and the exploration of the sources of the Niger. But there were hindrances of one kind and another, and when at length the caravan he intended to join was ready to depart Burckhardt was in no fit state to do so. Sickness had once more supervened, and in October, 1817, he died of dysentery at Cairo. And there he was laid to rest, as the holy *hadj* or pilgrim that he was, among the "true believers" in the Mohammedan cemetery.

FANNY'S FIRST RAILWAY JOURNEY

Opening of the Liverpool-Manchester Railway

WHAT A day it was, that fifteenth of September, 1830–it was a Wednesday, if you want to be even more precise–when the Liverpool to Manchester railway was opened to public traffic.

As soon as it was light the people started to stream out of Liverpool to where they might have a good view of the route. By seven o'clock the roads for seven or eight miles out of town were lined with dense crowds. Here and there large stands had been erected, to which the public were admitted at half a crown a head, and these were soon filled to capacity. Especially thick were the crowds round the entrance to the great tunnel which had been cut under Liverpool, a matter of a mile and a half, for here the locomotives were on the point of being marshalled.

Seven o'clock, eight o'clock, nine, half-past nine... Something is happening. The locomotives are being drawn out of their sheds, and with a great deal of puffing and blowing are shunted and pushed into their positions on the track. Ten o'clock, and there is a great burst of cheering. The military band placed in readiness crashes out the strains of "Here the conquering hero comes!", and the Duke of Wellington (who happens to be Prime Minister, although many among the crowd prefer to ignore that, remembering him only as the victor of Waterloo) drives up with his suite in an array of carriages. He gets down, and is conducted with all proper respect and ceremony to the siding where the splendid state-coach is waiting to receive him. Splendid is the right word to describe it: thirty-two feet long, carried on eight big iron wheels, and with a canopy borne aloft on golden pillars (which will have to be lowered when a tunnel looms ahead).

The excitement grows. The engines come snorting along the track, and those in the know point out to their neighbours which they are. The *Northumbrian* – that's the one the Duke is being led up to, and the railway company's directors and other distinguished visitors are to travel with him. ("That's Mr Huskisson over there, he's M.P. for Liverpool, and he's had some big posts in the Cabinet".) The *Phoenix*, that's the one with a green flag on the front; *North Star*, yellow flag; *Rocket* (most famous of them all), light blue flag; *Dart*, purple; *Comet*, deep red; *Arrow*, pink; and, bringing up the rear, *Meteor*, sporting a brown flag.

Much hissing of steam, puffings and snortings, excited shouts, wheels rumbling, doors banging, hats waving ... "they're off!"

On issuing from the tunnel (so we learn from a contemporary report of the great day's proceedings) the *Northumbrian* took the south or right-hand line of railway, drawing behind it three carriages, the first containing the band, the second the Duke of Wellington and other persons of distinction, and the third the railway company directors. The other seven engines proceeded along the north line. The *Phoenix* and *North Star* led the way, drawing five carriages apiece, crammed with passengers; the *Rocket* drew three, and the *Dart, Comet, Arrow,* and *Meteor* four carriages each, all of them equally packed. Altogether there were 772 persons being conveyed.

Puff-puff, chug-chug, clank, rattle ... at a steady speed of fifteen or sixteen miles an hour they went along, with the exception of the *Northumbrian* which, having a track to itself, was speeded up and slowed down from time to time, just to show the Duke of Wellington what she could do. Broad Green, Huyton, Rainhill, St Helens, Earlstown, Newton, Parkside ... Here a halt was called to enable the locomotives to replenish their supplies of water. And this seems a good opportunity to make the acquaintance of one of the passengers who has managed to keep her bonnet on her head and the smuts out of her eyes and has stored up in her mind all the details of a day that *she* never forgot and was able to put down on paper— to our great advantage, let it be said.

Fanny Kemble her name is; she is twenty, bright-eyed and keen-witted, and only last year she had made her debut as an actress on the stage at the Theatre Royal, Covent Garden. She had played Juliet–and what a first night it had proved for Fanny! "Stunned with the tremendous shout that greeted me . . . I stood like a terrified creature at bay, but in the balcony scene I *was* Juliet . . . the poetry sounded like music to me as I spoke it . . . I did not return into myself till all was over, tumultuous storm of applause, congratulaton what she could do. Broad Green, Huyton, Rainhill, St Helens, was as good as her aunt, Mrs Siddons. Since then she has been on tour–Edinburgh, Dublin, Liverpool–and it is not surprising that she has been offered a ticket for the opening of the railroad, as it is called; and, being a spirited, intensely curious young thing, has jumped at it. But let her speak for herself. First, a letter in which she describes meeting some weeks previously with George Stephenson, the redoubtable and justly renowned engineer, who designed the *Rocket* and built the Liverpool to Manchester line.

"My dearest Harriet," Fanny writes on a day in August, 1830, to her bosom friend Harriet St Leger, from Liverpool, where the Kemble company was then performing. "A common sheet of paper is enough for love, but a foolscap extra can alone contain a railroad and my ecstasies. There was once a man, who was born at Newcastle-on-Tyne, who was a common coal-digger! This man had an immense constructiveness, which displayed itself in pulling his watch to pieces and putting it together again; in making a pair of white shoes when he happened to be some days without occupation; finally–here there is a great gap in my story–it brought him in the capacity of an engineer before a committee of the House of Commons, with his head full of plans for constructing a railroad from Liverpool to Manchester. It so happened that to the quickest and most powerful perceptions, to the most indefatigable industry and perseverance, and the most accurate knowledge of the phenomena of nature as they affect his peculiar labours, this man joined an utter want of the 'gift of the gab'. He could no more explain to others what he meant to do and how he meant to do it, than he could fly; and therefore the members of the House of Commons . . . dismissed Stephenson as a visionary. Having prevailed upon a company of Liverpool gentlemen to be less incredulous, and having raised funds for his great undertaking, in December of 1826 the first spade was struck into the ground."

Now Fanny breaks off to describe an excursion she had made

the day before, together with a number of other visitors, to the scene of the railroad excavations. They had been ushered into a large courtyard where, under cover, stood several carriages of a very peculiar construction. One of these was prepared for their reception. It was a long-bodied vehicle with seats placed across it, back to back, as in "a sort of uncovered *char-a-banc*". The wheels were "placed upon two iron bands, which formed the road", and along which they could be made to "slide without any danger of hitching or becoming displaced". The carriage was set in motion by "a mere push".

So much for the carriages, and now for the locomotives. "We were introduced to the little engine which was to drag us along the rails. She (for they make these curious little fire-horses all mares) consisted of a boiler, a stove, a small platform, a bench, and behind the bench a barrel containing enough water to prevent her being thirsty for fifteen miles—the whole machine not bigger than a common fire-engine. She goes upon two wheels, which are her feet, and are moved by bright steel legs called pistons. They are propelled by steam, and in proportion as more steam is applied to the upper extremities (the hip-joints, I suppose) of these pistons, the faster they move the wheels ... The reins, bit and bridle of this wonderful beast is a small steel handle, which applies or withdraws the steam from its legs or pistons, so that a child could manage it ... This snorting little animal, which I felt rather inclined to pat, was then harnessed to our carriage, and Mr Stephenson, having taken me on the bench of the engine with him, we started at about ten miles per hour."

What a lucky girl! On they went, along the level, through deep cuttings, across that terrible Chat Moss whose masses of peat had almost defeated the world's finest engineer, until they came to a ravine, where Stephenson made her alight and gave her a lecture on the mechanics of railway construction, the workings of a steam-engine, and the geological origins of the landscape. But what enthralled her was the motion of travelling at such a tremendous speed. "You cannot conceive what that sensation of cutting the air was," she wrote.

Towards the end of the letter she adds "a word or two about the master of all these marvels, with whom I am most horribly in love. He is a man of from fifty to fifty-five years of age (in fact, Stephenson was then forty-nine). His face is fine, though careworn, and bears an expression of deep thoughtfulness. His mode of explaining his ideas is peculiar and very original, striking and forcible. Although his accent indicates strongly his north-country birth, his language has not the slightest touch of vulgarity or coarseness. He has certainly turned my head." Then Fanny tells her correspondent that the opening of the railway has been fixed for the fifteenth of next month, and that she supposes that "there will never have been a scene of more striking interest... The directors have kindly offered us three places for the opening, which is a great favour, for people are bidding almost anything for a place, I understand". She feared that they might have to decline, since her father had arranged to take her brother to school at Heidelberg before the next season opened; but as things turned out she and her mother *did* go to the opening, and so it is that she was enabled to provide us with a first-hand account of the events of the famous day.

Now we are back again at Parkside station, where the locomotives have been taking in water.

Before leaving Liverpool everybody had been particularly requested not to leave their carriages, and printed notices were displayed to the same effect. But when the trains stopped several gentlemen felt the urge to stretch their legs and strolled about the track. Among these was Mr Huskisson, who having descended from the *Northumbrian* walked along to where the Duke of Wellington was seated. They had been on not very good terms of late, but the Duke stretched out his hand in friendly greeting. They shook hands most cordially, and just at that moment the *Rocket* was perceived to be rapidly approaching on the other track.

"Get in! Get in!" several people cried, and while some scrambled up the side of the carriage–there were no steps–others made their way round to the back, Mr Huskisson, however, did neither. His friend, Mr Holmes, M.P., who had accompanied him to see the Duke and was now standing at his side, drew himself up as closely as he could against the side of the "Ducal car", and doubtless expected his friend to do the same. The space between the tracks was four feet, but the "Ducal car" overhung it by two feet and the *Rocket* by six inches; even so, this left a clear space of eighteen inches–quite sufficient to allow a person to stand with his back to the carriage without risk of injury.

Mr Holmes, flattening himself against the carriage, saw that Huskisson was still undecided what to do. He called out to him, "For God's sake, be firm, Mr. Huskisson!" But Huskisson apparently thought that there was not room to stand between the lines while trains were passing. A door in the carriage was open just above him. He reached up and grasped its handle, but before he could struggle up into the carriage the *Rocket* struck against the open door, with the result that this swung rapidly round and knocked Huskisson on to the line. The engine moved on, crushing Huskisson's right leg beneath it.

Mr. Holmes, with Lord Wilton and some other members of their party, hurried up as soon as the engine had passed, and endeavoured to raise Huskisson from the ground. Obviously he was in a very bad way. "I have met my death—God forgive me!" he is reported to have said in his agony.

At his stage we may return to Miss Kemble who, it will be understood, was following along in one of the other carriages. Writing as before to her "dearest Harriet" she tells her that: "We started on Wednesday last, to the number of about eight hundred people. The most intense curiosity and excitement prevailed. Though the weather was uncertain, enormous crowds of densely packed people lined the road, shouting and waving hats and handkerchiefs as we flew by them. What with the sight and sound of these cheering multitudes and the tremendous velocity with which we were borne past them, my spirits rose to the true champagne height, and I never enjoyed anything like so much as the first hour of our progress. I had been unluckily separated from my mother in the first distribution of places, but by an exchange of seats which she was enabled to make she rejoined me when I was at the height of my ecstasy, which was considerably dampened by finding that she was frightened to death, and intent upon nothing but devising means of escaping from a situation which appeared to her to threaten with instant annihilation herself and all her travelling companions."

While Fanny was "chewing the cud of this disappointment, which was rather bitter", since she had expected her mother to be as pleased as she was herself with their excursion, a man suddenly hurried past their carriage, calling through a speaking-trumpet that they should stop the engine, since somebody in the directors' carriage had been injured. They were stopped accordingly, and presently a hundred voices were heard exclaiming that "Mr Huskisson has been killed!"

"The confusion that ensued is indescribable," continues the girl; "the calling out from carriage to carriage to ascertain the truth, the contrary reports which were sent back to us, the hundred questions eagerly uttered at once, and the repeated and urgent demands for surgical assistance, created a sudden turmoil that was quite sickening."

Later she learnt from Lady Wilton, who had been in the Duke's carriage and was within a few yards of the spot when the accident happened, some details of the ghastly occurrence. While the engine was taking in water, Lord Wilton, together with Count Batthyany, Count Matuscewitz. Mr Huskisson, and other distinguished folk had got out and were standing talking on the middle of the track, when "an engine on the other line, which was parading up and down merely to show its speed, was seen coming down upon them like lightning. The most active of those in peril sprang back into their seats. Lord Wilton saved his life only by rushing behind the Duke's carriage, and Count Matuscewitz had but just leaped into it, with the engine all but touching his heels as he did so. Poor Mr Huskisson, less active from the effects of age and ill-health, bewildered, too, by the frantic cries of 'Stop the engine! Clear the track!' that resounded on all sides, completely lost his head, looked helplessly to the right and left, and was instantaneously prostrated by the fatal machine, which dashed down like a thunderbolt upon him, and passed over his leg, smashing and mangling it in the most horrible way. Lady Wilton said that she distinctly heard the crushing of the bone..."

For a few moments, apart from that ghastly "crushing" noise and poor Mr Huskisson's piercing shriek, not a sound was heard or a word uttered. Then the work of rescue began. Lord Wilton was the first to raise the poor sufferer's head, and, since he had fortunately made some amateur study of surgery, he was enabled to put a tourniquet with his handkerchief on the limb and so prevented death from loss of blood. The *Northumbrian* was then detached from its carriages, Mr Huskisson was gently lifted on to it, and together with Lord Wilton, George Stephenson, and two medical gentlemen, was conveyed "with the greatest possible speed" to Eccles, about ten miles farther on.

The little party arrived at Eccles about half-past one, and Huskisson was taken off the train, laid on a couch which had been hurriedly fetched from the vicarage, and conveyed thither, where Mr Blackburne, the vicar, offered every assistance in his power. A bed was made ready upstairs, but Huskisson was in such a bad state that he could not be moved, and in fact he remained on the couch in the drawing-room until he expired between nine and ten o'clock that same evening.

As he lay dying, he was heard to say that: "The country has had the best of me. I trust that it will do justice to my public character. I regret not the few years which might have remained to me, except for those dear ones (and here he grasped his wife's hand as she crouched, grief-stricken, beside the couch) whom I leave behind me."

William Huskisson's fame is indeed secure, but there is irony in the fact that he is chiefly remembered nowadays, not for what he had managed to accomplish as a far-seeing statesman, especially in economic matters, but because he was the first passenger to be killed in a railway accident in England.

What in the meantime had been happening to the rest of the procession? The Duke of Wellington had at first urged that the proceedings should be terminated without more ado, but for once he was overruled. The railway directors pointed out to him that they had spent a great deal of money on the venture, and their success had already been jeopardized by this most unfortunate accident. They felt that they had a public duty to perform, and besides, the people were in a very dangerous mood; they had assembled for a day's outing, and they might well make themselves a dangerous nuisance if they were deprived of the rest of the pleasure they had anticipated. So the *Northumbrian*, which by this time had returned from its trip to Manchester, was re-attached to the Duke's carriage, and the whole procession resumed its progress as originally arranged. The Duke arrived in Manchester at about a quarter to three in the afternoon, and the rest dribbled in later.

Here we may take up the story again as told by Fanny Kemble: "After this disastrous event the day became overcast, and as we neared Manchester the sky grew cloudy and dark and it began to rain. The vast concourse of people who had assembled to witness the triumphal arrival of the successful travellers was of the lowest order of mechanics and artisans, among whom great distress and a dangerous spirit of discontent with the Government at that time prevailed. Groans and hisses greeted the carriage, full of influential personages, in which the Duke of Wellington sat. High above the grim and grimy crowd of scowling faces a loom had been erected, at which sat a tattered, starved-looking weaver, evidently set there as a *representative man*, to protest against this triumph of machinery, and the gain and glory which the wealthy Liverpool and Manchester men were likely to derive from it.

"The contrast between our departure from Liverpool and our arrival at Manchester was one of the most striking things I ever witnessed. The news of Mr Huskisson's fatal accident spread immediately, and his death, which did not occur till the evening, was anticipated by rumour. A terrible cloud covered this great national achievement, and its success, which in every respect was complete, was atoned for to the Nemesis of good fortune by the sacrifice of the first financial statesman of the country."

The "Liverpool to Manchester" was open, however, and in the first week the directors had the satisfaction of learning that they had carried 6,104 passengers, an average of 763 per day, and that the receipts added up to the very satisfactory total of £2,043 11s. They rubbed their hands. Yes, no doubt about it, there was a bright future ahead. The railways had come to stay...

THE OREGON TRAIL

"The White-top Wagon Road"

"It is four o'clock a.m.; the sentinels on duty have discharged their rifles—the signal that the hours of sleep are over—and every wagon and tent is pouring forth its night tenants, and slow-kindling smokes begin largely to rise and float away in the morning air. Sixty men start from the corral, spreading as they go through the vast herd of cattle and horses that make a semi-circle around the encampment, the most distant perhaps two miles away.

"The herders pass to the extreme verge and carefully examine for trails beyond, to see that none of the animals have strayed or been stolen during the night. This morning no trails led beyond the outside animals in sight, and by five o'clock the herders begin to contract the great, moving circle. In about an hour five thousand animals are close up to the encampment, and the teamsters are busy selecting their teams and driving them inside the corral to be yoked. The corral is a circle one hundred yards deep, formed with wagons connected strongly with each other; the wagon in the rear being connected with the wagon in front by its tongue and ox chains. It is a strong barrier that the most vicious ox cannot break, and in case of an attack by the Sioux would be no contemptible entrenchment..."

And so began another day, a day in which, if all went well, the travellers along the "Oregon Trail", as it was beginning to be known, might make twenty miles with their ox-drawn wagons, averaging two miles an hour. This day, described by one of the travellers, Jesse Applegate–*A Day with the Cow Column of 1843*–was a comparatively easy, uneventful one. But if conditions of weather, or hostile Indians or animals slowed them, they might make only four or five miles in the entire day. Or none at all.

Indians were a real hazard, and there were occasional massacres of emigrants by them: diseases like cholera could strike and wipe out half a column in a few days. But perhaps the most terrifying incident on the march was a stampeding herd of buffalo. William Case, another traveller of the 1840s, described his own experience:

"As the two divisions were moving along deliberately, at ox-speed, in the usual parallel columns, the drivers were startled by a low sound to the north as of distant thunder. There was no appearance of a storm, however, in that or any other direction, and the noise grew louder and louder and was steady and uninterrupted. It soon became clear that there was a herd of buffalo approaching and on the run. Scouring anxiously the line of hills rimming the edge of the valley, the dark brown outline of the herd was at length descried, and was distinctly made out with a telescope, as buffaloes in violent motion and making directly for the train. The front of the line was perhaps half a mile long and the animals were several columns deep and coming like a tornado. They had probably been stampeded by hunters and would now stop at nothing. The only apparent chance of safety was to drive ahead and get out of the range of the herd. The oxen were consequently urged into a run and the train itself had the appearance of a stampede. Neither were they too quick; for the flying herds of the buffalo passed but a few yards to the rear of the last wagons, and were going at such a rate that to be struck by them would have been like the shock of rolling boulders of a ton's weight."

Obviously the path was beset with hazards. Why then did these thousands of men, women and children risk their lives on such an expedition? Why would people leave an east coast which was still under-populated, rich and fertile, to head into the unknown?

There were many reasons and, indeed, many destinations: not all who travelled the Trail went to Oregon. Some went to California; some, notably the Mormons, went only as far as the Great Salt Lake in what is now Utah. The Mormons went to escape religious persecution, to find a land where they could worship and live as they pleased without interference from their neighbours. Before them, at the start of the nineteenth century, had been the missionaries, going into an almost unknown wilderness to spread the word of God, as they saw it, among the savages.

But in the beginning it had been hunters who blazed trails. Without the courage–and often greed–of these almost incredibly hardy men, who followed, broadened, the paths of wild animals, made other more direct ones between their camp sites, and occasionally came back, with their skins, to report on what they had seen, it would have been many years before the West began to be opened up. In fact it has been said, without too much exaggeration, that the west of America was opened by the fops of England: it was they who demanded beaver pelts, for their handsome, fashionable, beaver hats. Years later, when these same fops had decided the silk hat, not the beaver, was the height of fashion, trappers went out of business. But by this time the Oregon Trail and others like it were fixtures on the map.

After the trappers, the missionaries, the persecuted, came those who simply wanted a new home with land available for the taking. Travellers' tales had inspired them to set out and grasp this new life for themselves: some were encouraged in the move by the economic depression which hit the United States, particularly the Middle West, in 1837. Over-confidence had bred a whole litter of extravagant schemes for railways, new cities, chains of banks–and suddenly, as would happen again in 1929, it was all over: high hopes vanished in a puff of smoke. There was a sudden desperate shortage of money, a horrifying drop in the price of farm products, and half the Middle West, it seemed, went bankrupt overnight. For them, and others not yet in their predicament, a new life in the Far West was indicated. So they set out, in their hundreds, driving ox-carts, corralling each night, as we have seen, cheerfully facing the hazards of the trail in the certainty of a better life at the far end–if they reached it.

And a little later, the mad rush of 1849, the "forty-niners" stampeding west by every possible means–Oregon Trail, ship round the Horn, trekking across the Isthmus of Panama to get ship in the Pacific–in order to get rich quick on the gold just discovered in California.

In this first half of the nineteenth century all roads led, as once they had to Rome, towards the frontier capital of St Louis. It was, and is, but a third of the way across the great North American continent: it was the end of civilization. The trappers had moved out from St Louis to the rich hunting grounds of the far North-west, and those that survived came back, with their furs. The paths they took, all of them going through one gap in the Rocky Mountains, the "South Pass", branching out on either side of it, eventually coalesced into the Oregon Trail. The route was the natural, obvious one, dictated by the lay of the land, the easiest mountain slopes, the least dangerous river crossings, the necessity for fodder and water and fuel.

We know it now as the Oregon Trail, but in its day it bore many names, from "The Emigrant Road" to the "Overland Trail"; even, as the Indians put it, "The White-top Wagon Road".

St Louis, though the frontier capital, was not the outpost: there was a flourishing community life for several hundred miles to the west. The Oregon Trail, with all its hazards, really began near the site of present-day Kansas City. For its first forty miles it was the same as the Santa Fé Trail down to Mexico, but near what is now the town of Gardner in Kansas it set off north-west, crossing the Kansas river, then the Platte, to wind on to Fort Laramie in Wyoming. Then on to Soda Springs, Idaho, skirting near present-day Boise in the same state, up to Walla Walla, on to the west coast.

Probably the first fair-sized group of people to travel the Trail were members of Wilson Hunt's expedition to the new "Astoria". John Jacob Astor had set his heart on opening up a community in the far north-west, had already sent a party round by sea and now despatched another overland, under Hunt. The overland party suffered every sort of privation and ill-luck, and only a few weary men reached the Columbia river. But they made it, and although it had not occurred to anyone that a comfortable crossing by wagon was feasible, there was a notice in the *Missouri Gazeteer* of 15 May, 1813, stating that "it appears that a journey across the continent of North America might be performed with a wagon, there being no obstruction in the whole route that any person would dare to call a mountain..."

It was in May, 1792, that Captain Gray of Boston, having sailed round the Horn in his vessel *Columbia*, had come to the mouth of a mighty, rushing river in the far north-west of the North American continent. He named the river after his ship, and it is as the Columbia river that we know it today, but for many years it retained the Indian name for the whole of that territory, "Oo-raggon", or "Hoo-raggon", soon to be crystallized in writing as "Oregon". From Gray's brief investigation of the river mouth it appeared that all manner of skins and minerals might be available for the taking, and he returned to the east with this verdict. Soon men were arriving at this river mouth–men from his own country, from Spain, Britain, France and even Russia, each group believing it had claim to the territory. The American "Astoria" community was one of the first. It fell into English hands during the war of 1812, but by 1818 was back as American territory, though now as "Fort George".

But even under a new name, "Astoria", that ill-considered Utopia was doomed to fade away: it was, as we have seen, missionaries who made the first permanent colonies in this new Oregon. From Captain Gray's first visit in the *Columbia*, men of God had been interested in this new land and very soon the Presbyterians had chosen a site near the river mouth. But they were two very different things, choosing a site and occupying it. Nothing was done for years; and then, surprisingly, it was a request from the Indians themselves that got the project moving. In 1831 a four-man delegation from the "Hoo-raggon" area made their way to St Louis and demanded a Bible and teachers to explain this new Christian religion to them. They were made welcome, taken round a number of churches, made passengers on the first steamboat ride up the upper Missouri; but the white man's life and his food disagreed with them and after short illnesses only one survived to go back and tell his Oregon fellows what the delegation had learnt. It was a strange life, he told them, but a good faith: the missionaries would be coming.

True to their word, they did. There were setbacks, some caused by the very Indians the white men had come to convert; Indians who, it transpired, were rather less eager than the earlier delegation. Missionaries were butchered; missions closed almost as soon as they had opened. Yet by 1840 there was a white, mission, population in the Oregon area of a hundred men, women and children. Probably most of these intended to return some day to the east, or to Europe, but before they could do so the great emigration began, of men fleeing from poverty, religious persecution, or simply humdrum, unrewarding life. They found themselves staying to minister to their own kind.

By 1842 emigration had started in earnest, and the population of Oregon doubled during that year. A still larger emigration took place in the following year, many hundreds of men and their families, leaving with them huge quantities of cattle–but no sheep. This, as a contemporary newspaper report pointed out, was a mistake: "Sheep are indispensable for Oregon".

This 1843 migration, "The Great Emigration" as it was called, succeeded, despite the absence of sheep (made good in later years) and despite quarrels among those taking part. The great herds of cattle were owned by a minority of the migrants and these felt, with some justification, that all men, including those without cattle, should take a turn at guarding them against Indians and wild beasts during the night halts: after all, the cattle would multiply, be for the good of the whole community. But those without animals refused to accept this point of view, staunchly refused to have anything to do with guarding the herds. The factions were finally held together by the remarkable Dr Marcus Whitman, a man of character, courage and great ability who played much the same role in this Great Emigration as Brigham Young was to do with the Mormons and their trek a few years later. He had no sooner resolved the differences of his flock than they encountered a swollen Laramie river, flooding over its banks and quite impossible to ford. The only way of crossing it would be to join the wagons into a ferry, drag this over by a rope. But who would get the rope over and make it fast? Marcus Whitman seized it, plunged into the icy water and swam over. A few hours later the advance party of the Great Emigration was on its way.

He found that many of those travelling liked to rest by the wayside, to "gather strength", but this he refused to allow. His advice was constantly: "Travel, travel, travel; nothing else will take you to the end of your journey; nothing is wise that does not help you along; nothing is good for you that causes a moment's delay."

Whitman, by being so largely responsible for this Great Emigration, can take a measure of credit for the establishment of the Oregon colony. The size of the '43 emigration, its obvious determination to stay there and prosper after all its hardships, was the deciding factor in persuading England to relinquish her claim (through a Hudson's Bay trading post) to the region. After much dispute, the 49th parallel of latitude was agreed on as the boundary separating all this new territory, from the Great Lakes westward, into English and American possessions. By the time this happened, in 1846, there had been still more emigration, but the die was cast in 1843.

From now on emigration was continuous, reaching a peak in '47, with some migrants branching south to found colonies in California. It had begun to look as if the process would continue peacefully for all time as industrious men and women hacked out new lives for themselves on the land.

But then came 1849.

"Forty-nine" is one of the most remarkable years in American history. For years men had found minute quantities of gold in riverbeds and streams of the west, but expert opinion held that this would never be found on a larger scale. Expert opinion was wrong indeed.

It was left to a Swiss-born emigrant, Captain John Sutter, to build himself a saw-mill in California and to find in his own mill-stream a solid rock of gold.

But this was ridiculous. Gold did not exist in this sort of bulk anywhere in the world: Sutter must be mistaken. The San Francisco *Californian*, in March of that year, 1848, ran a straightforward, factual story about the discovery and was ridiculed by all who read it. Not a man in California—with the exception of Sutter and one or two of his intimates, who were understandably anxious not to spread the story—believed a word of it.

But the story got, somehow, to the east coast and there, for some reason, it was instantly believed. By this time the good ship *California* had already sailed from New York to inaugurate a mail service to the west coast. She was carrying cargo as well as mail, but her considerable passenger accommodation, perhaps because it was more expensive than the journey overland, was completely empty.

To the astonishment and delight of her master, she was besieged in Callao harbour, Peru, by thousands of men desperate to be taken to California: it was now December, 1848. All passenger accommodation was instantly filled.

A few weeks later, in January of the fateful 1849, she had reached Panama and more thousands besieged her. Somehow, three hundred of these were loaded on board, like cattle, some paying the fantastic figure of a thousand dollars for the journey north to San Francisco.

The owners of the *California* might have been feeling elation at this quick profit, but it would have been dampened on arrival at

San Francisco: entire crew, including officers, deserted and rushed inland, axes in hand.

Obviously one now needed money or influence, or both, to travel by sea. The great majority of hopeful prospectors from the east began to set off along the Oregon Trail. But these were, for the most part, greedy, hasty men who made inadequate preparation: by April, 20,000 of them were camped along the Missouri river, waiting for weather which would allow them to press westward. Morale was abundly high, the wagons, though empty of many items which would be needed, were painted brightly with legends like "Ho, for the diggings!" and some flew flags and were decked with streamers.

For many of these overland prospectors this silly season of waiting was to be almost the end. They set off in their hundreds, and their lack of adequate preparation was rewarded by, among other things, a terrifying epidemic. As one who survived was to put it: "The name of *cholera* in a multitude—unorganized and unnumbered—is like a leak in the bottom of a ship whose decks are thronged with passengers. The disturbed waters of the ocean, the angry elements of nature, when aroused to fury, are but faint illustrations of the terror-stricken mass of humanity, when in their midst are falling with great rapidity their comrades, the strong, the young and the old. All this filled our ranks with the utmost terror and gloom. This terrible malady seemed to spend its most deadly force on the flat prairie east of and about Fort Laramie.

"One of the most appalling effects of this disease was to cause the most devoted friends to desert, in case of attack, the fallen one. Many a stout and powerful man fought the last battle alone upon the prairie. When the rough hand of the cholera was laid upon families, they rarely had either the assistance or the sympathy of their neighbours or travelling companions.

"There was one feature mixed with all this terror that afforded some degree of relief, and that was that there was no case of lingering suffering. When attacked, a single day ordinarily ended the strife in death or recovery. A vast amount of wagons, with beds and blankets, were left by the roadside, which no man, not even an Indian, would approach or touch through fear of the unknown, unseen, destroyer.

"While there were sad instances of comrades deserting comrades in this hour of extreme trial, I cannot pass this point of my story without stating that there were many instances of heroic devotion to the sick, when such attention was regarded as almost equivalent to the offering up of the well and healthy for the mere hope of saving the sick and dying."

Of the 42,000 people who rushed headlong into California that year, 33,000 were Americans (the rest came from all parts of the world), and 25,000 of these travelled the Oregon Trail. This number must have far exceeded the sum total of earlier emigrations—and without cholera the figure would have been much higher still.

(But though the Oregon Trail was used, to the point at which one way branched southward into California, the vast majority of those using it went to the southern colony: gold had not yet been found in Oregon.)

Gold and the gold rush petered out and now the Trail began to support the amazing Pony Express mail service. Kit Carson had started off the first United States Overland Mail in September, 1846, but it was 1860 before the service became regular. Shortly after that it was supplanted, for urgent messages, by the new Overland Telegraph, and for bulkier matter—like passengers—by the Stage Coach.

By now, though there were occasional perils to be faced when travelling by Stage—Indians, buffalo and, during the Civil War, the occasional Confederate raider—the original hazards of the route had all but vanished. Soon the railway, which had been creeping from east and from west (and many feared might never meet, so eager was each team to lay track right across the continent) was complete. The history of the Oregon Trail was—almost—over.

Not quite. There were those unwilling or unable to pay the rail fare, and these continued in covered wagons. The numbers diminished and we have no record of when the last of these "prairie schooners" made its bumping way along the Trail, but we know that a number were still travelling it in the closing years of the last century.

The Trail was unique: it was the longest road in America, travelling areas of staggering diversity and, here and there, great natural hazard. Although it was the best route available, and the one the railway engineers, with their more sophisticated instruments and calculation, were to follow, it was bounded by treacherous, snow-capped mountains, crossed by rushing torrents and shrouded for mile after mile in dense prairie dust. Yet men persevered, in their thousands, forcing a way into this new and unknown land, opening it up, revealing it, as one of the brightest jewels of the North American continent.

And to this day we can be grateful to the thousand of men and women who risked and often lost their lives in the pursuit of a new and better one for their descendants. Without their courage, along the Oregon Trail, a great part of a great continent would still be unknown.

JOURNEY TO LHASA

Father Huc's Adventures in Tibet

IN JANUARY, 1846, two young French priests, Fathers Gabet and Father Huc, travelled to Lhasa in a caravanserai of Buddhist dignitaries, humbler lamas, Chinese merchants and soldiers, which came from Mongolia, from the north, to Tibet. All ways of reaching Tibet, whether through the Chinese province of Szechwan or from India across the Himalayas, are difficult and dangerous; the northern route particularly so, the mountains being nearly as high as the Himalayas, the desert plateau, swept by icy winds, of immense length.

When the two priests joined the caravanserai at the Koukou Nor, the Blue Lake, to the north of the mountain barrier which they had to cross into Tibet, they were told that they were hardly likely to survive the regours of the way. In the course of the journey more than forty men of the caravan were abandoned still living, without the slightest possibility of anyone aiding them. They were carried on horse-back or camel-back so long as any hope remained but, when they could no longer eat or speak or hold themselves up, they were left by the wayside. The general body of the caravan could not stay to nurse them. As a token of sympathy, a wooden cup and a small bag of barley meal were sometimes placed beside the frozen but still living man. Looking back, one could see the crows and vultures that hovered over the caravan pouncing down on the unhappy creature who retained just enough of life to feel himself torn and mangled by these birds of prey. Father Gabet nearly died during the journey, losing the use of his nose and his ears at one time for several days, and for a long while he travelled strapped to his camel, almost an inanimate object.

The last stage of the journey to Lhasa, which took some fifteen days, was more clement. There were legs of mutton to be bought and these, as Huc says, fortified their stomachs and invigorated their emaciated limbs. Just before reaching Lhasa the caravan halted to re-organize at a place called Pampou, in Tibet. Father Huc states: "We availed ourselves of the opportunity to arrange our toilet as well as we could. Our hair and beards were so thick, our faces so blackened with the smoke of the tent, so ploughed up with the cold, so worn, so deplorable that, when we had the means of looking at ourselves in a glass, we were ready to weep with compassion at our melancholy appearance. Our costume was perfectly in unison with our persons."

When they arrived at Lhasa, the two Frenchmen set off at once to find themselves a lodging. After some searching, they found two rooms in a large house which contained in all fifty lodgers. Their abode was at the top of the house and to reach it they had to ascend twenty-six wooden stairs without railings and so steep and narrow that in order to prevent breaking their necks they found it prudent to use hands as well as feet on the stairs. Their apartment was one great square room and one small closet which they honoured with the appellation of cabinet. The larger room was lighted on the north-east by a narrow window, provided with thick wooden bars and, above, by a small skylight which served for a variety of purposes. First, it gave entrance to the light, the wind, the rain and the snow; secondly, it gave issue to the smoke from their fire. To protect themselves from the winter's cold, the Tibetans place in the centre of their rooms a small vessel of glazed earth in which they burn dried dung. As this combustible diffuses more smoke than heat, those who desire to warm themselves found it advantageous to have a hole in the ceiling, which enables them to light a fire without incurring the risk of being stifled by the smoke. "We were thus," writes Father Huc, "placed at once on the full level of Tibetan civilization."

As can be seen, the two priests were not exactly well-breeched travellers. Enjoined by their ecclesiastical superiors to visit various scattered Christian communities in Mongolia, their travelling equipment, even their clothes, had been bought second-hand. Their guide, companion, cameleer and servant was a young Mongol convert called Samdadchiemba, one of whose characteristics was an unbounded faith in his own knowledge of geography, a faith which many times since they had left their small missionary settlement just outside Peking, had led them nearly to disaster, to nights on marshes or hillsides without water, having come many miles in the wrong direction.

It was their intense curiosity and their spirit of adventure rather than the direct orders of the Church which had led Huc and Gabet to decide that Lhasa, as the centre of Buddhist faith and knowledge for most of the Far East, was also the most appropriate place to found a new Christian centre. Indeed they were not experienced travellers nor even learned in the geography of the unknown regions through which they had travelled. But they had two assets. One was a knowledge of Chinese and of the language and dialects of Mongolia, and an acquaintance with Tibetan, even though in this last tongue they needed an interpreter to convey anything other than simple daily business. The other asset was that they were considered by the Mongols and Tibetans as lamas or holy men, not in fact different from other travelling Buddhist priests, and as worshippers of "the Lord of Heaven" to be helped and treated with respect. The gates of the lamaseries—the centres of civilization in Mongolia as the monasteries of northern Europe were in the Middle Ages—were open to them for repose, refreshment and study. Indeed they were treated on a par with the many holy wanderers they met with.

Huc describes these wandering lamas: "They spend their time vagabondizing about like birds of passage, travelling all over their own and adjacent countries and subsisting upon the rude hospitality which in lamasery or in tent they are sure to receive throughout their wandering way. They enter without ceremony, seat themselves, and while the tea is preparing for refreshment, give their host an account of the places they have visited in their rambles. If they think fit to sleep where they are, they stretch themselves on the floor and repose until the morning. After breakfast, they stand at the entrance to the tent and watch the clouds and see whence the wind blows; then they take their way no matter whither by this path or that, east or west, north or south as their fancy suggests. Sure of having no destination before them, they never lose their way. Travelling without any end in view, the places they reach are always those they sought. The story of the Wandering Jew who is forever a wanderer is exactly realized in these lamas. They seem influenced by some secret power which makes them wander ceaselessly from place to place. God seems to have infused into the blood which flows in their veins something of that motive power which propels them on their way without allowing them to stop."

The two Christian priests and their follower were not quite as aimless and abandoned to the wind that blows, but they were birds of a feather. They would undoubtedly have perished many times but for the fact that they appeared to be members of a familiar Mongol community, and they would certainly have died in the mountains and plateaux of northern Tibet if they had not been able to spend a fortnight in the great lamasery at Koumboum before starting on the last stage of their journey to Lhasa.

Huc and Gabet were by no means the first Europeans to have visited Tibet. Yet this mysterious country was, in the mid-nineteenth century, one of the least known parts of the globe, as it is still today. Their descriptions of Tibet and the Tibetans were far more vivid than those of their predecessors, so vivid indeed that, until later travellers confirmed what they wrote, it was considered a sort of fairy tale. Other travellers have looked at and lived with the Tibetans from a position of strangeness; these two, as men and brothers. Nor did the fact that Tibet was governed by a priestly caste and devoted so much of its human and material resources to religion appear curious to them. Constantly they refer to the close similarity between Buddhism and the Roman Catholic Church, and the theocratic system of the country ruled by the Dalai Lama was essentially similar to that of Europe in the Middle Ages and perhaps even to the Papal States of the nineteenth century. The forty-six days which the two priests spent in Lhasa were not to be without stresses and disappointments; but they were days of enchantment. They were *en rapport* with the spirit of Tibet from the beginning.

The first days were spent in exploring Lhasa. The principal streets they found were broad, well laid out and tolerably clean, at least when it did not rain. The suburbs were filthy. The houses were large, lofty and handsome in the centre of the town, built some with stone, some with brick and some with mud, but all so elaborately covered with limewash that there was no distinguishing the

319

kind of material. In one of the suburban districts the houses they saw were built with the horns of oxen and sheep.

They went to visit the palace of the Damai Lama which merited, they thought, the celebrity which it enjoys throughout the world. The Potala is perched on a great hill from which the Living Divinity could contemplate his innumerable adorers advancing along the plain or prostrate at the foot of the Divine Mountain. The Tibetans, they found, were always humming psalms or popular songs as they walked about the streets. "Generosity and frankness enter largely into their characters," Huc writes. "Cleanliness is of small estimation among them, but this does not prevent them from being very fond of display and rich, sumptuous clothing."

At the time Huc visited Lhasa the government had been much concerned about increasing immorality among the population of Lhasa. The Tibetan women submitted at that time to a custom that was probably unique and altogether incredible to those who have not actually witnessed the operation. Before going out of doors, they rubbed their faces over with a sort of black glutinous varnish not unlike currant jelly; the object was to render themselves as ugly and hideous as possible. They daubed this disgusting composition over every feature in such a manner as no longer to resemble human creatures. But it was not, Huc observed, unusual to meet in the streets women who set law and decency at defiance by actually having the impudence to show themselves in public with their faces unvarnished and such as nature made them. Such women, however, were obliged to take care to keep out of the way of the police.

After being in Lhasa a few days they decided they ought to present themselves to the authorities. They accordingly went to the chief of police and declared to him that they belonged to a great kingdom called France and that they had come to Tibet to preach the Christian religion, of which they were ministers. Huc writes: "The person to whom we made this declaration was cold and inpenetrable as became a bureaucrat. He phlegmatically drew his bamboo quill from behind his ear and began to write, without the slightest observation, what we had told him. He contented himself with repeating twice or thrice, between his teeth, the words 'France' and 'Christian Religion' like a man who does not know what you mean. When he had done writing be wiped his pen, still wet with ink, in his hair and replaced it behind his right ear, saying 'Yak Poze' (very well). 'Dwell in peace', we replied, and putting out our tongues at him, we left him, delighted at having placed ourselves on a proper footing." Putting out the tongue is the polite greeting in Tibet. From what they knew of the country already they were quite sure that as foreigners they would not suffer the many vexations which foreigners suffered in China. They felt that they were in a hospitable land and able to breathe a free air.

But they were not to be left alone. In their humble room they were visited first by an exquisitely dressed Chinese merchant who came to see, apparently, what they had to sell. The two priests were inclined to wish to sell their saddles, for which they thought they would have little further use. The first visitor was followed by four more, two Chinese and two Tibetan lamas. The visits were clearly a pretext to find out who they were. Then as they sat down to their dinner (from a pot in which a good cut of beef had been boiling for some time) they were summoned by the police to see the Regent of Tibet, the head of the council which governed the country in the name of the Dalai Lama.

They had to leave their dinner and go at once. The Regent gazed at them for a long while in silence, with minute attention. He turned his head alternately to the right and to the left and smiled at them in a half-mocking and half-friendly manner. This sort of pantomime appeared to them to be so funny that they could not help laughing. They said to each other in French: "This gentleman seems a good enough fellow, our affairs will be all right." The Regent asked in an affable voice what language they were speaking in and what they had said. The two priests told him and he laughed. "You are right," he said. "I am kind, for kindness is the duty of a nobleman. I must be kind towards my people and also towards strangers."

The Regent asked them a number of questions and appeared to be very little informed about where France was. He said "Can you write?" The Regent then asked them to write some words on a piece of paper which he gave them. "Write something," he said, "in your own language." Huc took the paper on his knee and wrote this sentence: "What avails it to man to conquer the whole world if he lose his soul." The Regent was very interested in the French characters and he asked for the translation of what they had written. When it had been translated to him he said: "I have not been deceived, you are obviously men of great knowledge. You express thoughts as profound as those we find in prayer books."

Even before their first talk with the Regent was over the Chinese

Ambassador, Ki Chan, arrived and demanded to see the two priests. Ki Chan's attitude was far from benevolent, though, in his dealings with them, he was invariably courteous. He was, however, determined that their stay in Lhasa should be short. It was Ki Chan who ordered that their luggage should be publicly examined, as was the practice in Tibet with foreigners, though not by any means usually observed. However, when it was found that they had maps in their possession—and the friendly Regent already charmed by his two visitors grew pale when the maps of China and Mongolia were produced—Ki Chan was fair enough, as a man of the world and acquainted with European affairs, to admit that these maps had been printed in France.

The line that Ki Chan took thereafter with the Regent was that the two missionaries, although clearly not spies, were in fact acting against the laws of the Emperor of China and of the Dalai Lama in trying to convert the Tibetans to a new faith. Ki Chan argued that their avowed purpose was to substitute their religious belief for Buddhism. What would become of the Dalai Lama, he asked, when he had no worshippers? The introduction into the country of the religion of the Lord of Heaven would lead directly to the destruction of the Lama hierarchy and of the Tibetan government. The Regent did not agree. He maintained that the presence of the two priests in Lhasa could not in any way be prejudical to the Tibetan government. If the doctrines which these men held were false, he argued, the Tibetans would not embrace them. If, on the contrary, they were true, what had they to fear? How could truth be prejudicial to men? Can we, he asked, make ourselves guilty of an actual and certain injustice towards these travellers through an imaginary fear of some possible evil to come?

Ki Chan was, one imagined, amused at the *naïveté* of the Regent. He himself was simply determined to expel the two Christians because the laws of China were at that time directed against Christian missionary efforts and particularly French ones. It was an interesting sidelight on the relations between Tibet and China at that time that Ki Chan had his way and the two priests, almost to the chagrin of the Regent, though no doubt he was secretly relieved, resolved that they would depart voluntarily. Ki Chan refused to allow them to use the road to the south, to India, but said that they would travel in the greatest comfort with a mandarin and a Chinese escort back to China by the shortest eastern route to Szechwan.

For the fortnight in which they remained, the Regent's friendship for the two travellers made their stay in Lhasa agreeable and useful; but their very success–they were allowed to open a chapel in a small house which the Regent had put at their disposal–made their forced departure the more bitter. The Regent provided them with a tutor to learn Tibetan. He was very fond of talking about France and asked a number of questions about the manners, customs and productions of the country. He was told about steamboats, railways, balloons, gas, telegraphs, industrial production: all this amazed him.

Huc had with him a microscope. Whilst adjusting the instrument, he tried to give the Regent some notions about optics but, seeing that the theory did not excite much enthusiasm, he proceeded at once to practise. Huc asked if one of the company would be kind enough to provide a louse. The article, says Huc, was easier to find than a butterfly. A noble lama, secretary to the Regent, had merely to put his hand under his silk dress, to his armpit, and an extremely vigorous louse was put on the plate of the microscope. When it was seized with the nippers, the lama opposed this proceeding and insisted upon putting a stop to the experiment on the ground that they were going to cause the death of a living being. The Regent had no such strong religious scruples and told the lama to be quiet and to allow the experiment to proceed. The louse was fixed in the microscope and Huc then asked the Regent to apply his right eye, shutting his left, to the glass at the top of the machine. "Heavens above", exclaimed the Regent, "the louse is as big as a rat." After looking at it for a moment he raised his head and hid his face with both hands, saying it was horrible to look at. He tried to dissuade the others from examining it, but did not succeed. Everybody in his turn looked through the microscope and started back with cries of horror. The lama secretary, seeing that his little animal scarcely moved, advanced a claim in its favour. The nippers were taken off and the louse fell into the hands of its owner. Alas, the poor victim did not move. The Regent said laughingly to his secretary, "I think your louse is unwell; go and see if you can get it to take some physic, otherwise it will not recover."

The Regent had arranged for the two priests to go to the Potala and to see the Dalai Lama. They were on the point of making this visit when an alarm was started that the Dalai Lama might be given the smallpox. This illness had in fact just manifested itself at Lhasa and the people declared that it had been brought from Peking by the great caravan which had arrived some time before with the two priests. The Tibetans had a particular fear of smallpox. They never mentioned its name even without a sort of stupor, as though they were speaking of the greatest scourge that could possibly afflict mankind.

The day came for departure. They were to travel with an official escort under the orders of an elderly military mandarin called The Pacificator of Kingdoms, whose premature senility was the result not, as they supposed at first, of opium but of brandy. He was going back to China for good, and the travellers witnessed his farewell to his wife. A strong-limbed Tibetan female, very fairly dressed, she presented herself just before the party rode off. The Pacificator of Kingdoms had been married to her for six years and was about to leave her for ever; he had only one child by her which had died in its infancy. As these two conjugal halves were never again to see each other it was but natural that at the moment of such a separation there should be a few words of adieu. The thing was publicly done and in the following manner, as Huc writes: "'We are going to part,' said the husband. 'Do you stay here and sit quietly in your room'. 'Go in peace,' replied the wife. 'Go home in peace and take care of the swellings in your legs.' She put her hand before her eyes to make believe she was crying. 'Look here,' said The Pacificator of Kingdoms. 'They are odd people these Tibetan women. I leave her a well-built house and plenty of furniture, almost new, and yet she is going to cry. She is not content.'"

The way back to China was through a far less deserted country than the road from Mongolia and they often lodged in comparative comfort in inns. They neither starved nor went without drink. But in certain parts it was an excessively dangerous road. The most difficult section was about half-way, once the highest mountains had been passed. Travellers were obliged to pass between two enormous walls of vertical rock and to pass by following, at a great height, a very narrow ledge, so narrow that the horses frequently found only just enough room to plant their feet.

Huc writes: "As soon as we saw the oxen of the caravan making their way along this horrible path and heard the low roar of the waters rising from the depths of the gulfs, we were seized with fear and dismounted but everyone told us immediately to remount saying that the horses, accustomed to the journey, had surer feet than we; and that we must let them go their own way, contenting ourselves with keeping firmly in our stirrups and not looking about us. We recommended ourselves to God and followed in the wake of the columns. We were soon convinced that in point of fact it would have been impossible for us to keep our equilibrium on this slippery and rugged surface. It seemed as though at every moment an invisible force was drawing us towards the bottomless abyss. In case we should get giddy we kept our heads turned towards the mountain, the declivity of which was sometimes so perpendicular that it did not even offer a ledge for the horses to plant their feet on. In some places we passed over large trunks of trees supported by piles fixed horizontally in the mountainside. At the very sight of these frightful bridges we felt a cold perspiration running from all our limbs. It was essential however to advance, for to return or to dismount were two things beyond possibility."

It took two days before they at length got clear of this route, the most dreadful and dangerous imaginable. On hearing that the caravan had passed without any loss of life, a local Head Man expressed his opinion that the caravan had been stupendously fortunate. The Pacificator of Kingdoms then admitted that he had never passed this defile without witnessing frightful accidents.

After thirty-six days of travelling from Lhasa they had arrived at Tsiamido, still in Tibet but where the Chinese maintained a military mission. There were still mountains to cross. The Pacificator of Kingdoms fell seriously ill. The fatigues of the journey had made his legs swell so he could not mount or dismount. The physicians and sorcerers whom he consulted at Tsiamido said that he ought to continue his journey in a palanquin. A Chinese mandarin offered to sell him one and to engage the carriers for it. The advice was good but the Pacificator of Kingdoms protested that he could not afford such a thing and so he travelled on horseback in spite of his discomfort. However, the going was too rough for him and before they reached the town of Lithang, where there were a number of celebrated lamaseries, the poor mandarin died. His place was taken by a civilian mandarin, one with only an inferior White Button. "A young man of a puny stunted person," says Huc, "all pointed, smiling face with a shrill treble voice and trifling manners which gave him the air of a shop boy and not in the least like a proper mandarin." He was a prodigious talker and the two priests at first found him amusing but later rather boring.

Towards the Chinese the two Frenchmen adopted a quite different method of speaking than to the Tibetans. To the latter they were extremely polite and friendly; with the former, they found that it was better to be very much on your dignity and rather demanding. Shortly before the end of the journey they insisted on travelling in palanquins since their legs really would go no farther on horseback. So finally it was in a palanquin that they were conveyed, at the public expense, to the capital of the province of Szechwan where, by order of the Emperor, they found they were to undergo a solemn judgment before the Grand Mandarins of the Celestial Empire. This ordeal they surmounted, triumphantly even, and left behind them an atmosphere of goodwill. They then travelled across China to Macao, arriving there in the early part of October, 1846. Both died comparatively young as a consequence of their long, painful but infinitely rewarding odyssey, rewarding both to them and also to us.

JOURNEY UP THE AMAZON

The Experiences of Henry Walter Bates

A NATIVE of Leicester, Henry Walter Bates was educated at Creaton's boarding school, Billesden, which he left at the early age of thirteen to work as a hosier's apprentice. Thereafter he was self-educated.

Even as a boy he displayed a more than ordinary interest in insects. He had put together an impressive collection and had already read extensively about the subject when he met Alfred Russel Wallace, an English master at the Collegiate School in Leicester, who was also a keen entomologist. The two enthusiasts became firm friends, and when Wallace proposed a joint expedition up the Amazon to study the natural history of the region, Bates accepted with alacrity.

They sailed from Liverpool in a small trading steamer towards the end of April, 1848. Wallace was to return four years later, deeply disappointed because most of his collections were lost in a shipwreck. Bates was destined to stay away for an additional seven years and to bring back with him about fifteen thousand species, nearly half of which were new to science. He suffered many setbacks and his health was adversely affected, but his account of his travels, *The Naturalist on the River Amazon,* remains one of the durable monuments of English descriptive literature.

The first thing that struck Bates about the Amazon was its sheer immensity. Even seventy miles inland at Pará (Belem), where his series of journeys really started, the river was twenty miles wide. In view of the possibilities of exploration in the immediate neighbourhood, it is not surprising that Bates made Pará his headquarters for the next three years.

The two naturalists stepped ashore into the hot moist air of Pará on 28 May. Bates's impressions of the city itself were favourable. White, red-tiled houses, picturesque religious buildings, palm trees, a vivid blue sky, all these contributed to the cheerful aspect of the great Brazilian seaport. It was only later that he noticed the human poverty, the indolence and general seediness, the swampy patches and unweeded areas.

But for two or three days it was a question of getting all the baggage and equipment ashore, for practical entomologists require more than the average amount of gear. During this period and for a further couple of weeks they stayed at a friend's country house, and while they were settling in they walked round the suburbs, especially where they merged into the forest that hems in Pará. There they saw green parakeets, vultures, finches, tanagers and fly-catchers. They found the lizards unpleasant, but admired the exquisite butterflies. They were most fascinated, however, by the ants, some of which were over an inch long, and devoted several hours to a close study of the Saüba ant, the scourge of Brazil. In his book Bates describes how these pests operate in columns, robbing valuable trees of their leaves and making agriculture almost impossible. Even more active at night, they march into houses and bear away precious foodstuffs from store rooms.

Then Bates and his companion moved into a rented house in the village of Nazareth, just beyond the city limits and close to the forest. For several months they were busy with their ornithological and entomological researches, collecting specimens and compiling notes. In August they shipped their collections to England and began their preparations for a journey up the River Tocantins. The third largest of the rivers that form the Amazon system, the Tocantins flows roughly south from Pará for a distance of fourteen-hundred miles to its source in the Sierra des Pyreneos. They proposed to explore as far as Arroyos. Beyond that point a number of cataracts discouraged navigation.

The vessel they hired for the trip was a specially large canoe with two masts, a flat prow and a particularly broad beam that would enable her to survive rough seas. They took aboard enough food for three months, made sure their papers were in order, and with a crew of four set sail on the evening of 26 August, 1848. A stiff breeze and a fast tide carried them along at a good pace for roughly five or six miles. They dropped anchor when the tide turned, curled up on mats under the arched awnings fitted to the *vigilinga* and slept till sunrise.

They glided with the tide along the bay of Goajará and by midday had entered the Mojú, a river about the size of the Thames. Sometimes rowing, sometimes relying on the wind, they eventually swung into an artificial canal that linked the Mojú with a tributary of the Tocantins. Winding their way through a maze of narrow channels, they at last burst into the "Great River", as one of the crew called it. At the point where they emerged, the Tocantins was so wide that they could only just make out the far shore.

The crew rowed across to an island and there they landed to make tea and relax under tall palm trees with huge fan-shaped leaves. "The crowns, which were densely packed together at an immense height overhead," writes Bates, "shut out the rays of the sun; and the gloomy solitude beneath, through which the sound of our voices seemed to reverberate, could be compared to nothing so well as a solemn temple."

At midnight, when the tide was running favourably, they sailed slantwise across the river and eight hours later the *vigilinga* arrived at Cametá, an important town on the left bank of the Tocantins. Situated as it was on fairly high ground, Cametá offered a splendidly panoramic view of the river and its many palm-covered islands, of the tiny bays and creeks and sandy beaches. The beauty of the place was such that within a year Bates was back again.

This first visit, however, proved a short one. The party left the same day (30 August) making for Vista Alegre, a Brazilian planter's residence fifteen miles south of Cametá. As they were asked to stay there for two days, they had a splendid opportunity to comb the neighbouring forest for birds and insects not found at Pará.

When they left there was very little wind, so the men had to row. Bates observed that although the houses along the banks were all supported on piles, at high water the river still reached floor level. Their owners, however, did not appear to worry about the possibilities of flooding. They were cheerful, healthy people, but lazy and poor. Most of them were content to scrape along with a bare livelihood. All they asked of life was an undisturbed independence.

329

On 3 September they reached Baiao, a small fishing village of about four hundred inhabitants. As the mud-plastered, palm-thatched huts were perched on a high bluff, they had to climb a long ladder fixed against the river bank. Once again the travellers were struck by the unhurrying easy-going attitude of the villagers. The doors and windows of their houses gave on to the street and were a constant invitation to people to wander in and out as they pleased. There was nothing offensive about these intrusions. The callers were simply being sociable.

From Baiao they sailed to a creek with a wide stretch of beach where hundreds of sandpipers were running around. One of the Indians, an expert hunter named Alexandro, went ashore with Bates, and before they had gone very far they came across the spoor of a jaguar in the sand. By following a turtle's tracks they also found a nest from which they collected over a hundred eggs. After taking a quick swim, Bates was startled to see an alligator emerge from the water at the very spot where he had been bathing.

After a brief halt at a tiny settlement called Patos they crossed the river to Trocará, a delightful encampment occupied by half-breeds who had come from Cametá, eighty miles away, to fish and laze about during the summer months. Hunting and fishing supplied their daily wants and the weather was always sunny. The men "sometimes collect a little Indiarubber, salsaparilla, or copaiba oil, to sell to traders on their return; the women assist in paddling the canoes, do the cooking, and sometimes fish with rod and line". Bates remarked that this custom of setting out annually on a sort of protracted picnic was popular throughout the province.

The expedition sailed on, drawing closer and closer to the cataracts near Arroyos. After occasional halts for sightseeing ashore, they could take their large craft no farther because of the rapids. Anchoring the *vigilinga* near an island, they made their approach in a smaller vessel they had borrowed. From time to time they had to drag the canoe over tumbled masses of rocks and other obstacles. For ten hours they proceeded in this manner until at four o'clock in the afternoon they arrived at Arroyos, a staging-place for men travelling between Pará and the mining districts of the interior. They landed, had a meal and then battled against the dangerous currents as far the first cataract. Climbing to the top of a mound, they could see the angry waterfall cascading down a steep slope, swirling round huge boulders and crashing with a deafening roar into the furious waters below.

They made their way to the *vigilinga* early in the morning of 17 September. Controlling the light canoe with their paddles only, the crew raced down the swift river, shooting the rapids with great dexterity in spite of eddies and whirlpools. They transferred to the bigger boat and started their return journey to Pará. As they had done on the ascent, they made frequent landings, thus enabling Bates and Wallace to make their observations and add considerably to their collections of birds, insects and shells.

There was one memorable evening spent with other visitors in a large riverside residence. As there were no chairs or tables, meals were served on a mat on the floor and the guests squatted round and helped themselves. There were no beds either, so everybody used hammocks. For hours they lay there in the glow of the wood fire, telling stories and describing personal experiences. One old man employed expressive mime to overcome the language barrier when he was relating how he killed a jaguar. He jumped out of his hammock, "seized a bow and a large *taquará* arrow to show how he slew the beast, imitated its hoarse growl, and danced about the fire like a demon".

Then, on 26 September, they were clear of the islands and watching the dolphins roll in the broad mouth of the Tocantins. For the past day or two flocks of frigate birds had been wheeling overhead, a sure sign that they were in the river's lower reaches. Once again they wound their way through the labyrinth of channels between the "Great River" and the Mojú, and four days later they sailed into Pará.

After a couple of minor trips on his own to Cametá and Caripí, Bates spent three months in Pará and then set out on another journey into the interior. On 5 September, 1849, he sailed from his base in a trading schooner with the intention of staying for a time at some village on the northern shore of the Lower Amazon. He took with him such essentials as cooking utensils, crockery, cutlery, ammunition and such food items as would not be available where he was going. Because he was hoping to find new and interesting specimens for his collections, he also included plenty of store-boxes and his natural history books. Luco, "a short, fat, yellow-faced boy", who had worked for him before in Pará, went along as Bates's servant.

The owner of the schooner, who was obviously not in any hurry, began by putting in at Cametá, his native town, where he visited friends and relations and had a good time ashore. Taking advantage of a strong evening breeze, the schooner moved on twelve days later and sailed without incident until early on 24 September. The forty-ton vessel passed Entre-as-Ilhas on the morning tide and then attempted the fifteen-mile crossing to the eastern shore, a passage fraught with danger owing to the extensive shoals and fresh wind that had sprung up. The ship rolled and pitched all the way, but at length she was in safer waters and heading westwards along the southern coast of the island of Marajó.

A day's sailing brought them to the River Breves, and they sighted the village of the same name during the afternoon of the following day. From then on, until they joined the Amazon proper, their course lay through an intricate series of channels. The narrower ones, less than a hundred yards wide, were flanked by forest trees towering up to eighty feet or so. Slowly they advanced along the Jaburú and Macaco channels, past a cluster of islands, and round about midnight on 3 October the schooner was bounding forward before a spanking breeze. Although the stream they were on was at least two miles in width, it was only a minor branch of the mighty Amazon. The river's total breadth thereabouts was no less than twenty miles, but a number of large islands divides it into three separate water courses.

Bates was given a chance to land at Gurupá village and have a quick look at the plant life and glossy blue butterflies of that region. Then, after passing the mouth of the Xingú, another long tributary of the Amazon, they had to weather a sudden storm that lasted only half an hour and soon afterwards found themselves becalmed. For two days they endured the suffocating heat, waiting for the trade-wind to blow again. Unfortunately, when it *did* return it drove the schooner aground on a lee shore. It was an unnerving experience that might have ended disastrously if the bottom had not been of soft mud. Only by the combined efforts of crew and passengers did they manage to haul themselves clear.

For the next hundred and thirty miles they followed the southern coast as far as Santarem, a pleasant town of about 2,500 inhabitants just inside the mouth of the Tapajos. Its air of prosperity could be attributed to its advantageous situation, four hundred miles inland and yet accessible to big ships from the Atlantic. During his brief spell there Bates made a few inquiries about Obydos, another fifty miles up-river. The information he received convinced him that a prolonged stay there would be advisable. Consequently, when the schooner put in at Obydos a day later, he had all his luggage and equipment taken ashore and arranged to spend five or six weeks in what proved to be one of the most agreeable towns on the river. The old-established families who lived there entertained him lavishly. There was little in the forests to interest the ornithologist, but the many varieties of monkey and the rich diversity of insect life kept Bates fully occupied.

When Bates heard that a trader from Obydos intended sailing as far as the Rio Negro with frequent stops on the way, he lost no time in obtaining a passage. They left Obydos on 19 November pursued by a light wind, moving along steadily past wildly desolate scenery until darkness began to descend. Under no circumstances would the owner of the boat sail at night. He made fast to a tree at about nine o'clock, hammocks were slung on deck and everybody slept till dawn.

Apart from a violent squall on the 22nd, they proceeded in this manner until there was a welcome break in routine at Villa Nova, a little village of seventy houses, mostly mud huts, and there they stayed for four days. Naturally Bates explored the area as extensively as possible, noting among other things plenty of flowering shrubs and small attractive butterflies. He also found a forest pool swarming with water-fowl and fringed with tall trees harbouring macaws, canaries, hawks and eagles. Once when returning home he heard a pattering noise close to him, coming from the ground. He looked down and "a heavy gliding motion betrayed a large serpent making off almost from beneath my feet". It was his first rattlesnake.

The trading ship resumed her journey, sailed past a big island, lingered ten days at a settlement where Bates attended a festival in honour of Our Lady of Conception, hurried through a mosquito-infested area, and reached Serpa in time for the Christmas celebrations. Then, on beyond the mouth of the Amazon's greatest tributary, the Madeira, a river two thousand miles in length, until on 8 January they anchored off Matarí, a depressing little place with no more than twenty mud huts, occupied by ignorant and untrustworthy Múra Indians.

Shortly after leaving Matarí, in pelting rain, they called at several riverside settlements for trading purposes. Despite the inclement weather, Bates never failed to study the birds and insects in the boundless forests. Advancing in this way they gradually drew nearer to the mouth of the Rio Negro, completing the last few miles under full sail to take advantage of a brisk east wind. They crossed the river (to Barra Manáos), the end of the voyage as far as the Obydos trader was concerned.

Wallace, who had been exploring in that district, had arrived at Barra three weeks previously. The two friends enjoyed their daily rambles in the surrounding forest and were made extremely comfortable in the well-run town, but it was not long before they were again restless to see more of the Amazon and its natural wonders. They finally agreed that Wallace would explore the River Negro, while Bates would go up the River Solimoens as far as Ega, the first important town on that lengthy continuation of the Upper Amazon.

All the specimens he had collected between Pará and the Rio Negro Bates shipped back to Pará. He himself embarked on 26 March, 1850, in a *cuberta*, a type of large canoe, that was bound for Ega and was crewed by ten hard-working Cucáma Indians. They were on their way back from Santarem, where they had been delivering a cargo of turtle oil and were eager to return to their wives and families. They left at eight in the evening, pulling smoothly at the oars (all except one who was lying on the wet boards dead drunk after a mild debauch in Barra).

On a calm clear night they made good time across the wide mouth of the Rio Negro and on the following morning were maintaining a steady speed along the left bank of the Solimoens. Bates could not evoke any enthusiasm for the uninspiring scenery they were passing. The rainy season had begun and most low-lying areas were already under water. Uprooted trees and all manner of floating plants were swept along by the swift current. The immediate prospect was unutterably miserable. Furthermore, they were tormented during the daytime by the *motúca*, a bigger and more formidable fly than the mosquito. Then again the sultry atmosphere was unhealthily oppressive, especially after the comparatively dry, airy conditions Bates had known on the Lower Amazon.

The outlook became even more monotonous after passing Manacápurú, where many citizens from Barra had built country houses on the high rocky bank. Once this straggling settlement had been left behind, they travelled nineteen days through flat, featureless country without glimpsing a single human dwelling. As was the custom on such voyages, everybody had brought his own provisions, but more often than not it was a case of share and share alike. The crew took it in turns to fish and added anything they caught to the common larder. One day they harpooned a manatee, or sea-cow, about ten feet long. Bates could not stomach the greenish-coloured fat. The lean meat, he wrote, "had the taste of very coarse pork".

One morning he saw a most unusual sight. Heralded by a terrifying series of explosions, rather like peals of thunder, a *terra cahida*, or landslip, suddenly started about three miles away on the other side of the river. Over a distance of nearly two miles, "large masses of forest, including trees of colossal size, probably 200 feet in height, were rocking to and fro, and falling headlong one after the other into the water". Bates had heard the first crash just before dawn. The destruction was still going on two hours later.

On 30 April they reached the mouth of the Teffé, a smooth dark-water river mercifully free from pests, and next day Bates landed in Ega. He was at a point more than half-way across the South American continent. He was also in the town that was to be his headquarters for four and a half years.

He first made it his business to meet Ega's principal residents, the *Delegado* of police, the military commandant, his fashionable wife Donna Anna, an almost pure-blooded Indian vicar, a Director of Indians, and a wise old native merchant who was prepared to place his house and store at Bates's disposal. The naturalist, however, moved into a small dry cottage, reserving the best room for his workshop and study.

Once he was installed he settled down to a regular routine. He would rise with the sun, bathe in the river, spend five or six hours hunting specimens in the forest, and then from three in the afternoon until six he would concentrate on preparing and ticketing his collections and on bringing his notes up to date. Outside his normal working hours he could always find suitable diversions. There were parties, dancing, festivals, processions and occasional masquerades. The local inhabitants enjoyed merry-making, basing their recreational activities on a strange mixture of Indian and Portuguese religious rites.

But Bates's journeyings were far from over. First of all, because he fell ill he had to go back to Pará. After he had recovered he made Santarem his base for three and a half years during which period he explored the not easily navigable Tapajos. Then he returned to Ega and went on a series of short trips to examine the natural phenomena within striking distance of the town. He saw turtle pools in the forest, admired the skill of Indians netting an alligator, tasted the fruit of the giant *Pupunha* tree, listened to the reedy notes of cicadas, caught his first glimpse of the rare umbrella bird, watched the poisonous sap ooze from the bark of the *Assacú* tree.

On other excursions he studied the habits of monkeys, vampire bats, birds and insects. Then, going farther afield, he travelled two hundred and forty miles to Tunantins, a village of about twenty mud huts surrounded by swamps, and spent nineteen days there in search of new specimens. From Tunantins a trading schooner took him to the mouth of the Sapó and Bates visited a number of Indian settlements in the neighbourhood. He spent six weeks at Fonte Boa, the headquarters of mosquitoes, and on 5 September, 1857, he sailed nearly three hundred miles to St. Paulo de Olivença, a primitive village occupied by half-castes and Tucúna or Collína Indians. He stayed there five months, but if he had stayed five years he would not have exhausted the wealth of zoological and botanical treasures in that locality.

Bates would certainly have journeyed even farther west, but over-work, excessive exposure to the tropical sun, coupled with the indifferent food he had so often been obliged to swallow, eventually shattered his health. He returned to Ega, where he rested for a while, but he never recovered sufficiently to resume his investigations. He had to go back to Pará and there, on 2 June, 1859, he boarded the North American trading-ship, *Frederick Demming*, and on the following day, as the vessel headed seawards, he looked for the last time at the vast forest where his journeyings had started and ended.

For eleven years Henry Walter Bates had been travelling through "a magnificent wilderness, where civilized man has, as yet, scarcely obtained a footing". His dream of penetrating as far as the foot of the Andes would never be realized, for now it was farewell to what had surely been for Bates a naturalist's paradise, a land of perpetual summer.

WITH BURKE AND WILLS

Pioneers Across Australia

FLOUNDERING ACROSS the marshland went the two white men, dragging their poor horse behind them. Slithering on the sticky clay, knee-deep in water, falling into holes and clutching at the occasional tufts of grass to extricate themselves, they struggled on and on. Now they came to a pebbly ridge, and here the going was better. There were traces of a track made by the blackfellows' naked feet, and they followed this until they came to a small clearing in which a camp-fire was smouldering. As they drew near, a blackfellow who had been coiled up on the ground, his gin and picaninny (woman and child) beside him, got up to stretch his legs. He caught sight of them, stared at them in amazement, then dropped on his haunches and, accompanied by his jabbering companions, shuffled away into the undergrowth.

Still the two white men pushed ahead until they emerged at length from the scrub. They reached a strip of higher ground, and from there looked across an apparently limitless marsh. Water lapped round their ankles. They dipped their hands in it, and raised some to their lips. Brackish. Too salt to drink... They strained their eyes to see what lay beyond the marsh, but the only things that caught their gaze were hundreds of wild geese, plover and pelicans enjoying themselves in the water-courses. Again they raised the brackish water to their lips, and still they gazed north-wards. They knew what lay out there, even though they could not see it. Almost they could hear its waves beating on the shore, they felt the sea-breezes ruffling through their hair. The sea-birds rose into the air with frightened flapping of wings. Yes, there was no doubt about it. They had done it, done what they had been sent out to do, all those many weary months before, at the farther end of those two or three thousand miles of struggle and striving, hard-ship and danger, burning sun and dreadful thirst. As they stood there, they had the exultation of tremendous achievement. Although they could not catch even a glimpse of the ocean which lay only a mile or two beyond them, they had not the least doubt that they had accomplished the great object of their mission–that they were the first to have managed to cross the Australian continent from south to north.

The water – tidal water – lapped about their feet. The birds went on feeding. With one last look northwards, the two men–haggard, travel-worn, emaciated, desperately weary–turned in their tracks and set out along the way they had come, the way that led to the "home" they would never reach . . .

Our story opens in Melbourne, on a day in August, 1860, when an expedition of ten Europeans and three Indian sepoys, with horses and camels (brought over specially from India), and equipped with everything else that was considered necessary, set out on the long trail northwards. The leader of the expedition was one Robert O'Hara Burke, an Irishman born in 1821 in Co. Galway, who had commenced his career as a military cadet at Woolwich Academy, but who when still hardly more than a youth had joined a regiment of Hungarian hussars in the Austrian service. When this was disbanded in 1848 he obtained an appointment in the Royal Irish Constabulary, but in 1853 exchanged this for one in the police force of the Australian colony of Victoria.

When the Crimean War broke out he had hastened back to England in the hope of obtaining a commission and seeing active service, but arriving too late he had returned to the Victorian police, in which he was now an inspector. When the Philosophical Institute of Victoria, spurred on by reports of exploring expeditions sent out by some of the other Australian colonies, resolved on des-patching an expedition into the unknown heart of the immense continent, Burke seemed just the man to lead it, so full of daring was he, possessed of such an adventurous spirit, experienced in leadership and full of resource.

Second-in-command of the expedition was William John Wills, a native of Totnes in Devonshire, and a former student of medicine at St. Bartholomew's Hospital in London. When the news of the great gold discoveries in Australia reached England he had set out in 1852 for "down under". He practised for some years at Ballarat, but his tastes leaning towards astronomy and meteorology he was appointed to the staff of the Surveyor-General in Melbourne. The committee in charge of the arrangements thought that he would be very suitable for the scientific side of the expedition, and indeed he proved an excellent choice. Among the other members of the little band were a former seafaring man named Gray, and John King, who had served in the army in India.

The instructions given to Burke by the Exploration Committee were expressed in very general terms, and indeed in the then state of knowledge they could not be otherwise. He was "to explore the interior of Australia". A district known as Cooper's Creek, far to the west of the Darling river, which had been reached by the explorer Charles Sturt in 1845, was suggested to him as the most suitable base of operations, and he was to form a depot there and make arrengements for keeping open a channel of communication with Melbourne. He should thence explore the country intervening between it and the track that had been followed by Ludwig Leichhardt, another of the great pioneers of Australian discovery, who in 1843–45 had conducted an expedition from Moreton Bay, near Brisbane, to the Gulf of Carpentaria. (In 1847, it may be added, Leichhardt had again left Moreton Bay, this time in an attempt to cross the continent from east to west, and nothing was heard of him after April, 1848.) Very sensibly, however, the Exploration Committee stated that the details of the route would be left to Burke himself, and he was entrusted with "the largest discretion as regards the forming of depots, and your movements generally, but it is requested that you will mark your routes as permanently as possible, by leaving records, sowing seeds, building cairns, and marking trees at as many points as possible..."

Leaving the Royal Park at Melbourne on 20 August, 1860, the expedition reached Menindie, in New South Wales, on 23 September, and here Burke established his first depot. About a month later they moved on, under the guidance of a Mr. Wright, who had been for three years in charge of a cattle station on the Darling and professed to have a good knowledge of the country. They arrived at Torowoto, about two hundred miles farther on, and there Wright left them on 31 October, with instructions "to return to Menindie, and bring up the stores (that had been left there) as rapidly as possible to Cooper's Creek".

Again the march was resumed, and Burke kept a careful record of the camps they formed as they went along. On 11 November they were in the Cooper's Creek district. They travelled slowly down the creek, in order to preserve the strength of the animals, and on 20 November established Camp 63. But after a fortnight they were "driven out by the rats", and moved to Camp 65, where Burke established a permanent depot. "The feed upon this creek is good," wrote Burke in his despatch written on 13 December, "and the horses and camels have greatly improved in condition; but the flies, mosquitoes, and rats which abound here render it a very disagreeable summer residence. From Camp 63 we made very frequent excursions, in order to endeavour, in accordance with instructions, to find a practicable route northward... but without success. Mr. Wills, upon one occasion, travelled ninety miles to the north, without finding water, when his camels escaped, and he and the man who accompanied him were obliged to return on foot, which they accomplished in forty-eight hours. Fortunately, upon their return, they found a pool of water. The three camels have not been recovered... I am satisfied that a practicable route cannot be established in that direction, except during the rainy season, or by sinking wells, as the natives have lately abandoned that part of the country for want of water..." In these circumstances, Burke decided to divide his party into two. He himself would push on with Wills, King, and Gray, while the rest should remain behind under the command of Mr. Brahé. The course of events may be followed from the notebooks that were kept by Mr. Wills.

"*Sunday, 16 December, 1860.* We started at 6.40 a.m., for Eyre's Creek, the party consisting of Mr. Burke, myself, King, and Charley (Gray), having with us six camels, one horse, and three months' provisions. We followed down the creek to the point where the sandstone ranges cross the creek... Down to this point the banks of the creek are very rugged and stony, but there is a tolerable supply of grass and salt bush in the vicinity. A large tribe of blacks came pestering us to go to their camp and have a dance, which we declined. They were very troublesome, and nothing but the threat to shoot them will keep them away; they are, however, easily frightened, and although fine-looking men, decidedly not of a warlike disposition. They show the greatest inclination to take whatever they can, but will take no unnecessary risk in so doing. They seldom carry any weapons, except a shield and a kind of boomerang, which I believe they use for killing rats, etc.

Wednesday, 19 December. Started at a quarter-past eight a.m., leaving what seemed to be the end of Cooper's Creek ... At fifteen miles we halted, where two large plains joined ... Finding two or three water-holes of good milky water, we camped for the night. This enabled me to obtain an observation of the eclipse of Jupiter's satellite ...

Thursday, 20 December. We did not leave this camp till half-past eight, having delayed to refill the water-bags with the milky water, which all of us found to be a great treat again. There was a large camp of forty or fifty blacks near where we stopped. They brought us presents of fish, for which we gave them some beads and matches ...

Monday, 24 December. We took a day of rest on Gray's Creek, to celebrate Christmas ... Our camp was really an agreeable place ...

Saturday, 5 January, 1861. On leaving Camp 84 ... we came to a creek with a long, broad, shallow water-hole. The well-worn paths, the recent track of natives, and the heaps of shells, on the contents of which the latter had feasted, showed at once that this creek must be connected with some creek of considerable importance. The camels and horses being greatly in need of rest, we only moved up about half a mile, and camped for the day."

So the entries in Wills's Diary or Field Books continue all through January, and then we come to the first entry for February, 1861, contained in Fieldbook No. 9, when they thought they were "almost there".

"Finding the ground in such a state from the heavy falls of rain that the camels could scarcely be got along, it was decided to leave them at Camp 119, and for Mr. Burke and I to proceed towards the sea on foot. After breakfast we accordingly started, taking with us the horse and three days' provisions. Our first difficulty was in crossing Billy's Creek, which we had to do where it enters the river, a few hundred yards below the camp. In getting the horse in here, he got bogged in a quicksand bank so deeply as to be unable to stir, and we only succeeded in extricating him by undermining him on the creek side, and then lunging him into the water. Having got all the things in safely, we continued down the river bank... A great deal of the land was so soft and rotten that the horse, with only a saddle and about twenty-five pounds on his back, could scarcely walk over it. At a distance of about five miles, we again had him bogged in crossing a small creek, after which he seemed so weak that we had great doubts about getting him on. We, however, found some better ground close to the water's edge... and soon came on some table-land where the soil is shallow and gravelly, and clothed with box and swamp gums..."

A few hours later, and they had arrived at the place already described. (It was the estuary of the Flinders river, that runs into the Gulf of Carpentaria.) The tidal waters—the sea-birds—the smell of the ocean... They pitched camp in "one of the prettiest neighbourhoods we have seen during the journey". They had accomplished their mission, yes; but now there was the way back...

Since their provisions were running short, it was imperative that they should return to Cooper's Creek as soon as possible, and on 13 February, having rejoined King and Gray who had been left at Camp 119 with the camels, they all started off. The weather was very wet, for it had been raining continually, and the camels were up to their knees in mud, so that their stages for a considerable time did not exceed four or five miles a day. They had at first five camels—one had already had to be left behind—and the horse "Billy", but it was not long before they had to kill three of the camels as well as the horse: the poor beasts were so knocked up, and besides, their flesh was needed to save the party from starvation. Two of the men walked and two rode, so as to spare the remaining camels as much as possible.

Gray was the first to complain and crack up. He said he was suffering from dysentery, although his companions could see no telltale traces of it. On 8 April there is an entry in Wills's diary: "Halted fifteen minutes to send back for Gray, who gammoned he could not walk." But the poor fellow was not shamming, as they had supposed. There comes the entry for 17 April: "This morning, about sunrise, Gray died. He had not spoken a word distinctly since his first attack, which was just as we were about to start." Although they were extremely weak, his companions buried him as decently as they could, scooping a shallow grave out of the sand.

As it happened, this delay of a day to bury their comrade was to cost Burke and Wills their own lives.

The three survivors pushed on, nerved by the thought that they could not be so very far now from Cooper's Creek. For fifteen days they had had no provisions beyond the horseflesh that they had dried, and of this only a pound and a half remained when at length, on 21 April, they staggered into their old camp. On that day they had travelled thirty miles, Burke riding on one of the camels and Wills and King on the other.

How excited they were, to think of the happy meeting with their companions! Burke was a little in advance, and he often turned round to the others and said: "I think I see their tents ahead." When they were almost there, he called out the names of the men who had been left behind, and who surely would be making ready to welcome them. Fresh clothes, plenty of food, and a good sleep . . . There was no answer. They entered the camp. It was deserted.

At first they were too bewildered to do anything. Then Wills noticed that a tree had been marked with the words: "DIG. 21st April, 1861." He and King immediately set to work to open up the ground beneath the tree, and just below the surface they came on a box containing some provisions that had been left for them by Brahé, and a bottle in which there was a note. This was handed up to Burke, and he read it aloud. It stated briefly that Brahé and his party had left–that very morning!–to return to the Darling and so get into the track along which they had come. "Two of my companions and myself are quite well," the message continued; "the third–Patten–has been unable to walk for the last eighteen days, as his leg has been severely hurt when thrown by one of the horses. No person has been up here from the Darling. We have six camels and twelve horses in good working condition. *William Brahé*."

The entry in Wills's diary for that day strikes a somewhat bitter note. "Their camels and horses all well and in good condition. We and our camels being just done up, and scarcely able to reach the depot, have very little chance of overtaking them. Brahé has fortunately left us ample provisions (so Wills wrote ironically) to take us to the bounds of civilization, namely, flour, 50 lbs.; rice, 20 lbs.; oatmeal, 60 lbs.; sugar, 60 lbs.; and dried meat, 15 lbs. These provisions, together with a few horse-shoes and nails and some odds and ends, constitute all the articles left, and place us in a very awkward position in respect to clothing. Our disappointment in finding the depot deserted may easily be imagined–returning in an exhausted state, after four months of the severest travelling and privation, our legs almost paralysed, so that each of us found it a most trying task only to walk a few yards."

Why had Brahé decided to leave, they wondered? And what on earth had happened to Wright, who had been ordered to bring up fresh supplies from the base camp as soon as possible? They were not to know that Brahé, after waiting more than four months and with one of his men dangerously ill, had postponed his departure until the very last moment. So he had left a cache of such provisions as he could spare, and then departed in the hope of meeting Wright half-way (as in fact he did). Perhaps Burke and his companions gave a thought to the fact that if they had not spent a day burying Gray they would have reached Cooper's Creek just before Brahé set out. But as it was they made the best of a bad job, and "were not long in getting out the grub that Brahé had left, and made a good supper of some oatmeal porridge and sugar".

In point of fact, Brahé's note had given a much too favourable picture of his condition. None of his party was *quite* well, and neither were the camels and horses in such a good state as he had represented. If, then, the next morning, refreshed by a good night's sleep, Burke and his party had made their way back *along the same track as they had come*, they might have caught up with Brahé. This is, indeed, what Wills urged, but Burke decided otherwise, and Burke was the man in charge.

This was Burke's first great mistake. It was followed immediately by another. He placed a paper in the same place as they had found Brahé's note, in which he briefly outlined their plans. But he made no alteration in the inscription on the tree! So that when they quitted the place there was nothing to indicate that they had ever returned there ...

For the next couple of months the party remained in the vicinity, living on seeds and berries and roots when their stock of provisions had been used up. Occasionally they encountered blackfellows, from whom they were able to beg a few fish. One of the camels got bogged, and they were too weak to dig him out. So they shot him, and lived on the dried flesh. Then one evening the other camel—Rajah—became ill, and Burke ordered he should be shot likewise. King did so, and "we cut him up with two broken knives and a lancet". Twice they made attempts to reach a spot named Mt. Hopeless, where there was a cattle-station and they might have found a route southwards to Adelaide. But they could not manage it, and they continued wandering about Cooper's Creek, living mostly on the seeds of the nardoo plant and what they could get from the blacks.

In Wills's diary the entry for 30 May reads: "Reached the depot this morning, at eleven o'clock. No traces of anyone except blacks having been here since we left. Deposited some journals, and a notice of our present condition..."

But there *had* been someone else there. On 8 May, twenty-two days before, Brahé, who had by this time been joined by Wright with his supply-train, had returned to Cooper's Creek. Brahé had noticed the sign he had cut on the tree: DIG. It looked just as it had looked when he left it weeks before. He never thought to dig up the hole where he had buried the provisions, and (as we have seen) Burke and Wills had not thought it necessary to leave any obvious marks behind them...

The final entry in Wills's diary is dated Friday, 28 June:

"Clear, cold night; slight breeze from the east, day beautifully warm and pleasant. Mr. Burke suffers greatly from the cold, and is getting extremely weak. He and King start tomorrow up the creek to look for the blacks; it is the only chance we have of being saved from starvation. I am weaker than ever, although I have a good appetite and relish the nardoo much; but it seems to give us no nutriment, and the birds here are so shy as not to be got at. Nothing now but the greatest good luck can save any of us; and as for myself I may live four or five days if the weather continues warm. My pulse is at forty-eight, and very weak, and my legs and arms are nearly skin and bone. I can only look out, like Mr. Micawber, 'for something to turn up.'..."

But nothing did turn up for Wills. He had just sufficient strength to sign his name; and then, or not much later, he died, alone.

Meanwhile Burke and King were wandering about, looking for the blacks who might perhaps be able to give them a little food. But then Burke's strength began to fail him. He complained to King of great pain in his legs and back. This was on 29 June. The next morning he seemed to be a little better, and said he thought he was getting stronger. But after moving on another couple of miles he told King he could go no farther. King urged him to keep going, and at nightfall they camped beside a large sheet of water. Now we take up the story from King's account.

"From the time we halted Mr. Burke seemed to be getting worse, although he ate his supper (of nardoo seeds). He said he felt convinced he could not last many hours, and gave me his watch, which he said belonged to the Committee, and a pocket-book to give to Sir William Stawell [Chairman of the Exploration Committee], and in which he wrote some notes. He then said to me, 'I hope you will remain here with me till I am quite dead; it is a comfort to know that someone is by; but when I am dying, it is my wish that you should place the pistol in my right hand, and that you leave me unburied as I lie.' That night he spoke very little, and the following morning I found him speechless, or nearly so; and about eight o'clock he expired. I remained a few hours there, but as I saw there was no use in remaining longer, I went up the creek in search of the natives. I felt very lonely ..."

After resting two days in a native shelter, King returned to where they had left Wills. "The natives had been there and had taken away some of his clothes. I buried the corpse with sand, and remained there some days." But when his stock of nardoo had run out, he tracked some natives and lived with them as one of themselves, treated with the utmost kindness, until about a month later, when one of the tribe "came and told me that the 'white fellows' were coming'". It was the rescue party under Mr. Howitt which had been sent out when Brahé had arrived back in Melbourne and reported that he had no news of Burke and the rest.

Having loaded the kindly natives with presents, Mr. Howitt led his party back down the homeward trail. Of the four men who had set out from Cooper's Creek on that morning in mid-December, 1860, only King remained alive, and he now indicated to his rescuers where he had left the bodies of his companions. First they found Wills's remains, which they carefully re-interred. Then after a long search they came upon Burke's skeleton, lying under a clump of box trees. The revolver lay near by, partly covered with leaves and earth and corroded with rust. "We dug a grave close to the spot, and interred the remains wrapped in the union jack—the most fitting covering in which the bones of a brave but unfortunate man could take their last rest." And on a box tree at the head of the grave they carved Burke's initials, with the date, 21. 9. 61.

When Mr. Howitt returned to Melbourne, bringing with him the note-books and other relics of the dead explorers, there was a great outburst of popular indignation. The Exploration Committee held an immediate inquest, and this was soon followed by the appointment by the Governor of a royal commission to make a thorough investigation. The commission published its report in due course. "The conduct of Mr. Wright," it states, "appears to have been reprehensible in the highest degree"; he had disobeyed his leader's orders to bring up supplies to Cooper's Creek as soon as possible; had delayed a matter of months before setting out: "to that delay are mainly attributable the whole of the disasters of the expedition, with the exception of the death of Gray"—and he had failed to give any satisfactory reason for it. Brahé was blamed for leaving the depot at Cooper's Creek without orders—but it was allowed that he had waited four months for Wright and he had a very sick man on his hands. About Wills and King nothing but good was said, but Burke came in for some severe criticisms. He ought never to have appointed Wright to a position of such responsibility when he knew so little about him; he ought to have made arrangements for keeping open a channel of communication with Melbourne, as he had been instructed; he ought not to have left Cooper's Creek before the depot party had arrived from Menindie, he ought not to have undertaken so extended a journey with an insufficient supply of provisions, in the course of which he "was forced into the necessity of overtaxing the powers of his party, whose continuous and unremitting exertions resulted in the destruction of his animals, and the prostration of himself and his companions from fatigue and severe privation". Furthermore, he had failed to keep any regular journal, and had given no written instructions to his officers, with the result that they had been able to plead unsatisfactory and contradictory verbal orders and statements.

"We cannot too deeply deplore the lamentable result of an expedition," the report concludes, "undertaken at so great a cost to the colony; but, while we regret the absence of a systematic plan of operations on the part of the leader, we desire to express our admiration of his gallantry and daring..."

Burke and Wills were the pioneers, and they paid the all-too-frequent price of pioneering. Within a year or two expeditions were invading Australia's heartland from all directions, and the continent was crossed from south to north and north to south. But who knows the names of the successful explorers? Burke and Wills were the failures, and (such is the way of things) their names are imperishably enshrined in a great new nation's story.

C. M. DOUGHTY'S TRAVELS IN ARABIA

A Victorian Abroad

"It was afternoon when a few Arab friends bade me Godspeed, and, mounted with my camel-bags upon a mule, I came riding through Damascus with the Persian, Mohammed Aga, and a small company. As we turned from the long city street, that which in Paul's days was called 'The Straight', to go up, through the Medan, to the Boabat-Allah, some of the bystanders at the corner, setting upon me with their eyes, said to each other, 'Who is this? Eigh!' Another answered half-jestingly, 'It is someone belonging to the Persian'."

And so, in November, 1876, the imperturbable Victorian, Charles Doughty, passed through the Gate-of-Allah and began one of the most remarkable journeys in history. Starting this way, along the Route-of-Allah, the path of the annual Moslem pilgrimage to Mecca, he would spend two hazardous, uncomfortable and action-packed years in the desert of Arabia, to debouch in August, 1878, at the port of Jeddah and set sail, with his bursting note-books, for England.

From Damascus to Jeddah, as the crow flies, is rather less than nine hundred miles–but Doughty's trip was about as unlike the flight of that bird as it is possible to imagine. His wanderings about the desert of Arabia can be traced today on a map, like the recording pencil of a barograph, up and down and along, with sudden plunges in one direction or another, as whim, curiosity or desperate need made him alter course. During those two years he underwent great hardship, nearly lost his life on a number of occasions and indeed was so often a mere sword's length from death that, putting down the second and final massive volume of his journal, one is unable to recall the half of them.

C. M. Doughty's *Travels in Arabia Deserta* is still the bible for any serious student of Arabia and Arab affairs, though it was written more than eighty years ago. Not only is it an account of a remarkable journey by an Oriental scholar who was able to bring back priceless information of what he had seen and experienced, but it is one of the great prose works of our literature. As T. E. Lawrence, a later wanderer over some of the same territory, who relied extensively on what Doughty taught him, wrote about the book, it is "written in a style which has apparently neither father nor son, so closely wrought, so tense, so just in its words and phrases, that it demands a hard reader". And to the adventurous "Lawrence of Arabia", Doughty's book was the greatest adventure story ever written.

Ned Lawrence, in the Oxford High Street, or in London, or at the Versailles peace conference, always looked the part of the intrepid explorer–and went to some pains to maintain the image. Charles Doughty, son of a Suffolk clergyman, could hardly have looked less like one. He was poet, explorer and scholar, and he looked the archetype of the last, with his critical frown, his bag-laden eyes and his wandering beard; and a distinct air of not suffering fools, either gladly or at all. He was born in 1843 and almost immediately, it seems, was filled with a wild urge to travel. He scraped together the time and money to start doing so at an early age, and by the time of his death, aged eighty-three, he had journeyed as widely in Europe, Africa and Asia as any man before him, and with considerably more understanding of what he had seen.

To get some idea of what Doughty did we must consider just what "Arabia" was in the eighteen-seventies. It was a far less hospitable area than it is today. Turkey had control of a large part of it; there was a vague unease throughout the land, with no man trusting his neighbour, far less a stranger: in most of the villages Doughty was to visit no European had ever been seen. As a despised "Nasrani", or Christian, he found, as he knew he would, that most men's hands were against him, that, given the opportunity, half the people he met would gleefully cut his throat. And, knowing this, he set out to spend two years with them—and survived.

Classical authors have divided that huge peninsula—largest in the world—into "Arabia Felix", "Arabia Petraea" and "Arabia Deserta". The division was largely a political one, dating from the first century A.D. The first Arabia was independent, the second under the control of Rome, and the third, which Doughty set forth to investigate, under that of Persia.

Very few of the people with whom Doughty discussed his plan thought he had the slightest chance of surviving such a journey. They pointed out that to the climatic horrors of scorching heat and absent rain would be added the hostility, the murderous inclination, of Arab tribesmen. Quite apart from an understandable urge to eliminate a Christian, they would enjoy killing him for his wristwatch, his pen, the un-used pages of his note-book.

Doughty would have none of this: he would go, whatever they said, and win the trust, perhaps the grudging affection, of the Arabs he met, by offering treatment for their physical ills from his little medicine chest. Although he spoke almost perfect Arabic—and rather better than most of the bedouin he would meet—he would not try to pose as an Arab. He would wear Arab clothes because they seemed most suitable, but he would stoutly maintain his Christianity, make no bones about being an Englishman.

But no, said the cultured Arab friends he made in Damascus: that would be madness. He must assure all who asked that he revered Allah and only Allah; his Christianity must be a dark secret in his own heart. This was quite permissible: why, even the Koran urged this upon true Moslems travelling in hostile, non-Moslem lands; they should keep their beliefs well-hidden.

Ridiculous, said Doughty. If they will not accept me as a Christian, I will move on. He knew his Arabs well enough to realize that there would always be men prepared to welcome him for his medicine chest, even for his conversation, in the lonely depths of the desert. The people of Arabia fell into two distinct groups, bedouin and city-dweller, and he fancied he knew as much of the former as did his well-meaning, city-bred advisers. He would meet no more city-folk, apart from those who might travel with him in the Haj camel train, until he presented himself with his note-books to the British Consul at the port of Jeddah.

The bedouin with whom he would be living were men always

on the move, searching out food and water for the camels which were their livelihood. They were people brought up in the desert, who probably saw no other landscape throughout their short, hard, lives. Their living was the breeding of "ships of the desert", who thrived best on the plants, cacti and thorns of the barren lands where no other beast could survive. From this pitiful diet they could extract sufficient moisture and nourishment to make it unnecessary for them to drink water for weeks on end. The bedouin in charge of them lived in tribes, partly through family relationship, partly because the great hostile emptiness of the desert made men congregate in as large bodies as possible for mutual support. They lived in tents, raised on long stakes hammered into the ground, with rectangular strips of woven camel's hair across them for a roof. Sometimes there were walls of the same material, more often only open sides, with a hanging cloth dividing each tent into a part for women, a part for men. For furniture there would be a few cushions and carpets. For diet, milk and cheese, with a little coffee.

It was Sunday, 13 November, when Doughty set off, travelling with the pilgrim (Haj) caravan down the long Derb-el-Haj, the Pilgrims' Road. He had persuaded people to help him, as he knew he would, for "the hope of silver brought me five or six poorer persons, saying all with great 'By-Gods' they would set their seals to a paper to carry me safely to Medain Salih". (Here Doughty proposed leaving the caravan.) He was soon "clothed as a Syrian of simple fortune, for thus, mingled with the Persians in the Haj journey, I should be the less noted, whether by Persians or Arabs".

The Derb-el-Haj is not a made road, only a multitude of cattle paths, beaten down under the flat, soft feet of generations of camels, the heel-and-toe of generations of pilgrims. Yet the pilgrimage set off in the highest of spirits—six thousand people in a procession two miles long, singing, laughing, shouting, in anticipation of the holiness in which all survivors would be bathed. Not all the hopeful would arrive: there were old men, cripples of all ages, stumbling along, sometimes in single file, sometimes in a column eighty or ninety yards wide, and many of these would fall by the way, to be hastily buried by their friends, and almost immediately dug up by jackals and vultures.

For Doughty, whose health was never robust, discomfort began on the first night, when he found himself encamped in a filthy, dung-strewn field, as the scorching heat of day gave place to a startling, death-like chill. But he had little time to consider his situation, for at three in the morning the column moved off. There had been no stones where they camped, and the cooking pots had been set above holes dug in the sand. Now the pots were loaded up on camels and mules and the procession clanged its way into the daylight.

The next day's journey was longer, the one after that longer still, as men and camels were "broken in" to the hardships of the march. At this rate, they would make good progress and he anticipated reaching Medain Salih in a very few weeks.

Suddenly, one night, there was a scream—the most blood-curdling sound he had heard. It went on, mounting higher and higher, broken by gasps and the dreadful thudding of a club, on the body of a human being. He leaped from his rug, tore out into the night, following the sound through the darkness, up the column, till he came to the huge tent most of the Persians were using. It was able to hold a hundred sleeping men, and the cries, now grown fainter, seemed to come from its centre. He made his way in, in the darkness, stumbling over bodies which cursed him, standing men who cuffed him as he elbowed past.

There were oil-lamps flickering in the centre of the great camels-hair pavilion, and by these he could make out the quivering, bony form of a small man, held down by four others, one at each limb, while a fifth was beating him, beating with all his strength. The cudgel rose and fell, but the victim was no longer screaming; only a whispered groan emerged each time the blow came.

"Eigh," said a man beside him, "this will do it. Four strong men have wearied themselves in beating the villain. Now, with this fifth, the wretch will confess."

Aghast, Doughty watched for a few moments, then shouted out, "Stop!"

Everyone turned and looked at him, even the man with the club, who nevertheless went on with his steady, rhythmic work. A man spat.

"Stop! This man may not bear more. Hold—or he will die!"

The beating went on. Men turned and looked, in mingled surprise and disgust, at Doughty. The beating went on.

Then, suddenly, it was over. The fifth flagellant dropped his cudgel, exhausted, and the men at each limb let go, for there was no longer a need. A moment's pause and the man—but was he man or corpse?—was carried off.

The next day a tall, commanding Persian, came up to Doughty and addressed him in an Arabic much inferior to his own. "You were foolish, friend. You should not have interfered. Take warning, and do not try to do so again."

"But–but the man?"

"He has confessed." The episode was ended.

They were still in the ancient "Arabia Petraea", several days, march from "Arabia Deserta". They came to the city of Petra, with its monuments, and he was back, body as well as spirit, in the Old Testament. The valley in which he stood was still, to the Arabs, "The Valley of Moses".

As the days wore on, the curiosity of his companions grew and he began to hope for a speedy arrival at the "Cities of Salih", where he would leave them. His watch, his pen, they understood, but that dial which pointed to the north star, the other dial which climbed as they did, staggered with them, jerk by jerk as they ascended the bare hills of Arabia–what were these? He carefully explained his compass and his aneroid barometer, and they shook their heads. Each day he was recording the readings, making a three-dimensional map of considerable accuracy, which was to be a boon, for many years, to later travellers.

He was also writing his voluminous journal. And writing poetry.

They came to a mirage, for all the world like a sea of clear blue water, which vanished, tantalizingly, as they drew near, leaving golden, throbbing desert behind. Now they started leaving behind them the bodies of elderly pilgrims. Not a day went by without its little donation of skin, bones and flesh to the jackals and the vultures. And yet to die in this manner was in itself an honour: one had perished on the way to holiness, one was a martyr, a "Shahud".

They left behind them, as they trudged south, the well-trodden "Arabia Petraea", entered–though there was no boundary stone, no sign–the emptiness of "Arabia Deserta". The marches had reached a maximum length now, many hours of marching broken only by a rifle shot at noon to announce a pause of less than half an hour. Nothing was unloaded, the beasts stood still in their swarms of flies, under their groaning burdens. Usually a corpse was left behind.

Exactly four weeks after setting out the procession came to the spot where Doughty had planned to leave it, Medain Salih, "The Cities of Salih". Here there were monuments of great antiquity, with inscriptions in several languages, all that remained of what might once have been a flourishing urban community, now a wind-swept desert.

The Haj went on: Doughty stayed behind. Somehow he managed to persuade a local sheikh to allow him to live with the tribe for a few months. After some doubt, Sheikh Zeyd agreed. Slowly he raised his thin brown arm and, eyes on the Englishman, pointed out the barren land, stretching miles into the distance. "He watched to see if the townling were discouraged, in viewing only the empty desert before him. And he said, 'Hear, O Khalil; so wilt thou live here with us–and we will give thee a maiden to wife. If any children be born to thee, when thou wouldst go from hence, they shall be as mine own, and remain with me'."

Surely no offer could be fairer. One gathers that Doughty accepted, though his book, so minutely, painstakingly accurate in almost every respect, is less than explicit on this point. The Englishman adds, rather lamely, that "also of his stock he would give me a camel".

And so, with Zeyd he remains, living in almost every detail the life of a bedouin. The only point at which he resolved to differ from his hosts was in his staunch assertion of his Christian religion. The Sheikh respected him for it, but there were those in the tribe who did not, and on more than one occasion he heard angry talk of punishing the Nasrani for his faith. Usually Doughty sailed in with a retort before any conspiracy could be launched, and with his large vocabulary–which grew a little larger every day, as his note-books and his sketch-books filled–and with his gift of imagery he was soon able to discomfit his persecutors, so that they were laughed at or insulted by their fellows. All the while he was painstakingly translating inscriptions, sketching monuments, taking notes. Some of his sketches are as good, for accuracy of detail, as photographs.

The pilgrims came back, months later, from their journey to Mecca, and Doughty saw them pass, a far smaller procession now, far smaller, heading back to Damascus. By now he was accepted by almost everyone he met, in the changing society of the desert, as an Oriental of some sort, and a wise and learned one at that, who professed the Christian religion. The comparative pallor of his skin was on more than occasion explained away by the fact that he was "obviously a leper" and that the disease, no longer active, had bleached his skin.

And so the months went by. He cured men, women, and children of ailments, real and imaginary, cured them with rather greater success than he was able to cure himself; for Doughty, never a strong man, was several times very ill indeed, but managed, by sheer guts and determination, to force himself back to health.

The climax of his wandering came near the end— and what might have been the end in quite a different sense. Nearly two years had gone by since his departure from Damascus. He had travelled literally thousands of miles with different bedouin tribes, when he reached the settlement of Taif, not far from his ultimate destination of Jeddah. He had noticed a certain sullen reserve among those around the fire one evening. Suddenly, as if by predetermined plan, half a dozen men turned on him, spitting out abuse. They urged each other, in the Arab tradition, to do something about eliminating this infidel. Knives were drawn, pistols appeared from nowhere.

"Kill him—kill the Nasrani! And now!"

"Eigh—he must be killed, the infidel."

It was obvious to Doughty, by the careful scrutiny they had been giving his clothes and his belongings, that the matter of his religion was the flimsiest of excuses for setting upon him, robbing and killing him. Particularly they seemed to covet a fine carbine, a weapon superior to anything the bedouin possessed.

"Yes," he said. "I am an infidel in your eyes, and an Englishman. And you see this fine gun—and that cloth you are wearing, and this, and this, fine thing. What are they? They are things from England."

Taken aback, they stopped their abuse. Out of the corner of an eye he could see one man creeping up on him from behind. He fiddled with the trigger of the carbine and the man scuttled off.

"We will still kill him," said a voice, but with markedly less enthusiasm.

As Doughty remarks elsewhere in his book, out of every three Arabs, one is a mediator: the sudden wild emotion which makes men want to kill, to punish, to steal, dies soon in the desert. One of these now spoke up. "Why should we kill him? Let him give us all he owns, and we will treat him as a brother..."

The suggestion was well received and Doughty, realizing himself outnumbered and outgunned, suffered himself to be robbed of his money and his valuables. He warned them that he was expected hourly in Jeddah—which was true, for he had sent messages ahead— and that powerful sheikhs, to say nothing of the British Consul, would punish all who harmed him. One or two of his possessions were then hastily returned and there was a muttered discussion about whether it would not be wise to kill him now and deny all knowledge of him on arrival at Jeddah.

The decision had been taken. Men fingered their knives.

Then, somehow, the decision was abandoned. Doughty escaped with his life, and even, in the last few days before reaching Jeddah, had his possessions returned to him. He got there, a thin, brown, startling figure, well content with himself. His note-books were bulging, his haversacks were stuffed with minerals and carvings and other trophies, and he committed himself to "the open hospitality of the British Consulate".

It is impossible to précis the journey, for Doughty travelled rapidly for weeks, then seemed to stand still in contemplation for a month or more before setting out again in some unexpected direction, like a fly wandering over the surface of a table. Much of his journeying was through places not shown on any map. But the information he brought back, the superb little sketches, the scholarly translations from a number of ancient languages, and the delightful style which makes us read on, page by page (there are more than 1200 of them), put this journey in a class of its own. To travellers in Arabia it is still a bible, for Doughty tells the full truth of a situation which has changed little in a thousand years.

Few travel books can have been written with less bias. With all their intrigue he loved the Arabs, and the fact stands out clearly between the lines of his book: in the lines themselves we can see he has made every effort to be accurate, dispassionate. If there is a bias in the book, it is not bias against his Arab friends.

Doughty went among the people as one of them, studied them while he shared their life, and was in perhaps a greater, more prolonged, intimacy with them than any other European before or since—including the very different Lawrence of Arabia. He was Arab in manner, yet European, Christian, in mind: able to view his hosts objectively and dispassionately. At the end of his two years—he reached Jeddah in August, 1878—his note-books were full of the soul of the desert, never captured before, full of the magic of a strange, self-sufficient community, cut off from the rest of the world.

Only one major change has taken place, since the writing of Doughty's book; and that happened, quite suddenly, during the First World War. In Charles Doughty's day there were only Christians and Moslems, or at least, in Arab eyes, Moslems and infidels, to take account of: a man was either one thing or the other. But during the First World War the European idea of nationality crept in, so that western Arabs were fighting, without sense of its incongruity, against their own Caliph, the Sultan of Turkey, in order to achieve an "independence" which has been the catchword ever since.

Yet, despite this, a man set down in the heart of what is now Saudi Arabia with Doughty's work (and a strong camel to carry it) would find little altered in the lives of the bedouin people Doughty knew so well–and described so incomparably.

THE TREK OVER THE ORANGE RIVER

The Boers Move North

THERE WERE many migrations in the mid-nineteenth century: men and women travelling by land or sea to make a new life for themselves in a new land. The Victorian era may have been peaceful and smug and self-satisfied in England, but in other parts people were moving restlessly from one place to another. Some, like the Mormons of the United States, were driven by a religious persecution which drove them relentlessly to found a new community for themselves in the west; others travelled much the same route, but farther, to the west coast, along the Oregon Trail, looking for land which was fertile—and free—a land they had heard of, where beaver pelts, minerals, even gold, could be had for the taking. And from the Old World to the New there was a steady stream of emigration over the wide Atlantic.

To some extent, all this movement was inter-related. But thousands of miles away to the south, in a half-understood land where winter was summer and summer perversely winter, a quite different emigration had begun. Superficially, it bore resemblance to the mass migration over the Oregon Trail, for those who travelled did so, for the most part, in covered wagons not unlike the American "prairie schooner". But the motives underlying this migration were quite different.

Men have moved in ox-drawn wagons, bearing all their possessions, for thousands of years: it took the Boers of South Africa to
give the activity the short, sharp name which has entered the English
vocabulary, but they were by no means the first to engage in it.
Nor was their "Great Trek" particularly great in terms of the number involved, or the hardship encountered. Many parties of well
over a hundred wagons set out westward from the American frontier station of St Louis, but few indeed were convoys of this size in
South Africa. And as for distance, the Mormons who went only as
far as the Great Salt Lake, not to the west coast like so many others–
had over a thousand miles to negotiate: the Boers, trekking from
their start-point just south of the Orange River, had to cover only
five hundred to reach Port Natal–which is now Durban–or a mere
three hundred to settle on the far side of the River Vaal. Even to
reach the furthest extent of possible colonization, the North-east
Transvaal and the valley of the River Limpopo, was but six hundred miles.

As for hardship–the Americans moving west had high, snow-
covered mountains to deal with, and waterless desert: they were in
constant danger from well-armed, mounted Indians, Indians who
often had better fire-arms than they themselves carried, far better
horses. The Boers for the most part travelled lush and hospitable
plains and found that most of their route had been cleared of African natives by intertribal wars, that most of those they encountered
were passive, prepared to accept their invasion. And armed only
with assegais.

But, as we will see, there were occasional, horrifying hazards.

The Great Trek deserves its name, for at least one reason: it
carried with it the high proportion of one white person out of every
fifty from the old Cape Colony on the south-west coast. And it
established a new land, quite unlike anything else in the world.

The beautiful cape at the foot of Africa was first rounded by the
Portuguese Bartholomew Diaz, in 1488, and though it had been
known for some time as the "Cape of Storms", King John of Portugal now proudly titled it "Cape of Good Hope". Storm or no storm,
it was from the beginning a landmark of beauty, with a soft and
inviting climate. Sir Francis Drake called it "the fairest cape we
saw in the whole circumference of the earth". And yet more than a
century and a half elapsed before anyone thought of settling there.
Even then, in 1652, it was only a small watering point that the
Dutch East India Company established, a tiny Dutch population to

assist in watering, rationing, vessels on their way to the Indies. Gradually they built themselves a fort, at the foot of Table Mountain.

But when France attacked Holland and the latter appealed to England, English troops were sent to keep the Cape in safe custody for the Dutch. At the Peace of Amiens, they got it back. Four years later a larger British force helped themselves to it a second time, ostensibly to forestall French moves to seize it. By now it was a growing colony, and the Dutch were unwilling to allow this British incursion. Eventually they capitulated–and from then on the Cape Colony was generally recognized as being a British possession.

By the latter part of the eighteenth century some five-thousand Europeans were living in the Colony and rather more than twice that number in the land farther back. Particularly in these more remote country areas, the overwhelming majority of population was Dutch, and though these resented British rule, they were prepared to endure it: after all, they were many miles from the seat of colonial government in Cape Town and could do much as they liked. They had their slaves (not local Africans, who were often in much the same position and called "apprentices", but other negroes imported by sea in the days of the Dutch East India Company, when the Cape was all but deserted) and they could enforce any justice they cared. And it was justice that these hard-bitten "Boers" imposed: harsh, but according to their beliefs absolutely just. Woe betide any Boer who failed to honour its code.

In 1834 the British Government, which had been growing more sure of itself, more determined to govern, right to the farthest bound of this expanding African territory, decreed an emancipation of all slaves at a not-too-distant date, and the "un-apprenticing" of the local Hottentots to put them on an equal footing with whites. Not content with this drastic interference with Boer economy, they declared an intention to substitute English for Dutch–the Boer language–in all courts and schoolrooms.

The Great Trek was a direct result of these blows to, firstly, prosperity (for who could hope to prosper without slaves or at least "apprentices" on a peppercorn wage?) and, secondly, Dutch sentiment. It began, as these things do, quite slowly, but within its first decade, from 1835 to about 1845, some fourteen thousand Boers trekked away into the wilderness. In those few years the European-settled lands of southern Africa more than doubled.

The Trek was the third stage of European expansion. From the first Dutch settlement and the building of the castle, in mid-seventeenth century, until the start of the eighteenth, no man had ventured more than one hundred miles from the sea. During the eighteenth century expansion was rather more rapid, and by the start of the Great Trek, in 1835, there were isolated farms and homesteads as much as four hundred miles inland. But with the Great Trek these isolated posts would become part of a far larger, denser, community; the boundaries of that extend still farther.

The Boers who set out on their Trek were cheerful, hospitable folk, faithful to the beliefs and customs of the Dutch Reformed Church, jealously proud of their evolving language which they had begun to style "Afrikaans". Most were pastoralists, owning upwards of six thousand acres of grazing, two or three acres of which they set aside for subsistence farming, growing their own fruit and vegetables. By the 1830s, though, other types of men had arrived or developed: shop-keepers, artisans, missionaries, ministers, school-masters. They had all been moving slowly, steadily, away from the Cape Colony over the years, much to the distress of the Dutch East India Company and then the British, for both of these wished to have a prosperous, compact community, like, say, Virginia on the North American continent, which the Cape much resembled, with its soft, Mediterranean climate, the fertility of its soil. But as migrants came—and there were few enough of these—so the community pressed outwards, dissipating itself inland. Many had braved the mountain passes to get away to the north, had liked what they found there, and had no intention of doing the journey in reverse.

And then came the British legislation. Indigenous Hottentots were no longer required to have passes, could move freely wheresoever they wished. After years of half-hearted restriction on keeping slaves, intended—but without success—to discourage Boers from owning them, the Government decreed, in 1834, that slaves would become, like Hottentots, "apprentices" to whom a wage must be paid. Four years after that, the whole lot would be free.

This was too much, too appalling, to contemplate. Apart from the danger, in Boer eyes, of having free and unrestricted savages wandering about the countryside and in the villages, the economic effects of being denied slave labour would be crippling. The message went round that a real "trek", a one-way journey, not a "tog" or visit, was imminent, if the Boer community were to survive. Frontiers would have to be pushed back; the community would have to spill out in its thousands to new land, far from the influence of a stupid and alien government.

It was a brave idea, but the land was not entirely unexplored. Ivory traders had made a way inland from Port Natal on the Indian Ocean, had pushed on into the very land the Boers now hoped to exploit. And, using the northward route the emigrants would follow, there had been hunters and missionaries. Zion would not be unknown. And perhaps no people on earth knew more about travelling by ox-cart. Many Boers lived permanently in them, not bothering to build homes, taking possessions and families in the wagon to a suitable spot to control flocks, moving when grazing grew poor.

The Boer women were almost as hardy as their men, and even more determined to move. They bitterly resented slave emancipation and Hottentot equality for, among other things, they would have great difficulty in keeping servants. In the new legislation there was also a bill entitling anyone, regardless of colour, to bid for land; the thought of having idle, shiftless blacks in direct competition with their sons for the best land was too hideous to contemplate.

So by the end of 1835 parties were on the move. A year later larger ones had followed, and these contained, among their number, men who were travelling not only through discontent with a colony where–in their eyes–a divinely appointed colour-bar could be flouted, but for the thrill of adventure, the hope of making a new, clean start. The greed for new, free, land. For many there was the fear of loneliness and worse when the others had gone.

Most of the intending migrants were able to dispose of their property at a profit (hardly surprising, as most of the land had originally been a free grant) and were able to assemble a fine collection of more portable goods and load them into wagons, many of them constructed just for the Trek. At least one housewife had three wagons all to herself: one full of provisions, a second bursting with bedding and materials, a third full of her family's clothes. Men crammed in their furniture, ploughs, tools, fruit trees (carefully wrapped against the heat), seed–and, of course, many pounds of the gunpowder without which life in the wilderness would be impossible. Without fresh game to eat, the average Boer family would sicken. Besides, there was always the remote possibility of hostile natives.

So they set off, in their wagons, with cattle, sheep and horses between. The wagons were drawn, depending on the terrain, by anything up to two-dozen oxen, which slowly moved it on its four broad, iron wheels. Semi-circular wooden hoops held up the double canvas canopy: a waterproof outer one, thickly painted, and a white one, for coolness, inside. The patient beasts in front were not driven, for Boer carts had no reins, but were directed by shouts—each animal had a name, and knew it—and by occasional flicks of the long stock-whip. Sometimes, when the trail was difficult, or there was water to ford, a boy would walk in front, leading.

The intention shared by all these migrants was that they should cross the Orange River, continue north. Time enough later to consider whether to settle in coastal Natal or inland Transvaal. Unlike the great fleets of "prairie schooners" which at that very moment were moving westward over the North American continent, the Boers would travel in small groups: "trekkies", each under its own leader.

One typical party—though not typical in all that befell it—set off early in 1836 with two dozen wagons. They were cheerful and resolute, for Boer families were large and the entire party was composed of relatives, and a few neighbours for good measure. They reached the Orange River and found it in flood, but there was little difficulty in swimming the cattle and horses across, making a stout willow raft for the wagons. From a contemporary account of this "trekkie" we learn that the women-folk sang lustily from psalm books as the raft took them over their southern Jordan. (They could not use hymn-books; hymns not contained in the Bible were, to their ideas, immoral and an abomination.) They were happy, not only because they were entering a Promised Land, but because they could and would take their time over it. This is one more difference between the American and South African journeys: whereas the migrating Middle-Westerners knew that speed was the essence, that they had to make it before Indians or cholera or starvation caught up, the Boers, shooting for the pot, finding clear fresh water at almost every halt, could take their time. When ewes lambed, they stopped for a week or more. Illness was another respected reason for delay.

Now the "trekkie" joined up with another, and the pair went on, crossing (and naming) a number of lesser rivers, the Modder, the Vet, the Caledon, the Sand. They entered wonderful sheep-and-cattle country, the "High Veld", pressed on to find a Promised Land beyond. They came across peaceful native tribes; some of them, thanks to eager and courageous missionaries, were already ardent Methodists and Presbyterians. From the Sand River a party of them took a detour to explore a route eastward to the sea, for it was important, if the new Boer community–indeed, the new state, republic, for it was thus that they saw it–if this were to flourish and prosper for all time, that a seaport be found on the Indian Ocean, free from British control. There was, of course, Port Natal: perhaps this might serve the purpose.

They had just found peaceful natives working local iron and tin when frightening news arrived. Most tribes, as we have seen, were peaceful; but not the Matabele. These awesome, blood-drenched warriors were a proud branch of the Zulu race, and feared all over southern Africa. Their king, whose very name, Msilikazi, could start a stampede, was a ruthless man of many gifts who could put an army of twenty thousand into the field at a moment's notice, an army strictly disciplined, well-trained, and deployed into regiments.

Everyone knew–just as we all know, without necessarily having seen one, exactly what a ghost looks like–the terrifying appearance of the Matabele warrior. He wore a high feather head-dress, short leopard-skin kilt, with the leopard's tail dangling down; he had tufts of ox-tail at ankle, knee, elbow and wrist; he carried a huge ox-hide shield, oval with sharp ends, behind which a man could be completely hidden if necessary. A youth's shield was black-and-white, a grown man's, red-and-white. Each warrior carried a wooden cudgel, two or three light throwing-spears or assegais, and a shorter, heavier one, used as a dagger. They closed with this short one, hissing like swarms of insects, to stab and thrust.

Msilikazi had got on reasonably well with the Government at Cape Town. It sent him messages of nervous friendship to which he proudly, courteously, replied. He had no objection to missionaries entering his own domain, would in fact allow in almost anyone, for he was curious, eager for knowledge. But his visitors had to come singly.

The trekkers were advancing, albeit peacefully, in large numbers: Msilikazi sized up the situation and mobilized a regiment. That evening, when fortunately the trekkie had made its "laager" for the night, had formed the wagons into a tight circle, six hundred be-feathered warriors swooped down on it.

The Boers held their own while the screaming savages besieged their laager for six hours, trying to hack a way inside; eventually, having failed, withdrawing to leave two hundred of their men on the veld, victims of Boer marksmanship. Only two Boers were dead.

As soon as he heard of this insulting defeat, Msilikazi rushed another regiment to where a second trekkie was settling in. These, caught almost unawares, lost many white men and women with their "coloured," mixed-blooded, servants. Three white children were led away into slavery.

By now the alarm had spread and a number of small trekkies were able to laager together on a hilltop. The Boers set to work with a determination born of near panic and soon there were fifty heavy wagons in a circle, lashed together, bushes of thorns woven through the spokes of each wheel. Four more were lined up in the centre of the ring, roofed with wood as a shelter for women and children. While they waited, they melted down lead for bullets.

There was not long to wait. One moment the veld was empty save for a few prancing springbok; the next, five thousand Matabele were advancing, shoulder to shoulder. The Boer leaders rode out, rifle in hand, but before they could try and parley, the warriors attacked. Firing calmly, with precision, the Boers withdrew, yard by yard. Black warriors dropped, but the great force came on.

The Boer leaders got within their laager and closed the entrance. For a while the Matabele sat and watched, squatting in the long grass, feathered head-dresses flicking in the gentle wind. The tension in the laager mounted, minute by minute. It became unendurable, and a man seized a long whip, tied a red rag to it, waved. The Matabele leapt as one man to their feet and charged.

The Dutchmen waited till they were within range and opened up, with deadly accuracy, firing from behind the wagons. Dozens of black men dropped, writhing in death, but others got to the great ring of wagons and tried, screaming, to tear away the thorns. Others flung assegais into the air, to land them inside the fortified circle.

The Boers won the day. But as they were congratulating themselves, their women-folk beginning to strike up a psalm, a dreadful realization came upon them. A black army was in retreat, leaving its hundreds of black corpses behind, but the Dutch sheep and cattle were going with it. There had been room in the laager for horses: not for sheep and cattle.

A party charged out of the laager on horseback to catch up with the retreating Matabele, and the beasts. And as they did, other men, with their remarkable Boer eyesight, began to pick off "corpses" that were sweating, for dead men do not sweat.

The horsed party caught up with the black men, engaged it, shot down more of them. The enraged Matabele drove them all the way back again, losing many more warriors. Another short and futile siege of the laager and the survivors withdrew again–still with the sheep and cattle.

This was disaster: several men killed and all draught animals gone, to say nothing of the sheep. But they were able to contact another party and obtain oxen–just enough to move them.

A little later a punitive expedition set out. Not only would it retrieve what had been stolen and avenge the dead; it would inflict the most terrifying reprisal it could and ensure for all time that Msilikazi and his savages kept their distance. The punitive expedition was only two hundred strong–but every man was a hand-picked marksman.

At dawn, after a night of moving silently over the veld, it attacked. The biggest Matabele encampment in the area, a small town of thousands, was just waking when the Boers arrived. Within minutes thousands of black men were running headlong into the bush and the Boers had encircled no less than eleven thousand cattle. Half an hour after that the cattle–far more than had been lost in the first place–were being headed to the trekkie camp. Four hundred Matabele lay dead on the ground.

The trekkie completed its journey, arrived successfully north of the Vaal River and settled. The path had been cleared and others followed, confident now that there would be little interference from the Matabele. The emigration, the Trek, grew.

The trekkers had left the Cape in search of new land, of security in which to graze it, independence from British rule. They might, in the eyes of the world, be still a British colony, but no British colonialist stood a chance of ruling it: they were too far away. They set up their virile communities on both sides of the Vaal River and, with great hopes, in the sea-girt region of Natal. But this, as a wise old man had forecast as he headed his wagon to the east, away from the coast, was disaster: the British followed, by land and sea, bringing their hateful laws and customs. The great, hated, "tide of red and black"–red-coated soldiers, black natives–swept into Natal. Sadly, angrily, the Boers yoked up their cattle again, drove up into the wide-open spaces above the Drakensberg, unpopulated, forbidding.

Here–and they were right–few Englishmen would follow.

A CYCLE OF CATHAY

Sir Aurel Stein in Chinese Turkestan

AUREL STEIN was a many-sided man. Besides being one of the foremost British archaeologists of his day, he was a brilliant Oriental scholar and possessed a genius for travel which led him to make the most daring raid upon the long-buried secrets of an ancient civilization ever attempted by any archaeologist.

It was during the 1890s, when Principal of the Oriental College at Lahore, that Stein came across a copy of the *Si-yu-ki*, a book written in the seventh century A.D. by a Chinese Buddhist monk named Hiuen-Tsiang, a devout man of questing mind who yearned to visit Buddha's birthplace and trace his travels through India. With this end in view, Hiuen-Tsiang spent much time trying to map out the ancient trade route from China through the kingdom of Cathay to Bactria (Afghanistan), along which the caravans laden with goods had plodded westwards, passing the pilgrims toiling eastwards bearing the tidings of the Buddhist faith. Around the year A.D. 650 he set forth on his journey, though the route had long fallen into desuetude. Earth tremors had altered the watershed and the rivers had dried up; violent winds had brought sand from the Gobi to smother the once fertile lands, yet somehow Hiuen-Tsiang struggled on and the *Si-yu-ki*, in which he recorded his observations, is highly prized by Chinese officials even today.

367

As the centuries passed, legends about this ancient trade route grew and multiplied until it was commonly believed that the whole thing belonged to the realm of faery. A handful of men, however, Stein among them, knew the facts behind the myths and were convinced that priceless historical treasure lay buried in the territory known as Chinese Turkestan. The *Si-yu-ki*, with its meticulous descriptions, provided Stein with much valuable information about places on the fabled route linking east and west and he determined to follow in the monk's footsteps. In 1899 he approached the Government of India and obtained financial backing for his expedition, so in the early spring of 1900 he retired to Kashmir in order to make his preparations.

Stein had no illusions as to the magnitude of his undertaking, but felt sure that his "patron saint", as he always called Hiuen-Tsiang, would lead him safely through a territory which had been virtually cut off from the world for upwards of a thousand years. The region he sought was bordered on the north by the Altai mountains, beyond which lay the Gobi; and on the south by the Kun-Lun range, beyond which lay Tibet. There were a few oases, sites of once-famous cities, but over stretches 1,500 miles long and 250 miles wide there was empty desert. To the east this inhospitable land merged into China proper and the only approach to it from the west led over the Pamirs, the "roof of the world".

To accompany him as surveyor Stein had chosen Ram Singh, a wiry young Moslem from the Indian Survey Department, and the two spent a hectic month unpacking and sorting and re-packing all the stores and equipment needed for an expedition planned to last well over a year. It would be possible to replenish food supplies at Kashgar, on the eastern side of the Pamirs, but they had to carry all their surveying instruments and excavating tools. The porters were sturdy hillmen who had proved their worth on some of Stein's earlier expeditions and the pack-animals were sure-footed mountain ponies.

By mid-May the party was completed by the arrival of Ram Singh's personal servant, an efficient Rajput, while Stein had persuaded Mirza Alim, an itinerant Turki trader met with in Kabul, to act as interpreter and cook. Their start was delayed, however, since a crate of medical supplies had not yet been delivered and it was during this waiting period that Stein discovered to his dismay that Mirza Alim's culinary abilities were nil! Fortunately this problem was solved by the unexpected arrival on 28 May of another

Turki sent by George Macartney, the British Agent in Kashgar. His name was Sadak Akhun, and he was not only an excellent cook but a most colourful addition to the party. He was over six feet tall and wore a fur-lined cap, a long unstained azure coat and huge red leather boots. Almost simultaneously the medical stores were brought up by boat and on 31 May the expedition set forth.

Through the warm spring days they climbed steadily until they reached Minimarg, altitude 10,000 ft. Then began the zigzag descent into the Kishanganga valley and here they ran into trouble, for both men and ponies slipped and slithered on the shaley ground, and the snow-bridges spanning the hundreds of rivulets crumbled when they set foot on them. This involved endless detours, during one of which Dash, Stein's black-and-white terrier, who was so beloved by the porters that they called him Yolchi Beg, or "Sir Traveller", nearly lost his life in a melting snowdrift. Thereafter he had to be carried as the party laboriously ascended the far side of the Kishanganga, an indignity he much resented.

The next valley was the Astor, a very different proposition, for it was carpeted with short springy turf starred with wild flowers and they were able to walk by the clear stream which, during its long journey southwards, was to become the mighty Oxus river. Ahead of them, to the north, towered the icy mass of Rakiposhi, and as they drew nearer to the mountain the brilliant sunlight streaked its sides with violet and gold and rose, while at night Stein could lie snugly wrapped in his *yurt* (felt tent), with the flap open so that he could watch the play of the moonlight on its glittering peak. All too soon, however, they left the shelter of the Astor to journey through the bleak Hunza region where the families scratching a living from the poor soil looked askance at their cavalcade and even the children scuttled off at a stranger's approach.

The ground was stony so progress was slow and by the time they reached Nilth, the first Nagir village, they were all tired out. The headman was surly, and it is doubtful if he would have granted Stein's request for water, and the dried grass roots called *burse* for fuel, if it had not been for "Sir Traveller", who proved an excellent ambassador. He licked the headman's hand, wagged his stumpy tail, and finally sat up on his hind legs begging so imploringly that the Nagirs were captivated by his antics.

The following morning they entered the Nilth gorge, a dark,

forbidding place strewn with boulders among which the ponies had difficulty in picking their way. They were now in the foothills of the Pamirs and an icy wind blew in their faces as they struggled forward until at last the walls of the gorge fell away and they emerged on to what was known as the Shirin Maidan, or Milky Plain, beyond which rose Taghdumbash, the giant mountain they had to cross.

The crossing of the plain was a tricky business, as the boggy ground was covered by a deep crust of soft snow, and all were soaked to the skin before they scrambled on to a small rocky plateau at the entrance to the Kilik pass. After a much needed rest Stein checked all the baggage loads and proceeded to pay off the Hunza porters, since they and their ponies were now returning home, a task which took an unconscionable time as convention demanded that each man should haggle over the money owed him. When everyone was satisfied the formalities had to be observed; the head porter made a speech praising Stein as an employer, Stein replied with a short eulogy on the willing co-operation shown by the porters and their leader and lips were smacked over bowls of tea flavoured with rancid butter.

The new porters engaged for the actual crossing of Taghdumbash were Sarikolis, who brought their yaks as pack animals, and the ease with which these lumbering beasts negotiated precipitous slopes, glaciers, crevasses and snowdrifts while carrying heavy loads never ceased to amaze Stein. For the humans of the party the ascent through the Kilik was gruelling enough, but as they emerged on to the mountain face conditions grew steadily worse, for wild blizzards raged without ceasing. Blinded by swirling snow, buffeted by violent gusts of wind, they were unable to avoid the hazards which beset them. Time and again a jerk on the rope which linked them signified that one of their number had either floundered into a drift or fallen into a crevasse, and the whole column had to halt while those nearest rescued their unfortunate companion.

By the time they reached the mouth of the Mintaka pass they were exhausted, half-frozen and utterly dispirited, and Stein realized that a prolonged rest was absolutely necessary. After a search he found a shallow cave which gave some shelter from the elements, and with the remnants of their strength they dug it free of snow.

For two days they lay inert, huddled together for warmth, since even fur coats and sleeping-bags provided little protection from the biting cold. The only lively creature was "Sir Traveller", who had made the most comfortable ascent of the Pamirs ever known, in a basket strapped to a yak's back. It was his frenzied barking that announced the unexpected arrival of a Russian officer who had crossed Taghdumbash from its eastern side. He gave Stein much valuable information about the descent to Kashgar, then asked diffidently if his host could supply him with any powder or lotion which would destroy lice. When he added that he had bought his fur coat from a Sarikoli, Stein was not surprised by his request, as these tribesmen had their wives sew them into their coats in early September and did not take them off until the following June!

They bade farewell to the Russian and began their nightmare crossing of the Mintaka at an altitude of 20,000 ft. Owing to the rarefied atmosphere progress was pitifully slow; one assistant surveyor was struck by snow-blindness and had to be guided by Mahammed Yusuf, the head porter, while Ram Singh was in such poor shape that he had to be supported by two Sarikolis. According to Sadak Akhun, who knew the mountain well, it was the worst crossing of Taghdumbash he had ever experienced. There was no *burse* available for fuel, no respite from the icy wind that funnelled through the narrow pass, and if it had not been for Stein's faith in his "patron saint" and his overwhelming desire to uncover the secrets of Cathay the whole party would likely have perished, for the Sarikolis were superstitious folk and were sure that the mountain gods would put a curse on them if they advanced farther. With superhuman energy Stein cajoled, exhorted and bullied, driving the men forward until they reached the end of the pass. Most were in a state of collapse, but he permitted them only a brief rest for he knew that if allowed to relax completely they would never get to their feet again. He confessed afterwards that he remembered little of the descent. Numb with cold and exhaustion the party groped and slithered their way down between jagged spurs of rock until, just below the snowline, they came to Karakul lake which appeared to Stein as a great steel barrier between him and his goal. The long detour round its southern end added many miles to their journey, but on a day in August the bedraggled group limped wearily into the courtyard of George Macartney's Residency in Kashgar.

For the first time in over two months they were able to enjoy a

thorough rest, though Stein was up and doing again in forty-eight
hours, for he had many arrangements to make. First he had to pay
off Mahammed Yusuf and his Sarikolis with their yaks; then he
had to engage Turki porters, buy camels and ponies and replenish
food supplies. His old friend Macartney, who had been several
years in Kashgar, proved a tower of strength, and in the evenings
he passed on to Stein all the knowledge he had been able to glean
about the ancient trade route that lay just north of the Kun-Lun
range. The oases were few and far between, and while he felt sure
that in them Stein would unearth valuable relics of Cathay, he
stressed the fact that they were separated by vast stretches of barren desert and advised him to carry enough water and fuel to see
them through what he called "this abomination of desolation".
Stein, who had experience of many deserts, thought privately that
his friend exaggerated a little: he was soon to know the wisdom
of Macartney's words.

Towards the end of August they set out for Yarkand, marching
through a bleak, featureless landscape with no sign of vegetation.
The soil was of gravel and a cold north wind blew relentlessly, but
the sun shone from a clear sky and through the bitter nights they
kept warm enough huddled in furs and sleeping-bags inside their
yurts. As they progressed, the going became more difficult as the
gravel was now smothered in soft shifting sand which grew deeper
with every mile. When they reached Yarkand Stein found it hard
to believe the place had ever been a populous city, for at first sight
it consisted merely of a collection of dilapidated huts surrounded
by fields from which the inhabitants were laboriously gathering
their poor crops. Since he was now in Chinese territory Stein at
once paid a courtesy visit to the *ambun* in nominal charge of the
district and craved permission to start excavations. Mollified by
constant reference to the "patron saint" the Chinese gave gracious
assent and work began at once.

The results exceeded Stein's wildest hopes. Buried deep in sand
he found the remains of houses, built of timber frames filled in with
reeds and coated with plaster both inside and out, the ground floors
of which were in a remarkable state of preservation. From these
he took hundreds of records written on birch-bark, palm-leaf, silk
or thick paper, in a bewildering variety of languages. Many were in
the Indian Brahmi script used by the Kushana rulers of the Punjab;
some were in Aramaic, the language of Persians from Bokhara and
Samarkand; many again were in Kharoshthi, a script he knew from

coins discovered in North-west India; some were in Chinese, while others were in languages he was unable to identify.

The brief Turkestan summer had long departed and the temperature stood at twelve degrees below zero by the time Stein decided to move on to Khotan, once the capital city of Cathay. Their way led through the Taklamankan desert, which looked as he imagined the far side of the moon must look, a dead world of shifting sand-dunes with here and there a bare twisted tree silhouetted against the grey sky. This was the place Marco Polo had called "the Desert of Lop", and Stein reflected grimly that the Venetian's horrific description of it was in no way exaggerated. The north wind shrilled ceaselessly about their ears; frequently they had to stop and muffle their faces while a swirling sand-storm raged and as Stein shuffled forward nearly knee-deep in powdery sand Tennyson's line rang through his head like a recurrent jingle: "Better fifty years of Europe than a cycle of Cathay". Sand filled their ears, nostrils and mouths. They were parched with thirst and, despite strict rationing, their water supply ran out some fifteen miles short of their goal. Only "Sir Traveller", who enjoyed travelling by camel, retained his high spirits.

There were frustrating delays before Stein could begin the Khotan dig. The men had skin sores and blisters which needed treatment; the oasis inhabitants, intrigued by sight of the medicine chest, lined up outside Stein's yurt and beseeched the *hakim* (medicine man) to cure their ills. Sadak Akhun had accumulated a store of rice-spirit on which he got roaring drunk; the *ambun* thought the white man with the little dog was mad and it took a week of argument before he gave a reluctant consent—and even then he posted Chinese guards round the dig.

Somehow they got started and soon Stein realized that a veritable treasure-trove lay beneath the Khotan sand. The houses he unearthed were far larger and grander than those of Yarkand and the frescoes on their walls showed what a cosmopolitan place Cathay must have been, for some were unmistakably Roman in origin, while others were Greek or Persian. He also found innumerable reliefs of Graeco-Roman heads. One was a replica of Athena's shield bearing the Gorgon's head, and another a perfect miniature of a Roman legionary. Several Buddhist shrines were unearthed and these contained documents in Kharoshthi script written on oblong tablets or long slips of wood. The tablets had been placed in envelopes of bark which bore classic Roman seals, while the slips were bound together in pairs which were secured with similar seals. They could have continued to dig indefinitely, but time and money were pressing problems and in mid-winter they resumed their journey eastwards.

The cold was so intense that the ink froze in Stein's fountain-pen. Conditions were appalling and the shifting sand-dunes more treacherous than ever, but somehow they struggled from oasis to oasis. All yielded articles of value, but the find that pleased Stein most was in a Buddhist shrine unearthed at Miran. Here the walls were covered with glowing frescoes in a perfect state of preservation. At first glance they seemed identical with the famous murals in the Ajanta caves of central India, but close inspection revealed strange differences. One scene, for example, depicted three figures; an indubitably Persian girl, a typical Roman man and a boy with a pure classic head. Another illustrated an Indian Buddhist legend, but one of the figures was that of a youth of Levantine appearance wearing a Phrygian cap which bore the symbol of Mithras, the Anatolian god worshipped by Roman legionaries. More astonishing still, a short inscription written in Kharoshthi on the hind-quarters of the elephant in the picture, read: "This fresco is the work of Titus, who received 3,000 pieces of money for it." In simple terms, some time before A.D. 250 when Miran was smothered by sand, an itinerant Roman artist named Titus was commissioned to decorate a Buddhist shrine in the heart of Asia!

The party, now dog-weary, were nearing the narrow approach to China proper when Stein was intrigued by the presence of tall circular pyramids of sand which rose out of the desert at mile-long intervals. He set about clearing the sand from them and found they were ancient watch-towers built of mud bricks with guard-houses attached. He at once set about excavating the desert between each tower and uncovered an Old Wall which began nearly 200 miles north of the famous Jade Gate in the Great Wall of China. This Old Wall was made of slim bundles of reeds cemented together by clay and was eight feet thick. In places protected from the devastating north wind it rose to a height of twelve feet and Stein traced it for about a hundred miles.

The wealth of documents discovered in the guard-houses proved that the wall had been built in the second century B.C. to protect the trade route from attacks by the marauding ancestors of the Huns. At that time the emperors of the Han dynasty extended their empire to the farthest limits it has ever known, but by about

50 B.C. desiccation of the region was beginning to set in, though China continued to man the wall for roughly another 300 years. From the documents Stein learnt that the officers had been Chinese and the men, always alluded to as "barbarians", Indo-Scythian mercenaries armed and clad like Chinese regulars. Communications from the Commander-in-Chief of the Western Regions repeatedly urged the need for reducing rations and ordered that the "barbarians" be made to grow their own crops and cereals. Later documents showed how isolated and out of touch the garrisons became, and one dated "in the sixteenth year" of a certain emperor's reign was, in fact, written fourteen years after his death.

The year 1901 had but a few months to run when Stein most regretfully abandoned his excavations and led his party westwards since the time and money allocated by the Government of India were dwindling fast. A long train of camels carried nearly a hundred packing-cases filled with the treasures he had amassed, and by some miracle the caravan reached Kashgar without the loss of one man or beast. From here they struck north, crossing the Altai mountains into Russian Turkestan, where Stein supervised the loading of the cases on to a Turk-Sib railway train bound for Novosibirsk, at which point he and his load travelled by Trans-Siberian to Moscow and thence across Europe to London, where he handed over his precious cargo to the British Museum before returning to his usual duties in India.

Thoughts of all the sites he had been forced to leave untouched nagged at Stein continually and he beseeched the Government of India to allow him to return to Cathay. Early in 1906 he received their permission to do so and he made a second expedition, again with Ram Singh as companion. This time they crossed the Pamirs from Afghanistan and, as they had been given ample funds and two years' leave of absence, they were able to make new "digs" as well as to extend those already made at Khotan, Miran and other places.

Stein kept to the last the project dearest to his heart. Towards the eastern end of the trade route were many places where Buddhist cave-temples had been hewn out of the cliff-face above some former river by devout monks, and instinct told him that somewhere, could he but find it, was one which held a close connection with Hiuen-Tsiang. Most of the temples were empty and deserted, though south of T'a-shi, the "Valley of the Myriad Buddhas", he found a great number kept in good repair by a small community of priests who made their abode in them. Alas, they held no relics of value, so Stein pressed on to the little town of Tun-huang, where he was told of the Caves of the Thousand Buddhas just beyond it. These ruined shrines were occupied by a few Taoist monks, the leader of whom had collected enough money to repair one of the temples, and rumour had it that during this work the monk had found a walled-up chapel containing ancient documents.

Without delay Stein called upon this Taoist, accompanied only by his Chinese interpreter, and asked if he might see over the restored temple. The delighted monk showed him the newly decorated temple and the first thing Stein's eye lit on was a garish fresco depicting Hiuen-Tsiang, mounted on a pony laden with bundles of manuscripts, crossing a flooded river! This was surely a good omen, so Stein told the Taoist how he had long worshipped his "patron saint", how the holy man had watched over him on his travels, and how he had clearly guided his disciple to the temple so that he might blazon the news which had been brought from India some 1,100 years ago to the western world of the twentieth century. Deeply impressed, the Taoist led his guest through a rocky passage to the main cells, "and I could not help", wrote Stein later, "glancing to the right where an ugly patch of unplastered brickwork masked the door of the hidden chapel".

With supreme tact he went on discussing Hiuen-Tsiang's work, but when he bade the monk farewell his interpreter stayed behind and at last persuaded the Taoist to allow his master a glimpse of the hidden documents. Late in the evening the man came to Stein's *yurt* with a great bundle of manuscripts, which proved to be Chinese translations of holy Buddhist books written by Hiuen-Tsiang himself. Each bore a note to this effect and a reminder that the books had been brought all the way from India and transcribed so that mankind should benefit from their study. All night Stein pored over the writings and in the morning went to see the Taoist once more.

All day the two argued; Stein reiterating that his "patron saint" had guided him to recover these manuscripts from their ancient hiding-place for the express purpose of having them published abroad, the Taoist explaining his fears that the local folk who had helped him renovate the temple and his fellow monks might feel he had betrayed his sacred trust if he gave any manuscripts to a stranger. Finally he yielded, confessing that he truly believed Hiuen-Tsiang had sent his disciple; then led Stein to the now unblocked doorway. Beyond it, stacked together without any attempt at order, were 500 cubic feet of bundled manuscripts and scrolls!

For the next seven nights Stein and his interpreter toiled back and forth transporting the treasure, and when packed it filled twenty-four cases, while five more contained priceless religious pictures painted on silk. Stein told the Taoist that he would surely acquire divine merit and, tactfully and quietly, left him a large donation towards the restoration of the other cave-temples.

The party were inured to the harsh climate, but on their return journey they ran into such fearful weather that Stein lost some of his toes through frostbite and had to be carried over the Kun-Lun mountains to Tibet for treatment. Somehow he managed to forget all the pain he was suffering by concentrating on all the knowledge he had gained of the political history of Cathay. He saw the Han emperors guarding the country with Indo-Scythians who had originally been driven out of Turkestan by the northern Huns. The Kushana kings of the Punjab were of Scythian stock, and it was through them that the Buddhist faith first spread to Turkestan. He saw the fall of the Han dynasty about A.D. 200 and the gradual lessening of control by the Tang emperors until about A.D. 750 when the Tibetans seized and held for a hundred years a region that was by then virtually dead. He saw, too, the Greeks, the Romans, the Persians who had exerted their influence on this far land and, above all, the holy men like Hiuen-Tsiang stumbling their way across the vast desert.

The treasure from the Caves of the Thousand Buddhas eventually reached the British Museum in safety. Honours were heaped upon Stein and in 1912 he was made a Knight Commander of the Indian Empire. He was, however, a man to whom honours meant little, and until his death at the age of eighty-one in 1943 he preferred to think of himself as the disciple of Hiuen-Tsiang, the long-dead monk who had guided him to Chinese Turkestan and enabled him to uncover a whole cycle of Cathay.

TSCHIFFELY'S RIDE

Ten Thousand Miles

from Buenos Aires to New York

BORN IN Switzerland in 1895, Aimé Felix Tschiffely, after a fairly uneventful boyhood, began his professional career as a schoolmaster and taught in a number of schools in England, winding up as a temporary headmaster of a High School in Buenos Aires. Still young and physically fit, he felt the time had come to put into operation a plan he had been considering for several years. He believed it was a practical proposition to ride on horseback from Buenos Aires to New York, a distance of ten thousand miles.

When he first voiced his intentions, most people thought him crazy, but Tschiffely ignored public opinion and calmly went ahead with his preparations for the journey. He decided that he would make the attempt with two native Argentine horses. Through the good offices of the editor of *La Nación*, Argentina's leading newspaper, he was put in touch with Doctor Emilio Solanet, who was not only a breeder of Creole horses but also an authority on their habits and capabilities. The doctor confirmed that for long marches and for sheer stamina Creole horses could not be beaten. Descended from fine Spanish horses brought to Argentina in the first half of the sixteenth century by Don Pedro Mendoza, they were strong, patient animals with amazing powers of endurance. They could walk for incredible distances and would not be particularly disturbed by climatic changes and adverse travelling conditions. So enthusiastic did the doctor become about Tschiffely's project that he offered to supply the ideal horses for the trip.

Eventually Tschiffely assumed control of Mancha and Gato, a couple of far from docile creatures that had been broken in with great difficulty. Mancha was piebald; Gato had a coffee-coloured coat. Both had short, thick necks, strong shoulders and sturdy legs. They looked tough, as if they could give a good account of themselves even under the least favourable circumstances. They did not take kindly to being saddled, but once the saddles were comfortably fitted, Mancha and Gato calmed down and gave no further trouble.

At last, on the morning of Saint George's Day, the expedition set out, with Tschiffely riding Gato and Mancha serving as packhorse. After recent heavy rains the dirt road leading out of Buenos Aires had become a river of mud. It was by no means easy going, but the two horses jogged along quite unconcernedly, indifferent to a sudden downpour that tried to dampen their ardour. Mancha, indeed, had sufficient spare energy to kick Tschiffely's dog into a pool of water, shattering its shoulder-blade and forcing its master to leave the stricken animal in Moron, his first staging-place.

As there was no proper stabling in Moron, Tschiffely left Mancha and Gato at the local police station. He provided them with a bale of hay and then made for the nearest hotel, where he had to share a room with three other men. Armies of bugs launched such a vicious offensive that sleep was out of the question. In the end Tschiffely pitched the bug-infested mattress on to the floor and spent the rest of the night lying on the wire framework of the bed.

Next day he resumed his journey, heading across flat open country in the direction of Rosario. The dusty road lay between wire fences and ran straight as an arrow. More rain made the surface so treacherous that Mancha slipped and slithered beneath his load. The biggest nuisances, however, were motor-cars, some of which passed dangerously close to the two horses.

A heavier storm than usual drove Tschiffely to seek shelter and warmth at a wayside ranch. Attentive as always to the needs of the horses, he first turned them loose in a good field and then joined a party of men who were drying themselves by a fire inside a wooden out-building. This friendly gathering crouched beside the flames and shared a gourd of *yerba*, a stimulating Paraguayan tea. They also ate *asado*, a kind of meat slowly roasted and served in strips. Although the room was full of smoke, everybody stretched out on the floor and slept there.

Fortified by an unbroken night's sleep, Tschiffely moved on again, always across the vast, uninteresting plain. Occasionally villages or roadside inns broke the monotony. There was never any problem of finding covered accommodation at the end of each day's slog. The weather continued bad, but Tschiffely's plan was to reach the Bolivian border as the dry season was beginning. The daily drenchings were depressing, but there was consolation to be drawn from the fact that the farther he advanced, the more friendly and hospitable people became. Everywhere he met with the old-type settler's custom of welcoming strangers with an ever-open door. And if he happened to call at a house while a *fiesta* was in progress, then Tschiffely was invited to take part in the merry-making. At one *estancia*, for instance, he saw men and women in gala attire, feasted on roast lamb and sucking-pigs, washed this delicious fare down with wine of beer, and was a fascinated spectator at the exhibition of bare-back riding that followed the *siesta*.

As he drew nearer to Santiago del Estero, the countryside seemed even more barren. The land now was covered with pampas grass and giant cacti through which wandered big herds of goats. Here and there were primitive settlements of dark-skinned Indians living in miserable huts. Those who could spare it gave the dusty traveller dried goat's meat to eat.

But soon the semi-desert of Santiago del Estero was left behind and Tschiffely's appreciative eye was noting the hills and forests and irrigation canals. At farmhouses in the forest clearings he could obtain alfalfa in abundance and plenty of fresh water for Mancha and Gato. For himself there was a spotlessly clean village inn where he enjoyed an excellent meal and was able to relax in a comfortable bed.

Before undertaking the long trek to the foot of the Andes, Tschiffely stayed for several days at a farm not far from La Banda, an important town near Santiago. One night his generous hosts took him to see a travelling circus. The performance ended with a dramatic presentation, the closing scenes of which Tschiffely found unintentionally hilarious. The hero was killed "on a stage strewn with dead or dying friends and enemies, some having been stabbed, others shot, clubbed or strangled in a regular hurricane free-for-all fight".

Tschiffely's route northwards now passed through the fertile part of the Argentine that is devoted to the sugar industry and led him to the delightful little town of Tucuman. There he was lodged in the comparatively new military barracks and both officers and men put themselves out to entertain their unexpected guest. While in the "Eden" of the Argentine he seized the opportunity of visiting the historic house in which the document declaring Argentina to be a federal state had been signed over a hundred years previously.

Ahead loomed the mighty Andes, but before tackling the mountainous country north of Tucuman, Tschiffely and his equine companions (with whom he was now on the very best of terms) made their way through endless acres of sugar-cane fields where *mestizos* were cutting down the cane with machetes. He saw pretty, well-dressed girls, men drinking copiously at the end of their day's labours, ostriches and pumas, fast-flowing rivers and cockfights in Jujuy, just below the Tropic of Capricorn.

As for Mancha and Gato, they looked as fresh as ever, but Tschiffely was well aware that the two horses had not yet been fully extended. Although he was still confident that they would never let him down, he knew that certain adjustments would have to be made if they were to cross the mountain barrier successfully. To start with, he changed the pack-saddles completely. He also ensured that loads were kept to a minimum. He decided not to include a tent or a sleeping-bag, but to concentrate on such essentials as a cooking-pot, a kettle, items of food and drink, one large mosquito net and another small one to protect his face. His close attention to details at that particular stage suggests that he viewed the passage of the Andes as the toughest phase of the whole trip.

From Jujuy the road went due north between high mountains. Strewn with loose rocks and boulders, the irregular surface presented a stiff challenge to Mancha and Gato. Fortunately most of the rivers were dry; only a few held water where the currents were sometimes dangerous. Although the two horses faltered and stumbled occasionally, they somehow managed to overcome all obstacles, even in the sinister main valley, the Quebrada de Humahuaca, with its mysterious beehive graves and relics of a bygone age.

While he was examining one of the graves, a small thorn pricked Tschiffely's finger and subsequently blood-poisoning developed.

He was advised by a village medical expert to return to Buenos Aires, but this remarkable young man refused to acknowledge defeat. He pushed on as far as a mountaineer's hut and there was treated by an Indian herb-doctor who drew out the poison with a brew of simples and put his patient on his feet again within five days.

Shortly after this incident Tschiffely fell in with a party of Indians who said that they knew a short cut. The encounter saved him many miles of really rough travel. He parted with them at a side valley and continued in a northerly direction until he reached the unattractive border village of La Quiaca. When crossing the highest pass (11,000 ft.) at Tres Cruces, he had suffered from nosebleeds, but Mancha and Gato had not been affected by the rarefied atmosphere. Although they had covered thirteen hundred miles, they showed no traces of fatigue. Tschiffely's policy of placing their comfort before his own was undoubtedly paying dividends.

Feeling better for a brief rest in La Quiaca, Tschiffely was soon passing through a beautiful valley in Bolivian territory. His first "hotel" in Bolivia was no more than a mud hut with no ventilation whatsoever, but he was tired and slept soundly enough until he was awakened next morning by a prolonged beating of drums and a high-pitched cacophony produced by whistles and flutes. The villagers were celebrating the feast day of Saint Roque, the patron saint of dogs. With the band playing outside, all the dogs, gaily decorated with ribbons and coloured wool, were taken to church to be blessed. Later, in accordance with tradition, every dog in the village was turned loose to enjoy a few hours of freedom. Tschiffely's reactions to the resultant mass dog-fights are best described in his own words. As he sat outside his hotel room: "Suddenly a regular whirlpool of canine warriors of all colours and sizes came fighting up the street. During the heat of the battle one big growler knocked me off my chair, and while this was happening other retreating fighters took refuge in my room where a regular battle-royal ensued. One mongrel had obviously mistaken one of my saddle sheepskins for one of his enemies and dragged it outside, all the time shaking it and snarling viciously as if he were holding one of his foes by the throat, and had I not thrown my chair at him he would probably have torn my precious sheepskin to pieces."

A long day's ride brought Tschiffely to Tupiza, where he witnessed another *fiesta*. Then, instead of following the railroad to La Paz, he took a mountain route across the Bolivian highlands.

Among the many difficulties he ran into were tumultuous rivers, precipitous climbs and a shower of hailstones as big as pigeons' eggs. He also had to endure scorching heat during the day and freezing temperatures after sunset.

His next stop was at Potosi, the centre of a mining district at the foot of a mountain of the same name. The houses, with their quaint balconies and small grille-protected windows, had not changed much since the days of the Spanish invaders. In the Spanish mint, built of hardwood beams that were growing in the forests of western Brazil over three hundred years ago, the early minting machines still remained in a perfect state of preservation.

But the cold weather had started and Tschiffely could not afford to linger, for now he had to follow the old Spanish gold trail over the mountains towards Lake Popo. For Mancha and Gato the rocky uneven track was full of pitfalls. It was also necessary to take into account the fact that the territory was inhabited by the bloodthirsty Aymara Indians, a surly, unfriendly people, inimical to whites. The only disturbing incident for Tschiffely, however, occurred in an Indian settlement when he was forced to hide from a drunken chief. After spending an uncomfortable night under an oven, he was relieved to find the Indian in a more co-operative frame of mind on the following morning.

From Lake Popo, eleven thousand feet above sea-level, Tschiffely enjoyed the magnificent view across the Bolivian *mesa*. Thereafter his journey was mercifully downhill along a less exacting route, which passed through a few small villages and led to the busy little town of Oruro, where he discovered a reasonably clean hotel facing the main square. Mancha and Gato were accommodated in the public corral.

A few days later Tschiffely rode into La Paz, a colourful city presenting a curious combination of colonial and modern architectural styles. He called at the Argentine Embassy, where he was warmly received by the Ambassador and his staff. Mancha and Gato, in surprisingly excellent condition after their unwonted exertions, were made much of and given the best stabling available. Their master meanwhile sampled some of the amenities La Paz had to offer. One local custom did not impress him too favourably. At four o'clock in the afternoon everybody ate *picante*. This highly seasoned dish of turkey, chicken or other meat was so hot that he felt he "had taken a mouthful of glowing charcoal".

Much refreshed after his agreeable break at La Paz, Tschiffely now steered a course past the historic ruins of Tiahuanaco, and after spending an indifferent night in a squalid hotel he carried on as far as Guaqui, on the shore of Lake Titicaca. As the guest of a Bolivian regiment quartered in the lakeside village, he passed an amusing evening at a dance organized by the enterprising officers.

On the following day Tschiffely crossed a narrow bridge at the outlet of the lake, thus stepping out of Bolivia and into the Republic of Peru. It was not long before he was made uncomfortably aware of the strained relations that existed between Peru and Chile. Mistaken for a Chilean in one village where he halted, he came very close to being manhandled by the inhabitants. Awed by the distinctive seal on his documents, however, his would-be attackers quickly changed their tune. "Viva la República Argentina!" they shouted and urged him to stay in the village as long as he liked. Although he did not take advantage of their generous offer, he *did* accept their invitation to eat something. Mancha and Gato also benefited, for the contrite villagers provided them with a plentiful supply of fodder.

The next place of any consequence was Cuzco (the old capital of the Incas), a city of eighty thousand inhabitants, renowned for its many churches, its fine architecture and its picturesque ruins. It was there that Tschiffely met an Englishman who had spent much of his life in the Argentine and was interested in Inca relics. When his new acquaintance asked if he could join the expedition, Tschiffely reluctantly agreed and the two travelling companions moved off together; but within a few days the Englishman had completely lost his taste for adventure. Badly stung by mosquitoes, physically exhausted and uneasy about the possibility of violence from bandits, he wanted to get back to civilization. When they reached Ayacucho, a poverty-stricken town full of Indians and half-breeds, he was taken to the railway terminus by lorry and put on the train for Lima, thus terminating a partnership that had never been satisfactory.

The Englishman's departure heralded the start of the rainy season. Torrential downpours resulting in floods and landslides put paid to Tschiffely's intention of travelling by the regular road. He decided to go over the mountains to the west, but he was warned by the natives of Ayacucho not to attempt such a detour without the services of a guide who knew the area. The man he eventually hired conducted him part of the way and then disappeared with all the food supplies. Undeterred by this setback, Tschiffely pushed on as far as Pancara, where he obtained food and a bed for the night. From Pancara he dropped down to a pleasant valley through which ran the Central Peruvian Railway. Via a small railway terminus, the prosperous market town of Huancayo, a deviation through Tarma, he at length crossed the third Andean range and was able to look down on Lima, the capital of Peru. From those tremendous heights (16,500 ft. above sea-level) it took him two days to descend to the hot plains near the Pacific coast.

Naturally this man in heavy leather clothing, with his face badly chapped and in need of a shave, who came riding into Lima on one dusty perspiring horse, with a second equally travel-stained animal in tow, created something of a sensation. The crowd that quickly collected might have proved an embarrassment, but fortunately an intelligent policeman took control of the situation until the Argentine minister arrived to welcome Tschiffely. Stabling for Mancha and Gato was given top priority. Then Tschiffely himself, after bathing, shaving and changing into more suitable clothes, was shown the sights of the city. He saw Pizarro's remains well preserved in a glass coffin in the cathedral, the Bishop's palace, a gory but colourful exhibition of bull-fighting, and visited one of the officially sanctioned opium dens.

At last he was ready to move on. Mancha and Gato were acclimatized to the blistering heat and their thoughtful master had modified his equipment to suit the tropical conditions. Tschiffely was now committed to a long coastal journey almost as far as the border of Ecuador. Although the route lay across vast sandy deserts separated by wild dangerous rivers, he carried no water. He knew that the horses could satisfy their thirst in the streams rushing down from the mountains. For his own requirements he had two flasks, one filled with brandy and the other with lemon juice to which salt had been added.

On this coastal trek he frequently bedded down for the night in police stations, stabling the horses in prison yards. There was a certain monotony about the Peruvian diet of boiled rice, beans, fried bananas, eggs and black coffee and he found the villages insufferably hot and lacking in hygiene. His worst experience was crossing the hundred-mile stretch of desert (the *Matacaballo* or "Horse-Killer") between two rivers. Well aware that his only chance of success lay in breaking the back of the journey during the hours of darkness, Tschiffely set off at sunset and rode all through the night. The next morning was a scorcher, but he and his horses kept going until, early in the afternoon, the river was in sight. He was convinced that few other horses could have coped with that twenty-hour plod across the *Matacaballo*.

Tschiffely's route now lay through Trujillo, a town that did not appeal to him despite its exciting history, through the fertile Chicama valley, across the turbulent River Santa, then over the River Macara and into Ecuador. To avoid the Sechura desert he chose a fair trail threading the dense tropical forest-land to the foot of the Andes. For several days he zigzagged over high passes and down green valleys. At one of the villages where he stopped, a small Indian boy named Victor attached himself to the expedition. He made himself so useful that Tschiffely bought him a mountain pony and appointed him mule-boy.

Quito, only a few miles from the Equator, proved quaintly attractive with its antiques, military bands and thriving markets. Tschiffely found a first-rate hotel and rewarded Mancha and Gato with a liberal feed of alfalfa. Two days after leaving the city the horses were given a second treat. This was to celebrate crossing the line into the northern hemisphere.

Soon the little party was jogging along steadily in yet another country, Colombia. On the whole the road was good, but as they were passing through an area of volcanoes and earthquakes, there were patches of broken country and many tiring ascents. There had been no rain in the district for eight months and consequently fodder was expensive. The villages, too, had little to offer other than filthy hostelries and dilapidated huts. At this stage of the journey the heat was suffocating, so Tschiffely wisely resorted to night marches.

After a side-trip to Bogota to collect geographical data, Tschiffely was obliged to take ship to Colon. He first made for Medellin, capital of the state of Antioquia, and from there went to Puerto Berrio, a tiny port on the Magdalena river. It was a hot muddy place where cattle were being packed into flat-bottomed boats, without food and water. Although Mancha and Gato and Victor's pony had to travel in a barge alongside the passenger ship, they suffered no ill-effects from the three-day voyage to Calamar. Nevertheless, everybody was glad to get ashore.

The overland trip to Cartagena passed off uneventfully and soon Tschiffely was waving farewell to South America from the deck of the Dutch vessel *Crynnson*. The only casualty when the ship docked at Colon on the following afternoon was the boy Victor. Seriously ill with malaria, he had to be left in the hospital as he was in no fit state to support the unhealthy climate of Costa Rica, the next country on Tschiffely's itinerary after leaving Panama.

Held up for some time in the Canal Zone because Mancha had gashed his near hindleg on a wire, Tschiffely could not keep to the timetable he had worked out so methodically. He had intended to tackle the jungle and continental divide during the dry season, but owing to the delay he ran into torrential rain. To reach San José, the capital of Costa Rica, he had to negotiate Death Mountain, but once again Gato and Mancha (who was fit again) did not flinch from the formidable task that confronted them. For forty-eight hours they struggled along in cold, wet weather, patiently fighting their way up to and beyond the timber line and cautiously making the tricky descent during a veritable deluge.

It was still raining when Tschiffely rode into San José and called at the Argentine Legation to announce his arrival and to pick up the back mail that was waiting for him. The officials congratulated him on his achievements since leaving Buenos Aires, but advised him not to proceed via Nicaragua. The country was torn by revolution and no foreigner would be safe there. If he wanted to get to San Salvador he would have to go by sea.

Once more adjusting his gear to meet the exigencies of the ride ahead, Tschiffely made for Puntarenas, an unpleasantly sweltering port, and boarded the S.S. *City of San Francisco*, destination La Union. It was an anxious moment for him when Mancha and Gato, neatly crated, were swung from shore to lighter and then from lighter to ship, but the two horses survived the air-lift. The fuss lavished on them by the ship's officers and passengers more than compensated for any inconvenience they had suffered.

Glad to be back on dry land, the inseparable trio trudged through the stifling heat to San Salvador's densely populated capital. The outskirts of the city were dirty and depressingly poor, but the centre was clean with well-paved streets and charming little parks. As in most southern republics, although the upper classes were bright and lively conversationalists, they were fundamentally shallow and superficial, fond of making rousing speeches but reluctant to take positive action. The workers had to exist on starvation wages and a daily diet of beans and *tortillas*.

From the city of San Salvador to the border proved an easy trip. The frontier officials were evidently expecting Tschiffely, for they waived all formalities and went out of their way to facilitate his entry into Guatemala. Soon Mancha and Gato were ambling through the Mita valley, with its lush grasses and scented fir trees and sugar-loaf hills of volcanic origin. In spite of cold rains and thunder-storms, all three travellers were feeling happy and contented. The most arduous part of their long march now lay behind them.

Compelled by the foul weather to spend a night in Guilapa, a village with an unsavoury reputation, Tschiffely prudently chose to stay with a contingent of soldiers stationed in that locality. Mancha and Gato had to bed down on straw in the backyard. For many years Guilapa had been notorious for the number of murders and assaults committed there. Apart from a few stray shots after dark, however, nothing unusual happened and next morning Tschiffely again braved the pelting rain and headed for Guatemala City.

It was still pouring down when Mancha and Gato splashed their way into the capital. The streets were like rivers. The *Hotel Palace* provided Tschiffely with up-to-date accommodation and there was excellent stabling for his horses. As a relatively new capital, Guatemala City had little of interest for the sightseer, but visitors could always dance to the insistent rhythm of the many marimba bands. The people were courteous and affable and during his stay there Tschiffely made plenty of friends.

After leaving Guatemala City, Tschiffely followed the coast road via Antigua, through the missionary village of Tzanjuya, up to the top of a mountain and down a steep descent to the Mexican border. The steamy air and rich vegetation were characteristic of the tropical region through which he now had to pass. Guatemalan border officials met him at the Rio Suchiate and pointed out the small steel bridge that would take him into Mexico.

For the next fifteen hundred miles both Tschiffely and his horses were warmly welcomed wherever they appeared. As often as not there would be an enthusiastic escort to guide them from one staging point to another. Then, disaster struck. At a village hotel where the expedition halted, Tschiffely had no alternative but to corral the horses in a yard at the back of the building. When he went down in the morning to attend to them he found that a late arrival had tethered his mule alongside Gato. During the night the mule must have kicked out, caught poor Gato a nasty blow on the knee and started a terrible abscess. For a month the suffering animal received the best possible treatment, but the climate militated against a cure. In the long run Tschiffely was obliged to send Gato to Mexico City by train.

With the rainy season in full flood, Tschiffely thought it advisable to take a guide to help him cover the two hundred and fifty miles of swampland and jungle that lay between the Guatemalan border and Tehuantepec. The man he selected, Angel Riso, had not travelled far along that route, but luckily he turned out to be a great help. Tschiffely bought two horses, one for the guide and another to carry the pack and, happy to be astride Mancha once more, he was ready for the difficulties ahead.

On the curious caravan went, through forest and swamp, along muddy tracks and over swollen rivers, escorted by the military through the bandit-infested country in the State of Chiapas. Soaked to the skin and plastered with mud, they continued towards the Isthmus of Tehuantepec. By following the railroad in the direction of the Pacific, they at length rode safely into Tehuantepec, where they were accommodated in the City Hall.

After four wonderfully relaxing days in the old Mexican town, Tschiffely would have crossed the isthmus to Port Mexico, but because of the fighting over on that side he had to change his ideas and travel by way of the rugged, mountainous, uninhabited Sierra Madre, a formidable trek. It was indeed a sorry procession that limped into Oaxaca on the occasion of the town's annual *fiesta*.

A week later, however, with a fresh escort, the indefatigable Tschiffely was bound for Mexico City. He passed through Tehuacan, Tepeaca, Puebla and San Martin. At one stage he was plodding along mechanically, sick with malaria, but by the time he could see the snow-capped volcanoes, Ixtaccihuatl and Popocatepetl, he was beginning to feel better. His aches and pains were completely forgotten when, among the crowd assembled to welcome him, he saw Gato, fully recovered and overjoyed to be re-united with his master and with Mancha.

Tschiffely slept solidly for twenty hours and then was whirled through a varied programme of banquets, excursions, *fiestas*, bullfighting and theatres. It was with a heavy heart that he rode away from Mexico City, but he was to find the same warmth and hospitality wherever he stayed in Mexico–San Juan del Rio, Queretaro, San Luis Potosi, Saltillo and right through to Monterey. It was as if the Mexicans best appreciated the significance of Tschiffely's magnificent performance.

Then came the special thrill of crossing the Rio Grande and setting foot on the rich soil of Texas. From Laredo onwards the concrete roads and garages offered but cold comfort to Mancha and Gato. Tschiffely, on the other hand, was genuinely pleased to be in the United States and close to the finishing line of his ten-thousand-mile journey. He knew he could count on the full co-operation of the Texan Rangers, on the friendliness of the good people of Oklahoma, Missouri, Illinois, Indiana, Ohio and West Virginia. There would be flying at Fort Sam Houston, a visit to the MacAlester State Prison, a trip through the wooded Ozarks during the strawberry season, an excursion to the Blue Ridge Mountains and the passage of the Cumberland Narrows. But soon he would be seeing what he set out to see two and a half years ago, the dome of Washington's mighty Capitol.

Tschiffely's intention had been to finish his journey in New York, but he saw little point in risking serious road accidents along the short stretch between Washington and New York City. He had no wish to expose his incomparable horses to any further dangers. After all, they had brought him safely from Buenos Aires to Washington and had more than proved their worth.

THE PEKING-PARIS MOTOR RACE

The Golden Age of Motoring Pioneers

"AS LONG as a man has a motor-car," proclaimed the Paris newspaper *Le Matin*, "he can do anything and go anywhere." This statement, which even today would not be accepted without some reservations, was made in 1907, when the roads in most parts of the world were intended for the use of travellers using four-footed rather than four-wheeled methods of conveyance.

But 1907 was also "the golden age of motoring". The automobile was beginning to prove its capabilities, and France was in front of the field. Motoring, however, was still regarded as a sport rather than a practical and convenient method of transport, particularly over long distances. And so *Le Matin* issued its now classic challenge to motorists to drive from Paris to Peking, and thus prove that the motor-car had a potential far beyond its existing circumscribed use in racing circuits and minor rallies.

Le Matin's challenge produced an immediate response: entries for the race poured in from automobile manufacturers and enthusiastic motorists all over Europe. Because of weather conditions in China it was decided to run the race from Peking to Paris instead of the other way round. Rules were drawn up and schedules planned. An entrance fee of 2,000 francs (about £400 at present-day values) was fixed, and it soon became apparent that the over-all cost of the trip was going to be high, something like £20,000 for each car. This formidable hurdle, plus other practical difficulties of terrain and maintenence, caused many of the original entries to be scratched. In the end there were only five starters in the great 10,000-mile race.

One of these was Prince Scipione Borghese, an Italian nobleman who was well known as an adventurous mountaineer, motorist and man of action. He ordered from the Itala automobile works a new 40-h.p. four-cylinder touring car and proceeded to make detailed plans for the race, arranging through his wide diplomatic connections for dumps of fuel and spare parts to be left at strategic points along the route. He decided to take with him his dedicated mechanic, Ettore Guizzardi, who had served him from the age of fifteen.

The Marquis de Dion, president of the de Dion-Bouton Motor Corporation and founder of the Automobile Club of France, entered two of his cars. They were identical 10-h.p. two-cylinder de Dion-Boutons, and were to be driven by Georges Cormier and Victor Collignon, accompanied by their mechanics, Lelouvier and Bizc. Cormier and Collignon were both experienced drivers, but Cormier, a car dealer retained by de Dion to drive in endurance trials, had the more dominant personality.

Another French manufacturer, Contal, had entered one of his little 6-h.p. two-stroke *mototris*. This was little more than a glorified tricycle with a single rear driving wheel. The passenger sat in a bucket-seat over the front wheels, while behind him the driver was uncomfortably poised on a saddle-type seat. But the Contal had done well in various track events in France, and it was to be driven by Auguste Pons, with Octave Foucault (nicknamed "The Apache" because of his rather sinister features) as his mechanic.

Finally, there was the joker of the pack, Charles Godard. A former jockey, Godard was fanatical about motoring. He was a cheerful, brash, optimistic character, always the life and soul of the party and always short of money. Although completely broke, Godard was determined to take part in the race, and he was able to talk Jacobus Spijker, a partner in the Dutch Spyker car manufacturing concern, into entering a car which he, Godard, could drive. A Spyker car was duly provided, together with a comprehensive set of spare parts and spare tyres.

In due course all the contestants and their cars arrived in Peking. Prince Borghese, who had already spent some time surveying the route in his systematic way, reported that parts of the road were clearly impossible for motor vehicles, and that large and expensive gangs of porters would be necessary to haul the cars through and over obstacles.

The Chinese had been difficult over the question of issuing passports for the motorists to enter Mongolia, and at one point it looked as if the race might have to be abandoned. Prince Borghese, however, announced his decision to drive with or without a passport. The other drivers backed him up, and in the face of this unanimous decision on the part of the "foreign devils" the Chinese Imperial Grand Council finally gave way and issued passports.

On the morning of 10 June, 1907, the great Peking-to-Paris motor-car race got under way. After a celebration the night before and another farewell party in the morning, the contestants at last set off for the gate out of the city, followed by an admiring crowd and an official on horseback who had apparently been detailed to keep a watchful eye on the foreigners. The teams had agreed to drive in convoy during the arduous first stage of the journey as far as Irkutsk, so that they could help each other in the event of illness, breakdowns or other difficulties. This mutual-aid service was very quickly brought into operation, for the leading cars had hardly left Peking when they noticed that the Contal and Collignon's de Dion were already missing. Prince Borghese was furious, and insisted on continuing. It was Godard in the Spyker who agreed to go back to find the missing cars. He traced them in due course, having learned that they had taken a wrong turning in the city, and it was some three hours before they were all back in the race.

The road was made of ill-fitting blocks with many ruts, and before long the Contal was in trouble. The bad road surface persistently forced its front down and lifted its single driving wheel from the ground so that it could make only slow and erratic progress. The accompanying cars, not being in any great hurry at this stage in the long journey, frequently stopped and waited for the Contal to catch up.

Well ahead, Borghese in the Itala encountered the first formidable obstacle of the race, the once-beautiful marble bridges over the Cha Ho river. The bridge surfaces were of marble blocks, but they had subsided and fallen away from each other, leaving hazardous gaps and cavities. The steep approaches to the bridges had eroded away, leaving only narrow pathways of dried mud suitable, perhaps, for pack-animals, but not for heavy cars. Borghese, however, had brought with him specially made steel tracks which had been fitted on the Itala in place of mudguards. With the tracks under the wheels to provide a firm surface, and porters to push from behind, he was able to coax the car up the approach to the bridge, which was fifteen feet above the level of the road.

The other contestants, not having steel tracks, had to solve the problem by using block and tackle and manhandling their cars from road to bridge, all except Auguste Pons in the Contal, who had returned to Peking. He had had persistent trouble with his rear driving wheel over the rough roads and terrain, and the other drivers had agreed that, since the first stage of the journey was notoriously the worst, he would not be disqualified if he put the Contal on the train at Peking to the next stage of the journey at Nankow.

Borghese and Pons were, therefore, the only drivers to reach Nankow, forty miles from Peking, that night. The other teams pushed on long after dark until, exhausted, they decided to camp for the night, despite pouring rain. They did not realize that they were only one mile from Nankow.

The next day all set off on the gruelling climb over the three mountain ranges they had to pass to reach Kalgan, on the Mongolian border. It was over this stage that the porters proved their worth, for the cars had to be dragged, lifted and pushed through narrow gorges, over immense boulders, up steep gradients and far more dangerously down them again. The track was a camel-caravan route, and at times was only just wide enough to allow the cars to pass between the sheer rock walls of the gorges.

To add to the frustration, the porters would periodically give up and disappear to smoke pipes of opium. The so-called inns in which the travellers stayed were primitive and dirty, but the people were friendly and fascinated by the strange machines which the "foreign devils" had dragged with them. In due course, having passed through the Great Wall of China, and ploughed through rivers, mud and flooded paddy-fields in which the cars inevitably stuck and had to be dug out, they reached the plateau on which Kalgan was situated.

Prince Borghese in the Itala reached Kalgan a day ahead of the others; with his efficient equipment and very early starts each morning he consistently made the running. Kalgan had once been an important frontier town through which the camel caravans of the tea trade used to pass, but the opening of the Trans-Siberian railway had taken much of its commerce away. With the Russian-Chinese bank in Kalgan as their hosts, the teams were fêted and entertained, and their cars were thoroughly overhauled. They stayed there for two days, and left at four o'clock on the morning of 17 June for the final ascent of the plateau, after which the porters would no longer be needed.

In the seven days of the race so far the expedition had covered about 200 miles, and there were still over 9,000 miles to go. The next thousand miles, across Mongolia and the Gobi desert, were regarded as the most dangerous. Although petrol dumps had been laid down at the telegraph relay stations in the desert, if any of the cars broke down no help could be expected from anyone apart from other members of the party. The cars themselves had to carry adequate food and water supplies, and as much petrol and spare parts as possible, and anything that was not absolutely essential had to be jettisoned to reduce weight. The delighted porters, passing soldiers, and caravan drivers, gathered around to collect what they could of the goods being discarded by the car crews, including a case of champagne which Godard reluctantly threw out.

Godard had, with characteristic generosity, committed himself to assisting Auguste Pons who was still having serious trouble with his three-wheeled Contal: due to the weight carried at the front, the rear drive wheel would lose its grip on uneven ground. There-fore, to reduce the weight on the Contal's front wheels, Godard took on to his Spyker all Pons's food, petrol, tools and spare parts, and had to leave behind not only his champagne but also some of his own petrol stock. He blithely assumed that if he ran out of petrol before reaching Udde, the next desert petrol dump 370 miles away, he would be able to borrow a few litres from the other drivers.

The going, though rough at first, improved rapidly, but other hazards of a different kind were to arise. The poor little Contal still lagged well behind the others and arrived late at the next camping site, near to a small village, where all the teams spent the night together for the first and last time and planned the next stage of the journey.

In a desperate effort to make some headway, Pons in the Contal started off at three o'clock the next morning, but it was soon caught up and passed by the de Dions and the Spyker. In due course all the cars were passed by the Itala, going great guns, which had made a late start due to some trouble in stowing luggage. They roared across the empty desert, following the line of telegraph poles which marked the route to the distant telegraph station.

Early in the day's chase three of the cars made a mistake in direction which wasted some time, so that when it was observed that the Contal was nowhere in sight, the drivers assumed that it must have pulled ahead during the temporary diversion. However, they stopped for a while and waited to see if the Contal turned up, and when it did not they carried on towards Udde.

In fact, the Contal had run out of petrol, and was stranded in the middle of a baking wilderness. With neither fuel for the car nor water for themselves, Auguste Pons and his mechanic Foucault waited all day in the blazing heat for the other drivers to return to their aid, but they waited in vain. At the next camping post, when it was realized that the Contal was missing rather than late, Borghese persuaded the teams that there was no point in any of them going back to find the stranded car. Pons was still in an inhabited area, he pointed out, and he could get help locally.

Next morning they set off on the remaining 170-mile dash across the desert to Udde and the petrol dump. Before departing, Godard left behind two of his own precious cans of petrol to assist the Contal if it ever got so far. Then he drove off in the wake of the others, knowing full well that he had not enough petrol to get even half-way to Udde, but hoping to borrow some from the de Dions.

Pons and Foucault went in search of help, but found none. They then decided to drag their useless vehicle across the desert to the next camping post, or until help was found. For two days they struggled on, ill, exhausted, and without food and water, until finally they collapsed. Eventually they were discovered by nomads, who tended them for a while until they were well enough to be handed over to a troop of horsemen sent out from Kalga to look for them. It was the end of the race for Pons and Foucault. Leaving the Contal to rust away on the plain they returned to Peking, bitterly denouncing their companions who, they said, had betrayed them.

Meanwhile, Godard's petrol, as expected, ran dangerously low about half-way to Udde, and he begged the de Dion drivers to lend him some. This time they were less co-operative, however, and refused to part with more than a few litres. When the Spyker inevitably sputtered to its final halt they merely drove on after promising to send a supply of petrol out to Godard as soon as they reached Udde.

It was now the turn of Godard and his companion du Taillis to suffer the desert discomforts of blazing hot days and almost freezing nights. They had little food and water, and Godard sardonically regretted discarding his case of champagne. Two days and nights went by before they were able to make contact with a troop of warlike tribesmen. Godard, using sign language and waving money, managed to persuade them to ride to Udde and bring back cans of petrol, and this they did. Thus, after three days in the open desert, with cracked lips and sunburnt faces, exhausted but undaunted, Godard and du Taillis triumphantly drove the Spyker into Udde.

The others had been and gone, and were now well ahead. After their ordeal in the desert the two men should have rested for a while to recoup their strength, but Godard was determined to press on without delay. The next stop was Urga, on the opposite fringe of the desert, where the other contestants were to wait for him. In a grimly stubborn mood Godard completed this stretch of 385 miles in 24 hours with only one hour's rest—a record performance.

Godard's pleasure at this splendid effort outweighed his displeasure with the de Dion drivers who, he felt, had been responsible for stranding the Spyker in the desert. He greeted them warmly, and learned that Borghese had already left after an early morning start. The French drivers had slept late after a magnificent banquet given in their honour by the manager of the Russo-Chinese bank in Urga. The men were further entertained during the day, and visited the Grand Lama of Urga, a personage only slightly less holy than the Dalai Lama of Tibet.

Meanwhile, Prince Borghese in his single-minded way was pushing on across the 300 miles of Mongolia which still separated the Itala from the Siberian frontier. There was no road or obvious track to follow, and trouble lay ahead. Taking an easy-looking route across a lush green plain, the Itala suddenly became bogged down in swampy ground and began to sink. In great haste Borghese hired a team of horses to extricate the car from the quagmire before it was completely swallowed up.

Later, rounding the foothills of mountains on the way to Kiakhta, the next destination, Borghese inadvertently put the car into a quicksand. This time the crew frantically unloaded the car and even unbolted the body from the chassis in order to slow its descent. Eventually, with the aid of some Mongol peasants and a team of oxen, they were able to pull it out. Progress continued to be maddeningly slow. Interminable rivers and swamps had to be crossed or circumnavigated. Often it was necessary to remove the magneto and bind the engine with oily rags in order to get the car through the water without damage.

After the swamps and rivers came soft sand, which had to be dug down to a firm bed for the tyres, and sandstorms—and then the Itala and its crew reached Maimachen, the last town in China. Here the men were entertained with all the warmth of Chinese hospitality that they had encountered previously. Then, "cleaned, wined and dined", they crossed the border into Siberia and Imperial Russia.

At Kiakhta the petrol stocks which should have been laid down had not materialized. Prince Borghese managed to obtain enough petrol to reach Verkhne-Udinsk, the next stage, from a man in the town who had a motor-car, but there was no guarantee that he would find petrol there either, and in the event there was none. But Borghese, always resourceful, discovered a supply of petrol in the little town which was normally sold for dry-cleaning, and he bought the lot, some fifty litres.

Through rain, seas of mud and swollen rivers the Itala ploughed on to reach Lake Baikal, a huge inland sea. There was no ferry, so Borghese set off round the southern perimeter of the lake on a track which no longer existed, and across rotting bridges, one of which actually began to break up as the car crossed it. It seemed inevitable that they should finally come to a bridge that was completely broken, and that it should span a swift, impassable river. A local woodman thought that the bridge could be repaired in a week, but the Prince was not prepared to wait that long. On a sudden and daring inspiration he returned to the last town they had passed through and sent a message to the Governor-General of Siberia requesting permission to drive along the single-line track of the Trans-Siberian railway. Astonishingly enough, permission was granted.

And so the Itala joined the railroad. At a monotonous and uncomfortable pace of ten miles an hour the car bounced along the railway track, one set of wheels bumping over the sleepers between the lines and the other set outside the rails. The crew took with them a railway time-table, so that they could get clear of the track when trains were due to pass by on the single line, and a policeman with a red flag, who was authorized to stop trains if necessary. All went well, in a jolting way, until the time came to leave the track to give right of way to an imminent train. At a siding they pulled off the main line and went back to the road, with the intention of rejoining the railway at a level crossing a few miles farther on.

They came to a wooden bridge over a ten-feet deep torrential river. At this point the policeman, from intuition or experience of the area, decided to leap out of the car. Prince Borghese inspected the bridge with care, but it looked no worse than many others which the Itala had crossed safely enough. With his crew-members, Guizzardi and Barzini, he drove on. Disaster overtook them in the middle of the bridge. The wooden planks under the back wheels of the car splintered and collapsed, leaving a hole through which the Itala fell backwards and downwards, to land vertically on the bed of the river with its bonnet pointing upwards.

The crew managed to get clear, although Borghese and Barzini were bruised and slightly injured. Their escape was lucky, for the car had landed on the stack of spare tyres strapped vertically on its back, and this had acted as a concertina-like cushion, reducing impact and damage. Meanwhile the policeman, who had so prudently baled out before the catastrophe, dashed back to the railway and re-appeared shortly with about twenty platelayers. They immediately got to work with ropes and tackle, and in a remarkably short time had hoisted the Itala out of the water and back on to dry land. Guizzardi, the mechanic, made a thorough overhaul of the engine. Miraculously there was nothing seriously wrong, and within five hours of the accident the car was back on the road, and presently back on the railway.

As they came near to the port of Tankhoy, which was to be their night-stop, they were nearly run down by an approaching freight train, and only managed to lever the car from the track with seconds to spare. Despite this narrow escape, Prince Borghese decided to return to the tracks for the final run in to Tankhoy. There they learned that there would be no further railway hazards, for the Itala had now been scheduled as a special "train" in its own right, and worked into the time-table. However, despite the temptation of an "easy" but slow run to Irkutsk, the incessant bumping of the track sleepers was steadily shaking the car's fabric to pieces, and the Prince settled for a ferry trip on a ice-breaker, across the narrow neck of Lake Baikal, and thence by road through driving rain to Irkutsk to a warm welcome, banquets and festivities which lasted the better part of two nights.

a man named Stephan who was a skilled automobile mechanic sent out specially from Amsterdam by Spijker complete with a case of

In the meantime, Godard and the de Dions had left Udde in pursuit of the Itala. They encountered the same wearying succession of bogs and quicksands, and the same difficulties with bridges, but they did not drive along the Trans-Siberian railway track. In due course they, too, crossed the Siberian frontier to be met with an enthusiastic welcome and gay hospitality, but they were by now nearly three days behind Borghese, and still a long way from Irkutsk.

When they reached Lake Baikal they received a message from the Prince warning them that the path around the lake was impassable and that they should, if possible, take a ferry. But there were no regular ferrycraft plying on the lake, so the drivers put their cars on goods wagons and travelled by rail to Irkutsk. They arrived there on the evening of 3 July to find that Prince Borghese had left the town only that morning.

Festivities and celebrations in Irkutsk delayed them for two days before they could get under way again, but now the Spyker was giving trouble, and Godard was becoming worried. He plugged an oil leak in the back axle with a piece of raw bacon as a temporary measure, but a few hours later the magneto failed. Horses were hired to drag the Spyker to the nearest town. The de Dion mechanics worked for four hours on the magneto, but without success. Godard then asked the de Dions to continue, while he proposed to send the car by train to Tomsk, where it was certain to be serviced, and the return by train to the point of the breakdown and start again. Du Taillis, as representative of *Le Matin*, decided to go on with the de Dions as the main body, but first Godard borrowed money from him to pay for the train fares and car repairs.

So the de Dions pressed on towards Tomsk through the glutinous thick black mud of the Moskovy Trakt, skidding over country paths made of logs, many of which had been removed by local peasants for their own purposes, and becoming bogged down time and time again. In Tomsk they found Godard with the Spyker at last repaired, but while they drove on westwards, Godard had to put his car on a train and return to the spot where he had broken down, and then set off anew to catch up with the de Dions. He was now about ten days behind them.

Godard drove furiously and he also had a card up his sleeve. At a small village between Omsk and Tomsk he stopped to pick up spare parts for the Spyker. Thus reinforced, Godard belted on-wards like a bat out of hell to narrow the gap between the Spyker and the de Dions.

For the de Dions the roads improved but conditions deteriorated. They had to cut their way through a prairie fire, and then drive through unending rain and mud into the Ural mountains. When they reached the border separating Asia and Europe they drank a bottle of champagne which du Taillis had reserved for that moment. Then they struggled on through Birsk, where they rested for three days, to Kazan, still driving through rain, but now on a proper metal-based road.

In a Kazan inn they fell into an exhausted sleep, but were awakened at four o'clock in the morning by an unexpected noise. Rushing out on to the balcony they saw in the courtyard below the Spyker with two apparently dead men in it. One they recognized as Godard; the other, not known to them, was Stephan the mechanic. Godard, in a mood of stubborn determination, had finally made up the ten-day gap. And he had done it by driving for twenty hours a day non-stop, grudgingly snatching a few hours sleep when it became absolutely essential. His hands were raw from the steering wheel, but he had kept up the gruelling pace, making only one night stop at an inn in the Urals. The last stretch of the journey, which the de Dions covered in four days, Godard had done in less than one, even though both he and Stephan were ill with exhaustion and dysentery.

Prince Borghese had passed through Kazan two weeks earlier, and the remainder of the journey across Russia and into Germany on proper roads was relatively simple. The only delays now were caused by the crowds that turned out at each town and city to welcome them and invite them to social functions and receptions which, especially in Moscow, they were expected to attend unceasingly. Finally Prince Borghese, an inveterate planner, announced when the end was in sight that he would enter Paris on 10 August, just two months after the start of the race at Peking. He was as good as his word. On the appointed day he was halted in the Itala just outside Paris while a procession, headed by a charabanc carrying a thirty-piece brass band, was lined up in front of him. Finally, to a tumultous welcome from enormous crowds, the winner of the great Peking-to-Paris Motor Race reached his final destination.

At this time the two French de Dion teams, plus Godard and Stephan in the Spyker, despite their illness and exhaustion, were hot-footing it through Russia towards Europe. The rain poured down and the road was a bog. On the first day they covered only twenty-four miles. It continued to rain incessantly for four days on the unprotected drivers in their open cars. But at last they reached Nijni-Novgorod, from which point there were real hard-surfaced roads, and somehow the rain did not seem to matter any more.

The three cars arrived in Moscow on 14 August to a reception that was, perhaps, even more impressive than Borghese's. Two days later, after the cars had been thoroughly serviced and the crews had been thoroughly entertained, they set off again on the final lap into Europe. Everyone was cheerful and gay. At this point Godard, with his superior speed, could easily have pulled ahead of the de Dions, but he preferred to stay with his companions.

But there was trouble ahead for determined but irresponsible Godard. Some of those financial deals he had organized in Peking to raise money by pledging Spijker's credit had been rejected by Spijker, although later he had changed his mind when he realized the extent of the prestige which Godard had achieved for Spyker cars. But the executives of *Le Matin* did not know about the reconciliation between Spijker and Godard. They feared that Godard might pull ahead of the de Dions in order to enter Paris first, and so take the glory from the French cars. Consequently, producing evidence to the police of "false pretences" in China, the newspaper's managing director, Jules Madeline, had Godard arrested.

Godard's friends had got wind of the plot and had already engaged a lawyer to secure Godard's release. Spijker, also in the know, had brought another driver from Germany to take over the Spyker if the worst happened, then he and his associates returned to Amsterdam in disgust.

The cars went on without Godard, but at Enghein, a small town about eight miles from Paris where the cars were again halted for an official reception, Godard reappeared. As the crews prepared to set off Godard jumped into the Spyker with all his old brash insouciance, determined to drive into Paris. But it was not to be. Despite all du Taillis could do to stop them, four of Madeline's men appeared and dragged Godard from the car. The police joined in the fracas and poor old good-natured Godard, who always had more determination and drive than money and circumspection, was taken away. The cars then drove into Paris to another tumultuous reception from which *Le Matin* extracted the maximum amount of publicity without Godard.

In the event Godard was ordered to repay some of the money he had obtained from the Dutch diplomatists in Peking, but he did not go to prison. Some time later he entered, on borrowed money, a new *Le Matin* motor race, from New York to Paris, via Japan, but dropped out due to mechanical trouble before he had reached San Francisco.

Auguste Pons, who had driven the three-wheeled Contal, also entered the New York-to-Paris race, but he too had to retire before reaching the west coast of America. Later he settled down and married. His daughter was Lily Pons, the opera singer.

The Peking-to-Paris race was never repeated, despite an attempt to revive it on its fiftieth anniversary. Today, political boundaries offer greater hazards than geographical terrain.

THE CAVES OF ICE

Norbert Casteret's Discoveries

MOST OF us at one time or another have explored a cave, even
if only as tourists conducted by a guide. We have seen stalactites
and stalagmites, and other weird and often beautiful formations
which have been created over the centuries from mineral deposits.
On a more professional level the world's "caverns measureless to
man" are systematically being measured and mapped by spelaeologists and pot-holers who penetrate the strange underworld of
eternal darkness with the same kind of dedicated enthusiasm that
impels men to climb forbidding mountains simply because they are
there.

But in the ice caves which Norbert Casteret discovered in the
Pyrenees, officially recognized at the time as the highest ice caves
on record, the fantastic fairy-like sights which met his eyes were
formed not from deposited rock but from frozen water. The stalactites and stalagmites, the pillars and bizarre outcrops, were all of
solid ice, revealing in the artificial light of his lamp and flares a
translucent beauty of form, reflection, shadow and colour far trans-
cending that of ordinary caves of mundane rock.

The caves of ice were virtually on Casteret's own doorstep, but
he did not come upon them until he was nearly thirty years of age.
A native of the upper Garonne valley in the northern foothills of

the Pyrenees, he spent all his life in the region, apart from the war years and various expeditions to caves in other parts of Europe and North Africa. He has for decades been acknowledged as one of the world's top experts on spelaeology, and an authority on the strange, highly specialized forms of life that dwell in the perpetual darkness of caves including all species of cave-living bats. He found time to write a number of books on cave exploration which have been translated into many languages. His individual talents have not gone without recognition; he was not only appointed a Chevalier of the Legion of Honour in France, but became also the only French author to be a laureate of all four Academies–Française, des Sciences, des Sports and des Jeux Floraux.

It was in July, 1926, that Norbert Casteret first discovered the wonderful cave which was subsequently named after him, La Grotte Casteret. It lay nine thousand feet high in the uppermost tiers of the Marboré massif, on the Spanish side of the frontier, above Gavarnie in the Pyrenees. It seems likely that Casteret was the first human being ever to penetrate the cave to any depth, but on the first occasion he had no equipment with him and so postponed the preliminary exploration until the following month.

With his young wife, Elizabeth, Casteret returned to the cave a few weeks later. With axe and rope they made their way through a succession of ice galleries, frozen waterfalls and an underground glacier to emerge on the south side of the mountain peak among a chaotic area of rock, ridges and fissures, known to geologists as a *lapiaz*. Here they rested for a while, and Casteret's wife fell asleep.

Casteret himself was in a restless mood, convinced that the cave system they had just explored, though spectacular enough, was merely a foretaste of something much more magnificent. So, while his wife slept, he set off to explore the *lapiaz* to its northern limit, where it ended in a snowfield. Beyond rose a steep cliff, and at the foot of the cliff was a fissure which he was convinced, from experience was the entrance to a cave.

Naturally, no spelaeologist could resist the temptation to investigate farther. Without hesitation Casteret crawled in, lit a candle-end which he had in his pocket, and looked around. He was in a cavern in which he was able to stand upright. At his feet an expanse of granular snow (a *névé* of the kind that feeds a glacier) sloped downwards into the darkness. He followed it carefully, descending some sixty feet, until he found himself standing on a sheet of ice. Here the glimmer of the candle was reinforced by a shaft of daylight coming through a chimney in the roof of the cave. He saw that the ice-covered walls of the cave were of a fantastic sea-green hue.

Casteret was in a vast gallery of ice which was impenetrably dark beyond the shaft of light and the minute glow of the candle. He continued cautiously until he noticed that the floor of the ice immediately ahead looked darker than that on which he stood. Crouching down and holding the candle at arm's length he discovered that the darker line marked the edge of an abyss, and it was impossible to see what lay beyond.

He abandoned the exploration at that stage and went back to his wife to tell her what he had discovered. Although they were both eager to continue the investigation, other commitments made it impossible. Casteret vowed that one day soon he would return to complete his exploration of the ice caves, but for Elizabeth there was to be no return.

Twenty-four years went by before Casteret was to return to the Marboré massif and the ice caves which bore his name. Meanwhile his wife had died, and when in 1950 he finally returned to La Grotte Casteret he was accompanied by two of his five children, his elder daughters Maud and Gilberte. It was to some extent a sentimental as well as a scientific journey.

Casteret escorted his daughters through the first cave system. It had not changed in a quarter of a century, except that some of the stalactites and stalagmites had possibly grown by a fractional amount. He watched with amusement as the girls searched enthusiastically for some extension of the cave or other feature which might have escaped their father's notice. At one instant, Maud, prostrate on the ice, was energetically forcing her way through a narrow opening close to the floor. Only her feet were still visible when Casteret saw her suddenly spread her legs and try frantically to brake with her heels against the rock above. He leaped forward immediately, caught her feet and pulled her back. Maud, quite unruffled, explained that the ice floor just beyond the opening plunged into a sheer drop, over which she had almost slipped. To test the depth of the abyss she threw a lump of ice over the edge. The listeners could hear only the long-drawn-out sound of its fall fading into silence. Maud had narrowly escaped almost certain death.

The single rope which Casteret carried was obviously inadequate for the negotiation of such a deep cavity, so he wisely postponed its exploration. Instead, the party made their way up the mountainside to the other fissure higher up in the *lapiaz* which he had discovered and tentatively probed in 1926. Here, too, he had been stopped by an ice precipice, but this time, on a rope anchored by the point of an axe driven into the ice, he climbed down into the abyss. The depth was not as great as he had imagined, and soon he landed on a sheet of rough granular ice, and set off to explore.

In the light of his lamp he could see that the floor spread out around him like a frozen lake. Behind him towered the wall of ice he had just descended, and on either side were perpendicular rock faces. The floor ahead sloped upwards in a series of hummocks and then continued horizontally. Slipping and sliding, for he had left the crampons off his shoes on the top of the ice wall, Casteret finally succeeded in climbing the hummocks and so broke through to the gallery beyond—another circular lake of ice so clear that he could see stones embedded many feet below the surface. A giant stalactite of pure ice hung down almost to the floor, and the walls were hung with frozen cataracts.

Close to the entrance of this gallery he found several others: the Snow Cave, an enormous hall with a thick carpet of snow which fell through an opening in the roof; the Grotte du Névé, with a sloping floor of frozen snow rising at the far end to a huge mass of broken rock; and a third gallery which, after a long walk over the level surface of an ice river, terminated in a large hole too deep to descend and a frozen waterfall too high to scale with the available equipment. Casteret decided to call a halt to the exploration, for the lamps were reaching the end of their useful life, and the below-freezing temperature added greatly to the over-all strain and fatigue. He knew only too well that the return journey to the surface could be every bit as hazardous and exacting as the more exciting inward penetration.

One week later Casteret and his two daughters returned to the massif to explore the deep shaft which Maud had so sensationally and dangerously discovered in La Grotte Casteret. This time they took with them a steel-wire ladder. A single piton was driven deep into the ice floor of the cave by the low opening in the base of the wall. This was the anchor point for the ladder, which was then pushed through the opening until it unrolled into the abyss. Then Casteret slithered backwards through the narrow hole, his chest pressed to the ice floor, his back scraping on the rock above. Holding the ladder he allowed himself to slide over the edge of the abyss, then cautiously climbed down the swaying rungs. He was face to face with a perpendicular wall of ice, as smooth and transparent as glass, some sixty feet deep and about one hundred and fifty feet wide.

The ladder was not long enough. It terminated six feet above the sloping ice floor of a large gallery. Casteret was not to be put off–he let go and jumped. Landing safely, he called for Maud to join him. She made the descent in complete darkness so that he could take a photograph of her with the aid of a magnesium flash. Gilberte was less fortunate; she reported that the piton holding the ladder had loosened under their weight, and Casteret thought it advisable that she should remain above to superintend the return journey.

Casteret and Maud proceeded to inspect this new fantastic grotto. In the centre of the sixty-yard gallery was an immense column of pure transparent ice, broad at the base and tapering up to the remote ceiling. Access to what appeared to be other galleries was cut off by mounds of thick ice. But the most astonishing feature of the cave was the vast vertical ice wall down which they had descended. Casteret himself described it as a "frozen Niagara", but it was a smooth, polished and transparent Niagara in which pebbles could be seen embedded to a depth of ten feet, and in which Maud discovered the mummified body of an ermine, perfectly preserved, which had long ago suffered the fate that nearly overtook Maud a week earlier and had become entombed in the ice for ever.

They regained the ladder–no easy task as the foot of it was six feet from the floor–and climbed up to the Grotte Casteret, while Gilberte grimly held on to the loose and shifting piton. Casteret and his daughters camped among the rocks of the *lapiaz* during the bitterly cold night, and were astir early the next morning. Their breakfast was delayed by the unexpected appearance of half a dozen leaping chamois, whose agile beauty delighted the party. On impulse Casteret decided that the caves in the area, whose existence had never before been suspected, should be named Les Grottes des Isards (Caves of the Chamois). This was geographically in character since it was adjacent to a ridge already named Col des Isards.

Maud, who had been scanning the mountainside through binoculars, suddenly announced that she thought she could see the mouth of a new cave that they had not so far explored. This was enough to trigger off a new expedition. Up a steep *névé*, with its hard-packed frozen snow surface, Casteret, Maud and Gilberte toiled laboriously. The *névé* disappeared, curving beneath a low arch of rock. Maud crawled into the opening to make a preliminary reconnaissance, but returned almost at once with the news that ice began just beyond the entrance and continued for some distance.

They put on their crampons and, carrying lighted torches, crawled into the grotto and set off along the ice-floored path. Very soon the ceiling dropped lower and lower until they were obliged to crouch and even lie down and drag themselves along with great difficulty. They emerged at last into a big circular chamber of small significance, and from there progressed through another passage, with a floor of wet ice, into a lofty cavern where twin columns of ice ascended to the distant roof. Beneath the floor they could hear the sound of running water. Farther on, the water they had heard emerged as a tiny stream at the bottom of a deep, narrow crevasse.

The crevasse followed a gentle downward gradient towards the centre of the mountain. The roof again became progressively lower until the explorers were obliged to crawl flat against the ground, pushing their haversacks before them. All the time a film of water ran over the ice, soaking elbows, knees, chest and abdomen, and to add to the discomfort the gradient became steeper and more unmanageable. The danger of being swept willy-nilly over a yawning gulf seemed very real. Finally, to add insult to injury, an icy wind suddenly rushed up from the depths of the cave, lashing their faces and howling so that they had to shout at each other to make themselves heard.

In spite of the adverse conditions, they forced their way through the narrow tunnel until the ceiling rose and the wind died away. Now they were in a wide corridor with a gentle gradient, and they were able to stand up. They took time off to wring out their clothes before pursuing the course of the underground river. All were numb with cold in the frozen heart of the Marboré massif, even though outside, on the surface of the mountain, the sun was blazing with the dry heat of midsummer.

In due course a steep downward slope led to a spacious glittering cavity embellished by a towering column of ice which had probably never before been seen by human eyes. From this point the frozen river continued, passing through a high gallery with vertical walls on either side. The Casterets walked on, stopping from time to time to massage frost-bitten fingers and toes. Down the centre of the river of ice ran a rivulet of clear water, seeking its way into the interior of the massif. It was merely a shadow of what in former times must have been a raging underground torrent tearing its way into the heart of the mountain.

A sharp turn, and the ice floor plunged abruptly into a chasm thirty feet wide, whose depth it was impossible to judge. It was certainly too deep for the limited amount of equipment which the Casteret party had been able to bring with them, and proved to be an impassable obstacle. They turned back and retraced their steps some twenty yards to an equally impassable obstacle of a different kind—a cascade of ice falling like a petrified waterfall from an enormous height.

To climb is frequently easier than to descend, however, and Casteret decided to use his ice-pick to cut steps up to the top of the cascade. Slowly, with the aid of axe and crampons, Casteret reached the top, watched by his daughters down below. At the top the cave continued and forked into two diverging galleries which held the prospect of further fascinating exploration which he was unable to resist, even though they had already spent too long in the caves and were beginning to suffer from the persistent and unrelenting infiltration of cold.

He flung a rope down to his daughters and helped them to climb the cascade. They set off down one of the galleries, lined with dry crystal ice, in the direction of the faint sound of a distant waterfall. Presently they came upon a curious phenomenon: in a subterranean world where everything was frozen solid a powerful jet of water came plunging down through an opening in the roof and disappeared in a cloud of spray through a kind of trap-door in the floor. The mystery of the source and final destination of this water could not be solved, however, for fifty yards farther on they encountered another frozen cascade, a falling curtain of ice which filled the gallery from side to side and from roof to floor, completely halting any further progress.

The party retraced their steps and tried the second gallery. They found themselves in a corridor of exciting proportions which led directly to another obstacle in the form of a long precipitous slope, the depth of which could not be seen in the limited range of the torchlight. They employed the usual primitive means of reconnaissance, rolling boulders down the slope and listening for the sounds of impact. The boulders bounced and bounded along with plenty of noise, fell over a silent drop, and then could still be heard slithering on into the distance, accompanied by the tinkle of breaking stalactites. The sounds became fainter and fainter, but there was no indication that the boulders had come to rest.

In the end the only way to survey the slope was to try it for size, in person. As it was evidently a long slope, Casteret tied the wire ladder and the two ropes end to end. He was just about to start his descent when Gilberte pointed to a huge chandelier of ice poised above their heads from the roof. Shaped like the canopy of an enormous four-poster bed, this vast stalactite ice-formation seemed so precariously suspended that only by a miracle did it remain in place. The slightest sound or vibration might bring it crashing down on their heads. At this terrifying sight Casteret almost called off the whole venture. He studied the ice canopy for a long time and finally decided that it would, in terms of chance, be unlikely to fall during the few minutes that they took to pass beneath it. The risk was accepted, and they proceeded to descend the steep ice incline.

The slope down which the boulders had been hurled ended in a vertical drop which led to another steep incline of smooth ice. Casteret and his daughters pushed on with the aid of the ropes and the ladder. The gradient duly levelled off into a shallow bowl in which were scattered the rocks that had been rolled down from above.

In front of him Casteret found yet another cascade of ice, but beside it was the aperture of a narrow tunnel in the ice. Into this he forced his way, but was finally brought to a halt by an impassable plug of solid ice which marked the ultimate limit of the cave that it was possible to reach, though beyond the ice the tunnel continued downwards into the mountain, following the path that had been excavated thousands of years earlier by the underground river. Unable to make any further progress, he began to retrace his steps. Stiff with cold, but fortified by a hot drink he had brought down with him, he made the arduous climb back, by rope and ladder, to where Maud and Gilberte awaited him, stamping their feet in an effort to keep warm.

But it was not yet the end of this fantastic journey of discovery; returning along the broad ice river which ended in the unfathomable abyss, the party stopped to admire an impressive column of transparent ice. Casteret walked around the perimeter of its massive base, and thus, by accident, caught sight of an opening some six feet up in the rock wall. He promptly climbed up to it, and the girls joined him. Despite the surfeit of visual wonders that they had already witnessed and photographed, all three cried out in amazement. Before them was a gallery adorned with a wealth of sparkling ice crystals of a beauty and elegance such as they had never seen—a veritable Aladdin's cave. The crystals which bedecked this subterranean ice-palace were eight to ten inches in diameter, perfectly transparent, octagonal in shape and reminiscent of certain spiders' webs. Perhaps the most remarkable feature of this new and final grotto was a "bush" of ice, three feet high. Its base was white and opaque, but it had spread upwards and outwards in some inexplicable way, becoming translucent and then transparent with a delicate slender tracery of branches and twigs of intricate and incredible elegance. Casteret suspected that the ice formations in this gallery were thousands of years old and probably fossilized.

Farther along the gallery the fragile crystals were replaced by a film of sparkling hoar-frost. Casteret, striding ahead and bemused with admiration, was brought to an abrupt standstill by a violent impact which shook him from head to foot and knocked the torch from his hand. Completely bewildered, he looked around and realized that he had walked straight into a thin hanging curtain of transparent ice, so flawless as to be invisible, which now lay in fragments on the floor around him.

It was an occasion for laughter, and also regret at having damaged such a rare natural phenomenon, but proceeding with more caution Casteret came upon further curtains of ice and pure, virtually invisible stalactites. Before long he was forced to halt before a baffling green luminosity, like light seen through thick foliage from inside the mouth of a cave. Putting out his hand he found that he could actually touch this light. It was, in fact, another solid curtain of ice, similar to the one through which he had broken, but this time several yards deep. The green light was the natural colour of perfectly pure ice reflecting the light of his torch. It was an emerald door sealing off the gallery and making any further progress impossible.

In a way it was a disappointing ending to the most exciting phase of the exploration, but it was more than compensated for by the magnificent crystal beauty of the gallery as a whole. Casteret named it the Gallery of the Ice-Flowers (*La Tonnelle des Fleurs de Glace*).

The journey was over for the day. Norbert Casteret and his two daughters wearily and painstakingly retraced their steps to the surface via the dangerous and arduous paths that had led them into this frozen fairyland–through the glacial caverns where the eternal silence was broken only by the mournful howling of an icy wind.

The Grotte des Isards is there to this day, unchanged and unchanging, but it is an adventure for professional spelaeologists and not tourists. The full extent of the caves has not been explored, and much remains to be discovered beyond plugs and barriers of deep ice. The requirements, apart from adequate equipment, are tenacity and endurance, which Casteret had in full measure, and without which he could not have completed his long and fantastic journey.

Even so, the Marboré massif will inevitably yield more of its secrets to single-minded spelaeologists like Casteret, but of a younger generation, in years to come.

THE BRAZILIAN MYSTERY

The Disappearance of Colonel Fawcett

THE DISAPPEARANCE of Colonel Fawcett in the Brazilian jungle is one of the classic mysteries of modern journeys. Fawcett was a seasoned explorer who knew South America better than most, and he was fired with a romantic quest for a lost city in the Brazilian hinterland. In 1925 he went into the jungle with his son Jack and a friend, Raleigh Rimell, and they did not return. The many stories and rumours which filtered through to civilization during the decades which followed converted a not unusual disappearance in these remote and savage regions into an enigma for which there may never be an answer.

Fawcett was first and foremost a traveller, a lone wolf who spent most of his life in the distant backwaters of the vast South American continent, gladly suffering its discomforts, facing its dangers, and witnessing its horrors, its brutalities, its beauties and its splendours. Fawcett went to the South American rubber forests at the time of their greatest disrepute, at the beginning of the century, when European rubber companies were forcing the natives to collect rubber by such barbarous methods that it caused a world-wide scandal.

Born in 1868 at Torquay, Percy Harrison Fawcett entered the Army from Woolwich and served in Ceylon, Malta and Hong

Kong. He did secret service work in North Africa, learned surveying, and in 1906 began his life of exploration in South America
when he went to Bolivia under the joint auspices of the Royal
Geographical Society and the government of Bolivia. This was the
beginning of years of wanderings.

In 1924, just before he left on his last great journey, he wrote
that, of his twenty-four years of married life, he had spent only ten
of them with his wife. Four years were spent in the Great War
and ten in the great forests. "Yet my wife has never complained.
On the contrary, her practical help and her constant encouragement
have been big factors in the successes so far gained, and if I win in
the end the triumph will be largely due to her."*

On his first visit in 1906 Fawcett found in South America a
mixture of grandeur, romance and horror. Off the west coast, from
the deck of a ship rolling in a huge Pacific swell, he saw the Cor-
dilleras towering in snowy splendour behind the coastline of Peru.
Then followed a fabulous mountain journey from La Paz down
into tropical Bolivia, along perilous mountain paths with a breath-
taking panorama revealed at every turn. This journey was made
on sure-footed mules which on the narrow mountain ledges always
chose to walk nearest to the precipitous edge with the rider, heart
in mouth, looking down a sheer drop of thousands of feet into the
canyon below. Sometimes a pack-mule's load would catch on a
jutting rock, the impact of which would send the unfortunate beast
screaming over the edge of the precipice.

Down in the steaming, unhealthy jungles of Bolivia were to be
found horrors both of nature and of man. In 1906 the scandalous
oppressions of the rapacious rubber companies were only just beginning to trouble the conscience of mankind. Fawcett saw these
atrocities at their worst, just before Roger Casement's visit to the
Putumayo district of Peru, and the world-wide scandal which
resulted from his report of conditions there.

But in the Amazon nature itself was raw, full of terrors and
highly inimical to man. The snakes were fearsome creatures.
Anacondas of immense size—the largest from sixty to eighty feet in
length—lived in the swamps and were terrible enemies of man, with
their fetid, supposedly stupefying, breath, and fatal bite. The
surucucu, or bushmasters, were particularly aggressive and were
known to hunt a man down. They were lightning strikers, always
aimed hip-high and their bite was usually fatal.

* Exploration Fawcett by P. H. Fawcett (Hutchinson).

The river itself was infested not only with vicious anacondas and crocodiles, but the very fish were deadly. There were six-feet-long electric eels with a shock sufficient to paralyse and drown a man. The loathsome *candiru*, a fish two inches long with swept-back barbs on its body, which sought to embed itself in the natural orifices of any other animal, or human, and which caused fearful agony and even death, as once inside it could not be extracted because of its barbs, was another peril risked by anyone who swam in or fell into the Amazon. Yet another fearsome fish was the flesh-eating *piranha*, which was attracted by blood or open wounds. Piranhas attacked in shoals and were known to have stripped a carcass to the bone in seconds. A man swimming in the Amazon could have the flesh of his legs torn off him by these terrible little fish before he could scramble to safety. To be caught by a swarm of these vicious and blood-thirsty creatures where they infest the riverside abbatoirs could be practically instantaneous death. A mode of torture in those days was to put a bound man with a small cut on his body in the river to be eaten alive by *piranhas*.

The upper reaches of the Amazon were plagued with monstrous spiders of the tarantula type, called *apazaukas*, which could be the size of a dinner plate and whose bite could mean death. By the sultry river banks the plagues of insects were sometimes more than sanity could stand. At sunset the skies were darkened by huge and voracious mosquitoes, and night-time brought great vampire bats which would even gnaw through mosquito nets to get at their human victims.

The very air was laden with disease and decay. Life was short. Mortality was unbelievable. Humans took to alcohol to escape the burden of existence. Fawcett would arrive at villages and find every soul in the place either ill or drunk. Natives chewed a cane which contained a high proportion of cocaine, which after a time made them practically immune to pain. It also gave immunity to many of the forest diseases.

It was not really surprising that such a place brought out the worst in man. When Fawcett journeyed down from the Andes into the hot rain-forest of Bolivia, he was prepared to meet nature at its most formidable and dangerous, but he was not prepared to meet his fellow white man at his most wicked, most cruel and depraved.

It was the heyday of the rubber companies' exploitation of the forests of the Amazon basin. The rubber could only be collected by native labour, and the natives not unnaturally did not wish to do this; they had their own primitive economy, and the rewards offered by the white man were insufficient to tempt them to change. The result was enforced labour, slavery, beatings, floggings, nameless atrocities and wholesale murder. The rubber was produced at the cost of endless suffering and thousands of lives. The companies employed the most brutal and depraved managers and overseers, the sweepings of the slums and prisons of Europe. The use of inhumanity was in the circumstances the only way of getting rubber. The result was a scandal of an enormity which could be compared with the Nazi concentration camps thirty years later.

Slaving raids were frequently made upon Indian villages during which all the adults were seized or slaughtered and the children's brains were dashed out against the trees. The Indians in reprisal killed every white man on sight. The Government were gravely concerned about the situation, but were unable to do anything about it. Their underpaid officials, far from the seat of government, in a wild an lawless district, were bribed and bullied into acquiescence.

Fawcett found that slavery was openly carried on in the Amazon during the first decade of the century. He knew a German who bought a young Indian girl, had her educated in Europe and then married her. Fawcett found the girl attractive, a charming hostess who spoke four languages, and the mother of a delightful family. She was one of the fortunate few.

The poor opinion the white men had of the Indians—many regarded them as wild animals to be slaughtered—was not always shared by the white women. At Riberalta Fawcett met an Austrian woman, whom he described as vivacious and handsome, and who regularly went off into the forest alone to live with the Pacaguaras Indians, who had given her a fine collection of tooth necklaces and other savage jewellery in return for her favours. And there was the story of the wife of a Bolivian Government official who got lost on the river during a native attack. The Indians cared for her for years, and she was finally restored to her husband by a band of slave-raiders, together with her four half-caste children. The shock killed the husband, who had in the meantime married his step-daughter, but the lady survived for many years and was proud of her remarkable experience.

Fawcett was glad to get away from Riberalta, where he could

hear the sounds of flogging all day long in the police compound, and where even white people were sold as slaves in order to pay off the crushing debts they had incurred with the rubber companies whose ruthless credit system gave them enormous power over their employees. Fawcett was prepared to endure the beastliness of nature, but not that of man. He got on well with the forest Indians, who, he found, only became savage when they came into contact with the "savages" from the outside world.

Percy Fawcett was more than just a traveller and explorer. He was a dreamer, and he fell completely under the romantic spell of the South American continent. Few dreamers are men of action, pioneers and practical investigators; but Fawcett was. He was a talented and in many ways a brilliant man. He excelled at everything he took up—soldiering, engineering, yacht-designing, drawing. He wrote with distinction and style. He even played cricket for his county. He was something of a mystic and had an interest in the occult. Indeed a man of many parts.

Everyone who travels in South America becomes interested in its lost and abandoned cities. With Fawcett they became an obsession.

Most of these cities are Inca remains, the most celebrated being Machu-Picchu, a fortress city straddling a mountain ridge 8,000 ft. above sea-level, north-west of Cuzco in Peru, which was discovered in 1911.

There are many stories of lost cities in South America, and it was in search of one in Brazil that led Fawcett to make his last fatal journey into the unknown Matto Grosso. This particular city was supposed to be located in the eastern part of Brazil, in the mountainous district which lies to the east of the Sao Francisco river. Fawcett gave its position as 11° 30′ S. and 42° 30′ W. He first heard about it in an old document preserved in the archives at Rio de Janeiro. It was written by an unnamed and unknown Portuguese pioneer, whom Fawcett, for the sake of identification, calls Raposo.

In the year 1753 Raposo and a few hardy companions set off into the trackless hinterland in search of the lost mines of Muribeca—the story of which is a strange tale in itself. For years they wandered deep in this unknown country in untiring search for the fabulous Muribeca treasure, surviving many dangers and hardships. Eventually they had to admit failure and the disheartened party started to make their way eastwards towards the coast settlements.

They travelled through swamps and bush, and then came across some jagged mountains, the rocks of which were made of crystal quartz, not unusual in that part of Brazil. The mountains glittered in the sun, and to Raposo and his men it looked as though they were studded with gems. They thought they had found the Muribeca treasure at last, and they pressed forward eagerly. When they reached the foot of the mountains they saw precipices rising sheer and unclimbable above them. They spent hours trying to find a way up. The place abounded with deadly rattlesnakes, against whose bite they knew no remedy.

Not until evening, when they had decided to camp for the night, did they discover the chink in the mountain's armour, and this quite by accident when two of the party were looking for firewood and came across a cleft in the face of the precipice which was fairly easily climbable. The party clambered up the crevice, which seemed in places to be artificially made, and emerged at the top on to a ledge high above the plain below, and stood there gazing in stupefied amazement at a large city stretched before them beyond the lip of the plateau.

Their first reaction was one of fear, for they thought the place was inhabited. They thought it might be the last stronghold of an ancient civilization, such as the Incas in Peru, still holding out in this impregnable fortress against the European who had invaded the continent. As they gazed from behind the crest they could see no sign of life, no wisp of tell-tale smoke. The city lay wrapped in complete silence. It was all very frightening and unnerving, and night fell quickly with them lying huddled together, talking in whispers, afraid to light a fire, unable to sleep, each a prey to his superstitious fears. The Indians in the party were no less afraid, and could throw no light on this strange place. To them it was just taboo.

The next morning Raposo sent an Indian to make a reconnaissance, and the man returned in a state of fear, saying that the city was one of the dead, uninhabited at least by the denizens of this world. And so Raposo and his men cautiously entered the deserted city. As they reached it they saw it was in a state of ruin, but the ruins were massive—huge arches, megalithic temples, tumbled columns, all belonging to an age so long past that their minds reeled. They came to a great square, in the middle of which was a huge column of black stone upon which stood a majestic statue of a man with one hand pointing towards the north. They went into a vast ruined temple where millions of bats winged in circles among the eroded frescoes and carvings.

They walked through streets of two-storeyed houses, the stone walls of which were made of blocks which fitted together with great accuracy, and in the building of which no kind of mortar had been used. One part of the city was in complete ruin, just mounds of stone and masonry, in some cases half buried by earth. Here they found great chasms and openings in the earth as though made by an earthquake.

The Portuguese explorers spent some time in this ruined city, exploring it, although their superstitions would not allow them to sleep in the place at night. They found gold coins and the sealed-up entrances of what looked like mines. They decided to return to civilization and then come back with a properly equipped expedition to remove all the treasure from the city and open and examine the mines.

Raposo and his party eventually got back to Bahia on the coast, where Raposo wrote a report and gave it to the Viceroy. It was pigeon-holed and forgotten. What happened to Raposo, whether he returned to the lost city or not, is unknown. The document eventually found its way into a government archive in Rio de Janeiro. In the nineteenth century a half-hearted and unsuccessful attempt was made to investigate the story, after which the document was again forgotten until Fawcett dug it out when he was at Rio.

He was convinced of its authenticity. What impressed him was Raposo's remarkable description of the city, particularly such details as the statue of the man pointing north and the mortarless joins of the great stone blocks of the buildings. Raposo could not have known about any of the ancient cities of old Peru, thought Fawcett, which had not been discovered in his century. The fact that he was able to describe the city as he did showed that he could not have invented it. The statue on the black pedestal was seen in another such lost city discovered in 1913.

Fawcett believed that in the very dawn of history a great civilization had arisen in South America which was overwhelmed by a cataclysm that completely destroyed it. This catastrophe is reported in many folk legends. There was a tradition that the Atlantic Ocean on the European as well as the American side was made unnavigable owing to the tempests resulting from it. Fawcett even suggested that this catastrophe caused the Andes to form, although geologists say that the Andean range was formed during the Tertiary period, which was long before the appearance of man upon the earth.

However, convinced that the 1753 lost city existed, Fawcett set out to find it early in 1925. A letter was received from him dated 20 May, 1925, and was sent from Baciary Post, Matto Grosso, in which he said he expected to be at his main objective in August. "Thereafter our fate is in the lap of the gods." The last message came back with returning natives from Dead Horse Camp (Lat. 11° 43′ S. and 54° 35′ W.) saying that he, Fawcett, and his son Jack were well, but that he was worried about Raleigh Rimell, who was having trouble with his leg, but refused to go back. Fawcett added: "You need have no fear of any failure."

Since then nothing has been heard of them, and their fate remains a mystery to this day.

About two years later the rumours started. In 1927 a French civil engineer named Courteville claimed that when he and his wife were motoring through the province of Minas Gerais in Brazil they met a ragged old man sitting by the wayside. The old man told them his name was Fawcett. He looked ill and confused, said Courteville, as though he had suffered terrible hardships. Courteville said he knew nothing about Colonel Fawcett until he returned to civilization and reported the incident. Had he known he would have brought the old man back with him.

In 1928 Commander G. H. Dyott led an American expedition which retraced Fawcett's route. In the region of the Kuliseu river they came across evidence which suggested that Fawcett and his party had been killed by Indians. The Fawcett family, however, refused to accept their findings. In 1930 a journalistic expedition went into the jungle to try to solve the mystery, but in vain.

A sensation was caused in 1932 when a Swiss trapper, Stafan Rattin, arrived at Rio de Janeiro with the story that Fawcett was being held a prisoner of an Indian tribe in the Matto Grosso, and that he had met him and spoken to him. But the description Rattin gave did not satisfy Fawcett's family, and the old white man, who said he was an English colonel, and was dressed in skins and had a long yellowish white beard, did not actually say that he was Fawcett.

More credence was given to the statement of an Indian woman in 1933 of the existence of three white men answering to the description of the two Fawcetts and Rimell, living with the Aruvudu tribe in conditions of captivity. They had gone native, according to her. Fawcett was looked up to as a leader and a doctor, and Jack

Fawcett had married a native girl who had borne him children. The white men were unable to escape, she said, because they had run out of ammunition, and the district was surrounded by fierce tribes. If they had tried to escape, she said, even the friendly Indians would have killed them, for they followed them and watched them wherever they went. She inferred that the white men were making the best of their situation.

It is known that wild Indians acquire great prestige among neighbouring tribes by holding a white man captive, and there have been a number of reports of white men living in such circumstances in the little-known parts of Brazil. White men who venture into the interior usually have a knowledge of medicine, a knowledge which the Indians find very useful, and this is an additional reason why they are unwilling to let them go.

Another search for the Fawcett party was made by two brothers, Patrick and Gordon Ulyatt, in 1935, but natives prevented their going into the district where it was thought they were living. The Indians robbed them of all their equipment, except their rifles, and sent them back. The Ulyatts when they returned reported that rubber workers had heard quite a lot about Fawcett, and that the area where he was supposed to be was surrounded by unfriendly tribes.

In 1937 a lady missionary came up with another report of Fawcett and his son living with an Indian tribe, this time in another part of the Matto Grosso. Now a boy purported to be the son of Jack was produced, but not accepted by the Fawcett family. As the years passed interest in the Fawcett mystery increased rather than died down, and many attempts were made to solve it, a number of them palpably bogus, regardless of the feelings of the Fawcett family.

In 1951 a dramatic death-bed confession of an Indian chief was produced. This chief said he had clubbed the three white men to death following a quarrel. After the chief's death the tribe were persuaded to disclose the burial place, and the bones were exhumed, examined by anthropological experts in London and declared not to be those of Colonel Fawcett.

Other solutions and theories have been put forward, but no one has solved the mystery. Like many other such disappearances, that of Colonel Fawcett may always remain a mystery, even though the true explanation may be simple and prosaic.

What of his quest?

Colonel Fawcett stated pretty exactly where he believed the lost city was, but this area had been regularly flown over by air lines and systematically examined from the air, and no trace of an ancient city has been found there. This particular area in fact is well settled by civilized inhabitants, and was so at the time Colonel Fawcett left on his last journey.

It is difficult to see why so well informed a man as Fawcett was deceived into thinking the lost city existed at this spot, or why he should risk his life in the pursuit of an obstinate, romantic belief.

There does exist in that region a peculiar weather-worn sandstone formation which, from a distance, could be mistaken for old ruins. It is believed that the Portuguese pioneers of two hundred years ago saw this, and the rest of their tale was fashioned in their bemused imaginations. The ancient cities were not unknown in those days, and the descriptions which so impressed Fawcett may have been interpolated in the report kept for so long in the Brazilian archives.

Whatever the truth of it, the story of Colonel Fawcett is certainly one of the most romantic travel stories of the century.

LINDBERGH CROSSES THE ATLANTIC

Epic Journey of the Air

IT WAS, and it remains, one of the epic journeys of history: it ranks, in its own way, with the first flights into space. For Charles Lindbergh's flight across the Atlantic in 1927 was a flight into the unknown. "Outer space", by the time man entered it some three decades later, had been assailed and investigated by dogs, monkeys, portable television stations, every manner of scientific instrument. Lindbergh was embarking, alone, with one engine (built into a highly unsuitable little aeroplane), on a journey almost twice as long as that completed by the world-famous Alcock and Brown eight years previously.

But Lindbergh's flight, once it was over and the sceptics had been won over, gave rise to the greatest campaign of hero-worship, deification, the world had ever known. An American newspaper pointed out that Lindbergh had performed "the greatest feat of a solitary man in the records of the human race" and no one saw fit to disagree. Another paper devoted no less than one hundred columns of text and pictures to him; even the staid *New York Times* set aside the whole of its first five pages to a description of the man and his feat. President Coolidge of the United States despatched a cruiser to France to bring this young private citizen back home with his aeroplane. The Western Union telegraph company provided form messages of congratulation for the aviator and 55,000 of these were sent to him. From Minneapolis came one singleton telegram bearing 17,500 signatures, printed on a scroll 520 feet long, and this was carried during the civic welcome and parade in New York by some ten messenger boys, lurching under the weight.

Lindbergh was commissioned colonel and was awarded his country's highest military honour, equivalent to the British V.C., the Congressional Medal of Honour. He was offered every sort of distinction and financial consideration by the governments of foreign countries, while, at home, his signature sold for sixteen hundred dollars.

A few weeks previously this shy young man had been almost unknown. There had been a flutter of interest when he entered the big race to be first in crossing the Atlantic in a heavier-than-air machine, a slightly greater interest when it become known just how he proposed doing it, and much more when it became known that he had actually set out.

But it was as the extraordinary journey was nearing its close that the world's imagination took fire; took fire rather more spontaneously than that of the American ambassador in Paris, Myron T. Herrick. Herrick was a kind and thoughtful man whose interests and duties had taken him, on the day of Lindbergh's take-off, to Saint-Cloud, where he watched a tennis match between America's hero, Big Bill Tilden, and the French champion, René Lacoste. The next morning it was announced that the young aviator's "stunt" had carried him past Newfoundland, out over the Atlantic; but the whole affair still seemed foolish, unnecessary and doomed to failure. In view of the disappearance over this same Atlantic of the Frenchmen Nungesser and Coli, engaged on the same foolhardy exploit, but in the opposite direction, this American attempt was in poor taste. Or so Herrick reasoned. In some quarters there was still a hope that the Frenchmen would somehow be found, alive; while this possibility existed, any other attempt to fly the Atlantic and win the Orteig prize was in the poorest of taste, and Herrick feared for Franco-American relations, already in pretty poor shape.

But it was during the second afternoon's tennis at Saint-Cloud that Herrick was quietly informed of Lindbergh's passage over Ireland. Furthermore it now seemed that the French public, far from feeling resentment, was working itself up to a pitch of hero-worship. The young American had already covered the worst part of his journey: even if he crashed now, he would still have achieved more than any other flyer in flying's short history. The newspaper *Liberté* wrote breathlessly of uniting "in one fervent thought the names of Lindbergh, Nungesser and Coli. If Lindbergh should disappear in the immensity of the ocean, we shall think of his mother and shall join the same pious thought—mother of Lindbergh, mother of Nungesser, mother of Coli".

But Lindbergh did not disappear: he kept on coming, and the American ambassador, hurrying to his office from the tennis court, suddenly realized that the French people were as emotionally involved with the young American stunt pilot as were his own people back in the States.

Lindbergh had been seen over Cornwall, over the English Channel, over France. Mr Herrick gulped his dinner, headed in his car for Le Bourget airport. Already the roads were packed solid with other cars, heading the same way, and the Ambassador quietly cursed himself for not having realized the significance of the occasion, not having started a great deal earlier. But he got there, found the field packed with vehicles and humanity, etched out in the brilliance of arc lamps. An area at the centre of the great field had been kept clear for the landing, but to the Ambassador it looked ominously as if the crowd would surge out and obliterate even this, inadequate-seeming, landing place.

And then he heard it. A distant buzzing, like a homing bee. The Ambassador glanced at his watch, saw it was just ten-fifteen. He looked up, looked all round the heavens, saw nothing but swirling cloud. Then suddenly Lindbergh was over the field, banking hard only a few feet up, coming in on his approach. The proud name *Spirit of St Louis* was clearly visible, just behind the radial engine. Half a minute later the tiny aeroplane was on the ground and the crowd, roaring its enthusiasm, had broken through the police cordon, submerged and hidden it. Fearful of his young compatriot's safety, yet unable to do anything about it, Herrick retired to an upstairs waiting room where a number of French officials had already gathered. He was holding a bouquet of red roses, wondering if he would have a chance of handing them over.

Suddenly a downstairs window broke and a dishevelled head appeared, framed in it. The French officials down there realized instantly who it was: the young Monsieur Lindbergh had managed to escape tho crowd–oh, but how they had loved him. His tie was hanging loose, his shirt torn, he was gasping.

Mr Herrick also took in the situation at a glance. Beaming, he handed over the roses.

"But I'm *not* Lindbergh!" said the angry young man.

The Ambassador was not in a mood for frivolity. "Of course you are," he said, giving the roses a final shove into the unwilling hands of his young compatriot. Surely this was carrying modesty too far.

But of course it was not Lindbergh. The unfortunate American who had joined the thousands at Le Bourget to welcome the flyer had been unlucky enough to catch Lindbergh's flying helmet when someone threw it into the air. In the darkness and confusion, this was good enough for the crowd: there could not be *two* young Americans at Le Bourget with flying helmets. They mobbed the unfortunate Mr Wheeler, embraced him, tore half his clothes off his back.

The comedy of error was resolved and Charles Lindbergh, a little dazed and deafened by the thirty-three and a half hours he had been travelling behind a noisy radial engine, was rescued from the adoring crowd at the other end of the field and taken away by the Ambassador. "Young man, I'm going to take you home with me and look after you."

And so the extraordinary flight ended. But the adulation was to go on for another decade and more. The hero-worship which began with headlines in all the world's papers, varying from the *Denver Post's* LINDBERGH LANDS IN PARIS GREAT OVATION GREETS AIR HERO GIGANTIC CROWD RUSHES ON FIELD AND PULLS HAGGARD FLYER FROM HIS AIRPLANE, to the London *Observer's* CAPTAIN LINDBERGH'S TRIUMPH. PARIS REACHED AT 10.22 P.M., was to grow ever more hysterical.

Who was this young man, and what had he done to deserve such adulation?

He came from the Middle West of America, land of open fields and waving corn, and he had taught himself to fly. With a partner he had given demonstrations of stunt flying and parachuting, had taken passengers up for trips, dropping down into any convenient field to collect them, and using the money they gave him to pay off the aeroplane he was buying for his own use. He had then learnt that the United States Army was anxious to train men as combat pilots, and that if he were accepted by them he would get a full year of the finest flying in the world, in more powerful machines than he could ever hope to purchase for himself. He was accepted, did well on the course—only a very small percentage got through—and was commissioned into the United States Army. Then, in common with almost all the others, he resigned and went on the Reserve. A little later he was an Air Mail pilot, flying mail about the Middle West with the same panache and bravura that had characterized his early days as stunt flyer.

One can only hazard a guess as to what Charles Lindbergh's future might have held had Raymond Orteig not offered his handsome prize of twenty-five thousand dollars for the first non-stop flight between New York and Paris—in either direction. He was a rich man—he owned both the Brevoort and Lafayette Hotels in New York—and the sum he put up, though a fortune to the men who now considered whether to risk everything for it, was a small one to Orteig. And it seemed unlikely that it would ever be awarded. There had been the Alcock-Brown flight of 1919 from St John's, Newfoundland to a bog in Ireland, but this was a mere 1,960 miles as against the 3,600 between Paris and New York and for the first few years after the 1919 offer of the prize, there were no takers. Orteig, now an old man, retired to his native France (the "bringing-together of the two nations in service of aviation" had been his prime motive) and announced that the prize was still there, waiting for the right men. Men in the plural: no singleton would be able to stay awake at the controls of a bucking plane for the time required to cross the Atlantic. And by 1927 there were several teams of men who had decided, in the light of greatly improved engine performance for aeroplanes, to have a go.

We need not concern ourselves with them. Some failed tragically, like Nungesser and Coli, others failed because of quarrels, mechanical disaster or just bad luck, to get off the ground at all. By the morning of 20 May, 1927, there was only one competitor prepared and ready to take off. Lindbergh had entered as "C.A.Lindbergh, Air Mail Pilot" and now he and his diminutive monoplane had arrived in New York. Without adequate financial backing he had found difficulty in getting a suitable aircraft. The bigger manufacturers were markedly unhelpful, stipulating that even if Lindbergh had the money to buy one of their craft they would probably not want it entered for a flight across the Atlantic. And in any case, they would reserve the right to nominate their own crew.

Out of the blue he came upon the tiny Ryan Airline. They were eager to do business and they agreed to deliver within sixty days a plane costing only six thousand dollars–far less than the figures quoted by the big firms–into which he could insert any engine he wished. He chose a Wright J-5, which would give him an absolute maximum range of 4,000 miles, travelling at one hundred miles an hour. Work began. To the Ryan company's surprise, the young pilot insisted on supervising every stage of the design. No, he would not have radio or sextant: too heavy. For the same reason he would not have fuel gauges, though he would have larger tail surfaces than the designer had stipulated. At first he planned to have a landing gear which could be dropped once the plane was airborne, and save precious weight while cutting down wind resistance: then on calculating the extra weight of the device of releasing the gear, weight he could not afford on take-off, he rejected the idea.

Eventually, in a remarkably short time, for the Ryan staff had become imbued with enthusiasm, determined that their plane and its "Flying Fool" of a pilot would win the prize, the *Spirit of St Louis* was ready. It had a wing-span of forty-six feet (ten feet more than the standard model), stood nine feet eight inches high and was twenty-seven feet eight inches long. Empty, it weighed 2,150 pounds and was designed to have a fully loaded weight of 5,180–but Lindbergh planned to exceed this by more than a hundred pounds in filling his petrol tanks to the brim and not to the recommended mark.

On 28 April the *Spirit of St Louis* made its maiden flight. Adjustments were needed, but Lindbergh was well pleased. A little later aircraft and pilot were at Curtiss Field, New York. Two other aircraft, far larger than his, were to hand: the *America*, with Commander Byrd, of North Pole fame, in command, and the *Columbia*, to be piloted by either Clarence Chamberlin or Lloyd Bertaud, with the other as assistant. The owner of *Columbia*, who was neither of these men, refused to make up his mind, and had now got himself involved in litigation with backers. Commander Byrd was still recovering, with his crew, from a disastrous test flight of an intended trans-Atlantic aircraft, and was still in bandages.

And yet, though it became obvious that neither *Columbia* or *America* would take off in the near future, no one seemed able to believe the tiny, diminutive *Spirit of St Louis* capable of getting even half-way across the Atlantic. Those newspapers which editorialized about Lindbergh's chances were unanimously gloomy. Someone suggested that the prize should be withdrawn: too many good men had already perished in the attempt to win the prize and this "Flying Fool" should not be allowed to join them. It was true that his many escapes as stunt pilot had earned him a second nickname, "Lucky Lindy", but one needed far more than luck and a tiny, single-engined aeroplane to get across the Atlantic.

Despite this there was a sizeable crowd which had gathered, in response to rumour, on the airfield as dawn broke on the 20th. Lindbergh, looking first at them and then at his overloaded aircraft with its bulging tyres, bit his lower lip. Weather reports had been variable, but it had seemed that if he were ever going to start, today's weather was as he would get in the foreseeable future. He talked with a few good friends and helpers, stuffed a packet of sandwiches in his pocket, climbed in.

At 7.52 he revved-up the engine, and the plane, groaning under its weight, started to crawl forward. To the watching crowd, the few reporters and the man with the movie camera, it seemed impossible that it would ever gather sufficient speed to get off the ground. And to Lindbergh the problem was just as apparent. He had put a small flag half-way up his proposed take-off path, with the intention of throttling back and turning for another attempt (or abandonment) if his wheels had not unstuck by the time he reached it. They had not, but he gritted his teeth and willed the *Spirit of St Louis* into the air. It responded, waddled upwards, inch by inch, and he pulled the nose round to the right to clear the lowest of the row of trees in front.

He cleared the trees by inches, and, rather better, some overhead wires. He was confident now: the people below were dark grey ants, and he was free of them, heading out for the open sea, alone with the wind and the sun.

And the storm. As he steered north-east on his Great Circle course over Newfoundland he hit a bad one, found himself without warning in a towering cumulus cloud, with ice forming, great lumps of it on his wings, struts, fuselage, as he watched. With so little fuel to spare, he yet had to turn about, head back to where he knew there had been sunshine and warmth, get back there before the added weight stalled him and he crashed. He fought his way back, got into the clear air and watched as the treacherous ice began to melt. Then, taking a different course, he went on.

Meanwhile, back home, word had flashed along the wires that Lindbergh had started, and suddenly the entire population of the country went mad. The madness, the enthusiasm, grew. That night, with Lindbergh out over the Atlantic, having been last sighted heading east from Newfoundland, forty-thousand boxing fans rose to their feet at the start of the Sharkey-Maloney match in the Yankee Stadium to "pray for Lindbergh". Men who had never prayed for anyone, ever before, stood there with bowed heads. All over the United States, gatherings were being interrupted for news of the flight and pious hopes for its outcome. The huge annual banquet of the American Iron and Steel Institute was interrupted by the toast-master, who announced that he was "thinking of a young American boy who left this morning for Paris with a sandwich in his pocket".

By the next morning, when the plane was sighted over Ireland, the press had taken up the story, was working itself up to the enthusiasm which would culminate in the next day's editions, after the landing at Le Bourget. The radio gave progress reports all day, interspersed with knowledgeable interviews and talks on the subject of flying, the chances of success in this venture.

And while all this was going on, Charles Lindbergh was fighting tiredness. He had slept badly the night before take-off (and in any case, he had been called at a little after two in the morning) and he was now exhausted. He worked out a scheme for keeping himself awake. He would fly at varying altitudes, one minute up in the clouds, the next skimming the waves. It used up more fuel, but it kept him awake. He was distressed to find that the smelling-salts he had brought, in the hope that they would revive him when he flagged, seemed to have no smell or effect at all.

He had been airborne for twenty-seven hours when he saw specks on the water in front. Boats! Grinning with delight he lost altitude, dived down over them, circled one. A man's head stuck out of a porthole and Lindbergh shouted, "Which way is Ireland?" The man, impassive, pulled his head in, and Lindbergh flew on. An hour later he was over Ireland and, to his delight, at the exact spot–Dingle Bay–which he had planned.

Six hundred miles to go. Tiredness vanished. In a few more minutes, even if forced down, he would have broken the world's record for long-distance flying, and if he reached the coast of France he would qualify for the Orteig prize (and, oh, how he needed the money!) which had been re-stated to permit a landing anywhere in France. He tried one of the sandwiches, found it tasteless, stopped eating.

And, hours later, he saw the Eiffel Tower. He searched for the airfield, found it, was horrified at the lack of illumination. The feeble arc-lamps lit up only a tiny area, and half of that was filled with what seemed a seething mass of humanity. He began to doubt whether his senses would function correctly on landing, whether he would level-out at the correct height or crash ignominiously.

A moment later, at 10:24 p.m. on Saturday, 21 May, 1927, Charles Lindbergh landed at Le Bourget airfield, after thirty-three and a half hours in the air. The little plane was in perfect condition and in fact he had fuel in the tanks for nearly another thousand miles' flying. The damage to the aircraft would be done by the enthusiastic crowds milling around it, tearing off pieces of fabric. He stayed in the cockpit, wondering how he might ever escape from the mob, and at last two officials fought their way to him. One of them seized his flying helmet and to his annoyance hurled it into the crowd.

Then Lindbergh saw the reason. The mob chased off after it, like mad dogs after a bone. He was helped out of the cockpit, taken to safety.

And so ended one of the bravest journeys of the twentieth century—the journey of "Lucky Lindy", who in fact, as he pointed out angrily, had devoted a great deal of hard thought to his venture and most definitely had *not* relied on his luck. The flight of the *Spirit of St Louis* was a brave one, almost incredibly brave—but Charles Lindbergh had known exactly what he was doing, and he did it with skill and precision.

He needed more than luck—and he had it.

FLIGHT TO AUSTRALIA

Amy Johnson, Woman Pioneer

AMY JOHNSON was the first woman to fly solo to Australia, but it was only through her own burning ambition and dogged determination that she even started on her hazardous flight. It seemed to her that every possible obstacle was placed in her path before she eventually took off from Croydon Airport on her epic flight on 5 May, 1930, a flight which gained her world-wide fame and which made a large contribution in the speeding up of air communications between England and Australia.

Born in Hull, Yorkshire, in 1904, she was the eldest daughter of a trawl-fish merchant, who as a young man had taken part in the Klondyke gold rush. Amy's interest in flying had started when as a child she persuaded her younger sister to go with her on a five-shilling joy flight; ever afterwards she had wanted to fly her own aeroplane. Educated at the Boulevard Secondary School, Hull, she was a talented pupil and good at all sports. She passed the Oxford Senior Local Examination with first-class honours in Latin, and in 1922 went to Sheffield University, where she graduated as a Bachelor of Arts.

Her passion for flying was undimmed, but there was no flying club in Hull. The interest in light planes in Great Britain was only just beginning and had not spread much beyond London, so Amy went to London where she took a job as private secretary to a company of solicitors. All her spare time was spent at Astor House, Aldwych, as voluntary typist and secretary to the Air League of the British Empire. Towards the end of 1928 she joined the London Aeroplane Club and at week-ends and evenings she learned to fly.

Her total of 15 hours 45 minutes flying time before passing for her licence was the average. In her training over the fields beyond North London she had early experience of bad weather conditions. She took the Air Ministry test as a pilot in July, 1929, and gained her "A" licence with ease. Not content with the elementary instruction about the engine which she received as part of the training course, she joined the mechanical section of the London Club at Stag Lane and before long became a thoroughly qualified mechanic, and was the only woman in the world to hold a British ground engineer's licence.

The aeroplane Amy Johnson chose for her epic flight was the De Havilland Moth. It was not a new one. Its original owner was Captain W.L.Hope, who used Moths for a European air-taxi service, and had twice won the King's Cup Race around Great Britain in one. He had already flown 35,000 miles in the one Amy Johnson bought from him, and it cost her, including alterations, about £600.

This little plane was one of the most successful light aircraft ever built, and a version of it is still in use. It was a biplane with a wing-span of 30 ft., but the wings folded to enable the plane to be stored in a space of 10 ft. The Moth was considered easy to fly, especially for women pilots, and the Hon. Lady Baily used one for her solo flight around Africa of 18,000 miles. The Moth was 23 ft. 11 in. long and 8 ft. 9½ in. high, and its speed was about a hundred miles an hour. It had a stalling speed of 41 m.p.h., and if fitted with Handley Page automatic slots it could be landed at even lower speeds, and was thus a very safe and manoeuvrable little aeroplane. There were two seats arranged tandem fashion, and for the long flight, which Amy began to plan as soon as she bought her machine, she had an extra 35-gallon fuel tank fitted in the front seat. Another 25-gallon tank was fitted in the rear fuselage behind the pilot's cockpit, in addition to the usual 19-gallon centre-section tank. She was thus able to carry 79 gallons in all. With a cruising speed of about 80 m.p.h. and a petrol consumption of approximately 5 gallons per hour, she thus had a range of over a thousand miles.

Between preparing her plane, working at her office job during the day and at Stag Lane in the evenings, Amy tried to get support for her project of flying solo to Australia, for it was imperative that the trip should pay for itself. This was towards the end of 1929, but her idea was received without interest. No one would take her seriously. Newspaper editors were sceptical. The flight to Australia had been accomplished before and the public were beginning to weary of fliers who aspired to heroism. Lindbergh had already flown the Atlantic solo. Such flights were no longer miracles.

Amy went to see Lord Wakefield, but he was not impressed by this rather ordinary young woman, who was small and feminine, with fair hair and blue eyes. He thought the idea of her going on this lonely and dangerous flight was impossible. She then went to see the Australian Minister for Trade and Customs, then visiting London, who told her that if she wanted to go to Australia she should go by steamer. She next tried the High Commissioner, Sir Granville Ryrie, but got nowhere with him either. Amy's father, impressed by her determination, told her that if she could not find a backer he would help her himself.

Amy Johnson was not easily put off. She next went to Air Vice-Marshal Sir Sefton Brancker, Director of Civil Aviation, who had championed many amateur pilots, and who believed in encouraging adventurous young people. Impressed by her, he persuaded Lord Wakefield to guarantee her petrol supplies. Amy was delighted, for the fuel for her flight would have cost at least £300 even in those days.

Fleet Street, however, remained uninterested. Flying to Australia was not very original. She went to see the editor of the *Daily News*, but saw instead his secretary, the great man being out. Amy had taken some trouble with her appearance and wore long dangling ear-rings which seemed to be at variance with the proud, almost masculine set of her head, and the complete independence she showed. She said she was making the trip for her own pleasure and was not interested in newspaper publicity. When she returned from her journey her story would be of great value, she had been informed, but she did not care about that. All she was interested in was in flying to Australia and that she meant to do in May of that year.

When the newspapers made an announcement of her forthcoming flight, saying that she wanted to beat Captain Bert Hinkler's existing record to Australia, she protested that she had expressed no such ambition. She said that she was not making a high-speed flight and did not intend to make 1,000-mile non-stop hops. Utterly disgusted with the lack of interest, the polite rebuffs and the prejudice she found against flying amateurs, Amy Johnson turned her back on the older generation and set about making her own preparations for the flight.

She had her machine painted her favourite colour, green, and christened *Jason*, her family's trade-mark derived from her grandfather who was a Dane. She wore a green helmet and flying suit, and it amused her that her friends found the colour unlucky. It was both cool and serviceable and she liked it. She studied hard at navigation, which was unusual for an amateur flyer. She had decided to take the direct route across Europe, going via Vienna, Constantinople, across the Balkans and Asia Minor where uncivilized tribes were in the habit of taking pot-shots at passing planes. After that she would cross the desert to Baghdad, then across the Persian Gulf to Karachi, thence over India to Calcutta, Rangoon, down to Singapore, the Dutch East Indies (now Indonesia) and to Darwin. She had to obtain passports for every country over which she intended to fly, an irritating and time-wasting formality.

Her flight was finally fixed to begin on 5 May, and three days before she decided she ought to wear a parachute, a wise decision, in view of the weather she would meet *en route* and the fact that her small craft would be overloaded with fuel. The harness of the parachute had to be made smaller for her, and she learned how to use it in about half an hour, though she did not have a practice jump. She wore the parachute throughout her trip, even on the shortest flights, and her sensible nature also prompted her to take a spare propeller which had to be tied to the centre section struts on the port side of the machine.

Just before eight o'clock on the morning of 5 May she took off secretly on her great flight from Croydon Aerodrome, with only her father, a few friends and the airport officials to see her off. She had never taken off with a full load before and she did not allow herself sufficient distance for the take-off run at first, and had to make a second attempt before she finally became airborne and made off into the Surrey mists, accompanied for a short distance by five machines from the London Aeroplane Club.

The first stage of her flight was 800 miles to Vienna. It took her ten hours. She flew a further 800 miles the following day, arriving at Constantinople not at all tired, after twelve hours' flying, to an enthusiastic reception. The world began to take notice of the lone girl flyer who had never even crossed the Channel before–nor had she flown more than 200 miles before in a straight line. The world was impressed by her courage and ability.

Amy decided to press on with as much speed as possible. So far everything had gone to plan. From the Turkish capital she flew over the Bosphorus and to Asia Minor, landing at Aleppo on the third day, a distance of 550 miles. In three days she had spent about 27 hours in the air. On the fourth day she had to fly nearly 500 miles across the desert to Baghdad, and now for the first time she ran into trouble and danger.

The thing she most dreaded in that forsaken spot happened. She had to make a forced landing in a blinding sandstorm. The little machine was in danger of being nosed over by the force of the sand-laden gale which Amy had to fight against when she pushed her way out of the cockpit with her luggage, piling it against the wheels to make it more stable. Then she waited for the storm to die down, her revolver in her hand, ready to use it if any unfriendly Arabs turned up in this desolate spot, thankful that she was a good and experienced shot.

The storm lasted for two hours, apparently forcing the desert's inhabitants to keep under cover, for they did not put in an appearance. As soon as the storm abated, Amy hurriedly replaced her luggage and climbed back into the cockpit, expecting any moment to be attacked by a nomad tribe. She was intensely relieved to be airborne once more and winging her way to the city of the Caliphs.

She arrived at Baghdad on 8 May, and it was then realized that this inexperienced girl flyer was after all going to challenge Bert Hinkler's record flight to Australia. After four days' flying she was ahead of him by a few hundred miles, as she had taken a shorter course from England. The world was already agog with excitement. Her dream had come true, and what others had thought impossible was well on the way to being accomplished.

But she had still a long way to go, and on the fifth day her long spell in the air was causing concern at Basra, at the head of the Persian Gulf, where she was anxiously awaited, and which was known for its sudden wind-storms and bad visibility. It was thought that she might have pushed on to Bushire. Actually Amy had flown some 600 miles down the eastern side of the Gulf to Bander Abbas, passing over Basra, some 830 miles from Baghdad. The whole of the flight along the Persion Gulf was fraught with danger, and there were no safe landing places on a rugged coastline where no machine could land without crashing or being engulfed in the muddy waters.

On 10 May, her sixth day, she was at Karachi, the gateway to India. It had taken Hinkler eight days to get there. By now all the world was breathlessly watching this girl-wonder from Yorkshire as she flew across India to Calcutta. But Amy was now feeling the strain. She knew she was expected to continue to beat the record of Hinkler, who had flown the rest of the route to Port Darwin without a break, only stopping at the usual places for refuelling. But Amy knew she could not continue ot this pace, even if she wished to break Hinkler's record. It would be dangerous and difficult, and hardly worth attempting, when she was so tired. She made for Allahabad in central India, a flight of 1,000 miles, escorted part of the way by an R.A.F. aircraft and another D.H. Moth piloted by Wing-Commander Crosbie, the De Havilland Company's Indian representative. However, after 700 miles she ran out of petrol and had to make a forced landing at Jhansi, where she spent the night. She continued the next day across the great Indian plains to Allahabad, where she stayed only a short time before going on to Calcutta, a distance of 450 miles, She was still two days ahead of Hinkler, with about half the journey accomplished. In eight days Amy Johnson had flown 7,000 miles.

Rangoon was to be her next landing place, 650 miles away over the massive Yomas mountain range, one of the most dangerous stages of her flight. It was her ninth day and the date, 13 May, was an unlucky one for this courageous young air-woman. There was fog near Calcutta. Conditions improved as she approached the Burma coast, but not for long. The stormy crests of the Yomas now loomed in front of her, and the little Moth was soon buffeted by raging headwinds and lashed with heavy rain. Climbing to 12,000 feet, she met bad visibility and had to come down to 150 feet. The fact that there were few emergency landing places did nothing to console her, as she used the railway line as well as the coast to guide her to Rangoon.

Visibility was still bad when she thought she sighted the racecourse at Rangoon, which was used as the flying field, but what she really saw were the playing fields of Insein, just outside the Burmese capital. However, seeing that the area was too small for landing, she continued farther south, still looking for the mist-covered race-course. She must have been a little unnerved as she searched without success for the one safe place to land. With some trepidation she decided to return to the small playing field at Insein, and brought her plane down between the goal posts with accuracy and skill. But once more her luck deserted her, and while taxi-ing over the unknown ground she ran into a ditch and damaged the plane's undercarriage and wing.

Disconsolately she wandered over to a building in the adjoining field and her spirits were raised when she found that it was the workshop of the Government technical institute, whose immediate help was enlisted. Willing hands worked hard to repair the damage all the next day. Even so, precious time was lost. Amy was anxious to be off again, but had to contain her impatience even longer as it was impossible for her to take off from the small playing field. The Moth had to be taken to Rangoon by road.

Two days later she took off from that elusive race-course at Rangoon *en route* for Bangkok in Siam, 356 miles away. By now she had lost her two days' gain on Hinkler, but the excited world still watched and waited and everyone on her route was keyed up to give her every assistance.

The bright dawn of 16 May suddenly changed for the worse and during a short sea flight to the coast the newly repaired Moth was again buffeted by heavy rain. Turning inland, with rain clouds still blotting out visibility over country which was impossible for forced landings, Amy was in constant danger. She climbed to 10,000 feet, flying blind over dense jungle forest and mountain ranges, looking for a clear patch of sky, and when she found one she found she was still on the wrong side of the mountain ranges. The one pass through these mountains was only safe in good visibility. It took her seven hours to get through and she landed at the Siamese Air Force base of Don Muang, twelve miles north of Bangkok, on her twelfth day. Despite her physical exhaustion, she immediately set about preparing her plane for an early start, for her time was now about the same as Hinkler's and she felt that circumstances were compelling her to press on. The watching world, in fact, demanded it of her. The enthusiastic Siamese airmen, full of admiration for her achievement, could not do enough to assist her.

On the 13th day weather was still bad, and she flew down the Malay peninsula battling with strong head-winds and rain-storms, hoping to reach Singapore, but after six hours she had to land at Singapore and did not reach Singapore until the following day, having now dropped behind Hinkler's time. Two machines from the Singapore Flying Club came out to meet her and escorted her to

Singapore, where she received a tumultuous welcome. That night the R.A.F. entertained her in royal style, and nearly everyone in the civilized world now knew the name of Amy Johnson. She was behind Hinkler's time, but she had achieved a miracle of flying for so inexperienced a pilot.

Before her lay perhaps the most dangerous leg across the stormy East Indies and the treacherous Timor Sea, to Port Darwin, 2,500 miles away.

The flying club at Singapore operated Gipsy Moths like Amy's, but theirs had floats for emergency sea landings. If Amy could have afforded such floats, the risks attached to the final stages of her flight would have been somewhat lessened, but the cost, somewhere in the region of £300, made such a "luxury" impossible. As it was she needed a new lower wing for her plane, which the club fitted for her before she took off on the 15th day to cross the Java Sea to the Sumatra coast, hoping to reach Sourabaya.

However, the same pattern of bad weather again dogged her flight over the lonely Java Sea, where she battled against the fury of the storm, arriving at the Sumatra coast to find herself over dense jungle and mangrove swamps, getting short of fuel and faced with the prospect of making a forced landing. She finally had to make a rough landing at a sugar plantation at Tjomal, the little plane ploughing its way through fruit sticks which pierced the wing.

However, from the local factory willing workers arrived to patch up the holes, just as anxious as she was to get the Moth on its way, so thrillingly and urgently had her story gone around the world. Amy spent the night as a guest of the sugar plantation manager, and the following morning she accomplished a very difficult take-off of only 240 yards long, over soggy ground. Her luggage had been removed to lighten the machine and she landed at a better field, where her luggage had been taken and from which she was able to resume her flight to Samarang, only 60 miles away. Here she refuelled and continued to Sourabaya, a further 200 miles on the route, where she was escorted in by the regular Dutch Air Mail plane.

It was the 16th day, and though she had lost all hope now of matching Bert Hinkler's time, she looked quite happy, with a gay flower in her button-hole as she acknowledged a big ovation from a large crowd at Sourabaya.

She had a few hours' rest before returning to her machine to make preparations for the last highly dangerous stage of her flight across the Timor Sea. The engine of the Moth had not been running smoothly and she found that there was magneto trouble, which made the following day's flight even more risky. The islands of the Dutch East Indies were mostly covered with thick jungle, with emergency landing fields belonging to the Dutch mail service. After that she would be faced with hours of lonely flying over the Timor Sea with its extremes of tropical weather where engine failure would mean little chance of survival.

But she was determined to push on and she made a start at six in the morning, hoping to reach the Timor island of Atamboea which would shorten her flight over the sea to Port Darwin. About mid-day she was sighted over Bima, on the island of Sumbawa, and then nothing more was heard or seen of her for the rest of the day.

When night fell there was still no news, and the whole world waited anxiously, fearing that this young, courageous air-woman had at last fallen victim to the forces of nature she had so bravely challenged. The communication systems of the Dutch administration were kept working all night throughout the islands, but no hoped-for late message came in, and the worst fears were entertained.

Early the next morning preparations were started for organized searches over the sea and on the islands. The Government steamer *Gemma* had been ordered to search the Timor Sea. Local garrisons were alerted, and as Dornier Wal flying-boats were being prepared for the Timor search, news came through that Amy had landed safely at Haliloelik, a remote village just twelve miles short of Atamboea, where there was no telephone. Amy had managed to get transport into Atamboea to find somewhere to sleep, and not until she was able to send a telegram did the relieved world hear the happy news that she was safe.

Many thought that Amy should finish here and not tempt providence further, but she was determined to carry on across the Timor Sea. Bert Hinkler had had a rubber boat attached to the back of his machine, but Amy had to rely entirely on her plane and her own ability to keep it in the air. Fortunately this time the weather was kind to her and she had a comfortable flight. Half-way across she sighted the Shell Oil tanker *Phorus* which was on the look-out for her and wirelessed her progress to Port Darwin.

The waiting world breathed again.

It was her nineteenth day out of England and her final stage had been from dawn until three o'clock in the afternoon. During the flight she had averaged 600 miles a day and had flown 12,000 miles in all. Her navigation had been perfect. She carried no wireless, and with the whole coast of northern Australia ahead of her, and many hours over an empty sea, she could easily have missed her target. But she flew to it straight as an arrow, and to a tumultuous reception richly deserved. A number of aircraft had set out to meet her from Port Darwin, where an enormous crowd was waiting to welcome their heroine, the Yorkshire lass from England.

Her flight was the astonishment and wonder of the world. She was appointed C.B.E. and the *Daily Mail* made her a gift of £10,000. The children of Sydney raised a sum of money with which she bought a gold cup now offered annually for the most courageous juvenile deed of the year.

In 1932 Amy Johnson married James Allan Mollison, a pilot, with whom she made a number of record flights. In 1936 she made a record solo flight to the Cape and back, the last of her long flights. There were no children of her marriage, which was dissolved in 1938 when she resumed her maiden name.

In aeronautical circles she has always been regarded as a woman of unusual intrepidity and presence of mind, qualities she retained when in 1939 she joined the Air Transport Auxiliary. She was lost over the Thames Estuary on 5 January, 1941, when ferrying a plane with material for the Air Ministry. Her death was presumed by the Probate Court in December, 1943.

She will always be best remembered for her remarkable solo flight from England to Australia. She caught the public eye because, for all her deeds of daring, she never lost her feminine charm.

VALLEYS OF THE ASSASSINS

Freya Stark's Journey

ALTHOUGH FREYA STARK admits unashamedly that she travels for fun, her journeys have added considerably to the geographical knowledge of the Middle East, and at least one of them has been backed financially by the Royal Geographical Society.

She was a happy traveller, loving every minute of it, and a true traveller. No obstacle was too great to overcome. Nothing would stop her. She climbed the Elburz mountains in northern Persia to get a close view of the legendary Throne of Solomon when she should have gone to hospital after a violent attack of malaria, and she set off to the Valleys of the Assassins alone and with a mere £2 in her pocket.

This was a truly romantic quest in search of the ancient haunts of the Assassins, their ruined castles and their gentle descendants, many of whom had never seen a European woman before.

The Assassins were founded by Hasan-i-Sabbah in the eleventh century and were a branch of the Isma'ili sect who broke away from the Mohammedan faith and evolved a kind of free-thinking religion of their own. Hasan, a young Persian, invented a politico-religious philosophy in which murder was to be used as a legitimate weapon of the State. Under him the Assassins became a powerful

443

secret society in Syria and Persia. So successful were they in removing their enemies by the assassin's knife that they acquired great power and were widely feared.

In 1090 Hasan seized the fortress of Alamut in the Elburz mountains in northern Persia where he and his successors held powerful sway for a hundred and fifty years until they were crushed and massacred by the Mongols under Mangu Khan in 1256.

The Assassins proper were a band of young men, the *Fida'is* (the devoted ones), who gave blind, unquestioning obedience to Hasan. The word assassins is derived from *hashishin*, which in turn comes from *hashish*, the hemp drug, or bang, which points to the fact that these young fanatics were addicts of this drug. Their supreme ruler was called *Shaydh-al-Jabal,* which hal been commonly translated the Old Man of the Mountains.

Europeans first came into contact with the Assassins during the Crusades, and the legend of the Old Man of the Mountains who overcame the scruples of the young assassins by transporting them drugged to his secret "Paradise" in the mountains, which was replete with milk, honey and obliging maidens, was sung by troubadours all over medieval Europe.

It was Hasan-i-Sabbah's mountain stronghold of Alamut which Freya Stark sought when she set out from Hamadan in May, 1930, with, she wrote to her best friend, Venetia Buddicom, two pounds in her pocket–"the only comfort is there will be the less to rob". She went by road to Qazvin, travelling alone, her luggage consisting of her bed and saddle-bags. She had only a vague idea where Alamut was. There was a district of Alamut marked on the map, and there was an Alamut river, but no Alamut village. Hasan's castle was supposed to be at a place called Qasir Khan.

At Qazvin she was in another world, where Hasan-i-Sabbah was a household name and the days of the Assassins might have been yesterday. Eight hundred years meant nothing to these simple and delightful folk, to whom it was the most natural thing in the world that a young lady should travel all the way from England just to see the fabled castle of Alamut.

A muleteer named Kerbelai Aziz from Garmrud, in the valley of Alamut, undertook to be her guide. She paid him four shillings a day for his services, which included food and travel facilities. Despite the discomforts of the mode of travel, it cannot be said that she was overcharged. The caravan included not only Aziz's two subordinates, Ismail and Hujjat Allah (the Refuge of Allah), but also Aziz's small son Mohammed, who was sick, and Aziz's mother, a cheerful old lady in her seventies, who leaped streams with surprising agility.

Miss Stark was agreeably surprised to find herself treated with courteous charm and consideration by her escorts. They told her stories, sang her melancholy ballads and even gathered flowers for her as they climbed out of the plains into the foothills and valleys of the distant Elburz mountains. Travelling with these wild, simple and peaceful people, to whom the everyday and the miraculous were hardly separate worlds, she realized how easy a prey their ancestors must have been to the cunning wiles of the Old Man of the Mountains who gave them a dream of Paradise in exchange for their souls.

The little caravan continued through the empty Persian landscape towards the mountains. ". . . the solitude and the slow dreamlike travelling in the sun already made it seem as though we were remote from the world's business in some little backwater of time," wrote Freya Stark.*

The people had long forsworn the outrageous and heretical doctrines of the Old Man of the Mountains, and when Aziz arrived among them with the European infidel, they begged him not to drink out of her cup, a sentiment which she fully reciprocated for different reasons.

They climbed northwards towards the Chala Pass, the valleys drenched with sun and bright with flowers, ahead the snow-crested ridges of the Elburz. Here they met mule trains coming in the opposite direction laden with Caspian rice, a trade which had gone on uninterruptedly and in the same way for two thousand years, the small bells tinkling on the mules' hindquarters as they had done through the unchanging centuries.

At last, across the Chala Pass, she looked upon her goal, the Alamut country, stretching before her and below her, ridge upon ridge. From the darkening valleys, streaked with glinting river bends, she lifted her eyes to the gleaming ridges, and, towering above all, the snowfields of Solomon's Throne, its great arms black against the sky. From here they climbed down into the Valley of the Assassins. This was the place described by Marco Polo as a beautiful valley enclosed between two lofty mountains, and where Hasan-i-Sabbah had his "luxurious garden stored with every delicious fruit and every fragrant shrub that could be procured", in

* *The Valleys of the Assassins* (John Murray, 1934).

445

which he had constructed his "earthly paradise". Hasan's paradise was in a valley–a hidden and secret place–and no trace of it could possibly have survived the centuries. Freya Stark only found roses and jasmin and fragrant shrubs to remind her of the unforgotten legend. The fortresses of the Assassins, however–there was more than one–were built as usual on hilltops and their ruins had remained. The Rock of Alamut was the most famous, and the goal of Freya Stark's journey.

Down into the valley, the party crossed the Alamut river by a flimsy and dangerous bridge which had transported uncertain travellers for centuries. Along a dusty road they came to the village of Badasht, which meant Garden of the Desert, a suggestive and intriguing name in view of the nature of her quest. They traced the river valley along an ancient road to Shutur Khan, above which the Rock of the Assassins stood impressively on the mountainside like a black sentinel. The road itself had born the travellers of a thousand years and more, and had carried the merchants and envoys of China, India, Egypt and Syria. It was used in the days of Rustum, during the wars with the early Persian kings, and along it went the Assassins on their missions of murder, while Hasan waited and watched in the castle fastness on the Rock above.

Freya Stark spent the night at Shutur Khan, where she was surprised to find herself confronted by a young Persian policeman, who had heard about her arrival in his territory, which included the districts of Alamut and Rudbar, and had come to investigate this strange young Englishwoman who had made this unlikely journey into the Valleys of the Assassins.

She found him charming and intelligent, though determined to make a thorough search of all her luggage and belongings in the interests of the security of Persia. He was fascinated by the maps she had made of the country. "So these are the pictures you take in your black box and show to no one," he said, and he found it impossible to comprehend her explanation that the camera was for taking pictures and she drew the maps by hand. The young policeman lived a lonely life and his work consisted mainly of settling the quarrels of the inhabitants. The arrival of Freya Stark was an exciting diversion for him.

The following morning, leaving her luggage to be examined by the curious policeman, who naturally had to satisfy himself that she had no sinister intent in coming into his territory, she set off for the Rock of the Assassins after a pleasant breakfast of tea, bread and honey.

Though accompanied by Aziz and a guide from Shutur Khan, when she arrived at Qasir Khan, just below the Rock, it was essential that the ascent should be made under the guidance of the man who always guided strangers to the Rock. As only two parties of strangers had been here sightseeing during the past two years, it was hardly a tourist centre, but the ways of Persia were unalterable, and so a red-bearded old Assassin joined the party, carrying with him pick-axe and shovel, with which to hack steps on the dangerous mountain slopes. Something of a mountaineer herself, Freya Stark had no need of assistance in the ascent of the Rock of the Assassins, to which here and there clung the remains of Hasan's ancient castle–"ruined beyond the power of imagination to reconstruct".

It was a grim place. Behind it rose the granite precipices of Mount Haudegan. The fastness looked down upon the village of Qasir Khan, a thousand feet below, with its fields and trees, the valley with the Alamut river glinting away towards the snow-covered ridges of Elburz.

Here, eight centuries ago, lived Hasan-i-Sabbah, the Old Man of the Mountains, free-thinker, freebooter, terror of the land of Persia. Hasan threw away his Moslem customs and traditions and claimed divinity for himself. He abolished the prayers to Allah, renounced the allegiance with Egypt, grew vines and encouraged the drinking of wine in the valley. He grew also hashish, with which he drugged the *Fida'is* who became his assassins. A whole library of heretical books was collected by the Assassins during the time they flourished in Alamut.

The castle and its enclosure, judging by the remains, was a good size, though it was impossible to gain any picture of what the place looked like in the days of the Assassins. It was half-covered with wild tulips, yellow and red, and it was likely that in the time of its habitation cultivation of all kinds was undertaken in the castle precincts. Water was plentiful from a spring in the slopes above and brought down in conduits to the castle.

Here Hasan-i-Sabbah looked out over his lands, which stretched below him in the valley, peaceful and well cultivated. Here also he awaited the return of his *Fida'is* from their missions. Here too, it was said, Omar Khayyam used to visit him, and poet and Assassin discussed philosophy and mathematics. Persian civilization at this

447

time was more artistic and intellectual than that of its neighbours, and it certainly reached a higher culture than that of the more conventional Mohammedans.

This culture was wrecked by the invasions of barbarian Mongols in the thirteenth century, a hundred years and more after Hasan-i-Sabbah had looked for the last time across his valley from his castle above Qasir Khan. He died in 1124 at an advanced age. The Mongols came into the Alamut valley in 1256 under Hulagu, the brother of Mangu Khan. After a siege the Rock capitulated, and was utterly destroyed by the Mongol horde. The heretical library begun by Hasan, and perhaps contributed to by Omar Khayyam, was burnt and lost for ever. The Mongols massacred 12,000 Assassins before they passed on to more conquests, and the power of the Assassins was broken in Persia for ever.

It was said at Shutur Khan that, in the lower part of the castle where rooms and a water-tank were dug out, the Assassins' treasure was guarded by seven black dogs which breathed fire. But it would have required climbing-boots to have made the descent, and Miss Stark had not brought them with her and was not able to investigate the unlikely legend. She had to be content with an Assassin's bouquet of the roses of Hasan which grew on a narrow ledge on the Rock.

They found shards of pottery lying on the ground below, which were left there apparently by people who had occupied the castle in the eighteenth century and of whom little or nothing is known. Freya Stark and her guides then descended to Qasir Khan, where her return was celebrated by the villagers reciting stories of Hasan, but these seemed to her to be merely repetitions of travellers' tales. They told her that the Rock was originally built by Kaiumars, a legendary king of Alamut.

She returned to Shutur Khan, where her luggage had been thoroughly examined in her absence by the friendly young policeman, who was even more cordial when he had satisfied himself of her complete innocence of any sinister intent. In the policeman's office they discussed the Assassins' castles, of which there were several in the neighbourhood, and all of which had been reduced by the Mongols.

The following day she continued with Aziz and his family to their home at Garmrud, a unique and picturesque village at the foot of an immense precipice which formed an impressive exit to the Valley of the Assassins. Above Garmrud towered the second lofty mountain, which enclosed the valley described by Marco Polo as being the home of the Assassins.

The flat-roofed houses of Garmrud were built on the slope of the hill, so that the front door of one opened on to the roof of another. It was set among trees and lush vegetation. Beans and lettuce grew in the tiny walled gardens, and the drowsy valley was bathed in sunshine and peace. Here Freya Stark was received into the bosom of the Aziz family, who, seeing that she had travelled with him, claimed her as one of the family and engulfed her in a wave of true Persian hospitality and friendliness.

Above Garmrud, at the top of 3,000 feet of sheer rock, stood the Castle of Nevisar Shah, a visit to which was arranged for the following morning. Led by a mountain guide and accompanied by Aziz and Ismail, she climbed up the steep path, over shale and grass and slabs of granite, along precipitous paths where a sideways glance revealed the sunlit valley far below, and in the distance the mountain above Qasir Khan where she had climbed to the Rock of Alamut. Here they found the same pottery remains as before.

They found nothing left of the Castle of Nevisar Shah excepting a few remains of walls. A portion of the keep was standing, near the top of which was a loophole. On the crest of the hill she saw masses of ruined masonry which suggested that there were once houses as well as the castle. On each side the mountain wall dropped sheer. Beyond were snow-capped mountains. It had been a natural fortress of great strength, but it, too, had fallen to the terrible Mongol hordes, and all its defenders slain to the last man. No one knows how the Mongols, who were fighters of the plains and unused to mountain warfare, managed to get into the Assassins' Valley, which should have been impregnable.

In the Assassins' country there were fifty castles and strongholds, all of which were destroyed by Hulagu in 1256. Two of them put up a strong resistance and took many months to reduce. They were Girdkuh and Lamiasar.

Lamiasar was in the Shah Rud Valley, to the west of the Alamut Valley, and was captured in 1083 for the Assassins by Kiya Buzurg-Ummed, the successor of Hasan-i-Sabbah. It must have been a particularly formidable stronghold to have withstood the onslaught of the Mongols for so long, for the Mongols had brought with them Chinese engineers and every scientific siege machine of the day.

Freya Stark completed her exploration of the Valleys of the Assassins by journeying to Lamiasar in 1931. From Qazvin she went to Rashtegan and then to Siahdasht on the Shah Rud river. She travelled with the muleteer Ismail, taking two mules. Her favourite guide, Aziz, was unable to accompany her, being kept at Garmrud by the illness of his small son.

Of Ismail, Miss Stark says he was villainously untidy and stupid. He had a flattened head which made him look like the caricature of a convict, and his daily food consisted of an ancient piece of cheese which he carried around his neck on a goatskin and which "made him very trying at close quarters".

When the head-waiter of the Grand Hotel, Qazvin, saw who her travelling companion was, he exclaimed: "Into the hands of God may you be entrusted." However, such were the exigencies of travel in the lesser-known regions of Persia in the 1930s, and Freya Stark went forward with a similar pious wish in her heart.

They climbed northwards towards the Elburz and came once more to the Valleys of the Assassins, where there were huge bushes of wild roses among the barren rocks and the landscape was silent, immense and grey, and mysterious with unwritten history.

But the inhabitants were as friendly as ever.

"Lamiasar?" said an old man on a donkey, a load of grass under one arm, a sickle in his other hand. "Lamiasar is there." He pointed with his sickle across the Shah Rud to a fold in the hills. "You can get to it from here in one day."

She stayed the night at Mirg with Rustum Khan, a Kurd who owned the village, a prosperous man who had been educated in Teheran. Everyone slept on the flat roofs of the houses under the stars.

The next day she crossed the Shah Rud and followed its banks to Shahristan. Mosquitoes were everywhere, by day as well as by night. It was impossible to escape from them. They could only take quinine and hope.

This remote valley was very beautiful and rich with vegetation. The inhabitants cultivated cotton, rice, castor oil, tobacco, walnuts, fruit and vegetables. The place was hot and unhealthy, and Ismail, tired and indignant at being made to come here, complained bitterly.

They stayed the night at Inman Muhammed, from where, in the clear evening light, Miss Stark examined the ruins of Lamiasar through her field glasses. The place was on a truncated hill to the north, about one and a half hours' away. Leaving their luggage with the honest villagers, they started for Lamiasar in the morning.

It was about two miles north of Shahristan, on the banks of the Naina Rud.

After crossing muddy rice-fields, they had to climb a steep ravine, with the battlements of the castle looming above them, finally scrambling up a slope of blackish rock to the western gate of the fortress.

Lamiasar had been built on a truncated cone of a hill which was a sloping surface about 1,500 ft. long by 600 ft. wide. The walls and battlements had crumbled, but still impressively dominated the landscape. On the western side the immense precipice provided its own defence. But on the south and east the ramparts still stood. The weak point of the castle defence was to the north, where it was connected by a neck of rock to the mountainside behind it. This was the obvious way of attack, for the enemy had only to take the north gate, which had doubtless been massively fortified, now completely ruined, and then the rest of Lamiasar, sloping away downwards, would be at their mercy.

The southern gate, five hundred feet lower down the slope, was fairly well preserved, with the actual doorways and the ruins of the guard-house being discernible. There were a number of ruins in the enclosure itself, some of them of recent construction. In one of the ancient buildings, just below the north gate, there were twelve rooms and a tower. Some of the doors, with pointed arches, were still standing. In the vaulted buildings were places in the stone for vaults and the walls were nearly four feet thick. The buildings were clumsily constructed and were composed mainly of roughly-hewn boulders. Some care had been taken in the maintenance of the water supply. Water had been conducted from the nearby village of Viar and was stored in the castle in large rectangular cisterns which had been made in the solid rock.

On the eastern side a steep tunnel led down to the river, about which a remarkable tale was told. It was said that at the river entrance rams were put into the tunnel with skins of water tied to their bellies, and then wolves were put in behind them. The terrified rams rushed up the tunnel pursued by the wolves, and thus provided the castle with water. From this it must be assumed that a ram, even when handicapped by a load of water, can run faster than a wolf.

Leaving this important Assassin stronghold—one of the only two which had stood long sieges before their final destruction by the Mongol hordes—Freya Stark fell ill with a severe attack of malaria which she had contracted during her march in the mosquito-infested valley of the Shah Rud. She was attended by a Persian doctor and advised to go to hospital. Instead she continued her journey and climbed the slopes of the Elburz to the great mountain of Solomon's Temple.

But this was not part of her journey to the Valleys of the Assassins, which was one of her most romantic and intriguing adventures and the title of her most famous travel book.

OVERLAND FROM PEKING TO KASHMIR

Peter Fleming and Kini Maillart

DURING 1935 a young Englishman, Peter Fleming, and a young Swiss girl, Kini Maillart, travelled overland from Peking to Kashmir in northern India. The journey of 3,500 miles took them seven months and, although they went by train to Langchow in eastern China, the time they took to cover the total distance was about the same as Chang Chun in the thirteenth century took over an equivalent distance from Peking to Samarkand.*

For political reasons, the travellers had to take a far more difficult route than the normal way to Kashmir via Sinkiang (Chinese Turkestan). They had to go by the high mountains separating Tibet from Mongolia and Sinkiang, following, at the beginning, in the path of Father Huc.** In these mountains, the mode of travelling had not changed with the centuries and maps did not adequately cover the country. European travellers of note had crossed Mongolia and all this region and had brought back much knowledge, but still the greater part of Mongolia and Chinese Turkestan was country to be crossed only after careful preparation.

Peter Fleming, who wrote the book about this journey, *News from Tartary*, was twenty-eight, and had been educated at Eton and Oxford. He was fairly hard working, very keen on field sports

* See page 45. ** See page 316.

and an excellent shot, and had been working for *The Times* as a roving correspondent in Manchuria and China for a couple of years. His approach to life in general was, at that age, imbued with casualness; he played at being the ignorant amateur who drifts about and almost by accident finds himself in the wilds of Manchuria; he wrote in an easy, sometimes slangy, manner and practised the English habit of under-statement. For all that, he was a man of action with the qualities of such a man. He liked adventure and living hard, which he knew how to do. He had met Kini Maillart first in London, where he fancied she disliked him, and then in China where they had, in Fleming's phrase, "pottered about the backwoods of Manchuria" together. He discovered that she, as he, had decided to travel across Asia to India and, after considerable reluctance on both sides, they decided to do this together.

Kini Maillart's background had been very different from that of Fleming. Born in Geneva, the depression of the 'thirties found her teaching French in Wales. She did the odd bits of journalism and film work, was a ski-ing international and had sailed for Switzerland in the Olympic Games. She had travelled a lot in Russia, had written a book called *Turkestan Solo,* about travel in Turkestan and Bokhara, which had been a success, and she had been sent by a French newspaper to China. Fleming's last book incidentally had been called *One's Company*. It is not difficult to understand why these two characters joined forces rather suspiciously.

It was *The Times* which sent Peter Fleming on this journey, even though the adventure took him out of journalism for quite a while. On the other hand, it was part of his job, and of Kini Maillart's, as they both conceived their jobs, to find out what was happening in Sinkiang, the most westerly province of China, bounded by the Soviet Union on the north and the west and by India and Tibet in the south. No European traveller had come out of Sinkiang for eight years and, as Fleming writes: "In 1925, Sinkiang, if you substitute political for physical difficulties, shared with the peak of Everest the blue ribbon of inaccessibility."

Early in 1966 Sinkiang leapt into the news as the province in which Mao's China and Kosygin's Russia directly confronted each other. In 1935 the situation was similar in that the Chinese thought, with more reason probably than in 1966, that the Soviet Union was about to grab Sinkiang; it was similar, too, in the complex nature of the forces in play on the Chinese side. Since the downfall of the Manchu Dynasty in 1911 and the break-up of the Republic of Sun

Yat-sen, all China had been the scene of continuous civil war between Chinese war lords. Gradually a Nationalist Government, the Kuomintang, of whom the chief was Chiang Kai-shek, overcame the war lords by force and guile and established a government at Nanking. But a Chinese Soviet Republic was formed in the middle of China in 1931 and Manchuria was then attacked by the Japanese. The Nanking Government could overcome neither enemy. In 1933, Chiang had launched a massive attack and started an economic blockade of the Communist area in the south; but the Communists still remained in the mountains and a Communist army, under Mao, were to march north and establish themselves in Yenan, in Shensi Province.

Peter Fleming had gone home via America in 1933. To him, and to the rest of the world, it seemed unlikely that the Nanking Government could conquer the Communists, but equally unlikely that the Communists could conquer China. He decided to make his journey westward to far-distant Sinkiang because this province was still of considerable interest to British India, being one of the trade routes towards China and containing quite a number of British subjects, with a large and important consulate at Kashgar, in the west of the province. British opinion was, of course, much concerned to know what the Russians were up to. Moscow, like London, was alarmed by Japanese imperialism. Was China about to disintegrate? Were the Russians going to scramble for their bit of China? Already they had secured complete economic domination of Sinkiang Province, the Governor appointed by Nanking seeming to be completely in their pocket.

The establishment of a "People's Republic" in Sinkiang would bring the Soviet Union to the passes of India and Tibet, and of course would enable her to supply the Chinese Communists with arms. There was another party in this struggle. The Tungan rebels held the south part of the province. They, although professing loyalty to Nanking, were at odds with the Provincial Government and with the Russians, even though one of their first leaders had been enticed into Russian territory and was being entertained in Moscow.

Not all of this picture was clear to Peter Fleming when he began his journey; but enough was clear to make him decide that he and Kini Maillart would have no chance whatever if they went by the normal Silk Road across Asia into Sinkiang. By travelling south along the mountains they hoped to be able to descend into the part of Sinkiang in the hands of the Tungan rebels, where the absence of proper Nanking visas would not matter. For as soon as they had arrived at Langchow by rail from Peking they had realized they were in for official difficulties. The authorities were much concerned about the threat from Chinese Communist armies and were taking no risks whatever about allowing foreigners access to Sinkiang.

Apart from the not inconsiderable hazards of normal travel in China, from the difficulties of braving Chinese Governors and officials in the search for passports, the real journey began when they left Tangar, having failed to get any Chinese passport other than one permitting them to travel in the Chinghai Province, which took them only to the borders of Sinkiang.

They were travelling light. They had engaged a young Chinese named Li, an excellent man who had charge of the four camels that were to stay with them only, unfortunately, until they reached the mountainous barrier which separated Teijnar from Sinkiang. On their four Bactrian camels they were carrying exactly what they would have carried had they been Mongols. The chief items were two big sacks of barley for the horses, flour, rice, mien, tsamba, sugar, a few onions and potatoes, some little indestructible cubes of biscuits and a certain amount of garlic; add to this a few rather leprous dried apples, a sack of raisins, a small keg of Chinese spirit which had a bad smell, and one cooking pot, and one diminutive tent.

Tsamba is the staple food of Tibet. It is parched barley meal and in can be mistaken for sawdust. It is eaten in tea with butter, if you have got butter, or with melted mutton fat if you haven't got butter. The shallow wooden bowl is filled with tea, the butter is melted in the tea, and then you put a handful of tsamba in. Fleming describes tsamba as sustaining, digestible, and cheap. For nearly three months they ate tsamba for breakfast and tsamba for lunch and the diet was neither as unappetizing nor as monotonous as it sounded. "He would not," he writes, "go so far as to say that you never got tired of tsamba, but you would get tired of anything else much quicker."

Another thing the camels carried was various forms of currency. They carried the minimum of coins—six or seven hundred dollars secreted in different places among their gear. They had bought in Langchow a 12-oz. bar of gold which, besides being easily concealed, had the advantage of being negotiable anywhere. For the remoter communities, who often had no use for gold or silver, the travellers took with them eight bricks of tea and a good deal of cheap, coloured cloth, one of the other of which was always legal tender. Their supplies and equipment, though they would have been considered most inadequate by a respectable modern expedition, proved completely satisfactory. There was nothing they seriously lacked, though they could have done with a primus stove, and it was a pity that they had failed to procure a basin, for this reduced them to washing in the frying pan, when they washed at all. But Peter Fleming notes: "We had no single thing with us which proved superfluous. No single thing which, as the journey dragged on, provoked us to wonder, with growing exasperation, what the hell we had brought it along for."

Their personal belongings were few—some books, two compasses and two portable type-writers, two pounds of marmalade, four tins of cocoa, six bottles of brandy, one bottle of Worcester sauce, one pound of coffee, three small packets of chocolate, some soap and a good deal of tobacco. They also had a small store of knives, beads and toys by way of presents, and a rather scratch assortment of medicines which, as they went along, were very much in demand by friendly Mongols. They also had two Leica cameras and Fleming had with him a ·44 Winchester rifle with three hundred rounds of pre-war ammunition of a poorish vintage which was not worth firing; and a second-hand ·22 rook rifle which surpassed itself by keeping them in meat, when there was anything to shoot.

After a night at the Kum Bum lamasery where Father Huc and Father Gabet had stayed in 1846, they joined a caravan belonging to the Prince of Dzun which was collecting nearby. When they rode up to the caravan they were surrounded by the wildest crowd of men one could wish to see—Mongols garbed unwieldly in great sheepskins with a bare shoulder, one hand on the hilt on a Tibetan broadsword; Chinese Moslems, more trimly dressed, but still barbaric with hard, cunning, cruel faces. Their servant Li parried a torrent of questions: "No, they are not missionaries." Missionaries were the only kind of foreigners the crowd knew about. Whilst they were unloading their stuff and pitching their tent they received a summons from the Prince. The Prince's tent, though large, was anything but magnificent. The floor was covered with dirty felts, bundles and boxes were stacked around the perimeter. Half a dozen men were squatting around a dung fire. They made room for Fleming and Kini Maillart and gave them the place of honour, which was at the left of the back of the tent as you go in. The Prince greeted them non-committally. He was a young man, probably in his early thirties, and he wore a cap lined with squirrel fur and a voluminous scarlet robe, also fur-lined. He was a man of little ceremony, but although he received from his followers few outward signs of respect his writ appeared to run effectively. "Exactly what he was Prince of," Peter Fleming writes, "we never rightly discovered."

Tsaidam, which was the territory into which they were now penetrating, had been less visited by foreigners than any area of comparable size in Asia. When the Prince asked where the travellers were going, Fleming said to Teijnar, which was the next place of importance after the Prince's own headquarters at Dzunchia. The travellers gave him their cards and presently showed him their various Chinese passports, which he could not read but which looked good and had their photographs on them. They were very much on their best behaviour. They produced their gift, which was a small second-hand telescope, and with that went the flimsy light-blue ceremonial scarf which has to accompany all presents. The Prince, who had never seen a telescope before, spent a long time peering through it, his face contorted in an effort to keep one eye shut. At first they were a prey to some misgivings because they feared the Prince might not manage to see anything from the telescope. But at last he got the focus right and there were grunts of amazement and delight as a distant camel was brought magically nearer.

After this interview Fleming, on a splendid afternoon, went out and shot some three bar-headed geese. He wanted to present one to the Prince, for he thought this would be an appropriate and charming gesture. Fortunately their Mongol servant stopped him in the nick of time, for Buddhism, as interpreted in those parts, forbids the Mongols the flesh of geese, ducks and hares, although it allows them antelopes and pheasants. It would have been a frightful solecism to have given the Prince the goose. The next day he dragged back to the camp a large buck antelope which he had shot with his rook rifle. The antelope, he writes, made a profound impression on the caravan—the tiny ·22 bullets were passed from hand to hand amid exclamations of amazement. Fleming became the devil of a fellow. What else could the little gun kill? Yaks? Wild horses? Bandits, he said, and got a cheap laugh. They skinned the antelope, gave the four quarters away and Kini Maillart made schashlik on the cleaning-rod while the antelope's liver was boiling. That night they could be said to have dined sumptuously.

They travelled for seventeen days with the Prince of Dzun. It was a period of comfort and peace compared with what was to follow. Li used to wake the travellers in the grim half-light, thrusting under the flap of the tent what he called "eye-wash water". Cramped and cursing they dragged themselves out of their sleepings bags, made some pretence of washing in the frying pan, cleaned their teeth and pulled on their boots. It was far too cold to undress much at night. They were usually bad-tempered in an amiable sort of way. Then Li would bring the tea and they would swill it down and mix their tsamba, all the time struggling to pack their things against the coming of the camels. "Kini," Fleming writes, "was a slower eater than I was. I retain a vivid picture of her protesting as vainly as Canute protested at the waves, combing her hair with a lump of tsamba held between her teeth and a mirror balanced on her knees while I dismantled the tent about her and Mongols dragged away the box on which she was leaning. Our camels were always among the last to be loaded."

The caravan wound, stately and methodical, through the bleak and empty land, two hundred and fifty camels pacing in single file. At the head of it, leading the first string, usually rode an old woman on a white pony, a gnarled and withered crone whose conical fur-brimmed hat enhanced her resemblance to a witch. Scattered along the flanks went forty or fifty horsemen. The little ponies were dwarfed by the bulging sheepskins which encased their masters. Everyone carried, slung across the back, an ancient musket or a matchlock with a forked rest, and a few of the Chinese had repeating carbines. Some people wore broadswords as well.

For the first two or three hours they would get off their horses and walk on account of the cold to restore circulation. Sooner or later, every day, the wind got up. It came tearing out of the west and scorched them without mercy. It was enough to drive you mad. You could not smoke, you could not speak, and after a time you could not think consecutively. The wind did them no harm except to chap their faces, but it plagued them and got on their nerves. They would travel as a rule from early morning until about two or three in the afternoon. "It was always one of the best moments of the day," Fleming writes, "when we had got our tent pitched and the things stowed inside it and we could plunge in and lie luxuriously on our sleeping bags out of the wind. Out of the wind, it made such a difference. The air still roared outside and the thin walls bulged in upon us; but we could talk and smoke and rub butter on our chapped and burning faces and feel at peace. Presently there would be tea with red pepper in it and tsamba to abate the gnawing in our bellies. It is really impossible to describe how snug and comfortable we felt."

In the afternoon Fleming would go out looking for game, whilst Miss Maillart read or wrote or darned or slept. It was Miss Maillart who went out into the cold and cooked the evening meal. When it was ready, a great black pot was put just inside the tent and Li brought his bowl and the travellers got out their plates and dinner was served—rice or a kind of noodles or whatever meat Fleming had managed to obtain. How they ate! They did not speak. They shovelled food down until the pot was empty and they were distended. As soon as they had finished eating they felt sleepy. They wriggled into their flea-bags and covered themselves with their overcoats. They made pillows of rolled-up sweaters on a foundation of boots and field-glasses. Just outside, their horses munched their barley, making a sound as charming and as soporific as the sound of running water or of waves upon a beach. The tiny tent looked warm and cheerful in the candlelight. "One of us," said Fleming, "would perhaps grow suddenly talkative, theorizing about the future or reminiscing about the past. But conversation became increasingly one-sided; monosyllables received by grunts, and grunts by a profound indifferent silence."

During a part of their journey they reached nearly 14,000 feet above sea-level, and then, at Dzunchia, they came down on to comparatively low ground. The new world was flat and featureless, but at least it was warmer. They ate and basked luxuriously. They spent three days in a fort; but they did not take kindly to sleeping under a roof again. They had a long, squalid, hot, uncertain journey from Dzunchia to Taijnar, which they reached on 8 May. Here it was that they had to part with Li and his camels. They had great difficulty in obtaining camels from the Prince of Taijnar, who treated them in a somewhat unfriendly manner. On the other hand they were exceedingly fortunate to meet a White Russian called Borodishin, about whom they had heard in Langchow. They knew nothing about how to cross the high mountains between Taijnar and Sinkiang, nor the most favourable route to take into the forbidden province.

They crossed high mountains in a much less secure or comfortable manner than during their period with the Prince of Dzun. They went through miles of desert country until finally, exactly four months after leaving Peking, they entered the oasis of Cherchen in Sinkiang. "Wonder and joy", Fleming writes, "fell on them." The earth offers no greater contrast except that between land and sea than the contrast between desert and oasis. They had stepped clean out of one world into another. One moment they were stumbling in the open river bed, plagued by glare and a grit-laden wind, and the next they were marching down a narrow path under the murmurous protection of poplar and mulberry and ash. Everywhere water ran musically in the irrigation channels. A girl in a bright pink cap washing her baby in a pool veiled her face swiftly at the sight of the infidels. Low houses with mud walls and wooden beams stood under the trees, round courtyards half-roofed over. A cock crowed. The familiar sound, unheard for nearly three months, asserted their return to a world where men had homes and they began to think gloatingly of eggs. They wound deeper into the oasis in a kind of trance.

Now, for them, what seemed of the greatest importance was their reception by the Tungan rebels or whatever troops they would find in this war-torn country. It was not long before they met Tungan troops, an officer and a private soldier with a rifle. The officer, who wore a little film-star moustache and held himself well, asked them their business and identities. They were dismayed to see that the officer and the soldier wore Chinese Army flashes and therefore they expected that he would be very difficult about their failure to have a Chinese visa. Fleming switched on his Chinese technique, such as it was, and answered the officer in gay and deprecating terms. No, no, they were not Russians, that was wholly incorrect. He was English and she was French. His humble name was Learned Engraver on Stone, hers was Horse of International Goodwill. Here were their cards. His business was the affair of Extra Special Correspondent Officer to the Newspaper for the Enlightened Apprehension of Scholars, a great English newspaper. The officer looked blank and unimpressed. Of course they had the correct passports and Fleming gave a merry laugh at the mere idea that their papers might he out of order. We are for it, he thought.

The officer took them to a building which might have been an inn or a prison in the centre of the town and said their passports would be examined.

News of their arrival had spread and soon there came a sea of curious faces around them in the bazaar. Skull-caps, turbans, hats edged with lambskin bobbed up and down in efforts to secure an uninterrupted view of what was in most cases the first white people they had ever seen in the region. Quite soon the officer rode back and informed them that their passports were in order, and a little red stamp was fixed on the document delivered them in Chinghai. Then a greater surprise arrived. A tall, venerable Afghan with a dignified carriage and shrewd eyes saluted them respectfully and seemed genuinely pleased to see them. He was the local representative of the British Consulate-General in Kashgar. He said they were to lodge in his house. Once more their animals were loaded and they started for an hour's ride through pleasant, well-cultivated country. They came to a large new house which was to be their home for several days. A wall surrounded a garden of apricot trees and vines and over the gateway, over the wall, there hung, home-made, unorthodox in design but infinitely reassuring, no less an emblem than the Union Jack. They entered premises owned, in the last analysis, by His late Majesty, King George V. There could scarcely be a sharper contrast to the long bleak struggle over the uplands.

After this the travellers were virtually certain that they would reach the shelter of the Consulate-General in Kashgar, and from there the journey to India would have few problems. The match game was over and, in Fleming's phrase, they were now "playing the bye". All the same, their journey across long stretches of desert in southern Sinkiang was painful, at times exhausting. But they were now journalists, not merely adventurers. There were towns: in Khotan and Yarkand they were received by General Ma Ho San, the C.-in-C. of the Tungan army, and the half-brother of General Ma Chang Ying, who had gone off to Moscow. The C.-in-C. was vague about his half-brother's political position; he made it clear that he was expecting help from the Kuomintang against its own Provincial Government, now regarded as having gone over to the Russians. The General said his army would shortly advance over the route Fleming and Kini Maillart hoped to take, and cut off Kashgar and all the south of Sinkiang from the capital, Urumchi.

They were allowed to take photographs and to inspect the Mint where the Tungans were hand-printing their bank-notes on soggy paper made from mulberry fibre, quite without a penny of capital or credit to back them. On their route they talked with many Chinese officials and Russian-speaking Turks (Kini Maillart spoke good

Russian better than Fleming's fairly elementary Chinese) and gathered the information which made Fleming's subsequent articles in *The Times* one of the most brilliant pieces of reporting of the period. In Khotan and Yarkand they found their first back-numbers of British newspapers and learnt, along with much else, of the death of T. E. Lawrence, whom rumour, just before, had connected with Sinkiang.

As they were coming to the new city of Kashgar they saw something which resembled a station "fly" and, in charge of it, a turbanned orderly in khaki. A young man, immaculately dressed with a topee and mounted on a grey polo pony, greeted them. "I am sorry to have dropped out of the blue like this," said Fleming. "You see, we couldn't give you more than a day's notice." "It wasn't as unexpected as you think," answered the young man. "We've had an enquiry about you from the Secretary of State." At this, the travellers were momentarily aggrieved. "I don't know whether you drink beer," said the young man when they had reached the Consulate. He very soon knew that they did.

They spent a fortnight in the hospitable British Consulate in Kashgar, during which time they were entertained by a Chinese general in the pay of the Russians, who had been educated by the Y.M.C.A., swam and played tennis with most agreeable Russian diplomats, and learnt much. Then off to India, refreshed, through the Pamirs and the Himalayas. Here were higher passes to be crossed than any before, and a route which, though well recognized, still took its toll of lives.

But, for them, it was child's play, this passage to India. There were Rest Houses set up by the servants of the British Raj, and, on their way, they were entertained by the rulers of the mountain kingdoms of Hunza and Naga and helped by British Political Officers who appreciated what they had done. The journey, however, was anything but a prolonged picnic and now they were both longing for good beds, good food and letters from home. At Srinagar, they were told, there was "a very decent hotel" and they pictured themselves eating in a quiet dining-room in the company of officers on leave for hunting–congenial people.

The reality was different. The Srinagar hotel was large and luxurious, even flash. As they crossed the hall, the guests in evening dress were assembled for dinner. They were horribly aware of dusty clothes and blackened faces. "Anglo-India, starched and glossy, stared at us with horror and disgust. A stage clergyman with an Oxford voice started as though he had seen the devil. A hush through which on all sides could be heard the fell epithet "jungle" descended on the assembled guests. We were back in civilization." They went to register. "With a last poor attempt at swagger we both wrote in the Where from column Peking, but it might have been Poona for all the impression it made on the clerk. We turned back to the alien and hostile lounge." "That's that," said Kini Maillart, and sighed. The journey was over.

THE TALL SHIPS HAVE GONE

The Big Grain-Race of 1939

THE TALL ships have gone. Here and there one survives–as a training ship, perhaps–but she is, can only be, a memory of a vanished past. The day of the tall ship is over.

Yet on the eve of the Second World War there were still at least thirteen of these great vessels, propelled entirely by sail, operating commercially. They were not rich men's toys; they operated purely and simply as a means of making money for their owners, as cargo carriers–and in direct competition with steamers.

How was this possible? Surely, the greater speed and capacity of the average tramp-steamer put it in quite a different class? For certain cargoes, yes. But not, in 1939, and for generations before, on the grain run from Australia where a unique set of conditions operated. On that run, even if a sailing ship went out in ballast, carrying no cargo and therefore earning no money, and took four months on the return, loaded with South Australian grain, her owners made a tidy profit.

There were several good reasons. Grain was not perishable, nor was it a seasonal commodity, like fruit; it therefore made little difference when the voyage was made, or how long it took. It could be, and was, arranged when wind and weather would be most suitable. And the primitive loading and docking arrangements in some of the South Australian ports, like Port Lincoln, which would have made a steamer captain give up in despair, made little difference to the cheaply run, fuel-less, sailing vessel, with her low-paid crew. She could afford to wait calmly for four, five or six weeks, while grain in sacks was brought out to her in lighters—there being no jetty—and slung aboard. She could afford to do this and then take upwards of 120 days, if things went badly, on the trip to Britain—and make a profit.

With running costs so low—senior crew members might get two pounds sterling a month—the chief incentive for making fast passage was pride: a captain's and a crew's pride in the vessel and their ability to sail her, carrying every possible inch of sail, through the roughest weather.

It still makes little difference how long a cargo of grain takes to negotiate the oceans of half the globe: it still doesn't rot or perish. But other conditions have changed. Merchant shipping is less profitable today: wages are far higher, and the cost of literally everything has soared, as all of us know too well. And the port facilities of Australia, and other southern countries, from Chile to New Zealand, have improved so that a steamer can load a cargo at speed and get out again.

Already the writing was on the wall and there were many taking part in what turned out to be the "Great Grain Race of 1939"—though it sprang up naturally and by accident—who feared it would be the last.

In March of that year, when so many ships were due to return from the southern hemisphere, a race was inevitable. There was real incentive to do well, to break all records, leave a fine—and final—mark.

In the last century, average time for the clipper ships on the run was a hundred days. But the actual record, a remarkable one and never equalled, was a mere sixty-three. *Thermopylae* set it, on her maiden voyage in 1868: two months for 15,000 miles under sail. She was planned, though, for the tea-trade from China, and it was for this that her rival was launched the following year.

That rival, the famous *Cutty Sark*, arrived just too late: the Suez Canal opened in 1869 and it became cheaper to send China tea in steamers through it, where no sailing ship could go. The two clippers were transferred to the Australian wool trade, and later to grain. In the ten years 1885-1895, *Cutty Sark* averaged 80½ days outward from Britain to Australia round the Cape of Good Hope, and 82½ days for the return carrying on in the same direction, round Cape Horn, with prevailing winds. As for *Thermopylae*, though she never repeated her incredible maiden voyage, she managed to beat *Cutty Sark* regularly on the outward voyage–and to be beaten as regularly on the return.

These two were clippers, long, narrow, graceful, greyhounds of the sea. The barque was less attractive to the eye, though still beautiful in comparison with a dumpy, dirty, steamer. She was broader than the clipper and, instead of the clipper's three masts, might have anything up to five. Often she was of steel–built for strength and capacity. Yet barques did remarkable times. And it was partly to prove this that the thirteen contestants in the 1939 race–all of them barques–took part.

Most, as the names reveal, were Scandinavian. All but two were four-masters, only the *Winterhude* and *Killoran* having three. The other eleven were *Abraham Rydberg, Lawhill, Viking, Archibald Russell, Olive Bank, Pommern, Passat, Pamir, Padua, Kommodore Johnsen* and *Moshulu*.

In 1939 Captain Gustav Erikson of the port of Mariehamn, on an island in the Baltic off Finland, owned the largest fleet of these vessels in the world, with, in addition, a quantity of smaller ships busily employed in North European waters. One of his big ships was the graceful *Moshulu*. She had been launched in 1904 at Port Glasgow, for German owners, under the name *Kurt*, but after changing hands a number of times she had joined Erikson's fleet under a new, more musical, name.

And it was to Erikson that a young Englishman wrote in 1938, asking to be given the chance to sail as crew on one of the Finn's fleet. We can be grateful that he was given the opportunity, for Eric Newby has written a vivid and exciting account–and in places an uproariously humorous one–of his round trip from Ireland to Ireland via Australia.

He signed aboard *Moshulu*, after his father had paid a premium of £50 in order that he might do so. His contract as apprentice stated that he would be bound to the owner, Erikson, for eighteen months or the round trip, whichever was shorter. If he deserted in any foreign port the premium would, of course, be forfeit. If he died *en route* his parents could claim a repayment. Strictly *pro rata*, of course. He would be paid the equivalent of ten shillings a month and be subject to Finnish law. Young Newby was delighted.

Moshulu sailed on the outward voyage from Belfast on 18

October, 1938, her destination Port Lincoln, South Australia. She sailed with a cargo of ballast, part of which was sixty tons of drinking water, intended to last the whole round trip, for it cost £5 a ton in Australia. Even with this unprofitable outward cargo, *Moshulu* stood to make a fair profit for Erikson.

It was a hard, rough life, and Newby was introduced to it immediately–even before sailing. On his first day, with the ship still in Belfast docks, the Second Mate took a dislike to him and ordered him up the rigging:

"We were standing amidships by the mainmast. He pointed to the lower main shrouds which supported the mast and said simply, 'Op you go, then.' I could scarcely believe my ears. I had imagined that I should be allowed at least a day or two to become used to the ship and the feel of things, but this was my introduction to discipline. I looked at the Mate. He had a nasty glint in his eye and I decided I was more afraid of him than of the rigging. If I was killed, it would be his fault, not mine, I said to myself with little satisfaction. Nevertheless I asked him if I could change my shoes which had slippery soles.

" 'Change your shoes? Op the rigging.' He was becoming impatient.

"At this time *Moshulu* was the greatest sailing ship in commission and probably the tallest. Her mainmast cap was 198 feet above the keel. I started towards the main rigging on the starboard side nearest the quay, but was brought back by a cry from the mate.

" 'Babord, port side. If you fall, you may fall in the dock. When we're at sea you will always use the weather rigging, that's the side from which the wind blows. Never the lee rigging. And when I give you an order, you repeat it.'

" 'Op the rigging,' I said."

And so Eric Newby, just eighteen, goes "op" it, a harrowing trip even for the reader, with hair-raising slips, ratlines which break, grease over everything–until after a series of peremptory, broken-English orders from the deck, he is out on the yardarm, 160 feet above the Belfast sheds into which *Moshulu* is unloading 62,000 sacks of grain before replacing them with ballast for the outward trip. The roofs of the sheds are of glass, and he shudders. Weak with fright, he is ordered to the very top of the mast, 198 feet above the keel. There is no rope here, only bare, slippery pole, and he takes off the unsuitable shoes, the socks as well, wedges them under the jackstay. Taking a deep breath, closing his eyes, he negotiates the last six slippery feet, grasps the round hardwood cap at the top. Ignoring the Mate below who is screaming up at him, telling him to sit on the cap, he comes down.

Perhaps it is a good initiation—for soon, very soon, he will be doing the same thing in storms, with a wind of seventy miles an hour trying to pluck him from the rigging.

The ordinary work of the ship, the painting, the washing and so on, began at six every morning and went on until the same hour in the evening. The handling of the ship, of course, never stopped, and this was divided into watches, calculated so that no man did the same watch on two successive days. But as Eric Newby and the other uninitiated members of the crew were to find out, everything altered in rough weather: if sail had to be taken in, the watch on duty stayed and did it, however due for relief.

There was no race at stake in the outward journey, though it was filled with thrills and terrors, and we can dismiss it as an 82-day trip, without sight of land, between October, 1938, and dropping anchor off Port Lincoln, 8 January, 1939.

Two months later, fully loaded with 4,875 tons of grain in 59,000 sacks, *Moshulu* set sail on the homeward voyage, round the tip of South America. It was half-past six on the morning of Saturday, 11 March, and her destination was Queenstown in Ireland.

The first vessel in this unofficial but very real race had left nearly a month before: *Viking* sailed from Australia on 16 February. The race was against clock and calendar, so times of departure were irrelevant. Two other ships had left when *Moshulu* weighed anchor: *Pamir*, on 8 March, and *Passat* on the 9th.

Slowly, with the moon still shining and a wind from the north strengthening, gust by gust, *Moshulu* slipped out into the Gulf as her crew loosed the great square sails—no less than eighteen of them on fore, main and mizzen, plus a bewildering assortment of spankers and jibs at bow and stern. The moon faded, the sun rose up in the sky behind and, for *Moshulu*, the Great Grain Race was on.

Among the ship's company were three small black pigs purchased in Australia and christened Auguste, Filimon and Fabian, plus one large white female, too dignified to be christened at all and therefore eaten long before Cape Horn. The three little black ones spent most of their time out of their tiny hutches, for the crew had a grudging affection for them, used to let them out to snuffle about the deck, covering themselves with red lead, eating all temporarily

469

discarded clothing, as well as paint-brushes, sail-canvas and sea-boots.

All day, as they sailed south and then east, the wind mounted and soon it became clear that their first, fine day was degenerating into a storm. A mountain of cloud appeared from nowhere, poised itself over the ship: the barometer began to fall, almost visibly. Captain Sjögren ordered the royals taken in—the topmost sail on fore, main and mizzen mast. The wind grew stronger and the next sails down—upper topgallants—were taken in. Even now, "under low top-gallants", or with only four out of six square sails on each mast, *Moshulu* was plunging ahead at thirteen knots, water completely flooding the decks, sweeping out again through the scuppers.

By noon of the next day they had made 247 miles—a fine start. The storm had died, but there was a good wind, shifting slowly from north-west to south-west, and back. The crew were busy pre-paring for *really* bad weather, gales which were bound to come as they ran on into high latitudes to round the Horn. Lifelines were rigged, for a man to seize if being washed overboard; hatches were reinforced. As if to mock them, the wind died away to nothing, and in twenty-four hours they made only 76 miles. At this rate, far from breaking records, they would take seven months to reach Ireland.

18 March; south and east of Tasmania, 47° South Latitude and Longitude 153° East. Weather getting noticeably colder—and five thousand miles to Cape Horn.

Their first issue of rum, a lethal distillation, four degrees over proof, and almost every member of the crew very drunk. The wind mounted again and on 20 March they were off the Snares, a group of uninhabited islands south of New Zealand. Four days later, making good time now, they crossed the 180th meridian, the Inter-national Date Line, where the traveller from west to east earns another day. For *Moshulu*'s crew this was Friday, an unpopular choice (why couldn't it have been Sunday, a day of at least partial rest?), as a hard day, and probably unlucky to boot.

The barometer started to fall again a high wind shifted to the west and they ran before it. Sails were squared, spankers and gaff topsail taken in. There was no doubt about it now—this would be a storm to remember—if they lived that long.

At 5 p.m. on the first of the two adjacent Fridays, the heavy chain to the fore-royal, top sail on the foremast, parted, and they just manged to get the canvas in before it blew to pieces in the gale.

The other two royals were feverishly taken in, but the captain, determined not to waste any wind, however dangerous, kept on upper topgallants, the sails just below them. Suddenly an enormous wave, the sea like a mountain. It was dawn on the second Friday.

"There was just time to take a turn with the clewline round my middle and a good hold, the next moment it was on top of us. The rope was not torn from me; instead, it was as though a gentle giant had smoothed his hands over my knuckles. They simply opened of their own accord and I unravelled from it like a cotton reel from the end of a thread and was swept away. As I went another body bumped me, and I received a blow in the eye from a seaboot. Then I was alone, rushing onwards and turning over and over. My head was filled with bright light like a by-pass at night, and the air was full of the sounds of a large orchestra playing out of tune.

"No more obstructions now but still going very fast and still under water, perhaps no longer in the ship, washed overboard, alone in the Southern Ocean."

But Eric Newby was still aboard.

By noon on the second Friday, the second, 24 March, they had covered 296 miles, the best day's sailing any man could remember, and in fact the best done by *Moshulu* since 1909. Then, under her original German owners, she had run 300 miles in a day, between Australia and South America.

A force 9 gale, and now, to the alarm of half the crew, Captain Sjögren, gazing up at the canvas billowing aloft, says, "We'll see what she can stand." They go aloft and break out the main lower topgallant. The verdict among the crew is that the ship will never stand it. The crew is right and two hours later a sail below the one they have set carries away, has to be taken in, together with the lower topgallant. They are plunging on faster and faster, steel hull groaning.

" 'This Kapten is proper strongbody for vind,' said Sandell after an issue of rum and a good dinner of lobscouse–a sustaining hash made from pounded hard biscuit, potato and 'Buffalo'.

" ' – the Kapten,' replied Sedelquist, who was absolutely cynical about all men. 'Vonts to get his name in the papers, I shouldn't wonder.'

" 'We'll be in it too, if he does,' I said.

" 'Yes, in the bloddy paper but on the front with beeg black lines all round, "missing". That's what we'll be.' ".

There is ice about–just to add to the hazards of the biggest storm many of them have encountered.

By noon on Saturday, 25 March–no more dreadful "double days" now, Sunday will follow Saturday and so on till the end of time–they are at 50° 7′ South, 164° 21′ West: in the past three days they have run 296, 282, and 241 nautical miles. Were it not for the violence of the sea they would have covered considerably more. The barometer, incredibly, goes right on dropping. They are now 2,000 miles east of New Zealand with 3,000 ahead of them to the Horn, and Tahiti 2,000 to the north. To the south there is nothing but winter darkness, and somewhere inside it the Antarctic continent. The decks are awash, more like a reef than a ship, with winches and hatches only occasionally putting in appearance above the surface. There are sudden, terrifying lulls when the wind seems to vanish entirely for two or three seconds before coming back in still greater force, and in these lulls there is the frenzied screaming of pigs.

"At six o'clock, we cleaned out their sties, a difficult job in a ship running before a great gale. It took three of us to do it.

" 'For Chrissake don' let them go,' grunted Tria, as we levered the iron troughs through the door of the sty with crowbars.

"He had no sooner said this than Auguste and Filimon, believing that the ship was about to founder, charged the barricade of hatch-covers with which we had fenced them in, intent on finding a place in the boats. The barricade collapsed, and Filimon, who was leading, shot between Tria's legs, upsetting him in the nasty mess we were shovelling up. Auguste followed him closely, and they both went glissading away on their behinds into the lee scuppers, from which we had difficulty in rescuing them.

" 'Better eat them before they go overside,' I said as we struggled with Auguste, who was threshing about under water.

" 'I don' care how soon we eat that Filimon,' Tria said."

And so this epic storm goes on into its final phase. The ship is still carrying her sail. It is impossible to stand on the forecastle, but standing beneath it one can look aft and see the sea astern, higher than a three-storey house. Newby, off duty now, takes the courageous–or foolhardy–decision to climb the foremast and take pictures from that great, plunging height, of the ship below. Picking his way, he gets to the cross-trees 130 feet above the deck; "In a wind blowing 70 miles an hour, the noise and unearthly scream. Above me was the naked topgallant yard and above that the royal to which I presently climbed. I was now used to heights but the bare yard, gleaming yellow in the sunshine, was groaning and creaking on its tracks. The high whistle of the wind through the halliards' sheaf, and above all the pale blue, illimitable sky, cold and serene, made me deeply afraid and conscious of my insignificance.

"Far below, the ship was an impressive sight. For a time the whole of the after deck would disappear, hatches, winches, everything, as the solid water hit; and then, like an animal pulled down by hounds, she would rise and shake them from her, would come lifting out of the sea with her ports spouting.

"Opening my camera, I attached the lens hood, but the wind blew it into the sea. The mist of spray rising all about the ship made it almost impossible to see anything through the viewfinder. There was no need for the rangefinder. I simply set the scale to infinity and pressed the button, and even that was difficult enough."

And this brave photographic expedition, which produced good and startling pictures–and wrecked the camera–marked the end of the storm. In the early hours of Monday, 27 March, as barometer climbed and wind fell, they put on more and more sail: when dawn came up over the port bow they were in full sail.

The white pig was killed and eaten. With no refrigeration, she had to be consumed more or less at a sitting, or at least over a very few days in which everyone ate pork, pork and more of it, accompanied by blood pancakes. None of the white pig, the dignified lady, was wasted.

And then, on Easter Sunday, 9 April, after weeks of seeing nothing but sea and sky–wild, uncontrollable excitement. Dense cloud to the north, but suddenly it lifted; there, fifteen miles to port, was another barque, like themselves. Everyone rushed to the rail.

It could hardly be *Viking*, for she had sailed three weeks before them and it would be too much to hope they had overhauled her. It might be *Passat*, which had left Port Lincoln a day before them, or even *Pamir*, which had sailed a day before that, on 8 March.

Captain Sjögren, peering through his telescope, saw that the other ship was carrying topgallants but not royals. A moment later three crewmen on *Moshulu* were climbing aloft as fast as they could go, casting off the gaskets to let her royals be set.

An hour later they noticed the other ship had set royals. And a little later the First Mate, way up in the rigging, announced she was *Passat*.

Suddenly the race was real. They crammed on every inch of sail, willing *Moshulu* forward, scarce daring to take eyes off *Passat*, noticing with delight that she was slipping farther away astern. The sun sank away behind them, and they never saw the other barque again.

The next day, 10 April, they rounded Cape Horn, out of sight but marked by the island of Diego Ramirez and a sudden mass of birds which blotted out the sky. Each day's progress was now a matter of concern to the entire crew. And in the South Atlantic, heading north towards the Equator, spirits rose. Each day, men knew, would get warmer, and though the process would irritatingly reverse itself after they crossed the Line, there would be no more of the numbing winter cold of latitude fifty south. In fifty north, when they got there, spring would be half over and summer coming up over the horizon.

The weather grew warmer; the sea changed from grey, through green, to blue. And on 20 April, when it seemed the race might be won, the journey all but over, another storm hit them. Sheets parted, sails were wrecked, they were under water again on deck.

Suddenly the wind stopped completely. The ship was as silent—and as sinister—as it had ever been. It had been raining heavily a moment before, and now that too stopped, as if through Divine intervention. Most of the crew were amazed, delighted: not the captain. His voice roared at them and they frenziedly hauled down sail.

Seconds later it hit them: a colossal wind that brought one gigantic wave to engulf the entire ship. A sail exploded.

Moshulu weathered the storm, raced on northwards, into the South-east Trades. Days grew warmer, skies clearer and they strained eyes looking for sight of other competitors in the race. Confidence was high and no man expected to see any of the ships which had set sail after them: *Moshulu* had overhauled *Passat*, seen her drop away behind; perhaps she'd done the same with *Pamir*. *Viking* had left three weeks earlier, and they had hopes of catching her too.

And on 1 May they were hopelessly, utterly, becalmed. Cursing, almost weeping with frustration, they took the risk of swimming over the side, hoping to avoid sharks. They saw one, caught it on a hook baited with a bit of Augusta and gave up swimming. A bit more wind, then an agonizing crawl, doing 38, 78, 80, 70 miles on successive days.

But the race, as they hoped, was won. They arrived off Queenstown at noon on Saturday, 10 June, having negotiated the 15,000 miles in 91 days. *Viking*, who had worried them, had been sighted crossing the Equator after 90 days. (She would drop anchor after a voyage of 119.) No one seemed to worry that those sailing behind might beat their time, and in fact they were being given a good run for their money: *Padua*, *Pamir* and *Passat* would all do the journey in under one hundred days.

And so, though no one knew it, they had won not only the 1939 Grain Race, but the last real Race of all time. A few ships under sail would negotiate the distance after the war, and the incredible Francis Chichester, single-handed in his own small boat, *Gypsy Moth*, would astonish the world by doing an outward journey of 107 days, a return in 119. But the Grain Races would be over. No man is likely to consider building a four-masted barque in the latter half of the twentieth century—and if he did, it would be commercially almost useless.

A chapter—a fine one—has ended, in the tale of man's fight for speed.

THE VOYAGE OF THE "KON-TIKI"

A Modern Exploration of an Ancient Theme

HE LOOKED at his watch. Ten-to-ten. Automatically he looked for the sun, but it was bounding back and forwards in the sky and he realized that he was hanging to a wildly shaking rope, for dear life. In front—or was it behind, one couldn't tell on the bounding, leaping raft—was the vivid white of breakers. Beneath these, though as yet unseen, were the savage razor-blades of coral.

Kon-Tiki suddenly lifted up, as if by some giant hand, and almost capsized. The anchor slithered along the bamboo deck, gained speed and plunged overboard. A second later, with a sickening jerk, the raft stopped dead. Then she swung round, faced out to sea again, stern against the reef.

Torstein tapped out a final, urgent, message. Listen every hour: if we are silent for more than thirty-six of them, tell the Norwegian embassy in Washington. The American "ham" operator, thousands of miles away, acknowledged.

By now the roar of the breakers was deafening. They cut the anchor rope and *Kon-Tiki* began to move again. At first it was a gentle drift and for a moment it seemed as if they might be deposited gently on the reef with their vessel, would be able to dislodge it again at high tide, carry on to a final destination—wherever that might be.

But with a sudden fury the waves grasped them, lifted them up, seemed about to flip them over, hurl *Kon-Tiki*, like some great pancake, against the reef, smash her to a thousand pieces. It was as if they were at the top of a green glass mountain, ready to fall.

Then they were deep inside the mountain, blind under tons of water, clinging desperately, each man to his rope. It seemed minutes that they clung there, submerged. Then the green about them grew lighter. And it was over. *Kon-Tiki* lay, almost a total wreck, impaled on the reef, dead and still. They were clinging to her, sun beating down on their bodies, coral reef all about them. And in the deafening roar of breakers, somehow, it was peaceful.

And so, in this moment of battered triumph ended one of the most remarkable journeys on record, a journey taken to prove a theory—and which proved so much more.

It had begun a little over three months previously. Or had it begun a decade before that? Before the Second World War, when a young Norwegian scientist was working on a remote Pacific island in the Marquesas group. Thor Heyerdahl had been there with his wife, the only white people on the island, and they had spent a year studying its ancient culture, collecting specimens of rock, mineral, animal life, anything which would help build up a complete picture.

Many nights the young couple would sit, when the day's work was over, watching the waves in the moonlight flinging silver spray on the sand. And they noticed, remarked on it, that the breakers, the really big ones, were always on the island's east shore, never on the west.

A theory was born.

Heyerdahl had often pondered the origins of the cheerful Polynesian people. They were a type found only in these Pacific islands, different racially and in every other way from the black-skinned aboriginals of Australia, from the brown inhabitants of Indonesia and Asia. And there were stone monuments in the islands, particularly on Easter Island, quite different from anything in Asia, yet oddly reminiscent of some he had seen in South America. He knew that the islands had been uninhabited before A.D. 500, when a people with a Stone Age culture, ignorant of metal, had moved in. And in A.D. 500, the only people in the world who still possessed a Stone Age culture were the "Indian" inhabitants of the Americas. But the pleasing theory that these South Americans had sailed westwards across the ocean, sailed four thousand miles to settle in the islands of Polynesia, was knocked on the head by the fact, long established, that they had no ocean-going boats.

And suddenly, watching surf burst on the eastern shore of his island, Heyerdahl conceived his theory. The men from South America might have been incapable of making a large boat, but they could lash a few logs together. And rafts, made this way out of the light balsa wood which grows–has always grown–on the west coast of their continent, could easily be taken by the prevailing wind and current, right across the sea.

Like these breakers.

And in the fullness of time, while their passengers caught fish to eat, collected rainwater to drink, the rafts would deliver to one or other Pacific island a new race of immigrants, bringing their unique Stone Age culture, their weirdly carved gods, with them.

The more he thought of it, the more likely this seemed. The languages of Polynesia, for example: there were thousands of miles between, say, Hawaii and Tahiti, and there could have been no question of communication between the two. Yet the language was the same–as it was on every island of the vast area. Obviously, all had been colonized by the same people, and sufficiently recently for the language not to alter significantly.

Heyerdahl had plenty of time to ponder this theory, as the war broke out a little later.

Five years in the Norwegian Army; then peace and a renewed determination to prove the theory. He finished the treatise he had written on the subject, headed for America: surely, *there* he would be able to interest people? But in the United States academics were strangely unimpressed.

Thor Heyerdahl made up his mind. His money was running out and he moved to the Norwegian Sailors' Home in New York. Here, night after night, and in the public libraries, he studied maps and charts, read books. With the aid of a Norwegian friend, an ex-sailor, he calculated the speed at which the raft he had in mind would drift, the route and distance it would travel before reaching the Pacific islands. The number of days it would take. It would take ninety-seven days. He was sure of that.

His enthusiasm began to infect others. Before long he had received offers of financial backing and equipment–sleeping-bags, scientific equipment, cooking stoves, the rest of it. Manufacturers, the Army Department, even the British Ministry of Supply which had somehow got news of the venture, were delighted to provide all sorts of items, including rations, to be tested in the course of this extraordinary voyage.

More important than all this, he managed to assemble, by telegram, letter, personal contact, a team of five other young Scandinavians who would accompany him, sail under his command, in the good ship *Kon-Tiki*. For this would be her name: *Kon-Tiki*, the "Sun-God": the ancestor, as tradition had it, of all the Polynesian people, the great red-bearded being who had come from the east.

From various parts of the world, by plane and by ship, the expedition converged on New York. This was thousands of miles from the projected start-point, but it was the best place to get things organized. The six met, began to infect each other all over again with their enthusiasm, but the first problem, the building of a raft, seemed insurmountable. Fine balsa-wood grew in Peru–and this for a multitude of reasons had to be their start-point–but it grew inland and there was no means of getting the huge logs to the coast. The answer would be to do as the Peruvians must have done: move up the coast into Ecuador, where the trees grew to the water's edge, collect the wood, take it down to Peru.

They got to Ecuador. But now there was no longer any large balsa growing near the coast: it had been cut down during the war, fashioned into aeroplanes. If they wanted good-sized stuff, they would have to go many miles inland, cut the trees there and float them down a river to the coast. They did. Then, on the coast, they loaded them aboard a coastal steamer, got them to Peru. A little diplomacy and much persuasion and they got permission to build their raft, safe from the depredations of souvenir hunters, inside the dockyard of Callao harbour.

They did the work with axes and long knives, trimming the nine thickest, longest, logs to form the hull. No nails or wire could be used: that would be an anachronism, cheating. The nine logs were dropped into the water, side by side, the longest, of forty-five feet, in the middle. After they had settled into their natural floating position they were lashed together with hemp rope and the outline of the craft began to take shape. The forty-five footer at the centre formed a sharp bow, with the shorter logs outboard of it, giving sides thirty feet long. A block of balsa wood was fastened to the stern as mounting for the long steering-oar.

When the nine big logs were in place, thinner ones, a foot in diameter and eighteen feet long, were laid across them at right angles. Above these went a deck of bamboo, and aft of centre, a cabin of bamboo. Forward of the cabin: a triangular mast, two twenty-nine foot spars of mangrove wood, legs apart and joined securely together at the top. A big rectangular square-sail was fastened to this. In the chinks between logs they lowered fir planks, more or less wherever there was room, to act as centre-boards, prevent the flat raft from drifting sideways.

Heyerdahl at first objected to the idea of a radio, but when one of the others pointed out to him that unless they actually used it to ask for help, they would not be infringing the unwritten rules of the expedition. They could send valuable weather information about an almost unknown region, to be gratefully accepted by meteorological offices all over the world. Heyerdahl agreed–the authorities were enthusiastic–and a radio transmitter and receiver were installed in the cabin.

At this point, with the raft structurally complete, they ran into shocked, incredulous opposition. Why, a thing looking like that couldn't possibly survive in the open sea! And didn't they know that balsa only remained buoyant for a few weeks? Water would seep in, it would sink. The Peruvian Minister of Marine took one horrified look at the vessel, with its gaudy representation of Kon-Tiki himself on the sail, insisted they sign a paper forthwith, freeing him of all responsibility.

On 27 April, *Kon-Tiki* was ready to sail. The six-man crew: Haugland, Danielsson, Hesselberg, Raaby, Watzinger and Heyerdahl himself, took a final trip up into the mountains of Peru, got a last feel of land at 12,000 feet to compensate for months of living at sea-level. The next morning they embarked.

A tug had agreed to take them out of the bay, and after linguistic difficulties, which resulted in the raft being towed out minus half its crew, then being boarded by a pack of pretty girls, who were finally exchanged for the missing crew members, *Kon-Tiki* set out.

They were towed all night and by the next morning they were in the open sea, fifty miles off shore and at a latitude of twelve degrees South. The tug halted and Hesselberg, Danielsson and Heyerdahl rowed to it in the rubber dinghy which was to be a vital part of their equipment. The tug captain confirmed their position, pointed out that they would need lights for the first few nights, as they were in a shipping lane. After that they would see no ships, see nothing at all: He embraced them warmly. They rowed back to *Kon-Tiki* and sat on boxes of supplies watching the tug disappear toward the mountains of Peru. And then, for long, long hours, they remained absolutely stationary.

At last a wind came, a gentle zephyr from the south-east. The sail filled, the raft began to move. One of them took hold of the nineteen-foot oar. They threw screwed-up bits of paper on the water, timed the raft as it sailed slowly past each one, tried to calculate their speed.

4,300 miles to do. And 97 days to do them in.

It took, as we shall see, exactly that time—an incredible piece of calculation. And for none of those ninety-seven days, and the few that followed between landfall and shipwreck, were they bored. For a start, they were to spend nervous days wondering if the ropes which held them together would part, leaving them to collapse in mid-Pacific, become a bundle of logs floating off in all directions, the crew to be eaten by sharks or worse.

But now to their delight they saw just what the ancient coastal mariners of Peru had seen: the balsa wood, being soft, wore slowly and the ropes, instead of fraying, bit slowly into it, then lodged firm, in a stouter joint than even bolts would have made.

The mountains had gone. They were alone.

They were soon to become experienced sailors. Every man began on a rota of two hours on the steering-oar, three hours' rest; but as the weather grew worse and seas mounted, this became impossible. No man or even pair of men could manage the long oar for more than an hour. They changed to one hour at the oar, an hour and a half's rest.

They had brought with them, as last-minute addition to the crew, a green parrot in a cage, and it sat on the deck looking up at them with mingled sympathy and contempt (or so they felt) while they struggled and were sea-sick. *Kon-Tiki* bucked and twisted, yet somehow sailed majestically over the top of most waves, refusing to be swamped, even when great walls of water, twenty and more feet above them, seemed about to smash her to pieces.

They took their position regularly with a sextant, and a week later, with the water calmer, turning to blue instead of green, they saw they had been averaging almost exactly fifty-five miles a day. They had cured their sea-sickness. In any case there would have been no time to consider it, sending and receiving signals, checking position, steering, catching fish and cooking. There seemed hardly enough hours in the day to complete the day's tasks. But they found occasional moments of leisure when a pair of them could get in the rubber dinghy and paddle a little way off to take photos and laugh at the spectacle–odd even to themselves–of a raft in mid-Pacific with a lot of bearded men on board and another painted on her sail.

But one day, when two of them were doing just this, the wind got up. A moment before they had been paddling happily alongside: now, within seconds, they had been left behind, and the gap was growing greater. With a gasp of astonishment and dismay, the two men in the dinghy started to paddle with all their might. The other four, horrified, began to lower the great sail. It took time, and even when it had collapsed on the deck, *Kon-Tiki* sped on over the smooth water, almost as fast as before.

But with a frantic burst of speed, born of panic, the two in the dinghy caught up and were dragged to safety by their companions. From this day on the dinghy was never launched without a rope joining it firmly to the raft.

More and more fish began to come aboard. Usually these were flying fish, and as they seemed to arrive most plentifully during the night, they made a fine breakfast, cooked on the Primus stove. But early one morning, long before thoughts of breakfast, Raaby as he lay on the deck put out a hand in the dark. Something slithered up his arm, touched his cheek. Something cold. He jumped to his feet, lit a match. There, lying on the deck, was something like an eel, but with vicious teeth projecting from its jaw. As he watched, first one large fish came out of the creature's mouth, then another. The other men, wakened by the noise, studied the eel, decided it was the extremely rare Gempylus. This was the first one ever to be seen alive.

From this night on they slept less soundly, conscious of all the things which might jump, swim or clamber aboard to join them. One very real fear was of the giant squid, the octopus whose arms could pluck a man off the deck, take him below for a meal, without their owner even getting aboard. Sharks were constant, stupid, companions and gave them little trouble. They were able to kill a great many, until the novelty of destroying a vicious, greedy enemy wore off. One day they encountered the rare whale shark, biggest fish in the world, and over fifty feet in length. It swam slowly underneath *Kon-Tiki* and they looked down in apprehension at the vast brown body with its small white spots. A moment later it dived, was never seen again.

They had been getting some remarkable photographs, from the dinghy and from *Kon-Tiki* herself, but suddenly they found themselves unable to develop them correctly: the negatives were streaked and useless. They sent a radio message to a "ham" asking for advice, and a little later it came back: "Your developer's too warm." They devised an ingenious method of cooling water—even producing one small piece of ice. There was no further trouble with the developer.

They noticed that their raft had become a garden. All sorts of seeds and little plants they had brought with them were sprouting, growing bigger, greener, almost as they watched. The green coconuts had become trees a foot tall, with Johannes, the tame crab who had come aboard and been befriended, walking happily, sideways, between them. But it was almost as if fate decreed this ark must not support more than one beast at a time: while they made much of Johannes, fed him with scraps of fish and tinned meat, a wave came up and took the luckless parrot away, in its cage.

One evening they heard a shout of alarm. A wind had got up and the sound came, soft and indistinct, against it. To their horror they saw Watzinger in the water, the raft racing past him. He had reached for his sleeping-bag as the wind plucked it away, and had fallen overboard.

They grabbed a lifebelt, threw it at him, and the wind threw it back. By now Watzinger was behind them, in a position where experience had shown nothing that fell off the raft could be retrieved. They made more efforts to throw a lifebelt. Each time it came back to them. And then, with a splash, Knut Haugland was in the water, swimming with powerful strokes towards the vanishing Watzinger, and dragging with him a lifebelt, at the end of a rope. As they watched, hearts in their mouths, he reached the man, flung an arm round him and allowed them both to be dragged in. As they pulled at the rope, the other four noticed a large fish—perhaps a shark—nudging the sleeping-bag along the surface behind the two men. It got steadily closer; they pulled the harder.

Then, complete with sleeping-bag, it vanished in the depths.

And now, with more than half the journey gone, they caught each other surreptitiously tearing off soggy bits of balsa wood from the logs which supported them, dropping them into the sea. Each time they sank.

But Heyerdahl plunged his knife into one of the logs and found to his relief that the centre was dry and solid: only the outer two

inches were water-logged. As much by good luck as good management, they had used the less buoyant, green, logs. Had they used
the dry balsa–had any, in fact, been available–the most gloomy
prophecies of their end would have come true. The water would
slowly have penetrated right to the centre. With green logs, the
sap at the centre kept it out.

They weathered a number of terrible storms, endured hours on
end when it seemed *Kon-Tiki* would not survive another minute,
but somehow the gallant craft always managed to stay afloat, right
way up and in one piece.

It was the end of July when they saw the first birds and, a little
later, heard their cries. Raucous as it came, the sound was music
to their ears, for now they were near land. At six o'clock on the
morning of the 30th–ninety-three days after setting sail–they
saw on the horizon an island: with one voice they cheered it.
This, they calculated, was Puka-Puka, first island of the Tuamoto
group. They sailed slowly past, and as the island vanished again
beneath the horizon they noticed a tall pillar of smoke rising
from it.

And it was the ninety-seventh day, exactly as calculated, that
they found the island of Angatau, right in their path. By the evening, they were close to it, only prevented from landing by the
encircling reef. There were men and women on shore, and as they
sailed by Heyerdahl saw a boat set out from the shore.

The two men in it approached, got through the narrow gap in
the reef; caught up with the drifting *Kon-Tiki.*

"Goodnight!" The language was English. "Er, goodnight" they
replied.

"Goodnight, goodnight!" It was the only European expression
the man knew. "Goodnight. Goodnight. *Good* night."

But they were unable to land on Angatau, and on they sailed,
for another three days and nights, realization slowly dawning
that with every island encircled by its atoll or reef their ultimate
landfall would be, quite simply, shipwreck.

And, as we have seen, it was.

They were rescued from their coral reef, taken to Tahiti–after
a moving, wonderful reception on the little island of Taroia,
whose inhabitants, all one hundred and twenty-seven of them,
wept when they left. And from Tahiti, where the battered *Kon-
Tiki*, which had been towed this distance from its resting place on
the Taroia reef, was lifted aboard the ship, they sailed for Europe.

So ends a journey, embarked on almost light-heartedly by six young men (and a parrot), a journey which for sheer impudence equals almost any other in history. To Thor Heyerdahl and his companions the theory of Polynesian settlement was proved. Not all scientists are prepared to accept it, even now. But the information obtained—about weather conditions, marine life, survival at sea—more than made up for any shortcomings in a young man's theory.

VOLUNTARY CASTAWAY

Survival at Sea

ONE MORNING in 1951 the bodies of 43 fishermen lay in the hospital of Boulogne-sur-mer. To one young doctor, Alain Bombard, the tragic sight brought home the full horror of disaster at sea. Of the fearful pictures that formed in his mind that of the castaways who die in agonies of hunger and thirst in open boats was the most terrible of all.

From now on Alain Bombard, who had been studying the resistance of the human organism to extreme privation (famine, for instance), concentrated on the plight of the shipwrecked. From statistics he learnt that the search for survivors was almost invariably called off after ten days, as it was then assumed that there was no hope of finding them alive. This brought Bombard up with a jerk. The ocean, after all, is not sterile; might it not provide castaways with sufficient sustenance to keep them going until they were sighted by a passing ship or until they reached land? True, a man deprived of water will certainly die in ten days, but the few elementary experiments Bombard carried out to discover the nutritional properties of fish provided an answer to this problem. The liquid in fish, he found, contained so little salt that it was perfectly safe to drink. Thus castaways had a drinking supply on tap, so to speak. Bombard now became excited; if, by acting as a voluntary castaway, he could prove that it was possible to live off the sea, he might save countless lives. The trouble was that he lacked the money for further research.

A few weeks after Bombard had formed the opinion that castaways had the means of survival, a friend of his asked him to come for a trial run on a new type of lifeboat which a wealthy Dutchman, an expert in life-saving equipment, had asked him to try out. The *Hitch Hiker*, a rubber dinghy with an outboard engine, proved her stability and rode a stormy sea with ease; a larger version of this craft minus the outboard engine would be ideal for the guinea-pig journey he longed to make, thought Bombard. When they landed, his friend introduced him to Meinherr X. Bombard, who found him sympathetic, began to talk to him about Project Castaway, and so aroused his interest that he volunteered to finance the work of research. If, he said, Bombard could prove that it *was* possible to live off the sea, he would gladly act as his backer.

On top of the world, Bombard went to Monaco, and was given the use of a laboratory at the Museum of Oceanography. Here he carried out countless experiments and through these and chemical analyses found that fish would provide him with protein and fat, and the vital vitamins A, B1, B2, and D. Vitamin C was present in plankton, which also contained sugar; there was glucose in the livers of certain fish. With regard to water, Bombard discovered that fish are made up of 50%–80% of liquid, and he calculated that a catch of six to seven pounds would yield him a day's drinking supply. But supposing he did not catch any fish for three or four days, what then? He must on no account allow his body to become dehydrated, so he would have to drink sea-water. Bombard had now to establish the amount he could drink with safety, for too great an intake would cause nephritis and certain death. An analysis of the composition of sea-water led him to the conclusion that 1½ pints a day for not more than five days would do no damage to his kidneys.

Once Bombard had satisfied himself that he could count on a reasonably well-balanced diet, Project Castaway was on. As the whole point was to attract the maximum amount of attention, Bombard decided to make an Atlantic crossing and follow the route taken by Columbus on two of his journeys: from the Canaries via the Cape Verde Islands to the West Indies. As he wished to land on French territory, he would make for Guadeloupe. Bombard now made an intensive study of the fish he would find in the Atlantic, of maps and charts, favourable winds and currents.

Well-publicized by Meinherr X., Bombard's projected voyage had aroused the greatest interest. Photographs of Bombard appeared in the press, and reporters who came to interview him respectfully addressed him as "professor". Would-be castaways eagerly volunteered to accompany him; to Bombard's amusement, one of them offered to allow himself to be eaten if the worst came to the worst! As it certainly would, sailors assured him. Live off the sea, indeed! Such a belief was not only crazy, it was utterly heretical!

When Meinherr X. presented Bombard with the craft for his voyage, he was completely taken aback. It was a kind of water-scooter, very similar to those in which holiday-makers at Mediterranean resorts disport themselves. His sponsor proposed a trial run to Portugal and back, but when Bombard had it towed out to put it through its paces a leeboard broke, it turned turtle, and that was the end of that!

From the ridiculous, Meinherr X went to the sublime, and produced plans for a large catamaran with a cabin and galley–hardly the sort of vessel on which castaways were likely to find themselves. Bombard decided that the only thing to do was to present his sponsor with a *fait accompli*, and promptly wrote to the designer of the *Hitch Hiker*. In May, Bombard proudly took possession of his "personal, transatlantic liner".

The *Hérétique*, as Bombard had aptly named his craft, was as unorthodox as he himself, and had not even been officially approved as seaworthy. She was a horseshoe-shaped inflatable rubber dinghy some fifteen feet long by six feet wide. Her rubber floats were divided into three compartments by hermetically-sealed rubber bulkheads. The open end of the dinghy was closed by a wooden stern-board over which fishing lines could be trailed without damaging the floats. *Hérétique*'s deck was barely three feet in width, and her sail was too far forward to allow her to sail into the wind; two leeboards, however, gave her a certain amount of manoeuvrability. Like *Kon-Tiki*, she had to be towed out to sea.

Amongst the would-be castaways was an Englishman, Jack Palmer, to whom Bombard had taken a particular liking. Palmer was a skilled navigator which he himself was not, and if he came along on the voyage the Atlantic crossing would be far less hazardous. But would Jack be as congenial at sea as he was on land?

In order to find out, Bombard invited him to come on a trial trip on the Mediterranean.

On 24 May, 1952, from the little port of Fonvielle, *Hérétique* set off on her maiden voyage. For twelve days Bombard and Jack, who proved to be a most delightful companion, lived off sea-water, fish, fish-liquid and plankton which tasted rather like crab or lobster purée. Jack developed a rash and Bombard a nasty abscess on the gums, but otherwise they were in good shape when they reached Majorca. They had broken the record for survivors by two days—the experiment had been a complete success.

From Majorca, *Hérétique* was transported to Las Palmas, the point of departure for the Atlantic journey. To familiarize himself with the navigational instruments, Bombard made two short solo voyages; finally, as Jack failed to show up, and the season of the favourable north-north-east winds would soon come to an end, Bombard decided to delay no longer. His equipment consisted of the barest necessities: two spare lee-boards, a spare sail, tubes of rubber solution for running repairs, several coils of twine, a carton of matches, needle and thread, a battery wireless set, writing materials, a few books. Two cases, one filled with tins of food, powdered milk, etc., the other with medical supplies, were put aboard *Hérétique*; a list had been made of the items the cases contained, and both had been officially sealed. Bombard was absolutely determined to leave these seals intact for as long as humanly possible.

On Sunday, 19 October, 1952, *Hérétique* was towed out of Santa Cruz. Bombard was given a rousing send-off; from sailing-craft of every kind came shouts of "Good luck!" and all the ships in the port sounded their sirens. When they were clear of the harbour, Bombard dropped the tow—from now on, he was on his own.

The weather was clear, and *Hérétique* made three knots until nightfall when the wind died away. After Bombard had lashed a lighted lantern to the mast to warn passing ships of his presence, he bedded himself down with his head on a couple of lifebelts. His last waking thoughts were of his wife, Ginette; poor Ginette, she'd been so brave, but he knew what an ordeal he was putting her through.

Morning came, but there was still no wind. The following day was equally calm. *Hérétique* was drifting south, but how far south Bombard could not calculate; this was to throw him out in all his reckonings. The third day dawned. Still no wind. As Bombard had been unable to catch any fish, he drank his allowance of sea-water. That evening, the trade wind blew up again and soon reached gale force. Fully assured of *Hérétique*'s stability, Bombard settled down for the night. Settled was hardly the word, for he awoke from a frightful nightmare of being awash–good God! he *was* awash, he was in the water *above Hérétique*! The dinghy had been submerged by a giant wave and only her floats were visible. Frantically Bombard began to bale her out with his hands, and after two hours, how he never knew, managed to right her. Numbed with cold, completely exhausted, he clambered in; luckily, his equipment was in water-tight containers. *Hérétique*, however, had been turned into a regular salt-marsh, and he himself was en-crusted with salt which he had no means of washing away.

When day broke, misfortune struck again: the dinghy sail was torn across by the wind. Bombard threw out his sea-anchor and rigged up the spare sail, but half an hour later a gust whipped it away. He let go the anchor once more, and laboriously mended the torn sail, but he was far from sure that his stitches would hold, and from then on, whenever he looked at the black cobble, he trembled with apprehension.

On the next morning, blue and green stains on the water told Bombard that a harvest of fish was drawing near, and sure enough a shoal of dolphins appeared. Lashing his knife to an oar, after jabbing several of them ineffectually, he succeeded in landing one –at last he had food and drink. Behind its gill-cover, the dolphin has a hook-shaped bone; the ingenious castaway fastened it to a length of twine, and lo and behold–a fishing line!

Bombard had believed that solitude would not affect him; it was only when he lost sight of land that he realized how presumptuous he had been. Wherever he looked there was nothing but sea and sky, and on the vast expanse of water he felt as if he had dwindled to a mere speck. On the Mediterranean, he and Jack had never been out of sight of a vessel of some kind, or a plane. On the route he was following across the Atlantic the chance of meeting a ship was remote, of spotting a plane remoter still. He was now part of a strange, silent world, a world which could not be measured in human terms.

The dolphins continued to follow *Hérétique*–even those he had gashed came along, though they prudently kept their distance. Flying-fish blundered into the mast at night and fell stunned on to the deck. When the castaway rose, there was his breakfast! The flying-fish tasted rather like anchovies.

Bombard's 28th birthday fell on 27 October, and he actually had a "treat". He landed a shearwater which had swooped down and taken the bait on his fishing line, and ate one half for his supper. That night he woke and was startled to see *Hérétique* lit by a ghostly glimmer. It was not, however, a spirit from the vasty deep, but the other half of the shearwater giving off a phosphorescent glow!

Next day Bombard broke the strap of his self-winding wrist-watch, and though he pinned it to his shirt, it refused to go. This was to have dire consequences, as he could no longer tell what progress he was making westward.

In order not to succumb to the loneliness which drove so many castaways mad, Bombard had imposed a strict routine on himself. At Sunrise he rose, sorted out the flying-fish and ate the largest for his breakfast; after that he fished for an hour or so, took his position (accurately, he hoped) at noon and carried out a minute inspection of the dinghy (this was vital, for if the rubberized canvas started to wear away, it would have fatal results). When he had had his mid-day meal, he did half an hour's p.t., read for a while, roughed out several pages of the book he had been commissioned to write about his voyage, and gave himself a thorough physical check-up. After supper he usually turned on the radio for a short while and tuned in to a concert. One night, curiosity made him flash his torch over the sea. The next moment a sudden buffet almost knocked him overboard, and to his horror he saw a huge shark butting its nose against the dinghy, plainly intent on making a meal of the floats. Fortunately the monster found them too large to tackle, for it finally made off, but never again did Bombard illuminate the sea! He was to encounter many sharks, but they were cowardly creatures, he found—he had only to hit them over the head with an oar and they were off.

The first effects of Bombard's diet soon showed themselves. He lost a toenail and came out in a rash, and his buttocks grew so sore that he could not sit down for long. It was to become more and more difficult for him to find a comfortable position; as the rolling of the dinghy made it impossible for him to stand, he was obliged to squat, balanced against one of the floats. To prevent himself from toppling overboard he secured himself to the mast with a length of twine knotted round his waist.

In spite of his discomfort, Bombard's optimism was unlimited. The trade-wind was bowling *Hérétique* along at a spanking pace,

491

and he was quite convinced that he would sight land in another three weeks at most. True, he had realized by now that navigation was by no means a simple affair, still, he flattered himself that he knew as much about it as Christopher Columbus. He was utterly and hopelessly wrong...

On Sunday, 7 November, the voyage nearly came to an abrupt end as far as Bombard was concerned. He dropped his air-pillow overboard, put out the sea-anchor, dived in and swam astern to retrieve it, but when he turned it was to see *Hérétique* scudding away at a great rate–the anchor had fouled. Bombard was a powerful swimmer, but in his weakened state he had no hope of catching the dinghy up–it looked as if she were going to cross the Atlantic without him! Luckily, the cords of the sea-anchor disentangled themselves, *Hérétique* slowed down and came to a stop.

On the morning after this incident, Bombard actually saw a ship. Much to his disappointment, she did not sight him–"Pity the poor castaway," he thought. He would have given anything to have been able to send a reassuring message to Ginette. As the ship disappeared from sight, the solitude seemed to close in on him, and he felt as if his heart were beating in the midst of nothingness. Just to hear the sound of his own voice, he started talking to the dolphins, but this only had the effect of intensifying the silence.

On 5 November a flock of shearwaters circled over *Hérétique*. Bombard, who had read that if a large number of birds appear, land is not far away, was completely mystified. He had no idea that the Cape Verde Isles lay only some sixty miles to the southeast, and even had he known it it would have done him no good at this point as, owing to the prevailing wind and current, he could not possibly have headed for them.

Bombard now went down with parotitis, a mild form of mumps, but his physiological functions remained normal. He was counting on reaching the West Indies some time between 23-30 November–it never entered his head that December would find him still at sea...

The faithful dolphins continued to Keep *Hérétique* company, and every afternoon, a small stormy petrel regularly appeared. On 8 November, to Bombard's dismay, the radio, which had been growing fainter and fainter, went completely dead.

On 11 November the wind suddenly dropped; soon there was not even a breath of breeze. The sea had become as smooth and sleek as oil. Aat once Bombard realized what this meant. "Rain! Rain!" he shouted exultantly, and stripping off his clothes lay flat on a float, gripping an inflatable rubber mattress between his knees. Down came a tropical downpour, and while it did not last for long, it filled the mattress with three or four gallons of precious water. Bombard took huge gulps of the nectar, but his attempts to scrub away the salt with which he was encrusted proved vain–he was to remain pickled in brine for the rest of the voyage.

The blessing of the rain was followed by a hideous experience. To Bombard's horror, a huge and most determined swordfish dealt the rudder a violent blow. As he prepared to spear it, *Hérétique* lurched and he dropped his weapon overboard. The next twelve hours were an agony of suspense–the persistent swordfish kept charging at the floats, but each time that it appeared certain it would strike them it suddenly changed course. Finally it tired of these tactics, and to Bombard's immense relief took itself off.

In the morning it began to pour again, and for the next three days the rain fell in a continuous sheet. It would be too ironic, thought Bombard, if he were to drown in fresh water! As he baled out, he reflected that he had become the first castaway to empty the precious liquid into the sea.

The inky sea, the sullen, oppressive sky weighed heavily on Bombard's spirits. He was now suffering great discomfort, for hard lumps filled with pus had formed all over his body. There were antibiotics in the sealed case, but Bombard was still determined not to open it. Pockets of matter formed under most of his fingernails–lancing them without an anaesthetic was agony. Three more of his toenails dropped off, and great strips of skin peeled from his feet, leaving them raw and bloody.

The rain stopped at last and the sun broke through. As Bombard had not been able to take his position for three days he had no idea where he was. He was now able to do so, and found that, according to his reckoning, he was still on the 17th parallel of longitude. Up bubbled his optimism. "In a week or, at the outside, a fortnight, I shall land somewhere between Guadeloupe, Monserrat and Antigua," he told himself. The wind, however, was capricious, and *Hérétique* made little progress. On 23 November his "outside" date, there was still no sign of any island. That morning, after an uneasy, brooding calm, day suddenly turned into night, and a violent typhoon unleashed its mighty force. Bombard wrapped the main-sheet of the sail round his wrist, which dripped with blood, as

Hérétique tore through the water at over five knots. The typhoon did not rage for long, but was terrifying while it lasted. "Thank God, the worst is over," thought Bombard, but the worst was still to come...

The typhoon was followed by a period of almost complete calm, and *Hérétique* made practically no headway–at this rate it looked as though he never would reach the land which *must* be near. Must be, because he had seen all those signs which, according to the Raft Book, the castaway's guide, were indications that the coast was not far away. Pieces of driftwood, a gossamer thread which a spider had spun, a butterfly, a fly, a gannet, several frigate birds... Frigate birds and gannets, said the Raft Book, rarely fly more than a hundred miles from the shore. It was certainly strange that there were no ships...

No wind. The sun blazed pitilessly down on Bombard till his brain seemed to be boiling in his skull. It was now 4 December, and he was suffering from violent diarrhoea. On 6 December he made his will, in which he bequeathed his notes to Ginette and asked that legal steps should be taken against authors of handbooks which gave false information to hapless castaways about signs of the proximity of land. The entries he made in his log became shorter and shorter, and his handwriting was almost undecipherable. When he thought of what Ginette's feeling must be his torments became almost intolerable. The diarrhoea was wearing him out–he yearned for a long cool drink of milk, and it was all he could do to force himself to swallow his nauseous diet. To make matters worse, only a pint or so of fresh water remained, and he would soon have to drink sea-water. Another frigate bird–he should have reached land by now, even at this crawl. Damnation on the Raft Book. God! Surely the wind would rise tomorrow–or tomorrow–or tomorrow...

Bombard was almost at his last gasp when at 10 a.m. on 10 December he saw a ship on a course which brought it across his own. Through the loud-hailer the captain shouted: "Do you want any help?" "Just my exact longitude, please?" croaked Bombard. "49° 50′ W," the captain told him. Bombard felt as though he had been sandbagged–he was ten degrees out in his estimated position; in other words, he was still 600 miles from land. In a daze he accepted the captain's invitation to come aboard the *Arakaka* and have a shower. As he caught sight of himself in the mirror, he recoiled with horror: was this gaunt, hollow-eyed apparition, covered with running sores, half of its face and chest invisible beneath a dense, matted tangle of beard, really Alain Bombard? What would Ginette say if she could see him now? Thank God he could send her a message to say he was safe.

Although the captain suggested taking him and his dinghy to Georgetown, Bombard decided to continue his voyage. The captain took him into the chart house, showed him his exact position and gave him a few of the reasons that had led to his making such an error in his position—plainly, a little knowledge of navigation had been a very dangerous thing . . .

On the day before Christmas, Bombard reached Barbados. Landing was extremely hazardous, for he might easily have been dashed to pieces on the rocks, but he made it safely. He had lost 55 1b. in weight, he was seriously anaemic, his blood pressure was dangerously low, he had developed grave defects of vision, but—he was alive. Alive after 65 days at sea—the indomitable Alain Bombard had become the living proof that castaways should never despair.

INTO THE DEPTHS

The Exploration of "Inner Space"

Now that man has reached the second half of the twentieth century, the world has become familiar and almost commonplace. All the important mountains have been scaled, jungles tamed and deserts of sand or snow traversed. In his restless search for fresh worlds to conquer, man must go upwards, into outer space, or down into the deep oceans–into "inner space".

As a consequence, the concept of exploration has changed. Man's inquisitive mind still plays an essential part in every new endeavour, but the fantastic cost of probes into either realms of "space" is such that they can only be mounted by governments utilizing experts and specialists from a bewildering variety of associated fields.

The headline-making achievements in outer space have dominated scientific thought for several years, but it is difficult to separate a genuine desire for knowledge from the seemingly implacable rivalry–both scientific and political–between the two great protagonists in this field, Russia and the United States of America.

The less spectacular, but probably far more rewarding, probing of the ocean's depths has generally been undertaken with the benefit of all in mind, rather than one specific nation. There is nothing new in underwater exploration–Alexander the Great is said to have spent some time in a diving bell examining the bottom of the

Mediterranean–but as an exact science it is less than a hundred years old.

It really began in 1872 when H.M.S. *Challenger*, with a team of scientists led by Professor Charles Wyville Thomson, set off on a round-the-world voyage of research and marine exploration. It was sponsored by the Royal Society and British Admiralty and, for three and a half years, Thomson and his team made hundreds of soundings, recorded water temperature at different depths and collected thousands of animal, plant and mineral samples, some of which were dredged from depths of more than 3,000 fathoms (18,000 ft.). The findings of this great expedition revealed a fascinating undersea world, a world of hitherto unsuspected mountains and deep valleys contrary to the general impression of the time–for it had always been believed that the sea bed was uniformly flat–and that it was similar to that of the land, only on a much vaster scale.

Interest quickened and many more soundings began to be made, compared and published. It is only during the past forty years, however, that the great undersea mountain ranges and incredibly deep chasms have been plotted with speed and accuracy, thanks to the introduction of the echo-sounder. Such important data, however, was not enough. Investigation of life in the lower depths–if life existed at all, that is–could only be complete when man himself descended into these depths to see for himself what actually existed there. To do this, of course, a suitable means of protection had to be developed against the tremendous pressure of the water, which, at the greatest depths, is equal to *nine tons* to the square inch! A diving suit was not sufficient; something more robust, in which the inhabitant could move about, survey the outside "world" and note down his findings was required.

There were many pioneers. A Spaniard, Cervo, is the first recorded person to lose his life whilst demonstrating a device of this nature. He descended in a wooden sphere in 1831, but, presumably, the pressure crushed his vehicle. Whatever the reason, he never returned.

Perhaps the greatest pioneer in this field was the American, Dr William Beebe, who collaborated with an engineer from New England, Otis Barton, to design a metal sphere capable of descending into the black and silent world of the great deeps. The sphere was built of steel, with walls one and a half inches thick, and was fitted with a port-hole of rock crystal. When finished, Barton remarked that it looked like "an enormous, inflated and slightly cockeyed bullfrog". It was lowered into the sea by means of an inch-thick steel cable from a tender and this bathysphere, as it became known, took Beebe and Barton down to a record depth of 250 fathoms in 1930.

Two years later they passed the 1,700-ft. mark, descending into a strange dark world, for light cannot penetrate beyond this depth. Writing of his experiences in a fascinating book, *Half Mile Down* (New York, 1934) Beebe says: "From here down, for two billion years, there had been no day or night, no summer or winter, no passing of time until we came to record it."

Although there was no sunlight, Beebe was amazed to find that the world outside his tiny porthole was not wholly black, for, swimming past, was a procession of strange, luminous creatures which slid past "twinkling and winking like a thousand stars". They varied considerably in size, shape and means of self-illumination, for some carried but one large, single light whilst others displayed hundreds of glittering points which were massed together to form patterns.

The bathysphere continued to descend until it reached 2,170 ft., each minute of its drop revealing new and exciting creatures. Two strange fish, each six feet long, with glowing, pale-blue sides and with red and blue lights glittering from their tails, caused Beebe, with his inimitable sense of humour, to name them as Untouchable Bathysphere Fish.

In 1934 a new and improved bathysphere was built and Beebe prepared for his greatest-ever dive. He and Barton started to descend again, dropping down, down into the still depths, seeing more incredible creatures until they came to a halt at last, some 510 fathoms (3,060 ft.) down, the full extent of their cable. Here, with the sea floor still more than a mile below them, the bathysphere was subjected to a pressure of more than a ton to the square inch. As both men stared out into the dark, yet brilliantly illuminated world that surrounded them, they had a moment of stark horror, for there came a sudden jolt which caused them to believe that the cable had snapped and that they were heading for the ocean bed where, as Beebe drily remarked: "We would have had an awfully long time to make observations!"

It was merely a swell on the surface, however, which had caused their tender to roll and pitch, jerking at the cable and, later, both men regained its deck in safety.

Exciting and rewarding as these dives had been, they revealed an inherent weakness in the principle of the bathysphere–it could only descend as far as its cable would allow. Obviously, a vehicle was needed that could be independent of such a restraining umbilical cord. The inventive mind of Professor Auguste Piccard produced the answer. He had already become famous for his probes into outer space, reaching a height of 55,557 ft. in a stratosphere balloon known as the FRNS-1, which used the initials of the Belgian Government research fund (or Fonds National de la Recherche Scientifique) and he applied the principles of this device in the design of a deep-sea boat, the FRNS-2.

Its basic idea was brilliantly simple. The spherical bathysphere was retained, but its walls were greatly strengthened and it was attached to a cigar-like float which was filled with petrol. As a balloon utilizes lighter-than-air gas, so the bathyscaphe (from the Greek *bathy*–"deep", and *scaphe*–"boat") used lighter-than-water petrol to give buoyancy to the heavy sphere which enclosed the crew. Petrol, in addition to providing this buoyancy, also prevents the float from being crushed by the pressure of the water, being very difficult to compress. For "ballast", the bathyscaphe carried large quantities of lead-shot in silos, causing it to sink; then, when it was time to come up again a quantity was jettisoned (exactly like sand from a balloon's gondola) and the vehicle ascended at a regulated speed.

By 1948 the bathyscaphe was ready and moved to the coast of West Africa for the first dives. A depth of 4,600 ft. without occupants, was registered and both sphere and float operated well when submerged. Unfortunately, the float was not seaworthy and was wrecked by a surface swell when being towed back to base.

Piccard's team had been strengthened by the famous submariner, Jacques-Yves Cousteau, leading the Undersea Research Group, and Cousteau persuaded the French and Belgian Governments to combine in order to produce another bathyscaphe to be called the FRNS-3. The design was much superior to the previous vessel and work began. There were several irritating delays, however, and Piccard finally resigned from the committee and began to organize the building of yet another bathyscaphe, this time under Italio-Swiss patronage, which would be entirely under his control. He decided to name it *Trieste*.

Work went on at Toulon where the FRNS-3 was under construction and something of a race developed between the two organizations. In such a revolutionary field, however, nothing could be rushed, and as men's lives were at stake, neither could anything be left to chance. The French bathyscaphe finally came off the stocks and began a series of test dives. She was now under the command of two Frenchman. One was a naval officer, Commander Georges S. Houot; the other a young and dedicated engineer, Pierre-Henri Willm.

Houot was posted to the FRNS-3 in 1952 to take over command from Cousteau and at the first meeting he confessed to the latter that he felt himself unsuited for the post. He had contracted polio some years before and had been forbidden to go swimming–or even get wet! Shaken by this information, Cousteau conveyed the news to Tailliez, the officer commanding the Undersea Research Group, and both men tried to have Houot relieved. The French Admiralty was adamant, however, and he was confirmed in his position–a very wise decision as it turned out.

When most of the preliminary dives had been completed, the FRNS-3 was shipped to Dakar, where everyone waited for suitable diving weather. Both men were determined to go deeper than any man had been before and the waiting must have been most nerve-racking for them, especially as Piccard announced from Italy that the sphere in their bathyscaphe–the original he had built in 1938–was defective. X-rays showed that there were minute flaws, but the Admiralty confirmed that the sphere would nevertheless stand up to the pressures of a 2,000-fathom dive, but left the final decision to Houot and Willm.

Both decided, without hesitation, to go ahead as planned.

At midday on Saturday, 13 February, 1954, a small convoy put to sea. It consisted of the *Elie Monnier*, the bathyscaphe's tender, the *Tenace*, a tug towing the FRNS-3, and the *Beautemps Beaupré*, carrying a number of journalists and a radio transmitter which would broadcast direct to Paris a commentary on the dive. The latter ship reached the diving ground first, and reported the depth of water under her keel and that the bottom shelved only very slightly.

Houot and Willm transferred from the *Tenace* to the bathyscaphe dressed in shorts and pullovers, taking sandwiches and a bottle of wine with them. Then there was a last-minute hitch. It was necessary to use aqua-lung divers to remove the special clamps that were bolted over the electromagnets controlling the shot silos, and one of them emerged to report that the safety clamp on number

4 silo was jammed, closing the magnetic field. To remove this meant that a quarter of the ballast would slide away into the sea and be lost. It had to be done, however, and more shot was ferried across from the *Elie Monnier*. This was a hazardous job as a high sea was running and the transference was done in rubber rafts. Indeed, two of the first four sacks slipped off the float and disappeared into the swirling water, but the rest was got across safely and the FRNS-3 was ready to submerge.

The hatch was bolted shut and a young midshipman, Michaudon, stayed on the float to follow orders relayed to him by a portable telephone which also linked the men inside the sphere with Commandant Ortolan in *Elie Monnier*.

Houot, in the stirring book he subsequently wrote with Willm, entitled *Two Thousand Fathoms Down* (Hamish Hamilton & Rupert Hart-Davis, 1955, and Penguin, 1958) described the departure:

" 'Michaudon, the hatch is closed. Cast off the towline.'

"Commandant Ortolan called from his ship saying, 'Final reading of the echo-sounders, 4,050 metres (13,365 ft.). Your towline has been cast off.'

"Willm then told Michaudon to open the vents of the air-tanks and, from inside the sphere, they could hear his footsteps as he walked across to do so. There was a pause, then, 'All vents open'.

" 'Open the safety valve of the air-lock.'

"The sound of a wrench being operated was followed by the midshipman's last report, 'Open'.

" ' Good. *A bientôt*. Get off in the dinghy,' Willm replied, then added, 'Hallo *Elie Monnier*, bathyscaphe calling. We are ready to dive. Let us know when the personnel is away from the float.'

"There followed a long pause, seeming almost an eternity to the two tense men in the sphere, then, 'Hallo bathyscaphe, you can dive,' came Ortolan's voice."

The first two valves were opened and the FRNS-3 began to submerge. As it went, the men heard Ortolan's voice saying; "Your deck is going under. Water halfway up the bathtub. Your antennae . . .", then silence.

It was a little past ten o'clock in the morning and communication with the surface except for ultra-sound signals was at an end. From that moment, until the craft emerged again, no other person could help them, the two men were on their own. As Houot put it: "It was with a slight sense of intoxication that we felt ourselves the sole masters of our fate. This was how, in days gone by, mariners had sailed forth from a continent and launched out in search of unknown lands. They had still hoped to discover their own kind when they reached their goal. Willm and I were venturing into a world reserved for a special fauna, which no man had ever visited, even for an instant."

The bathyscaphe slowly descended, moving through a green photo-synthetic zone which became flushed with ultramarine and which, in turn, changed slowly to indigo. It moved downwards at a foot a second, and every half an hour Houot was expected to send ultra-sound signals to the surface using A for *Je vous Appelle* (Bathyscaphe calling), V for *Tout Va Bien* (All's well), and then a number which indicated the depth in hundreds of metres. He was supposed to receive an R in acknowledgement from the *Elie Monnier*, but throughout the whole dive none was received.

At 10.30 the message was sent, "AAA, V2 V2," indicating that the craft had reached the two hundred metre mark. Houot stared through the small porthole and noted that the water was unusually dark and turgid. A few minutes later, compass readings showed that the bathyscaphe was very slowly turning around as it sank lower and lower into the depths. As he stared out he felt something dripping on to his neck. For a moment he thought it was "raining", then realized that the stuffing box in the pressure gauge had given way. As they were heading for really great pressures he picked up a spanner and tightened the nut.

At 11.30 the depth-gauge showed that they had reached 2,000 metres and another signal was sent to announce this fact to their comrades in the pitching, rolling tender overhead. As usual, there was no reply.

By noon, Willm tapped out the message–"V30 V30"–they had reached three thousand metres and it was decided to slow down the rate of descent. A ton or so of lead shot poured out from the silos and the speed dropped considerably. More shot followed and the vessel came to a stop whilst the two men checked for leaks. There were none, despite the fact that something like 590 tons were pressing down on to the hatch-cover alone. The temperature of the water was 5° C., that of the petrol 13°. The men waited whilst the temperature of the latter fell and, as it did so, the bathyscaphe continued its descent.

At 3,300 metres Willm, who was logging every stage of the journey, noted that there was an abundance of life outside, with shrimps and the strange luminous creatures (or siphonophores).

3,500 metres down, and the echo-sounder was started, the stylus moving rapidly across the paper, although, as yet, no mark was seen. Then, at 12.55, the stylus began to bite and the first marks appeared. The curve began to swing upwards–the craft was descending too fast–so more ballast was shed until it almost came to a stop again.

At one o'clock the signal went out, "V40 V40". They had reached the fantastic depth of 4,000 metres, far deeper than man had ever ventured. 2,000-watt searchlights fitted to the hull of the float had been switched on and Willm suddenly exclaimed in a voice that shook with excitement: "I can see the bottom." He moved aside to let his companion stare through the port-hole as, ten metres from the sea-bed, a guide chain touched the bottom and the bathyscaphe came to rest, swinging gently on the chain, although the column of water which rested on her weighed more than 68,000 tons.

The lights illumined a large circle and showed very fine, white sand which became clearer as the petrol cooled, and the sphere drifted slowly down until, in a spurt of sand, it actually settled on the sea-bed. Willm was back at the porthole and gave a gasp of surprise, "Shark!" he exclaimed, "He's coming nearer." It certainly *was* a shark, but of a species never before seen by man. It swam slowly into the circle thrown by the lights and stared back at them with mildly curious, popped-out eyes.

It had been arranged that the FRNS-3 would spend three hours exploring the sea-bed, so the motors were started and the vessel began to move slowly along, whilst Houot and Willm began to take still and moving photographs. Suddenly there was a rumbling noise from overhead, followed immediately by another. The sea outside became inky black as the lights disappeared and the two men looked at each other in dismay. The two thirteen-hundred-pound batteries on top of the float had dropped away from their electro-magnets. Obviously a fuse had blown and the emergency cut-out had come into operation. The bathyscaphe, now lighter by more than a ton, began to ascend of its own accord.

M for *Je Monte* (I am ascending) was sent off and two very disappointed men began to pass the time before the surface was reached. As Houot says: "My friend's face reflected a profound gloom. He was the engineer and I could understand that he disliked mechanical breakdowns. The loss of our batteries upset him. I was equally vexed, without, however, attaching as much importance as he appeared to do this minor mishap in the course of our enormous adventure. The FRNS-3 had twice descended to more than 4,000 metres; the future looked wonderful."

"What's the matter, Willm?" he asked. "Your batteries will be replaced. In the meantime, we haven't had anything to eat since seven this morning; it's about time we looked to see what the cook's prepared for us."

As Houot began to open the dispatch-case containing the sandwiches, the regretful answer came: "This is my last dive."

Willm, the engineer who had so successfully carried out the long series of dives, was no longer required. Now that the final test had ended in triumph he would have to give way to scientists.

At 15.00 hours the call went out, "V13 M, V13 M", and twenty-two minutes later, after 5 hours and 14 minutes under the sea, the porthole revealed green water outside and the sphere started to rock. At this both men looked at each other, then sighed and said simultaneously: "It was so nice down there."

Willm then connected the radio-telephone and called to the tender. A reply came back immediately: "Hallo, bathyscaphe, *Elie Monnier* calling. Receiving you loud and clear. All your signals received. The flying-boat is over your heads and I'm on my way to join you. We congratulate you."

Similar messages of congratulation continued to pour in as the two men emptied the air-lock and, after opening its hatch, moved up the ladder. They shoved open the hatch above their heads and were soon blinking in the afternoon sun.

The "enormous adventure" was over.

JOURNEY INTO THE KALAHARI

Van der Post and the Bushmen*

BORN AND bred not far from the Great River, Laurens Jan van der Post grew up in what had once been the very heart of South Africa's Bushman country. As a child he had listened to enchanting tales about the original inhabitants of his native land. He had learned that the Bushman was small but beautifully made, that he was ultra-sensitive concerning his lack of inches, that the colour of his skin was apricot yellow, that he was, first and foremost, a hunter. Having no cattle of his own, and no interest in agricultural pursuits, he relied for his food on his skill with bow and arrow and spear. He fashioned traps for fish, set snares for buck and leopard, dug pits for big game, and allowed the honey-diviner bird to lead him to the hives of the wild bees.

Van der Post was also impressed by the irrefutable evidence of the Bushman's artistic achievements. Although the little man had left behind no written accounts of the stories he enjoyed, there was no doubt that a rich body of *spoken* literature had existed and that the Bushman had been a superb teller of tales. Moreover, if he could not translate experience into words, he could always convey it in terms of music and dance, for he was a born dancer. Finally,

* The account in this chapter is based on *Journey into the Kalahari* by Laurens van der Post (Chatto and Windus, Ltd.).

505

there were his cave paintings–magnificent representations, lovingly created in vivid colours, of the birds and beasts that flashed across the African scene.

The more information he gathered about the Bushman, the more difficult it was for the youthful van der Post to understand why these little people had been ruthlessly and systematically exterminated. His persecutors, black and white alike, had unwarrantably condemned the whole race as inferior, savage and needlessly aggressive. Basutos, Amazulu, Griquas, Korannas, the first Europeans who landed at the Cape in 1652, all of them had been determined to kill off the original owners of the land. To the invaders pouring into South Africa from the north and from the south, the Bushman was little better than a wild animal. He was a dangerous creature, a threat to civilization, a pestilential nuisance. As a matter of policy he had to be wiped out wherever he was found.

It soon became obvious to van der Post that all these preconceived notions about the Bushman were entirely without foundation. Despite his Stone Age weapons and apparently primitive behaviour, the Bushman was intelligent, knowledgeable, talented, resourceful and keenly aware of certain spiritual values. Far from being aggressive, he was a friendly little man until provoked. It was only when he found himself being hounded down by callous land-grabbers that he turned on his attackers and struck back.

The disturbing image of this golden-skinned manikin, with his bow and arrows, stubbornly defying men armed with European guns, aroused van der Post's sympathies and sense of fair play. He felt that a monstrous injustice had been done. He was especially concerned about the part his own ancestors had played in the inhumane slaughter of the First People of Africa. It was as if he personally had inherited some of their guilt. In his opinion, a crime had been committed and he wanted to expiate it. He grieved because they had killed off the Bushman without knowing very much about him.

Then, one day, a traveller who had journeyed across the Kalahari Desert visited van der Post's home. Describing his adventures in the desert, he mentioned casually that authentic Bushmen were still living there in conditions very little removed from those that had existed when their forefathers had occupied the territory close to the Great River. For van der Post it was a significant utterance. He was only eight years old at the time, but he made a secret pact with himself, recording it in his diary. When he was a man, he would go to the Kalahari and seek out the Buhman.

With the passage of years van der Post developed other interests, but he never forgot that entry in his diary. During his twenties, indeed, he made two unsuccessful attempts to locate the Bushman. His failure on both occasions could be attributed to inexperience and insufficient stamina. He returned from these expeditions with a practical knowledge of the vast wasteland and the conviction that if the Bushman existed anywhere at all, it could be only in the Kalahari.

The Second World War put paid for the time being to any further ventures into the interior, for van der Post was busy soldiering in Abyssinia, in the Western Desert and in the Far East. After spending the last two years of the war in a Japanese prisoner-of-war camp, he first joined Mountbatten's staff and later undertook a number of missions on behalf of the British Government, including an official trip to the Kalahari Desert in 1952. During his desert explorations he not only came across the characteristically tiny footprints of genuine Bushmen; he also had brief encounters with a few isolated men, women and children of that race. He was now confident that a community of Bushmen inhabited the Kalahari. He resolved to discover them and thus honour his childhood pact. At the earliest opportunity he would organize a journey into the desert.

Van der Post then made a wise decision. He reasoned that he was most likely to meet the pure Bushman if he travelled during the worst time of the year. In those months of heat and drought between the winter and the rainy period there would be a general movement of man and beast away from the inhospitable wilderness. Only the authentic Bushman would accept the grim challenge of a Kalahari seemingly without the means of sustaining life. None but he could suck water from the parched sand or find food in the dust and desolation of the sun-baked scrub-land.

An approach from the north towards the end of August offered the best possibilities. Van der Post made his plans accordingly. He was fully aware that for the journey he had in mind one of the most important factors would be his choice of travelling companions. He therefore began by inviting his friend, Wyndham Vyan, an experienced rancher from East Africa, who knew the country well and was familiar with its peculiar problems. He also wrote to another close acquaintance, Ben Hatherall, whose youthful accomplishments included shooting, hunting and horse-taming. Brought up on his father's farm at Ghanzis, on the edge of the Kalahari, Ben had been looked after by Bushman servants and had played with Bushman children. His knowledge of the language and habits of the little people would obviously prove invaluable to the expedition.

As for transport, van der Post decided to use Land Rovers. Their carrying capacity was smaller than he would have wished, but their performance over deep sand was most impressive. Additional petrol and water tanks would be wanted, but the Rover Company's headquarters staff promised to be responsible for the necessary modifications. With a view to producing a documentary sound film about the Bushman, van der Post enlisted the aid of the B.B.C. Told that he would have to organize his own film unit, he engaged a continental free-lance film producer named Eugene Spode. The B.B.C. generously made arrangements for Spode to visit their studios and examine their methods. At the end of his training he was to join the rest of the party in Africa on 21 August.

Meanwhile van der Post returned to Africa, carried out a programme of Bushman research, saw a number of officials, appointed his drivers and fixed various supply and fuelling points. He ordered the miscellaneous stores he required and made sure that all essential drugs and medicines would be available. On the whole his preparations were going smoothly. At that stage the only cloud on his horizon was Spode. People who knew him predicted that the temperamental film producer would succumb to the strain of such a tough journey. As a precautionary measure van der Post wrote to Spode and advised him to take on an assistant.

Towards the end of August, after Spode's arrival in Bulawayo, the Land Rovers were collected at Johannesburg, loaded and driven three hundred miles to Lobatsi, where Ben Hatherall was waiting to be picked up. Before moving on into the interior, van der Post enrolled two cooks, Jeremiah and John. Then the convoy followed the road leading north from Mafeking for over five hundred miles, leaguered in Francistown and at nightfall drove into Bulawayo. Two days later the expedition had reached the Victoria Falls. The drivers checked their vehicles and attended to any last-minute repairs. The main journey was about to start.

With Ben Hatherall in the lead, the four Land Rovers moved off at two o'clock in the afternoon on 3 September. A few days previously van der Post had seen a herd of eleplants in a clearing down by the river, a sure sign that the great withdrawal from the desert was already under way. The conditions he had insisted upon had been met. Buffaloes, wildebeests, zebras, giraffes and all the other fair-weather denizens of the Kalahari were falling back on the river before their dwindling drinking places shrank to nothing under the sun's concentrated glare.

For a time the expedition rolled westwards along a track running parallel to the river. Not until they reached the junction of the Chobe and the Zambezi did they change course, veering southwest and making for the frontier post of Kasane. There they rested for a while. The officer in charge drew van der Post's attention to the hazards of the next fifty miles and insisted that one of his men, Trooper Khgometsu, should join the party. Fearing a clash of personalities, van der Post evinced little enthusiasm at first, but after meeting Khgometsu he realized immediately that the smart young Bantu policeman was the very man he wanted. When they pressed on from Kasane, the new recruit was sitting alongside the leader of the expedition at the head of the convoy.

Throughout that day's travel they came across plenty of evidence that herds of elephant had recently passed that way. For fifty miles the sand was pitted with deep tracks that made driving a constant hazard. Eventually they camped on a rise dominating a stretch of the Chobe river. At two o'clock in the morning van der Post's slumbers were rudely interrupted by what sounded like a gun-shot. Just beyond the glow of their dying fire bulky shapes seemed to be advancing menacingly towards them. A regiment of elephants had encircled the camp.

Showing great presence of mind, van der Post yelled to awake the others, ran across to the fire and threw more wood on it. One of the cooks blew on the embers and quickly produced a blaze. As the flames flared up, the elephants lumbered away into the darkness. The crisis was over. No damage had been done, but if one of the herd had not warned van der Post by stepping on a branch of dead wood the consequences might have been serious.

When it was light they were off again, through the country of the fantastic baobab trees with their abnormally distended trunks, past an outpost in North Bechuanaland where sleeping-sickness was rife, and east of a vast swamp-land down to a level plain among the greens, reds and golds of the slender-trunked Mopani trees. They pitched camp in a clearing and next day turned southwards in the direction of the Shinamba Hills. After by-passing the

509

hills, they were again on level ground and there, half-hidden in the long grass, they saw thousands of animals peacefully grazing. Climbing on to the roofs of their vehicles, they were able to identify giraffes, zebras, wildebeests, hartebeests and many other wild creatures. There was, according to Vyan and Hatherall, enough food in that part of the country to feed an army.

That day they halted near two round water-pans brimful of water. Van der Post decided to stay there for a few days with a view to a closer examination of the area. Although it was September, the floods did not appear to be subsiding and somehow the expedition had to negotiate the treacherous marshes and ubiquitous waters. Probes to the east, to the south and to the west failed to discover a way through. To add to van der Post's wretchedness, Spode said he had reached breaking-point and asked to be sent back to Europe. Naturally the request was turned down, a circumstance that occasioned considerable unpleasantness.

A chance early-morning encounter with an old man and a boy determined van der Post's next move. Informed by the old man that there was no way westward through the flooded area and that there were no Bushmen on their side of the swamp, he resolved to make a detour of six hundred miles to Muhembo, on the Okovango river. They could then proceed by water and explore the district to the south-west, where he hoped to establish contact with a community of River Bushmen.

Shortly after breakfast the Land Rovers were speeding along the narrow track leading from the Zambezi to Maun, a small administrative settlement. They lunched at an hotel there and spent the night on a picturesque camp-site at the bottom of the District Commissioner's garden. On the following afternoon they resumed their journey and two days later they drove into Sepopa, a rest centre on the edge of the swamp. Van der Post knew that a race of dug-out men lived close by. He was relying on their chief, Karuso, to supply sufficient river craft and paddlers to transport him and his party to the Bushman country.

First he went to Muhembo and had a talk with one of the European officials, who stressed the danger of travelling by dug-outs at that time of the year and insisted on putting a launch at van der Post's disposal. It would thus be possible for the explorers to cover part of the perilous river trip in comparative safety. Only when the channel could no longer accommodate the launch would they have to transfer to the *makorros*.

Next day van der Post went in the launch to Tkwagga Bay, where Karuso and his dug-out men were waiting. After some lengthy bargaining, the chief said he would provide thirteen dug-outs and twenty-eight men to paddle them. A little grey-haired native called Samutchoso, who had never taken his eyes off van der Post's face during the negotiations, suddenly announced that he would like to join the expedition. As if prompted by some mysterious force outside himself, van der Post unhesitatingly agreed to take him.

That night the whole outfit stayed at the last African outpost on the northern edge of the swamp, about forty miles on from Maun. Ahead of them lay a vast unknown tract of marshland. An African headman tried to persuade van der Post to abandon the project, pointing out that the river was infested with crocodiles and hippos. Although the explorer refused to be put off by this vivid account of the risks that had to be run, he gratefully accepted the headman's offer to furnish him with a trustworthy guide who had an unrivalled knowledge of the swamps. The man was not only a guide; he was also a skilled trapper and a hunter.

Karuso and his dug-out team arrived next day, bubbling over with exaggerated tales of attacks by hippo bulls. Listening to their chatter, van der Post felt doubly indebted to the Muhembo official who had loaned him the launch. He could now appreciate the wisdom of not using the dug-outs until it became absolutely necessary. The best plan, he decided, was for everybody to travel in the launch and let it tow the dug-outs up-stream as far as was practicable.

The paddlers transferred their baggage and food to the launch, and to a melancholy accompaniment of farewell drum-beats the expedition started.

To begin with, the general direction was south-east, but soon the river was twisting and turning through swamp-lands, with masses of reeds and rushes on either bank. At night they moored the boat to a small island where they disembarked and lit their fires for cooking and to discourage mosquitoes. Their energies sapped by the heat of the day, they turned in early under a tangle of trees. The only sounds were the angry humming of mosquitoes and the occasional splashing and puffing of hippos.

Just before first light they sailed on through the desolate swamps, plunging deeper and deeper into the interior. As the day advanced they saw many a muddy tunnel among the reeds, marking the paths taken by hippos in search of shade. Giant crocodiles, sunning themselves on shallow sand-banks, slithered into the water at the launch's approach. For hours they glided past immense tracts of oozing marsh and heaving papyrus grass, until at last van der Post's heart gave a bound. He felt sure he had glimpsed a young Bushwoman's face peering at him through the tall rushes.

They carried on, however, to a large island standing well out of the water and crowned with a central clump of trees. They had reached that part of the steadily narrowing river where it was necessary to abandon the launch and take to the dug-outs. Since entering the swamp they had travelled two hundred miles.

Once they were safely ashore, van der Post organized three separate hunting parties. Although the other two outfits, led by Vyan and Hatherall, went into areas where game abounded, it was van der Post's own party that brought back meat for the pot. At a distance of a hundred and fifty yards, although only its head and throat were visible, van der Post shot an antelope.

Some days later, when he was on another hunting expedition with Samutchoso, his companion suddenly informed him that there were no Bushmen in the swamp. Van der Post naturally wanted to know why. According to Samutchoso, the Bushmen who used to be there had fled from the tsetse flies that infested the area. At first he would not reveal where they had gone, but after due consideration he admitted that he knew of a place where the Bushmen assembled every year. A great distance from his own home in the swamps, he said, out across the desert, were the Tsodilo Hills. These hills were honeycombed with caves in which dwelt the spirits of every bird, beast, insect and plant that had ever existed. The master spirit had his habitation in the central hill. On the rock faces all around were paintings of animals, and wild bees swarmed in the cracks and crevices. It was there, Samutchoso concluded, that the Bushmen met annually. He had seen them.

Deeply moved by these revelations, van der Post asked to be taken to the Tsodilo Hills. Samutchoso agreed to act as guide, but with two provisos. There would have to be no quarrelling among those who went, and shooting, even for food, was forbidden. After van der Post had promised that both conditions would be observed, they returned to the main camp.

Several more or less uneventful days elapsed, and then one morning before sunrise they all boarded the launch and made their way back to Sepopa. Spode, completely shattered by his experiences in the swamp, again begged van der Post to let him go back to

Europe, and this time, although the chances of finding a suitable replacement seemed slender, the harassed leader of the expedition gave his assent. In fact he went farther than that. He drove to Muhembo on the following day and made arrangements for Spode to be flown out.

From Muhembo van der Post flew to Johannesburg on what he thought would be a vain search for another cameraman. Luck was with him, however, for he secured the services of Duncan Abraham, a free-lance photographer who had made his own documentaries. Elated by his success, he caught the next plane to Muhembo, where Ben and Vyan were awaiting him. Duncan joined them a few days later and it was not long before they were all back at Sepopa. A guide took van der Post to Samutchoso's village in the swamp and soon all members of the expedition were bouncing along in the Land Rovers heading for the Tsodilo Hills.

That night they slept in the bush on the sands of the Kalahari. In the morning they were off again across the sun-baked plain rolling towards the distant hills. At last the Land Rovers were drawn up inside the crescent of towering rocks. The silence was uncanny. There was not even a breath of wind; only the overwhelming heat and a sense of the mysterious. Everybody felt uneasy during that first night among the Tsodilo Hills. They slept only fitfully, and shortly after sunrise they were attacked fiercely by swarms of wild bees. This visitation was all the more bewildering in that the bees ignored both their water supply and the sugar they had put out for their morning coffee. They concentrated exclusively on the men and their belongings.

They breakfasted in the eerie light of dawn and then, with Samutchoso leading them, they walked in single file among the foot-hills where, according to their guide, the Bushmen sometimes gathered. They were brought up short by a huge rock-painting of an eland bull, a female giraffe and a baby giraffe. The colours were as fresh as they had been when applied centuries ago. The hand-prints that served as the artist's signature identified the painting beyond all doubt. Only one man could have had such tiny hands.

The Bushman...

It was then that a strange thing happened. Duncan twice tried to film the painting, but on each occasion his camera jammed. After dealing with the stoppages, he made a third attempt. Again the camera was unaccountably thrown out of gear. Completely baffled, Duncan went back to camp to clear the magazines and collect his spares.

Meanwhile other rock paintings were discovered, mainly of animals. Then, a yell from Samutchoso announced that he had made an important discovery. He had stumbled on the site of a recent Bushman encampment. Gravely studying the grass, broken nutshells, old melon rinds, scraps of rabbit fur and the ashes of dead fires, Samutchoso declared that the Bushmen had left about a week ago.

When Duncan was ready for another filming session, a vital part of the camera refused to function. Samutchoso's explanation of the phenomenon was that the spirits of the place were hostile because they had been treated with disrespect. The leader of the expedition should have presented himself first to propitiate them.

Back in camp van der Post wrote a letter to the spirits of the Tsodilo Hills pleading for forgiveness. After all the others had signed the document, he placed it inside a bottle and buried it in a niche just below the painting of the eland. Samutchoso then assured him that there would be no further trouble. The hill spirits, it seemed, were satisfied.

Then began the arduous journey back to Maun. They dropped Samutchoso at his home *en route*. There were no aircraft available at Maun, so van der Post had a rough four-hundred-mile ride across the northern Kalahari in a diesel truck. At Francistown he picked up a plane for Johannesburg and there he had an incredible stroke of luck. A German, who was an expert precision-instrument manufacturer, volunteered to replace the broken camera part within a week. He also knew a man in the city who had a new camera of the same make. Van der Post tracked down the owner and bought it for a large amount.

A few days later he was back in the Kalahari with the other members of his party, planning the next move in their hunt for the Bushman. This time they had arranged a rendezvous at Gemsbok Pan, an administrative outpost on the edge of the Central Desert. According to Ben, they could not have chosen a more propitious moment, for only Bushmen who had been born and bred in the desert would be found there at that time of the year. Moreover, he had persuaded some friends of his to loan their Bushman servant to the expedition to act as tracker, interpreter and general adviser. The little man's name, he added, was Dabe.

When the Land Rovers had been loaded to capacity at the last supply point, the convoy drove off at dawn straight into the water-less desert. They followed a track that Ben and his father had used many years previously. A dim memory stirred in Ben that at the end of the track they had found some sip-wells. If a Bushman community existed, he argued, it would be grouped about those wells, the only source of drinking water in that part of the desert.

Under a pitilessly hot sun, bumping along over the parched sand, they plunged through scrub and bush, relying entirely on Ben's sense of direction. It was a leisurely advance, largely un-eventful until one day they ran into a handful of desert nomads hurrying towards the nearest cattle-post. It was encouraging to hear from these wanderers that there *were* authentic Bushmen in the desert ahead. They pressed on with renewed hope, always on the look-out for the vital sip-wells and for any sign of the little golden men who sucked water from them.

It was Dabe who eventually spotted what they were looking for. On a hot afternoon they had come up against a patch of particularly difficult scrub. Dabe had run on ahead to see if there was a way through. Suddenly he yelled to attract the attention of the others. When they joined him he pointed down to a set of small human footprints in the sand. They were only a few hours old and had obviously been made by a Bushman.

For mile after mile they followed the tiny tracks, but it was evening before they caught up with their quarry, a young Bushman wearing a loin strap and nothing else. His skin was characteristi-cally apricot coloured and from him emanated a distinctive odour. His name, Dabe discovered, was Nxou. While van der Post and the others watched, the youth probed in the sand with a hooked rod until he flushed a hare, which he swiftly despatched with a wooden club. He then collected all his gear, guided the explorers to a camping site, and after promising to return next day, vanished in the gathering darkness.

True to his word, Nxou was back the following morning, together with his friend whom he introduced as Bauxhau. Although they were both armed with bows and arrows and hunting spears, there was no doubt that they were friendly. With very little prompting they led the party to their simple settlement, which comprised several grass-roofed shelters constructed like out-sized bee-hives. There were not many Bushmen, but Nxou conducted van der Post to another small community about a mile away. There were roughly thirty Bush people in the second group, including men, women and children. One Bushman was busy tipping his arrows with poison. The women, who had been out in the desert in search of food, carried bundles of roots and tubers. They also had ostrich-egg shells filled with water, a circumstance that mystified van der Post and his companions until Bauxhau took them to the Bushman's secret water supplies.

These were the famous sip-wells—deep excavations in the sand into which the Bushman stuck a five-foot tube and sucked up crystal-clear water from beneath the desert's arid surface. The precious liquid was stored in ostrich shells, thus enabling the Bushman to exist between rains.

For several days van der Post and his team studied the life of the isolated community. They saw for themselves that the Bushman was well disciplined, industrious and an incomparable hunter. They also observed him at play, noting his love of music, singing and dancing. Regrettably the little people no longer painted. And all the time it had been getting steadily hotter until the earth was scorched and all vegetation shrivelled up and dead. Every day the Bushman searched the heavens for some hint of rain. It was a period of anxiety, but at last it came to an end. The skies gradually darkened and then, with dramatic suddenness, black clouds piled up around the horizon and thunder rumbled ominously nearer. In response to the challenge of the approaching storm, the Bushmen and Bushwomen began to dance. First they performed the Eland Dance and then the Fire Dance. At night the hero of the dancing picked up live coals from the fire, scattered them and prayed to the troubled night.

At that moment it began to rain.

All night it rained and next day it was as if the desert had been reborn. Flowers sprang up all around, trees blossomed and even the withered thorn budded. Birds were building their nests and beasts were mating. With the start of the rainy season the desert had put on its fairest face as if to persuade van der Post and his friends to stay longer.

But the records were complete, the filming was done and the hour of departure had struck. On the final evening the diminutive apricot-coloured remnants of Africa's First People assembled to receive their farewell gifts—beads and kerchiefs for the women; hunters' knives and tobacco for the men. Van der Post's cooks prepared gallons of coffee for the occasion and everybody drank.

Handing out the presents was a genuinely sad and moving ceremony.

The whole Bushman community was there next morning to see their visitors off. Van der Post was the first to leave. He drove slowly past the last few descendants of a race that had long since vanished from the land, past the undulating dunes, past the unique sip-wells. He stopped the Land Rover on a rise, jumped out and looked back. His journey in search of the elusive Bushman had been circuitous, exhausting and sometimes dangerous, but of one thing he was certain.

It had been worth while...

THE TONGAN TRAVELLERS HIT
MINERVA REEF

At one moment it was only the gentle sound of water moving
through the crippled hull, a splashing, humming little song with
a drowsy rhythm to lull him to sleep. He was trying hard to sleep
and it was not easy, propped as he was almost upright against a
vertical deck.

Suddenly he leapt up. As he did so there was a cry, almost a
scream, from the man on watch and in a moment their self-im-
posed prison which had been so completely still and silent was
alive, quivering and shaking, a bedlam of sound. "Fire!" he roared.
"Make fire! Quick, quick!" But already the others were stumbling
out from below deck, clutching brands from the ever-living fire.
One man fell in a shower of sparks; there was a cry of pain. They
were waving fire-sticks now, but it was hardly necessary: the plane
had seen them, was swooping low over them, its red and green
navigation lights growing bigger, like eyes, in the dark.

And suddenly it was daylight. It was as if the sun, gone these
past few hours, had swept right round the under-part of the world
and roared up into the sky again to explode immediately over
their heads. For a moment he thought something of the kind, some
supernatural sunlight, had arrived. Then he saw the "sun" hang
helpless at the end of a parachute harness, drop slowly to the sea.

518

Two more flares followed, flares that dropped straight into the sea and floated, and after them a sort of box, without light, which fell at the end of its parachute into the water at their feet.

So their prayers had been answered. Feverishly they tore open the para-pack, took out the bully-beef, the tinned sausages, the all-important tin-openers–the wonderful water. The accompanying note, telling them help was on its way, seemed almost unnecessary. They knelt, thanked God for their deliverance. And at dawn the aircraft returned, a monster bird-boat, a Sunderland which alighted smoothly on the water, almost vanished in white spray and came gently to a halt two hundred yards away from them. As they watched in wonder, a door opened and a rubber dinghy was pushed out. Five men clambered down a short ladder, got into the dinghy and headed it toward the reef.

When the little boat reached them, a man–who turned out to be the plane's pilot–got out first: Ve'etutu advanced and shook him by the hand. There was no need for words.

They showed the rescuers Fatai's grave, and a young, pale doctor examined it for a few minutes. Then they lifted up Fetaiaki's body in its blanket and began a shuttle service in the rubber dinghy, getting everyone, the living, the not-long-dead, out to the Sunderland flying-boat. In half an hour they were airborne. A bit after that the pilot was banking hard over an island, pointing it out.

"Kandavu!" he shouted over the noise of engines. "Kandavu– where your mates landed."

So this was what had happened to *Maloleili*, the boat they had built with their own hands–and little else–which had left them all those ages ago to find help. God bless *Maloleili*.

And so ended one of the most ill-starred journeys of recent times, yet one which demonstrated how the faith and simple courage of men can cling to life when clinging seems all but useless.

South Minerva Reef is a giant figure-eight in the South Pacific, between Fiji and the Tonga Islands. The shape comprises two circular atolls, forced up from the ocean-bed together and touching, with a total perimeter of fifteen miles. Like many other atolls, including its sister, North Minerva, some eighteen miles away, it is under water at high tide, a hidden peril lurking just below the surface of the sea, waiting to tear a ship's bottom out with razor-tipped claws of coral. A strange name for this pair of harpies–the name of a Roman goddess of "wisdom and good counsel", but given to them in memory of their first recorded victim, the whaler *Minerva* which sailed from Sydney in August of 1829, to perish on their coral on 9 September. There have been many wrecks on Minerva since, there will be more, but we are concerned now with the tale of the *Tuaikaepau*. Some ships that perished on North or South Minerva reef have been young, gleaming with fresh paint, like the *Strathcona*, which met an end there in her sixth day of life. None, surely, can have been as long in the tooth as *Tuaikaepau*, a cutter launched in 1902. She had led half a dozen different lives, under different names, before being bought in 1957 by a resident of Tonga, Tofa Ramsay, for the small sum of about £1,600 sterling. Ramsay spent the same sum again in re-conditioning her, fitting a new diesel engine, new sails and rigging. This took time, for the money was hard to come by, but eventually he found himself with a fine craft, 51 feet overall, capable of holding her own in any sea.

In March, 1962, Tofa Ramsay sailed his *Tuaikaepau* to Auckland in New Zealand, from her home port of Nuku'alofa in Tonga, managing the westward trip in thirteen days, the return eastward in nine. So successful and profitable was this round trip that he planned another, to start in July. This time, much as he loved his vessel, he would put her in charge of another man, for *Tuaikaepau* was almost capable of finding her own way by now, and Ramsay had business which made it inconvenient for him to go with her.

He chose as her captain a fine seaman, David Fifita, well over six feet tall and some twenty stone in weight, who commanded instant respect and obedience from all who sailed under him. The vessel would have a crew of seven, a passenger list of ten, the passengers paying a return fare of £43.

Two of David's sons were in his crew, Sateki and Lalo Fifita. With them were a ship's carpenter, David Uaisele, ship's engineer Fine, deck-hand Johnny Lousi. The mate was Ve'etutu. As for the passengers, these, like crew, were all Tongans and most were professional boxers, an export of which Tonga is justly proud. Their intention was to have a few bouts in New Zealand–some had already been arranged–make a bit of money and come back, wiser and richer.

There was also a taxi-driver, by name Teiapa'a Bloomfield, going simply to "investigate drinking facilities in New Zealand" and enjoy himself. And to round off the little party there was William Fa, an expert carpenter, going, like the taxi-driver, to enjoy himself, increase his knowledge of the world.

Tongans are proud of their nation and proudest perhaps of expert workers in wood—of whom there were two on this voyage—and of good boxers. There were hundreds of Tongans to bid farewell to their idols when *Tuaikaepau* set sail.

After some delay they set sail late on 4 July, straight into the teeth of a strong adverse wind, blowing straight from the land they hoped to reach. They planned to make a landfall on the small island of 'Ata by dawn the next day, but wind and high sea made nonsense of the scheme: they reached 'Ata at four in the afternoon.

'Ata is a fascinating place—too far, perhaps, from other islands to make the trip worthwhile, but well worth visiting on one's way to anywhere. Until the 1860s it was a happy, populated, Eden, with marvellous fishing, a wealth of carefully tended gardens and all manner of other good things. Then, in the latter half of the last century, slavers came and removed a sizeable part of 'Ata's population: the remainder wisely moved to another, less accessible island, leaving their gardens, their homes, behind.

Here, on the reef outside 'Ata, the men of the *Tuaikaepau* suffered their first mishap: the dinghy which five of them boarded to reach the shore was flung by a wave against a pillar of coral and wrecked. The remains were hoisted on board the bigger craft and both carpenters looked down at the torn wood, the sprung planking, and shook their heads. A boat-builder's yard might do something—they, most certainly, could not.

Minus a serviceable dinghy, plus a few fish they caught on lines over the side, they set sail from 'Ata. More accurately, they started up the diesel, for the wind was in exactly the wrong quarter. This was bitter disappointment indeed, and David Fifita looked anxiously at the sky for sign of change: if he were forced to run long on diesel, the fuel would soon be gone. Early next morning, though the wind had not changed in direction or velocity, he gave order to set sails, bring the ship close-hauled into the wind, hold her on a port tack. This would head them just south of the two Minerva Reefs, but it was less wasteful of time and patience than the starboard tack which would take them considerably farther from the treacherous reefs, to the north—and at the same time keep them farther from their intended course to New Zealand.

In any case, David reckoned, progress had been slow: Minerva Reef was miles and days away. And so it was—but the days, the miles, crept by. They sailed on through the 5th and 6th of July into the 7th.

Then it happened—the impossible. One minute they were sailing close-hauled, leaving Minerva Reef well to starboard, to the north, and the next moment they went over what at first felt like a submerged log and then, all too definitely, proved to be a reef. There was a second impact and the *Tuaikaepau* was suddenly on her beam-ends. Pandemonium broke out below deck, for it was dark and many of the crew and passengers had retired for the night. "Reef! Reef!" David screamed. Then he went below and ordered every man to put on a lifebelt, get on deck–despite its crazy angle– and surround the mast.

In the moonlight it was obvious they were lodged firm in the cleft of a coral reef. David counted dark forms around the mast, found he had all seventeen. Some were praying, others simply hanging on for dear life. Any moment the ship would burst open and they would be at the mercy of the waves and the wind and the coral, clinging to whatever flotsam they could find. They huddled closer round the mast.

The pounding went on, tremendous blows from the sea. At last, with a roar, the ship burst open from stem to stern. They were suddenly all in the water and, although several were pinned for a moment or two underneath pieces of the wreck, were convinced death was upon them, all were soon free–even able to stand, with water up to their necks, on the razor-sharp coral.

As dawn came it was clear that rising waters would dislodge them, that their only hope of salvation lay in building some sort of raft from the wreckage–and building it quickly. Frantically, using the 38-foot mast as a start, they set to work, lashing pieces of wood to it. First came the lid of the hatch, then the entire port side of their shattered vessel: if the pieces would hold together, some sort of raft would soon be ready. But where, with most of their rations and water lost, would they reach on a shapeless, engine-less, raft?

No time to think about this: they worked feverishly, up to their shoulders in water, getting the raft ready. The water, was falling slowly and David Fifita calculated it would be dead low tide by 6.30 a.m. . With luck, they might then be able to find some of their cargo, a few clothes, navigating instruments.

By that hour, sun up and water down, they were able to look about them, in mingled horror and fascination, at South Minerva Reef. Yes, there was no doubt: one could make out the odd figure-eight design, even when one was a part of it.

"Look," said someone. "What's that?"

Rather over a mile away, on the coral, was a strange, surprising, shape. It might almost have been a two-storey house. One of the passengers was sent off to inspect it while the rest carried on rescuing bits of equipment from the shallows. Hours later, as the waters were rising again, the man came back. His feet were bleeding from the savage coral, he limped and grimaced with pain, but he gave a cheery wave and they stopped work to talk with him. Soon, very soon, their hopes were high.

They loaded the treasures they had found among the coral, piled them high on their new-built raft, and began to push it along the surface, walking knee-deep in the rising water. If report were accurate, a few at least of their desperate troubles were over.

They reached the "two-storey house" and there was a faint cheer. For this, while not exactly a house, was a large wooden ship, some eighty feet in length by twenty-four. She had been thrown up on the highest part of the reef so that even at high water only a fifth or less of her was submerged. Defiant, a little foolish, she lay there, wedged firmly and safely on her side, mast and funnel sticking out almost exactly horizontal. Japanese letters adorned her stern, near the large, helpless rudder which swung to and fro in the breeze.

This—and what a Godsend it had been, how swiftly their prayers were answered!—would be their home until such time as rescuers came to Minerva Reef, took them off. Here, within the sturdy timbers of a well-built fishing boat, they would be protected from the elements, could even choose comfortable sleeping quarters, albeit up-ended. There was a shark cruising in a pool and within minutes they had taken a hook from the fishing boat, baited it with a convenient clam, caught the shark. Soon after that they had found matches, built a fire, cooked and eaten the great fish.

But there was nothing, not a drop, to drink.

No time to worry about this at first, for the Japanese ship was full of exciting things to be discovered, even though it was clear she had been abandoned in an orderly manner, her crew rescued by another ship, taking all major equipment with them. There was no end of fishing gear, there were cooking utensils, drums of fuel oil. There was a radio-transmitter with which the crew had probably called for help, and received it, but this was now useless. There were, in addition to other foodstuffs, five big tubs of delicious soy sauce, every man's favourite. But David Fifita forbade them to be broached: without adequate water supplies, men would go mad from thirst even earlier if they ate soy.

The next day was Sunday, 8 July, and they held a prayer meeting, thanked God for his goodness to them, prayed they might soon be rescued. Prayed that they be given strength to await their rescue like brave men, a credit to Tonga. In this little band of seventeen ship-wrecked seafarers there were Catholics, Wesleyans, Mormons, and now they prayed together for salvation. Then they caught small fish, which David commanded them to eat raw, in order not to waste the fresh water inside.

They painted, with the paint which abounded inside the Japanese vessel, a huge "S.O.S." on the side of the hull, the side looking up to the blue Pacific sky. They painted other, longer messages on fishing buoys and drums, cast them adrift. One read "SOS 17 men on Minerva Reef app 196 m. sw of 'Ata".

They lost no time in making a still from a convenient kettle and length of pipe. They had already lit a fire with one of the matches and David ordered that this fire never be let out, lest the matches get lost or spoilt and they have no opportunity of kindling another. Soon a thin trickle of warm, fresh water was coming from the end of the tube. It would not be enough, but it would help. And surely, within a week or so, their non-arrival at Auckland must be the signal for a search operation culminating in rescue?

Had any one of them known it would be more than three months before they were rescued, even their great faith in God and His goodness might not have kept alive the will to live. Yet perhaps this is an unfair judgment, for as days became weeks and then months, they prayed again and again, found comfort.

Soon they all began to feel unwell, despite ample food and a near-sufficiency of water. David, though he said nothing, knew this was caused by an absence of Vitamin "C": there was no fresh fruit or vegetable, and little chance of any drifting their way. He searched for seaweed, failed.

Gloomy consideration of this was interrupted by a phenomenon which, to less sophisticated islanders, might have been utterly terrifying, a foretaste of hell which would either frighten them to death or make them fight still harder for life, rather than face such an hereafter. Suddenly one night, the whole sky was lit up; it went green, then yellow, then pink and stayed, a throbbing mass of colour, for almost ten minutes. But the seventeen men from the *Tuaikaepau* were sophisticated, literate Tongans who had read their newspapers and knew the Americans would be firing their "rainbow bomb" that night. They watched, more in admiration than in wonder.

And had they but known it, a hope of rapid rescue was being dashed at that very moment. *Life* magazine was planning a Christmas issue on beautiful islands and atolls in the Pacific. Plans were well ahead to fly a camera team to North Minerva, one of the most photogenic reefs in the whole ocean. And although North Minerva is at eighteen miles distance from her southern sister, there had been a good chance that the aircraft would at least pass near South Minerva, near enough to see men stranded on her, waving. But at the last moment it was decided the expedition would be too expensive; some other, more accessible, reef would have to be—and was—found. For the men on South Minerva, though none of them could have guessed the gloomy fact, this was a sentence to three more months on the reef.

Morale was still high, for as prayers were offered, so valuable adjuncts to their life appeared from under the water at low tide. Rubber boots, drinking cups. But now, so great was their consumption of wood and diesel oil, that David, their captain, gave instructions for using much less—and distilling less water. They would have to eke out the fuel, even if they went thirsty.

And now the thieving began. The communal water-holder, though guarded at all times, mysteriously ran dry and they had to use precious fuel to distil more. Little delicacies which had been hoarded seemed to vanish. David was able to find the culprit in almost every case, make him confess his guilt and repent. But ingenious methods were used to effect the robberies. When water was transferred from still to container, via measuring glass—which the Japanese fishermen had used for their *saki*—a man might count "one, two, three, three, four—" and, on finding his "error" had not been noticed, be able to help himself to an extra glassful. Yet throughout their enforced sojourn on the reef, David as captain was able to keep control, settle disputes swiftly and firmly, while keeping thefts down to a minimum among men who were being slowly crazed by lack of water, absence of vitamins.

The first to fall sick was a passenger. They were able to find a thermometer among the fishing-boat's gear and by checking its reading in their own mouths ascertain where "normal" must be. By this device the sick man's temperature was shown to be as normal as anyone else's, but David gave him the benefit of the doubt, let him off the daily fatigues of distilling water, catching fish, collecting "treasure", cooking. He knew that soon there would be others, plenty of them, in worse plight.

And soon there were. The dreadful symptoms of scurvy became obvious. One man, constipated since leaving Tonga, was slowly and painfully distending, like a football, as the days slipped into weeks. They began catching bigger fish, smashing holes in the skull through which they could drink a fearful mess of blood, brains and water– but it gave strength and "sweet mouths". They never lacked food of a sort: on 27 July, three weeks after being wrecked on the reef, they caught 21 crays and 120 other fish in a few hours. Occasionally, with baited hook, they landed a shark, and it was the liver from one of these, eaten still hot from the writhing body, that succeeded in curing Pulu's agonizing constipation, just when it seemed he might die.

Each day they sent off more messages, composed differently on different objects which were to bear them away and get help, from a simple "S.O.S." on a fishing buoy to a long sentence about conditions on South Minerva, on a plank. The paint, the planks, were almost unlimited–though the ship which had begun as one of several cabins gradually metamorphosed into an "open-plan" living space, with everyone sleeping on the starboard wall, which was only five degrees from horizontal.

As the wecks lengthened to a pair of months, David realized that help might never come. As long as they prayed, they would get back somehow–those the Lord saw fit to return to their loved ones–but they would have to take matters into their own hands and make a boat.

There was no question of building one capable of taking all seventeen. No, David reasoned, a small boat, but strong and capable of taking three hand-picked men to some other island to seek help, was all they could manage. And as the nearest island, in the direction they would be taken by the wind, was well over two hundred miles away, the boat would have to be seaworthy.

They began to build one. Not a raft, but a real sailing boat, and the ingenuity they showed, in finding correct materials, cutting them to size, bending planks, was remarkable. They had virtually no tools–only a hammer–but by heating a long nail in the fire and literally burning a way through the wood, they were able to cut and smooth their hull with the greatest delicacy. It took shape rapidly: a blunt but workmanlike vessel 18 feet long, 4½ wide. They added a keel of 18-inch depth and even launched her–a mammoth undertaking down the vertical deck of their "shipyard"– before David decided she must be an outrigger, without keel. This entailed lifting the enormous weight back to another, improvised yard where they could work on it.

Eventually the *Maloleili*, or "Good Morning" as they had named her, was ready to set sail. David had instructed Ve'etutu in his duties as commander of the island party: he, David Fifita, with his son Sateki–the best swimmer in the party–and the ship's carpenter, the other David, Uaisele, would set sail in *Maloleili* and get help.

But before the brave little *Maloleili* and her braver crew, sadly weakened by a deficiency diet, could set sail, there were three deaths, in rapid succession. On 28 September the oldest passenger, Fatai, gentleman of leisure, aged forty-six, died quite suddenly. He had been ill for a long time, growing daily weaker, but his death when it came was a shock. Two days later, much younger men, the two Johnnies, died. Johnny Skimeti and Johnny Lousi died within minutes of each other, while working on last-minute preparations for the voyage of the *Maloleili*.

They were able to scratch a grave for Fatai in the reef, able to wind him tightly in a canvas shroud. As they had no adequate shroud for the others, but feared to bury them naked, lest the crabs and fishes devour them, and they, the survivors, become cannibals by eating crabs and fishes, they wrapped them in what blankets they could spare, buoyed them up with floats, and pushed them out to sea.

A few days later the *Maloleili* followed them. As we have seen, she made it, and the eleven men left living on South Minerva Reef were rescued by Sunderland flying-boat from Fiji. But *Maloleili*'s journey was far from uneventful. David remembered the bearing and distance from Tonga to the island he now planned to reach, the bearing and distance from Tonga of Minerva Reef. By plotting these carefully in a note-book he had worked out the course to sail in order to reach his island, Ono-i-lau, 220 miles almost due north. But somehow they missed it, sailed clean past, perhaps during the hours of darkness. There was no means of going back, so they turned to port and made for the big island of Kandavu, many miles to the north-west. However inaccurate their navigation, they would be certain to see Kandavu from a distance, have reasonable opportunity of altering course to it: Kandavu was more than thirty miles in length and up to eight miles across, with mountains reaching to nearly three thousand feet above the sea.

They were right, and a cheer rose up from the three exhausted men as they made out an island skyline. Then they headed for a break in the reef surrounding it. They found their break, a gap in the coral, three hundred yards across, but so vicious was the sea roaring through it, so huge the waves, that they were picked up bodily and flung, upside down, through it.

When he was able to see again, David found himself clinging to the upturned boat, and the others had vanished. Then he saw them, thirty yards away. They were inside the reef, nearer to the shore than himself, and he decided to leave the useless boat and join them in the long, mile and a half, swim to the shore.

And it was during this swim that David lost his son, his Sateki, the best swimmer in the crew, best swimmer in a family of swimmers. Sateki simply lacked the strength to make the distance. David tried again and again to buoy him up, drag him through the water, but it was useless. At last, clinging to his son, he breathed a last prayer.

Then he left him, swam with all his strength towards the distant shore, for if David delayed, the other David might lose heart and die. Perhaps he, David Fifita, would sink too—and then all the others on Minerva Reef would perish with them.

He took one last anguished look back. Sateki had vanished.

The two Davids reached the shore of the island, fell exhausted on the sand and lay there. Then, recovering a little strength, they saw coconut palms directly above them. They were able to pull down a few green coconuts and drink the juice till they were heartily, happily, ill.

There was a long walk ahead before they found other human beings, and then a deal of misunderstanding and confusion before the truth could be conveyed, that there were other men, dying, hundreds of miles away. Runners took a garbled message to the nearest radio transmitter, this was further muddled in transmission, and the information received at Suva was utterly meaningless.

But eventually, as the two Davids, now very ill, repeated their tale, again and again, the message got through. The rescue plane took off—and the story was over. One more man had died since the captain and his two-man crew had sailed away to get help: apart from that, life had been uneventful. They took the body with them in the plane.

The story—for those who had lived it, those who had died to make it—was over. But in the South Pacific, a tale of *Tuaikaepau* and her tiny offspring *Maloleili* will be told for many, many years.

Index

Acknowledgements

The editor expresses his acknowledgements to publishers for their courtesy in permitting condensations and quotations from the following books:

George Allen & Unwin Ltd., *The Kon-Tiki Expedition* by Thor Heyerdahl, *The Great Chinese Travellers* by Jeannolt Mirsky; Angus & Robertson Ltd., *Minerva Reef* by Olef Ruhen; Jonathan Cape Ltd., *News From Tartary* by Peter Fleming; Collins Publishers, *Arabia Felix* by Thorkild Hansen; J. M. Dent & Sons Ltd., *The Darkness Under The Earth* by Norbert Casteret; André Deutsch Ltd., *The Bombard Story* by Alain Bombard; George G. Harrap & Company Ltd., *The Mad Motorists* by Allen Andrews; Hamish Hamilton Ltd. and Rupert Hart Davis Ltd., *Two Thousand Fathoms Down* by Houot and Willm; William Heinemann Ltd., *Tschiffely's Ride* by A. F. Tschiffely; Hutchinson Publishing Group Ltd., *Amy Johnson* by H. S. Banner; John Murray (Publishers) Ltd., *The Valleys of the Assassins* by Freya Stark; Martin Secker & Warburg Ltd., *The Last Grain Race* by Eric Newby.